MODERN
PUBLIC
ADMINISTRATION

MODERN PUBLIC ADMINISTRATION

SECOND EDITION

Felix A. Nigro

University of Georgia

HARPER & ROW, PUBLISHERS
New York, Evanston, and London

To Lloyd

CONTENTS

Part III   BASIC PROBLEMS
                OF MANAGEMENT   167

PREFACE

The second edition of *Modern Public Administration* represents an extensive updating and revision of the materials in the first edition. Because the field of public administration changes so quickly, many new developments had to be incorporated. To improve the original coverage, two new key chapters are added: one on Organization Theory and the other on Collective Bargaining in the Public Service. In other chapters there is much new material on problems of the urban environment; administrative aspects of intergovernmental relations; new developments in decisionmaking and budgeting, such as planning-programming-budgeting; adjustment of civil service systems to meet the needs of the disadvantaged; and the Scandinavian institution of the Ombudsman as a means of making the bureaucracy more responsive to the needs of the individual citizen. The chapter bibliographies have been expanded to help those desiring to explore the particular topics in greater detail.

The essential characteristic of the book as a concise, comprehensive introduction to public administration that combines both theory and practice has been preserved. The author appreciates the suggestions of teachers and students who have used the book, and is again much indebted to his wife for her invaluable assistance in typing the manuscript and performing various related chores.

F.A.N.

PART I
NATURE
AND SCOPE
OF THE FIELD

CHAPTER 1
WHAT IS
PUBLIC
ADMINISTRATION?

ONE-SENTENCE definitions are desirable, particularly in textbooks, but, in the case of public administration, they have proved inadequate. Indeed, a review of the literature shows that where a one-sentence definition is attempted, the writer usually hastens to add to it in subsequent paragraphs. As Dwight Waldo has said:

> The immediate effect of all one-sentence or one-paragraph definitions of public administration is mental paralysis rather than enlightenment and stimulation. This is because a serious definition of the term . . . inevitably contains several abstract words or phrases. In short compass these abstract words and phrases can be explained only by other abstract words and phrases, and in the process the reality and importance of "it" become fogged and lost.[1]

Underlying these semantic difficulties is the fact that the boundaries of the field have never been precisely delimited, and that they have in recent years become increasingly indeterminate as both the practitioners' and the scholars' concept of the scope

[1] Dwight Waldo, *The Study of Public Administration,* New York: Doubleday, 1955, p. 2.

3

has broadened considerably. Present-day students of public administration get a substantially different version of the subject from their teachers, the literature, and public officials than those who took the first courses, read the first books, attended the first meetings of the American Society for Public Administration, and listened to the pioneering practitioners who sought recognition for the "new field of administration." Although such change has taken place in many fields of study and action, it has been particularly true of public administration.

Our approach will be to delay giving a definition until we have explored several different considerations that bear upon the determination of the proper scope of public administration. The advantage of this procedure is that it will show clearly why, when we come to the definition, we include some things and exclude others.

THE ROLE OF THE THREE BRANCHES

One approach is to identify public administration as it relates to the three traditional branches of government: executive, legislative, and judicial.

Legislative and administrative powers

In this conception, administration is execution, that is, carrying out the laws passed by the legislature. There is a clear distinction between legislative and administrative powers: The legislature possesses the former, but when it passes a law, what the executive branch does with that law becomes "administration." Although the legislative and executive branches are not completely separate entities, still it is the latter that has the administrative power, so it follows that public administration is "what the executive branch does." The judiciary stands apart from "administration," deciding cases between private parties but also restraining the public administrators from unconstitutional, illegal, and arbitrary acts.

This kind of definition emphasizes "who does what," but as the hearings of the Senate Subcommittee on Separation of Powers make very clear, the Constitution makes no statement of differences between legislative and administrative powers.[2] This Subcommittee, whose reports are recommended reading for all serious students of American government, has been investigating "the extent, if any, to which any branch or branches of the Government may have encroached upon the powers, functions, and duties vested in any other branch by the Constitution of

[2] *Separation of Powers,* Hearings Before the Senate Subcommittee on Separation of Powers, 90th Congress, 1st Session, Washington, D.C.: Government Printing Office, 1967.

the United States."[3] One of its particular concerns has been the dispute between the legislative and executive branches over the constitutionality and wisdom of so-called legislative vetoes that require some form of prior approval in Congress, either by committee or by one or both Houses, before administrative agencies can take certain action. The legislative veto is not new, but it "has developed largely since 1950" and has been written into more than 25 recent statutes.[4] One such statute, the Small Watershed Protection and Flood Prevention Act of 1954, became a major issue between President Johnson and the Congress in 1967.

Like Presidents Eisenhower and Kennedy, Johnson became concerned over what he considered a dilution of executive power represented by "coming-into-agreement" requirements. He had vetoed the Pacific Northwest Disaster Relief Act of 1965 because it contained a provision preventing the expenditure of funds on a project to restabilize the banks of the Eel River in northern California without the advance approval of the Senate and House Public Works Committees.[5] The President argued that "The executive branch is given, by the Constitution, the responsibility to implement all laws—a specific and exclusive responsibility which cannot properly be shared with a committee of Congress."[6] A requirement in the Small Watershed Act that no appropriation could be made for projects to which the federal government would contribute construction funds in excess of $250,000, or which would provide more than 2500 acre-feet of total capacity, without prior approval of designated committees in the House and Senate, had been observed by the Eisenhower and Kennedy Administrations, but proved particularly distasteful to Johnson. He announced that in the future he would disregard this provision, and proposed instead an amendment that would require project plans to be filed with the Congress, with a waiting period of 30 days before federal participation in the project could begin.[7]

The argument of the Johnson Administration, ably stated by Assistant Attorney General Frank M. Wozencraft, was essentially that the selection of particular projects was an executive act with which Congress, if it held to the Constitution, should not interfere.[8] Subcommittee Chairman Sam J. Ervin, Jr., of North Carolina repeatedly asked why, if Congress could make the coming-into-effect of legislation contingent upon conditions to be determined by the executive branch, could it not in other cases make one of its committees the agent for this purpose? Representatives of the Johnson Administration answered basically

[3] *Ibid.*, p. 1.
[4] *Ibid.*, p. 188.
[5] John H. Averill, "House Passes Revised Flood Relief Measure," *Los Angeles Times*, June 16, 1965.
[6] *Separation of Powers, op. cit.*, p. 114.
[7] *Ibid.*, pp. 77–83.
[8] *Ibid.*, pp. 201–233.

that such action by Congress would not be "legislative," although obviously Congress had the right to check up later on what kinds of decisions the executive branch had made on particular projects, and to pass new legislation canceling or authorizing certain projects.

Ervin and others did not accept this interpretation of the limits of legislative power in relation to project approval. They saw no provision in the Constitution that says where legislative power ends, which to them puts the burden of proof on the executive branch to demonstrate that its refusal to observe a coming-into-agreement provision is not a wilful violation of the Constitution.

Thus the interpretation that "administration" is execution, and that there is a clear distinction between legislative and administrative powers, breaks down. One can side with the Presidents or with Congress, but the Ervin Subcommittee hearings make very clear that Congress does not consider itself limited to criticism, after-the-act, of decisions in the implementation of legislation. It views its role in some cases as codirection with the administrative agencies concerned of the particular programs, not simply legislative authorization, appropriation, and post-review.[9] This is one important reason why any definition of public administration cannot leave out the legislature, but there are also other reasons.

Other involvement of legislatures in administration

Actually, it is frequently overlooked that legislatures directly oversee the activities of some administrative agencies; examples at the national level are the Government Printing Office, the Library of Congress, and the General Accounting Office.[10] Thus not all law-implementing agencies are in the executive branch, which is further evidence that "administration" is not all contained within that branch. More importantly, as indicated previously, in the American scheme of government, legislatures are responsible for maintaining a close watch on what goes on in the administrative agencies under the Chief Executive, whether President, Governor, or Mayor. This is the function known as *legislative oversight*, now very crucial because of the great growth of the executive branch and the expansion of the powers of the Presidency.

Many people are concerned that Congress, under present conditions, can do very little to make the critical examination that should be made, in the public interest, of the functioning of the

[9] See Morton Grodzins, "American Political Parties and the American System," *Western Political Quarterly*, XIII, No. 4 (December, 1960), 980–982.
[10] *United States Government Organization Manual*, 1968–69, Washington, D.C.: Government Printing Office, pp. 30–42.

executive agencies, a problem discussed in detail in Part VI of this book. However effective legislative post-review of entire programs or activities, the individual Congressmen and their staffs spend considerable time making contacts with agency officials on behalf of their constituents, whether it be to speed up a pension check, get an answer to a letter, or otherwise obtain action in countless situations where the citizen understandably goes to his Representative for help. Known as Congressional "case work," the result is that every day's work in an administrative agency is characterized by very close relationships between the executive and legislative branches, a pattern of continuous executive-legislative interaction that is also found in state and local governments.[11] To photograph the executive branch "in action" would capture the faces of many legislators beside those of the "bureaucrats," and not particularly in the background, either.

Considering administration *as a process*, that is, as a body of knowledge and techniques for the effective management of any enterprise, it is needed in legislatures, just as in other entities. Legislatures should be properly organized. For example, the number of committees should not be excessive, and their respective jurisdictions should be clearly defined. The committees and the individual legislators should have the staff required for doing the best possible job; satisfactory space, equipment, and other housekeeping services should be provided. In short, if they are to function satisfactorily, legislatures must constantly improve their own internal organization and procedures; their failure to do so accounts for much of today's dissatisfaction with lawmakers. Thus, looking at the legislature from the "inside," we find that it needs good "administration."

The judiciary

Far from standing apart, the judiciary is a powerful force in shaping public administration. When the courts pass upon the constitutionality of legislative enactments and administrative acts, they are determining what kinds of public services can be rendered and under what conditions. The federal courts established the requirement for school desegregation, declared unconstitutional numerous attempts to get around it, and are seeing to it that the schools are kept open on a desegregated basis. There are limitations to their enforcement authority, as indicated by the need on several occasions to send federal troops. But the courts' interpretation of the United States Constitution stands, notwithstanding any conflicting provisions in state constitutions and statutes, and any

[11] See Grodzins, *op. cit.*, 984–985.

contrary views of federal, state, and local government officials.

Currently there is concern that court decisions hamper law enforcement. Whether the charge is true or not, it is clear from such controversies that the daily activities of policemen and other public employees are greatly influenced by court decisions. Furthermore, the courts also protect against *ultra vires* acts, that is, when officials exceed the authority granted to them in the statutes. In the policymaking area, the federal courts can nullify the decisions of regulatory commissions, such as the Federal Communications Commission (FCC) and the Federal Power Commission (FPC) to name only two.

Panel discussions on judicial administration have been fairly frequent at meetings of public administration professional societies and other groups; the need to relieve congestion of court dockets and otherwise improve the "administration" of justice is considered a high-priority "administrative" problem. More than half the states now have court systems with administrative officers who in effect are business managers, as much careerists in public administration as officials in the executive agencies.

The Administrative Office of the United States Courts has existed since 1939, and in early 1968 President Johnson signed legislation establishing a Federal Judicial Center to serve as a research and training agency for the federal judiciary.[12] One of the responsibilities of the Center is to apply computer technology to the task of improving court records and procedures; it is holding seminars for new judges and will develop training programs for court clerks and other personnel.[13] Like the legislature, the judiciary has a great impact on public administration, and also needs to apply the best available management techniques in its own internal functioning. Thus the obvious conclusion is that all three branches of government are a part of the study and practice of public administration.

POLICY AND ADMINISTRATION

[12] See *United States Government Organization Manual, 1968–69, op. cit.,* pp. 51–52.

[13] Bill Andronicos, "New Unit Attacking Court Congestion," *Federal Times,* March 20, 1968.

The administration-policy dichotomy is the basis for another attempt at definition: Policy is made by the legislature in the form of laws, and is carried out by the executive branch. At first glance this interpretation may seem identical with the attempted distinction between legislative and administrative powers. The Johnson Administration did not say that it had no role in policymaking; rather, it insisted that once the Congress had passed a statute, the lawmakers had no right to exercise a veto over administrative discretion in carrying out the law.

Separation of powers is subject to many different interpretations, depending on one's objectives. Assistant Attorney General Wozencraft went back to 1825 to quote Chief Justice John Marshall's statement that "The difference between the departments undoubtedly is that the legislature makes, the executive executes, and the judiciary construes the law." In Wozencraft's opinion:

> Marshall's words are as true today as they were when he pronounced them. Within this framework, there are necessarily situations where these functions may overlap. Congress has the initial choice of legislating in terms of broad statements of policy to be implemented by the executive, or with such particularity that little discretion is left to the executive. Once the Congress has legislated, however, it is for the executive branch—not the Congress—to implement the legislation.[14]

In our complicated, problem-ridden society, the executive branch and the President have developed so much power that it would have been ludicrous to have told the Ervin Subcommittee that all administrative officials did was simply to carry out policies made by the Congress. Yet the early writers in public administration did make a distinction between policy and administration. One reason is that they were anxious to keep "politics" out of administration; the legislators represented "politics," and, with their allies in the party organizations and their influence on the administration in power, they could prevent the professionalization of the public service. Accordingly, the concept of a neutral, nonpolicymaking bureaucracy was developed. The "separateness" of administration was stressed in the effort to gain acceptance of it as a new, untarnished field essential for proper, efficient management of the government's business.[15] Furthermore, although Woodrow Wilson stressed the growing complexity of American society when in 1887 he wrote his famous essay on "The Study of Administration,"[16] the policy role of the executive branch, while it existed, was hardly as great as it is today. The policy-administration dichotomy was always fiction, but not an outright absurdity in the period when legislatures still retained strong initiatives in policymaking and the executive branch, while growing, was much smaller than it is today.

The growth of administrative discretion

Execution of the law always requires some discretion. Leonard D. White in his book *The Federalists* shows how attempts were made to keep administrative discretion to a minimum during the

[14] *Separation of Powers, op. cit.,* p. 202.

[15] Waldo, *op. cit.,* pp. 40–41.

[16] Reproduced in Peter Woll (ed.), *Public Administration and Policy,* New York: Harper & Row, 1966, pp. 15–41.

administrations of George Washington and John Adams, and how this could not be accomplished even in the relatively simple society of the first years of the new Republic. For example, when Congress decided to raise money by taxing carriages, it wrestled with the problem of establishing a uniform classification of the carriages for tax purposes, but in the end it had to "recognize a substantial degree of administrative leeway." The problem was how to differentiate between chariots, coaches, four-wheeled carriages, and similar vehicles with the unstandardized structural features characteristic of the times. Congress did the best it could in trying to describe each class of carriage in the law, "but added that in cases of doubt any carriage should be deemed to belong in that class to which it bore the greatest resemblance." Exercising this discretion, the New Jersey collector applied the tax to wagons of farmers going to market.[17]

As long as the great majority of Americans lived in the rural areas and economic and social relations did not require much regulation by government, the discretionary powers of public officials could be kept relatively modest. At the same time, while new laws and new policies were recommended to the Congress by the executive branch, it was not possible to say, as it is today, that "the bulk of public legislation passed by Congress does not originate there, but rather in the particular administrative agency or agencies concerned with the legislation."[18] Congress, and state and local governing bodies as well, now find it necessary to legislate in highly complicated areas where expert knowledge of the programs concerned is essential, and this usually is best supplied by the administrative officials who specialize in such programs.

Undoubtedly the developments in physical and social technology which, beginning with the latter part of the nineteenth century, have created a highly interdependent economy, largely account for the greatly enhanced policy role of administrative officials. The regulatory commissions are frequently cited as examples, because of their powers to fix charges, set standards of service, and otherwise control in the public interest the activities of gas, electric, telephone, and other utilities. It is correctly stated that the policy decisions of these commissions have a greater effect on citizens and their pocketbooks than those of many of the nonregulatory agencies, but the latter have also accumulated very significant policy roles. In such departments as Health, Education, and Welfare, Agriculture, and Interior, countless decisions are made every day on applications for pension payments, grants, loans, permits to use government facilities, and other requests.

[17] Leonard D. White, *The Federalists*, New York: Macmillan, 1948, p. 452.

[18] Peter Woll, *American Bureaucracy*, New York: Norton, 1963, p. 8.

The Defense Department lets contracts for billions of dollars, and in the process makes determinations that affect economic conditions in numerous communities throughout the country. With the development of new inventions and technologies, a subject explored in detail in the next chapter, the scope of the discretion of existing agencies increases. Thus the Federal Communications Commission now regulates television, as well as radio, and it has complex decisions to make on equal time for political opponents, pay TV, and the noise decibels of commercials. New agencies, like the Federal Aviation Agency, are given more extensive policy roles than their predecessors because of the need to cope with new problems such as the danger of plane collisions in mid-air.

The latest phase of administrative policymaking

As the 1960s came to an end, it was clear that administrative policymaking had, along with the entire government, moved into an even more crucial stage. Important as are economic regulation and control of the new technologies, a new dimension, ever so much more complicating, has been added: substantial societal change. There is a great difference between the Work Projects Administration of Roosevelt's New Deal and the Office of Economic Opportunity, which directs the war against poverty. The New Deal was a social and political revolution, but its objective was economic recovery, not the elimination of the ghettoes, reconstruction of the cities, changing of citizen attitudes, and massive government involvement in meeting the health, education, leisure-time, and other needs of all sectors of the population. Until recently, these were entertained only as distant objectives; America did not have the economic means to give much thought to such huge programs. Whatever the exact reasons, the levels of expectations of many citizens have risen sharply: They want a better life, as quickly as possible, and this is as characteristic of a young white trade unionist as it is of a low-income Negro, although, of course, the economic deprivation of the latter usually creates a more intense feeling against the existing order. Public administration today must deal effectively with problems of social disorganization and intense citizen desires for satisfaction of needs that are felt to be legitimate and within the power of an affluent society to meet.

The times require that public employees be creative, both in their policy-recommending and implementing capacities. Presently there is general dissatisfaction with existing public assistance programs, particularly Aid to Dependent Children, the cost of which has risen greatly. Various substitute programs have been suggested, such as the negative income tax and a guaranteed minimum income. Obviously, legislators as well as administrative officials are applying their brainpower to the weighing of these alternatives. Only the legislature can authorize any new programs, but based on past experience, the experts in the administrative branch will be relied upon to work out the details of the legislation, and then will take the responsibility for making it a success in practice. It is clearer now than ever before that these programs will not succeed, no matter how well-supported financially, unless the administrators make sound decisions in initiating and carrying out the different projects.

The Demonstration Cities and Metropolitan Development Act of 1966 is a good example. Its rationale is that for urban renewal to be successful, it should proceed on the basis of integrated physical and social rehabilitation in whole neighborhoods. In approving this legislation, Congress endorsed the approach as worthy of trial. It is up to the Department of Housing and Urban Development, with cooperating state and local governments and private groups, to make it a success.

Ventures in social planning must take into account many different factors and be based on deep understanding of the human element. Congress can criticize, make suggestions, and give additional financial support, but as a practical matter, its policymaking function cannot extend to many of the most crucial decisions in program implementation. This is also illustrated in the community action and other programs of the Office of Economic Opportunity; the money appropriated so far has been much too little, but it is obvious that the problem is so difficult to deal with effectively that many more billions could be spent—and wasted.[19] Furthermore, the intended beneficiaries of these programs, and the taxpayers who pay the bill, expect relatively quick results.

NEW CHALLENGES FOR ADMINISTRATIVE DISCRETION

[19] See Peter Marris and Martin Rein, *Dilemmas of Social Reform: Poverty and Community Action in the United States,* New York: Atherton, 1967.

The classroom examples that used to be given of administrative discretion were how the postal clerk used his judgment in deciding to weigh a letter, and the public health sanitarian in recommending the closing of a restaurant. These are still valid examples, but such decisions do not tax ingenuity as do persuading people to accept family planning, stop smoking cigarettes, move back to the rural communities, shed their racial and other prejudices, and be effective ambassadors for the United States when on vacation abroad. These used to be considered purely personal matters, and certainly they should be dealt with on the basis of persuasion rather than coercion; actually, it is improbable that these new outlooks and attitudes could be imposed on the people anyway.

The police officer on duty in the ghettoes must be intelligent and sensitive, as well as physically strong and agile; there is very little margin for mistakes, as riot records demonstrate.[20] Laws can be passed to help remedy the deficit in the balance of payments, but they cannot, except under a system of rigid government controls, be expected to deal with all facets of the problem. Private groups and individuals must be persuaded to cooperate with the government, under conditions where such cooperation may entail real sacrifices. In our highly interrelated society one problem impinges upon another, and coordinated action is necessary on numerous different fronts, with the public officials playing an important role in such coordination.

THE STRAIN ON THE ADMINISTRATIVE MACHINERY

In 1940 Charles Beard, the historian, observed that the tasks of legislation were relatively easy as compared with those of administration.[21]

In late 1966 James Reston, the newspaper columnist, found an "administrative monstrosity" in Washington; the 89th Congress alone had "passed 21 new health programs, 17 new educational programs, 15 new economic development programs, 12 new programs for the cities, 17 new resource development programs, and 4 new manpower training programs."[22] It could not "absorb" so many new, far-reaching and varigated programs: "As President Johnson starts his fourth year in the White House, one fact is not only clear but undisputed: his Administration is poorly organized to administer the domestic programs he has introduced, and the administrative chaos of the state and local governments is even worse."[23] The legislative box score was impressive, but the administrative machinery was in creaking, overloaded condition. What Beard found difficult in 1940 seemed close to impossible in 1966, so greatly had the load on the administrative branch increased.

THE ADMINISTRATIVE BRANCH AND "GOAL CONFLICTS"

As new programs are created and assigned to existing agencies, the policy responsibilities of officials put them at the center of controversies legislatures cannot, or would rather not, resolve. Public lands, parks, and forests can be used for several different purposes, but an increase in one emphasis usually means a decrease

[20] On police discretion, see *Report of the National Advisory Commission on Civil Disorders*, New York: Bantam, 1968, pp. 312–314.

[21] Charles Beard, "Administration, A Foundation of Government," *American Political Science Review, XXXIV*, No. 2 (April, 1940), 232.

[22] James Reston, "Washington: Johnson's Administrative Monstrosity." *New York Times*, November 23, 1966.

[23] *Ibid.*

in another. An expansion in tourist facilities often is at the expense of nature lovers; currently there is constant pressure to provide more recreational outlets for a rapidly growing, leisure-conscious population. The way out for the legislature is to mention in the authorizing statutes the different uses of the particular resources, and then leave it to the administrators to try to satisfy all the various segments of the population clamoring for attention to their needs.

The legislative mandates are often vague and even contradictory; note this statement in the California Wildlife Conservation Act of 1947: " 'The preservation, protection, and restoration of wildlife . . . is an inseparable part of providing adequate recreation for our people in the interest of public welfare.' "[24] But "recreation" for the bird watcher is not the same as that for the hunter and fisherman, and consequently it is no wonder that the California Department of Fish and Game has been bewildered as it "listened to a multitude of voices urging it to act in many different and at times contradictory ways."[25]

The resolution of "goal conflict" is passed on to the administrative agencies, which actually is a common occurrence in day-by-day administration: Decisions must be made among competing claims where the discretion is great but the possibilities of satisfying all client groups remote.

TWO RECENT DEVELOPMENTS

Two very recent developments affecting administrative policymaking should be mentioned: planning-programming-budgeting (PPB) and collective bargaining between public agencies and employee organizations. (These are dealt with in detail in Chapters 17 and 15, respectively.) The purpose of PPB is to define program goals, establish priorities, and achieve maximum work results at the least cost. Over the years new responsibilities have been added to old ones, to the point where many administrative agencies are not sure just which activities they should be emphasizing. PPB calls for continuous comparison of the merits of all agency programs, old, new, and proposed; thus, it requires policy planning on a comprehensive, rigorous basis. If PPB succeeds, administrative policymaking will be more rational, the decisions sounder, and consequently the role of the administrators even more significant.

Rarely in the past have organized employees been able to participate in the formulation of agency policies. Now, in such fields as teaching and public welfare, collective agreements are

[24] John R. Owens, "A Wildlife Agency and Its Possessive Public," in Frederick C. Mosher (ed.), *Governmental Reorganizations: Cases and Commentary*, Indianapolis, Ind.: Bobbs-Merrill, 1967, pp. 109–110.

[25] *Ibid.*, p. 115.

being negotiated that provide for joint decisionmaking by management and the employee organizations in program areas such as class size and case loads. It is one thing for administrators to decide agency policies; it is another for them to work them out jointly with the employees. Policy determination over the bargaining table is a very new development for which public management was not at all prepared. The bargaining requirement may be unsettling not only to administrative officials but also to scholars who have stressed rationality as the basis for decisionmaking. Yet the employee organizations claim that sounder, fairer, and therefore more rational policies will result from bargaining than from unilateral decrees by management.

LIMITATIONS OF LEGISLATION

The present period also provides convincing examples of how legislatures cannot solve certain problems with laws, anymore than administrators can with regulations and edicts. Perhaps the best example is public employee strikes, which are occurring despite the laws against them (see Chapter 15, pages 330–336). Theodore W. Kheel, one of the most highly regarded labor mediators, has said: "In the end, labor relations must depend on the human factor. The most elaborate machinery is no better than the people who run it. It cannot function automatically. With skillful and responsible negotiators, no machinery, no outsiders, and no fixed rules are needed to settle disputes."[26]

If negotiations break down, governments can supply skilled mediators and otherwise try to get the collective bargaining process to function; the administrative branch must flexibly employ all available techniques for resolving the dispute and innovate with new methods. Laws do not come packaged with sure, automatic enforcement features.

ABUSE OF POLICY POWERS

Although allegations that administrative officials disregard legislative intent have long been made, they have become much more frequent in recent years. The complaint is that if the bureaucrats do not agree with a policy statement in the law, they simply pay no attention to it; further, if they find a statute too restrictive, they simple issue administrative regulations that permit them to proceed at will. Charges of this kind were heard by the Ervin Subcommittee; the entire problem is discussed in detail in Chapters 20 and 21. Suffice it to say here that the question in the minds of some people is not whether administrative officials have policy

[26] *New York Times,* February 23, 1968.

powers, but whether they have far too much, to the point where they even ignore the legislature.

ADMINISTRATION AND POLITICS

It follows from the above discussion that there is no separation between administration and politics. As Wallace S. Sayre states, "The exercise of discretionary power, the making of value choices, is a characteristic and increasing function of administrators and bureaucrats; they are thus importantly engaged in politics."[27] Any participation in the formulation of public policies means, *ipso facto*, involvement in politics; it is a political act when an administrator recommends legislation and when he makes policy decisions in carrying out a law. Furthermore, since politics is "the process by which power and influence are acquired and exercised,"[28] public officials move in this environment, because, for one thing, they seek power and influence with legislators and pressure groups, in support of the programs they administer.

Social scientists do not limit the use of the term *politics* to political-party activity or even to governmental affairs. Policy-making and power struggles take place in many areas of human activity. A *political* approach—which, in everyday usage, means being shrewd and engaging in "horsetrading"—can take place in any kind of organization. Under merit systems (see Chapter 12), *partisan politics* cannot dictate the filling of positions; only in this sense is administration separate from politics.

A single example from the current scene will show administrators are squarely in politics. Title 2 of the Economic Opportunity Act of 1964, as originally passed, defined a community action program as one "developed, conducted, and administered with the maximum feasible participation of residents of the areas and members of the groups served." This language is vague, and when mayors in cities such as Chicago, Los Angeles, and Syracuse appointed local community action boards, the poor people protested that they were not adequately represented. This put Sargent Shriver, Director of the Office of Economic Opportunity, in the middle, between the pressures of the local city halls and of the militant poor. One newspaper correspondent wrote, "Mr. Shriver amiably says he is no politician. But in his spot . . . it would seem he can't be anything else."[29] On several occasions Shriver withheld federal funds until the mayors included poor people on the local boards; on others, he urged the poor to cooperate with the local political structure. In the process he made far more significant political decisions than many an elective official.

[27] Wallace S. Sayre, "Premises of Public Administration: Past and Emerging," *Public Administration Review,* XVIII, No. 2 (Spring, 1958), 104.

[28] John M. Pfiffner and Frank P. Sherwood, *Administrative Organization,* Englewood Cliffs, N.J.: Prentice-Hall, 1960, p. 311.

[29] Joseph A. Loftus, "The Poor Are Going into Politics," *New York Times,* December 12, 1965.

PRIVATE AND PUBLIC ADMINISTRATION

Any definition of public administration must deal with the question of how it is similar to or different from private administration. The similarities are great, for administration as a process is by no means limited to the public sector. Factories, hospitals, labor unions, charitable agencies, churches—in all these and every other kind of human organization, the key to successful operations is the effective utilization of human and physical resources. This is the work of administration or, as it is also frequently called, management. Another way of expressing this is that administration is cooperative group effort, in a public or private setting. While the common factor is the element of cooperation, the purposes or goals of human organizations naturally vary, as is evident from the preceding examples. Furthermore, the problems of all public organizations are not the same, just as the problems of private ones vary from company to company. Each organization, public or private, must meet the challenges of its particular environment. The risk element, for example, in a private atomic-energy plant is at present greater than that in a telephone company. The military regiments the individual soldier in ways that would be considered intolerable in civilian public agencies. The exact form of administration varies, depending upon the kind of undertaking.

From the standpoint of organization planning, Harvey Sherman, Director of the Organization and Procedures Department of the New York Port Authority, in his excellent book argues that the difference between public and private entities has been greatly exaggerated. Far more meaningful to him are "the specific differences in objectives among or between different enterprises, whether they be government agencies, private companies, or a mixture of both."[30] Yet he notes that "the organization of many government agencies is set by legislation and is not subject to major changes by the agency head,"[31] which creates undesirable rigidity.

Because the legislature and the general public are directly concerned, no public organization can ever be exactly the same as a private one. The peculiar element in public administration is that everything a government agency does is the public's business. Tax money is being used, so every citizen has the right to know how it is spent and to criticize public officials with whose decisions they do not agree. As has often been said, the public official operates in a "goldfish bowl"; he is subject to searching and

[30] Harvey Sherman, *It All Depends: A Pragmatic Approach to Organization*, University, Ala.: University of Alabama Press, 1966, p. 23.

[31] *Ibid.*, p. 30.

constant outside scrutiny. In fact, it is a cardinal principle of democratic government that civil servants be guided by public opinion. Although the officials of a private company also have important public contacts, they are not operating in a "goldfish bowl." Companies want satisfied clients, and they are also increasingly subject to government regulation, all of which makes *public relations* an important element in business success. Nevertheless, companies still remain private in character, and their internal operations are relatively their own business and not that of the general public.

James Forrestal once said that "the difficulty of government work is that it not only has to be well done, but the public has to be convinced that it is being well done. In other words, there is a necessity both for competence and exposition, and I hold it is extremely difficult to combine the two in the same person."[32] This is why some businessmen fail in government positions. Impatient over the need to justify their decisions to the public, and accustomed in their companies to giving orders that quickly produce action, they complain that in the government they are thwarted by red tape. Yet it is the public that insists on this paperwork because it is their money that is being spent. Civil service, conflict of interest, and numerous other laws and regulations must be observed. This is what creates the red tape so exasperating to the typical businessman. Some of the red tape may safely be eliminated, but a sizeable residue will always be necessary to protect the public interest.

It is sometimes bluntly stated that a public official needs a thick skin. Criticism of government workers has been so intense from time to time that Senator Jacob Javits of New York has suggested creation of a new Congressional committee to function as a kind of public defender for maligned federal employees.[33] Along with other members of the Senate Subcommittee on National Policy Machinery, he had listened to numerous witnesses testify that the government was handicapped in its efforts to recruit scientific and other valuable personnel because of the savage attacks on public employees. Such concern by a legislator for the feelings of administrative officials is rare, so it is not surprising that such a "public-defender" committee has not been established.

Government is also different because no private company can equal it in size and diversity of activities. Federal employment is now close to three million; no one firm, including even the giants such as General Motors and the American Telephone and Telegraph Company, employs anywhere near this figure.

[32] Quoted in John J. Corson, "Distinguishing Characteristics of Public Administration," *Public Administration Review*, XII, No. 2 (Spring, 1952), 124.

[33] Senate Subcommittee on National Policy Machinery, *Mobilizing Talent for Government Service*, 86th Congress, 2nd session, Washington, D.C.: Government Printing Office, 1960, pp. 422–423.

Even more important is the great scope of governmental activities, affecting the entire economic and social structure of society. Furthermore, the comparison need not be made with the federal government alone. State and municipal governments have also greatly expanded their activities. These range from much bigger educational systems and multimillion dollar superhighways to air- and water-pollution programs, urban redevelopment, manpower training and retraining, educational television, airports, heliports, picnic areas, public housing, and many other programs. The billion-dollar mark in some state, county, and municipal budgets was passed some time ago. At the same time, for reasons discussed in the next chapter, the outlook for the future is for a continued increase in the load on government at all levels. The variety of skills required in public employment in state and local governments is usually much wider than that found in private business, except for a few multipurpose corporations such as General Electric.

THE PUBLIC–PRIVATE PARTNERSHIP

Whenever comparisons are made between public and private administration, the impression may be given that each is opposed to the other and occupies a separate, distinct field. Actually, much of what takes place in public administration is accomplished with the collaboration of numerous private groups and individuals; indeed, in recent years the line between "private" and "public" has become so blurred that doubt is even raised that it is possible to "tell where government leaves off and private business begins."[34]

Government-by-contract

One important reason for the difficulty in separating government and private business is the great use made by the federal government of private contractors. These contractors spend billions of tax dollars and employ millions of workers who, while technically not government employees, are really part of its work force. In one recent year, each of five private corporations, as contractors, spent more than $1 billion in federal tax funds, a sum greater than that expended by any one of five of the cabinet-level departments. In that same year, the 100 private corporations with the largest net value of prime military contracts spent more of the government's funds than all executive-branch civil agencies, excluding interest on the national debt. Furthermore, "in carrying out these programs, the Government in a number of cases has contracted

[34] Sherman, *op. cit.*, p. 25.

with private corporations for the planning, research, and technical direction of entire systems. It has even created several corporations, such as the Rand Corporation—supported largely by Federal funds—that are carrying on functions similar, if not identical, to programs carried on directly by Government agencies in other instances."[35]

Most of these contracts are let by the Defense Department, explaining the concern about the "military-industrial complex." However, as Erwin D. Canham, the editor of the *Christian Science Monitor*, points out, if the huge defense expenditures were no longer necessary, "some sort of government-industrial complex would continue." He believes that the "United States has moved into a form of crypto-socialism in which a great deal of industry is working for government . . . ," and that "Even when we get around to cleaning up the cities, if we want it well done we might consider contracting out the job to the great systems-management corporations which are able to swing such tasks efficiently."[36]

Currently public and private agencies are joined together in close, cooperative relationships required for effective attack on difficult social problems. Again, the war against poverty is an excellent example: In many cases, community-action programs are run by private nonprofit agencies such as church organizations, through contract arrangements with the Office of Economic Opportunity.[37] Federal, state, and local governments are anxious for businessmen to make investments in the slum neighborhoods and to train and employ the "hard-core" unemployed. Such large infusions of capital and so massive an effort are required, that large-scale cooperation with business and other private groups is essential.

All over the country, new arrangements between government and local groups are being fashioned; for example, a National Alliance of Businessmen has been formed to help make a success of the Job Opportunities in the Business Sector (JOBS) program, proposed by President Johnson in January, 1968, with the goal of finding jobs for the unemployed in 50 major cities. Evidencing the role of imaginative planning, the Defense Department has initiated a program whereby representatives of private companies, assigned to the military bases, give vocational training courses to Negro servicemen awaiting discharge. The objective is to provide these men, who came to the service from the ghettoes, with the skills that will enable them to find jobs in nonslum areas. The network of community organizations is expanding; in such cities as Chicago there is a multiplicity of private neigh-

[35] "The Role of the General Accounting Office in Business-Government Relationships," address by Elmer B. Staats, Comptroller General of the United States, at Ceremonies Marking Dean's Day, New York University, New York, N.Y., December 2, 1967.

[36] Erwin D. Canham, "It's Taxpayers' Money," editorial page, *Christian Science Monitor*, March 4, 1968.

[37] See *Catalog of Federal Assistance Programs*, Office of Economic Opportunity, Executive Office of the President, Washington, D.C.: 1967.

borhood groups with paid staffs that urge local governments to improve public services, and themselves take the initiative in getting programs of different kinds started. Without this "grass-roots" support, it would be much more difficult for public officials to deal with many pressing problems. All these, however, are only more recent examples of the public–private partnership; it has long existed in functions such as health protection, recreation, education, and many others.[38]

DEFINITION OF PUBLIC ADMINISTRATION

We have traveled a long way in the search for a satisfactory definition of public administration, but why we had to do so can now readily be appreciated. No condensed definition can encompass all of the preceding points. They can, however, be presented in the form of a brief summary that will constitute the definition.

Public administration:

1. is cooperative group effort in a public setting
2. covers all three branches—executive, legislative, and judicial —and their interrelationships
3. has an important role in the formulation of public policy and is thus a part of the political process
4. is different in significant ways from private administration
5. is closely associated with numerous private groups and individuals in providing services to the community

THE STUDY OF PUBLIC ADMINISTRATION

In closing this chapter, an explanation will be given of the statement made earlier that public administration as a field of study is substantially different today from what it was at its inception. This difference involves not only the offerings at academic institutions but also the subjects dealt with in the literature of the field and discussed at meetings of the professional societies.

The early period

The study of administration is as old as history, but in its modern phase it begins in the late nineteenth century and the beginning of the twentieth. The change from a predominantly rural to a complicated urban civilization, the rapid developments in physical technology, and the consequent need for more orderly processes in both the private and public sectors were all factors in

[38] See Morton Grodzins, *Trends in American Living and Outdoor Recreation*, The Outdoor Recreation Resources Review Commission, Study Report 22, Washington, D.C.: Government Printing Office, 1962.

the emergence of administration "as a self-conscious study."[39]

The mental climate in America came to emphasize efficiency and the "scientific" approach, symbolized in the scientific management movement. This movement was pioneered by Frederick W. Taylor, who believed that in any undertaking scientific analysis would lead to discovery of the "one best way" of carrying out each operation.[40] Originally applied to shops in private establishments at the turn of the century, the Taylor techniques were later, from about 1910 on, introduced in government. New philosophical approaches took hold that gave impetus and a more realistic character to political and administrative reform; pragmatism emphasized the study of government as it actually worked and led to thorough analyses of the facts of political life and public administration. Summarizing these developments, Waldo writes, "The rise of public administration . . . is an attempt to make government work under the new and more demanding conditions, by increasing the amount of systematic study of the problems of government and the competence and training of those entering government service."[41]

In the universities, political science developed "as a separate and substantial area of academic research and teaching,"[42] and it was in the political science departments that the first courses in public administration were taught. These courses, and the first textbooks,[43] described the structure of administrative organization in government, and placed a great deal of emphasis on management services such as personnel and financial administration. Some attention was given to intergovernmental relations, regulatory functions, the role of the chief executive, relationships of administrative agencies with legislators and the general public, and the nature of the programs carried out by the executive branch. The stress on the administrative housekeeping functions responded not only to the need at that time to strengthen them in government, but also to pave the way for careers in the public service for college students with general backgrounds. Administrative policymaking was given little attention; indeed, it generally was left out as part of the separate field of politics. Problems of organization were treated within the scientific management mold, and attempts were made to formulate "principles" as to the best way of structuring and managing administrative agencies.

In retrospect, the contribution of this early period was to focus attention on the administrative function as such and on improving organization, procedures, and the quality of public service personnel. The successes were many, because public administration did achieve recognition as a new field, and the

[39] Waldo, op. cit., p. 19.

[40] Frederick W. Taylor, The Principles of Scientific Management, New York: Norton, 1967 (originally published in 1911).

[41] Waldo, op. cit., p. 19.

[42] Ibid.

[43] Leonard D. White, Introduction to the Study of Public Administration, New York: Macmillan, 1926, and F. W. Willoughby, Principles of Public Administration, Washington, D.C.,: Brookings Institution, 1927.

public service was improved. Graduates of public administration programs were among the large numbers of college-trained people entering the federal service and state and local governments during the New Deal period. In 1939 the American Society for Public Administration was established; its purpose is to "advance the science, processes, and art of public administration," and its membership includes public employees from all levels of government, teachers, researchers, consultants, civic leaders, and others united in this objective.

The period since World War II

After World War II the whole concept of public administration expanded. The administration-policy split was rejected, thus opening a large new area for study: administrative policymaking. The value judgments of administrators, goal conflicts, power struggles, and the relationships with pressure groups and legislators became essential elements to administrative study.[44] New dimensions were added to administration as a process, in particular the analysis of decisionmaking and communications. The preoccupation with organization charts and formal lines of authority was replaced by a much broader focus, namely the consideration of organizations as social systems in which the workers interact in many different ways, frequently at variance with the directives and conceptions of those in official charge.

So many questions were raised about the "principles" approach to administration that the word itself came into disrepute.[45] Although the best of the management experts had been careful to condition the application of the "principles" to the special facts of each case, some had confidently defined certain "universals" of administration. Generally, these universals were presented as discovered through personal experiences, or as desirable models to follow in any case. They were not based on empirical research, and they rested on premises of organizational logic rather than on documented facts of human behavior in organizations. The repudiation of the "principles" approach did not, however, signify the abandonment of the search for a true administrative science. This quest was resumed on a new basis: behavioral research testing various hypotheses in different kinds of organizations.[46] As yet, there is no agreement upon such an administrative science, but the new approach is generally regarded as much sounder than the previous one.

As the examination of the human factor became a principal concern, public administration dropped its original stance of

[44] Such aspects are illustrated very well in Frederick C. Mosher (ed.), *Governmental Reorganizations: Cases and Commentary, op. cit.*

[45] See Herbert A. Simon, *Administrative Behavior: A Study of Decision-Making Processes in Administrative Organization,* New York: Free Press (second edition), 1957, pp. 20–44.

[46] See Robert Presthus, *Behavioral Approaches to Public Administration,* University, Ala.: University of Alabama Press, 1965, pp. 17–40.

separateness, to the point where it now applies the knowledges and insights of the social sciences, particularly sociology, social psychology, psychology, and anthropology. References to findings in these fields are now commonplace, both in the theoretical works and in discussions of "practical" problems in administration. A recommended list of materials for any good public administration library, prepared by one of the best-known graduate schools of public administration, includes titles in these and many other fields.[47]

As Figure 1 shows, both the scholars and the practitioners are primarily concerned with the substantive programs of government, not the "tool" subjects like personnel and finance. It is not that the latter are no longer considered important; indeed, they are viewed more broadly, reflect the human relations emphasis, and take into account important new developments. In 1967 the National Academy of Public Administration, which functions in association with the American Society for Public Administration, was established. Its purpose is to "bring administrators and scholars together in a two-way exchange of ideas . . . to foster both research and education in public administration, to serve as an effective agent for the intellectual interests and energies of the profession (scholars, administrators, and men of stature in public affairs), and to be a trustworthy source of advice on problems of public administration."[48] It will accomplish its work through staff studies, committees, panels, seminars, study groups, and other suitable procedures, and will concentrate on "public problems" rather than "demonstrating abstract truths."[49] Indicative of the subject areas in which it will deal are the following:

1. delegation of authority (to private contractors and to state and local governments)
2. intergovernmental administrative relationships
3. administration of overseas programs
4. university programs in public administration
5. development of programs of training and research in public administration in foreign countries
6. control and integration of the activities of different professional groups (engineers, chemists, medical doctors, and many others)
7. the personal equation in administrative leadership and the management function
8. the governmental employer and the unionized employee
9. interface with business administration and business operations
10. state administration in transition
11. urban innovation

[47] David Mars and H. George Frederickson (compilers), *Suggested Library in Public Administration: With 1964 Supplement,* Los Angeles Public Administration Center, School of Public Administration, University of Southern California, June 1, 1964.

[48] The National Academy of Public Administration, Interests and Program, February, 1968, p. 2.

[49] *Ibid.*

*Fig. 1. The 1968 National Conference
on Public Administration**

Topic	Panel Sessions
I. Administration and Regionalism: Interstate and Intrastate	1.1 Intergovernmental Relationships in the United States: A Quarter Century of Evolution 1.2 Regionalism: An Approach to Development Planning 1.3 Interstate SMSA: Response to Regional Problems 1.4 The Regional Council of Governments in Metro-Urban Politics 1.5 Water Resources Management: The Inter-Governmental Decision-Making Process 1.6 Urban Highways: The Impact of State Decision-Making on Local Government
II. Administration: Inner-City and Inter-Urban Problems	2.1 Other Governments: What is Their Contribution toward Solving Urban Ills? 2.2 The Urban Complex: What are the Alternatives for its Management? 2.3 Urban Administration and the Urban Crisis (Panel of Mayors) 2.4 Specialized Problems: Challenges to Intergovernmental Machinery 2.5 Organizational Response to the Federal Metropolitan Review Requirement 2.6 The Citizen and His Concerns: Are Urban Administrators Effective Communicators?
III. Administration and Innovation: Technical, Social, Political	3.1 The Ombudsman: Appraisal of a Political-Administrative Solution 3.2 Administering State Constitutional Revision 3.3 Challenges to Education for Public Administration 3.4 Innovation in County Government 3.5 Innovative Uses of Private Institutions in the Uses of Public Policy
IV. Administration and the Assault on Poverty	4.1 Administrative Responses to the Conduct of the War on Poverty at the Local Level 4.2 The OEO [Office of Economic Opportunity] and Interagency Coordination at the Federal Level: A Top and Bottom View 4.3 The Poverty Program and the States: Organization and Role Responses

Fig. 1. (continued)

Topic	Panel Sessions
V. Administration: The Concept of Social Service	5.1 The Model Cities Program: Weaving the Strands Together 5.2 Labor Relations in the Public Service 5.3 The Older Americans Act of 1965: New Administrative Patterns for Positive Social Goals 5.4 Administration of New Systems of Neighborhood Services 5.5 Medicare/Medicaid: Penetrating Administrative Thickets
VI. Administration and a Changing World Environment	6.1 Comparative Metropolitan Government 6.2 International Civil Servants and International Loyalty 6.3 Administration and Innovation in Europe 6.4 Education for Administration: The Clerk Mentality in Post-Colonial Society 6.5 Developmental Models for Public Administration in Latin America 6.6 The Administration of the Treaty for East African Cooperation
VII. Administration: New Concepts in Management	7.1 Scientific Management—1970 7.2 Intergovernmental Approaches for Information Systems Development 7.3 Program Focus: A New Problem for O & M [Organization and Management] 7.4 Planning-Programming-Budgeting Systems 7.5 Participative Management in Public Service 7.6 Planning-Programming-Budgeting Systems and Decisionmaking
VIII. Administration: The Education Complex	8.1 Coordination of Public Higher Education Planning and Development 8.2 University Presidency, 1968: The President's Job 8.3 Education for Academic Administration 8.4 A Fresh Look at the Bureau Movement: Prospects for Developing an Urbanized Philosophy for the Years Ahead

* Program of The American Society for Public Administration, Boston: March 27–30, 1968.

Like the 1968 program of the American Society for Public Administration, this listing of topics naturally emphasizes areas currently deemed of particular importance; neither is intended to give a complete picture of administrative study. A reading of both lists, however, should make more concrete the scope of public administration today.

BIBLIOGRAPHY

Boyer, William W., *Bureaucracy On Trial: Policy-Making by Government Agencies*, Indianapolis, Ind.: Bobbs-Merrill, 1964.

Butler, Warren H., "Administering Congress: The Role of Staff," *Public Administration Review*, XXVI, No. 1 (March, 1966).

Dahl, Robert A., and Lindblom, Charles E., *Politics, Economics and Welfare*, New York: Harper & Row, 1953.

Gaus, John M., White, Leonard D., and Dimock, Marshall E., *The Frontiers of Public Administration*, Chicago: University of Chicago Press, 1936.

Gaus, John M., *Reflections on Public Administration*, University, Ala.: University of Alabama Press, 1947.

Gittell, Marilyn, "Professionalism and Public Participation in Educational Policy-Making: New York City, A Case Study," *Public Administration Review*, XXVII, No. 3 (September, 1967).

Goldstein, Herman, "Police Discretion: The Ideal Versus the Real," *Public Administration Review*, XXIII, No. 3 (September, 1963).

"Higher Education for Public Service," a symposium, *Public Administration Review*, XXVII, No. 4 (November, 1967).

Jacobs, Clyde E., and Gallagher, John F., *The Selective Service Act: A Case Study of the Governmental Process*, New York: Dodd, Mead, 1967.

Krislov, Samuel, and Musolf, Lloyd D., (eds.), *The Politics of Regulation: A Reader*, Boston: Houghton Mifflin, 1964.

Mosher, Frederick C., (ed.), *Governmental Reorganizations: Cases and Commentary*, Indianapolis, Ind.: Bobbs-Merrill, 1967.

Nelson, William R., (ed.), *The Politics of Science: Readings in Science, Technology, and Government*, New York: Oxford University Press, 1968.

Presthus, Robert, *Behavioral Approaches to Public Administration*, University, Ala.: University of Alabama Press, 1965.

Redford, Emmette S., *Ideal and Practice in Public Administration*, University, Ala.: University of Alabama Press, 1958.

Rourke, Francis E., *Bureaucratic Power in National Politics*, Boston: Little, Brown, 1965.

Sayre, Wallace S., "Premises of Public Administration: Past and Emerging," *Public Administration Review, XVIII*, No. 2 (Spring, 1958).

Sayre, Wallace S., "Trends of a Decade in Administrative Values," *Public Administration Review, XI*, No. 1 (Winter, 1951).

"Science and Public Policy: A Symposium," *Public Administration Review, XXVII*, No. 2 (June, 1967).

Separation of Powers, Hearings Before the Senate Subcommittee on Separation of Powers, 90th Congress, 1st Session, Washington, D.C.: Government Printing Office, 1967.

Simon, Herbert A., *Administrative Behavior: A Study of Decision-Making Processes in Administrative Organization*, New York: Free Press (second edition), 1957.

Stein, Harold, (ed.), *Public Administration and Policy Development, A Casebook*, New York: Harcourt, Brace & World, 1952.

Tullock, Gordon, *The Politics of Bureaucracy*, Washington, D.C.: Public Affairs Press, 1965.

Waldo, Dwight, *The Administrative State*, New York: Ronald, 1948.

Waldo, Dwight, "The Administrative State Revisited," *Public Administration Review, XXV*, No. 1 (March, 1965).

Waldo, Dwight, *Perspectives on Administration*, University, Ala.: University of Alabama Press, 1956.

Waldo, Dwight, *The Study of Public Administration* (Doubleday Short Studies in Political Science), New York: Doubleday, 1955.

Woll, Peter, *American Bureaucracy*, New York: Norton, 1963.

Woll, Peter, (ed.), *Public Administration and Policy*, New York: Harper & Row, 1966.

CHAPTER 2
ENVIRONMENT
OF PUBLIC
ADMINISTRATION
IN THE UNITED
STATES

A SPECIFIC INDICATION was given in the preceding chapter of the kinds of problems with which public administration is concerned today. As changes take place in the physical and human environment, efforts must be made to reorient government programs accordingly. There is always some lag in the governmental response to new conditions, but a comparison of the programs, actual and proposed, most widely discussed at the end of the 1960s, with those given high priority at the beginning of the decade, will show some very clear new emphases. Domestically, the "problems of the cities" now command the greatest attention, as they should. As certain problems in the environment become more acute, many more people become concerned and demand immediate action: air and water pollution are good examples. What are the outstanding characteristics of American society today, and how do they affect public administration? No exhaustive treatment will be attempted, but several of the most important factors will be discussed in detail.

POPULATION CHANGES

Although the national birth rate declined recently to an all-time low, the "population explosion" was expected to continue because of a substantial increase in the number of women of childbearing age.[1] On November 20, 1967, the United States Census Bureau announced that the population had reached 200 million. The Bureau's 1960 census had shown 179,323,175, although, interestingly, it later reported that it apparently had failed to count about 5.7 million Americans, including some 2.1 million nonwhites. Significantly, the "undercount" occurred primarily in urban slum areas; one of every six Negro males between the ages of 20 and 39 was missed. In late 1967 the Bureau estimated that the 300 million mark would not be reached until 1990 at the earliest. Yet it took until 1915 for the population to become 100 million, and until 1950 for it to rise to 150 million.

Changes in composition

Not only has the population grown greatly, but its composition has also changed. The proportion of aged persons is much larger than previously, and this trend continues. By November, 1967, there were 19 million people over 65 years of age—close to 10 percent of the entire population. At the same time, there has been a sizeable increase in the number of young persons—106 million, well over half the population, were under age 25. About 85 million of the 200 million Americans were born after July 1, 1945.[2] In the case of those from 20 to 24, the anticipated increase from 1966 to 1975 is 37 percent; for those from 25 to 29 it is 50 percent. It is much less—27 percent—for those from 30 to 34 because of the low birth rates of the Depression years. In 1970, persons from ages 40 to 44 were expected to be "relatively scarce," and, in 1980, those from 50 to 54 were expected to be "scarce."[3]

As to the nonwhites, while their proportion of the total population has been increasing since 1950, it is now about the same as it was in 1900—12 percent. From 1960 to 1966 the number of nonwhites increased 14.2 percent, as compared with 8.6 percent for the whites. During the first part of the century, the higher fertility rate of Negro women had been offset by the higher death rate for Negroes as a whole, and by the large-scale immigration of whites to this country. With advances in medicine,

[1] *200 Million Americans*, U.S. Department of Commerce, Bureau of the Census, Washington, D.C.: Government Printing Office, November, 1967, pp. 13, 16.

[2] *Ibid.*, p. 7.

[3] *Ibid.*, p. 8.

the Negro death rate declined, and after 1920 restricted immigration policies cut off the flow of immigrants. Thus it was expected that by 1972 one in every eight Americans would be a Negro.[4]

Changes in geographic distribution

The "urbanization" of the population continues: two of every three Americans now live in a metropolitan area, and "perhaps even three out of four of us will be living in or around the cities in just another ten years."[5] Many of the central cities in these metropolitan areas are continuing to lose population; the "suburbs are growing five times as fast as the central cities and over twice as fast as the country as a whole."[6] In the first six years of the 1960s, the Negro population in the central cities increased by more than two million, while that of the whites decreased by one million. Almost all the Negro population growth is taking place in the metropolitan areas, mostly within the central cities. The proportion of Negroes in all the central cities rose from 12 percent in 1950 to 20 percent in 1966; elsewhere in the metropolitan areas, the proportion of whites had increased to 96 percent by 1966.[7] Unless present trends are reversed, by the end of the century the cities may be almost all black and the suburbs all white.

The farm population continues its precipitous decline. In early 1968 about 5.5 percent of the population lived on the farms, compared with 8.7 percent in 1960. Only slightly more than one in every 20 persons now lives on the farms, compared with one in three as late as 1910. Mechanization of the farms largely explains the mass migration of the Negroes from the South to other parts of the country, and, in the South, from rural areas to the cities. Even in the South, more than three of every five Negroes live in urban areas. Seventy-three percent of the country's Negroes now reside in the cities. Whether black or white, the young people continue to leave the farm and the countryside in large numbers because of a lack of jobs. Evidence of the Indians' abject condition is that in 1960 three-fourths of them lived in rural locations.[8]

Finally, the westward movement of the population continues, but on a somewhat decreased scale. While the percentage increase in such states as California is declining, in round numbers it is still very substantial because of the very large population base. The Western states, and other "sunny" parts of the country

[4] Report of the National Advisory Commission on Civil Disorders, New York: Bantam, 1968, pp. 237–238.

[5] 200 Million Americans, op. cit., p. 25.

[6] Ibid.

[7] Report of the National Advisory Commission on Civil Disorders, op. cit., p. 243.

[8] Federal Times, January 24, 1968.

such as Florida, are becoming congested, the jobs are not quite so numerous, and the attractions not as great as during the great migrations into these areas after World War II and in the 1950s.

Family incomes

The popular demand for and the support of public services is obviously related to income levels. The United States is acquiring wealth much faster than it is adding people: for example, in 1966 the output of goods and services increased 5.8 percent, compared with a population rise of 1.15 percent. The average family income in 1966 was almost $7500, about 2.5 times the 1947 figure of slightly over $3000. Allowing for price inflation, the increase in family purchasing power still was nearly 70 percent. Yet while those in the lower income brackets are earning more, their proportionate share of the aggregate income has remained about the same; in the early World War II years, it had increased. Those in the lowest 20 percent are still getting only 5 percent of the total income, the same as 20 years ago.[9]

Impact on public administration

Several years ago, thinking Americans were concerned about the rapid population increase in the underdeveloped countries. They still are, but the recent evidences of congestion, poverty in the midst of affluence, and intense pressure on public services have convinced them that the population is also growing too fast in the United States. Until very recently, population control was generally considered taboo for government. Currently, however, help in family planning is offered under such programs as the war against poverty and public assistance. The Department of Health, Education, and Welfare now has a Deputy Assistant Secretary for Population and Family Planning.[10] Apart from the problems of the poor, concern is felt that no matter how fast the gross national product grows, the "quality of life" will deteriorate unless the rate of population increase slows down.

Joseph C. Harsch believes that the "second industrial revolution" has made 30 million persons "unneeded"; these are the "poor people," displaced from the farms by machines, who have sought haven in the cities but too often found continued misery. Harsch writes: "The United States will have vast social problems at home until it finds ways and means of balancing the number of people in the country against the need for people. As of today, population is more out of balance in the United States than in

[9] *200 Million Americans, op. cit.,* pp. 59–60.

[10] Wilbur J. Cohen, Secretary of Health, Education, and Welfare, "Health Care for the Nation's Children," a talk at the Yeshiva College of Medicine Special Continuing Education Symposium, April 7, 1968, New York.

any other modern Western country. In this department, the United States equates with Asian countries, not with European."[11] One suggested solution is to reverse the flow of population back to the rural areas through imaginative programs to build non-metropolitan regions, but it would take some time for such efforts to be successful. Meanwhile, the central cities remain congested, and the Bureau of the Census confirms that there are 30 million persons in the urban and rural slums living in a state of poverty. (The "poverty level," as defined by the Social Security Administration, is currently $3335 for an urban family of four.)

The mass migration of former rural dwellers into the cities increases the load on the municipal government at the same time that its tax base is reduced with the out-migration of white families that are more prosperous. Up to now, the efforts to persuade the whites to remain in the core city areas have usually failed. When the tensions of the ghettoes are added to those of air pollution, traffic congestion, a shrinking tax base, and obsolescent governmental structure, it can readily be seen why the "problems of the cities" are so serious, although no one who has been in them needs to be convinced of this. Nor is all peace and quiet in the suburbs, for frequently, far from being "exclusive" sections, they are untidy, hastily laid-out settlements. The Bureau of the Census puts it aptly:

> In the first place, the suburbs have to run as if on a treadmill to try to keep up with their growth, and never quite manage it. There are never enough streets—or sewers—or schools—or firemen—or policemen—or even water to fill promptly all the needs and demands of the movers-in . . . what once were "wide open, low tax, no smog" areas sometimes wind up to be just exactly the opposite.[12]

Despite the slowing down of the "westward migration," in mid-1966 the Population Reference Bureau, a private non-profit educational organization, predicted a possible 1.5 billion people in California within 100 years, creating the prospect of "intolerable and impossible congestion." The "immediate threat" was pollution of air, water, and land. Air pollution is so severe as to cause chronic eye irritation in the heavily urbanized areas, and substantial crop losses in the agricultural zones.[13]

Apart from the problems of the poor and the movements of the people, the sheer increase in the total population places heavy burdens on all levels of government. Since domestic civilian services such as education, police and fire protection, and health inspections are still paid for primarily by state and local govern-

[11] Joseph C. Harsch, "Too Many People," editorial page, *Christian Science Monitor*, March 5, 1968.

[12] *200 Million Americans, op. cit.*, pp. 32–33.

[13] *Los Angeles Times*, June 19, 1966.

ments, the pressures on them have been very great. From 1955 to 1965, state and local government expenditures increased more than twice as fast as general federal expenditures, and state and local government employment rose by 58 percent, compared with a 9 percent increase in federal employment. The employment requirements of state and local governments were expected to increase nearly 50 percent between 1965 and 1975, and requirements for professional, administrative, and technical (PAT) positions alone to rise two-fifths. In 1965, state and local governments employed 3.8 million in the PAT occupations; the predicted requirement for 1975 was 5.4 million. The task of recruiting 1.6 million new workers over this period, besides replacing the 1.3 million expected to leave these jobs for one reason or another, evidences the great challenges presently confronting public administration.

There will be decreases in the recruitment of additional teachers, compared with the early 1960s, but the total demand for them will continue to rise because of growing student enrollments and reductions in pupil-teacher ratios. The greatest need will be for college teachers; employment requirements for them were expected to increase from more than 120,000 in 1965 to about 210,000 in 1975. Total state and local employment was 7.7 million in 1965; the forecast for 1975 was 11.4 million.

Apart from teachers, the demand for persons trained in the life sciences, engineering, physical science, technician occupations (such as draftsmen), and in the social sciences was expected to increase greatly, corresponding to the expansion of government programs requiring their skills. Biological and other life scientists will be needed for governmental research in medicine, agriculture, and forestry. Engineers and physical scientists will be needed for air and water pollution control; natural resource, highway, and urban development; and other construction-related activity. Social scientists will be needed for public welfare and urban research and related programs. Assuming an end to the Vietnam war by 1970, it was predicted that in 1975 federal expenditures would be over $200 billion. Expenditures of state and local governments were expected to be $129 billion, of which part would come from federal funds as all levels of government continued to cooperate in efforts to deal effectively with numerous domestic problems.[14]

Besides increased educational expenditures for the young, there are many other responsibilities that government must assume in respect to young Americans. For example, teen-age

14 *Federal Times*, July 5, 1967.

unemployment, particularly of Negroes, continues to be a serious problem,—the jobless rate for this group is more than triple the nation's overall jobless rate.

With the large numbers of aging and aged, many new, unprecedented programs such as Medicare and Medicaid are now part of "government services," with much thought being given to governmental initiatives that would help make life easier and more pleasant for the older people. Former Secretary of Health, Education, and Welfare John W. Gardner recommended mid-career clinics for those 10 or 15 years away from normal retirement to help prepare them for a useful and stimulating life after retirement. Senator Walter F. Mondale, chairman of a Senate subcommittee investigating psychological problems of retirees, has predicted that the average person will soon be spending from 20 to 25 years in retirement. Needless to say, with the longer vacations, the increased incomes, and the automobile and the jet airplane, the leisure-time activities of all Americans have increased, and governments are hard-pressed to provide the additional park, recreation, and other facilities.

ADVANCES IN PHYSICAL TECHNOLOGY

Inventions, scientific discoveries, and other advances in physical technology constitute a whole complex of factors that have greatly influenced American society.

The automobile age

The automobile is a case in point. As author Harrison Brown notes: "In 1920 automobiles were a luxury—few people could afford them. By 1930, however, the automobile had become a necessity for millions of persons. The new mode of transportation made possible new ways of life. And new patterns of life quickly evolved around the automobile."[15] He comments that the point seems already to have been reached where every person qualified by age to drive wants to have a car at his disposal. Eventually, he believes, there will be one self-propelled vehicle in existence for every person of driving age. In another 40 years, there may be more than 200 million private cars in the United States.

Governments have long provided facilities such as paved highways, and controls such as licensing of motor vehicle operators, in the attempt to maximize the benefits and lessen the dangers of the automobile. Not easy in the 1930s, this task had become infinitely more difficult by the end of the 1960s. The automobile

[15] Harrison Brown, "The Prospective Environment for Policymaking and Administration," in *The Formulation and Administration of United States Foreign Policy*, Senate Foreign Relations Committee, 86th Congress, 2nd Session, Washington, D.C.: Government Printing Office, 1960, p. 145.

has created, or greatly contributed to, the need for new government programs; here, as elsewhere, the federal government is becoming increasingly involved in matters long considered "local."

There are two good examples of the increasing federal involvement. One concerns air pollution caused by automobile emissions. California pioneered with smog-control devices, but when it became clear that national action was necessary, Congress passed authorizing legislation whereby the Department of Health, Education, and Welfare ordered all new cars, beginning with the 1968 models, to be fitted with equipment for reducing carbon monoxide exhausts. The second area of federal involvement concerns highway safety. For many years it had been hoped that it would not be necessary for the federal government to regulate highway safety, but when traffic accidents increased sharply, Congress approved the National Traffic and Motor Vehicle Safety Act of 1966. This Act requires safety standards for motor vehicles and equipment, including tires. The Federal Highway Administration, in the Department of Transportation, issues these standards.

The automobile has made possible the movement to the suburbs and is largely responsible for the great decline in the number of railroad commuters. This decline, together with other factors, has caused many railroad commuter lines to go out of business. People in the cities also prefer to use their cars, rendering local bus service an unprofitable venture and creating a particularly difficult problem for lower income families dependent on public transportation. Here, too, federal action became necessary. In 1961 Congress appropriated funds for exploratory studies of urban transportation problems, and, since 1964, it has been providing funds for loans and grants to the cities for improvement of mass transit facilities, including development of high-speed intercity railroad service, such as between New York and Washington, D.C.

The streets and roads are congested with countless vehicles carrying people to and from work, and the parking problem has become particularly vexatious. Traffic control is a bewildering problem that produces many frustrations for both local officials and private citizens. Leaving the city, the private car takes millions of Americans every year to numerous vacation points within the country. These vacationers support the tourist industry, bolster the economy, and therefore increase government tax yields, but also overload the capacities of parks and other public recreation facilities. The automobile population is so great that governments are hard put to deal with the public nuisance of numerous abandoned cars and unsightly vehicle "graveyards."

The airplane

With most long-distance, inter-city passenger transportation now being provided by the commercial airlines, and with the number of persons traveling by plane constantly increasing, the "Air Age" is also at a new point in its development. The Federal Aviation Agency (FAA), created in August, 1958, in recognition of the importance of air travel and of the need to provide coordinated control of the skyways, is no longer a "new agency." Flights are so numerous that there are long delays while crews and passengers wait in the planes for clearance to take off from extremely busy airports. The air safety record is good, but the possibilities of mid-air collisions are always present, and there is great uncertainty about the adequacy of government programs and spending for meeting the problems of the future.

The sophistication of the Air Age is evidenced in the increased use of helicopters to carry passengers to, from, and between airports. With more persons in the affluent society owning their own planes, there is increasing concern over inadequate government control of such aircraft and their pilots. The airlines, co-operating in the efforts to close the "dollar gap," are reducing fares for visitors from other countries, and preparing to put into service new, huge planes that will carry hundreds of passengers at speeds far exceeding those of the "conventional" jets. Stewardesses are going to court to challenge the legality of company rules requiring them to give up their jobs at age 32. Some people roundly criticize the Congress for spending billions on the development of a supersonic civil airliner when other programs such as the war against poverty are being curtailed. "Airport management" is an indisputably major local government service, as cities and counties endeavor to improve and expand their publicly owned airport buildings and facilities.

The Civil Aeronautics Board (CAB) regulates the commercial aviation industry, acting upon requests for rate increases, changes in service, and mergers, just like the Interstate Commerce Commission (ICC) for the railroads. State Aeronautics Commissions regulate small airlines and private aircraft operating within the particular state. The partial airline strike in the summer of 1966 added to the criticisms of existing federal legislation and programs for dealing with labor disputes in the transportation industry.

Congressional defenders of the manned bomber continue to urge the Defense Department and the President to spend for the development and production of new types of such aircraft. The President and other officials travel thousands of air miles, attending meetings and making appearances impossible before the full-blown development of air transport.

The communications revolution

When in August, 1967, President Johnson sent a message devoted entirely to communications policy, he "looked toward the day when telephone calls would be carried routinely by satellite to every part of the world, when schools in all lands could be connected by television, and when global consultations with voice and pictures could summon specialists in any field anywhere in the world."[16] Much had happened since the launching of the first Telestar; the United States was a member of Intelsat, a multination consortium for developing an international satellite communications system, and Johnson recommended a domestic network that would be compatible with Intelsat. There had been a long debate in Congress on the issue of public as against private ownership before approval in 1962 of legislation creating Comsat (Communications Satellite Corporation) to establish a commercial satellite system in cooperation with other nations via Intelsat. As finally decided in the authorizing legislation, Comsat is privately owned but with some stock sold to the general public.

Comsat and such private companies as the International Telephone and Telegraph Company, the American Telephone and Telegraph Company, and the Radio Corporation of America all had their points of view on what national communications policies should be approved, such as in the use of satellites for educational TV. There was concern about monopolistic control in the communications industry, a problem area for the Federal Communications Commission (FCC) and the Justice Department long before the development of the satellites. In 1967 Congress authorized the establishment of a public corporation to provide aid to noncommercial educational television and radio broadcasting. The decisions of the Corporation for Public Broadcasting, as it is titled, are expected to have a great influence on the future development of educational TV in this country.

Discussion continues over the proper role of the FCC in licensing television and radio stations and in regulating their activities. License renewal is no longer automatic, and the FCC has been criticized for its interpretations of the "equal-time" rules for

[16] Neil Stanford, "U.S. to Scan Policy on Communications," *Christian Science Monitor,* August 16, 1967.

political candidates. Some people urge that Congress repeal the rule outright, but many are much more concerned about the huge bills for TV during political campaigns, a powerful indication of the importance of "money in elections." The availability of quick, dramatic TV news reporting worries some people; they believe, for example, that this might be a contributing cause to the spread of riots.[17] TV advertising for cigarettes, a subject discussed in some detail in Chapter 10, is a controversial issue. In general, communications are more abundant and faster than ever before, but there are many unresolved questions of government policy.

The agricultural revolution

At the beginning of the century, one farm worker could produce enough food for seven people. By 1935 he could feed about 10—and today the figure is almost 40.[18] This indicates the continued rapid pace of the improved farm technologies: Tractors and electric energy have replaced horse and mule power, and improvements are constantly being made in fertilizers, hybrid seeds, and scientific methods of cultivation. Crop yields have increased greatly, far fewer farm workers are needed, and the "small, general-purpose farms that once formed self-sufficient units" are being replaced by the "new family farm, a larger, more specialized enterprise demanding great technical and managerial skill to operate and vastly increased investments to turn a profit."[19]

Although food production has increased much faster than the population growth, reports show that millions of Americans are ill-fed and even starving. Huge farm surpluses are now a thing of the past; under new policies approved by the Congress, the Department of Agriculture is increasing acreage allotments and buying food supplies commercially to meet the needs of underdeveloped countries under the Food for Peace program. With an anticipated world population of four billion by 1975, it is estimated that world food production will have to be increased by about 35 percent to sustain even the admittedly insufficient existing per capita food consumption levels.

The National Food Commission on Food Marketing, authorized by Congress, has recommended strong action to control further concentration in the food-processing industry; by 1966, the cost of processing and marketing food had risen one-third since 1950, absorbing 68 cents of the consumer's dollar and leaving only 32 cents for the farmer. Collective bargaining to enable farmers to obtain better prices from the processors has become

[17] On this, see *Report of the National Advisory Commission on Civil Disorders, op. cit.,* pp. 369–374.
[18] *200 Million Americans, op. cit.,* p. 45.
[19] Donald Janson, "Era of Prosperity Looms for Farmers," *New York Times,* February 14, 1966.

an issue. A National Farm Bargaining Board, with much the same functions as those of the National Labor Relations Board for labor, has been proposed. National, state, and local governments are concerned over the piteous condition of migrant farm laborers and their families. There is great contrast between affluence and abject poverty; former Secretary of Agriculture Orville L. Freeman predicted a "farmer of the future who will operate from an air-conditioned office, drawing on computerized information to plan how many acres to plant," with field work "fully automated and supervised by television scanners on towers."[20]

Automation and the computer revolution

Largely because of automation, white-collar jobs are now substantially more numerous than blue-collar ones; in late 1967 the figures were 33 million and 27 million respectively.[21] With the tight labor market, the fears that automation would cause mass unemployment were dissipated, at least for the time being. Manpower retraining programs, authorized by Congress in 1962 and supplemented with additional ones under the war against poverty, are equipping thousands of workers displaced by machines, and others entering the labor market for the first time, with the skills essential for finding jobs.

In the midst of job abundance for those possessing the qualifications, the education-deprived Negroes constitute a large part of the "hard-core" unemployed. A National Commission on Technology, Automation, and Economic Progress, established by Congress, has recommended 14 years of free public schooling and a commitment to provide every qualified person with a college education, as well as immediate programs to find jobs in government and industry for the unemployed.

Although organized labor did not fight automation as such, it has stressed the need to alleviate the disruptions it causes and to provide new jobs for displaced workers. Adjusting to the changed composition of the work force, labor has launched organizing drives among white-collar workers, making special efforts to recruit new members in government. Conscious of their increased numbers, professional workers in both the public and private sectors have become increasingly militant.

Rapid advances in computer technology have contributed further to the "information revolution." Primarily, computers are being used on paperwork such as issuance of pay checks, preparation of utility bills, storage and retrieval of data about persons on welfare, inventory control, and finance and personnel

20 *Federal Times,* January 24, 1968.
21 *200 Million Americans, op. cit.,* p. 7.

records.[22] The use of magnetic tape makes possible the quick, convenient storage and retrieval of vast "data banks" of information. Interagency and intergovernmental systems for sharing and exchanging data are being developed; for example, "information centrals" are being planned by state governments to meet the needs of all public agencies in the state.[23] Increasingly, external data is being stored (that is, data relating to the environment served by governments, such as information about housing and family conditions of citizens). Computers monitor both the environment and an agency's internal operations, "observing and tabulating reported events and alerting management when some variation from a preestablished norm occurs," such as "a third fire in a single location or a person's repeated application for public assistance in different counties."[24]

"Simulation," re-creating within the computer a "fairly accurate image of what happens in the outside world," is being used to experiment with solutions to such problems as traffic control. "The computer found that cars should not be allowed to enter the Holland Tunnel as quickly as the toll booths could process them"; if they were "held up periodically for a short time, the total flow through the tunnel increased!"[25] In such simulation, the computer's ability to make complicated mathematical calculations with great speed permits the testing of numerous variables, so that "within one week of computer simulation we could acquire the equivalent of five years' experience."[26] Countless possible uses of computers to aid in decisionmaking have been projected, although it is realized that humans will have to make the decisions, and that the quality of the advice given by the computers will depend on how they are programmed by other humans. The end of the 1960s finds the computer revolution really only beginning.

Atomic energy

Atomic energy has had an immediate and direct impact on government. The atomic bomb itself was developed by the War Department, but after the war the principle of civilian control was established with the creation in 1946 of the Atomic Energy Commission (AEC). Within the AEC there is a Military Liaison Committee through which the Commission advises the Defense Department on matters related to the military application of atomic energy. This arrangement seems to have worked out well, and the issue of civil versus military control has faded into the background.

[22] See George Terborgh, *The Automation Hysteria*, New York: Norton, 1966, pp. 28–32, and John C. Kemeny, "The City and the Computer Revolution," in Stephen B. Sweeney and James C. Charlesworth (eds.), *Governing Urban Society: New Scientific Approaches*, Philadelphia: The American Academy of Political and Social Science, 1967.

[23] Edward F. R. Hearle, "The Scope of Management Information Systems in Governmental Administration," in Sweeney and Charlesworth, *op. cit.*, pp. 206–207.

[24] *Ibid.*, p. 204.

[25] C. West Churchman, "The Use of Science in Public Affairs," in Sweeney and Charlesworth, *op. cit.*, pp. 54–55.

[26] *Ibid.*, p. 54.

Substantial progress has been made in developing nuclear energy for domestic purposes, and the prospective development of breeder nuclear reactors has prompted predictions that mankind could be kept on an energy budget 50 times that of today. The breeders produce more nuclear fuel than they consume, and also make it possible to "burn the rocks and the dirt"[27] whereas the first reactors required enriched uranium fuel, extracted from ores at great cost. According to one expert, there is enough uranium and thorium in the granite rocks of the earth to make possible " 'agro-industrial complexes' in the world's ocean-side deserts, where vast nuclear plants would provide cheap electricity, desalt ocean water, and produce hydrogen for fertilizer and the production of heavy chemicals. . . ."[28]

The public is concerned over radiation hazards, and the AEC has, on occasion, been charged with issuing public statements minimizing these dangers. Since it runs the atomic-energy program, some people feel that the AEC finds itself compelled to put out reassuring statements. For this reason it has been recommended that the Public Health Service, as a neutral body, be given complete responsibility for a comprehensive, nationwide program of radiation safety. Since 1959 there has been a Federal Radiation Council that advises federal agencies on the formulation of radiation standards and on the establishment and execution of programs of cooperation with the state governments. Serious as fallout is after the testing of nuclear weapons, it is anticipated that the hazards of radioactive wastes from peacetime atomic energy will be far greater. These wastes are put in underground storage tanks, but this is only a temporary solution because of the huge amounts of radioactive wastes expected to accumulate and the need to isolate them for hundreds of years.[29] State and local governments need to protect citizens from sources of radiation in atomic plants and other places where radioactive materials are stored or handled. Several fires have already broken out in such places, and firemen are being trained in the special methods of fighting such conflagrations.

Missile and space technology

The government is also very much involved in missile and space technology. Responsibility for the military phases rests with the Defense Department—particularly the Air Force—while the National Aeronautics and Space Administration (NASA) is in charge of the civilian space program. So long as international tensions continue, budgets for military missiles and antimissile defense sys-

[27] Evert Clark, "15 Billion People by Year 2000 Forecast," *New York Times*, April 23, 1967.

[28] *Ibid.*

[29] *Possible Nonmilitary Scientific Developments and Their Potential Impact on Foreign Policy Problems of the United States*, Senate Foreign Relations Committee, 86th Congress, 1st Session, Washington, D.C.: Government Printing Office, 1959, p. 20.

tems will continue to be high. Communications satellites and weather satellites are already operational. Expenditures for space exploration run into the billions (although recently reduced somewhat) and constitute a sizeable part of the federal government's budget.

ADVANCES IN SOCIAL INVENTIONS

The American environment has been radically transformed by advances in not only physical but also *social* technology. Man invents not only physical devices but also social ones, and the latter have a great impact on public administration. Pointing out that the atomic bomb was "*as much an achievement on the human side as on the side of physical science*,"[30] Dwight Waldo comments:

> Because we have lived from birth in a society with an advanced technology of cooperation and have learned so much of this technology without awareness, we accept the miracles of human cooperation all about us as though they were natural or indeed inevitable. But they are not. . . . This technology was achieved through incalculable human industry, much systematic thought, and the flashes of inspiration of occasional geniuses.[31]

Government itself is an example of social invention, but we will concentrate instead on the institutions and devices that have grown up in the environment that surrounds it. A list of social inventions could be endless, for it might range from double-entry bookkeeping to international organizations such as the United Nations. Therefore only a few of the most important ones will be mentioned.

The corporation

Let us put the corporation at the top of the list, as did John M. Gaus when he wrote his landmark essay on the "Ecology of Government."[32]

The corporation is, of course, no recent social invention. Max Lerner comments:

> . . . A discerning anthropologist, studying characteristic American inventions, such as the dating pattern, the success system, and judicial review, might seize on the corporation as the most important of all. Reaching into every area of life, it has become the instrument by which Americans organize and project demanding group effort, impersonality, continuity beyond the

[30] Dwight Waldo, *The Study of Public Administration,* New York: Doubleday, 1955, p. 1.

[31] *Ibid.,* p. 2.

[32] John M. Gaus, *Reflections on Public Administration,* University, Ala.: University of Alabama Press, 1947.

individual life, and limited liability. It is striking that a highly individualistic people should accept a transformation of its life wrought by so impersonal a social invention.[33]

Corporations have continued to grow, and the nation is still plagued by the dilemma of how to retain the advantages of large-scale operations and at the same time preserve competition, protect the smaller businessman and the consumer, and avoid regulatory policies that unjustifiably slow up economic expansion. The number of antimonopoly cases brought by the government, some 30 a year, is large enough to make clear that the threat of monopoly is very real. While eliminating the loopholes in the laws has been important, the real problem has always been in the area of administering the law. Before the Federal Trade Commission and the Justice Department can take action that they can reasonably expect to be sustained in the courts, they must collect much detailed information in complicated areas of the economy. The enforcement problem is staggering, and the budgets of the regulatory agencies, no matter how much increased, never seem equal to the task.

The government-industrial complex has already been discussed in Chapter 1. This complex raises such questions as these: Should a larger share of the contracts go to smaller companies? Do the "giants" have too much power? Should both the Defense Department and Congress do something about curbing the influence of these "giants"? If so, what specifically should be done? How can the public be sure that military procurement officers are making fair decisions in awarding these contracts? Is it fair to refuse to give more defense business to efficient producers just because they already are so very large?

Relationships between the government and the big corporations have become so close that doubt is now expressed as to the validity of Lerner's evaluation made in 1957. He wrote: "The American corporation as a power bloc . . . while it may sometimes control and even cow specific officials or agencies of the government, is not in itself the government. Along with the other power institutions, it presents on the American landscape a plurality of power groupings which are the better for their dispersal."[34] In the opinion of Harvard economist John Kenneth Galbraith, some of the big companies are becoming so dependent on government orders and planning that they " 'will eventually become a part of the administrative complex within the state,' " and he predicts that " 'in time the line between the two will disappear.' " He points out that the officers of a " 'firm which does all its business

[33] Max Lerner, *America as a Civilization*, New York: Simon and Schuster, 1957, p. 284.

[34] *Ibid.*, pp. 288–289.

with the United States Government are not more likely in public to speak critically, or even candidly,' of the government agency on which they depend 'than is the head of a Soviet combine of the ministry to which he reports.' "[35] As an editorial writer concludes, "the danger would appear to be that, given the economic ties that bind, the countervailing power of government and business can no longer be counted on to hold each other in check. It is a situation that bears watching."[36]

Labor unions

The union is another social invention now very prominent on the American scene. Previously weak in comparison with corporate power, the unions received a great boost with the passage in 1935 of the Wagner Act, which required employers to bargain collectively with the workers. Union power grew so greatly that in 1947 Congress passed the Taft-Hartley law, which sought to restore the balance and to curb certain labor abuses.

The scandals of the International Teamsters and certain other unions led to the Landrum-Griffin Act of 1959, which introduces government into unprecedented supervision of the internal affairs of the unions. Under this Act, unions must submit reports to the Labor Department on their constitutions, bylaws, officers, loans, investments, and financial status. The government's role, however, goes beyond the mere processing of reports. Under a "bill of rights" provision, union members may complain to the Department if they feel that their privileges to vote, to run for office, and to speak up at meetings have not been respected by union officers; the law also requires periodic election of union officers by secret ballot. The purpose of these requirements is to curb such abuses as rigging of union elections and punishment of members who defy dictatorial or corrupt leaders. This brings the government directly into the management of union activities, just as it has been drawn into the vital role of making decisions affecting the corporations. In general, government today is as much concerned with the unions as a "power cluster" as it is with business.

In recent years the Presidents have faced difficult problems in determining policies and tactics for heading off inflationary wage settlements and avoiding major strikes. The wage-price guideposts were tried and finally abandoned, but the White House, with varying intensity, has continued to apply pressure on labor and management to control wage and price inflation. The emergency strike provisions of the Taft-Hartley law have been invoked on occasion, but there is general dissatisfaction with these procedures

[35] *Christian Science Monitor*, editorial, December 28, 1966.

[36] *Ibid*.

and much difference of opinion as to what to substitute for them.

The rapid growth of the union movement in government poses new problems for chief executives, legislators, and public administrators. With the rank-and-file membership, both in government and industry, freely rejecting contracts negotiated by the union leaders, there is concern over the whole future of the collective bargaining process.

Pressure groups

Both business and labor are examples of pressure groups, the last itself constituting an important social invention. Pressure groups are of many different types—economic, social, professional, and philanthropic. But in every case they join together individuals who have a common interest and who want to influence public policy accordingly. Frequently a tripartite alliance is formed between an administrative agency on the one hand, a pressure group, and sympathetic legislators. If the agency is big and powerful, the interest group equally so, and the legislators in question highly influential, such an alliance can wield tremendous power. The agencies themselves are pressure groups, since in their fight to survive and expand they develop all the power they can with legislators, economic and other groups, and the public.

As stressed in Chapter 1, administrative officials have much discretion in their actions. Thus pressure-group representatives often spend more time with them than with legislators. At the same time, the administrators use these representatives as communication links for determining reaction to both existing and proposed new policies. As a social invention, the pressure group is now highly sophisticated and well organized. Forward-looking policymakers both in the legislative and executive branches face the problem of how to piece together the public interest out of a welter of frequently conflicting private pressures. For the general public, the problem is to be sure that the "regulated" interests do not take over the government agency, a charge that has often been leveled against the regulatory commissions, unfortunately with some substantiation.[37]

37 See Bernard Schwartz, "Crisis in the Commissions," in Samuel Krislov and Lloyd D. Musolf (eds.), *The Politics of Regulation*, Boston: Houghton Mifflin, 1964.

Technical-assistance programs

Turning to international relations, a social invention now much used is *technical assistance*. Throughout history, nations have borrowed from one another, taking advantage of significant discoveries and advances in other lands. Since World War II, numerous bilateral and multilateral programs have been developed for the interchange of skills and knowledge between the peoples of the world. With the impetus of the Point IV program under President Truman, the United States has sent many experts to help the underdeveloped countries, and has also provided training in the United States for thousands of foreign nationals. The Soviet Union and Red China have conducted their own programs in the competition to win the support of the "uncommitted" nations, and many other governments, small as well as large, have entered this field. The developed nations realize that the deep, widening gap between their affluence and the poverty of the underdeveloped world could, as the historian Arnold Toynbee has predicted, lead to a "catastrophic collision."[38] Multilateral technical assistance is a major activity of the United Nations and of the specialized international agencies such as the World Health Organization and the International Labor Organization, as well as of the regional agencies such as the Organization of American States.

The next chapter, Administration and Culture, discusses the challenges in offering effective assistance of this kind to sovereign nations; for more than two decades now, intensive efforts have been made to improve the techniques used and to perfect what has become one of the most important areas in international cooperation. Undoubtedly, public administration will be concerned with this problem for the foreseeable future, because the need for such programs and their improvement continues great.

THE IDEOLOGICAL ENVIRONMENT

The *ideological* environment refers to the ideas and beliefs of the American people. Government is what a people living in a particular place, with certain traditions and viewpoints, decide to make it. If this seems an overly simple statement, remember that people do not develop physical or social inventions unless they want them. The factors of human aspirations and preferences have thus been present in all of the developments already mentioned in this chapter.

Individualism

The American tradition of individualism has always been a principal element in this ideological background. During the colonial period, "government" was associated with British rule and "executive power" with the tyranny of the British Crown. When independence was achieved, those who drafted the state consti-

[38] *St. Louis Post-Dispatch* editorial section, January 3, 1960

tutions were anxious to protect the nation against abuses of government power. Although by the time of the Constitutional Convention in 1787 a counterreaction had developed, and there was much support for a stronger national union, the writers of the Constitution were, in general, believers in limited government. American individualism is not only derived from the ideology of the Revolutionary War, but also from the thinking of the frontier period, when everybody was supposed to help himself rather than to rely on the government.

Political leaders in both major parties still find it necessary to disavow any belief in "big" government. This term generally refers to the building up of governmental power, particularly in Washington, presumably merely for the sake of making government "big." Americans do not want that kind of government, but the real question is whether, in fact, the expansion of governmental power is the result of a conspiracy of the bureaucrats. The frontier has long passed from the American scene, and, in practice, it is increasingly recognized—even if still grudgingly by some—that under conditions of modern living, many people cannot be expected to help themselves. The mythology of individualism and self-help still persists, however. No matter how big we have found it necessary to make government, we do not believe in "big" government. Extracts from an interview with John Kenneth Galbraith when he was economic advisor to President-elect John F. Kennedy are very revealing:

> *Question.* Doesn't this all mean a larger role for the federal government?
>
> *Answer.* Yes, it could mean that. One tendency—in some ways, I think, the most unhappy tendency of the last 20 years—has been to take an ideological view of the role of the federal government, and to say that we must, by all odds and by any possible devices, minimize that role.
>
> This in turn leads others to defend the federal government for any and all functions. The argument, then, is not over the desirability of the individual functions of government but over government per se.
>
> *Question.* Does it not come down to a question of how big the government should be?
>
> *Answer.* No. We must think of the issue in practical terms. If we're going to produce automobiles, we must produce roads, and we will get roads, as we have learned, only with a substantial federal subsidy.
>
> If we're going to have better cities and fewer slums, then we must tear down the slums and redevelop the land, and we

have learned that this happens only with federal financial assistance and federal leadership.

And so it goes. I regard these not as questions of ideology, not as matters of religion, but as essentially practical problems. How do we know what must be done? I'm constantly shocked that a nation which regards itself as inherently practical should endeavor to decide so many questions on such essentially theological grounds.[39]

Only a few years after the Galbraith interview, at the urging of President Johnson, Congress had authorized a whole series of new programs greatly expanding the role of the federal government in such traditionally "local" activities as education. Most people did not question the need for the federal grant money, but many argued that the new programs were faltering and could succeed only if the state and local governments and individual citizens were given a larger role in them. They felt that individualism and "localism" were enduring values that federal administrators had failed to take into account sufficiently.

Our business civilization

Our business civilization and its values have also greatly influenced our thinking about government. The example of business, with its machines and its efficiency, is constantly held up to the government official. So admired is the business example that, as Dwight Waldo believes, "probably the most pervasive and important model in American administrative study in the Twentieth Century is the *machine model*."[40] In his words: "Achieving efficiency in administration is conceived analagously to achieving efficiency in machine performance. There must be good design—organization charts equal blueprints—parts must be adjusted properly to one another; friction must be reduced; power loss prevented, and so forth."[41] The practical—rather than theoretical—nature of Americans leads them to want to imitate the corporate executive.

> . . . one reason for the speed with which the bureaucratization of social life proceeds is that to the modern mind no other way of looking at organization seems sensible. For example, a close correlation exists between the pragmatic attitude of Americans toward organization and their propensity for bureaucratizing social relationships. For bureaucracy is above all a triumph for the deliberate, calculated, conscious attempt to adapt means to ends in the most rational manner.[42]

39 "Interview with John Kenneth Galbraith," *U.S. News & World Report*, November 21, 1960, p. 93.

40 Dwight Waldo, *Perspectives on Administration*, University, Ala.: University of Alabama Press, 1956, pp. 30–32.

41 *Ibid.*, p. 32.

42 Robert A. Dahl and Charles E. Lindblom, *Politics, Economics, and Welfare*, New York: Harper & Row, 1953, p. 245.

While many businessmen have long supported efforts to make government more efficient, such as by contributing funds to municipal research bureaus, "all too often" business organizations have opposed new government programs, both state and federal, "on the ground that the best government was the least government."[43] The quoted words are from the 1967 annual report of the Advisory Commission on Intergovernmental Relations, in which it is also stated:

> The year [1967] just closed, however, saw a "crossing of the Rubicon." The Committee for Economic Development, the United States Chamber of Commerce, and the National Association of Manufacturers took important steps to marshall support in the business community for grass roots efforts to strengthen and modernize state and local government and to utilize the fiscal resources needed at those levels to deal effectively with emerging problems.[44]

As discussed in Chapter 1, the business community was cooperating with governmental agencies in various antipoverty programs, and even retired executives were contributing their efforts, for example, as consultants to private companies under the State Technical Services Act of 1965, and as technical assistance experts overseas.

Business, however, also drains talent away from government. To date, it has been the business career that has been preferred by college graduates and others with marketable skills or potentialities. This is dealt with in greater detail in Part IV, but it must be mentioned here as one of the negative consequences for government of our business civilization.

Peculiarities of the political system

Certain peculiarities of the United States constitutional and political system have also shaped public administration in different ways. Since they reflect American thinking about government, they constitute an important part of the ideological environment.

There is, for example, the long-standing rivalry between the executive and the legislative branches. As indicated in Chapter 1, it is never clear just what the exact dividing line between the two branches really is. Both strive to lead—and frequently department heads and employees of the executive establishments in general are caught in the middle. They have not one "boss" but two—in fact, three, if we count also the element in the general

43 *Advisory Commission on Intergovernmental Relations, Ninth Annual Report,* January 31, 1968, Washington, D.C., p. 7.
44 *Ibid.*

public that seeks expression. There is nothing wrong in having so many "bosses" provided they speak with one voice, but often they do not. One consequence is that a chief executive cannot possibly maintain the same control over his subordinates as the general manager of a private company is able to do. The gain in responsibility to the public may, in the long run, offset the damaging effect on administrative leadership, but the latter consequence is a very real one nonetheless.

If we compare our system with that of the British, we will readily see the differences in the framework in which public administration operates in each country. In England the legislative and executive powers are fused, while the Cabinet, as an inner committee of the Parliament, clearly exercises the leadership in defining public policies. Political parties, unlike those in the United States, are tightly disciplined and generally do what their leaders have first decided. As Dahl and Lindblom state, "The governmental policy is so organized that in so far as the cabinet itself can be coordinated, governmental policy can be coordinated, and against a unified cabinet there is slight opportunity for minority leaders to obstruct cabinet policy, exercise a veto, or compel bargains that seriously conflict with important cabinet policies."[45] It should be no surprise, then, that in England the reverse criticism is frequently heard: The Cabinet leads too much and parliamentary control is too weak.

The divided leadership that is characteristic of the American system greatly facilitates the operation of pressure groups. If chief excutives controlled disciplined party representatives in the legislatures, interest groups would not be able to exert influence at so many different points. Instead of being able to operate simultaneously on legislators, department heads, and lesser administrative officials, they would have to concentrate their attention on the chief executive and his principal advisers. This would not necessarily make them any less powerful, but it certainly would radically change their mode of operations.

The great burdens on chief executives

The great burdens placed upon chief executives in the United States, particularly upon the President, are another important aspect of our political system. Ceremonial, political, executive, and other responsibilities are combined in one office, whereas in other countries some of the load is carried by other officials and groups. The British Prime Minister is generally relieved of ceremonial duties by the Crown, and is greatly aided in political policymak-

[45] Dahl and Lindblom, *op. cit.*, p. 345.

ing by the other members of the Cabinet. It is no wonder, then, that an appreciable part of the literature of public administration in the United States is devoted to the chief executive and his problems.

A unique American contribution—federalism

The influence of another peculiarly American institution, judicial review, has already been discussed in Chapter 1. Federalism, however, has not been discussed as such, although the discussion of individualism necessarily included some reference to "localism." In the past, the system of division of powers between the national government and the states has worked so well that scholars have singled out federalism as the unique American contribution to the science of government. "Cooperative federalism," whereby administrative officials at all levels of government have pooled their efforts, seemed to be working very well, but the unprecedented strains of the past few years are subjecting the federal system to its severest test in the present century. As the Advisory Commission on Intergovernmental Relations states:

> Through the Nation's history a distinguishing feature of the federal system has been its remarkable capacity—with but one failure—to adapt to changing circumstances and shifting demands. But now the rate at which circumstances and demands shift and change is of a totally different magnitude and imposes a new dimension.
>
> Despite this new dimension, many states and localities still cling to policies and practices that hardly satisfied the modest requirements of a bygone era and are grossly unsuited to cope with today's urgent challenge. Despite this new dimension, some policies and attitudes of the Federal establishment continue more attuned to the problems and solutions of the thirties and forties, than to the horizon of the seventies and eighties.[46]

The federal structure has always provided the framework in which public administration in this country has functioned; the present task is to improve and adjust this structure so that it can meet the new problems.

As can be seen from this description of some of the principal elements—physical, social, and ideological—in the environment of public administration in the United States, physical change comes quickly, but against a background of certain enduring ideas and traditions. Certainly no one can doubt that public administration has an extremely important role to play in modern American society.

[46] *Advisory Commission on Intergovernmental Relations, Ninth Annual Report, op. cit.,* pp. 13–14.

BIBLIOGRAPHY

Beaumont, Richard A., and Helfgott, Roy B., *Management, Automation, and People*, New York: Industrial Relations Counsellors, 1964.

Catalog of Federal Assistance Programs, Washington, D.C.: Office of Economic Opportunity, 1967. A description of the federal government's domestic programs to assist the American people in furthering their social and economic progress.

Charlesworth, James C., (ed.), *Leisure in America: Blessing or Curse?* Philadelphia: The American Academy of Political and Social Science, 1964.

Commager, Henry Steele, *The American Mind*, New Haven, Conn.: Yale University Press, 1950.

Elazar, Daniel J., "Federal-State Collaboration in the Nineteenth-Century United States," in Wildavsky, Aaron, (ed.), *American Federalism in Perspective*, Boston: Little, Brown, 1967.

Freeman, J. Lieper, "The Political Ecology of a Bureau," in Altshuler, Alan A., *The Politics of the Federal Bureaucracy*, New York: Dodd, Mead, 1968.

Gaus, John M., "American Society and Public Administration," in *The Frontiers of Public Administration*, Chicago: University of Chicago Press, 1936.

Gaus, John M., *Reflections on Public Administration*, University, Ala.: University of Alabama Press, 1947. See Chapter 1, "Ecology of Government."

Greer, Scott, *Urban Renewal and American Cities*, New York: Bobbs-Merrill, 1965.

Grodzins, Morton, "American Political Parties and the American System," in Wildavsky, Aaron, (ed.), *American Federalism in Perspective*, Boston: Little, Brown, 1967.

Grodzins, Morton, "Centralization and Decentralization in the American Federal System," in Goldwin, Robert A., (ed.), *A Nation of States, Essays on the American Federal System*, Chicago: Rand McNally, 1961.

Grodzins, Morton, "The Great Schism of Population," in Williams, Oliver P., and Press, Charles, (eds.), *Democracy in Urban America: Readings on Government and Politics*, Chicago: Rand McNally, 1961.

Lerner, Max, *America as a Civilization*, New York: Simon and Schuster, 1957.

McConnell, Grant, *The Modern Presidency*, New York: St. Martin's Press, 1967.

Report of the National Advisory Commission on Civil Disorders, New York: Bantam, March, 1968.

Reynolds, Harry W., "Local Government Structure in Urban Planning, Renewal, and Relocation," *Public Administration Review, XXIV,* No. 1 (March, 1964).

Schechter, Alan H., "The Influence of Public Service on Businessmen's Attitudes Toward the Federal Government," *Public Administration Review, XXVII,* No. 5 (December, 1967).

Senate Foreign Relations Committee, 86th Congress, 1st Session, *Possible Nonmilitary Scientific Developments and Their Potential Impact on Foreign Policy Problems of the United States,* Washington, D.C.: Government Printing Office, 1959.

Sweeney, Stephen B., and Charlesworth, James C., (eds.), *Governing Urban Society: New Scientific Approaches,* Philadelphia: The American Academy of Political and Social Science, 1967.

200 Million Americans, U.S. Department of Commerce, Bureau of the Census, Washington, D.C.: Government Printing Office, November, 1967.

Waldo, Dwight, *The Administrative State,* New York: Ronald, 1948.

Waldo, Dwight, *Perspectives on Administration,* University, Ala.: University of Alabama Press, 1956.

CHAPTER 3
ADMINISTRATION
AND CULTURE

C ULTURE is "that complex whole which includes knowledge, belief, art, morals, law, custom, and any other capabilities and habits acquired by man as a member of society."[1] This chapter will take up in detail the relationship between administration and culture, a subject given intensive attention in recent years largely because of the development of the technical assistance programs referred to in Chapter 2. Since the objective is to transfer skills and attitudes from one country to another, the process is transcultural, making the function of the outside expert that of a cross-cultural change agent. While underdeveloped countries generally want to "modernize" their economies and to utilize the techniques of the developed world, they frequently find this extremely difficult because of the persistence of time-honored traditions that resist sharp changes. The first part of this chapter will deal with this problem, referring to the experience under different technical assistance projects and related programs.

Important as international relationships are, understanding of

[1] Edward B. Tylor, *Primitive Culture*, New York: Henry Holt, 1877, quoted in Sidney W. Mintz, "Puerto Rico: An Essay in the Definition of a National Culture," in *Status of Puerto Rico: Selected Background Studies Prepared for the United States-Puerto Rico Commission on the Status of Puerto Rico*, Washington, D.C.: Government Printing

the cultural factor is also essential in the formulation and execution of programs for different ethnic groups within a particular country. The second part of this chapter will be concerned with this aspect. Cultural barriers create numerous problems in relationships between public officials and such groups as the American Indians, the Mexican and Spanish Americans, and the Puerto Ricans. Of course, all of these people are Americans, and they represent one of the greatest values in our society—cultural diversity. In order to serve them effectively, public employees who have contact with them should understand why and how they are in some respects different from other Americans. We also include the American Negro in this discussion, because programs to help him will fail unless based on an accurate understanding of the Negro subculture within the total society.

CULTURE AND PUBLIC HEALTH ADMINISTRATION

The problems in persuading traditional societies to accept modernization are well illustrated by programs in the field of public health.

Examples from Latin America

In 1950, after eight years of cooperative health programs in Latin America, the Institute of Inter-American Affairs requested the Public Health Service to make a thoroughgoing evaluation of what had been accomplished. Cultural anthropologists were included in the survey team because of the conviction that "knowledge of the people is just as important in many aspects of a public health program as is knowledge of medical science."[2] The section of the final report containing the findings of these cultural anthropologists certainly bears out this thesis.

PREVENTIVE AND CURATIVE MEDICINE

It was discovered from this survey that many Latin Americans were reluctant to present themselves for periodic checkups in the health centers jointly maintained by the Institute and the host government. In their culture, to consult a physician was rare enough for most people; to do so before one became sick definitely broke with local habit. Thus, although the health centers offered both preventive and curative service, the survey team found that the average Latin American in most cases went to the centers, "not primarily to keep well, but to get well." The American health technicians, trained in a society that emphasizes the

Office, 1966, p. 342.

[2] *10 Years of Cooperative Health Programs in Latin America: An Evaluation,* conducted by the Public Health Service for the Institute of Inter-American Affairs, Washington, D.C.: 1953. Findings and recommendations on "Cultural Aspects" appear in Chapter 2, pp. 11–29.

advantages of preventive medicine, could not understand this. Yet, significantly, it was found that, in those countries where the centers were operated with "frank recognition that for a long time to come curative medicine must be an integral part of any public health program," the relations between staff members and the public were good. In those places where curative services were provided only grudgingly, this was not the case, and the cooperative health programs were far less successful.

FOLK MEDICINE

Latin Americans also cling tenaciously to their faith in folk medicine. The health center, with its physicians and other exponents of modern medicine, must compete with the native *curandero*, and the latter has a distinct edge in the esteem of the local masses. The people respect the *curandero* because they are impressed with his knowledge of the magical and other causes of illness as contained in the country's folklore traditions. He knows just which herbal teas and other folk-cure remedies to prescribe, and the people do not blame him if, as often happens, he fails to save the patient. They reason simply that the *curandero* was impotent against certain evil forces. The professionally trained doctor operates under a great handicap in such societies because the patients who do finally consult him are often in such advanced stages of illness that nothing can be done for them. When these patients die, the people become all the more convinced that the modern doctor is incompetent by comparison with the revered *curandero*.

Yet there are ways of utilizing these folk beliefs for the purposes of modern medicine. For example, in Chile the health-center doctors had to treat many cases of infant diarrhea. Although they knew that the cause of these outbreaks was a contaminated water supply, they also knew that the mothers probably would not heed instructions to give their babies boiled water to drink. As a solution, they decided to use the stratagem of prescribing herbal teas. Since this was a familiar remedy to them, the mothers gained confidence in the doctors, and, at the same time, some of the cases of infant diarrhea were cured in this way.

Another example can be found in Mexico, where isolation of the sick is well established in the culture. Usually this is because it is feared that visitors might make the sick person's condition worse; a visitor might carry with him the evil effects of "aire" (bad air), of "strong body humors," or of "strong blood." The real source of contagion, the patient himself who coughs up germs and can infect someone in the same room, is given little thought.

As the authors of the evaluation report write, "The nurse need not remark on the potential danger of 'aire,' but if she simply says that visitors are undesirable the chances are that the family will respect her recommendation, even though she is thinking in terms of contagion and they in terms of magic."[3]

These are happy examples, because it was possible to persuade the people to follow the treatments indicated by medical science. However, the impression should not be left that it is always possible to find a formula for converting folk beliefs into instruments of modern medicine. Yet much more progress is usually made when the health technicians—whether they are United States advisers or Latin Americans—understand the intricacies of folk medicine and the nature of the remedies that make sense to the people.

SOCIAL TRADITIONS AND MEDICINE

Knowledge of the social organization of the family in a particular environment is another key to obtaining acceptance of modern health programs. In Xochimilco, Mexico, the bride typically lives in the home of her husband's family, where she is closely controlled by her mother-in-law. The health-center staff in this town noted that some of the pregnant women who visited the center either were not following their recommendations or were experiencing some difficulty in trying to do so. When they investigated, they found that the patient's mother-in-law was telling her to disregard the advice received at the health center. Obviously, in such a situation, there is nothing that any outsider can do, so we can understand the quiet comment that "recognition of these and similar problems makes more intelligible the response of the patients."[4]

Compromise in India

The change agents are not always foreigners; they usually collaborate with local nationals who very much want their countries to modernize. National leaders such as Prime Ministers Nehru, Shastri, and Ghandi of India have made strong efforts to reduce the resistance to changes, and again health and medicine are a good example (although, of course, only one). In India, within the Ministry of Public Health, an adviser on indigenous medicine has functioned as a kind of mediator between modern doctors and practitioners of the two indigenous systems, known as *ayurveda* and *unani*. *Ayurveda* began about the tenth century B.C.; *unani* goes back to early Greek medicine, and in the tenth cen-

[3] *Ibid.*, p. 25
[4] *Ibid.*, p. 28.

tury A.D. was introduced in India by the Moslems. There is in each of India's 500,000 villages at least one practitioner of one or the other of these two indigenous systems; few modern physicians are willing to go into these villages.[5]

In an interview with a *New York Times* correspondent, Dr. Chandragiri Dwarkanath, serving in the advisory position when Shastri was Prime Minister, stated that 80 percent of the traditional practitioners were quacks but that, notwithstanding, there was a " 'valuable core of science' " in both which should be protected. " 'What good would we do if we drove out the quacks among them without bringing in somebody better? . . . Even the quacks have at least some glimmering of knowledge, often inherited from their fathers, who were also practitioners. They're better than nothing.' " He pointed out that 38,000 traditional practitioners had already been trained in Government colleges and were doing very good work in the villages.[6] Here, too, we see a pragmatic solution, a compromise between the "modern" and the "traditional." Evidence that folk medicine can be "right" is seen in the fact that Kainic acid, now a standard medical treatment for worms in the Far East, was discovered in a red seaweed long recommended for the same ailment by Japanese folk doctors.

CULTURAL DIFFERENCES
IN PUBLIC ADMINISTRATION PROGRAMS

Another area in which technical assistance has been given for some time now is public administration itself. From the very start of the foreign aid programs, it quickly became evident that the countries receiving such help could not effectively utilize it unless they were also assisted in improving the quality of their public services. The governments of these countries direct economic development and similar programs; it is exceedingly important that their administrative agencies be organized properly and that they function in an efficient manner. Yet, in practice, this has not been easy to accomplish; furthermore, this has been the case even when groups of local nationals, inside and outside the government, have pressed hard for administrative reforms.

People are efficiency-conscious only if their environment and traditions require them to be. An industrialized civilization creates the need for time schedules, elimination of waste, and everything experts from the developed countries associate with efficiency. Since the underdeveloped countries are, by definition, nonindustrialized, it is only natural that they do not think in these same terms. Americans believe that the government should employ

[5] J. Anthony Lukas, "Shastri Defends Traditional Medicine as Needed," *New York Times*, July 20, 1965.
[6] *Ibid.*

only that number of persons actually needed to get the work done properly. Naturally, we sometimes slip and put too many on the payrolls, but it is significant how violently the public reacts when this happens. In the underdeveloped countries the situation is very different. A large part of the population may eke out a bare existence by tilling the soil, but thousands of others will congregate in the cities and towns where jobs are very hard to get. The solution has been to put as many of the jobless as possible on the government payrolls. This is long-established practice in the Near East, Asia, and Latin America, and, of course, it means that the public agencies are often grossly overstaffed.

In Iran there are thousands of surplus employees, many of whom work only on payday.[7] In Egypt the "civil service corps seems to grow, rather than improve"; according to one recent estimate, the government rolls number some 600,000, not including the military and the nationalized industries.[8] Many other examples could be given, including those from Africa where the newly independent states have also had to find jobs in the government for those without other employment possibilities.

While leaders such as Nasser in Egypt have been critical of the oversized bureaucracies, in general this practice is justified as, in effect, a form of the welfare state. Conceptions of the government's responsibilities are also colored by traditional attitudes toward private employment; in some Asian countries the workers consider it the *obligation* of the company to provide them jobs and pay them wages unrelated to performance, "much as an American parent is responsible for meeting the expenses of his adolescent son."[9]

The intense competition for government jobs

Administrative experts from the developed countries are accustomed to the full employment that exists in their home environments, and they expect government jobs to be hard to fill. Yet it is common in the underdeveloped countries to have a large oversupply of manpower, even among professional and other white-collar workers. Furthermore, members of the educated classes compete, sometimes desperately, for government jobs. In the United States, many college-trained persons prefer industry. However, private employment is actually looked down upon in many foreign countries. For example, one of the major problems India has had to face in its industrialization program is how to combat the prejudice among those with formal education against any kind of job associated with using one's hands.

[7] Harlan Cleveland, Gerard J. Mangone, and John Clarke Adams, *The Overseas Americans*, New York: McGraw-Hill, 1960, p. 164.

[8] Jay Walz, "Nasser in Battle on Bureaucracy," *New York Times*, September 25, 1967.

[9] Saul W. Gellerman, "Job Attitudes in Asia," paper presented at Seminar on Staffing Overseas Programs, sponsored by Johnson Foundation and Agency for International Development, Racine, Wisc., February 8–10, 1967.

Every year in India the colleges graduate thousands of youths, prepared in political theory and English literature, who covet government service so much that they compete for jobs as *babus* (clerks with very limited responsibilities). So long as they are unwilling to train in such fields as engineering, chemistry, physics, and automative mechanics, the "major alternative is unemployment."[10] As to the private sector in India, Saul Gellerman states, "for the typical Indian employee, the overriding fact of life is the specter of unemployment."[11]

Of course, there is nothing wrong with public service having high prestige in these countries, but the mere existence of numerous applicants for government jobs does not ensure the establishment of a merit system. Unfortunately, the pressures in some countries are to make job security, rather than merit, the central consideration. Recruit and promote people solely on the basis of their ability and performance? Give equal pay for equal work? How can this be done if local traditions require strong deference to age, seniority, and social position—as is true in Asia?

Overstaffing leads to multiplication of "red tape," because small tasks justify many of the jobs. Note the following report:

> A foreign educator, still struggling to adjust to the bureaucratic maze, lamented . . . that he had to visit 18 offices and obtain 26 signatures before customs officials at Cairo Airport would release a package of catalogs shipped prepaid from abroad and having no local resale value.
>
> Inherent in Egypt's bureaucratic tangle is the conflict between welfare and efficiency. For years, the civil service has virtually guaranteed jobs to educated Egyptians who wanted careers in government.
>
> On the day that efficiency was being urged by Premier Mohieddine, the Government was announcing plans to make room for most of the 26,000 new university graduates in need of work.[12]

THE FAMILISTIC ORIENTATION

What Philip Hauser calls the *familistic orientation*[13]—the practice of helping one's relatives—is also deeply entrenched in traditional societies. This leads to nepotism in both private and public employment, and to what many Americans would consider disproportionate attention to family matters by both management and the workers. The family comes first, throughout one's lifetime.

In the United States most people spend their formative years within the family unit, but upon attaining maturity, generally

[10] Paul Grimes, "Nehru Aims Jolt India Traditions," *New York Times,* December 4, 1960.

[11] Gellerman, *op. cit.*

[12] Hedrick Smith, "War on Red Tape Pressed by Cairo," *New York Times,* November 14, 1965.

[13] Philip M. Hauser, "Cultural and Personal Obstacles to Economic Development in the Less Developed Areas," *Human Organization,* XVIII, No. 2 (Summer, 1959), 78–84.

leave it to lead a separate existence. In Latin America and Asia, the individual remains in close association with his relatives throughout his life. In these circumstances, nepotism—far from being the evil many of us consider it—is only the natural development of the human personality. When the element of job scarcity enters the picture as well, it is not difficult to see why this familistic orientation should be so strong.

THE ROLE OF FRIENDSHIPS

Different ideas as to the treatment of friends also often produce problems. Friendships are not unimportant in dealings in private and public agencies in the United States, but usually they do not play the same role as in many other societies:

> The American finds his friends next door and among those with whom he works. It has been noted that we take people up quickly and drop them just as quickly. Occasionally a friendship formed during schooldays will persist, but this is rare. For us there are few well-defined rules governing the obligations of friendship. It is difficult to say at which point our friendship gives way to business opportunism or pressure from above. In this we differ from many other people in the world. As a general rule in foreign countries, friendships are not formed as quickly as in the United States but go much deeper, last longer, and involve real obligations. . . .
>
> Friends and family around the world represent a sort of social insurance that would be difficult to find in the United States. We do not use our friends to help us out in disaster as much as we do as a means of getting ahead—or, at least, of getting the job done. The United States systems work by means of closely tabulated favors and obligations carefully doled out where they will do the most good. And the least that we expect in exchange for a favor is gratitude.
>
> The opposite is the case in India, where the friend's role is to "sense" a person's need and do something about it. The idea of reciprocity as we know it is unheard of. An American in India will have difficulty if he attempts to follow American friendship patterns. He gains nothing by extending himself in behalf of others, least of all gratitude, because the Indian assumes that what he does for others he does for the good of his own psyche. . . .[14]

The consequence is that one is expected to help his friends, which means making decisions on a personal rather than a "business" basis. The Tagalog word *pakikisama* expresses one of the basic ethics of the Filipinos: It "refers to friendships that have a sort of all-or-nothing quality. . . . To be the friend of a Filipino

[14] Edward T. Hall, "The Silent Language in Overseas Business," *Harvard Business Review*, XXXVIII, No. 3 (May–June, 1960), 91–92.

is to become, as it were, a member of his family: to have no secrets from him, to withhold no aid, to share his other friendships and his enmities."[15]

Accordingly, despite certain admiration for American managers, Filipinos frequently find them "impersonal, not entirely trustworthy because they value efficiency above friendship, and even somewhat ruthless in their insistence on performance."[16] Within organizations, *pakikisama* encourages division into cliques; Peace Corps volunteers were advised in training sessions that "Filipinos develop long-lasting mutual assistance alliances based on reciprocal obligations, which often override personal consequences, and often 'get in the way' of accomplishing specific technological or managerial tasks."[17] As recounted by one volunteer, the difficulty is that the trainee must be able to accept these points emotionally as well as intellectually, and too often he is unprepared to do so emotionally. Although Peace Corps workers are "doers"—nurses, teachers, auto mechanics, rather than advisers only—the record of their experiences is exceedingly useful for an understanding of cross-cultural work.

CULTURAL DIFFERENCES AND ADMINISTRATIVE RELATIONSHIPS

Whatever the kind of technical assistance offered, difficulties often arise in the personal relationships between representatives of the cooperating governments. Friction of this sort can arise in any relationship, public or private, calling for frequent contacts between nationals of different countries. The problem is not one that arises only in the context of aid programs; the expansion of these programs has simply served to bring to the fore many of the points of conflict.

Hall tells about an American expert sent to Egypt to teach modern agricultural methods to the farmers of that country. This expert requested his interpreter to ask an Egyptian farmer how much he expected his field to yield that year. The farmer became very angry. The interpreter, anxious to smooth over the situation, told the American that the farmer had simply said he did not know. The real explanation was that the "Arabs regard anyone who tries to look into the future as slightly insane. When the American asked him about his future yield, the Egyptian was highly insulted since he thought the American considered him crazy. To the Arab only God knows the future, and it is presumptuous even to talk about it."[18]

Another revealing case has to do with the natives of a South

[15] Gellerman. *op. cit.*

[16] *Ibid.*

[17] David L. Szanton, "Cultural Confrontation in the Philippines," in Robert B. Textor (ed.), *Cultural Frontiers of the Peace Corps,* Cambridge, Mass.: M.I.T. Press, 1966, p. 43.

[18] Edward T. Hall, *The Silent Language,* Garden City, N.Y.: Doubleday, 1959, p. 15.

Pacific island. In their hiring practices, the white supervisors had been employing too many natives from one segment of the island's population, unknowingly disrupting the power relationships between the different groups of natives. As a result, the whole island was infuriated. The head men of two factions met one night to discuss "an acceptable reallocation of the jobs." Finally, they reached a solution and, accompanied by their followers *en masse*, woke up the plant manager between two and three in the morning to tell him what had been decided. The American, knowing "neither the local language nor the culture nor what the hullabaloo was all about, thought he had a riot on his hands and called out the Marines."[19] He did not know that, to the natives, being awakened in the middle of the night did not imply the extreme emergency it does in the American culture.

The tendency of the American to be frank in his statements also creates problems. The foreign national is not accustomed to such directness and is both taken aback and resentful. In Latin America, children are taught to demonstrate their *educación*, meaning good manners, and to be polite and deferential in their relations with others. To tell a virtual stranger just what you really think is not an accepted part of the culture pattern. So, to the American, Latin Americans may seem uncooperative and even evasive, while the American, in turn, strikes them as someone who apparently could use some *educación*. Peace Corps field representatives made the mistake of advising the volunteers to be " 'perfectly frank' " with the Filipinos:

> What they failed to realize is that the Filipinos just don't behave that way. . . . Philippine social interaction is, to an impressive degree, based on what the Volunteers later came to call "SIR," or "smooth interpersonal relationships. . . ." Among the leading American scholars of Philippine culture . . . is Dr. Frank Lynch, S.J., who comments on "SIR" as follows: "For the American newly arrived in the Philippines, the most striking quality manifested by Filipinos is their pleasantness, and among Filipinos getting their first full taste of American ways, a recurrent complaint is that Americans are often 'brutally frank.' "[20]

Democratic attitudes of the progressive-type American manager often fail to produce a response because the local culture demands unquestioned respect for the employer. Appeals to the employees to speak up meet with disbelief and may even cause lack of confidence. Writing about Thailand, Daniel Wit com-

---

[19] *Ibid.*, p. 25

[20] George M. Guthrie, "Cultural Preparation for the Philippines," in Robert B. Textor (ed.), *Cultural Frontiers of the Peace Corps*, Cambridge, Mass.: M.I.T. Press, 1966, pp. 28–29.

ments that "excessive subservience and deference to superiors . . . leads individuals to devote more attention to pleasing and cultivating their bosses than to efficient and productive job performance."[21]

Strict conformism is the pattern even in so highly developed a country as Japan:

> It is surprising . . . for an American to discover that the educated young Japanese very often does not seem to have any opinion at all on questions which presumably affect him directly. . . . As far as he is concerned, firm opinions are the prerogatives of his elders and his leaders. To think matters through to the point of stating an opinion of one's own would, for the younger Japanese, be presumptuous. He is not even neutral: he is simply unopinionated. The testimony of his own experience is not very convincing when pitted against the opinions of those who are entitled to have opinions. As a result, one encounters Japanese who profess to believe things that their own experience has never supported, and may even have contradicted. . . . The young Japanese prefers to defer.[22]

Americans also deplore what Hauser calls *atomism* in the underdeveloped countries.[23] He means by this the loose structure of such societies, as manifested by such phenomena as the extreme competition for top positions in both private and public employment; the bitter feuds between rival factions; the tendency to "mind one's business" instead of cooperating together; the emphasis on personal rather than organizational ends; and, in general, the lack of discipline.[24] While these are factors identified with countries in South and Southeast Asia, they are commonly found in most *traditional* societies.

Naturally, management experts from the highly developed countries find these serious obstacles to improvement, as they certainly are. Yet each of these negative factors has a ready explanation in terms of the local environment. Respect for "organizational ends" cannot realistically be expected in countries in which modern, large-scale organizations do not exist, and whose people, therefore, do not understand their advantages. As a start is made in the transition to a modern society, the culture itself begins to change, and some of these tendencies recede into the background. Thus, one of the keys to success in dealing with the peoples of other countries is to understand the relationship between these obstacles and the present state of their economies. Possibly some of the countries receiving assistance from the United States or

[21] Daniel Wit, *Thailand Another Vietnam?*, New York: Scribner, 1968, p. 142.

[22] Gellerman, *op. cit.*

[23] Hauser, *op. cit.*, pp. 82–83. See also Richard W. Gable, "Culture and Administration in Iran," *Middle East Journal, XIII* (Autumn, 1959), 407–421.

[24] See Wit, *op. cit.*, p. 143.

another source will never modernize; the cultural and other barriers may prove too strong. On the other hand, there is no evidence that changes will be impossible in any of them, and generally speaking, experience so far strongly suggests that, in time, the obstacles can be surmounted.

BLINDNESS OF ETHNOCENTRICITY

In this area of differing national characteristics, it is easy to make dangerous generalizations and to be unaware of one's own prejudices. A common blindness is to feel sure that the best attitudes and practices in one's own culture represent the national standards, and to assume that the worst cases in a foreign country are typical of that country's standards. Called by the sociologists "ethnocentric thinking," this clouds many of the discussions of administration and culture. Fortunately, much of this "ethnocentric thinking" is disappearing as nationals of different countries get to know one another better.

On the question of frankness, anyone who has had really close contacts with nationals of other countries knows that they can, in time, be so frank as to be devastating. Their critical faculties may be held in reserve, but when released, they have real force. Straightforward expressions of opinion, privately given to friends, are not as rare as some outsiders all too prematurely conclude. Indeed, one author says that, in India, one sign of real friendship is "speaking one's mind." This bewilders the American who finds that "as he gets to know people in India better, they may become more critical of him."[25] The price of becoming real friends is exposure to a good deal of blunt criticism, whereas when he did not have this status, the foreigner was treated with polite formality.

The point still remains, however, that while some of the dissimilarities are sometimes exaggerated, "the actual behavior of men is not the same the world over. For instance, a Japanese, when insulted, might behave differently from one of us. He might be less belligerent at the moment but much more concerned about 'losing face.' "[26] Cultures differ profoundly, but only because the different societies of men possess "in different degrees characteristics that are present in all."[27] In other words, people around the world manifest the same qualities, but to a lesser or greater extent. Frankness in initial contacts is a characteristic of Americans, but frankness as a quality is far from nonexistent in other parts of the world.

25 Hall, "The Silent Language in Overseas Business," *op. cit.*, 92.
26 George C. Homans, *The Human Group*, New York: Harcourt, Brace & World, 1950, p. 191.
27 *Ibid.*

THE CULTURAL FACTOR
IN DOMESTIC PROGRAMS

During recent hearings of the Senate Subcommittee on Indian Education, the Reverend John F. Bryde, Jesuit superintendent of the Holy Rosary Mission School in Pine Ridge, South Dakota, testified, "We haven't made a dent on the Indian mind." His judgment was that the reservation schools imposed a "cultural conflict" on the Indians, causing them to "feel anxious, depressed, and socially isolated." He pointed out that the system of rewards and punishments in these schools reflects the values of the white administrators and therefore contributes to much of this conflict. The Indians, he stressed, are not striving for middle-class status but rather to preserve their " 'Indianness.' "[28]

We need not be concerned here with the total history of government Indian policy. There have been several stages: the original approach of forced assimilation; the emphasis on the needs of the Indian culture ("the Indian New Deal") when John Collier was United States Commissioner of Indian Affairs (1933 to 1945); the swing back to "putting the Indian on his own" with Congressional Resolution 108, passed in 1953, providing for ultimate termination of federal responsibility; and the return again under the Kennedy and Johnson Administrations to Indian culture-oriented approaches.[29] When in 1966 the Senate Committee on Interior and Insular Affairs confirmed the appointment of Robert La Follette Bennett, this century's first Indian to be Commissioner of Indian Affairs, it in effect told him to ignore the termination resolution and redirect the Bureau of Indian Affairs toward more understanding policies. Indian leaders want to be consulted more by the Bureau, which in the past has been paternalistic and treated the Indians as "wards" incapable of participating in the decisions governing their destinies.

Under Collier, prominence was given to the Indian Personality and Administration Research program. This was a long-range undertaking of the Office of Indian Affairs and the University of Chicago's Committee on Human Development (the latter being succeeded by the Society for Applied Anthropology). The failures to understand the cultures of the different Indian tribes studied are analyzed in Laura Thompson's outstanding book, *Culture in Crisis: A Study of the Hopi Indian.*[30] Since they illustrate so well the relationships between administration and culture, Miss Thompson's findings are summarized below.

[28] Homer Bigart, "Tribal Leaders Tell Senate Panel Schools Alienate Children," *New York Times,* December 15, 1967.

[29] See Carey McWilliams, *Brothers Under the Skin,* Boston: Little, Brown, 1964, pp. 59–88.

[30] Laura Thompson, *Culture in Crisis: A Study of the Hopi Indians,* New York: Harper & Row, 1950.

A culture in crisis

The Hopi, a tribe of several thousand Pueblo Indians inhabiting arid lands of the northern Arizona highland, have a culture that is neatly balanced both internally and in its relations with the external environment. This balance, however, has been upset by patterns of conduct imposed on them by private groups such as the Mennonite missionaries and also by the Indian Service itself. The Hopi were suffering a crisis as the result of this imbalance, which could only be corrected by allowing them to find their own solutions to their problems through the unhampered functioning of their own culture. Miss Thompson explains, "Exotic, arbitrarily imposed types of administration may be expected, in the long run, to be unsuccessful and psychologically unhealthy in human terms because they attempt to superimpose arbitrary, rigid, and foreign culture structures on the community and tend therefore to dislocate critically indigenous structures and to engender culture crisis."[31]

The Hopi lived for centuries in a desert environment in which they had to struggle hard to survive. As a result, they developed a highly cooperative form of social organization in which each individual clearly accepted the need to join efforts in the interests of the group. Far from finding individualism a virtue, the Hopi actually frown upon it. Unaware of this, schoolteachers and other white American personnel made appeals to the individualistic, competitive spirit that they assumed the Hopi would have. One teacher sent a group of Hopi children to the blackboard to do arithmetic problems. In order to stimulate them to do good work, she asked them to turn their backs to the board as soon as they had finished. To her surprise, the child who finished first waited and looked around furtively. He did not turn his back until one of the other children had done so. The teacher was forced to abandon this practice, just as she had to stop designating the bright children as leaders of the classroom. They just would not accept this "honor." Hopi children are not competitively inclined, to the point that they do not even keep score when playing basketball or other games.

Miss Thompson's essential thesis is that "each society molds the potentialities of its constituents, but it can do so to their full potentialities only if allowed cultural autonomy."[32] Because the policy of assimilation by force was the direct opposite of permitting such "cultural autonomy," Miss Thompson and her colleagues believe that the Indian Service had a harmful effect on

[31] *Ibid.*, p. 181.
[32] *Ibid.*, p. 148.

the Hopi. Forced assimilation was wrong, because if the Hopi were not allowed to "remain essentially themselves," they could not be expected to retain "their integrity as individuals and as a group." This did not mean that the Hopi should not change their ways at all. To survive, cultures must adjust to new conditions. However, "every change adopted by the tribe must pass two tests: (1) it must have survival value in the arid environment; and (2) it must be reconciled or rationalized in terms of Hopi traditional values and world view."[33]

Some problems of Mexican and Spanish Americans

The term *Anglo*, as it is commonly used in the Southwest, means "the numerically dominant, natively English-speaking population whose culture is, with minor regional variations, that of the United States as a whole."[34] As anyone who has visited the Southwest knows, in some communities it is the Spanish-speaking group that is "numerically dominant," not the Anglos. Our discussion here will be very brief, particularly because there are great similarities between the behavior patterns of the Spanish and Mexican Americans and those of Latin Americans, discussed earlier in this chapter.

In his study entitled *Cultural Differences and Medical Care*, Lyle Saunders describes how irritated Anglo officials become because the Spanish-speaking people seem to be willing to accept a status of dependency on local government welfare services.[35] Americans are reared in a culture that emphasizes self-help; we feel guilty and ashamed if we have to ask the government to satisfy our vital needs for any long period of time. So when we have contact with someone who seems to think nothing of accepting such services and a prolonged status of dependency, we are prone to regard him as irresponsible.

Yet for many years the Spanish-speaking people have lived in social relationships where asking for help from others and expecting to receive it is the accepted mode of conduct. For centuries they lived in isolated, self-contained communities in which the members were drawn together by close family and personal ties. Most everyone had frequent face-to-face contact with his neighbors; there was no institution of government as we know it today, with its welfare services, hospitals, and the like. When someone was in trouble or needed something, he sought and received the protection and help of his relatives and friends. Many of the Mexican and Spanish Americans continue to live in relatively isolated communities where this same pattern of conduct is

[33] *Ibid.*, p. 187.

[34] Lyle Saunders, *Cultural Differences and Medical Care*, New York: Russell Sage Foundation, 1954, p. 249.

[35] *Ibid.*

preserved. Even those who have moved to the urban centers still basically maintain some of these same attitudes. Thus when government services of various kinds are made available to them today, they will accept such help in ways that indicate they see nothing wrong in doing so. To the Anglo who has no knowledge of their background of customs, this is "peculiar" behavior. To the Anglo who understands their traditions, it is just as normal as the typical American's uneasiness over accepting such help.

Saunders tells the story of the failure of efforts to establish and keep in operation a cooperative health association in Taos County. Despite the great need for this association, it failed, largely because the members were not accustomed to the responsibilities of participation in a formal organization. Membership in itself entailed the onerous obligations of attending meetings, electing officers, and being exposed to impersonal machinery with which they were not familiar. In the villages where their people had lived for so many years, almost everything was done on a personal basis. Formal organizations, such as the civic groups and associations that typically sprout up in an Anglo community, simply did not exist. It is therefore not surprising that they should find all of this uninviting and too demanding of their time and effort. When the costs of participation were low because of subsidies from the Farm Security Administration, they remained in the association; but when these subsidies were no longer available, they were not interested enough to want to continue their memberships. A similar health association failed in Costilla County for about the same reasons.[36]

Saunders' conclusion was that prepayment for medical services, acceptable to Anglos, is not feasible as a precondition for health programs for Mexican and Spanish Americans, at least in the early stages of such programs.[37] His basic reasoning is that these Americans, unlike the Anglos, are not much concerned with planning for the future. Specifically, Saunders recommends programs offering limited medical services instead of the whole battery of specialized medical and clinical care characteristic of the Anglo approach. Patients requiring the services of specialists would be taken to the cities for such consultations, and hospitalization would be kept to a minimum, thus conserving the time of the physicians. The greatest possible use would be made of members of the family and of friends in caring for sick persons. Clinics would be kept small, with the nurses—not doctors— treating minor ailments; similarly, maximum use would be made of visiting nurses to make home calls to check up on the patient's condition or to give follow-up treatments as recommended by

[36] *Ibid.*, pp. 175–189 for the stories of the Taos and Costilla County Health Associations.

[37] *Ibid.*, pp. 189–205 for Saunders' proposals.

the physician. Home deliveries would be made in uncomplicated cases by trained midwives who would be licensed by the State Department of Public Health. The people would not have to attend meetings and otherwise take an active part in the health program *as a prior condition for their qualifying for medical care.*

Above all, more personal relationships should be established with the patient. Rigid time schedules for appointments should not be followed, and if possible, all matters relating to a single illness should be taken care of during one visit. Doctors and nurses should be chosen not only on the basis of professional qualifications, but also for their personal qualities and ability to establish rapport with the patients. While "in the treatment of disease there can be no compromise with the highest professional standards . . . in the treatment of people there may have to be more compromise if the treatment relationship is to be accepted."[38]

These recommendations are in the nature of a compromise, and they suggest how some improvement can be made rather than none at all if the Anglos insist on complete acceptance of their values. Saunders' "minimum program" actually is a "maximum" one in terms of appreciation of the cultural factor.

The Negro subculture

The term *Negro subculture*, as used here, refers to the living patterns of the Negro as a response to his situation in the larger society. In no sense is it meant to imply a "style of life that has become a thing in itself"[39]; in no sense does it imply something that the Negro would prefer no matter what his economic and social position. Furthermore, it is recognized that much of what can be said about the Negro is true of lower income groups in general. Our intention is simply to explain briefly the kind of life that the Negro poor must live, and how governmental programs to help them will not succeed unless based on a firm understanding of the conditions that have dictated this kind of existence.

THE MOYNIHAN REPORT

In a commencement address at Harvard University on June 4, 1965, President Johnson called attention to the breakdown in the Negro family structure, caused by "long years of degradation and discrimination, which have attacked his [the Negro's] dignity and assaulted his ability to provide for his family." The

[38] *Ibid.*, p. 203.

[39] Hylan Lewis, "Agenda Paper No. V: The Family: Resources for Change— Planning Session for the White House Conference 'To Fulfill These Rights,' November 16–18, 1965," in Lee Rainwater and William L. Yancey, *The Moynihan Report and the Politics of Controversy,* Cambridge, Mass.: M.I.T. Press, 1967, p. 339.

President stressed that only a minority of Negro children age 18 have lived all their lives with both parents, and that at some time or another a majority of Negro children receive public assistance. Johnson argued that unless "we work to strengthen the family, to create conditions under which most parents will stay together," it would be impossible to "cut completely the circle of despair and deprivation." The responsibility to correct the situation was that of the whites, and, as a preliminary step, he would call a White House Conference whose "theme and title would be 'To Fulfill These Rights.' "[40]

The President was moved to make these remarks by a report prepared earlier by Daniel P. Moynihan, Assistant Secretary of Labor. Originally intended for limited distribution within the government only, its contents were "leaked" to the press and, because of the numerous inquiries about it, the Administration decided to release the entire text. Rather than a research document, it is a kind of position paper intended to arouse the Administration to an understanding of the "new crisis in race relations," resulting from the "crumbling" of the Negro family in the ghettoes. In dramatic terms it calls for a "national effort . . . directed to a new kind of national goal: the establishment of a stable Negro family structure."[41]

THE CENTRAL THESIS. Moynihan's thesis is that the civil rights movement had brought the Negro legal equality, but that because of his long-depressed social and economic position, he lacked equality of opportunity and thus could not make himself equal in fact with the whites. Taking "an unflinching look at the present potential of Negro Americans to move from where they now are to where they want, and ought to be,"[42] Moynihan saw the principal problem as the deterioration of the Negro family, evidenced in the following: nearly a quarter of urban Negro marriages dissolved and almost a quarter of Negro births illegitimate; as a consequence, the same proportion of Negro families headed by females; and a "startling increase" in the number of children requiring help under ADC (Aid for Dependent Children).[43]

If family units are to survive, the father must have a job, but this is what the Negro male so often lacked. Not only was Negro unemployment at "disaster levels," but the data for the years 1951 to 1963 showed a definite correlation between the Negro unemployment rate and the number of broken families; "cyclical swings in unemployment" had "their counterpart in increases and decreases in separations."[44]

[40] Rainwater and Yancey, *op. cit.*, pp. 130–131.
[41] *Ibid.*, p. 43.
[42] *Ibid.*, p. 50.
[43] *Ibid.*, pp. 51–60.
[44] *Ibid.*, p. 67.

Unable to provide decently for their families, the husbands leave, forcing the Negro community "into a matriarchal structure which, because it is so out of line with the rest of American society, seriously retards the progress of the group as a whole, and imposes a crushing burden on the Negro male and, in consequence, on a great many Negro women as well."[45] Without stable families and a father in the home, Negro children "flounder—and fail."[46] Moynihan cites research showing that Negro youths with fathers in the home score higher on intelligence tests than those from broken homes, as well as delinquency statistics relating the high incidence of Negro delinquency to the same factor. He refers to one study that concludes that delinquent behavior results from the need of children in fatherless homes to compensate by seeking immediate satisfaction of their desires.[47]

In his report, Moynihan does not make specific proposals for correcting the situation he describes; as he explains, the first step is to get people, inside and outside the government, to understand the basic problem: the "deep-seated structural distortions in the life of the Negro American" that have created a "tangle of pathology" that must be broken if the Negro is really to be equal. He concludes: "In a word, a national effort toward the problem of Negro Americans must be directed toward the question of family structure. The object should be to strengthen the Negro family so as to enable it to raise and support its members as do other families. After that, how this group of Americans chooses to run its affairs, take advantage of its opportunities, or fail to do so, is none of the nation's business."[48]

CRITICISM OF EXISTING PROGRAMS. With regard to existing programs to help the poor, Moynihan on previous occasions had expressed strong doubts about their wisdom. In his opinion, not only the long-established welfare programs but also the community-action projects of the recently launched war against poverty missed the mark, because they made available "surrogate family services" that are much better provided through the "traditional family arrangement."[49] He believed the government should develop policies and programs to strengthen the family structure of the poor, concentrating on employment, income maintenance, education, and better housing. Moynihan had studied the social programs of other industrial democracies and found that most of them emphasized the family rather than the individual. "Such measures as family allowances, differential unemployment benefits depending on family responsibilities, differential wages depending on the family status of the wage earner, tax policies that

45 *Ibid.*, p. 75.
46 *Ibid.*, p. 81.
47 *Ibid.*, pp. 82–85.
48 *Ibid.*, pp. 93–94.
49 *Ibid.*, p. 20.

take family size more realistically into account" were characteristic of their efforts.[50]

REACTION TO THE REPORT. Much of the press coverage of the Moynihan report stressed the "deterioration" of the Negro family, without adequately explaining the reasons given by Moynihan for the picture as he saw it. Some accounts interpreted the report to mean that the Negro should "do more for himself," leading to the implication that he was largely responsible for his situation. Negro sensitivities were injured; civil rights leaders feared that any redirection of efforts to concentrate on "family structure" would slow down the campaign to end segregation and discrimination; and, within the Government, those responsible for existing programs felt they were being blamed for inadequacies Moynihan saw in those programs. The Johnson Administration became absorbed with the Vietnam war, and although the White House Conference was held in November, 1965, only one agenda session was devoted to the family question as such because of the numerous criticisms of the Moynihan report.

FINDINGS AND RECOMMENDATIONS
OF OTHER SOCIAL SCIENTISTS

The social scientists are by no means in full agreement in their analyses of the problems of the poor and what the Government should do to reduce poverty. Independent scholars have challenged the accuracy of some of Moynihan's facts and interpretations, and certainly it is not our purpose here to endorse his or anybody else's point of view and recommendations. We do consider it significant that the National Advisory Commission on Civil Disorders stresses the impact of unemployment on the family. The Commission reports that "in 1967 the proportion of married men either divorced or separated from their wives was more than twice as high among unemployed nonwhite men as among employed nonwhite men," and that "among those participating in the labor force, there was a higher proportion of married men with wives present than with wives absent."[51] The Commission also notes that in 1966, among families with incomes under $3000, the proportion with female heads was 42 percent for Negroes but only 23 percent for whites; yet for families with incomes of $7000 or more, 8 percent of Negro families had female heads compared to 4 percent for the whites. Furthermore, the proportion of fatherless families is increasing in the poorest neighborhoods, such as the Hough section in Cleveland and Watts in Los Angeles.[52] Those Negroes who do find employment are

[50] Ibid., pp. 149–150. For Moynihan's views in greater detail, see his testimony, Federal Role in Urban Affairs, Hearings Before the Senate Subcommittee on Executive Reorganization, 89th Congress, 2nd Session, Part 13, Washington. D.C.: Government Printing Office, 1967, pp. 2639–2693.

[51] Report of the National Advisory Commission on Civil Disorders, New York: Bantam, 1968, pp. 260–261.

[52] Ibid., p. 261.

forced to take menial, low-paying jobs that cannot "sustain a worker's self-respect, or the respect of his family and friends."[53] The consequences are:

> Wives of these men are forced to work, and usually produce more money. If men stay at home without working, their inadequacies constantly confront them and tensions arise between them and their wives and children. Under these pressures, it is not surprising that many of these men flee their responsibilities as husbands and fathers, leaving home, and drifting from city to city, or adopting the style of "street-corner men. . . ."
>
> With the father absent and the mother working, many ghetto children spend the bulk of their time on the streets—the streets of a crime-ridden, violence-prone and povery-stricken world. The image of success in this world is not that of the "solid citizen," the responsible husband and father, but rather that of the "hustler" who takes care of himself by exploiting others. . . .
>
> Young people in the ghetto are acutely conscious of a system which appears to offer rewards to those who illegally exploit others, and failure to those who struggle under traditional responsibilities. Under these circumstances, many adopt exploitation and the "hustle" as a way of life, disdaining both work and marriage in favor of casual and temporary liaisons. This pattern reinforces itself from one generation to the next, creating a "culture of poverty" and an ingrained cynicism about society and its institutions.[54]

A highly praised study of Negro street-corner men reveals that many of them leave the home after constant quarrels with their wives over money matters. The wife wants the husband to be the real head of the family, to provide well for her and the children, just as any man does in the middle-class culture. But he is unable to find a job equal to these expectations, and so he "retreats to the street corner. Here, where the measure of man is considerably smaller, and where weaknesses are somehow turned upside down and almost magically transformed into strengths, he can be, once again, a man among men."[55]

This bears out the analysis of the eminent Negro psychologist Kenneth B. Clark, who explains that because of race discrimination the Negro male "cannot function effectively as a husband and father . . . [so] he often does not function at all." Clark writes: "Even his presence would not be significantly different from his absence. If he were present and unable to protect his wife and child, there would be psychological torment and the inevitable explosion into aggression. . . . Programs designed to end poverty, no matter how enthusiastically generated, will fail unless they acknowledge the realities of the interrelationship be-

[53] *Ibid.*, p. 260.

[54] *Ibid.*, pp. 260, 262.

[55] Elliot Liebow, *Tally's Corner: A Study of Negro Streetcorner Men*, Boston: Little, Brown, 1967, p. 136.

tween job discrimination and the psychological damage associated with the menial status of the Negro male, as well as the effects of these upon the stability of the Negro family."[56]

COMPARISON OF NEW AND OLD MIGRANTS

It is sometimes asked why the Negro cannot pick himself up from poverty as did so many immigrants from the Old World. Whereas the European immigrants arrived when there was an abundance of unskilled jobs, the "new migrants," for the reasons given in Chapter 2, find few such jobs available. Since their skins are black, their social mobility is much more restricted, and they are denied the escape from poverty available to the original immigrants. The latter allied themselves with powerful political machines that gave them jobs and other benefits in return for their votes; indeed, "Ethnic groups often dominated one or more of the municipal services—police and fire protection, sanitation, and even public education."[57] Most of these old-style political organizations have long since disappeared, and in recent years the patronage jobs have been scarce.

Strong family units, with many wage earners, were also a source of strength to the old immigrants. Since they had come from societies with very low standards of living, they "sensed little deprivation in being forced to take . . . dirty and poorly paid jobs," and the "men found satisfaction in family life that helped compensate for the bad jobs they had to take and the hard work they had to endure."[58]

Furthermore, they developed communal organizations "for the satisfaction of common social and cultural needs," such as mutual aid societies, churches, and fraternal societies.[59] "Fully functioning ethnic communities" were created that furnished the "individual with a medium through which he could understand the difficulties of the strange society around him and relate himself meaningfully to it."[60] By contrast, Negroes and Puerto Ricans in New York City "have not developed the integrated pattern of voluntary organizations that gave their predecessors understanding of the problems of metropolitan life and aid in dealing with them."[61] A principal explanation is that Puerto Ricans and Negroes have not felt as "strange" in their new environment as the European immigrant, who "knew that he had decisively severed his ties with his old home, that he would not return, and that his future was entirely in the United States." For the Puerto Ricans and Negroes, "migration was not the decisive break it had been for the Europeans." They moved "back and forth between the old home and the new," and not feeling the "complete and total sense

[56] Kenneth B. Clark, "Sex, Status, and Underemployment of the Negro Male," in Arthur M. Ross and Herbert Hill (eds.), *Employment, Race, and Poverty*, New York: Harcourt, Brace & World, 1967, p. 147.

[57] *Report of the National Advisory Commission on Civil Disorders, op. cit.,* p. 279.

[58] *Ibid.,* p. 280.

[59] Oscar Handlin, *The Newcomers: Negroes and Puerto Ricans in a Changing Metropolis,* Garden City, N.Y.: Doubleday, 1962, p. 18.

[60] *Ibid.,* p. 40.

[61] *Ibid.,* p. 106.

of foreignness that overwhelmed the European immigrants," did not find it necessary to "create the institutions which were the response to the shock of separation."[62] Above all, for them any stance of "separateness" could have been construed as willingness to accept segregation and racial inferiority.

THE SEARCH FOR SOLUTIONS

The National Advisory Commission on Civil Disorders recommended expanded federal programs to improve employment, welfare services, educational opportunities, and housing for the poor.[63] Such programs would, of course, improve the conditions of the Negro family, but the Commission did not make the question of strengthening "family structure" the key element in its proposals. Perhaps this was strategic, to avoid controversy such as that over the Moynihan report, but in truth the nature of the specific programs required to make the Negroes truly equal is not yet known. The nation's first experiment with the negative income tax—one of the proposed solutions—is taking place in New Jersey. Financed with federal antipoverty funds, some 1200 poor families, chosen from the largest cities in New Jersey, are included in the study. Under the negative income tax, the federal government would pay taxes to the poor, instead of the other way around. In the New Jersey project, money earned by a family in excess of an income floor was to be subtracted from the tax paid by the government, but not on a dollar-by-dollar basis. The objective was to find out whether a guaranteed income actually pushes more people into jobs, whether subsidized families stay together, and whether they seek better housing, and to measure the impact on the birth rate of the participating families and measure any cultural and social changes.

However it is viewed—as an indistinguishable part of the culture of lower income groups in general, or as a subculture of American society—the circumstances and characteristics of the Negro poor must be understood if remedial programs, public and private, are to be successful.

BIBLIOGRAPHY

Barnett, H. G., *Anthropology in Administration*, New York: Harper & Row, 1956.

Black, C. E., *The Dynamics of Modernization*, New York: Harper & Row, 1967.

Brown, David S., "Strategy and Tactics of Public Administration

[62] *Ibid.*, p. 110.

[63] *Report of the National Advisory Commission on Civil Disorders, op. cit.*, pp. 410–483.

Technical Assistance: 1945–1963," in Montgomery, John D., and Siffin, William J., (eds.), *Approaches to Development, Politics, Administration and Change*, New York: McGraw-Hill, 1966.

Caudill, Harry M., *Night Comes to the Cumberlands*, Boston: Little, Brown, 1963.

de Madariaga, Salvador, *Englishmen, Frenchmen, and Spaniards*, New York: Oxford University Press, 1928.

Esman, Milton J., "Japanese Administration—A Comparative View," *Public Administration Review*, *VII*, No. 2 (Spring, 1947).

Fayerweather, John, *The Executive Overseas*, Syracuse, N.Y.: Syracuse University Press, 1959.

Gable, Richard A., (ed.), "Partnership for Progress: International Technical Cooperation," *Annals of the American Academy of Political and Social Science*, *CCCXXIII* (May, 1959).

Hall, Edward T., *The Silent Language*, Garden City, N.Y.: Doubleday, 1959.

Handlin, Oscar, *The Newcomers: Negroes and Puerto Ricans in a Changing Metropolis*, Garden City, N.Y.: Doubleday, 1962.

Leighton, Alexander, *The Governing of Men*, Princeton, N.J.: Princeton University Press, 1945.

Liebow, Elliot, *Talley's Corner: A study of Negro Streetcorner Men*, Boston: Little, Brown, 1967.

McWilliams, Carey, *Brothers Under the Skin*, Boston: Little, Brown, 1964.

Millikan, Max F., and Blackmer, Donald L. M., (eds.), *The Emerging Nations, Their Growth and U.S. Policy*, Boston: Little, Brown, 1961.

Mintz, Sidney W., "Puerto Rico: An Essay in the Definition of a National Culture," in *Status of Puerto Rico, Selected Background Studies Prepared for the United States-Puerto Rico Commission on the Status of Puerto Rico*, Washington, D.C.: Government Printing Office, 1966.

Paul, Benjamin D., (ed.), *Health, Culture, and Community*, New York: Russell Sage Foundation, 1955. Case studies of public reactions to health programs in different cultural settings.

Rainwater, Lee, and Yancey, William L., *The Moynihan Report and the Politics of Controversy*, Cambridge, Mass.: M.I.T. Press, 1967.

Raphaeli, Nimrod, (ed.), *Readings in Comparative Public Administration*, Boston: Allyn and Bacon, 1967.

Report of the National Advisory Commission On Civil Disorders, New York: Bantam, 1968.

Ross, Arthur M., and Hill, Herbert, (eds.), *Employment, Race and Poverty*, New York: Harcourt, Brace & World, 1967.

Senate Foreign Relations Committee, 86th Congress, 2nd Session, *Economic, Social, and Political Change in the Underdeveloped Countries and Its Implications for United States Policy*, Washington, D.C.: Government Printing Office, 1960. Study prepared by Center for International Studies, M.I.T.

Textor, Robert B., (ed.), *Cultural Frontiers of the Peace Corps*, Cambridge, Mass.: M.I.T. Press, 1966.

Ward, Robert E. *et al., Field Research in the Developing Areas Studying Politics Abroad*, Boston: Little, Brown, 1964.

PART II
ADMINISTRATIVE
ORGANIZATION

CHAPTER 4
ORGANIZATION
THEORY

M UCH COOPERATIVE human effort takes place in formal organizations, of which government agencies are, of course, only one example. Other examples are private companies, trade associations, labor unions, churches and synagogues, the military, hospitals, political parties, foundations, parent-teacher associations, and patriotic societies. Public administration is concerned not only with the nature of public agencies as organizations, but also with the relationships of these agencies with the numerous other organizations in society. Political and administrative theory merge: Just as political theorists are concerned about the threat of "government" to the rights of the citizen, so are administrative theorists critical of the constraints placed upon individuals in the organizations where they earn their living, and in the other organizations with which they are associated, like the political party and the trade union.

What is included in organization theory depends upon the nature and scope of the conceptualizations behind the particular theory. As author Robert T. Golembiewski states, "The complex problem of organization derives from the two types of questions which must be treated: What is related to what in organizations? and, What relations are desirable and how are they to be achieved in organizations?"[1]

The first question is basically one of perception: Exactly what constitutes an organization? One observer sees certain phenomena as the principal elements in organizations, and he believes them to be related in certain ways. Another discerns other features and relationships that he finds much more important; perhaps he rejects completely the interpretations of the other person. The second question makes clear that, depending upon moral and other values, there can be many goal-based theories. Golembiewski, along with others, would like to see organizations structured and managed in such ways that the values of the Judaeo-Christian tradition can be respected; his views will be elaborated later in this chapter. While organizations are inevitable in modern society, the particular form they take is not, for this depends upon the wishes and preferences of the humans who create and manage them.

SPECIFIC THEORIES

Concepts of organization can be traced back to ancient history, with many significant ideas revealed. But it is only with the development of the factory system and large-scale economic enterprise that we see the beginnings of modern management science.[2]

The machine model

Toward the end of the nineteenth century, *scientific management,* based on the work of Frederick W. Taylor and his followers, came into prominence, and relatively soon provided the rationale for a general approach to organization frequently referred to as the "machine model." So-called traditional or classical organization theory derives in large part from the scientific management movement. Taylor did not himself attempt to study the entire organization of a plant; rather, he concentrated on intensive analysis of work processes at the level of the individual worker. From his experiments he developed the fundamental concept of the "one best way," a truly revolutionary one for his times.

It is well to explain Taylor's ideas in some detail, so as to make his thinking clear and explain why he has such an important position in the history of management thought.[3] Although his

[1] Robert T. Golembiewski, *Men, Management, and Morality: Toward a New Organizational Ethic,* New York: McGraw-Hill, 1965, p. 35.

[2] See Claude S. George, Jr., *The History of Management Thought,* Englewood Cliffs, N.J.: Prentice-Hall, 1968.

[3] See Frederick W. Taylor, *The Principles of Scientific Management,* New York: Norton, 1967 (first published in 1911).

basic approach is generally considered inadequate for today's problems, when he enunciated his "principles" he accelerated a movement that was to reorganize shop management on radically rationalistic lines, and to replace haphazard practices with the efficient ones we have long come to expect in modern organizations.

ABSENCE OF REAL MANAGEMENT

Orderliness was the keynote of Taylor's thought; he was reacting to the disorder he found in the typical plant of his day where, he relates, the workers themselves decided what work methods to follow and selected their own tools for each operation. They were not being managed; they were managing themselves. Instead of standard work procedures, discovered and prescribed for them by a management really fulfilling its role, each workman used rule-of-thumb methods, developed over the years in his trade. These constituted what Taylor called "traditional" knowledge as opposed to true science. The foremen and the superintendents basically did not know enough to be able to tell the worker what precise methods to follow; thus they could only urge him to use his " 'initiative' so as to yield the largest possible return to his employer."[4] Taylor's own words best convey how he reacted to this:

> . . . Now, among the various methods and implements used in each element of each trade there is always one method and one implement which is quicker and better than any of the rest. And this one best method and best implement can only be discovered or developed through a scientific study and analysis of all the methods and implements in use, together with accurate, minute, motion and time study. . . .
>
> . . . In almost all of the mechanic arts the science which underlies each act of each workman is so great and amounts to so much that the workman who is best suited to actually doing the work is incapable of fully understanding this science, without the guidance and help of those who are working with him or over him, either through lack of education or through insufficient mental capacity. . . . Those in the management whose duty it is to develop this science should also guide and help the workman in working under it, and should assume a much larger share of the responsibility for results than under usual conditions is assumed by the management.[5]

RELATIONSHIP BETWEEN MAN AND THE SYSTEM

Although Taylor did not ignore the human factor, he saw it in a certain relationship. To correct the absence of order, the sys-

[4] *Ibid.*, p. 32.

[5] *Ibid.*, pp. 25–26.

tem, not the man, should come first.[6] The "man" simply did not know enough; in his own best interest, he should follow the management-dictated "system." Taylor is severely criticized for viewing the worker as an instrument of production, a means rather than an end, and there are telltale references in his writings supporting this interpretation. For example: "Now one of the very first requirements for a man who is fit to handle pig iron as a regular occupation is that he shall be so stupid and so phlegmatic that he more nearly resembles in his mental make-up the ox than any other type."[7] Also, describing his experiments to improve the efficiency of female inspectors in a bicycle ball factory, he quickly dismisses the possible objection that the "girls were brutally treated" because they "were seated so far apart that they could not conveniently talk while at work."[8] After all, their hours of work had been shortened (from 10½ to 8½), and "we" had provided the "most favorable working conditions," and this "made it possible for them to really work steadily instead of pretending to do so."[9]

Nonetheless, Taylor's attitude toward the worker is basically kindly; indeed, "friendly cooperation" between management and the workers is one of his basic principles. However, since management determines the "one best way," it knows best, which of course means undiluted paternalism. The worker counts as a human being, but he is viewed as impelled by an inexorable logic to adjust to management's requirements. In effect, Taylor did deflate the worker, because he thought the latter had far too much freedom as an operative. Taylor went to the other extreme and persuasively recommended a status of dependency for the worker, which he assumed the worker would not mind because of increased earnings. Worker motivation was very simple to Taylor; speaking of Schmidt, "a mentally sluggish type," he states unequivocally that it is "high wages which he wants."[10] As to the bicycle ball factory, his scientific procedures would give the girls what "they most want, namely, *high wages*, and the employers what they most want, namely, the maximum output and best quality of work,—which means a *low labor cost*."[11]

Although he was against speeding up the work pace to the point of injuring the individual's health, Taylor basically posited an "economic man," to be used to the limit of his physiological capacities. He believed in the existence of "laws" (he never precisely defines the term) which, when discovered, not only fix the one best way for each work operation, but also for setting compensation. Collective bargaining would have been incomprehensible to him. He wrote, "What constitutes a fair

[6] *Ibid.*, p. 7.
[7] *Ibid.*, p. 59.
[8] *Ibid.*, p. 92.
[9] *Ibid.*, pp. 92–93.
[10] *Ibid.*, p. 46.
[11] *Ibid.*, p. 93.

day's work will be a question for scientific investigation, instead of a subject to be bargained and haggled over."[12] Indeed, he envisioned that scientific management and differential piece rates would remove "almost all causes for dispute and disagreement" between workers and management.[13]

SCIENTIFIC MANAGEMENT APPLIED TO THE STUDY OF ORGANIZATIONS

The full implications of Taylorism are seen in his statement that "the fundamental principles of scientific management are applicable to all kinds of human activities, from our simplest individual acts to the work of our great corporations, which call for the most elaborate cooperation."[14] The logical conclusion from this is that there is a one best way of building organizations, based on the discovery of certain laws or principles. The engineering, scientific approach could be expected to solve "all problems facing man"[15]; understandably, the first real management writings were published almost exclusively in engineering journals.[16]

Gradually, in both the private and public sectors, "principles" of organization were developed leading to a fully developed machine model, impregnated with the basic Taylorian values. These were the ruling beliefs, handed down to students of both private and public management and little questioned through the first three decades of the present century.

Those who developed these "principles" did not slavishly imitate Taylor since they were making a wider application of his precepts, but they never departed from his fundamental assumptions. The individual had to adjust to the organization; the design of the physical structure—the anatomy of the organization —came first and, indeed, was the principal consideration. This structure was the "organization," and efficiency depended upon the proper initial arrangement and later readjustment of the "parts," that is, the organization subdivisions. Like Taylor, they knew that the cooperation of the employees was essential, but like him they assumed this cooperation would be a by-product of the scientific approach, now carried to the level of structuring of the entire enterprise.

During the period when the machine model was being erected, it had much to commend it because of disorganization in the private and public sectors. Indeed, the scientific approach still has great application: with human imperfection being what it is, there is much room for tidying up organization structure and processes. In the case of government, there was increasing citizen concern over inefficiency and waste, and scientific manage-

[12] *Ibid.*, pp. 142–143.

[13] *Ibid.*, p. 142.

[14] *Ibid.*, p. 7.

[15] Golembiewski, *op. cit.*, p. 31.

[16] George, *op. cit.*, pp. 79–80.

ment provided the intellectual apparatus for making government more "businesslike." The administrative branches of governments were unwieldy and illogical: There were far too many agencies and their functions were poorly defined, with consequent overlapping, duplication, and confusion.

As the advocate of the scientific approach studied organizations, he was as dismayed as Taylor at the lack of order, and just as optimistic that proper restructuring would correct the situation. Historically, the contributions of scientific management have been considerable; without this "mental revolution," modern society could never have progressed as it has. Organization theories respond to the needs of the times; they do not necessarily meet all these needs effectively but, in retrospect, they may seem far more inadequate than they were when first developed.

THE "PRINCIPLES"

The basic principles of the machine model are as follows:

1. *Division of labor and specialization.* The functions of the organization are differentiated and placed in separate departments (departmentalization). Each department is subdivided into specialized parts (sections, units, whatever the nomenclature employed). The more specialization in individual work assignments, the better. As the organization grows, new departments are added, and existing ones may be subdivided further. If an organization is not functioning properly, the likely reason is that the principle of division of labor has not been correctly applied, and some rearrangement of the "parts" is necessary.

2. *Unity of command and centralization of decisionmaking.* For the "parts" to function correctly, there must be a unified command at the top of the organization. Similarly, the head of each organization subdivision must centrally direct all activities in that subdivision. This is the same bias as Taylor's: To provide order, superior officials must direct and monitor operations. As Daniel Katz and Robert L. Kahn state, although the organization was viewed as a machine, it was not considered "self-directing."[17] Just as Taylor had found central controls lacking in the shops, so did the governmental reorganizers find an absence of coordinated direction of the administrative branch. More effective control by the chief executive was considered essential.

3. *One-way authority.* As a corollary of the second principle, authority flows down the line of command, from the top of the organization to the bottom. Basically this doctrine is authoritarian and paternalistic, but no other approach to developing efficient organization seemed feasible. The delegation of

[17] Daniel Katz and Robert L. Kahn, *The Social Psychology of Organizations,* New York: Wiley, 1966, p. 72.

authority is not encouraged, for traditional theory "has a marked bias toward the centralized pattern."[18]

4. *Narrow span of control.* There is a limit to the number of immediate subordinates that any one individual can effectively supervise. Since supervision must be detailed, the number of such subordinates must be kept small. Sometimes this was expressed in mathematical terms. For example, a top figure of five or six might be recommended. The span of control should be narrow, not broad. A "flat" kind of organization is to be avoided; the "tall kind," characterized by various levels of supervision created to ensure a narrow span, is much preferable. The "tall" structure emphasizes the importance of hierarchy, for it possesses symmetry and order. The "flat" one is sprawling and disorderly. Many a consultant quickly seized upon an organization chart showing numerous units under one official as the probable source of reported difficulties in the organization.

Other Taylor-derived or related "principles" could be mentioned, but the real inadequacy of the machine model is its restricted focus. Since the humans in organization were assumed as givens, no attempt was made to analyze interpersonal relationships, role concepts, communication flow, and the decisionmaking process. No exploration was made of the relationship of the organization to its external environment: Its life and survival were apparently considered to depend only upon the mechanical arrangement of its internal parts.

TRADITIONAL THEORY AND MAX WEBER

Although his intention was not to prescribe forms of organization, Max Weber, the famous German scholar, has become closely identified with the machine model. Using his concept of an "ideal type," Weber "contributed the first fully developed theory of bureaucracy."[19] The ideal type is not intended to mirror reality perfectly; it extracts certain characteristics of given phenomena and accentuates them, in order to facilitate making comparisons. As Don Martindale writes, " . . . the whole purpose of the type is to isolate configurations of facts which have causal influence on the course of social events."[20]

Weber's ideal bureaucratic type is characterized by the following[21]:

1. Division of labor, with specified spheres of competence legitimized as official duties.
2. Hierarchical arrangement of offices, that is, each lower office under a higher one.

[18] Golembiewski, *op. cit.*, p. 262.

[19] Warren G. Bennis, *Changing Organizations: Essays on the Development and Evolution of Human Organization*, New York: McGraw-Hill, 1966, p. 66.

[20] Don Martindale, *The Nature and Types of Sociological Theory*, Boston: Houghton Mifflin, 1960, p. 383.

[21] See H. H. Gerth and C. Wright Mills, *From Max Weber: Essays in Sociology*, New York: Oxford University Press, 1946, pp. 196–239, and Talcott Parsons (ed.), *Max Weber: The Theory of Social and Economic Organization*, New York: Macmillan, Free Press Paperback.

3. Rules for carrying out the work, to be applied uniformly to individual cases.
4. Impersonality. The official is subject to an impersonal order and established norms of conduct, and he acts objectively in his contacts with individuals inside and outside the organization.
5. Officials selected on the basis of competence, not irrelevant considerations.

So defined, bureaucracy existed "in large-scale private organizations, in parties and armies, as well as in the state and the church."[22] In a fully developed bureaucracy, "the office hierarchy is *monocratically* organized."[23] (Italics ours.) In sum, bureaucracy was the "most rational known means of carrying out imperative control over human beings."

Weber wrote:

> It is superior to any other form in precision, in stability, in the stringency of its discipline, and in its reliability. It thus makes possible a particularly high degree of calculability of results for the heads of the organization and for those acting in relation to it. It is finally superior both in intensive efficiency and in the scope of its operations, and is formally capable of application to all kinds of administrative tasks.[24]

Weber's bureaucratic model clearly resembled scientific management in the emphasis upon rationality, predictability, impersonality, technical competence, and authoritarianism. It did not inspire the scientific management movement, which developed independently, but in recent years students of organization have tended to lump together Weber's writings with those of the "other traditionalists." Those who reject the machine model often express themselves as being against "bureaucracy." Actually, Weber himself eventually decried it.[25] He simply ably categorized what many people have come to dislike.

The human relations approach

In the late 1920s and early 1930s the Harvard Business School, under the leadership of Elton Mayo and his associates, conducted research at the Hawthorne plant of the Western Electric Company. This research was to "mark the beginning of an ideological revolution in organization theory."[26] Described in detail in the landmark volume *Management and the Worker*,[27] this research led to the first systematic conception of organizations as social systems, and destroyed some of the basic assumptions of the "machine model."

[22] Parsons, *op. cit.*, p. 330.
[23] Gerth and Mills, *op. cit.*, p. 197.
[24] Parson, *op. cit.*, p. 337.
[25] Bennis, *op. cit.*, pp. 6–7.
[26] John M. Pfiffner and Frank P. Sherwood, *Administrative Organization*, Englewood Cliffs, N.J.: Prentice-Hall, 1960, p. 101.
[27] F. J. Roethlisberger and William J. Dickson, *Management and the Worker*, Cambridge, Mass.: Harvard University Press, 1939.

In one experiment the activities of a small group of men engaged in making parts of telephone switches were observed. Following Taylor's assumption of a "mutuality of interest," the management developed a piece-rate system that it was sure would enable the workers to increase their earnings without subjecting them to undue physical strain. This stimulus was supposed to produce a logical response: Worker recognition of individual best interest and acceptance of the plan. Instead, they reacted illogically, not at all like "economic men." They refused to increase their output, agreeing among themselves to set it at a certain daily level which, in their judgment, was entirely adequate. They did not trust the management, fearing that if production went up, some jobs might be eliminated or wage rates cut. Although the management assured them this would not happen, and there was no evidence from past company practice that it would, the workers remained unconvinced. Investigating further, the researchers discovered that the workers were members of a small, closely knit group, governed by a code that rejected the "rate buster" (who does too much work), the "chiseler" (who does too little), and the "squealer" (who communicates detrimental information about others to the supervisors).[28]

In another experiment a group of girls engaged in assembling telephone relays were placed in a special test room, apart from all other workers. For a period of two years, changes were deliberately made in the physical conditions under which they worked to note the effect on their production. Sometimes the lighting was improved, sometimes made worse; rest pauses were introduced and then eliminated. Yet even when working conditions were changed unfavorably, production did not go down; in fact, it increased. It seemed as though the company could make almost any kind of change in the conditions under which the girls worked without their reacting negatively. This was just the opposite from the experience with the men working on the telephone switches; they seemed to react negatively to any new ideas of the management.

IMPORTANCE OF THE INFORMAL ORGANIZATION

It was only when the role of the informal organization in each group had been accurately diagnosed that the situation became clear. Because the girls had been selected for an important experiment and had been given special status by being placed in the test room, they felt much more important, and they were glad to cooperate with a management that treated them with

[28] *Ibid.*, p. 522.

such consideration. Unlike the situation with the men, the informal organization in this case had functioned in harmony with the formal (officially prescribed) organization.

In the future, management would have to weigh proposed changes not only in terms of their technological soundness but also of their impact on the informal organization. "Human relations" were important. The plant was a social organization, characterized by intricate patterns of interrelationships between the workers; they did not respond as isolated individuals.

THE SOCIAL ETHIC

The human-relations approach responded to certain changes in the environment. With the disappearance of the frontier, the continued expansion of large-scale economic enterprise, and the urbanization of the population, society became increasingly characterized by interdependence. The new conditions led to an increasing emphasis on cooperation and to a resultant social ethic that "affirms the value of human collaboration and social solidarity."[29]

Taylorism emerged during the heyday of the "individualistic ethic," according to which the " 'atomistic' person acting intelligently in pursuit of his own self-interest will eventually contribute the most to the good of the group."[30] This individualistic ethic has never been completely rejected, but it coexists with the social ethic that recognizes the need for tempering individual action, including that of employers. As William G. Scott observes, ". . . the conditions existing in pre-20th century America caused an ethic of individualism to make sense for management. Equally, the changed conditions in 20th-century America created a climate in which the social ethic has progressively enlarged its role in management philosophy."[31]

The attack on the "principles"

Initially, the Hawthorne studies did not have much impact; until the end of World War II the machine model was still very strong. In his classic study *The Administrative State* (1948), Dwight Waldo noted some recent writings evidencing "a wholly new interest in the massive emotional substructure of organizations and in the structure of 'informal organization.' "[32] But his comment on the public administration literature as a whole was that "people and organization parts are regarded more or less as though they were the interchangeable parts of

29 William G. Scott, *Organization Theory: A Behavioral Analysis for Management*, Homewood, Ill.: Irwin, 1967, p. 46.

30 *Ibid.*, p. 47.

31 *Ibid.*

32 Dwight Waldo, *The Administrative State*, New York: Ronald Press, 1948, p. 176.

modern machinery."[33] The following excerpt reveals Waldo's effectiveness in criticizing the "principles" approach:

> . . . Thus Urwick, in his "Organization as a Technical Problem," confesses that "personal factors intrude" and that they "cannot be ignored." Yet he insists that "individuals are the raw material of organization." "The idea that organization should be built up around and adjusted to individual idiosyncracies, rather than that individuals should be adapted to the requirements of sound principles of organization, is as foolish as attempting to design an engine to accord with the whimsies of one's maiden aunt rather than with the laws of mechanical science." This is a truly remarkable statement. Do the "laws of mechanical science" have an existence apart from the "idiosyncracies" of the metals, fuels, and lubricants that constitute an engine?[34]

The exponents of "principles" and "laws," although they often invoked the name of science, did not even come close to using scientific methods. Their "principles" were derived from "common sense" and/or the collection of facts, the assumption being that if enough data were accumulated, a science of administration would somehow emerge. F. S. C. Northrop's distinction between "observed fact" and "described fact" was not well understood: The former is noted without any relation to any theory, the latter is "observed fact" interpreted in terms of some theory.[35]

Waldo wrote:

> To use the apocryphal example of Newton and the apple, it was not because Newton saw many apples—or anything else—fall, that he was able to formulate in his mechanics the laws of gravitation. As Newton himself stated, the basic concepts of his system, such as mass and momentum, are not common-sense notions at all, but theoretical concepts. The heaping up of facts with a blind faith that a science must eventually emerge if the pile becomes large enough can only be characterized as naive.[36]

Waldo also emphasized that the organization theorists seemed to consider that structure was properly divorced from purpose, whereas in fact their recommendations reflected definite value judgments as to goals. One form of organization facilitates a certain objective; another form may thwart it. The value element in organization proposals was always there, and to pretend that it did not exist was hardly "scientific."[37]

Another young scholar, Herbert A. Simon, systematically

[33] *Ibid.*, pp. 173–174.
[34] *Ibid.*, p. 174.
[35] *Ibid.*, p. 179.
[36] *Ibid.*, p. 181.
[37] *Ibid.*, p. 175.
[38] Herbert A. Simon, *Administrative Behavior: A Study of Decision-Making Processes in Administrative Organization*, New York: Free Press (second edition), 1957, pp. 20–44.

attacked the "principles"; he found them mutually contradictory.[38] For example, the principle of a narrow span of control was considered "incontrovertible," yet according to another maxim efficiency required keeping to a minimum the number of supervisory levels in the organization. Simon uses the hypothetical example of a small health department. Under one plan, the health officer has all 11 employees reporting directly to him (undesirably broad span of control); under the second or "corrected" plan, an intermediate level of supervision is created, with the various program activities grouped and respectively placed under a medical officer, chief inspector, and head nurse. Under the second plan, there are delays in obtaining the health officer's approval on matters that must be referred to him by these intermediate supervisors; furthermore, the latter, good health technicians, must spend much time on administrative duties.[39] Thus, to follow one maxim is to negate the others, and, devastatingly, Simon pairs and shows the same contradictions in other widely accepted "principles."

As stated in Chapter 1, the most competent administrative consultants did not fall into this kind of trap; they did not need to be told that "it all depends" on the circumstances in each case. The extra level of supervision might be desirable in one organization but not in another, depending on the competence, personal characteristics of the people concerned, and other factors. Yet the theoretical literature in public administration had emphasized "principles," often stated resoundingly, and Simon unquestionably performed a valuable service in calling attention to the need to develop an administrative science along much sounder lines. Incidentally, as Harvey Sherman recently demonstrated, the "principles" approach is still present, but it is generally considered outmoded.[40] Simon's contribution was to reveal clearly the narrowness and sterility of the "traditional" approach, and to demonstrate persuasively that "before we can establish any immutable 'principles' of administration, we must be able to describe, in words, exactly how an administrative organization looks and exactly how it works."[41]

PERSISTENCE OF THE TRADITIONAL APPROACH

In practice, however, organizations are still constructed and managed in accordance with the fundamental postulate of the machine model: adjustment of the individual to the organization, not the other way around.

[39] *Ibid.*, pp. 26–28.
[40] Harvey Sherman, *It All Depends: A Pragmatic Approach to Organization*, University, Ala.: University of Alabama Press, 1966, pp. 39–65.
[41] Simon, *op. cit.*, p. xlv.

CRITICISM OF "HUMAN RELATIONS"

The contributions of the human relations approach are not denied, but recent reappraisals concur that it proceeded upon the mistaken assumption that all would be solved if managers expertly applied human relations skills in their dealings with the workers. Basically, the Hawthorne findings were congenial to many managers: There was nothing wrong with the basic organization of the work, and all that was necessary was to be aware of the informal organization and to guide it in accordance with company-determined goals. As practiced, "human relations" was management-oriented and paternalistic; Golembiewski notes that "the underlying tension" between the traditional theory and the social ethic is commonly resolved in favor of the former.[42] He writes:

> ... For example, the power of an informal group may thwart the purposes of some supervisor, as well as support them. The Social Ethic neglects such cases because it places faith in group processes per se: it does not specify which products of group processes are acceptable. The manager is not likely to be so careless. Consequently, his devotion to the Social Ethic is likely to be lukewarm and his approach manipulative. . . . Rather than freeing individuals from arbitrary power exercised over them, it can make individuals more willing participants in their own subjugation.[43]

As William F. Whyte pointed out in an appraisal made in the mid-1950s, if human relations skills were all that mattered, how could it be explained that of two companies with equally good supervision, one would have much more labor strife than the other?[44] He stressed that ". . . the way you build your organization has a great influence on its pattern of human relations."[45] Sears and other companies were using a flat, rather than a tall, structure and achieving good results, thus contradicting two pillars of traditional theory: narrow span of control and close supervision. Whyte said: "Instead of theorizing in *a priori* manner, we are beginning to carry on the empirical research that may some day enable us to plan the structure of the company so as to predetermine, in some degree, the nature of its human relations."[46]

Others have charged that Elton Mayo's entire approach was wrong because he sought to explain away human conflicts and trusted in an elite of industrial managers to maintain harmony. Reinhard Bendix and Lloyd H. Fisher have commented, ". . . the Goliath of industrial warfare cannot be slain by the David of

42 Golembiewski, *op. cit.*, p. 70.
43 *Ibid.*
44 William F. Whyte, "Human Relations—A Progress Report," in Amitai Etzioni (ed.), *Complex Organizations: A Sociological Reader,* New York: Holt, Rinehart and Winston, 1961, pp. 106–107. See also Sherman Krupp, *Pattern in Organization Analysis: A Critical Examination,* New York: Holt, Rinehart and Winston, 1961, pp. 20–50.
45 Whyte, *op. cit.,* p. 111.
46 *Ibid.,* p. 112.

human relations."[47] Mayo and his associates on the Hawthorne studies did not go into union relations; at that time, the Hawthorne plant had a company union only.

The goal of man-centered organization

Recognition of the inadequacies of the human relations approach concurrently with the intensification of bureaucratic patterns has led to specific analyses and proposals that constitute the latest stage in the development of organization theory. Although the emphases and detailed suggestions vary somewhat, the objective is the same: to redesign jobs and the work environment to meet the needs of human personality.

Referring to the private sector, Scott calls this "industrial humanism,"[48] of which he and others such as Douglas McGregor,[49] Chris Argyris,[50] and Rensis Likert[51] are leading exponents. In public administration, "man-centered organization," the term used by Golembiewski, is also gaining many adherents.

RECOGNIZING THE JUDAEO-CHRISTIAN ETHIC

Golembiewski's contribution is to show in detail how traditional organization conflicts with the values of the Judaeo-Christian ethic. These values, as applied to the work environment, are:

1. Work must be psychologically acceptable to the individual; that is, its performance cannot generally threaten the individual. . . .
2. Work must allow man to develop his faculties. . . .
3. The work task must allow the individual considerable room for self-determination. . . .
4. The worker must have the possibility of controlling, in a meaningful way, the environment within which the task is to be performed. . . .
5. The organization should not be the sole and final arbiter of behavior; both the organization and the individual must be subject to an external moral order. . . .[52]

The "principles" of traditional theory (see pages 88–89) are in strident conflict with these values. Minute task specialization makes the work repetitive and deadening; narrow span of control and centralized decisionmaking practically eliminate the opportunities for worker "self-determination." In the traditionally-conceived organization, management is all-powerful and the worker very much dependent, a status that Golembiewski believes the research evidence has established is acceptable to only a small minority of workers. He cites studies showing that

[47] Reinhard Bendix and Lloyd H. Fisher, "The Perspectives of Elton Mayo," in Etzioni, *op. cit.,* p. 125. See also George C. Homans, "Some Corrections to 'The Perspectives of Elton Mayo,'" in Etzioni, *op. cit.,* pp. 127–129.

[48] Scott, *op. cit.,* pp. 43–44.

[49] See Douglas McGregor, *The Human Side of Enterprise,* New York: McGraw-Hill, 1960.

[50] See Chris Argyris, *Personality and Organization,* New York: Harper & Row, 1957, and *Integrating the Individual and the Organization,* New York: Wiley, 1964.

[51] Rensis Likert, *New Patterns of Management,* New York: McGraw-Hill, 1961.

[52] Golembiewski, *op. cit.,* p. 65.

even assembly-line workers prefer varied rather than repetitive tasks,[53] and furthermore, he shows how jobs, work flows, and organization structure can be modified to permit realization of the Judaeo-Christian ethic.

Jobs do not have to be broken down to the point where they are very repetitive and require minimum training. Better results, both in terms of production and worker satisfaction, can be obtained by making the individual responsible for several operations rather than just one, and by organizing the work flow around complete, or fairly complete, work cycles (whole stages in the process of manufacture). When a group is made responsible for a complete work cycle, its members can change over and perform different operations in the cycle; furthermore, it is not necessary for one worker to step aside for someone else to come in and perform the next in a chain of highly specialized sequential tasks. Job enlargement, as this is known, is not applicable to all jobs, but it is to many, not only in industrial but also in clerical and administrative settings. Golembiewski maintains that job enlargement also serves the interests of profits and efficiency; both management and the worker benefit.[54]

Efficiency does not require close supervision, narrow span of control, and centralized decisionmaking. When individual workers and supervisors are given as much "wriggle room" (discretion) as they can manage, their performance tends to improve. The traditionalist notion that to delegate to subordinates is to lose power to them is fallacious. Both supervisor and subordinate gain in the process; actually, the most respected supervisors are often those who give the workers much freedom. The flat form of organization leaves subordinate supervisors free to develop their own solutions to problems, discourages them from passing the buck upwards, and encourages them to give more discretion to their own subordinates (they have power to share). Essentially, Golembiewski's point is that fundamental changes in the organization of the work are necessary but, fortunately, can be made; "moral sensitivity can be associated with satisfactory output and employee satisfaction."[55] Social currents also strongly point toward "man-centered" organization, for there is a "revolution of rising expectations expressed as demands by members for greater control over the organizations and institutions affecting them."[56]

DEMOCRACY IN ORGANIZATIONS

This latter quotation reflects the preference of the "humanists" for democratic values. Indeed, Warren G. Bennis believes that

[53] *Ibid.*, p. 141.
[54] *Ibid.*, pp. 128–142.
[55] *Ibid.*, p. 53.
[56] *Ibid.*, p. 206.

democracy is inevitable in present-day organizations.[57] He rests his argument on pragmatic grounds: "bureaucracy" no longer works. It did "for simple tasks under static conditions," but now organizations must compete for survival ". . . *under conditions of chronic change*."[58] The new conditions make adaptability and flexibility essential; "it is only when society reaches a level of technological development in which survival is dependent on the institutionalization of perpetual change that democracy becomes necessary."[59] He explains:

> . . . Stability has vanished. As Ellis Johnson said: ". . . the once-reliable constants have now become 'galloping' variables. . . ." One factor accelerating change is the growth of science, research and development activities, and intellectual technology. Another is the increase of transactions with social institutions and the importance of the latter in conducting the enterprise—including government, distributors and consumers, shareholders, competitors, raw-material and power suppliers, sources of employees (particularly managers), trade unions, and groups within the firms. There is, as well, more interdependence between the economic and other facets of society, resulting in complications of legislation and public regulation. . . . *The three main features of the environment will be interdependence rather than competition, turbulence rather than stability, and large rather than small enterprises.* [Italics added.][60]

Although Bennis refers primarily to industrial organizations, it should be recalled that Chapter 1 emphasized the fast-changing, unbelievably complex environment of government today. The autocratic, centralized structure that Bennis says has in the past characterized most industrial organizations has not been as prevalent in government (although some will disagree), but the bureaucratic rigidities have often been greater. Suffice it to say that if Bennis' thesis about the inevitability of democracy is valid for business, it is equally so for government.

EDUCATION, THE SCIENTIFIC ATTITUDE, AND THE PROFESSIONAL. Both business and government sectors draw from the same labor market, now made up of individuals with much more formal education than in the times of Frederick W. Taylor. Since there is "a positive correlation between education and need for autonomy,"[61] many of these workers are alienated by "bureaucracy." Furthermore, in our affluent society they readily find other employment if they are not satisfied.

Not only has the general level of worker education risen, but also professional men holding advanced degrees "are entering

[57] Bennis, *op. cit.*, pp. 16–33.
[58] *Ibid.*, p. 19.
[59] *Ibid.*, pp. 25–26.
[60] *Ibid.*, pp. 9–10.
[61] *Ibid.*, p. 11.

all types of organizations at a higher rate than any other sector of the labor market."[62] Hierarchy and bureaucracy are usually anathema to the professional; he draws his satisfactions from his work, and is loyal to his profession, not to his employer.[63] Above all, he has the "scientific attitude," which emphasizes the rights of free inquiry and dissent and can thus flourish only in a democratic environment. "Democracy and our new professional man identify primarily with the adaptive process, not the 'establishment'. . . ."[64] ". . . The institution of science is the only institution based on, and geared for, change. It is built not only to adapt to change but to overthrow and create change."[65]

Bennis and others believe that organizations of the future will be characterized by temporary project team arrangements to solve specific problems; instead of a hierarchical supervisor, the executive will function in a coordinating role, or as a " 'linking pin' between various project groups."[66] This "organic-adaptive structure,"[67] as Bennis calls it, will replace bureaucracy. His prediction is far from fanciful, as attested to by the patterns of relationships in the aerospace industry and research and development organizations in both the private and public sectors.

EXACT APPLICATION OF DEMOCRACY. On just how far the democratic principle should be carried—indeed, exactly what it means —there is, as might be expected, no agreement. Katz and Kahn conclude that "an organization in which all members had equal access to information, equal share in all decisions, would not be maximally effective."[68] Scott states, ". . . democratic leadership is a 'state of mind' in which the management is committed to the recognition of the dignity of employees as men and not merely as factors of production."[69] To Bennis, democracy is a "system of values" emphasizing:

1. Full and free communication, regardless of rank and power.
2. A reliance on consensus, rather than on the more customary forms of coercion or compromise, to manage conflict.
3. The idea that influence is based on technical competence and knowledge rather than on the vagaries of personal whims or prerogatives of power.
4. An atmosphere that permits and even encourages emotional expression as well as task-oriented acts.
5. A basically human bias, one which accepts the inevitability of conflict between the organization and the individual but which is willing to cope with and mediate this conflict on rational grounds.[70]

[62] *Ibid.*, p. 25.

[63] See Mark Abrahamson, *The Professional in the Organization*, Chicago: Rand McNally, 1967, p. 8.

[64] Bennis, *op. cit.*, p. 25.

[65] *Ibid.*, pp. 20–21.

[66] *Ibid.*, p. 12.

[67] *Ibid.*

[68] Katz and Kahn, *op. cit.*, p. 333.

[69] Scott, *op. cit.*, p. 338.

[70] Bennis, *op. cit.*, p. 19.

Collective bargaining has been a force for more democratic processes in the private sector, and now it is rapidly spreading in government. Note these words of one of the public-employee leaders: "Democracy means treating all people in society with equal decency with the emphasis on decency. Collective bargaining is not designed to misuse employers. It is the fruit of a dignified democracy. It means that employer and employees sit down and plan their economic and social gains."[71] (See Chapter 15 of this book.)

Open-system theory

Because of the need to adapt to the rapidly changing environment, the open-system conceptualization of organizations is increasingly preferred by contemporary organization theorists.[72] This approach is fully compatible with industrial humanism, man-centered organization, and democracy. It represents an analytical framework believed to be the most effective for adequately describing what an organization is, how it functions, and *how it should function.*

In open systems, energy *inputs* are taken in from the external environment and converted into *outputs*; these outputs then furnish the energy requirements for repeating the cycle.[73] In a factory, the machinery, materiel, and labor inputs enable the production of articles; from the sale of these articles new inputs are financed, and so the process continues. If it is a service that is provided, as is frequently the case in government, the tax money reenergizes the cycle; if a purely voluntary organization, the intrinsic satisfaction of the participants provides the reinvigoration.

COMPARISON WITH PHYSICAL AND BIOLOGICAL SYSTEMS

Organizations are socially contrived, which distinguishes them in important ways from physical machines or the human organism. In a biological system, the relationship between the parts is stable, and these parts cannot leave the organism. Whereas the input requirements (for instance, caloric intake) are clearly specified, they are much less so in the case of organizations; not enough is known about the ". . . motivations which will attract people to a social system and keep them functioning in it. . . ."[74]

Organizations are much more open systems than machines and biological organisms, a vital point missed by the classicists. They assumed that the machinery, materiel, and work processes

[71] *The Public Employee, XXXI,* No. 9 (September, 1966), 5.

[72] William G. Scott, "Organization Theory: An Overview and an Appraisal," in Robert T. Golembiewski and Frank Gibson (eds.), *Managerial Behavior and Organization Demands, Management as a Linking of Levels of Interaction,* Chicago: Rand McNally, 1967, pp. 12–35.

[73] The following description of the system and subsystems is taken from Katz and Kahn, *op. cit.,* pp. 1–109.

[74] *Ibid.,* p. 32.

were the only variables, and that the human factor remained constant. Thus not only did they fail to detect the constant "commerce" of the system with the external world, they also did not discern that within the organization were "subsystems," patterns of relationships often loosely structured but essential for understanding the whole system. It is no wonder that the traditionalists prescribed rigid structures; they saw only one aspect of the reality.

THE SUPER-SYSTEMS

It should be clarified that organizations are parts of "super-systems"; for example, the Department of the Army (system) is part of the Defense Department (super-system). Definition of both the system and super-system depends upon the vantage point: Defense is part of another larger system, the entire federal government. It is the interaction within and between systems and super-systems that constitutes organizational life. Survival and expansion are dependent upon the adaptive process in the confrontation with the rapidly changing external environment.

THE SUBSYSTEMS

Understanding of the system as a whole should be facilitated by briefly explaining the subsystems, which, as described by Katz and Kahn, are:

1. *Production or technical subsystems*, which is the part of the organization that transforms the input into the output (frequently referred to as *line operations*).

2. *Supportive structures*, of which there are two types: (a) procurement of raw material inputs and disposal of product outputs; (b) development and maintenance of good relationships with external structures (as through marketing research, advertising, and public relations).

3. *Maintenance substructures*, to ensure the necessary inputs of human energy, that is, the personnel function in all its ramifications (selection, indoctrination, and motivation). The purpose here is to maintain stability and predictability in the organization.

4. *Adaptive structures*, the functions of which are to meet the changing needs of the environment (for instance, planning and research and development groups).

5. *Managerial subsystems* (the "management"), the role of which is to coordinate the other subsystems, resolve conflicts between hierarchical levels, and relate external requirements to organizational resources and needs.[75]

75 *Ibid.*, pp. 39–47, 85–108.

COMMENTARY ON THE SYSTEMS CONCEPT

The systems concept, with the subsystems, provides an excellent social-psychological framework for analyzing the behavior of organizations and of the individuals in them. Looking at the system or super-system as a totality, the role of group norms and shared values can be analyzed; concentrating on the individual, his input potential can be assessed and developed. Surveying the total environment, the successes and failures of systems to cope with new external demands can be appraised.

Academic institutions are one example. They are currently under great stress in absorbing new kinds of inputs (students dissatisfied with the existing society) and in adapting to new concepts of their role in a troubled urban society. The quality of their processing of the input, and of the resultant outputs (inadequately trained graduates), is under sharp challenge. Their managerial subsystem, the "administration," is criticized as withdrawn from reality and blindly persisting in archaic ideas about students, faculty, and the function of education in society. Flexibility and adaptability are in short supply when the internal and external pressures for change are most intense. Screening out of undesirable inputs (too independent-minded students and faculty) is futilely attempted, and/or the rest of the world is told that the university will continue on the same basis as always (rejecting unwanted aspects of reality). The resultant closed character of the system invites disaster, because it gives external elements the excuse that the whole structure must be torn down.

Another example is school decentralization, pressure for which is great in cities such as New York where neighborhood groups and parents are convinced that the existing centralized system is unresponsive to their needs. This demand for "debureaucratization"[76] reflects the lack of system "openness."

CRITICISMS OF PARETO AND PARSONS MODELS

Under the human relations model, management's role was viewed as "that of maintaining the social system of the industrial plant in a state of equilibrium such that both the external and internal purposes of the enterprise are realized."[77] The Hawthorne researchers were influenced by Pareto in their concept of "an interaction of sentiments and interests in a relation of mutual dependency, resulting in a state of equilibrium such that if that state is altered, forces tending to reestablish it come into play."[78] Contemporary writers believe that the human relations concept of system is much too closed; they argue that Mayo valued

[76] On this concept, see S. N. Eisenstadt, "Bureaucracy, Bureaucratization, and De-bureaucratization," in Nimrod Raphaeli (ed.), *Readings in Comparative Administration*, Boston: Allyn and Bacon, 1967, pp. 354–372.

[77] Roethlisberger and Dickson, *op. cit.*, p. 590.

[78] See Scott, *Organization Theory: A Behavioral Analysis for Management, op. cit.*, p. 41.

stability above all and that consequently any potential disruptive internal or external elements in the system were disregarded. Opposition to management was assumed to be irrational; the possibility of basic conflicts of interest with the workers was denied.[79]

Talcott Parsons is criticized by a new school of sociology that believes his model has a "conserving orientation"[80] and does not adequately provide for the role of change. Walter Buckley argues that Parsons builds on the dominant, institutionalized structures, those that conform to role expectations, and that he treats "deviance and strains of various kinds" as residual and dysfunctional for the system. "In sum, we note that the model leads only to a consideration of such mechanisms as those of defense, adjustment, and deviance control, all aimed at adaptation of the *actor* to a given dominant structure, with no consideration given to the historically obvious mechanisms that adapt or change the system structure to accommodate the actor and maintain the total system."[81] Suffice it to say that contemporary writers emphasize the need to conceptualize adequately the role of change and conflict in organizations. Bennis' fifth point on the inevitability of conflict (see page 99) should be recalled.

Modern organization theory

As Scott states, "Modern organization theory is in no way a a unified body of thought."[82] The most "unifying thread," in his opinion, is probably "the effort to look at the organization in its totality." He mentions its "conceptual-analytical base,"[83] which emphasizes theory-building and empirical research to test hypotheses, and concurs with Golembiewski that it is more correct to speak of theories, rather than a single one.[84] He refers to the dream of creating a "science of organizational universals,"[85] but notes that apart "from the notion of the system, there are few, if any, other ideas of a unifying nature."[86] No one can quarrel with his statement, "Modern organization theory represents a frontier of research which has great significance for management."[87]

BIBLIOGRAPHY

Administrative Science Quarterly, X, No. 1 (June, 1965). Special issue on professionals in organization.

[79] Krupp, *op. cit.*, pp. 32–50.

[80] Walter Buckley, *Sociology and Modern System Theory*, Englewood Cliffs, N.J.: Prentice-Hall, 1967, p. 28.

[81] *Ibid.*, p. 30.

[82] Scott, "Organization Theory: An Overview and an Appraisal," *op. cit.*, p. 23.

[83] *Ibid.*, p. 22.

[84] *Ibid.*, p. 33.

[85] *Ibid.*, p. 28.

[86] *Ibid.*, p. 33.

[87] *Ibid.*, p. 35.

Administrative Science Quarterly, II, No. 4 (March, 1967). Special issue on universities as organizations.

Argyris, Chris, *Integrating the Individual and the Organization,* New York: Wiley, 1964.

Argyris, Chris, *Personality and Organization,* New York: Harper & Row, 1957.

Barnard, Chester I., *The Functions of the Executive,* Cambridge, Mass.: Harvard University Press, 1938.

Bennis, Warren G., *Changing Organizations: Essays on the Development and Evolution of Human Organization,* New York: McGraw-Hill, 1966.

Blau, Peter M., *Bureaucracy in Modern Society,* New York: Random House, 1956.

Blau, Peter M., *The Dynamics of Bureaucracy,* Chicago: University of Chicago Press, 1955.

Blau, Peter M., and Scott, W. Richard, *Formal Organizations,* San Francisco: Chandler, 1963.

Buckley, Walter, *Sociology and Modern System Theory,* Englewood Cliffs, N.J.: Prentice-Hall, 1967.

Etzioni, Amitai, *A Comparative Analysis of Complex Organizations,* Glencoe, Ill.: Free Press, 1961.

Etzioni, Amitai, (ed.), *Complex Organizations: A Sociological Reader,* New York: Holt, Rinehart and Winston, 1961.

George, Claude S., Jr., *The History of Management Thought,* Englewood Cliffs, N.J.: Prentice-Hall, 1968.

Golembiewski, Robert T., *Behavior and Organization: O & M and the Small Group,* Chicago: Rand McNally, 1962.

Golembiewski, Robert T., *Men, Management, and Morality: Toward a New Organizational Ethic,* New York: McGraw-Hill, 1965.

Katz, Daniel, and Kahn, Robert L., *The Social Psychology of Organizations,* New York: Wiley, 1966.

Leavitt, Harold J., (ed.), *The Social Science of Organizations,* Englewood Cliffs, N.J.: Prentice-Hall, 1963.

Likert, Rensis, *The Human Organization: Its Management and Value,* New York: McGraw-Hill, 1967.

Likert, Rensis, *New Patterns of Management,* New York: McGraw-Hill, 1961.

Litterer, Joseph A., (ed.), *Organizations: Structure and Behavior,* New York: Wiley, 1963.

McGregor, Douglas, *The Human Side of Enterprise,* New York: McGraw-Hill, 1960.

March, James G., and Simon, Herbert A., *Organizations,* New York: Wiley, 1958.

Merton, Robert K., (ed.), *Reader in Bureaucracy*, New York: Free Press, 1953.

Mooney, James D., and Riley, Alan C., *The Principles of Organization*, New York: Harper & Row, 1939.

Pfiffner, John M., and Sherwood, Frank P., *Administrative Organization*, Englewood Cliffs, N.J.: Prentice-Hall, 1960.

Presthus, Robert, *The Organizational Society*, New York: Knopf, 1962.

Scott, William G., *Organization Theory, A Behavioral Analysis for Management*, Homewood, Ill.: Irwin, 1967.

Sherman, Harvey, *It All Depends: A Pragmatic Approach to Organization*, University, Ala.: University of Alabama Press, 1966.

Simon, Herbert A., *Administrative Behavior: A Study of Decision-Making Processes in Administrative Organization*, New York: Free Press (second edition), 1957.

Thompson, James D., *Organizations in Action*, New York: McGraw-Hill, 1967.

Thompson, Victor A., *Modern Organization: A General Theory*, New York: Knopf, 1961.

Udell, Jon G., "An Empirical Test of Hypotheses Relating to Span of Control," *Administrative Science Quarterly*, XII, No. 3, (December, 1967).

CHAPTER 5
LINE
AND STAFF
SERVICES

IN A MUCH-QUOTED article, O. Glenn Stahl wrote some years ago: *"I find it convenient to think of the work of an enterprise as a network, a grid, or a checkerboard in which vertical program subdivisions are interlaced with horizontal supporting activities. The chief executive sits in a position at the top corner from which he holds both the vertical and the horizontal lines. They are all lines; for controls are exercised in both directions at once."*[1] Traditionally, the terms used to describe these "vertical program subdivisions" and "horizontal supporting activities" have been *line* and *staff*, respectively.

In classical organization theory, the distinction is maintained that line commands whereas staff advises only, thus making staff less important than line. In practice, staff frequently also commands and, in general, can hardly be said to carry out functions purely incidental to line. Nonetheless, many organ-

[1] O. Glenn Stahl, "The Network of Authority," *Public Administration Review*, XVIII, No. 1 (Winter, 1958), iii, iv.

izations still preserve in their rule books the myth of the command-advice distinction. The actual practice is not admitted. Stahl's analogy of the network or grid with its "program" and "sustaining" activities is realistic, for both kinds of activities are essential and neither is more important than the other. This will be brought out in the following description of the creation of the organization framework for a hypothetical city government. Through this example, the origins and nature of line and staff services can be made clear, and then will be related to the newer currents in organization theory described in Chapter 4.

In recent years whole cities have sprung up, and their administrative structures were developed virtually overnight. A good example is Oak Ridge, Tennessee, which was originally built by the War Department as the site for its Manhattan Atomic Bomb Project. Oak Ridge was constructed on a huge 59,000-acre tract from which some 3000 farmers were removed; by 1944 it had a population of 75,000. With the completion of the Manhattan Project, the population declined, yet Oak Ridge continues to be a sizeable community, with a 1965 population of 30,000. Cases could also be cited of small cities that quickly grew into relatively large ones as the result of large influxes of government and defense workers.

Let us assume that we have been asked to prepare the organization plan for a brand new city with an anticipated initial population of around 50,000. In newly created agencies, the first act of delegation is the initiation of the organizational structure itself. We may suppose that the decision has been made to hire a city manager, and that the new city will be organized according to a typical council-manager form of government. The manager, a professionally trained individual, is to develop plans for the rest of the administrative organization, and he is given the power to appoint all department heads. His first job is to prepare an *organization ordinance* for the approval of the city council; the purpose of this ordinance is to create the departments and the other major organization units of the city government and to define their responsibilities. The ordinance must take into account the different public services the municipality is expected to provide. Since cities vary somewhat in the kinds of services they make available to the community, no standard blueprint can be applied. However, certain kinds of activities are generally considered essential. These can be divided into the two types of functions mentioned above: line and staff.

LINE SERVICES

Line services refer to those activities that are *substantive* or *direct* in their contribution to the city administration's objectives, such as police and fire protection. The term *line* originated in the military, where it refers to the military commanders and other officers in direct charge of combat operations—in other words, those responsible for the substantive work of the armed forces. The line, or chain of command, extends from the top-ranking officer down to the lowest ranking enlisted man.

The police are responsible in this way for the maintenance of law and order and for the enforcement of the relevant ordinances. They will also have to administer the city jails. The fire department also functions substantively in a program of prevention and fire-fighting. Officials in this department are responsible for the enforcement of fire regulations and for investigating the causes of fires.

Since the city manager—the executive head of the municipality—has the responsibility for providing general direction of all functions of the city government, he is the chief line officer. Yet he has neither the time nor the technical proficiency required for either police or fire work. Therefore he must delegate this line responsibility to qualified subordinates.

There are many other line services that must be instituted by the city manager if the administration is to be effective in the community. For the development of the physical facilities of the community, the city manager provides for a Department of Public Works. The responsibilities of this department will include construction and maintenance of the streets and the sewer and storm drain system; garbage and trash collection; installation and operation of street lighting and other municipal electrical facilities; enforcement of building laws and regulations; maintenance and repair of public buildings; and traffic engineering. Similarly, to prevent outbreaks of disease and otherwise to protect the health of the city's residents, a Department of Public Health is essential. Still another direct service to the public is provision of park and recreation facilities, which necessitates a Department of Parks and Recreation. Finally, since the city council has decided that there will be a municipal library, the manager provides for a Library Department.

All of these line departments are shown in Figure 2. You may have wondered if the city manager expects the population to do without a water supply. Indeed, he does not; but since the city is in a large metropolitan bay area, the water is provided by a municipal utility district serving all the cities in the area.

Fig. 2. Line departments, City of X.

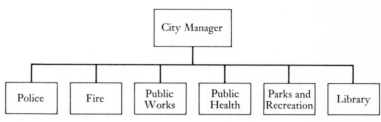

STAFF SERVICES

Before the line units can begin to function, they need manpower, money, equipment, materials, buildings, and various services. These services are *adjectival* in nature, or *indirect* in their contribution to the administration's objectives. Again, the city manager cannot personally undertake to provide all of these indirect services; he must also establish certain staff agencies— to be manned by specialists—in the particular fields concerned.

First is the task of finding qualified persons to fill the positions in the administrative branch. The basic employment policy will be outlined in a *civil-service ordinance* and approved by the city council. A complete personnel program consists of various elements and requires a good deal of specialized knowledge. Thus a Personnel Department is the first staff agency to be instituted. Its function will be to advise the city manager and the council on personnel policies, and to help the line officials to find and retain good employees. It will give competitive examinations, both for original entrance into the service and for promotion, plan and carry out in-service training programs, and provide leadership in stimulating the employees to contribute their best efforts.

Nothing can be accomplished by the municipal government without money, so there must be some provision for a Finance Department. The various components of the finance function include:

1. preparation and control of the budget
2. receipt and safekeeping of all municipal funds
3. assessment of real and personal property
4. administration and collection of municipal taxes and license fees
5. procurement of materials, supplies, equipment, and services
6. supply, property, and records management
7. financial estimating and fiscal accounting

As chief executive, the city manager himself will be responsible for financial planning, yet he will not have the time to exercise direct supervision over these tasks; he will need competent subordinates in immediate charge of each specialized function. Specifically, there should be a budget officer, a treasurer, an assessor, a tax collector, and a purchasing agent. Each official will, of course, have to be given the necessary complement of assistants and office help, and each will be performing a staff service in making it possible for the line departments to get their work done.

The city council has also advised the manager that it will create a Planning Commission. The manager, however, is to appoint a director of planning and to exercise general administrative control over him, just as he does over other department heads. The director of planning and his staff are to provide professional advice to both the manager and the Planning Commission on problems relating to the development of the streets, roads, park areas, bridges, and other physical facilities of the municipality. They will prepare master plans and other guides for the orderly growth of the city. Final adoption of these plans will be the responsibility of the city council, after hearing the recommendations of the city manager and the Planning Commission.

The planning staff itself will not assume direct responsibility for building these facilities. The Public Works Department will primarily be in charge of this, although with some participation by Parks and Recreation. The last department will have the responsibility for the construction and maintenance of roads, buildings, and other physical features of recreation and play areas.

The various departments of the government will need legal advice; the city must also have legal counsel to represent it in court, both as defendant and plaintiff. Expert legal assistance will also be required in the drafting of ordinances, resolutions, contracts, and other documents. The case then is complete for adding a fourth staff agency—the Legal Department.

It should be noted that each of these four units provides facilitating services for *all* the line departments. In other words, their scope of activities is citywide. They are not restricted to helping only the line agencies, but also mutually service one another, as when the city attorney gives advice to the personnel director, and when the Finance Department purchases materials and supplies for all three other staff units, as well as for itself and the line agencies. Because they make their services available to the entire city government, they are known as *central staff agencies*. Figure 3 shows the proposed administrative organization for the municipality, with these central staff agencies now added.

Fig. 3.   Proposed administrative organization, City of X. Top rows: staff agencies; bottom row: line agencies.

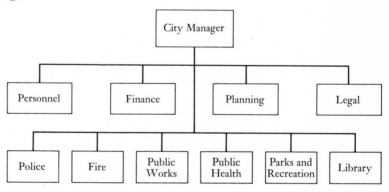

The city manager must organize his own immediate office in such a way as to discharge his responsibilities with maximum efficiency. He has already delegated important line responsibilities, and also provided for central staff agencies that should give him invaluable help. But he will also need an assistant city manager—someone to represent him in contacts with all department heads and also to act for him in his absence. Such a person will be a full-fledged deputy, empowered to give orders to the department heads and to exercise any other powers delegated to him by the city manager. This does not mean that the department heads will always have to deal with the manager through the deputy, but that the manager will designate certain business that they normally should first take up with the assistant city manager. This will free the manager's time for meetings with the city council; conferences with leaders of community organizations; negotiations with federal, state, and other local officials in the area; and similar activities. Since the assistant city manager will be directly in the chain of command between the manager and the line department heads, he will be the number two line officer.

Having a deputy will help the manager a good deal, but there will be some tasks that neither he nor the assistant city manager will have time to perform. Preparing drafts of speeches is one such task. Doing the same for press releases and keeping in touch with press representatives is another. Going over reports by the department heads and making preliminary comments is another. Looking up information and collecting data the manager needs is still another. Sometimes the designation "legman" is used to refer to aides who do such work. This, however, should not be interpreted to mean that the work itself is of an unimportant character. Whether or not the manager makes a good speech is certainly not a minor matter. So, in our hypothetical example, the position of administrative assistant to the city manager is also needed.

Will the person appointed to it be staff or line? On the basis of the duties just described, he will be staff. This is, however, a different kind of staff activity than that carried out by the central staff agencies, which will handle routine functions of the organization; that is, they will regularly take action and make decisions in the name of the top line officer. The administrative assistant to the manager is not expected to act for his superior—he is rather a personal aide and adviser. The city manager will make some decisions partly on the basis of information and advice supplied by the administrative assistant, but he will not ask the assistant to act for him in getting these decisions executed.

Apart from clerical assistance, our city manager now has all the help he needs in his immediate office. Figure 4 shows the overall administrative structure of the municipality as he has constructed it. The commissions and boards, such as those normally established by municipalities in such fields as parks and recreation, planning, and personnel are not shown, since this is not necessary for our purpose here.

Staff officials within the line departments

Let us turn our attention now to the internal organization of the line departments. Public Works will be quite large, combining

as it does the responsibility for several different functions. Therefore the position of assistant director of public works is authorized. This is a line position, because the assistant director will
serve as a full-fledged deputy, second in the line of command.
The department will also need to keep cost figures on its
various activities; in addition, the director of public works
will need someone in his immediate office to be responsible for
receiving complaints from the public. He will also require
someone to act as liaison to the City Personnel Department.

*Fig. 4. Proposed overall
administrative organization,
City of X.*

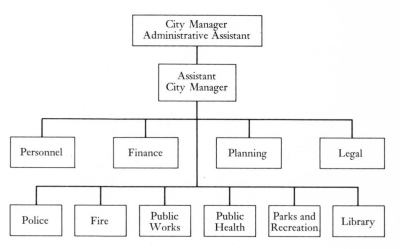

Clearly, then, there is enough work here for a departmental
business manager, who would perform all of the above-mentioned
tasks and assume responsibility for office-management functions
in general, such as records systems and care of machine equipment. The objective here is to facilitate the work of the line
supervisors in the Public Works Department.

Thus besides the central staff agencies there will be staff
officers such as business managers carrying out the same adjectival
functions within the line departments themselves. In fact, similar
positions may be created even within subdivisions of these
departments. Furthermore, more than one staff official may
be needed at the departmental level and in each subdivision.

This is not likely since our city will not be large, but it could happen in some departments. For example, perhaps in time the Public Works Department will require, in addition to the business manager, a full-time personnel officer. Establishment of such positions will not be limited to the office of the chief executive. Figure 5 shows how the Public Works Department, for example, would look in the framework of the total city government.

TRADITIONAL THEORY AND THE STAFF-LINE CONCEPT

From the previous description it is clear that certain kinds of staff officials do give commands; indeed, if they did not do so

Fig. 5.   Proposed administrative organization, City of X. Internal organization of one department.

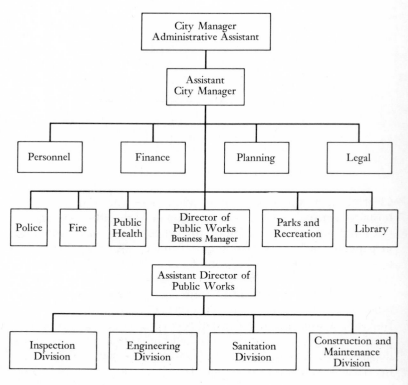

their jobs could not be justified. The personnel director is expected to approve or disapprove line official requests, depending upon the conformance of these requests to the civil-service ordinance, the personnel regulations, and the policies of the city manager. The manager would achieve very little by hiring a personnel director if he still had to make all the decisions himself, despite his lack of expertise in the area and all the other pressures on his time.

Traditional organization theory rationalizes the decision-making and action powers of the personnel director by reminding that the line official whose request is denied can appeal to the city manager. While this is true, the expectation is that successful appeals of this type will be rare, for otherwise the conclusion must be that the personnel director consistently makes poor decisions and is incompetent. Actually, if it is a question of interpretation of the civil-service ordinance, the personnel director derives his authority and decisionmaking power from the law itself, not from the manager, and is justified in proceeding independently. For reasons of diplomacy with the line, the personnel director may emphasize that his aim is to serve, not to control; but control he must if his correct advice, as he sees it, is not accepted.

Critics of traditional theory argue that if the distinction is supposed to be that staff advises only, but in practice it does command, then there is no difference between line and staff. This argument is irrefutable. However, if the difference is between program and sustaining activities, as explained by Stahl, then there is nothing wrong in continuing to speak of line and staff. Admittedly, just which functions should be considered line (program) and which staff (sustaining) will be a matter of opinion: for example, a neighborhood city hall to process the complaints of ghetto residents can be considered a direct service or program for the poor, or an aspect of one of the jurisdiction-wide indirect services—public relations. This is why Sherman writes:

> . . . Avoid talmudic discussions of "correct" staff-line theory and philosophy. Decide instead how your particular enterprise wants to work, what you want to be designated as staff and what as line, what their functions shall be, and how they shall interrelate. Then educate all concerned on your decision. It would be well to follow the advice of Humpty Dumpty who said: "When I use a word, it means just what I choose it to mean—neither more nor less."[2]

[2] Harvey Sherman, *It All Depends: A Pragmatic Approach to Organization,* University, Ala.: University of Alabama Press, 1966, p. 73.

The command or advice myth persists because it is needed to prop up traditional organization theory, which, as noted in Chapter 4, emphasizes specialization, hierarchy, and centralized command at the top of the organization.[3] Line specializes in command; staff in advice. Within the organization, there are separate hierarchies for line and staff, with higher level line and staff officials directing counterparts at lower levels. This vertically fragments the organization, separates line from staff, and tends to make them opponents rather than collaborators. The supreme decisionmaking power is in the line; staff is definitely subordinate. Staff understandably resents this status of inferiority, particularly because it does in fact make or at least influence important decisions.

In a penetrating analysis, Golembiewski shows the inadequacies of the Neutral and Inferior Instrument Model assigned to staff under traditional theory. The Colleague Model is what he recommends, one in which teams of program and sustaining officials, at different levels in the organization, assume joint responsibility for all operations. This ties in with his concept of organizing around complete work flows (see pages 96–97), with staff mostly assigned to the lower levels of the organization. There, as team members, they truly cooperate with program officials, rather than check up on them from on high. His basic argument is that traditional organization creates the relationships that lead to some of the worst tensions between line and staff officials. These conflicts are not simply to be explained by personality or cultural differences; they derive from the way in which the work is organized. But it is this very fact that gives hope, because the organization can be restructured to produce integration of line-staff activity through the colleague or team concept.

STAFF-LINE CONFLICTS

The Colleague Model is still the exception, and staff-line conflicts do exist. Pending structural changes, some success can be achieved in lessening these conflicts.

Specific resentments of line officials

The line frequently resents the *controls* exercised by the staff officials. Line officials generally will not propose illegal or improper actions, but sometimes they make requests that, in the best judgment of the staff experts concerned, should be

[3] See Robert T. Golembiewski, *Organizing Men and Power: Patterns of Behavior and Line-Staff Models*, Chicago: Rand McNally, 1967.

denied. Whether or not the purchasing agent's judgment is the best, the fact remains that as the city's expert in this field, he is authorized to accept or reject requests made by line officials. Thus the nature of the relationship is such that the sensitivities of the line officials are easily offended. Obviously, the more tactful the staff expert is, the better the relationships with the line. But advising him to be tactful will not remove the source of the difficulty; so long as he exercises a veto over the line official, resentments of this type are bound to occur.

Line officials feel even more bitter when they reflect upon the recency of the creation of the staff units. In modern organizations, many of the staff units were established only in recent years. Line officers naturally do not like to receive orders from the representatives of these new staff units, particularly if the latter are younger and have more education than those in the line group. In the past, many line supervisors started their working careers without extensive educational backgrounds, and by dint of hard work they gained posts of high responsibility. In many cases, their advancement was slow, something they find hard to forget. Their resentment increases when they see college graduates recruited directly from school into well-paying jobs in staff departments, where promotion is often more rapid than it was for them when they started out. To cap it all, these young men are placed in positions where, despite their limited work experience, they can give orders to the line men.

Line officials also sometimes fear that the staff man will discover deficiencies in their work or procedures. Since it is the nature of the staff's job to check on operations and to recommend improvements, the line naturally is afraid that the staff experts will succeed in effecting major changes in the accustomed ways of doing things. Since resistance to change is a human characteristic, it is not strange that the line should suspect the staff of being insensate "innovators."

Further, line officials are frequently jealous of the influence they believe the staff man has with the "boss." An individual serving as assistant to an organization executive, as one example, arouses such feelings. The assistant functions as a personal aide to his superior, and thus he is in a strategic position to become influential with him. Perhaps he may never become really close with him, but there is always that strong possibility. In any case, the suspicion persists that the mission of the staff man is to obtain information to be used with the "boss" against the line subordinates. Bluntly, he is a spy, and not to be trusted despite all his protestations of "wanting to help."

Relationship difficulties of staff officials

The power relationship is not one-sided, however. Since frequently they are relatively new additions to the organization, staff men tend to be uncertain of their status. They feel that they must prove themselves, and are frustrated at the difficulties in showing objective evidence of their contributions. While it is true that staff activities in government are by now generally accepted, the services rendered seem intangible and are much harder to justify in terms of results than are those of the line departments.

For example, Public Works can point to the streets, roads, and sewers it builds and maintains. Parks and Recreation can cite impressive statistics showing the number of people in all age groups using its facilities. Public Health can demonstrate how its vaccination programs have reduced the incidence of such feared diseases as polio. While the staff departments can also cite statistics, their figures have less force. If Personnel reveals that it administered so many examinations during a given period, someone may question why it was necessary to give that many. The city manager may receive such good advice from the Legal Department that he considers its services indispensable, but he has no quantitative measurement to prove this. To refer to the number of legal opinions he has received from the city attorneys during a specific period does not prove anything. Furthermore, what evidence can he give to prove beyond the shadow of a doubt that he really needs to have an administrative assistant? And does the Public Works Department really need a business manager?

Since the staff man renders a service that is indirect in its contribution to the agency's objectives, his job, naturally, is frequently more difficult to justify than those of line officers. While whole staff departments are usually not eliminated in budget reductions, the staff people often do suffer greater job insecurity than do line men during times of financial stringency. If cuts must be made, staff specialists may go first. Even if funds are not short, staff groups may still have reason to feel insecure, particularly if their function is brand new. A good example would be that of a recently established planning staff. How long should it take this staff to develop their plans? Are they inefficient if a few months pass and they still are in the process of preparing these plans? And how can it be proved one way or the other that these plans, when finally ready, are sound? It is no wonder that some staff men should feel uneasy about their status. Usually there are at least some line men who either opposed or were lukewarm to the institution of the new staff activity in the first place.

Because they are anxious to establish themselves, some staff men push too hard in their relationships with line officials. They put pressure on them to accept their recommendations, and they may not conceal their annoyance when the line men seem unconvinced. If these staff people felt more secure, some of their overaggressive conduct undoubtedly would disappear. It is up to the management of the agency to give the staff people assurances that will reduce such psychological tensions.

Another area of conflict arises from the tendency of some staff officials to look down on the line men. If their educational background is superior, as it frequently is, some of them will develop a condescending attitude. Indeed, a few may even have the idea that they constitute the "brains" of the organization, in contrast to the line people who, from their viewpoint, are unimaginative, sometimes crude, and, in any event, indisposed to look ahead and to plan their work properly. This is a stereotype that has no basis in reality. There is no reason to believe that staff experts have a monopoly on brain power. The line department head is not of feeble intellect simply because he needs help from staff advisers. Line officials are also decision-makers, and to make good decisions requires a high level of intellectual ability. The best way for the condescending staff man to find this out is for management to place him in a line position for a while and let him make some of these decisions. He would then probably realize that he was grievously mistaken about the nonintellectual nature of the line function.

Since many of the staff specialists do wield control, it is not surprising that some should become unduly negative and rigid in their outlook. A complaint often heard is that the staff is more interested in perpetuating itself and its paperwork than it is in helping the line organization. Outright lack of sympathy with the line is rare, but lack of flexibility in dealings with them is frequent. The argument here is not that the staff should always cater to the requests of the line without regard to existing regulations; it is rather that staff specialists should maintain a positive attitude in considering a line officer's requests. Since the organization's regulations cannot cover every situation that arises, the staff man can, when appropriate, occasionally yield to a line request. The line is justifiably infuriated if it has cause to feel that staff units are predisposed to look disfavorably upon *any* request they might make. Unfortunately, some staff people are so minded; some may even themselves be unsure as to what the regulations mean, and may take the safe side in denying the line man. On the other hand, line officials frequently make sweeping condemnation of all staff agencies on the basis of only one or two negative experiences.

The conscientious staff officer faces a real dilemma. He wants to preserve his integrity and to be respected by his colleagues, such as those in personnel, finance, or planning. There is no quicker way to lose their esteem than to be seen constantly capitulating to indefensible requests of line officials. However, neither should he be so unbending as to impede the work of the line men. The problem, then, is how to achieve this happy balance.

Finally, the staff man is sometimes accused of living in an "ivory tower." The charge is that the staff specialists seem virtually to lock themselves in their offices, where, divorced from reality, they develop impractical plans. Unfortunately, some staff men do seem to isolate themselves from line officials. In some cases this is attributable to the analytical nature of some of staff work itself; the specialist wants a quiet atmosphere in which to develop his plans. Whatever the explanation, it is professional suicide for a staff official to maintain a posture of aloofness. A line man could hardly be expected to place his confidence in someone he does not know, and who apparently is not interested in knowing him. If staff units are to succeed, they must use "salesmanship" and persuasion in developing close working relationships with the line. The staff man who circulates freely throughout the line organization, who has numerous face-to-face contacts with operating officials, and who convinces them that he wants to help is on much more solid ground than one who holds himself aloof.

These are some of the causes of the friction between line and staff. Numerous cases can be cited where the line man was at fault, but just as many can be described where the responsibility lay with the staff man. While these cases may be revealing as to the cause of the trouble, they tend to reflect the bias of the person who relates the "facts" as he sees them. A much more constructive approach would be to explore the different proposals that have been made for improving staff-line relationships.

IMPROVING STAFF-LINE RELATIONSHIPS

First, the superior officer should make entirely clear to both staff and line subordinates the exact nature of their responsibilities. This may seem elementary, but all too frequently superior officers do not specify their subordinates' responsibilities.[4] The staff specialist should not be given vague assignments, because this not only leaves him uncertain as to his duties but is also apt to increase any resentment among the line men. We have seen that some staff men are overanxious to establish themselves. If their purpose is not specified, the danger is that they may go too far in pressuring the line to accept their recommendations. Conversely, line officials who refuse to cooperate with the staff men have no excuse if the chief has made clear that they themselves will be expected to cooperate in certain clearly defined areas.

Second, staff and line officers should be encouraged to become better acquainted, and absence of frequent contact between them should be an immediate source of concern to the agency head. We have already mentioned the tendency of some staff men to withdraw into an "ivory tower." Line supervisors, similarly, may not relish too much contact with the "college punks." The management of the agency should impress upon the heads of staff departments the need for their men to establish rapport with the line organization. Actually, the best staff director is one who does not need to be told this. So long as the agency management makes clear that this kind of close relationship between line and staff is desired, any number of methods of accomplishing the objective can be employed. The executive's own staff meeting provides him with an excellent opportunity to bring together staff and line subordinates at regular intervals and to encourage them to work together. It has been suggested that line heads invite representatives of the staff to their departmental conferences, and vice versa. Informal luncheon meetings with members of both groups present have in the past also contributed to better mutual understanding.

Efforts should also be made to provide travel funds and other inducements for staff officers to visit the actual sites of line operations. The line man may be on sound ground when he criticizes the staff specialists for infrequency of visits and for seeming to develop their recommendations in a vacuum. Impressions formed at headquarters may prove entirely erroneous when the true field

[4] See Ernest Dale and Lyndall F. Urwick, *Staff in Organization*, New York: McGraw-Hill, 1960, pp. 166–167.

situation is studied. The military discovered this a long time ago; Dale and Urwick write:

> Almost the first lesson taught to a young general staff officer serving with troops is to go and see for himself the conditions under which soldiers are living, to get to know personally the officers with whom he deals. . . . The only effective safeguard against "bureaucracy," the insidious breakdown of effective understanding which invariably ensues when officials rely on "paper" communications unsupported by personal contact, is for administrators of all grades to have or make time to go and see for themselves. The first sign that a general, or any other executive, is no leader is when he becomes "chair-borne." He is content to fall back upon penmanship about circumstances with which he has no direct experience, to rely on the written word to do duty for the deed undone.[5]

Third, rotation of staff and line assignments, whether as temporary details or indefinite transfers, should be practiced. The objective is to assure that those in staff jobs at any particular time appreciate the point of view of the line men, and that the latter have the same tolerance for the staff specialists. People frequently change their outlook when they go into a different kind of job. The man who was bitter against the staff units when he served in the line organization suddenly starts to talk a different tune when he is rotated to a staff assignment. Similarly, the staff man who switches to a line assignment, or from a central staff agency to a staff position in a line agency, will grow to appreciate the reality of problems he once thought imaginary or highly exaggerated. Wherever possible, rotation should, in fact, be part of the individual's internship. Staff recruits in such fields, for example, as personnel, finance, and planning can profitably be detailed to work in the line departments as part of their initial training. Similarly, arrangements could be made in some cases for line recruits to spend part of their learning period in one or more staff offices.

Some skepticism has been expressed about the advantages of rotation; for one thing, "Rotation into highly technical positions such as legal and medical . . . is generally not feasible."[6] Furthermore, the anticipated changes in attitudes may not materialize; Sherman points out that staff units are usually just as " 'tough' " with other staff units as they are with the line.[7] Yet that the outlook can change is seen clearly in a recently published case, "The Coming of Age of the Langley Porter Clinic."[8] A budget analyst in the California State Department of Finance is transferred to the Clinic to serve as head of its Business Services Division:

[5] *Ibid.*, p. 101.

[6] Sherman, *op. cit.*, p. 74.

[7] *Ibid.*

[8] Frederick C. Mosher (ed.), *Governmental Reorganizations: Cases and Commentary*, Indianapolis, Ind.: Bobbs Merrill, 1967, pp. 251–300.

Coming as he did, directly from the Budget Division of Finance, Wensel was thoroughly familiar with budget procedures and with what was needed to provide an adequate basis for administrative policy consideration. He was also able to provide an effective channel of communication from Langley Porter to the state government and the Legislature. . . . He also increasingly gave the Clinic the kind of solid support from the business function that the survey team had hoped for.

Wensel himself had undergone a change of attitudes since coming to the Clinic. As he put it, "When you are a budget analyst in Finance, you sometimes think you understand an agency, but you really don't. You only find out by working in one." Before coming to Langley Porter, he had not believed the Clinic really needed some of the increases it was asking for in maintenance staff; since working there he had "found out I was wrong. We really do need them."[9]

Fourth, the character of the person's academic preparation is of great importance. Taking the staff men first, there is a great danger that the programs of study they pursue may be too narrow. Since they will be dealing constantly with the line organization, they should not only be technically competent in their fields but also have a proper grounding in the substantive work of the organizations with which they are employed. Specifically, this means that those preparing to enter the service in such posts as personnel and finance should also receive appropriate training in the social sciences, such as economics, sociology, and anthropology. Without this kind of background, they will not fully understand the role of their employing organization in modern society. In this connection, it is well to remember that habits of thought, first developed as the result of inadequate university training, naturally carry over into the graduate's actual conduct on the job and become more deeply embedded in his outlook as the result of continuous contact with persons similarly trained. One of the damaging consequences is the failure of the staff man to become sufficiently interested in the details of line functions. Such a failure is particularly unstrategic for good relations with the line organization, for the easiest path to gaining the confidence of the line official is to demonstrate interest in, and the desire to learn more about, the program activities of which he is in charge.

Many line men enter the public service as economists, lawyers, medical doctors, social workers, engineers, and statisticians. In the past quite a few have in time come to occupy the key program-administration posts, such as the positions of line department and division heads in our hypothetical city government. Although

_____

[9] *Ibid.*, p. 289.

trained in one of these areas, they are placed in posts where their primary responsibility is for administration, not for the direct performance of professional tasks in the particular field. This, for example, has been true of engineering graduates for some time now. Consequently, some training in administration is also highly desirable so that they will not be completely at sea when they are later appointed to directive posts. Broad training is thus highly desirable for both staff and line workers. Basically, it is narrowness of viewpoint that in the past has made it so difficult for them to develop effective working relationships.

Fifth, an "overall management climate" should be established "which emphasizes results, teamwork, and loyalty to the enterprise as a whole rather than just to segments of it."[10]

In concluding this chapter, Sherman's reminder should be stressed: "Conflict between line and staff is desirable if it brings to bear on the solution of problems different perspectives and points of view, rather than merely jurisdictional jealousies."[11] Traditional theory seems on the one hand to deny the reality of such conflict, and on the other hand to assume that top line executives have a supreme wisdom that enables them to make the "best" decisions based on their perception of "all the facts." Conflict is realistically faced through the team concept and horizontal integration of the insights of line and staff at the levels in the organization where the problems are directly confronted. The Olympian view from up high is apt to ignore much of the reality, and to minimize, rather than maximize, the potential contribution of program and sustaining officials throughout the organization.

BIBLIOGRAPHY

Brown, David S., "The Staff Man Looks in the Mirror," *Public Administration Review, XXIII*, No. 2 (June, 1963).

Dale, Ernest, and Urwick, Lyndall F., *Staff in Organization*, New York: McGraw-Hill, 1960.

Dalton, Melville, "Staff and Line Relationships—A Study of Conflicts," in Dubin, Robert, (ed.), *Human Relations in Administration*, Englewood Cliffs, N.J.: Prentice-Hall, 1961.

Fisch, Gerald G., "Line-Staff Is Obsolete," in Golembiewski, Robert T., Gibson, Frank, and Cornog, Geoffrey Y., *Public Administration: Readings in Institutions, Processes, Behavior*, Chicago: Rand McNally, 1966.

Gaus, John M., "A Theory of Organization in Public Administration," reproduced in Nigro, Felix A., (ed.), *Public Admin-*

---

[10] Sherman, *op. cit.*, p. 73.
[11] *Ibid.*

istration, Readings and Documents, New York: Holt, Rinehart and Winston, 1951.

Golembiewski, Robert T., *Organizing Men and Power: Patterns of Behavior and Line-Staff Models,* Chicago: Rand McNally, 1967.

Gorlitz, Walter, *History of the German General Staff, 1657–1945,* New York: Praeger, 1953.

Learned, Edmund P., Ulrich, David N., and Booz, Donald R., *Executive Action,* Boston: Harvard Graduate School of Business Administration, 1951. Chapters X and XI.

Nelson, Otto L., Jr., *National Security and the General Staff,* Washington, D.C.: Infantry Journal Press, 1946.

Pfiffner, John M., and Sherwood, Frank P., *Administrative Organization,* Englewood Cliffs, N.J.: Prentice-Hall, 1960. Chapter X.

Sampson, Robert C., *The Staff Role in Management: Its Creative Uses,* New York: Harper & Row, 1955.

Sherman, Harvey, *It All Depends: A Pragmatic Approach to Organization,* University, Ala.: University of Alabama Press, 1966.

CHAPTER 6
THE GEOGRAPHY
OF ORGANIZATION

S ORGANIZATIONS grow in size, it proves impossible—or at least undesirable—to administer all activities out of a single office; besides the headquarters location, field offices are also needed. Even in our hypothetical city of 50,000, a few such branch offices will have to be established. The Public Health Department might have several district health centers, each serving residents of a demarcated zone in the city. This brings the service closer to the people, and also makes possible provision of special facilities that may be required in any one area. Similarly, park and recreational facilities will be constructed at different locations throughout the city, with each installation being manned by field representatives of the Department of Parks and Recreation. Other examples could be given, but let us now illustrate with an example where the need for field offices is much greater. This will introduce an element in organization planning not yet treated: the geographic factor.

THE CHICAGO PARK DISTRICT

The population of Chicago is more than three and a half million, which makes it 70 times larger than our hypothetical city. And as anyone who has been in Chicago knows, its physical area is extensive. It should be no surprise, then, that the Chicago Park District should have many different field locations throughout the city.

First, a few words about the Park District's legal status are in order. Actually, it is a separate municipality, independent of the city government. Originally a number of park districts were established in different neighborhoods of the city, in accordance with the provisions of state law. Each had its own taxing powers and was governed by an elective board of commissioners. In 1934 various civic groups, anxious to simplify the complicated structure of local government, were successful in obtaining the passage of a Park Consolidation Act. Through this legislation, the Chicago Park District was created and the 22 previously separate parks were placed under its jurisdiction. The Park District is governed by a five-man Board of Commissioners, appointed by the mayor with the approval of the city council. This is the only formal link with the city government, because the District still levies its own taxes and pays all charges for the operation, maintenance, and improvement of the parks.

Field activities are carried out at dozens of installations known as parks or playgrounds. The parks are bigger than the playgrounds and usually include sizeable buildings with separate gymnasiums for girls and boys, a swimming pool, game rooms, shops, and even auditoriums, in addition to outdoor facilities for sports. The playgrounds are smaller and usually have one or more small buildings with game rooms, plus outdoor facilities and equipment for different kinds of recreational activities.

The headquarters staff

Responsibility for the general direction of recreation programs at all these field locations rests with the Recreation Department, located in the District's Administration Building in downtown Chicago, where the headquarters staff of the District is located.

The headquarters-field office organization of the Recreation Department is shown in Figure 6. At the top we have the director and assistant director who have responsibility in the headquarters office for the city-wide recreation program. This headquarters staff formulates the broad policies governing the kinds of programs to be offered throughout the city. The program-planning staff consists of experts in the different recreational specialties who make their skills and knowledge available to the instructors at the field locations.

Fig. 6. Headquarters—Field Organization, Chicago Park District.

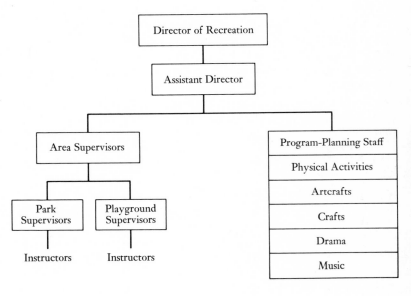

For example, the program expert on artcrafts supervises, from a technical standpoint, the activities of the field artcraft instructors, and helps them to develop programs that will stimulate park patrons to do creative work in the manual arts, weaving, rug making, knitting, sewing, fabric decoration, and pottery making. Another expert similarly advises the crafts instructors who teach techniques of working with leather, wood, metal, reed, plastic, and other media. There is also a dramatics expert who helps the field instructors plan and direct dramatic programs at the local parks. Physical activities, including games and sports of various kinds, are so extensive that the Recreation Department requires more than a single program expert; there is a staff of a dozen or so specialists who advise and instruct the physical-activity instructors in the field locations on how to organize and conduct indoor and outdoor physical activities and gymnastics.

As Figure 6 shows, the Recreation Department at Headquarters has divided the city of Chicago into a number of areas or zones. Since the director of recreation could not directly supervise each and every one of these zones, there are area supervisors who exercise administrative supervision over the parks and playgrounds in each zone. It is not necessary for these area supervisors to maintain offices in their areas; instead, they have desks at the Headquarters Office, but they do spend most of their time visiting the parks and playgrounds in their zones.

The area supervisor serves primarily as administrative coordinator of the various parks and playgrounds in his area, and as liaison between them and Headquarters, rather than as the direct supervisor for each recreation center in the zone. To fill this last capacity, there is a park supervisor to oversee the various activities and programs offered at each park, and a playground supervisor with the same function at each playground. These officials are a part of the field-office staff.

The field-office staff

It is the park supervisor to whom the people of the local community look for the development of recreation programs that meet the needs of the neighborhood. It is his job to develop a balanced program of recreational activities in the park that he supervises. In this capacity, he exercises administrative supervision over all personnel assigned to the park, including both the professional staff and the building-facilities maintenance employees (these latter are not discussed here, since we are concentrating on the program itself). In other words, the park supervisor is a *generalist*, that is, one who integrates and coordinates the efforts of the *specialists*, or the individual activity instructors (Figure 7).

For example, overzealous instructors may press for a disproportionate use of park facilities for their particular programs; two or more may try to reserve the same hours and space, leading to conflicts that can best be solved by a common superior. Thus the park supervisor makes the final decisions about the days, hours, and places that will be reserved for the different kinds of recreation programs. His extensive contacts with parents, children, adult park patrons, and many different civic groups, combined with his responsibility for administrative direction of a variety of programs, make the position an unusual one. From the viewpoint of the Headquarters Recreation Department, the park supervisor is its representative with the local community organizations and the general public, and it relies on him for the implementation of the rules and policies instituted at Headquarters. It also depends on him periodically to submit detailed reports covering the overall program at the individual park.

Fig. 7.   Recreation staff,
large park, Chicago Park District.

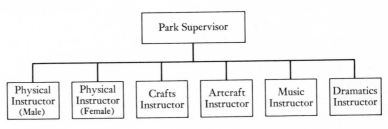

Although the park supervisor must know a great deal about the technical aspects of individual activities, he himself does not carry out or lead these activities. The professional or instructional staff already mentioned has this responsibility. Taking their direction from the park supervisor, these instructors also see to it that park property is properly taken care of, that park rules are followed by the public, and so forth. Of course, they keep detailed records of their activities for the park supervisor.

Relationships between the headquarters and field staffs

Since the area supervisors are the liaison officers between the field staff and the officials at Headquarters, the park supervisors communicate their points of view to the Recreation Department through the area supervisors, indicating the special needs and problems of the individual parks. In turn, the area supervisors transmit policy directives and instructions from the director of recreation to the park supervisors. This system does not obviate all direct contact between the director of recreation and the park supervisors, however. Certain urgencies necessitate dispensing with the formal, routine channels, and Headquarters officials—even the director of recreation himself—may telephone the park supervisor directly, and vice versa. In fact, it has been increasingly recognized that too much rigidity in formal communication systems is undesirable. So long as normal situations flow through the area supervisors, flexibility of operations is encouraged.

A more direct channel operates between the program-planning staff at Headquarters and the instructional field staff. It is not the area supervisor—nor even the park supervisor—who gives the field staff technical guidance, but the program-planning staff. Each specialist on this staff must do his best to cover the entire city, visiting all of the field locations in their turn. This is no easy task, but with competent instructors in the field, there is usually little need for the specialists to consult with them with great frequency. During his visit at a field location, the program expert assists in every way possible, advising on technical problems and clarifying program objectives. Naturally, this also entails a review of the instructor's performance and his efficiency.

Thus the instructional staff is subordinate to two types of supervisory official: the park supervisor with his interest in the overall program coordination and administration at the individual park, and the Headquarters program expert with his interest in the particular activity specialty and the city-wide coordination of the particular specialty. At the park level, the park supervisor and the instructors are part of the line organization; the Headquarters program-planning experts really constitute another kind of staff service, sometimes called "functional" staff to distinguish it from the "housekeeping" kinds of staff units described in Chapter 5 (such as personnel and finance).

Just as there are conflicts between "housekeeping" staff and line (see pages 116–120), so are there disagreements between "functional" staff and line. Let us assume that the park supervisor believes that a program-planning technician from Headquarters has given the incorrect technical instructions to one of the park staff. He can discuss the problem with the area supervisor who, in turn, can take it up with the director of recreation. The director, of course, makes the final decision. It should not be assumed, however, that differences of this type need always go up to the top line officer for final resolution. Perhaps the park supervisor can himself convince the program technician that he was wrong. If not, maybe the area supervisor will be able to do so. In other words, the incident need not develop into a major controversy.

By and large, the instructors at the parks function independently of the park supervisor in carrying out the technical details of their work. In the unlikely event that the park supervisor did rescind an instruction given by a program-planning staff specialist, the instructor can promptly advise the staff specialist of his dilemma. The matter then will be resolved between the park supervisor and the program-planning staff specialist or referred to the area supervisor—and, if necessary, to the recreation director—for final decision.

In general terms, this is the Chicago Park District's solution of the age-old problem of how to administer functional programs over a large physical area. This observer's impression was that its technical and administrative staff worked together very well. Perhaps an important reason for this is the similar background of many of the park supervisors, instructors, and Headquarters program technicians. Many park supervisors have previously served as physical-activity instructors or in specialized phases of recreation work. Their point of view is not apt to be out of line with that of the park staff or of Headquarters representatives; they are leaders of a professional group imbued with the same goals and possessing the same enthusiasms.

CENTRALIZATION AND DECENTRALIZATION

In Chapter 4 it was noted that there is a centralizing bias in traditional organization theory: Delegation of authority, whether to subordinate headquarters personnel or to field staffs, is not encouraged. In general, the advantages of decentralization are stressed in the newer theories, but not in absolute terms because again "it all depends."

In the first place, as has been observed by Paul Appleby, once an assistant to the Secretary of Agriculture, nothing can be decentralized until it has first been centralized.[1] Headquarters policies must first be defined, or there will be as many policies as there are field offices. This explains why an organization can be both centralized and decentralized; it has uniform policies that the local officials cannot disregard, while specialized situations at each of the localities necessitate policy decisions made at the field level.

Furthermore, programs are not static. Headquarters may be dissatisfied with the nature and scope of services offered at the field level, and find it necessary to assume direct responsibility for field programs until they are functioning satisfactorily. The case study "Health Centers and Community Needs"[2] relates that in Philadelphia the Department of Public Health originally had no generalized public health program; all its public health nurses worked in specialized fields only, such as child hygiene and tuberculosis and venereal disease control. Several private voluntary

[1] Paul Appleby, *Big Democracy,* New York: Knopf, 1945, p. 104.

[2] Mariana Robinson, "Health Centers and Community Needs," in Frederick C. Mosher (ed.), *Governmental Reorganizations: Cases and Commentary,* Indianapolis, Ind.: Bobbs-Merrill, 1967, pp. 61–103.

agencies also provided municipal nursing services, one of them offering "the only city-wide generalized nursing service."[3]

In 1952 the city-employed nurses were placed in a single, generalized service, and the director of the new Division was given the job of implementing the new plan. Reviewing the problem, "she found that the specialized nurses in each medical division did not even know each other."[4] Understandably, at first she was not a supporter of plans to decentralize the entire operations of the Department: The generalized nursing program had to be operational before it could be delegated to the field. Moreover, when the voluntary nurses were later integrated with the city force, this merger also had to be made effective before decentralization could be speeded. Once the new generalized, integrated program was functioning reasonably well, however, she was willing to decentralize, and indeed did so to such an extent that she felt that the nursing services "were more decentralized to district operations than any of the other programs in Community Health Services."[5]

Centralization may also be a necessity during crises or other periods of stress. Headquarters wants to hold the reins until the emergency is ended. This is explained by a British expert:

> When a ministry undertakes some new activity or adopts a substantial change in policy, it may be necessary, for a time, to retain complete authority and control at the centre. During this early period experience will be gained and precedents will be created which will enable top management to form and define its policy and intentions in more detail. When this point is reached, some measure of decentralization will become possible. At the start the delegated responsibilities may be limited but they will be increased as further experience and understanding of the subject is acquired throughout the ministry until, except for questions of the highest importance, decentralization of day to day administration is complete.
>
> This position may continue for some years, and then because the subject takes on a new importance, or attracts considerable political attention or possibly because public criticism reveals that conflicting or inconsistent decisions are being given, it becomes necessary to withdraw delegated authority and once more centralize decisions. After a further period of centralization when interest in the subject has abated or when the ministry has re-defined its policy or its aims, the process of decentralization will begin all over again.[6]

Field offices must prove that they can be trusted to discharge the responsibilities honestly and efficiently before headquarters is justified in decentralizing. A case in point is that of the

[3] *Ibid.*, p. 68.
[4] *Ibid.*, p. 73.
[5] *Ibid.*, p. 93.
[6] H. J. Kruisinga (ed.), *The Balance Between Centralization and Decentralization in Management Control,* Leiden: H. E. Stenfert Kroese N.V., 1954, p. 71.

Veterans Administration (VA). During the Harding Administration—when the agency was known as the Veterans Bureau—it was discredited by major scandals.[7] In addition, many field officials had been appointed because of their devotion to veterans' problems, rather than for their administrative leadership and understanding. When General Frank T. Hines became VA administrator, he took strong measures to bring the field offices under strict controls to prevent further scandals and malpractices. Thereafter until 1945, all personnel activity, no matter how routine, was subject to Washington approval; the regional manager could not even authorize the purchase of a pair of scissors, nor could he shift offices from one corner of the building to another without headquarters' sanction. While this policy of centralization went to extremes, in view of the history of scandals in the field operations there were decided advantages. Since 1945 all of this has changed, for the VA has expanded its activities greatly and consequently devolved much authority back to its field offices, and the latter now can be trusted to bear a good deal of the load for administering this expanded program.

The alleged reasons for decentralization sometimes are not the real ones and simply reflect the desire to avoid responsibility. To illustrate, local politicians may ask national administrators to relax certain controls over field offices simply because these controls prevent political infiltration. If the pressure is severe, an administrator may agree to "decentralize." When decentralization occurs for these reasons, it may actually be a cloak for cowardice. Influential politicians will sometimes even try to dictate the field structure of an agency. For example, some United States Senators prefer state to regional offices, because it is easier for them to control appointments to federal jobs in their own states. Having an office in each state may thus be justified as "decentralization" when a few regional offices would suffice and cost much less to maintain.

Granted all of the above, centralization frequently reflects over-bureaucratization and the desire to preserve the status quo. Let us return to the current pressures for school decentralization, mentioned in Chapter 4 (see page 102). *New York Times* editorialists have explained why they believe decentralization is a necessity for the New York City school system. First of all, "Decentralization is essential, not because it is demanded by any segment of the population, but because the present centralized system has proved itself incapable of responding effectively to the diverse needs of more than a million children in 900 schools." There is a great difference in the background of "well-to-do and deprived

[7] Gladys M. Kammerer, "The Veterans Administration in Transition," *Public Administration Review,* VIII, No. 2 (Spring, 1948), 104–106.

pupils," calling for "a greater variety of methods than any centralized bureaucracy can authorize, let alone devise and encourage." Furthermore, "the forces of the existing establishment —the Board of Education, the professional hierarchy, the civil service process of teacher licensing and placement, and the United Federation of Teachers—have fostered standardization instead of diversity." The net effect has been to create a centralized system which, "with its commitment to the *status quo*, functions in isolation from the community."[8] Summarizing, "the goal of school decentralization is to bring the administration of educational policies so close to the community and so to improve the quality of education that parents will regain confidence in those who teach their children. This goal can be accomplished only if the professionals—the district superintendents, principals, and teachers—have the power to respond to community needs, without waiting for directives and trends from a distant authority."[9]

Because minority groups and others find government remote and unresponsive to their needs, decentralization takes on new urgency. The National Advisory Commission on Civil Disorders recommended the establishment of Neighborhood City Halls that would "make information about government programs and services available to ghetto residents, enabling them to make more effective use of such programs and services and . . . expand opportunities for meaningful community access to an involvement in the planning and implementation of policy affecting their neighborhoods." The Neighborhood City Hall would help achieve "the democratic goal of making government closer and more accountable to the citizen."[10]

ADMINISTRATIVE RELATIONSHIPS AMONG LEVELS OF GOVERNMENT

So far we have discussed the geography of organization in terms of headquarters—field-office relationships of agencies at a particular level of government. However, this is only one aspect of the geographic factor in organization. Actually, administrative relationships among levels of government are even more important in terms of total program activity and the number of public employees involved.

For some time now, most important governmental activities have been the joint responsibility of all levels of government. In the past few years, however, federal grants to state and local governments have increased so greatly that the study of public administration in this country must largely be concerned with

[8] *New York Times,* editorial, July 11, 1968.
[9] *New York Times,* editorial, July 12, 1968. See Marilyn Gittell, "Professionalism and Public Participation in Educational Policy-Making: New York City, A Case Study," *Public Administration Review,* XXVII, No. 3 (September, 1967), 237–251.
[10] *Report of the National Advisory Commission on Civil Disorders,* New York: Bantam, 1968, p. 295.

intergovernmental relationships. The changes in the environment discussed in Chapter 2 have made clearer than ever before the need for greater collaboration between levels and units of government in coping with problems that cannot be dealt with effectively on a fragmented basis. Apart from reevaluation of the grant-in-aid, new partnership arrangements between federal, state, and local governments are being developed. The challenge is to meet citizen needs for new and expanded services, at the same time preserving a balance in the American constitutional system so that state and local governments do not end up as mere branches of the federal government.

In headquarters-field relationships, authority flows from a single source—headquarters—which can, if necessary, dispense with persuasion and mandate action at the field level. There are sanctions in intergovernmental programs; the dispensing agency can cut off grants-in-aid if the recipient agency fails to meet certain standards. Similarly, some interstate entities such as the Delaware River Basin Commission have the authority to force compliance with their decisions by the participating states. In practice, no grant-dispensing agency or interstate instrumentality can proceed just like the headquarters office of an agency within a single level of government. The essence of intergovernmental arrangements is the concept of equality of the partners, no matter how much more powerful one partner may in fact be (for instance, in tax resources). In practice, any available sanctions are usually not used; indeed, they may be self-defeating. To cut off grant funds penalizes the people in the nonconforming state or locality; to demand obedience by a sister state to a compact may simply drive it to withdraw from the agreement. Note this statement by William G. Colman, Executive Director of the Advisory Commission on Intergovernmental Relations (ACIR):

[11] Senate Subcommittee on Intergovernmental Relations, *Creative Federalism*, Part 2-B, The State-Local-Regional Level, 90th Congress, 1st Session, Washington, D.C.: Government Printing Office, 1967, p. 913.

In developing its proposals and in seeking their implementation, the ACIR has always been mindful of a fundamental fact that many tend to forget, namely, that program implementation in an intergovernmental context is unique and conforms to none of the models close to the hearts of public administration authorities. Its structure is not hierarchic but more like a series of interlocking circles. Responsibility does not flow up from one level to another; but up, down, and all around. Authority flows in many directions simultaneously, not from one level down to another. Such an administrative system places a premium on collaboration, not conflict, since conflict is always assured in this decentralized system. Finally, it emphasizes adaptability and practicality, not an inflexible adherence to a military model. . . .[11]

Grants-in-aid

Since the standard American government texts list the fields in which the federal and state governments provide grants-in-aid, no summary of these programs is attempted here. While the federal subsidies attract more attention because of the huge sums involved, the states themselves give substantial aid to local governmental units (for instance, to the school districts).

From less than $1 billion in 1946, federal aid to state and local governments had risen to an estimated $20.3 billion for fiscal 1969 (July 1, 1968 through June 30, 1969). The expectation was that by 1975 it would total between $50 and $60 billion. In January, 1967, Senator Edmund S. Muskie reported that "during the past six sessions, Congress has . . . appropriated more Federal-aid money than in all the previous Congresses going back to 1789."[12] In March, 1967, in a message to the Congress on the "Quality of American Government," President Johnson stated, "This year alone, some 70 per cent of our Federal expenditures for domestic social programs will be distributed through the state and local governments."[13]

There are more than 220 major federal-aid programs, based on some 400 Congressional authorizations; this aid is administered by 21 agencies, with more than 150 major bureaus and offices in Washington, and some 400 regional and subregional offices, participating in the process. An estimated 2.6 million federal employees contribute their efforts to these programs in one way or another.[14] Most of the aid goes to the state governments, which in turn allocate it to the local governments; some bypasses the states and goes directly to local government units. The "administrative monstrosity" referred to by *New York Times* correspondent James Reston (see page 13) is in large part explained by this sudden explosion of federally aided activities. It is difficult enough to administer vastly expanded programs like those in the Defense Department, whose budget nearly doubled with the Vietnam war; it is even harder to carry out a wide variety of grant programs in such fields as health, education, welfare, housing, transportation, and law enforcement since numerous arrangements must be entered into with state and local officials and cooperating citizen groups.

DEFICIENCIES IN GRANT ADMINISTRATION

In its continuing, thoroughgoing review of the grant programs, Senator Muskie's Subcommittee on Intergovernmental Relations has identified numerous problem areas, such as:

[12] Senate Subcommittee on Intergovernmental Relations, *Creative Federalism*, Part 2-A, The State-Local-Regional Level, 90th Congress, 1st Session, Washington, D.C.: Government Printing Office, 1967, p. 472.

[13] *Creative Federalism*, Part 2-B, *op. cit.*, pp. 954–955.

[14] *Creative Federalism*, Part 2-A, *op. cit.*, p. 473.

1. *Distortion of state and local priorities.* A long-standing criticism of the grant programs is that they influence state and local governments to spend in areas where federal money is currently available, rather than in those of greatest need. This was substantiated by testimony before the Muskie Subcommittee; note this report from Atlanta:

> The present programmatic nature of federal grants is considered to be disruptive of long-range planning to meet specific goals. "Part of our planning," the planning director said, "is to establish our needs, and schedule meeting those needs based on overall objectives, priorities, and availability of funds. Then along comes a new federal program which may not be top priority according to our plan. Obviously, if it's a question of the plan or the promise of a realized project, we ditch the priority planning and go hell bent for the new program."[15]

2. *Lack of policy initiative at state and local levels.* Professor Alan K. Campbell of Syracuse University testified that "there have been no major policy breakthroughs by the state-local parts of the governmental system. . . . On the whole, it seems fair to say that as the system now stands the policy initiatives come from the national part of the system while the administration of the new programs are left in the hands of state and local officials, with considerable supervision by the national bureaucracy."[16] The reasons are not entirely clear, but one of them certainly is the grant system as presently conceived and administered.

3. *Rigidity.* With few exceptions, and these very recent, the aid is "categorical," meaning that it is available for segments of programs rather than entire programs. For example, there are separate grant programs for aid to dependent children, the blind, the disabled, and the needy; there is no single, block grant for public welfare that would permit the states and localities to determine their own priorities for each kind of welfare assistance. "Florida found that a public health nurse, financed from the special heart fund, was not supposed to render aid to cancer and tuberculosis patients even when they were in a household she was visiting. Pennsylvania found that categorical distribution of public assistance grants results in needless administrative expenses. Federal reimbursement percentages vary between categories, and each category has its own restrictions, qualifications and required reports."[17] Apart from categorization, there typically are numerous conditions attached to the use of the federal money, the explanation in part being that when the subsidies were originally considered in Congress, those legislators opposed or lukewarm

[15] *Ibid.*, pp. 707-708.

[16] *Creative Federalism*, Part 2-B, *op. cit.*, p. 848.

[17] *Ibid.*, p. 822.

sought to protect the taxpayers by imposing these restrictions.

4. *Lack of coordination.* By and large, the numerous federal agencies administering grant programs function independently, with little disposition to coordinate their activities. As the Muskie Subcommittee learned from a questionnaire survey of federal grant administrator attitudes, the majority reflect a "narrowly defined functionalism" that "has deep roots."[18] The legislation establishing each grant program is the result of an alliance between administrators, pressure groups, and legislators, all dedicated to the specialized field concerned:

> . . . The approach followed throughout this legislative process is basically a functional one. It is geared to meeting specific, often urgent, problems. Relatively little consideration is given generally to the impact on other programs or on the state and local units which will administer it. . . .
>
> Further, there is not much likelihood that interlevel problems will be explored at any length after a program's enactment. The aid administrator is called upon to carry out successfully the specific goals of his program. . . . The functional bias once again reveals itself as aid administrators and satellite interest groups fight to preserve "the integrity of the program." They may view as intruders those legislative committees, top administrators, and commissions concerned with the broader problems of policy consistency, interlevel administrative procedures, interagency coordination, and structural reorganization.[19]

To add to coordination difficulties, several different federal agencies may administer grant programs in the same fields, such as recreation, economic development, and community water supply. The same local project may be supported by funds from these several agencies, each of which imposes separate and sometimes inconsistent requirements. Their regional offices may not be in the same cities, and they may or may not enjoy delegated authority from Washington. This obviously adds to the frustrations of state and local officials trying to deal with the federal government on particular projects.

5. *Poor communication.* Local officials complain that it is very difficult to obtain complete information about available state and federal grants; state and local officials agree that they often must make decisions on spending priorities without knowing about all the federal programs that might be tapped. Considering the vast number of governmental units and aid programs in the picture, the following statement is not surprising: "Our greatest difficulty . . . is communication, communication from our local governments through our state government to our federal

18 Senate Subcommittee on Intergovernmental Relations, *The Federal System as Seen by Federal Aid Officials: Results of a Questionnaire Dealing with Intergovernmental Relations,* 89th Congress, 1st Session, Washington, D.C.: Government Printing Office, 1965, p. 22.

19 *Ibid.*

government. Once we establish the communication we can usually work out our problems. But to get the communication through the state to the federal government takes a lot of doing."[20]

6. *Appropriation delays and uncertainties.* In recent years Congress has often failed to pass appropriation bills until several months after the end of the fiscal year. There is much uncertainty as to the amounts that will ultimately be approved for the various grant programs; in the meantime, state and local officials have to try to make plans, *not knowing how much aid they will get from the federal government and when.* Even if Congress acted before the end of the fiscal year, this is still very late for some programs such as education. The school academic year, September through June, does not coincide with the federal fiscal year, July through June. To obtain the best teachers, offers must be made in the spring, but Congress rarely acts this soon. Of course, the schools can, with the help of the appropriate federal aid officials, go ahead and estimate the amount of grant money they will receive, but this is hazardous:

> During the summer of 1966, the U.S. Office of Education advised us that we could safely inform the districts that their allocations would be approximately 85 percent of the prior year's allocation. Several school districts proceeded on this basis and are now in real trouble, and will have to go before the Board of Supervisors to exceed the school district budget to "pick up" the differences, or discontinue the program in the middle of the year.[21]

The gamble is great because, for one thing, teacher contracts run for the entire academic year; layoff before contract expiration is unthinkable.

Apart from the recruitment problems, educational and other programs require "lead time," during which sound project plans can be made so that when the federal money is appropriated and disbursed, it can be used promptly and effectively. Preplanning is particularly necessary because Congress has authorized aid in so many new fields where precedents and experience are lacking. Ironically, sometimes when Congress acts after long delay, state and local officials are urged to rush their plans and take advantage of the federal funds before they are "lost."[22] Unless the funds are committed before the end of the federal fiscal year, they lapse and are returned to the Treasury, despite the fact that much of the fiscal year may have passed before Congress acted.

State and local officials also are subject to great pressures by local groups that learn about the new federal-aid programs and

[20] *Creative Federalism,* Part 2-B, *op. cit.,* p. 743.

[21] *Ibid.,* p. 824.

[22] *Ibid.*

expect ample funding in their communities. Their expectations are high and their frustrations consequently great when it develops that the federal money is available only on a reduced basis or not at all. Local officials are close and so get much of the blame; suffice it to say that apart from the delays and inefficiency caused by the uncertainties in federal funding, some serious public relations problems are also created.

RECOMMENDATIONS FOR CHANGE

REVENUE SHARING. The most sweeping proposal is to abolish the present system and instead have the federal government share its revenues with the states, making block grants "with no strings attached."[23] There have been many such proposals; as one example, a bill that would return to the states "a straight 5 percent of the federal personal income tax."[24] The states could then determine their own priorities, and the administrative problems attributable to the present federal role would be eliminated. The argument here is that the states have the will and the capacity to develop sound programs in the areas now covered by the present grant system; what they have lacked is the funds. The revenue-sharing proposal has economic stabilization implications that will not be discussed here. However, the plan is favored by some largely as a means of doing away once and for all with that part of the "administrative monstrosity" represented by the present grant system.

The question is whether such a complete change is necessary and would not make the situation worse, all aspects considered. Many people doubt that the state governments would spend adequately for such purposes as construction of sewage treatment plants where the federal government started programs only because the states had not acted. Above all, they fear that state legislatures, based on their past record, would give inadequate financial support to the urban areas. Some revenue-sharing proposals would require the states to return a fixed percentage to the local governments, but skepticism is expressed that a formula could be agreed upon that would guarantee proper attention to the needs of the cities. Senator Muskie and others also doubt that the bureaucratic rigidities would be eliminated; they note that some of the sponsors of block grants are the same persons who in the past have argued for detailed state controls over local government spending of grant money.

In August, 1969, President Nixon sent a message to Congress recommending a beginning on revenue sharing. During fiscal year 1971, $500 million would be returned to the state and local

[23] *Congressional Record*, 90th Congress, 1st Session, Speeches of Hon. Melvin R. Laird in the House of Representatives, February 15, March 13, and April 10, 1967. Quote is from page 1 in reprint distributed by Congressman Laird.

[24] *Ibid.*

governments to spend as they saw fit, "without federal strings." This amount was to be augmented annually thereafter so that, beginning with mid-1975, $5 billion in federal revenues would be shared with the state and local governments. The allocation of the total annual fund among the 50 states and the District of Columbia was to be made on the basis of each state's share of the national population, adjusted for the state's revenue effort to provide a bonus for states that tax more than the national average. Each state would "pass through" a portion of the moneys received to the units of local government in the state, in accordance with a prescribed formula.

CONSOLIDATION OF GRANTS.   The first important step toward block grants was taken with the passage of the Partnership and Health Act of 1966, which authorized the merging of "some 16 previously separate health grants," thus giving the states ". . . broad discretion . . . to develop their own locally tailored comprehensive planning and services programs."[25] As President Johnson explained, "With that measure Congress . . . established for these activities a single set of requirements, a single authorization, and a single appropriation."[26] Senator Muskie's Intergovernmental Cooperation Act of 1968 originally contained a title empowering the President to propose grant-consolidation plans to the Congress, but this provision was not in the legislation as passed by Congress.[27] In April, 1969, President Nixon asked Congress to pass a grant consolidation act empowering the President to propose consolidations that would go into effect unless vetoed by one house of Congress within 60 days of transmission of the plan to Congress.

DEVELOPING COORDINATION.   The same legislation contains the statement of principle that "all viewpoints—national, regional, State, and local—shall, to the extent possible, be fully considered and taken into account in planning Federal or federally assisted development programs and projects. State and local government objectives, together with the objectives of regional organizations, shall be considered and evaluated within a framework of national public objectives, as expressed in Federal law, and available projections of future national conditions and needs of regions, States, and localities shall be considered in plan formulation, evaluation and review. . . . Each Federal Department and agency administering a development assistance program shall, to the maximum extent practicable, consult with and seek advice from all other signifi-

[25] *Creative Federalism*, Part 2-B, *op. cit.*, p. 909.
[26] *Ibid.*, p. 956.
[27] Public Law 90-577, 90th Congress, S. 698, October 16, 1968.

cantly affected Federal departments and agencies in an effort to assure fully coordinated programs."[28]

Another bill introduced by Senator Muskie, to establish a National Intergovernmental Affairs Council, has also been before the Congress.[29] The Council, to consist of the President (Chairman), Vice President, and "those Cabinet officials and agency heads whose programs have a major impact on state and local government," would be responsible for coordinating the grant programs, both in their planning and execution stages.[30] In effect, it would be the domestic policy arm of the Chief Executive: "The President would have the means of developing flexible and more direct relationships with State and local leaders. And the States and localities, in turn, could be secure in knowing that 'some one up there' in the complex of the Washington bureaucracy was concerned with their problems."[31]

At the state and local level, new arrangements are being made to improve coordination and generally to improve grant administration. A number of states now have offices or departments of local affairs, whose functions are to: ". . . assist in coordinating activities and services of state agencies which involve significant relationships with local governments . . . encourage and assist in efforts of local governments to develop mutual and cooperative solutions to their common problems . . . [and] . . . serve as a clearinghouse of information concerning state and federal services available to local governments."[32] There are more than 300 county development coordinators who serve as central points of information about grant programs and work toward "centralization, efficiency, and coordination of all grant activities in the county."[33] More than two-thirds of the states have state-federal liaison offices, either in the state capital or in Washington, or in both places.[34] Some counties and cities have liaison offices or representatives in the state capitals and/or Washington.

President Nixon's solution was to establish by Executive Order an Office of Intergovernmental Affairs under Vice President Agnew. The new office maintains liaison with state and local governments, and the Vice President also was given the responsibility for advising the Council for Urban Affairs on general governmental issues. The Council, also established by Executive Order of President Nixon, is chaired by the President, has as permanent members the Secretaries of Health, Education and Welfare, Housing and Urban Development, and Transportation, and the Director of the Office of Economic Opportunity. Its principal staff officer is the President's special assistant on urban

[28] *Ibid.*, pp. 5–6.
[29] See *Creative Federalism,* Part 2-A, *op. cit.,* pp. 472–479.
[30] *Ibid.,* p. 475.
[31] *Ibid.*
[32] *Creative Federalism,* Part 2-B, *op. cit.,* p. 810.
[33] *Ibid.,* p. 791.
[34] *Ibid.,* p. 811.

problems. The Secretaries of Labor, Commerce, and Agriculture participate in the discussions of the Council when invited to do so. Several federal agencies also have their own state-local liaison units.

COMPUTERIZED INFORMATION SYSTEM. Senator Edward M. Kennedy has introduced a joint resolution authorizing the Advisory Commission on Intergovernmental Relations to make a thorough study of the "desirability of developing and maintaining an information system making use of automatic data processing equipment, and other forms of advanced information technology, which system would be capable of collecting, storing, evaluating, sorting, and disseminating all relevant information necessary to enable the officials of states and localities, on a continuing basis, to assess areas of community need, assign priorities among such areas of need, and more effectively participate in federally assisted programs."[35] Senator Kennedy has in mind a "computer-based information system," with satellite centers which, based on profiles of each community, would furnish it with complete information on "what new programs are available, what programs have filled their quotas, what programs have changed, and what programs have been discontinued."[36]

Pending development of such a system, numerous handbooks and other materials have been developed at the federal level to guide the states and localities,[37] and new channels of direct communication have been opened.

THE FUNDING DILEMMA. The following exchange between Senator Muskie and Nassau (New York) County Executive Eugene H. Nickerson reveals how unlikely it is that the funding problems described above will be solved:

> *Mr. Nickerson*: Under our long-range federally supported air pollution program, we put up $1 locally for every three federal dollars. When we prepare our county budget, we must guess the matching requirements. How does Washington expect a local government to budget properly and do effective long-range planning under this kind of system? There should be advance commitments from the federal agencies in time for the preparation of local budgets when contracts are definitely going to be renewed.
>
> *Senator Muskie*: You are asking for back-door financing, and that is fiscally irresponsible. We must have an annual congressional appropriation, subject to all of the political pitfalls that they run into and all the political resistance they encounter. If we are to

[35] *Creative Federalism*, Part 2-A, *op. cit.*, p. 507.

[36] *Ibid.*, pp. 504–505.

[37] *Ibid.*, p. 503. See *The Vice President's Handbook for Local Officials: A Guide to Federal Assistance for Local Governments*, Office of the Vice President, Washington, D.C., November, 1967.

be fiscally responsible we cannot conceivably endorse that kind of commitment.[38]

Furthermore, Congress also views with disfavor appropriations for more than one-year periods. Even without advance commitments, if school districts, for example, could plan over a two-year period, this would be a distinct improvement. Up to now, however, Congress has with few exceptions been unwilling to make two-year appropriations for grant programs. The "political pitfalls" referred to by Senator Muskie have an air of inevitability about them, further evidence of how "politics" affects "administration."

The regional commissions

In the past few years a new instrument of intergovernmental cooperation has been developed: the regional commission. The first of these, the Appalachian Regional Commission, was authorized by Congress with the Appalachian Regional Development Act of 1965; the others, of which there are now several, such as the Ozarks and New England commissions, were established by the Secretary of Commerce under the Public Works and Economic Development Act of 1965.

Each commission is composed of a federal representative, appointed by the President subject to Senate confirmation, and of a representative of each of the participating states, usually the Governor. The federal representative serves as one cochairman, the other being designated by a majority of the state representatives. The function of each commission is to determine the region's public investment needs for economic development and to approve only those state and local requests for federal grant funds that are consistent with the commission's regional plans. This is an innovation, because under the traditional grant structure the federal agencies have usually dealt directly with state and local functional officials without going through the Governor. Under the regional commission arrangement, both the states and the federal government must be in agreement before a proposed expenditure can be made. Specifically, "affirmative actions of the commission must have a dual approval—a majority vote of the governor members and the 'yea' vote of the federal co-chairman."[39]

John L. Sweeney, the Appalachian federal cochairman, reports: "No project comes before the Appalachian Commission, and hence any federal agency, absent gubernatorial support and sponsorship. And there is no opportunity for the federal govern-

[38] *Creative Federalism*, Part 2-B, *op. cit.*, p. 766.

[39] Randy Hamilton, "The Regional Commissions: A Restrained View," in Albert H. Rosenthal (ed.), "A Symposium: Intergovernmental Relations: Insights and Outlooks," *Public Administration Review*, XXVIII, No. 1 (January–February, 1968), 20.

ment to unilaterally make an investment of Appalachian funds without full cooperation and support of the Governors."[40] Referring to criticism of the "federal veto," he says it has never been exercised on his commission, "and in my own personal judgment . . . it need never be."[41] Comparing the traditional and the commission approach, he states:

> In most instances, federal agencies must operate within rather rigid legislative mandates which restrict their flexibility of program and project decisions. Even more restraining are the rules and regulations which arise during many years on Federal administration of most grant-in-aid programs.
>
> . . . The sometimes artificial restraints are not the result of bureaucratic pettiness. They are really the result of a search for some national norm that would do the best job of satisfying the most and antagonizing the least. Unfortunately, such a national norm rarely can meet the precise problems that exist in a given area of the country. . . .
>
> The Appalachian program permits a far more flexible decision-making process; both the policy and procedures of the Commission are designed to honor the particular conditions found in each state.[42]

Experience with the regional commissions is too short for definitive evaluation. Some are apprehensive that they may merely be "window dressing for federally created, federally financed, federally operated and controlled new instruments and levels of government something more akin to a unitary than a federal system of intergovernmental relations."[43] Others point to the inherent technical difficulties in any form of public investment planning.[44] Clearly, however, the Governors have a more important role under the regional commission structure; from a relationship standpoint, this new administrative machinery has been helpful.

Interstate compacts

Interstate compacts are another example of "cooperative federalism," and though they are not as important as grants-in-aid in terms of size and variety of programs administered, they have become an important element in the American federal system and are increasingly used. As individual states find themselves unable to deal effectively with some of the problems mentioned in Chapter 2, they are entering into new compact agreements or strengthening the cooperative arrangements under old ones.

An example of a new compact is the one providing for the Educational Commission of the States, which carries out re-

[40] *Creative Federalism,* Part 2-A, *op. cit.,* p. 602.

[41] *Ibid.,* p. 604.

[42] *Ibid.*

[43] Hamilton, *op. cit.,* 22.

[44] Edward F. R. Hearle, "Regional Commissions: Approach to Economic Development," in Rosenthal, *op. cit.,* 17–18.

search on public education and serves as a center for exchange of information and ideas, and for consideration of new educational policies, to be adopted by the participating states as they see fit. An illustration of an expanded compact is the one between New York and New Jersey providing for an Interstate Sanitation Commission. Originally established to try to control water pollution, it is now also concerned with air pollution.

The compact agencies generally rely on education and persuasion to accomplish their purposes, because in very few cases do they have enforcement powers of their own. Typically, the agreements make clear that the findings of the compact agency will not be binding in the courts. Enforcement powers that do exist may only be exercised by the regular administrative machinery of the signatory states.

The water-apportionment commissions exemplify the use of persuasion. The responsibility of these commissions is to oversee the technical details of the allocation of water to the participating states. Stream-gauging stations are operated to obtain data for determining whether the states are keeping within the limits set by the compact as to the amount of water that may be stored or diverted. The commission cannot take action against a violating state; all they can do is report their findings to the appropriate state officials and try to convince them that they should take action to obtain compliance with the compact agreement within their state. As in the case of the other compact agencies, the members of the water-apportionment commissions argue their case before legislative and administrative bodies, and also conduct public relations programs to enlist the support of the public for making effective the compact agreement. "Public relations work has therefore assumed as much importance in compact agencies as it has in other segments of our national life."[45]

Even the New York Port Authority, the most successful of interstate-compact agencies, is without enforcement powers: The compact agreement states that the "two states shall provide penalties for violations of any order, rule, or regulation of the Port Authority, and for the manner of enforcing same."[46] However, an interstate agency like the New York Port Authority is not impotent because, in general, the participating states do provide effective means of enforcement, and the agency itself uses powerful tools of persuasion. Even among the few agencies that do have enforcement powers, primary reliance has been placed on persuasion and public education.

Essentially, the task is to work through state and local agencies to implement decisions made by the interstate agency.

[45] Richard H. Leach and Redding S. Sugg, Jr., *The Administration of Interstate Compacts*, Baton Rouge, La.: Louisiana State University Press, 1959, p. 92.
[46] *Ibid.*, p 96.

For example, while the comprehensive water resources use plan approved by the Delaware River Basin Commission is binding upon the compact members, for interagency coordination the Commission relies on the personnel of the participating agencies; it maintains only enough professional staff of its own "to effectively coordinate and interpret their work to keep our Commissioners sufficiently informed and to keep the many problems of the Basin in perspective."[47]

The metropolitan problem

Intergovernmental relationships are particularly complicated in the large metropolitan areas where so many Americans now live. The typical situation is one of multitudinous, overlapping, uncoordinated units of local government; there is no single entity responsible for planned development of functions such as transportation, economic development, location of open spaces, and air pollution control, which cannot be dealt with effectively except on a metropolitan-wide basis. As Dr. Alan K. Campbell of Syracuse University states, "All are agreed that metropolitan areas constitute interdependent economic and social units; yet they do not have . . . governments which encompass this area of social and economic interdependence."[48]

Historically, the federal government has contributed to the confusion by initiating or approving highway and other projects without consideration for integrated planning of all public services in an area; indeed, federally aided projects have sometimes conflicted with local plans. In the last few years, however, Congress has included provisions in several statutes conditioning approval of local projects upon the existence of a general comprehensive program for the metropolitan area. This is now true, for example, in the highway, airport, and open-space grant programs. Furthermore, the Housing and Urban Development Act of 1965 provides for federal grants for the establishment of voluntary metropolitan councils of governments, of which there are now many in various stages of development. The hope is that these councils will evolve into entities possessing sufficient power to develop and control the execution of integrated metropolitan development plans. One of them, the Association of Bay Area Governments in California, has been making decisions by majority vote of the participating local government units (it was created before the federal legislation referred to above).[49]

Various other devices are being used to promote coordination and improvement of government services within metropolitan

47 *Creative Federalism*, Part 2-B, *op. cit.*, p. 935.
48 *Ibid.*, p. 850.
49 *Ibid.*, pp. 885–905.

areas. For example, smaller local government units may contract with larger units for the provision of specified public services. The smaller units frequently cannot provide certain services as economically or as efficiently as larger jurisdictions; furthermore, if they enter into such contracts, this permits a large measure of uniformity in metropolitan administration. Los Angeles County, through contracts of this kind, provides municipal-type services to many cities in the county. The city of Lakewood, to illustrate, receives all its municipal services from the county; other cities contract for particular services, such as public health. The prediction that Los Angeles County "may well be entering an era in which it will be the major administrative unit in the metropolitan area, while policies with respect to standards and kinds of local services will be set by city councils for the county departments to follow"[50] has largely proved true.

Another arrangement is joint provision by two or more government units of a particular service, or the joint operation of a public facility, like a hospital. The objective here is for the boards of county commissioners and the city councils to appraise critically the quality of the public services their jurisdictions are providing. Depending on the findings, they might then agree to relegate to the county the responsibility for such functions as water supply and sewage disposal. Conversely, they might even find that the country should cease providing the municipalities with certain kinds of services.[51] About 30 states have granted "various kinds of permissive authority for cooperation to the local units."[52]

Other devices could be mentioned, but these will suffice to indicate the difficulties of providing administrative services in metropolitan areas. Problems bear little relationship to political boundaries. Metropolitan residents are confused by the bewildering pattern of local government, but as yet no firm sense of identification with the metropolitan community, as such, has developed. Thus local government officials must do what they can to provide efficient public services—a difficult task.

BIBLIOGRAPHY

Advisory Commission on Intergovernmental Relations, *Alternative Approaches to Governmental Reorganization in Metropolitan Areas*, Washington, D.C.: Government Printing Office, 1962.

Advisory Commission on Intergovernmental Relations, *Intergov-*

[50] Judith N. Jamison and Richard Bigger, "Metropolitan Coordination in Los Angeles," *Public Administration Review*, XVII, No. 3 (Summer, 1957), 164–165.

[51] House Committee on Government Operations, *Government Structure, Organization, and Planning in Metropolitan Areas*, 87th Congress 1st Session, Washington, D.C.: Government Printing Office, 1961, pp. 25, 30–31.

[52] *Creative Federalism*, Part 2-B, *op. cit.*, p. 854.

ernmental Relations in the Poverty Program, Washington, D.C.: Government Printing Office, 1966.

Advisory Commission on Intergovernmental Relations, *Periodic Congressional Reassessment of Federal Grants-in-Aid to State and Local Governments*, Washington, D.C.: Government Printing Office, 1961.

Beckman, Norman, "How Metropolitan Are Federal and State Policies?," *Public Administration Review*, XXVI, No. 2 (June, 1966).

Campbell, Alan K., and Sacks, Seymour, "Administering the Spread City," *Public Administration Review*, XXIV, No. 3 (September, 1964).

Foss, Philip O., "Reorganization and Reassignment in the California Highway Patrol," in Mosher, Frederick C. (ed.), *Governmental Reorganizations: Cases and Commentary*, Indianapolis, Ind.: Bobbs-Merrill, 1967.

Gittell, Marilyn, *Participants and Participation: A Study of School Policy in New York City*, New York: Center for Urban Education, 1967.

Goldbach, John, "Local Formation Commissions: California's Struggle over Municipal Incorporation," *Public Administration Review*, XXV, No. 3 (September, 1965).

Hebal, John J., "Generalist Versus Specialist in the Bureau of Indian Affairs," *Public Administration Review*, XXI, No. 1 (Winter, 1961).

Kaufman, Herbert, *The Forest Ranger: A Study in Administrative Behavior*, Baltimore: Johns Hopkins Press, 1960.

Modernizing Local Government to Secure a Balanced Federalism, a Statement on National Policy by the Research and Policy Committee of the Committee for Economic Development, New York, 1966.

Owens, John R., "A Wildlife Agency and Its Possessive Public," in Mosher, Frederick C., (ed.), *Governmental Reorganizations: Cases and Commentary*, Indianapolis, Ind.: Bobbs-Merrill, 1967.

Rosenthal, Albert A., (ed.), "A Symposium: Intergovernmental Relations: Insights and Outlooks," *Public Administration Review*, XXVIII, No. 1 (January–February, 1968).

Senate Subcommittee on Intergovernmental Relations, *Creative Federalism*, Part 2-A, The State-Local-Regional Level, 90th Congress, 1st Session, Washington, D.C.: Government Printing Office, 1967.

Senate Subcommittee on Intergovernmental Relations, *Creative Federalism*, Part 2-B, The State-Local-Regional Level, 90th

Congress, 1st Session, Washington, D. C.: Government Printing Office, 1967.

Senate Subcommittee on Intergovernmental Relations, *The Federal System as Seen by Federal Aid Officials: Results of a Questionnaire Dealing with Intergovernmental Relations*, 89th Congress, 1st Session, Washington, D.C.: Government Printing Office, 1965.

Senate Subcommittee on Intergovernmental Relations, *The Federal System as Seen by State and Local Officials: Results of a Questionnaire Dealing with Intergovernmental Relations*, 88th Congress, 1st Session, Washington, D.C.: Government Printing Office, 1963.

CHAPTER 7
THE POLITICS
OF ORGANIZATION

MANY PEOPLE believe that building an organization structure is strictly a question of logic; that no matter what the purposes of the organization, certain principles must be followed. Such people profess to see no relationship between the technical questions of organization and disagreements over objectives. Such an approach is unrealistic, to say the least.

In the first place, there is the inevitable controversy over whether there is or is not a need for a given organization *to exist* at all. Second, policy disputes may arise over the *formation* of the structure itself; one form may promote one purpose, whereas another might hinder the achievement of this purpose. These disputes originate in differences of opinion as to *which purpose* or *purposes* the organization is supposed to serve. One group may stand to gain from one set of goals; another group may have quite different objectives in mind. Further, political battles center around the question of who will have jurisdiction over the organization; those opposed to its creation in the first place often try to have it placed somewhere in the bureaucracy where its influence will be limited. Then, once an organization has been established, there is continuing debate over its reorganization, revision of goals and objectives, and whether or not the responsibility for its administration should be given to someone else.

Numerous recent examples can be cited. The legislation providing for the establishment of the Department of Housing and Urban Development was finally passed by Congress in 1965, after several years of debate between those who believed the interests of the cities were already adequately represented in the federal bureaucracy and those who did not.

THE MARITIME INTERESTS AND THE DEPARTMENT OF TRANSPORTATION

There also was a battle over creation of the Department of Transportation, approved by Congress in late 1966 but only after the original bill had been greatly weakened. As initially drafted and sponsored by the White House, the Secretary of Transportation was to have the power to set standards and criteria for the allocation of federal funds to the different modes of transport. Many Congressmen viewed this as usurpation of legislative power. Joining forces with the lawmakers on this issue were the shipbuilding, trucking, and air-transportation interests, each fearing that the Secretary might decrease "its share of the federal financial pie—for ships, highways, and air terminals. . . ."[1] The Bureau of Public Roads (formerly in Commerce), the Federal Aviation Agency and the Saint Lawrence Seaway Development Corporation (previously independent), the Coast Guard (from Treasury), and the Alaska Railroad (from Interior) were all transferred to the new Department. Because of the opposition of the shipping interests and the maritime unions, the Maritime Administration (in Commerce) was excluded.

The maritime industry urgently desires a continuation of ship construction subsidies; it traces the decline in the American merchant marine to a reorganization in 1950 that removed the responsibility for development and promotion of the industry from the United States Maritime Commission, and established a new unit in Commerce for this function, the Maritime Administration. The shipping industry claims that whereas it received strong support from the independent Maritime Commission, it has been neglected in Commerce, which is a multipurpose department and must divide its attention among many different programs. The shipping interests were "even less enthusiastic" about the proposed transfer of the Maritime Administration to

[1] John D. Morris, "Secretary of Transportation 12th Man Joining the Cabinet," *New York Times*, October 2, 1966.

the new Department of Transportation: "In such an arrangement, they feared, their interests—when weighed directly against those of highway, rail, and air interests, and by the same officials —would be even more subordinated."[2]

The tactics used to prevent absorption of the Maritime Administration into Transportation illustrate very well "the politics of organization." According to correspondent Tom Wicker, the " 'key-man' " was Paul Hall, president of the AFL-CIO Maritime Trades Department and a close friend of AFL-CIO president George Meany. Hall first appealed to Congressmen from districts with shipyard and seaport interests; he followed this up by gaining adoption of a strong AFL-CIO antitransfer resolution that put "heavy labor pressure on many members of Congress who had no specific interest in shipping or seafarers." Meany cooperated by sending two long telegrams to every member of the House; "In an election year, with many members in hard fights for political survival and campaign funds, this got the message across effectively." Hall then cleverly "played . . . on the fears of the relatively minor Merchant Marine and Fisheries Committee [in the House]. If maritime affairs were to be thrown into the vast new Cabinet department, might not the function and even the existence of the Committee be threatened? Even now, there is no comparable body in the Senate." The Committee members responded not only by unanimously opposing the transfer but also by supporting a bill to make the Maritime Administration an independent agency. As is often the case in such controversies, partisan politics intruded; seeing a chance "to claim a victory over President Johnson, and score some points with Hall and labor . . . ," the Republican Policy Committee in the House came out against the transfer.[3] Later it proudly related its role in defeating "an attempt to bury the Maritime Administration in the newly created Department of Transportation."[4]

Since opposition to reorganizations is based upon calculations that may prove wrong, it was not clear that the shipping interests had won a victory; Wicker believed that they might have added to their woes. The Maritime Administration remained a "redheaded stepchild" in Commerce, and now it would be unrepresented in a new Department responsible for developing a national transportation policy. The *New York Times'* interpretation was that the shipping companies and the maritime unions had "always found it comfortable to deal with the tame underlings of the Maritime Administration." They had demonstrated this "the one time that they were confronted by a bold and independent administrator, Nicholas Johnson . . ." whom they succeeded in get-

2 Tom Wicker, "Maritime Interests Outmaneuver Themselves," *Wilmington Evening Journal,* October 13, 1966.

3 *Ibid.*

4 *Congressional Record,* 89th Congress, 2nd Session, *112,* No. 181, Part 2, October 20, 1966.

ting removed. Thus "they much preferred to continue the present arrangement than to risk tangling with a Secretary of Transportation who will possess all of the prestige and support that goes with Cabinet rank." The *Times'* view, shared by others, was that shipping was in a "mess," and that the subsidy program had failed miserably.[5]

PROPOSED MERGER OF COMMERCE AND LABOR DEPARTMENTS

In his 1967 State of the Union Message, President Johnson recommended the merger of Commerce and Labor into a new Department of Business and Labor. His reasoning was strictly logical. Labor had originally been a given separate voice in the "highest councils of government" because the trade unions were "small and weak."[6] This was no longer the case; business and labor now had a common interest in such vital programs as manpower training, economic development, and international trade. These mutual interests could better be served in an integrated department that "would add a strong voice to the formulation of economic policy in government and would be the chief instrument for carrying out national policies affecting industry and labor."[7]

Big business either supported the President's plan or was neutral. Many small businessmen were opposed, because they feared "that the special offices looking after their interests would be swallowed up by the new department."[8] In particular, they wanted the Small Business Administration, created in 1953, continued as an independent agency, rather than absorbed, as planned, into the new department. The greatest opposition came from organized labor which, although accepting much of the President's logic, decided that it was best represented by a separate Department of Labor.[9] The President later announced that he was deferring action on the plan and referring it to his Advisory Commission on Labor-Management Policy for further study. He remained "convinced that the establishment of a new Department would in no way diminish the legitimate voice of business and labor in the councils of the Nation," but he respected "the considerations which lie behind these views to the contrary."[10]

THE ATTACK ON THE OFFICE OF ECONOMIC OPPORTUNITY

During the Johnson Administration, the Office of Economic Opportunity (OEO), established in 1964 and a symbol of the war on

[5] *New York Times,* editorial, October 17, 1966.

[6] Senate Subcommittee on Intergovernmental Relations, *Creative Federalism,* Part 2-B, The State-Local-Regional Level, 90th Congress. 1st Session, Washington, D.C.: Government Printing Office, 1967, p. 948.

[7] *Ibid.,* p. 949.

[8] Max Frankel, "Johnson Defers Cabinet Merger," *New York Times,* March 18, 1967.

[9] David R. Jones, "Johnson Asks Labor Not to Oppose Cabinet Plan," *New York Times,* February 22, 1967.

[10] *Creative Federalism, op. cit.,* pp. 949–950.

poverty, was under sharp attack by Republican leaders. They contended that the OEO had wasted much money, permitted irregularities in the use of funds, and generally been ineffective in dealing with the poverty problem. Their strategy in Congress was to try to dismantle the OEO and get its programs transferred to other departments, such as Labor and Health, Education, and Welfare. The Republicans said they wanted the federal government to deal more effectively with the poverty problem, but supporters of the OEO, while admitting its deficiencies, suspected that some of its critics basically did not sympathize with its objectives. Quite a few Democrats, including liberals such as Senator Wayne Morse of Oregon, were also very critical of the OEO's record, so the disagreement was hardly on straight party lines.

The Republican-sponsored "Opportunity Crusade Act of 1967," not passed, stated, "It is the finding of Congress that no independent agency of government can effectively coordinate the manifold and multiformed federal programs oriented to the elimination of poverty, and that such an objective can only be accomplished through the Office of the President."[11] The bill called for creation of a Council of Economic Opportunity Advisers, in the Executive Office of the President, "to formulate and recommend the national antipoverty policy" and "to develop and recommend policies to foster coordination among federal, state, and local antipoverty programs. . . ."[12] The Jobs Corps, Head Start, Vista (Volunteers in Service to America), and the community action programs, all directly administered by the OEO from its inception, were to be transferred to HEW.[13] While Johnson was President, the efforts to obtain these transfers failed, although some programs, like student work-study, were moved out, in this case to HEW (Office of Education).

In the summer of 1968 the Senate voted to transfer Head Start to HEW; grants were to be made to the states on a block basis rather than project-by-project as under OEO, and the Office of Education in HEW could not disapprove a plan without first giving the state educational agency an opportunity for a hearing. Senator Clark of Pennsylvania dubbed the proposal a "shotgun wedding," arguing that neither the OEO nor HEW wanted the change which, in his opinion, would "commit the program 'to the tender mercies of states that don't want it.' "[14] The Republicans also tried but failed to obtain the transfer of the Jobs Corps to Labor, to the relief of some OEO staff members previously employed in Labor: they said that "the Employment Service, which is controlled by the individual states, is not disposed in many states to do anything for the poor."[15]

[11] 90th Congress, 1st Session, H.R. 10682, pp. 3–4.

[12] *Ibid.*, pp. 4–6.

[13] For descriptions of these programs, see *Catalog of Federal Assistance Programs,* Washington, D.C.: Office of Economic Opportunity, 1967.

[14] Joseph A. Loftus, "Head Start Shift Voted by Senate," *New York Times,* July 18, 1968.

[15] Joseph A. Loftus, "Shriver Willing to Yield Power," *New York Times,* November 6, 1966.

The approach of Sargent Shriver, first OEO Administrator, while these proposals were being made and the bureaucratic infighting went on, was to maintain a posture of calm and dedication to the ideals of the antipoverty programs. He said he would not try to hold any program simply to preserve a bureaucratic empire; if it could be proved that another agency could do a better job of administering any OEO activity, he would "give it a sympathetic hearing."[16] Obviously, he did not want to see the OEO dismembered; his reasonableness probably made it difficult for his opponents to portray him as a power-hungry bureaucrat.

The approach of the Nixon Administration has been to change the mission of the OEO from operation of antipoverty programs to the development of new approaches to social ills. Programs developed by the OEO are being "spun off" to other federal agencies; the Job Corps has been shifted to the Labor Department and Head Start to HEW. The President does not oppose the antipoverty program, but rather has a different conception of the policies that should be followed and how they should be administered.

ILLUSTRATIONS FROM NEW YORK CITY

The politics of organization is not limited to the federal government, as John Lindsay's experience as Mayor of New York City demonstrates. On one occasion Lindsay proposed the elimination of the Division of Veterans Affairs, but veterans groups protested to the Board of Estimates and the City Council, which restored funds for the Division. The Mayor acquiesced.[17] Another time, he recommended the inclusion of a consumer protection division within a new superagency, the Economic Development Administration. But the Democratic-controlled City Council passed a bill providing for a new, independent Department of Consumer Protection, which the Mayor found it politically necessary to accept.[18] Consumer interests, at all levels of government, argue that the only way to obtain adequate protection of the consumer is through a separate department; to be represented by many different agencies as an incidental function means being given only minor attention. A councilman supporting the new department said that it "would become a clearinghouse for all consumer complaints, regardless of whether or not the city has jurisdiction."[19] "Everyone has a lobbyist except the consumer," said Councilman Edward L. Sadowsky. "Now he's going to have one with the necessary political clout to protect his interests."[20]

Lindsay's proposal for another superagency, the Health Serv-

16 *Ibid.*

17 Charles G. Bennett, "Mayor Fills Post He Sought to End," *New York Times*, August 16, 1966.

18 Charles G. Bennett, "Council Approves New Superagency," *New York Times, August* 21, 1968.

19 *Ibid.*

20 Charles G. Bennett, "Consumer Agency Due for City Soon," *New York Times*, June 28, 1968.

ices Administration, was approved over objections of the Health Department, which wanted to remain independent. It was combined with the Hospital Department, the Community Mental Health Board, and the Office of the Chief Medical Examiner. The opinion of the City Health Commissioner was that "The public health function would be cannibalized without one department to look after the total health of the citizens."[21] The Health Department feared that a single budget, covering both preventive and curative medicine, would be employed in the superagency, and that the funds for its area of responsibility—preventive medicine—would be reduced. The *New York Times* editorialized, "When budget funds are short, as they almost always are, the tendency in a single agency having overall responsibility would be to sacrifice the long-range needs of protective services in favor of the immediate needs of the critically ill."[22] Lindsay's judgment was that "the reorganization would invest the Health Services Administration with the executive responsibility and authority, the modern management techniques, and the internal flexibility" needed to provide adequate health care.[23]

A DETAILED CASE STUDY: U.S. FOREST SERVICE

The case of the United States Forest Service provides a more detailed example of the politics of organization. The struggle between the Interior and Agriculture Departments for jurisdiction over this agency covers many years, and demonstrates the role sometimes played by strong individual leaders in administrative politics; that is, when an individual has a personal interest at stake, he can sometimes win a great deal of political support by capitalizing on the public issues and utilizing the interest groups in the field of national policy concerned. A key figure in this struggle was Gifford Pinchot, whose personal interest in forest conservation was a dominant factor.

As late as 1891 there were no national forests. Ten years earlier, Congress had established a tiny unit, called the Division of Forestry, in the Department of Agriculture, as a result of a detailed report on the nation's forests. But Congress had not authorized national forest reserves. In 1891 Congress finally gave the President authority to set aside 13 million acres of forest land for such reserves, but it made no "provision for administering the reserves or for keeping them in good shape."[24] Unrestricted grazing was allowed, and "thieves often found it easy to cut and remove some of the finest timber."[25] Pinchot was among those who urged that this situation be corrected, arguing that even more

[21] Martin Tolchin, "A Dwindling Health Department Fights for Life in New City Setup," *New York Times,* May 22, 1967.

[22] *New York Times,* editorial, May 27, 1967.

[23] Tolchin, *op. cit.*

[24] M. Nelson McGeary, *Gifford Pinchot: Forester, Politician,* Princeton, N.J.: Princeton University Press, 1960, p. 36.

[25] *Ibid.,* p. 37.

timberland should be set aside, and that a plan should be developed for the efficient management of all the reserves. In subsequent years the nation's reserves were expanded, but in 1897 Congress passed legislation giving Interior, not Agriculture, essential control over all the reserves.

Pinchot was hired by the Secretary of the Interior to make a study of the reserves and to prepare a detailed proposal for organization of a national forest service. At first, Pinchot was not particularly concerned with the question of which department should have the responsibility for the timber lands; his primary concern was only that conservation measures be fully implemented. His experience in the Department of Interior, however, soon convinced him that this was not the place for his beloved forests. The more Pinchot "learned about the Department of Interior, however, the more distrustful he became of the general philosophy of its personnel. As the months and years passed he became convinced that, with exceptions here and there, the Interior Department tended to be more interested in methods of giving away government land than in protecting it for the general use and welfare."[26]

Shortly after Pinchot completed his report in 1897, a vacancy developed in the position of head of the still-existing Division of Forestry in the Department of Agriculture. The Secretary of Agriculture promptly offered the post to Pinchot, who accepted and immediately began a campaign to get the forest reserves transferred to the Department of Agriculture. Although he was successful in enlarging the Division and in increasing its budget appropriations, Pinchot was at first frustrated in his attempts to obtain control of the forests. Powerful interests opposed to conservation wanted the Interior Department to retain control over the reserves. Interior had the legal authority to prevent "timber grabbing and forest devastation," but it was lax in enforcing the law. "Those who stood to gain by unmolested sawing and cutting and grazing, sensing that forests under Pinchot would be more vigorously protected than forests under the General Land Office, strained every muscle to defeat the transfer."[27] The General Land Office was the unit in Interior that had been placed in charge of the reserves.

Undaunted, Pinchot and his followers devoted their efforts to convincing dozens of different associations to pass resolutions recommending the transfer of the reserves to Agriculture. Although these attempts met with increasing success, the picture brightened considerably when Theodore Roosevelt became President. Not only was Roosevelt an ardent conservationist himself,

[26] *Ibid.*, p. 44.
[27] *Ibid.*, p. 52.

but he was also an intimate friend of Pinchot. Even before Roosevelt moved into the White House, Pinchot went to see him, urging him to recommend to Congress that the Forestry Bureau (the title had been changed from Division to Bureau, due to its increased size) be given full responsibility for managing the government's forests. Roosevelt obliged, but Congress was not yet ready to act. Planning his moves carefully, Pinchot sought more allies for his point of view. In 1900 he organized the Society of American Foresters, whose meetings proved to be a "major factor in developing a sense of comradeship and an *esprit de corps* among the foresters attached to the Bureau of Forestry."[28] Further, now well-practiced in legislative contacts, Pinchot sought out key members of Congress.

Roosevelt cooperated at every turn. On one occasion he invited some Congressmen to lunch at the White House in order "to give [Pinchot] a chance at them on the transfer bill." On another, he invited one of the wealthiest lumber barons in the country to confer with him at the White House, with Pinchot present. This meeting was deliberately scheduled to take place one month before a convention of the National Lumber Manufacturers' Association. Roosevelt's plan was to get the movement for forest conservation to come from the lumbermen themselves, and he succeeded in persuading his guests to support the reserve policy.

Pinchot was astute in using support wherever he could get it. Bitter disputes frequently broke out between the different private interests using the national forests for grazing purposes. Land feuds, sometimes terminating in shooting or other forms of violence, were not uncommon. The cattlemen resented "encroachments" on their holdings by sheepmen and by small homesteaders. They erected fences to keep out the invaders and resorted to other strong measures, all of which shocked the public and led to a movement to stop all grazing in the national forests. Playing his cards carefully, Pinchot "joined in publicly denouncing big stockmen, but at the same time sought and obtained their support for the transfer."[29] Pinchot had never believed that the forest lands should simply be set aside and not used in any way by private interests. Since he favored continuation of grazing and even the legalizing of fences, "the cattle barons" now decided that it would be politic for them to support him in the transfer issue.

The high point in Pinchot's campaign came in 1905 when he organized a meeting of the American Forest Congress in Washington, D.C. Pinchot's real purpose has been explained as follows:

[28] *Ibid.*, p. 57.
[29] *Ibid.*, p. 59.

Billed as a kind of parliament for representatives of groups interested in forests, the Congress convened for five days. Among the delegates were influential foresters, lumbermen, miners, railroad men, wool growers, and men representing the grazing and irrigation interests. Pinchot, designating Roosevelt as honorary president of the Congress, induced his boss, Secretary of Agriculture Wilson, to act as president, and his father, James Pinchot, as first vice-president. The meeting, packed with persons favorable to forest conservation, was primarily a propaganda device for demonstrating to Congress and the country the sizeable amount of support that had been built up for practical forestry.

With the aid of the astute publicity unit of Pinchot's Bureau, news releases concerning the meeting were circulated throughout the nation. The *Brooklyn Daily Eagle*, for example, on the day before the Congress met, devoted an entire page to the meetings and to the general subject of forestry. Readers of the *Eagle* and of many other newspapers were reminded that if the current rate of timber cutting continued, the nation's forests would be exhausted in about sixty years.[30]

The Forest Congress passed a resolution favoring the transfer, and victory was finally at hand for Pinchot. Less than a month later, the transfer bill was passed in both houses of the United States Congress and quickly signed by President Roosevelt. Overnight, Pinchot "was transformed from a man with some foresters but no forests, into a man with 86 million acres of forest land." Shortly thereafter, the title of the Bureau was changed to United States Forest Service, and the reserves were designated as "national forests."

The later revival of the controversy

This was not to be the end of the issue, however. Years later, in the 1930s, it was revived when Franklin D. Roosevelt named as his Secretary of Interior Harold Ickes, a man of strong opinions and many enemies, but whose personal integrity was above question. Ickes was determined to erase the public image of Interior as a venal department; a hard worker, he set high standards for his subordinates and was strict in holding them to account. Under Ickes, Interior became a respectable Department. In the process of building it up, Ickes became convinced that it should become a Department of Conservation, with complete responsibility for all federal natural resource programs. Arthur M. Schlesinger, Jr., writes: "The keystone for such a department, as he saw it, had to be the Forest Service. From his first days in Interior, Ickes therefore embarked on an interminable campaign of intrigue, persua-

[30] *Ibid.*, p. 60.

sion, and pressure designed to recapture Forestry from Agriculture."[31]

At this time Pinchot was still very active in public life; in fact, when Franklin Roosevelt became President, Pinchot was the Republican Governor of Pennsylvania. Ickes and Pinchot were good friends, but as soon as Ickes' plan to take over the Forest Service became clear, the personal relations between the two men deteriorated. Pinchot never questioned Ickes' integrity, but he reasoned that Ickes could not live forever—and then what would happen to the Forest Service in an Interior Department so tarnished with past history of scandals? After all, Harding's Secretary of Interior, Albert B. Fall, had "auctioned off some of the nation's prize oil reserves" to private interests. Fall had tried to "recapture the Forest Service from Henry C. Wallace in order to increase the available loot."[32]

Ickes argued that this was all part of the past and should be forgotten. He felt strongly that so many programs had been taken away from Interior that few of its "vital organs" remained. A real fighter, he even proposed a trade of bureaus with Agriculture Secretary Henry A. Wallace. He was ready to cede to Agriculture such bureaus as Reclamation, General Land Office, Grazing, Soil Erosion, and Subsistence Homesteads in exchange for Forestry, Roads, and the Biological Survey. For a time in March, 1934, Wallace was inclined to agree to this most unusual proposal, but the Forest Service objected so strenuously that Wallace "turned against the package deal."[33]

It should be mentioned that Pinchot was doing his best to help the Forest Service in this fight. He completed his second term of office as Governor of Pennsylvania at the end of 1934. Defeated in his bid for the Republican nomination for the Senate, he had retired to private life, but still maintained his old interests. In June, 1935, Pinchot wrote in his diary: "Saw Harold who is red hot to get Dept. Cons. I'm again [sic] it strong." Back to work he went, trying to arouse the country against the Ickes' plan. In a letter to the newspapers, he warned that "the National Forests are again in danger." Before mailing the letter, he explained to Ickes that he "hate(d) like the devil" to be against him, but that he had to follow his conscience. However, as Ickes persisted in his plan, Pinchot dropped the amenities, and Ickes responded in kind. In a speech given in April, 1937, at the national convention of the Izaak Walton League, Pinchot charged that Ickes had allowed his ambition to impair his good judgment, and that it was his desire for more power that made him want the Forest Service.[34] Ickes inveighed against Pinchot as " 'the self-annointed

[31] Arthur M. Schlesinger, Jr., *The Coming of the New Deal,* Boston: Houghton Mifflin, 1959, p. 346.

[32] *Ibid.,* p. 344.

[33] *Ibid.,* p. 347.

[34] McGeary, *op. cit.,* pp. 410–411.

Messiah of conservation' who had posed too long 'as the infallible, the impeccable, and the omnipotent conservationist of all time.' "[35]

FDR's attitude during this controversy was basically to keep out of it. In principle he seems to have supported Ickes' side of the argument, but he did not think the matter important enough to make a major issue of it with Congress. In FDR's opinion, Interior had been created to take care of the public lands and Agriculture to help those farming privately owned lands; logically, this placed the Forest Service in Interior. The President did not think that anybody could any longer say that the Interior Department was "utterly black and crooked."[36] FDR appeared undecided for a long time, but as Schlesinger noted: "Yet, for all the troubles this competition created, it also spurred each Department to redouble its efforts in the conservation cause—a fact which may too have entered into Roosevelt's calculations."[37]

In 1938 Congress shelved a bill pushed by Ickes that would have converted Interior into a Department of Conservation and Works. The battle was almost over, but not quite. In 1939 Congress passed a Reorganization Act under which the President could make the switch by proposing a reorganization plan to Congress. In January, 1940, the President wrote Pinchot a letter suggesting that he might be leaning toward Ickes' point of view. FDR was irked because Pinchot had inspired faculty members of forestry schools to send the White House a batch of antitransfer letters.

Pinchot showed FDR's letter to Supreme Court Justice Felix Frankfurter, "who agreed that the President was angry but doubted if he would take any action. To make doubly certain, however, Pinchot addressed an antitransfer letter to every congressman and senator."[38] Finally, in February, 1940, newspapermen could assure Pinchot that the transfer move was dead. The battle was over, and Pinchot and his allies had again won.

A recent proposal

Just recently, Senator Moss of Utah introduced a bill to redesignate the Department of the Interior as the Department of Natural Resources. The Forest Service was to be transferred to the new Department, along with other units and programs from Agriculture, Interior, HEW, Defense, and the National Science Foundation.[39] Moss believes that under existing arrangements, responsibility for resource programs is diffused among many agencies, causing a "fragmentation" that "is preventing the quality

[35] Schlesinger, *op. cit.*, p. 347.

[36] *Ibid.*, p. 349.

[37] *Ibid.*

[38] McGeary, *op. cit.*, pp. 411–412.

[39] *Congressional Record*, 90th Congress, 1st Session, *113*, No. 18, February 7, 1967.

of conservation and management that the public interest requires. . . ."[40]

When a Senate subcommittee held hearings on the bill, most of the departments affected opposed the bill. Secretary of Agriculture Freeman said: "administrative organization, including the grouping of Government functions, should not be determined by abstract theory. . . . There were sound reasons for the transfer of the Forest Service to the Department of Agriculture, and those reasons are just as sound today as they were 62 years ago."[41] The opposition was so strong that when Senator Ribicoff of Connecticut asked Moss if he would settle for simply changing the name of Interior to Natural Resources, he said, "Well, maybe I should settle for anything I can get, from what I hear."[42] These hearings had again demonstrated that "organization theory in public administration is a problem in political strategy; a choice of organization structure is a choice of which interest or value will have preferred access or greater emphasis."[43]

BIBLIOGRAPHY

[40] *Ibid.*

[41] *Redesignate the Department of the Interior as the Department of Natural Resources*, Hearings Before the Senate Subcommittee on Executive Reorganization, 90th Congress, 1st Session, on S. 886, Washington, D.C.: Government Printing Office, 1968, p. 62.

[42] *Ibid.*, p. 118

[43] Wallace S. Sayre, "Premises of Public Administration: Past and Emerging," *Public Administration Review*, XVIII, No. 2 (Spring, 1958), 104.

Baldwin, Sidney, *Poverty and Politics: The Rise and Decline of the Farm Security Administration*, Chapel Hill, N.C.: University of North Carolina Press, 1968.

Carper, Edith T., "The Reorganization of the Public Health Service," in Mosher, Frederick C., (ed.), *Governmental Reorganizations: Cases and Commentary*, Indianapolis, Ind.: Bobbs-Merrill, 1967.

Creating a Department of Consumers, Hearings Before the House Subcommittee on Government Operations, 89th Congress, 2d Session, on H.R. 7179, Washington D.C.: Government Printing Office, 1966.

Creating a Department of Transportation, Parts I and II, Hearings Before House Subcommittee on Government Operations, 89th Congress, 2nd Session, on H.R. 13200, Washington, D.C.: Government Printing Office, 1966.

Dalton, Melville, *Men Who Manage*, New York: Wiley, 1959. Analyzes power struggles in a private company.

Davis, Vincent, *The Admirals Lobby*, Chapel Hill, N.C.: University of North Carolina Press, 1967.

Donovan, John C., *The Politics of Poverty*, New York: Pegasus, 1967.

Krislov, Samuel, and Musolf, Lloyd D., (eds.), *The Politics of Regulation: A Reader*, Boston: Houghton Mifflin, 1964.

Long, Norton E., "Power and Administration," *Public Administration Review*, IX, No. 4 (Autumn, 1949).

McGeary, Nelson, *Gifford Pinchot: Forester, Politician*, Princeton, N.J.: Princeton University Press, 1960.

Oslund, Margaret G., "The Guardians of La Loma," in Mosher, Frederick C., (ed.), *Governmental Reorganizations: Cases and Commentary*, Indianapolis, Ind.: Bobbs-Merrill, 1967.

Redesignate the Department of the Interior as the Department of Natural Resources, Hearings Before the Senate Subcommittee on Executive Reorganization, 90th Congress, 1st Session, on S. 886, Washington, D.C.: Government Printing Office, 1968.

Rosholt, Robert L., *An Administrative History of NASA, 1958–1963*, Washington, D.C.: National Aeronautics and Space Administration, 1966. Creation and history of NASA provide excellent illustration of power struggles for jurisdiction.

Rourke, Francis E., (ed.), *Bureaucracy, Politics, and Public Policy*, Boston: Little, Brown, 1969.

Rourke, Francis E., (ed.), *Bureauratic Power in National Politics*, Boston: Little, Brown, 1966.

Somit, Albert, "Bureaucratic Realpolitik and the Teaching of Administration," *Public Administration Review*, XVI, No. 4 (Autumn, 1956).

Stein, Harold, (ed.), *Public Administration and Policy Development: A Casebook*, New York: Harcourt, Brace & World, 1952.

Steiner, Gilbert Y., *Social Insecurity: The Politics of Welfare*, Chicago: Rand McNally, 1966.

Towards Postal Excellence, The Report of the President's Commission on Postal Organization, Washington, D.C.: Government Printing Office, 1968. Recommends establishment of postal service as a government corporation to take it out of politics.

PART III
BASIC
PROBLEMS OF
MANAGEMENT

CHAPTER 8
DECISIONMAKING

W HAT REALLY takes place in an organization cannot be understood unless one analyzes the decisionmaking process employed, the kinds of decisions that are made, and who makes them. The key to improving administration is to assure that better decisions are made. Obviously, this is an exceedingly difficult area; some of the major aspects will be reviewed.

THE RESPONSIBILITY FOR DECISIONMAKING

One of the misconceptions about modern organizations is that the most important decisions are unilaterally conceived and approved by a single "omnipotent" individual, presumably the "chief," whoever this is at the particular level of the organization.[1] "The all-powerful chief can maintain such control only to the extent that he is not dependent on others within his organization . . . ," and this is true only in "a situation of *modest complexity*," whereas so many organizations today are highly complex.[2]

1 James D. Thompson, *Organizations in Action*, New York: McGraw-Hill, 1967, p. 133.
2 *Ibid.*, p. 132.

169

The chief cannot decide everything unaided, because he is dependent on others for their specialized knowledge, as, for example, when the "complexity of the technology or technologies exceeds the comprehension of the individual" or "the organization faces contingencies on more fronts than the individual is able to keep under surveillance."[3] Furthermore, in our very interdependent society no one organization can act without consultations with numerous other organizations, which explains Harlan Cleveland's statement that "no one person 'decides' anything; each 'decision' of any importance is the product of an intricate process of brokerage involving individuals inside and outside the organization who feel some reason to be affected by the decision, or who have special knowledge to contribute to it."[4] Cleveland does not believe that in large-scale organizations the individual's opportunity to participate in decisionmaking is sharply limited. Rather, he states:

> A large and powerful organization has so many more important decisions to be made that there is proportionately more, not less, decisionmaking authority to go around. The larger the organization and the wider its reach, the more lateral contacts it has to make and maintain, the more complexities must be sorted out by experts on complexity—which is to say leaders. . . . The nearer you get to the top of the hierarchy the fewer unreviewed decisions you make. The man who buys writing pads and pencils for a government agency is virtually his own boss, but the President of the United States has to operate in a world peopled with countervailing organizations in and out of government which believe his every move is of concern to them, and must therefore be cleared with them. The more countervailing organizations have to be consulted, the more members of the internal staff must be assigned to deal with them—and must therefore "participate in major decisions."[5]

While responsibility for decisionmaking is widely diffused, "the types of decisions as well as the conditions change in character as we descend from the major executive to the non-executive positions in organization."[6] The top executives concentrate their attention on decisions relating to ends rather than means. Middle-level executives break these broad purposes into more specific ends. At the lower levels, the emphasis is on making decisions that effectively implement the policy directives received from above. This is of great importance despite the fact that the responsibility for it rests in the hands of the low-level personnel. If the wrong decisions are made at this point, the basic plans established by the top managers will prove to be failures:

[3] *Ibid.*, p. 133.

[4] Harlan Cleveland, "Dinosaurs and Personal Freedom," *Saturday Review*, February 28, 1959, 38.

[5] *Ibid.*, 14.

[6] Chester I. Barnard, *The Functions of the Executive*, Cambridge, Mass.: Harvard University Press, 1956, p. 192.

From the point of view of aggregate importance, it is not decisions of executives but of non-executive participants in organization which should enlist major interest. . . . It is here that the final and most concrete objectives of purposes are found, with the maximum of definiteness. There is no further stage of organization action. The final selection of means takes place at this point.[7]

AUTHORITY AND THE DECISIONMAKING PROCESS

Grants of particular kinds of decisionmaking responsibilities measure the power an individual or group has in the organization. *Power* has been defined as "the capacity to secure the dominance of one's values or goals."[8]

Formal authority must not be confused with power, because clearly the right to issue commands does not ensure that the commands will be heeded, while evidence of power is "to influence someone to behave in a particular way or to make decisions."[9] Herbert A. Simon writes:

Authority may be defined as the power to make decisions which guide the actions of another. It is a relationship between two individuals, one "superior," the other "subordinate." The superior frames and transmits decisions with the expectation that they will be accepted by the subordinate. The subordinate expects such decisions, and his conduct is determined by them.

The relationship of authority can be defined, therefore, in purely objective and behavioristic terms. It involves behaviors on the part of both superior and subordinate. When, and only when, these behaviors occur does a relation of authority exist between the two persons involved. When the behaviors do not occur there is no authority, whatever may be the "paper" theory of organization.[10]

Furthermore, power is not measured by position in the formal hierarchy alone. One who holds a high position on the organization chart may actually have very little influence in the organization. Membership in the cliques of the informal organization may be a much better measure of the individual's real standing in the structure. The name of an official's secretary may not appear on the organization chart, yet in reality she may be far more influential with him than are some of his fellow executives, and she may even participate in making decisions that are not at all a part of her job description. Conversely, some of the responsibilities spelled out in the job descriptions of other employees may never be

---

[7] *Ibid.*

[8] John M. Pfiffner and Frank P. Sherwood, *Administrative Organization*, Englewood Cliffs, N.J.: Prentice-Hall, 1960, p. 77.

[9] *Ibid.*, p. 25.

[10] Herbert A. Simon, *Administrative Behavior, A Study of Decision-Making Processes in Administrative Organization*, New York: Free Press (second edition), 1957, p. 125.

exercised. In other words, what the formal organization prescribes, the informal organization can modify or eliminate.

Sometimes those with the right to give orders may prefer to put their requests to the subordinates in the form of suggestions, a wise approach in gaining acceptance of authority, since a succession of formal orders may produce resistance. Too much order-giving may in fact be evidence that the supervisor is having difficulty in exercising effective authority. He fails to get the desired response, and makes the situation worse by seeking to compel compliance by reasserting his authority.

Normally, supervisory officers will depend a good deal on trusted subordinates and accept their judgments on many matters simply because they have developed confidence in them. Subordinates become "specialists" in the detailed responsibilities they have exercised over long periods of time. Their great familiarity with the problems encountered in carrying out their assignments leads the chief to believe they are in the best position to "know." In some areas, then, these subordinates hold the real authority.

THE DECISIONMAKING PROCESS

Some of the conceptions of decisionmaking have placed a heavy emphasis on rationality and the maximation of outcomes. In part, they have been based upon interpretations of the reality; often they have reflected ideas as to how decisions should be made, no matter what the existing practice. The "rational-comprehensive approach"[11] sees decisionmaking as a progression of logical steps: (1) recognition and accurate diagnosis of the problem, (2) determination of all possible alternatives, (3) thorough investigation and analysis of facts relating to each alternative, (4) comparison of the consequences of each alternative, and (5) selection of the *best possible solution* for the problem.[12] Anthony Downs cogently states that public officials "operate in a realistic world, not the 'perfectly informed' world of traditional economic theory."[13] He itemizes the following "inherent limitations of human decisionmaking":

1. Each decisionmaker can devote only a limited amount of time to decisionmaking.
2. Each decisionmaker can mentally weigh and consider only a limited amount of information at one time.
3. The functions of most officials require them to become involved in more activities than they can consider simultaneously; hence they must normally focus their attention on only part of their major concerns, while the rest remain latent.

[11] See Charles E. Lindblom, "The Science of 'Muddling Through,' " *Public Administration Review*, XIX, No. 2 (Spring, 1959), 79–88.

[12] See John M. Pfiffner, "Administrative Rationality," *Public Administration Review*, XX, No. 3 (Summer, 1960), 129.

[13] Anthony Downs, *Inside Bureaucracy*, Boston: Little, Brown, 1967, p. 75.

4. The amount of information initially available to every decision-maker about each problem is only a small fraction of all the information potentially available on the subject.
5. Additional information bearing on any particular problem can usually be procured, but the costs of procurement and utilization may rise rapidly as the amount of data increases.
6. Important aspects of many problems involve information that cannot be procured at all, especially concerning future events; hence many decisions must be made in the face of some ineradicable uncertainty.[14]

Consequently, in practice decisionmaking is far from being as logical as envisioned in the "rational-comprehensive" model; indeed, research shows that in some cases immediate attention is given to proposed solutions, without any prior careful collection of facts and evaluation of alternatives.[15] While this is understandable when circumstances such as crises require quick action, it also happens when such pressures do not exist. Furthermore, even when a logical sequence of steps is followed, the determinations made at each step fall far short of rationality in the perfect sense.

Influence of the organizational context

The organization itself, with its particular history, leadership, and desired patterns of conduct, largely explains why decisionmaking is restricted in many ways and cannot follow ideal patterns. This is brought out strikingly in Chris Argyris' study, *Some Causes of Organizational Ineffectiveness Within the Department of State*.[16] On the basis of his participation in a training conference with a group of senior foreign service officers, Argyris found that the "*living system* of the State Department in general, and of the Foreign Service in particular, . . . contains norms that inhibit open confrontation of difficult issues and penalize people who take risks." Further, this culture "rewards certain types of interpersonal styles, helps to create a perception of the Foreign Service as being a rather closed club, induces a degree of blindness on the part of the members concerning their impact on each other and 'outsiders,' and generates an intricate network of organizational defenses that makes the members believe that changing it may be very difficult if not impossible."[17]

The constraints on foreign service officers are perhaps best revealed in their conviction that to get ahead one should not disagree with superiors and "make waves." The supervisory officers defined leadership with such phrases as "respect for individuals"

[14] *Ibid.*
[15] Pfiffner, *op. cit.*
[16] Chris Argyris, *Some Causes of Organizational Ineffectiveness Within the Department of State,* Center for International Systems Research, Occasional Papers, Number 2, Department of State, Washington, D.C.: 1967.
[17] *Ibid.,* p. 2.

and "helping people take on more responsibility," but in describing their actual behavior, they impressed Argyris as emphasizing "domination and control" much more than helping "people to grow and take responsibility."[18] Although this lack of awareness between professed beliefs and actual behavior is characteristic of business and many other types of executives, and although the entire "living system" of the State Department is far from unique, the faculty selected for the State Department conferences were "unanimous, so far, that the . . . conferences are the most difficult to unfreeze, i.e., to help the participants to learn to be more open, to take risks, and to help others to do the same." They cited "as reasons for this difficulty, the participants' relatively strong discomfort in talking about interpersonal issues and feelings, in confronting problems openly, in being aware of themselves, in their willingness to be dependent upon the faculty, and in their strong tendency to intellectualize."[19]

Happily, although it is not easy, the "living system" can be changed—which is the intention of the State Department officials sponsoring these conferences. Argyris stresses that the key to success in this effort is to make the supervisors aware of how certain of their attitudes cause "organizational ineffectiveness," and to get them to change their behavior accordingly, thus setting the proper example for those below them.[20] How drastically this would change decisionmaking is seen in the present reliance on the "survival quotient of 'checking with everyone,' of developing policies that upset no one, of establishing policies in such a way that the superior takes the responsibility for them."[21]

OUTSIDE PRESSURES

There are many other organizational constraints besides the social conventions and leadership styles of the particular officials. Many of the pressures come from outside the organization, and consequently some decisions will be forced upon the administrators. The tenure-protected career official may feel that he can ignore some of these pressures, and this may also be the stand of the appointive and elective officials. Obviously, however, on many occasions the political leadership will judge it necessary or desirable to yield, in some degree at least, to the clamor. Since politics is largely "horse-trading," and politics and administration are not separable (as noted in this book so many times) the "rational-comprehensive" model of decisionmaking is all the more limited in the governmental environment.

If administrators are constantly making "political decisions,"

18 *Ibid.*, p. 12.
19 *Ibid.*, p. 17.
20 *Ibid.*, p. 46.
21 *Ibid.*, p. 33.
22 See Frederick C. Mosher (ed.), *Governmental Reorganizations: Cases and Commentary*, Indianapolis, Ind.: Bobbs-Merrill, 1967.

as the casebooks verify,[22] abstract logic cannot realistically be posed as the model for all governmental decisionmaking. This does not mean that administrators, political policymaking officials, legislators, and the public should not, to the extent possible, carefully study issues and use orderly procedures and rational judgments in coming to conclusions. It simply means that decisionmaking procedures cannot be shaped independently of the real world to which Downs refers.

"SUNK COSTS"

"Sunk costs"—the previous investment in money, other resources, and time—explain much of organizational inertia and conservatism. If substantial sums have already been invested in a program, administrators often stubbornly persist with it despite what appears to the critics to be overwhelming evidence that the original decision was wrong and should be changed. More is involved than the loss in money; long-established modes of conduct have been built around the existing policy, so to embark on a different one means much additional effort. In his private life the individual rejects change if the cost in terms of past effort seems too great; in bureaucratic organizations this tendency is greatly magnified. The difficulty alone of getting any consensus on a new policy is very discouraging, because agreements must be compromised to take into account the protective points of view of the different subunits, not to mention the "countervailing" organizations referred to by Cleveland (see page 170).

Administrators, indeed elective officials, often inherit these "sunk costs." To reject the old policy is to criticize one's predecessor in a visible way, which may be politically undesirable or at least awkward. The shifting nature of the governmental bureaucracy makes it possible for some few administrators at least to stick with poor policies because they themselves expect to depart their posts soon, and for their successors to continue with the same mistakes for fear that to admit a big error too long perpetuated would jeopardize their future careers. Other officials courageously fight for new policies, but it would be difficult to exaggerate the difficulties of moving a bureaucracy, *from within,* onto a completely new course. Outside forces (just noted) can be much more effective. When Congress is dissatisfied with the results, it will on occasion order the end of undertakings on which millions have already been expended, as it did with Project Mohole, the purpose of which was to drill a hole deep in the ocean floor to explore the mineral and other resources underneath.

Personality determinants

The kinds of decisions the official makes are naturally determined in large part by his own personality characteristics, developed before exposure to the particular organization. The recruitment process typically screens out job applicants with attitudes not in tune with the "living system"; at the same time, persons with the "right" attitudes are attracted to seek employment in the agency. Argyris believes that many foreign service officers chose the Service "because its norms and their values tended to be highly consonant."[23] Of course, the "living system" reinforces the original predispositions of the recruits. Personnel administration, discussed in detail in Chapters 12–15, is sometimes neglected in studying decisionmaking. This is both surprising and unfortunate, because the selection and shaping of the individual employee are crucial elements in the quality of the decisions made in any organization.

BUREAUCRATIC TYPES AND DECISIONS

There are endless relationships between individual personality and decision preferences. Down's framework will be followed here.

He identifies three factors in the formation of bureaucratic types: (1) the psychological predispositions inherent in someone's personality, (2) the nature of the position occupied, and (3) the probability of attaining the goals to which one is psychologically inclined.[24]

Using ideal types not intended fully to reflect the reality, he distinguishes first of all between *purely self-interested* officials "motivated almost entirely by goals that benefit themselves rather than their bureaus or society as a whole" and *mixed-motive officials* who "combine self-interest and altruistic loyalty to larger values." The first category he divides into *climbers* (after power, income, and prestige) and *conservers* (mostly concerned with convenience and security). In the second category he places *zealots* (intensely loyal to narrow policies such as the development of the nuclear submarine), *advocates* ("loyal to a broader set of functions or to a broader organization than zealots"), and *statesmen* (proponents of the general welfare).[25]

Illustrating the relationship between the three factors noted above, it is likely that the climber is an ambitious man who holds a job with enough content to permit him to exert pressure for the changes that will bring him advancement, and has a background of previous success in such efforts that keeps his expectations high. Conservers frequently are people who are "timorous, self-effacing, extremely cautious, plagued by inferiority feelings, or

[23] Argyris, *op. cit.*, p. 10.
[24] Downs, *op. cit.*, p. 89.
[25] *Ibid.*, p. 88–89.

just indifferent about their occupations." They are frequently found in the middle ranks of the bureaucracy, where they have reached the limits of their capacities, sometimes for reasons beyond their control, sometimes because of lack of ability or surrender to frustrations over past failures. Therefore they are "biased against any change in the status quo. It might harm them greatly and cannot do them much good. The only changes they strongly favor are those that reduce either their effort and inconvenience or the probability that any additional future changes will threaten their security."[26] They are afraid to make decisions on their own, so go by the rule book to avoid being blamed for anything which goes wrong.

Zealots press hard for change and "are even willing to antagonize their superiors to an astounding degree."[27] Advocates favor innovations because they want to build up the functions under their control, but they are against "changes that might benefit them personally but injure their organizations."[28] Unlike advocates, statesmen will not support a policy that in their opinion would injure society or the nation as a whole.

Significantly, Downs concludes that *"in every bureau, there is an inherent pressure upon the vast majority of officials to become conservers in the long run."*[29] In most cases, the longer an official is in the bureau and the older he is, the more likely it is that he will become a conserver. At any one time, most officials in an established bureau will have reached their "peaks," and will cling to the status quo. As to the statesmen, they are usually "misfits" in the bureaucratic way of life; "If everyone in an organization except one official advocates expanding his own functions, and that one official adopts a non-partisan view, his functions will probably receive an under-allocation of resources."[30]

INFLUENCE OF OUTSIDE REFERENCE GROUPS

One may not agree with this typology of officials, but it does show the relationship to decisionmaking. Another powerful force is the social environment of the decisionmaker—the kinds of people in society with whom he identifies. The executive tends to associate with groups "at his own level of power and status, or somewhat above it."[31] He is predisposed to give more weight to the ideas of these groups than to those of lower status.

The executive himself is typically unaware of this bias, but can be made conscious of it so that he can at least try to alter his behavior accordingly. For this reason, changes in institutional arrangements may be worth considering; for example, some public employee leaders are now making a case for final resolution of

[26] *Ibid.*, p. 97.
[27] *Ibid.*, p. 110.
[28] *Ibid.*, p. 109.
[29] *Ibid.*, p. 99.
[30] *Ibid.*, p. 111.
[31] David Katz and Robert L. Kahn, *The Social Psychology of Organizations*, New York: Wiley, 1966, p. 285.

employee grievances not by management-appointed civil service commissions as typically has been the case, but by outside arbitrators. They argue that no matter how fair the civil service commissioner tries to be, he represents the same upper class values as other members of the management, and cannot be expected to identify with working-class points of view.

OTHER PAST CONDITIONING

The individual's previous training may also influence *the way in which he makes decisions*. For example, the man who is a "bundle of fears" about both himself and others is prone to keep a tight control on everything. He is suspicious that subordinates may abuse any authority he delegates to them. On the other hand, they might perform so well as to outshine him, so why should he give away his job? Possibly it is simply a peculiar tendency; he has to dot every *i* and cross every *t* in the correspondence that goes out of his office.[32]

The individual's previous work history in the agency also has a direct bearing on the decisions he makes. Because he has such frequent contacts with the citizens of the community, a field office official may come to identify with their interests and to champion their point of view. Conversely, because of his remoteness from the scene of operations, a headquarters officer may make decisions that are unrealistic in terms of the situation in the field. This is why efforts are often made to put men with field experience in headquarters jobs, and vice versa. Job rotation can be justified as an excellent means of broadening the experiential base upon which decisions are made; "balanced decisions" are made by persons with "balanced" backgrounds.

In choosing the members of the work team, the administrator is really, to some extent at least, controlling the kinds of decisions the group will make. If he selects only persons with the same ideas, he reduces the possibilities of friction but he also creates the conditions for "conformism." The sage statement has been made that "when everyone in the room thinks the same thing, no one is thinking very much."[33] This is why some organizations avoid rigid "promotion from within" policies. If individuals are to be creative, the work atmosphere should be one in which new ideas can be freely presented.

COMMON ERRORS IN DECISIONMAKING

Certain errors in decisionmaking are so common as to warrant listing. They are: (1) "cognitive nearsightedness,"[34] (2) over-

[32] See Marshall E. Dimock, *The Executive in Action*, New York: Harper & Row, 1945, pp. 83–84.

[33] Robert Tannenbaum, Irving R. Weschler, and Fred Massarik, *Leadership and Organization: A Behavioral Science Approach*, New York: McGraw-Hill, 1961, p. 108.

[34] Katz and Kahn, *op. cit.*, p. 289.

simplification, (3) overreliance on one's own experience, (4) preconceived notions, and (5) reluctance to decide.

"Cognitive nearsightedness"

The human tendency is to make decisions that satisfy immediate needs, and to brush aside doubts as to their wisdom from the long-range standpoint. The hope is that the decision will prove a good one for the future also, but this really is to count on being lucky when the odds for such good fortune are poor.

As noted in Chapters 1 and 2, the problems confronting governments today are typically very complex in our rapidly changing environment, but a tempting immediate solution may create infinitely greater difficulties for the future. Furthermore, the complicated governmental environment in which officials function, exemplified by the discussion of intergovernmental relations in Chapter 6, encourages making decisions based on relatively narrow considerations of the moment. Many of the urgent problems described in Chapter 2 were clearly predictable quite a few years back. For example, the influx of the Negroes into the core cities, and the movement of whites to the suburbs, had already reached alarming proportions by the end of the 1950s.[35] To deal with such problems effectively requires coordinated action of officials representing all levels of government; lacking such coordination, each official feels justified in making only those kinds of decisions that satisfy the current needs of his agency. Furthermore, he can dismiss from consideration the future implications of his decision for another agency.

Expediency goes hand in hand with "cognitive nearsightedness." His own superiors may be just as insensitive as he is to future consequences; he may rightly conclude that it does not pay to think about long-range complications. Furthermore, even if there are later reverberations, many other persons will likely have participated in the original decision so that he can easily disclaim responsibility.

Oversimplification

An equally prevalent tendency is to deal with the *symptoms* of the problem, not its causes. For many people, the effective solution for the "riots"—short and long-range—is to suppress them and insist on "law and order."

Once riots break out, they must of course be brought under control, in the interests of all society. But the fundamental need

[35] See Morton Grodzins, "The Great Schism of Population," in Oliver P. Williams and Charles Press (eds.), *Democracy in Urban America: Readings on Government and Politics,* Chicago: Rand McNally, 1961.

is to eliminate the injustices that lead to the outbreaks. Race, labor, and other difficulties are frequently blamed on "trouble-makers" and "outside elements"; this simplifies matters and produces the satisfaction of having identified the "real culprits." That there is no magic formula for doing away with some problems once and for all is incomprehensible to many people. There must be a way of preventing strikes—but the reality is that in a free society no one has yet found it or likely ever will. When problems are so complicated and serious as to be terrifying (for instance, the situation in the American cities), many people are quick to favor some widely advertised remedy that in fact is like a fake medicine.

An official may reject such oversimplifications but still err in preferring a simple solution as opposed to a complicated one. It is easier for him, as it is for others participating in the deliberations, to understand the simpler one; furthermore, the latter kind is more readily explained to others and therefore more likely to be adopted. Of course, in some cases the less involved solution may be the better one. The point is that the decisionmaker is looking for any acceptable answer and takes the first simple one, no matter how inferior to other somewhat more complicated alternatives.

Overreliance on one's own experience

In general, practitioners place great weight on their own previous experience and personal judgment.[36] Although the experienced executive should be able to make better decisions than the completely inexperienced one, a person's own experience may still not be the best guide. Frequently someone else with just as much experience has a completely different solution, and is just as sure that he is the one who is being "practical." In truth, past success in a certain kind of situation may have been attributable to pure luck, not to the particular action taken.

This is why the official profits by consulting with his colleagues, subordinates, and others to find out about their experiences: Shared decisionmaking produces wiser decisions. It is also why training sessions, based on case discussions, are so valuable. During these discussions, one participant will confidently offer an opinion or solution based on his own experience, only to have someone else recount a completely opposite experience. Of course, no two situations are exactly alike, and the "case" in the book may be different in important ways from the "case" in one's experience. But still the two situations may be very similar, whereas the lessons of the experiences of the group are so varied.

[36] See Roger W. Jones, "The Model as a Decision Maker's Dilemma," in "Governmental Decision Making" (a symposium), *Public Administration Review*, XXIV, No. 3 (September, 1964), 158–160.

Participation in such discussions suggests new possibilities to the executive and, far from denying the importance of his personal experiences, enables him to put them in proper perspective.

Preconceived notions

In many cases, decisions are allegedly based on the "facts," but in truth reflect the preconceived ideas of the decisionmaker. This appears dishonest, and it is dishonest when the "facts" are doctored to justify the decision. However, in many cases the official is capable of seeing only those "facts" that support his biases. Anything else is not credible, and therefore does not qualify as a "fact."

Administrative decisions would undoubtedly be better ones if based on social science findings, but, as Alexander Leighton stresses, these findings are often ignored if they contradict the ideas of the decisionmakers. When the scientific approach is employed, "facts, observed events, and ascertained information play a dominant role."[37] By contrast, in administrative policy-making "conclusions are supported by a structure of logic that extends dangerously high on its mixed foundation of facts and basic assumptions. It is vast in proportion to the facts employed. Frequently the facts are insufficient to form any part of the foundation, and are fastened on the superstructure here and there for illustration."[38] Leighton states that the decisionmaker makes it appear that he has proceeded in an orderly way from consideration of the facts to conclusions logically derived from them. Actually, he feels, the conclusions come first, and then facts are found to justify them.

Reluctance to decide

Even when in possession of very adequate facts, some people will try to avoid making a decision. Chester I. Barnard speaks of the "natural reluctance" of men "to decide." He explains:

> The making of decisions, as everyone knows from personal experience, is a burdensome task. Offsetting the exhilaration that may result from correct and successful decision and the relief that follows the terminating of a struggle to determine issues is the depression that comes from failure or error of decision and the frustration which ensues from uncertainty.[39]

Some people believe that the environment in the government is such as to discourage the executive from making decisions. So

37 Alexander Leighton, *Human Relations in a Changing World*, Princeton, N.J.: Princeton University Press, 1949, p. 152.
38 *Ibid.*
39 Barnard, *op. cit.*, p. 189.

many clearances with other officials and agencies are required that he finds it easier to "pass the buck." Businessmen who enter the government service complain bitterly about the red tape. Accustomed to being able to take quick action in their companies, it is a frustrating experience for them to have to await approval of proposed actions by finance officers and others as prescribed in the laws and regulations. They are annoyed by the career government official's apparent unconcern over these delays, and they may even come to the conclusion that far too many of them are experts in escaping responsibility.

"Passing the buck" is, of course, a practice that exists in private companies as well. Both in government and industry, evading responsibility is the mark of the poor executive rather than the good one. Furthermore, there is no reason to think that any but a very small minority of public employees behave in this way. Yet the government environment is different, since it is the taxpayers' money that is being spent. Fear of public criticism may discourage the official from making certain decisions; sometimes the irresponsible nature of some of the criticism leads him to withdraw from the government decisionmaking scene. He prefers to make his decisions elsewhere. Others adapt to the government environment and find it both possible and exciting to participate in the formulation and implementation of public policies. However, Dahl and Lindblom write:

> Reluctance to render a decision combined with an effort to push the decision on to someone else—what Americans call "passing the buck"—is also inherent in bureaucratic structures. Specialization helps the specialist to make competent decisions within his domain of enterprise, but it also means that he may be incompetent outside it. What appears to be a weak-kneed refusal to come to the point may actually be a healthy limitation of the specialist's power. Hierarchy operates in the same direction, for one of the major purposes of hierarchy is to *prevent* subordinates from making decisions they ought not to make. In a complex organization, coordination would be impossible if the members did not know when to "pass the buck."[40]

While this is true, subordinates sometimes try to "pass the buck" upward; that is, to have their superiors make the decisions for them, as related by Argyris in the case of some foreign service officers. In discussions of delegation, it is sometimes overlooked that subordinates themselves sometimes resist the chief's efforts to get them to make some of the decisions. As Lawrence Appley points out, it is easy for someone to sit back and do nothing because a situation has arisen which is not covered by an

[40] Robert A. Dahl and Charles E. Lindblom, *Politics, Economics, and Welfare,* New York: Harper & Row, 1953, p. 249.

existing delegation of authority from his superior officer. That makes it even easier for the subordinate to decide that there is nothing that he can do. Appley condemns such inaction, and argues that, just as the manager must sometimes make decisions on the basis of inadequate facts, so must he sometimes act "with inadequate clearances."[41] Whether or not one agrees with him on this, certainly the least that the subordinate can do is to exercise the decisionmaking power that has been delegated to him.

DECISIONMAKING THEORY: THE PRESENT STATUS

These common errors in decisionmaking illustrate again how unrealistic is the "rational-comprehensive" model. Herbert A. Simon, who in the first edition of his *Administrative Behavior* made the "implicit assumption that the science of administration deals only with rational behavior . . . ,"[42] wrote in the preface to the second edition: "While economic man maximizes—selects the best alternatives from among all those available to him—his cousin, whom we shall call administrative man, satisfices—looks for a course of action that is satisfactory or 'good enough.' "[43] However, while the "rational-comprehensive" model has lost favor, disagreement exists as to the best substitute.

Incrementalism

Incremental decisionmaking, which enjoys wide support both as a normative and descriptive model, posits the following:

1. Rather than attempting a comprehensive survey and evaluation of all alternatives, the decisionmaker focuses only on those policies that differ incrementally from existing policies.
2. Only a relatively small number of policy alternatives are considered.
3. For each policy alternative, only a restricted number of "important" consequences are evaluated.
4. The problem confronting the decisionmaker is continually redefined: Incrementalism allows for countless ends-means and means-ends adjustments which, in effect, make the problem more manageable.
5. Thus there is no one decision or "right" solution, but a "never-ending series of attacks" on the issues at hand through serial analyses and evaluation.
6. As such, incremental decisionmaking is described as remedial, geared more to the alleviation of present, concrete social imperfections than to the promotion of future social goals.[44]

[41] Lawrence A. Appley, *Management in Action*, New York: American Management Association, 1956, pp. 102–103.

[42] Robert T. Golembiewski, William A. Welsh, and William J. Crotty, *A Methodological Primer for Political Scientists*, Chicago: Rand McNally, 1969, p. 208.

[43] Simon, *op. cit.*

[44] Charles E. Lindblom, *The Intelligence of Democracy*, New York: Free Press, 1965, pp. 144–148, as summarized by Amitai Etzioni, "Mixed Scanning: A 'Third' Approach to Decision-Making," *Public Administration Review*, XXVII, No. 5, (December, 1967), 386–387.

Incrementalism is criticized as "an ideological reinforcement of the pro-inertia and anti-innovation forces prevalent in all human organizations. . . ."[45] Yehezkel Dror stresses that *"marginal changes"* are not always *"sufficient for achieving an acceptable rate of improvements in policy-results. . . ."*[46] Amitai Etzioni believes that "the number and role of fundamental decisions are significantly greater than incrementalists state, and when the fundamental ones are missing, incremental decisionmaking amounts to drifting—action without direction."[47]

"Mixed scanning"

Etzioni recommends "mixed scanning," which he illustrates with proposed plans for establishing a worldwide weather observation system, utilizing satellites. Under the "rational-comprehensive" approach, very complete attempts would be made to survey weather conditions, using "cameras capable of detailed observations" and "scheduling reviews of the entire sky as often as possible." This would yield far too much data and likely "overwhelm our action capacities. . . ." Incrementalism would concentrate on areas of the world where in the recent past similar patterns had manifested themselves, "and perhaps on a few nearby regions." Under mixed-scanning, two cameras would be used: "a broad-angle camera that would cover all parts of the sky but not in great detail, and a second one which would zero in on those areas revealed by the first camera to require a more in-depth examination. While mixed-scanning might miss areas in which only a detailed camera could reveal trouble, it is less likely than incrementalism to miss obvious trouble spots in unfamiliar areas."[48] The idea is to flexibly employ the two levels of scanning, depending upon the problem: In some cases "high-coverage" scanning would be desirable, in others the more " 'truncated view' " would be in order. He explains:

In the exploration of mixed-scanning, it is essential to differentiate fundamental decisions from incremental ones. Fundamental decisions are made by exploring the main alternatives the actor sees in view of his conception of his goals, but—unlike what rationalism would indicate—details and specifications are omitted so that an overview is feasible. Incremental decisions are made but within the context set by fundamental decisions (and fundamental reviews). Thus, each of the two elements in mixed-scanning helps to reduce the effects of the particular shortcomings of the other; incrementalism reduces the unrealistic aspects of rationalism by limiting the details required in funda-

45 Yehezkel Dror, "Muddling Through—'Science' or Inertia," in "Governmental Decision Making" (a symposium), *Public Administration Review,* XXIV, No. 3 (September, 1964), 155.

46 *Ibid.,* 154.

47 Etzioni, *op. cit.,* 388.

48 *Ibid.,* 389.

mental decisions, and contextuating rationalism helps to overcome the conservative slant of incrementalism by exploring longer-run alternatives.[49]

Decisionmaking theory obviously is moving closer to the "real world," but, reassuringly, it is in no sense drifting back to the folklore stage of reliance on personal opinion and judgment. These latter elements remain as ineradicable, but the methodology employed in theory-building is constantly being improved, as are the techniques for verification through empirical research.

BIBLIOGRAPHY

Art, Robert J., *The TFX Decision: McNamara and the Military*, Boston: Little, Brown, 1968.

Barnard, Chester I., *The Functions of the Executive*, Cambridge, Mass.: Harvard University Press, 1956.

Downs, Anthony, *Inside Bureaucracy*, Boston: Little, Brown, 1967.

Etzioni, Amitai, "Mixed Scanning: A 'Third' Approach to Decision-Making," *Public Administration Review*, XXVII, No. 5 (December, 1967).

Glover, John Desmond, and Hower, Ralph M., *The Administrator, Cases on Human Relations in Business*, Homewood, Ill.: Irwin, 1963. Fourth edition.

Golembiewski, Robert T., Welsh, William A., and Crotty, William J., *A Methodological Primer for Political Scientists*, Chicago: Rand McNally, 1969. Chapter VII.

Gore, William J., *Administrative Decision-Making: A Heuristic Model*, New York: Wiley, 1964.

Gore, William J., and Dyson, J. W., (eds.), *The Making of Decisions: A Reader in Administrative Behavior*, New York: Free Press, 1964.

"Governmental Decisionmaking" (a symposium), *Public Administration Review*, XXIV, No. 3 (September, 1964).

Holland, Howard K., "Decision-Making and Personality," *Personnel Administration*, XXXI, No. 3 (May-June, 1968).

Katz, Daniel, and Kahn, Robert L., *The Social Psychology of Organizations*, New York: Wiley, 1966. Chapter 10.

Latane, Henry A., "The Rationality Model in Organizational Decision-Making," in Leavitt, Harold J., *The Social Science of Organizations*, New York: Prentice-Hall, 1963.

Lindblom, Charles E., "The Science of 'Muddling Through,'" *Public Administration Review*, XIX, No. 2 (Spring, 1959).

[49] *Ibid.*, 389–390.

Mosher, Frederick C., (ed.), *Governmental Reorganizations: Cases and Commentary*, Indianapolis, Ind.: Bobbs-Merrill, 1967.

Pfiffner, John M., "Administrative Rationality," *Public Administration Review*, XX, No. 3 (Summer, 1960).

Schiff, Ashley L., "Innovation and Administrative Decision-Making: A Study of the Conservation of Land Resources," *Administrative Science Quarterly*, II, No. 1 (June, 1966).

Scott, William G., *Organization Theory: A Behavioral Analysis for Management*, Homewood, Ill.: Irwin, 1967. Chapter 10.

Simon, Herbert A., *Administrative Behavior, A Study of Decision-Making Processes in Administrative Organization*, New York: Free Press, 1957. Second edition.

Simon, Herbert A., "Administrative Decision Making," *Public Administration Review*, XXV, No. 1 (March, 1965).

Stein, Harold, (ed.), *Public Administration and Policy Development, A Casebook*, New York: Harcourt, Brace & World, 1952.

Tannenbaum, Robert, "A Look at Formal Organization: Managerial Decision Making," in Tannenbaum *et al.*, *Leadership and Organization: A Behavioral Science Approach*, New York: McGraw-Hill, 1961.

CHAPTER 9
COMMUNICATIONS

THE ABILITY to speak, read, write, and communicate through a wide variety of sophisticated devices sets off man from animals, yet few organizations of humans are characterized by effective communication. Indeed, it would appear that of all human faculties, the ability to communicate is one of the least developed in relation to organizational needs.

Part of the difficulty is the "inadequacy of language to carry precisely the ideas of the sender . . ."[1]; certain words simply do not convey the same meaning to everyone. In many cases, however, the real problem is inability to select the right words and make one's meaning clear. Worse, the individual may not have clarified his own thinking: "If an executive cannot shape up in his own mind a clear concept of policies, objectives, programs, and organization structure . . . he is seriously handicapped."[2]

The size and complexity of modern organizations, with their numerous levels of supervision, makes the communications process —which is not easy in any case—a particularly difficult one. As

[1] William G. Scott, *Organization Theory: A Behavioral Analysis for Management*, Homewood, Ill.: Irwin, 1967, p. 302.

[2] Lawrence A. Appley, *Management in Action*, New York: American Management Association, 1956, p. 186.

187

noted in Chapter 1, much attention is now given to communications, and undoubtedly much of the recent improvement in administration is attributable to the stress on freer flow of information and, in general, better communication. Developing individual communication skills, however, will not solve conflicts rooted in basically opposed value systems. "Nor are management and the workers also able to communicate effectively with each other even though their messages may be exquisitely logical and beautifully reasoned."[3] Still, effectively exchanged communications may have the beneficial effect of pinpointing the issues, which, sometimes at least, paves the way toward accommodation and eventual agreement. In any case, knowledge of the communications patterns in an organization is indispensable for a proper understanding of how it functions:

> Let us suppose that a man is foreman in a factory, and that we are watching him at work. What do we see and hear? We watch him, perhaps, overseeing a battery of punch presses, going from one man to another as they tend the machines, answering their questions and showing them, if they have made mistakes, where they have gone wrong. We see him also at his desk making out records. That is, we see that he has a certain kind of job, that he carries on certain activities. We see also that he deals with certain men in the plant and not with others. He goes to certain men and talks to them; others come to his desk and talk to him. He gets his orders from a boss and passes on the orders to members of his own department. That is, he communicates or, as we shall say . . . interacts with certain persons and not with others, and this communication from person to person often takes place in a certain order—for instance, from the boss to the foreman and then from the foreman to the workers—so that we can say . . . that the foreman occupies a position in a chain of communications.[4]

TYPES OF COMMUNICATIONS

From the standpoint of the direction in which communications flow, three types can be distinguished: (1) downward, (2) upward, and (3) lateral. Let us discuss each of these in turn.

Downward communication

Downward communication refers to the directives and other messages that originate with the officials at the top of the organization and are transmitted down through the hierarchy—through the intervening levels of supervision—until they reach the lowest-

[3] Robert N. McMurry, "Conflict in Human Values," in Robert T. Golembiewski, Frank Gibson, and Geoffry Y. Cornog, *Public Administration: Readings in Institutions, Processes, Behavior,* Chicago: Rand McNally, 1966, p. 314.

[4] George C. Homans, *The Human Group,* New York: Harcourt, Brace & World, 1950, pp. 11–12.

ranking worker in the chain. The traditional approach to administration concentrated on this kind of communication and generally ignored the other two. It was assumed that the management was in a position to make decisions that were in the best interests of the workers. Once made, these decisions could be "dropped in the chute," so to speak, and be expected to slide smoothly down the hierarchy. If any hitch developed in the implementation of the decisions at any point in this downward chain, it was attributed to the shortcomings of the workers concerned. Furthermore, top management held the ultimate authority, so it could invoke means to force compliance with its instructions.

The Hawthorne experiments, referred to in Chapter 4, showed that downward communication was not so simple. Management could not make decisions that would be accepted at lower levels without first encouraging upward communication—that is, the transmission of information and opinions by the workers up the same hierarchy, traveling the reverse route. In large organizations, downward communication is difficult enough because orders must descend through numerous intermediate levels before the point of execution is reached. Misunderstandings can easily occur when instructions pass through so many people. If little upward communication exists, the difficulties are multiplied, because the orders themselves are apt to be unrealistic and to meet with worker resistance.

In any case, an excessive number of levels of supervision makes downward communication very difficult. A case study of the California Highway Patrol related how at one time there were five levels of command. "According to one story, Commissioner Crittenden once issued a statewide directive that was so variously interpreted as it passed down through the hierarchy that its meaning had become altogether different by the time he next encountered it on a remote patrol office bulletin board."[5] Later, the organization was "flattened" by eliminating three of these levels; coupled with greater delegation of authority, the result was that "members of the Patrol generally felt that the communications system was much improved."[6]

Upward communication

Many years have passed since the Hawthorne experiments, but few organizations have been able to develop really effective systems of upward communication—that is, messages that are passed from the lower levels of the hierarchy up to the management. There are a number of barriers to upward communication:

[5] Philip O. Foss, "Reorganization and Reassignment in the California Highway Patrol," in Frederick C. Mosher (ed.), *Governmental Reorganization: Cases and Commentary*, Indianapolis, Ind.: Bobbs-Merrill, 1967, p. 195.
[6] *Ibid.*, p. 206.

1. physical distance or inaccessibility
2. dilution or distortion at each level
3. the attitude of the supervisor
4. the inferior status of the subordinate
5. tradition[7]

Workers separated by great distances from the source of authority at the top of the organization have difficulty in communicating upward. A field worker, for example, may have relatively infrequent contact with the head of the field office. The latter, in turn, may have only limited opportunity to see his superiors at headquarters and to express his ideas fully to them. The same is true even when all the workers are located in the same area. The larger the organization, the greater the number of links in the supervisory chain, and the principle of "following channels" requires that no link in this chain be bypassed; everyone must deal through his immediate chief.

It is not surprising, then, that few messages that are voluntarily initiated by the lowest worker ever travel upward until they finally reach the desk of the top executive. Reports required by the top management must traverse this route, but they do not have the spontaneity that ideally should characterize the system of upward communication.

As information is passed up the hierarchy, it is subject to a filtering process at each level. Some of this is deliberate; a good deal is unconscious. The picture of operations as described by a subordinate may not square with the superior's conception of the situation, particularly when the subordinate reports that some things are not going well at all. "Problems" are disturbing, and a typically human reaction is to refuse to believe that they exist or are as serious as they are painted to be. (Good news ascends the hierarchy much more easily than bad news.) The tendency is to "edit" the reports to present a brighter picture. An agency head can sometimes appear to be unbelievably blind as to what is really going on in his agency. Yet based on the reports he gets, everything *is* fine; these reports simply do not present him with all the facts.

In theory, when a man becomes the head of an organization he acquires a vantage point that gives him a broader view of operations. In practice, however, the executive who is not afraid of problems and who wants the true picture is still apt to be the victim of a "conspiracy of smoothness," or the tendency of his assistants to "protect him against discomforts and to shield him from unpleasantness."[8]

[7] See Earl Planty and William Machaver, "Upward Communications: A Project in Executive Development," *Personnel*, XXVIII, No. 4 (January, 1952), 304–317.

[8] Appley, *op. cit.*, p. 195.

. . . Though his vision is broadened, he is less able to see what is going on at his very feet. Again it is the old story of his old associates and his intimates insisting on treating him differently. Somehow information does not get to him in the usual way; suddenly he does not know what the grapevine is saying; suddenly he isn't one of the old gang; suddenly he is wrapped in cellophane, insulated against certain realities, and, unless he works to prevent it, given special information in specially prepared forms. Various leaders who have told me of being victims of this process come from such widely separated walks of life as the church, business, government, and labor unions.[9]

To the subordinate, the executive represents someone who wields power and could damage the subordinate's prospects for advancement. This creates a communications block, for the subordinate is wary even though the superior may urge him to be frank. Subordinates who, for one reason or another, feel secure in their positions tend to be the most frank in expressing themselves to their superiors. For example, "From the very moment he assumes office, the dean will find a disarming and sometimes jarring frankness on the parts of those faculty members who are secure in their outside positions."[10] If the professor has published and enjoys high prestige in his field, he will normally receive job offers from other institutions and other invitations attesting to his value. Since his reputation is based largely on his outside standing, he does not have to worry too much about the reaction of his immediate superiors. There are limits to this, of course, but in general, upward communication is not as inhibited in the academic world as it is in many other environments. Frankness is also characteristic of research and development groups, and in the ranks of other professional workers in scarce supply.[11]

If the chief is not interested in hearing about problems, he in effect shuts off upward communication. There are some supervisors who sincerely want to encourage at least some upward communication, but who unwittingly discourage it. Their errors are of several different kinds. One possible difficulty is that they are not good listeners in any relationship, with subordinates or otherwise. These individuals are so tied up with their own problems and personalities that they find it difficult to concentrate on what the other person is saying. Either they interrupt to express their own viewpoints—sometimes abruptly changing the subject— or they give the other person little chance to say much. The net result is that there may be a good deal of communication of the superior's feelings, but little or no upward communication of the subordinate's views to him.

[9] *Ibid.*, p. 196.

[10] Harlan Cleveland, "The Dean's Dilemma: Leadership of Equals," *Public Administration Review*, XX, No. 1 (Winter, 1960), 25.

[11] See cases dealing with research and development organizations in John Desmond Glover and Ralph M. Hower, *The Administrator: Cases on Human Relations in Business*, Homewood, Ill.: Irwin (Fourth edition), 1963.

In recent years there has been a sprouting of books and articles in the management field on "listening." Belatedly, there is awareness of this previously neglected aspect of communications. Then, too, the superior may not know how to arrange his time so as to create the relaxed setting that will encourage the subordinate to speak up. Constant interruptions to take telephone calls and frequent glances at one's wristwatch make the subordinate feel ill at ease. He came in with something important to discuss, but somehow he never gets a chance to introduce the subject. The pity is that the superior officer may really have been interested in hearing about the problem.

The subordinate is handicapped at the outset of any upward communication, because he is not free to break in on the superior and intrude on his time. If the chief has something on his mind, he can, at any time, ask the subordinate to see him as soon as possible. In a sense, he controls their time; they in no sense control his. Rather, they must petition an audience with him. There are usually several who want to see the chief at the same time, and he is very busy as it is satisfying the other demands on his time. Further, the status symbols that set off the superior officers tend to discourage subordinates. The chief may be surrounded by personal aides and secretaries who are anxious to conserve his time; indeed, his secretary can function as a powerful obstacle to easy contact with him. Many subordinates meet with so many obstacles when trying to see the chief that they decide to drop the matter altogether.

Upward communication is in a very important sense "unnatural." It is like rowing upstream, against the current. Downward communication has the great force of tradition behind it. There is nothing at all unusual about communications originating at the top of the hierarchy and being routed downward. By contrast, upward communication is unconventional. In most organizations, it is not established procedure for the employees spontaneously to direct upward any large numbers of communications. The employee who attempts to do so may even take a risk. Further, the management that genuinely wants to encourage upward communication will have difficulty because the upward route will generally have been used so rarely in the past that the employees will remain reluctant to use it.

IMPROVING UPWARD COMMUNICATION

All of these obstacles are formidable, but the very awareness of them constitutes the first step in a program of improving upward communication. If it is so aware, management can embark on a program to stimulate upward communication. The management should not expect such communication to be spontaneous with the employees, nor is it enough simply to tell the workers that upward communication is desirable. Most of the employees will require clear evidence that the management really is interested in their opinions. Since an important change is being made in the worker's accustomed role, he understandably needs help and encouragement in making the shift from mere cog to full participant in the aims of the organization. Some workers may be so used to playing an insignificant role that they have become quite indifferent to the future of the organization. Thus the management must change the whole outlook of these workers if it is to succeed in getting them to participate in any system of upward communication.

Superior officers should follow a consistent policy of listening to their subordinates. This may involve adapting to a willingness to face bad news. The management should encourage its supervisors to do this, and the example set by the agency head in this respect will normally have a great influence on the other executives. If he encourages communications from below and accepts even negative reports, his key assistants are likely to do the same with their subordinates.

The most unfriendly atmosphere for upward communication is one in which the management seems to isolate itself, keeping information to itself and considering many matters "confidential" and not to be revealed outside the inner circle. A management that practices such limited downward communication automatically inhibits upward communication, and in effect builds a wall between itself and the rest of the organization. For subordinates to initiate upward communication in such an atmosphere would be almost tantamount to defiance. Fortunately, such an attitude by management is now considered old-fashioned and tends to be the exception rather than the rule.

The supervisor should exercise care in selecting his "communicators"—that is, those who provide him with information—and make sure that these communicators are not merely "reflectors" of what he is predisposed to seeing. Some executives make a point of surrounding themselves with at least one or two "no" men in a conscious effort to avoid the "conspiracy of smoothness" mentioned earlier. Selecting the "communicators" on the basis of pure convenience is a common mistake by superiors. The foreign national who knows English, for example, is easy to communicate with, but what he relays may be unrepresentative of the predominant beliefs in his society. The executive who obtains most of his field information from headquarters makes the same kind of mistake, even though it may be convenient for him to talk with the headquarters staff but inconvenient to visit the field offices for first-hand information.

As to distortion, executives can make appropriate use of the strategy of "counterbiases."[12] For example, "Every general was once a lieutenant and remembers the type of distortion he used when he forwarded information to his own superiors. Therefore, he develops a counterbiased attitude toward most reports received from his subordinates. . . . Insofar as he is correctly able to estimate these distortions, he can restore the information to its original form." Furthermore, even if the official has no background that permits him to identify the "type of distortion . . . incorporated into information he has received . . . ," he knows that "the more inherently uncertain any information is, the more scope there is for distortion in reporting it."[13] Aware of the tendency of subordinates to resolve uncertainty questions in their favor, he insists that they report results, to the extent possible, in terms of " 'measurable' " rather than " 'immeasurable factors.' "[14] The mere knowledge that he may decide to verify the statements and data in the reports will deter the subordinates from claiming what they might otherwise claim.[15]

The superior officer should also strive to correct any personal habits that prevent the subordinate from speaking to him freely. Again, the superior must first be aware of these mannerisms, and humans are typically blind when it comes to personal failings. Yet some self-prompting is possible once the supervisor has become aware of these tendencies and has really decided to encourage the subordinate. It should be pointed out here that superior officers frequently feel a compulsion to demonstrate their superiority to their subordinates. With some, this is a protective device; if they *appear* to know more than their subordinates, they can feel they are living up to their official roles in the organization. Other supervisors are vain and would in any case treat their subordinates with condescension. While the supervisor must never forget his responsibilities as a superior officer, his position hardly means that he is always better apprized of all the facts than is the subordinate. Once the supervisor recognizes that his subordinates are likely to possess information that he does not, he is much more apt to encourage subordinates to communicate freely with him.

Another common mistake is for the superior to state his own position before he listens to the subordinate, rather than inviting the subordinate to give his opinions on the particular problem.

12 Anthony Downs, *Inside Bureaucracy*, Boston: Little, Brown, 1967, p. 121.

13 *Ibid.*

14 *Ibid.*, p. 122.

15 Felix A. Nigro, "Control and Inspection for Better Government Operation," *Modern Government*, VI, No. 1 (January–February, 1965), 47–54.

There may be no intention on the part of the superior to force his views on the subordinate, but the latter is quickly placed in a difficult position: He must agree with the boss. Few people will want to challenge the chief so openly.

Encouraging subordinates to express their views also offers another advantage. As noted in the previous chapter, some workers prefer to leave all decisions to someone else in order to avoid the responsibility. Such an attitude generally serves to impair the caliber of the individual's work, which ultimately reflects on the supervisor as well as adds to his load of decisionmaking. If, however, the supervisor encourages free expression of ideas from his subordinates, he is likely to lead this sort of individual to develop his capacity for greater responsibility. The supervisor will never succeed in this if he merely asks his subordinates for reactions to his own ideas.

Where it is indicated and feasible, the superior officer should *use* the information given to him by his subordinates. Nothing is more destructive of free expression—and of upward communication—than the chief's failure to act upon the ideas and problems reported to him. The subordinates are led to believe that they are wasting their time, and may even wish that the superior had not gone through the formality of listening. The purpose of communication is to achieve organizational objectives. Action at some point is essential if subordinates are to continue to feel motivated in contributing to these objectives by communicating significant information to their superiors.

Lateral communication

Lateral communication is that which takes place among workers of the same level in the hierarchy, or among individuals of different levels who are not in a superior-subordinate relationship. Lateral relationships will frequently go from one agency to another, and are not restricted to intraagency relationships. We use the term *lateral* instead of *horizontal* in order to be able to include *all* across-the-organization contacts.

Traditional organization theory is based on the organization chart and the system of *scalar* authority it depicts. The scalar principle means that the different positions of authority are shown in descending order of importance. The limitations of the chart give the clue to the inadequacies of traditional theory, as is so well revealed in the following statement:

> The relation between the scheme of activities and the scheme of interaction in an organization is usually represented by the

familiar organization chart, which shows the organization divided into departments and subdepartments, the various officers and subofficers occupying boxes, connected by lines to show which persons are subordinate to what other ones. Every such chart is too neat; it tells what the channels of interaction ought to be but not always what they are. The pyramid-type chart is particularly misleading because it shows only the interaction between superiors and subordinates, the kind of interaction that we shall call, following Barnard, *scalar*. It does not show the interaction that goes on between two or more persons at about the same level of the organization, for instance, between two department heads. . . .

This kind of interaction we shall call lateral interaction, though we must remember that there are borderline cases where the distinction between scalar and lateral interaction disappears. The conventional organization chart represents the scalar but not the lateral interaction. *If it were not for the unhappy association with predatory spiders, the facts would be much better represented by a web, the top leader at the center, spokes radiating from him, and concentric circles linking the spokes. Interaction takes place along the concentric circles as well as along the spokes.* [Italics added.][16]

Traditional organization theory has emphasized coordination through command; that is, through the downward communications of the superior. This assumes that the superior knows enough about the detailed work activities under him to be able to give instructions that will automatically provoke coordinated action on the part of the subordinates.[17] Never sound, this concept is now clearly unrealistic because of the complex operations of modern organizations. Furthermore, there are serious limits to the coordination that can be imposed on the employees from above. Such coordination tends to be nominal, simply because it is forced on the worker, and, at best, he only grudgingly complies. Real team play is characterized by spontaneity. The individual wants to cooperate because he derives *personal* satisfaction from functioning as a member of the team.

In the previous chapter it was stated that in modern organizations, decisionmaking is not monopolized by just a few top people. Management depends on the specialized skills and knowledge of its subordinates, and modern administrations recognize this. Today, they invite workers to participate in the decisionmaking process; logically, this requires the encouragement of both upward and lateral communication. The wise superior finds it advantageous to encourage his subordinates not only to express their ideas to him freely, but also to settle as many problems as possible among

[16] Homans, *op. cit.*, pp. 104–105.
[17] See Victor A. Thompson, *Modern Organization*, New York: Knopf, 1961, p. 181.

themselves. If they are to cooperate in this manner, they must obviously be in close contact with one another.

OBSTACLES

Just as in the case of upward communication, the lateral pattern of interaction presents its difficulties. In some respects, effective lateral communication is even more difficult to achieve. In upward communication, the subordinate must adjust to only one person—his immediate supervisor. In lateral communication, workers must deal with several coworkers, and any one department head must try to work together harmoniously with all other department heads; he must also develop effective working relationships with department heads and other officials of outside agencies. Suffice it to say that since cooperative relationships must be established with many different officials—with the usual variation in personalities and modes of behavior—lateral communication is far from easy.

The very division of an organization into specialized parts creates barriers to lateral communication and coordination. Specialists typically develop strong loyalties, not to the organization as a whole but to their own areas of interest. The tendency is for them to regard members of other specialized groups as threats to their own positions in the organization. The members of each specialized group think its function is the most important in the agency. Furthermore, specialized professions have their peculiar frames of reference and technical language. The members of each can communicate among themselves effectively, but they frequently have difficulty grasping the point of view of outsiders.

As one example, if those in basic research in a research and development branch are perpetually at odds with those in development, the entire organization suffers. The basic researchers, desiring free play for their creative urges, want to work on projects that may promise no immediate results, whereas the development people prefer research effort that seems likely to pay off quickly.[18] Sometimes it seems that the only factor uniting different specialist groups is their common dislike for the "administrators," the alleged paper-shufflers who hold them down with budgetary and other controls. Actually, these administrators represent another specialist group, one trained in the *management* of enterprises, and, admittedly, this kind of training also produces a narrow focus.

Besides the frictions between specialists, there are rivalries and consequent tensions between the different organization units. Departments compete with other departments for bigger ap-

[18] See Evelyn Glatt, "The Demise of the Ballistics Division," in Mosher, *op. cit.*, pp. 219–249.

propriations and more prominent roles in the total government program. Similarly, within any one department the bureaus and other subdivisions fight for special status. The rival organization units eye one another with suspicion and sometimes with considerable hostility. Instead of freely exchanging information on operating plans, they may try to keep one another in the dark. Deviousness, instead of open discussion of mutual problems, may characterize the conversations between their respective personnel. The principal officials in each department may play their cards close to their chests, always afraid of being outmaneuvered by the other party. Or they may interchange polite but meaningless communications, just like suave diplomats who have no intention of coming to an agreement. The hostility between the different groups may be so great that they repress their feelings and communicate very little with one another until suddenly there is a big blow-up.

The very complexity of modern organization also creates difficulties, just as it does in the case of downward and upward communications. The more persons an official must consult, both within and outside the agency, the more complicated the process of lateral communication becomes. Often he is uncertain as to whom he should consult, because the lines of responsibility within the agency are not that clearly defined. If he must check with another agency, his problem becomes even more difficult, for he may be unfamiliar with the work assignments of the officials in that agency. Valuable time is lost before he can identify the particular individual with whom he should deal. Furthermore, in both intraagency and interagency contacts, physical separation may delay and impede communications, as is illustrated in communications between widely separated field offices.

Merely looking at the organization chart of a large public agency will give some idea of the complexities of lateral communication. Although the interaction between the numerous departments, divisions, and organization units is not shown on the chart, the very number of these horizontally placed units suggests the intricate pattern of interrelationships necessary for efficient operation. Naturally, the red tape increases as documents and other communications are directed laterally from points inside and outside the agency.

An example of confused lateral communications comes from the history of the United Nations Relief and Rehabilitation Administration (UNRRA). Its headquarters office in Washington, D.C., was making innumerable copies of cables as they were received from field officials stationed abroad. The so-called "action copy" of each incoming cable was routed to the headquarters division that was considered to be the most concerned with the subject dealt with in the message. The jurisdictions of the different divisions had been defined so vaguely, however, that in many cases there was much uncertainty as to which headquarters official was supposed to receive the action copy. Accordingly, the duplicating machines were kept busy making countless copies of all cables so that each division could get a copy of every incoming and outgoing communication—just in case the subject matter might be of interest to it. This illustrates how, when organization responsibilities are so poorly defined that anyone's business is everyone's business, communication channels become hopelessly clogged. The "veins" and the "arteries" of the organization were choked because the "brain" was not functioning as it should.

A further difficulty arises from the fact that the person initiating a lateral communication usually cannot exert the same pressure as can a supervisor on his own subordinates. In dealing with coequals, representatives of other agencies, or even the subordinates of others, the official must usually rely on persuasion. This may mean far more delay in lateral than in downward communication, where the traditional flow of authority does give the communication at least some ring of urgency.

IMPROVING LATERAL COMMUNICATION

The first step in developing efficient communications is to build a sound organization structure and to make clear everybody's responsibilities. In the UNRRA example, when the "brain" did clarify the responsibilities of the different headquarters offices, the communications channels were drained of the excessive paper flow. As to achieving coordination, George F. Gant stresses what he calls "unity by agency objective."[19] By this he means that employees at all levels will work together better if the leaders of the agency clearly explain the importance of the agency program and of their own particular contributions to it. Many different techniques can be employed in this effort, but obviously a very superior quality of leadership is required if the employees throughout the agency are to be induced to work together as a team. Why it takes time to build the team is seen in the following statement:

> We understand people easily through our experience with them, which teaches us their special use of words, the meaning of intonation and gestures, whether they are matter of fact or emotional, given to exaggeration or understatement, are reticent or voluble, and many other subtle characteristics of communication. Without the confidence that accompanies this kind of under-

19 George F. Gant, "Unity and Specialization in Administration," in Felix A. Nigro (ed.), *Public Administration, Readings and Documents*, New York: Holt, Rinehart and Winston, 1951, pp. 126–135.

standing, reticence, hesitation, indecision, delay, error, and panic ensue.

"Know your people" is nearly as important as "know your language" in the communication upon which organized effort depends. The difficulty of communication on matters of concrete action between individuals who have not known each other is a matter of common experience, but its importance with respect to organization seems to be forgotten because the organizations we know have, in fact, developed usually through long periods. At a given time nearly everyone has habitual relationships with most of those with whom he needs to communicate regularly.[20]

The agency head naturally wants his subordinates to cooperate and to pull together; yet it takes a real effort to get even the heads of organization units to work together properly. Above all, the agency head must be aware of the probable existence of at least some sensitive relationships between them. With this awareness, he is in a much better position to induce coordinated efforts. The staff conference is frequently mentioned as a valuable tool for achieving coordination, yet the experienced executive knows that some of his subordinates may come to these meetings determined to conceal their real thoughts and plans from the others. He will also be well aware that some of the positions taken may be reactions to certain individuals and their personalities, rather than to the objective situation. Subordinate A may react negatively to suggestions made by subordinate B simply because it is B who makes them. If C were to make them, his reaction might be different.

Thus if the executive is to be successful in improving lateral communication, he must first be effective in improving the interpersonal relationships among his subordinates. Unless he understands his role in this way, the kinds of communications he evokes from them will likely consist of mere words, unsupported by any real desire to cooperate. Obviously, there are limits to what the executive can do to promote better personal relationships between his subordinates. It is a certainty, however, that he will have very little success unless he is first able to interpret accurately the feelings behind the communications they initiate, both when in a staff conference or when conferring with him individually.[21]

It has been suggested that in committee meetings no one comment on what someone else has said until he has first satisfactorily repeated what he understands as the other person's meaning. This, of course, has only limited application in direct operations, since the time usually is not available to go through such a procedure. In administration, the communicators do not

[20] Chester I. Barnard, "Education for Executives," in Robert Dubin (ed.), *Human Relations in Administration*, Englewood Cliffs, N.J.: Prentice-Hall, 1961, p. 20.

[21] An excellent treatment of this problem is Warren H. Schmidt and Robert Tannenbaum, "The Management of Differences," in Robert Tannenbaum, Irving R. Weschler, and Fred Massarik (eds.), *Leadership and Organization: A Behavioral Science Approach*, New York: McGraw-Hill, 1961, pp. 101–118.

have to be polished speakers or great writers, but they do have to make themselves understood. In general, it can be said that too few supervisors in government have developed really satisfactory communications skills. Fortunately, current training programs give the subject a good deal of emphasis.

In assuring proper clearance, one technique is to require those who originate the action copies of outgoing letters and documents to obtain the initials, on the file copy, of representatives of certain other organization units with a legitimate interest in the matter. No purely mechanical procedure will solve this problem of lateral clearance, because the originating official must use his own judgment in deciding whose initials should be obtained in the particular case. When correspondence is prepared for his own signature, the official should examine the file copy before he signs the original. In this way, if important initials are missing he can return the correspondence to the originator with instructions to obtain the necessary clearances. The repeated failure of a sub-ordinate to forward correspondence that contains all the required initials will warrant the superior official to investigate. However, it is neither practicable nor desirable to have all outgoing letters signed by a higher official. Many will be signed and sent out by the originating officer. In such case, only a post-control can be exercised, as by reviewing files of correspondence already dis-patched. In the final analysis, however, no matter what the pro-cedural manual says, the effectiveness of the system of clearing correspondence will basically depend on the desire of the officials concerned really to cooperate.

INFORMAL COMMUNICATIONS

The formal communications network will always be supple-mented by an informal one. If clearances are difficult to obtain through the formal channels, contact can be made informally with a friend who can expedite things.

Although the "grapevine" admittedly can damage the organ-ization by carrying ugly gossip and false information, it also can play a constructive role. Valuable information that an individual will normally not be willing to communicate through the official channels is often transmitted to superior officers very rapidly through the grapevine. For instance, John Jones may be unhappy about a certain condition in his office, but he is not inclined to "jump" channels and complain to the management. He expresses himself freely to his friends, one or more of whom may have an "in" with the top officials in the agency. They informally communicate John Jones' dissatisfactions, whereupon management can look into a situation of which it had not been aware.

Thus the friendship ties characteristic of the informal organization remove some of the communication blocks in upward communication. They perform the same function in facilitating lateral and even downward communication: The superior officer may want to give a subordinate personal advice, but he feels that his official capacity does not permit it. He talks freely to another employee who is in a position to pass the advice on to the person concerned. Obviously, considerable skill must be developed in utilizing these informal channels if the desired results are to be obtained. The dangers are great, because information fed into the gossip mill can easily be distorted and do more harm than good.

Eugene Walton observes that the "organization's informal communications network begins to hum whenever the formal channels are silent or ambiguous on subjects of importance to its members."[22] This indicates that the management stands to profit from knowing what kind of information is being transmitted through the grapevine. If the employees learn about significant organization developments mostly through the grapevine, this is a clear indication that the official channels are not functioning as efficiently as they should. Of course, no matter how good the formal system of communications, the grapevine will still exist, but it should not have to do the job of advising employees of management policies. This is the responsibility of the formal organization.

The following words of Herbert A. Simon are very much to the point:

> No step in the administrative process is more generally ignored, or more poorly performed, than the task of communicating decisions. All too often, plans are "ordered" into effect without any consideration of the manner in which they can be brought to influence the behavior of the individual members of the group. Procedural manuals are promulgated without follow-up to determine whether the contents of the manuals are used by the individuals to guide their decisions. Organization plans are drawn on paper, although the members of the organization are ignorant of the plan that purports to describe their relationships.[23]

BIBLIOGRAPHY

Anderson, John, "What's Blocking Upward Communications?" *Personnel Administration*, XXXI, No. 1 (January–February, 1968).

[22] Eugene Walton, "How Efficient is the Grapevine?" *Personnel*, XXXVIII, No. 2 (March–April, 1961), 45.

[23] Herbert A. Simon, *Administrative Behavior, A Study of Decision-Making Processes in Administrative Organization*, New York: Free Press (second edition), 1957, p. 108.

Boyd, Bradford B., "An Analysis of Communication Between Departments—Roadblock and By-Passes," *Personnel Administration*, *XXVIII*, No. 6 (November–December, 1965).

Dorsey, John T., Jr., "A Communication Model for Administration," *Administrative Science Quarterly*, *II*, No. 3 (December, 1957).

Downs, Anthony, *Inside Bureaucracy*, Boston: Little, Brown, 1967.

Goetzinger, Charles, and Valentine, Milton, "Problems in Executive Interpersonal Communication," *Personnel Administration*, *XXVII*, No. 2 (March–April, 1964).

Katz, Daniel, and Kahn, Robert L., *The Social Psychology of Organizations*, New York: Wiley, 1966. Chapter 9.

Likert, Rensis, *New Patterns of Management*, New York: McGraw-Hill, 1961. Chapter 4.

Pfiffner, John M., and Sherwood, Frank P., *Administrative Organization*, Englewood Cliffs, N.J.: Prentice-Hall, 1960. Chapter 16.

Redfield, Charles E., *Communication in Management*, Chicago: University of Chicago Press, 1958.

Scott, William G., *Organization Theory: A Behavioral Analysis for Management*, Homewood, Ill.: Irwin, 1967. Chapters 7 and 15.

Senate Subcommittee on National Security and International Operations, 90th Congress, 2nd Session, *Specialists and Generalists: A Selection of Readings*, Washington, D.C.: Government Printing Office, 1968.

Simon, Herbert A., *Administrative Behavior: A Study of Decision-Making Processes in Administrative Organization*, New York: Free Press (second edition), 1957. Chapter VIII.

Simon, Herbert A., Smithburg, Donald W., and Thompson, Victor A., *Public Administration*, New York: Knopf, 1950. Chapters 10 and 11.

Vogel, Alfred, "Why Don't Employees Speak Up?" *Personnel Administration*, *XXX*, No. 3 (May–June, 1967).

CHAPTER 10
PUBLIC RELATIONS

L AWRENCE A. APPLEY writes: "Whatever an organization does that affects the opinions of its various publics toward it is public relations."[1] A given organization may not employ a public relations director or have any formal program for developing favorable public attitudes, yet it will elicit some kind of response on the part of the people who have contact with it. Thus it has public relations, good, bad, or indifferent.

A distinction should be made between *public relations* itself and *public relations administration*. If an organization is aware of the importance of its publics' opinions and develops a positive program intended to influence these publics intelligently and constructively, it has public relations administration. Appley refers to *publics*, plural, because modern organizations are constantly dealing with many different groups. This makes public relations administration difficult since favorable relations may be enjoyed with one group, but often at the expense of another.

[1] Lawrence A. Appley, *Management in Action*, New York: American Management Association, 1956, p. 53.

MULTIPLE PUBLICS

A private company's publics include not only its customers but also its stockholders, labor unions, trade associations, suppliers, and the other organizations with which it has contact. In government, the specific nature of an agency's publics will depend on the kind of programs for which it is responsible. The Department of Agriculture's publics, for example, include numerous commodity groups, large and small farm operators, manufacturers of agricultural machinery, owners of grain elevators, the starving peoples of the world, and even the American housewife. As indicated in Chapter 1, in many important fields of government activity great discretion must be entrusted to officials in the administrative branch. These officials must define the "public interest." When Newton Minow, a former Chairman of the Federal Communications Commission, called television a "wasteland," he did not endear himself to one of his publics—the broadcasters. On the other hand, he won the admiration of another—namely, numerous parents who are very disturbed by the emphasis on violence in television programs.

The ideal situation, of course, is to enjoy reasonably good relations with all or the majority of the agency's publics. This is difficult to accomplish, particularly when agency objectives are described vaguely or inconsistently in the authorizing legislation. Legislators hope that a bill will satisfy as many different groups and individuals as possible. Enforcement officials are faced with the formidable task of accomplishing this in practice. Legislators themselves constitute one of the most crucial publics for administrative officials. If it is displeased, the legislature can reduce the agency's budget and even abolish it. The agency typically has many publics within the legislative body. These are the appropriations and other committees that review its activities and pass upon its requests for additional funds and approval of new programs. Each member of the legislature is by himself a potential public, depending on where his interests lie.[2]

DEVELOPING THE PUBLIC RELATIONS PROGRAM

The management of any public agency should not only employ competent *media specialists*—those who handle press contacts, prepare news releases, write radio scripts, and carry out other information activities—but it should also create a favorable image of itself, both inside and outside the agency.

[2] For an unusually good example of disagreements between an agency's publics, see John R. Owens, "A Wildlife Agency and Its Possessive Public," in Frederick C. Mosher (ed.), *Governmental Reorganizations: Cases and Commentary*, Indianapolis, Ind.: Bobbs-Merrill, 1967, pp. 107-149.

Media specialists

Care should be exercised to keep the media specialists in their proper sphere. Primarily persons with journalism backgrounds, these men and women have contributed a great deal to the success of the programs of many public agencies. Using their special skills, they have often achieved excellent results in interpreting the agency's program to the citizenry. Department heads and other top officials usually do not have the time to write their own speeches, so every day in government talented members of the information staffs prepare drafts for them. The director of information has shrewd comments to make to the agency head about how to obtain public support for a proposed course of action.

But with few exceptions, these media specialists are not qualified to participate in the formulation of the agency's policies as such. Some people believe that this is a proper and necessary activity for the information staff; their argument is that no public relations program, no matter how artfully conceived, can remedy deficiencies in the agency's basic policies. Accordingly, they argue, the information specialist should play a leading role in the development of the substance or content of the agency program. Logically, this position means that the information head should have much the same abilities as the agency head. What else if he is to have such an important role in the formulation of agency policies? It is here that the argument falls down. Most newspapermen do not have a broad enough background to qualify as agency policymakers. They are neither trained administrators nor experts in the content of government programs. Furthermore, in most cases they themselves do not aspire to such a role; they are content to function as information specialists. Realistically speaking, if the management of an enterprise is incapable of developing policies that produce good public relations, it should be changed. The solution is not to cede the policymaking function to the information staff. In fact, there may be a tendency for an organization to think that it has done all it can do in the field of public relations when it hires a staff of public relations experts.

Nothing that has been said should be interpreted to mean that it is unnecessary or undesirable for the management to have a close relationship with the information staff. Public relations is a management tool, and this means that the information director should be fully advised of management plans and the reasons for new agency policies. Unless he is thoroughly familiar with the thinking of the management, he and his staff will be unable to do a good job of interpreting these policies to the agency's publics. Furthermore, while the information director may not qualify as a policymaker, he is equipped to give expert advice on probable public reactions to proposed policies and on how to present new policies with maximum effectiveness.

Employee morale and public relations

Above all, the agency management should understand the relationship between the morale of all its employees and effective public relations. Dissatisfied employees are by no means an internal problem only. They live in the local community; their neighbors identify them with the agency. If they seem little interested in their work or, with apparent justification, are even critical of their superiors, these neighbors and friends will form an unfavorable impression of the agency.

The relationship between internal personnel management and the agency's reputation in the community is very close. A high "quit" rate makes people wonder what goes on in the agency. Evidence of patent failure to impress upon the employees the need to deal courteously with local citizens will reinforce the notion that the government bureaucracy does not really care about the people. Some private companies have long recognized this relationship; the example comes to mind of the restaurant that prominently displays a sign, "This is a good place to work." The customers presumably are much more interested in the quality of the restaurant's food than in its personnel policies; but, of course, a place that can keep good employees is also one that takes pains to treat the customers well. This again demonstrates the breadth of the public relations field. In addition to its many other facets, it encompasses the important field of personnel administration, which is presented in detail in Part IV of this book.

Although the employees should be trained generally in public relations, a particular need is to develop their communications skills. Communications bears upon public relations in several important ways. For example, employees should be able to write intelligible letters in response to inquiries from the public. Also, the agency should have at least a few officials who are good speakers and who can explain its program to local groups. As we saw in Chapter 9, employees will be more likely to cooperate with the management if barriers to upward communication are removed. Inside and outside the organization, the agency will suffer if its personnel does not have some degree of competence in the area of communications.

Community relations programs

The positive approach emphasizes the need for community relations programs designed to gain acceptance of the agency in the community. There are many possible points of friction in the relationships with the local people; agency policies and activities should be continuously scrutinized to eliminate offending features, wherever possible. New organizations locating in a community can create difficult traffic, noise, and other problems; particularly if they seem indifferent to these inconveniences they may be causing, they may quickly find themselves without very many friends in the area. The first essential is to be aware in detail of how the community is reacting to the agency in all its aspects—personnel, policies, and concepts of civic responsibility. Having located the trouble spots, the management then knows what it must do to make itself better liked.

The numerous devices for maintaining good relationships include: (1) establishing contact with "local-thought leaders," such as prominent businessmen, heads of civic organizations, and newspaper editors; (2) exchanging speakers with local groups, such as the Lions, Rotary, or Kiwanis; (3) participating in community campaigns, such as the United Fund drive; (4) making buildings and other facilities available for meetings of civic groups; (5) arranging "clinics" and open houses to explain the agency's program; and (6) sponsoring special events, such as anniversary observances, demonstrations, and special days and weeks.[3]

IMPROVING RELATIONSHIPS IN THE GHETTOES

Currently, stress is being placed on programs to improve relationships with those living in the ghettoes. Chapter 6 noted the recommendation of the National Advisory Commission on Civil Disorders for the establishment of Neighborhood City Halls. Essentially, the function of the Neighborhood City Halls, some of which are operating in cities such as New York, is to establish more direct and more effective communication between ghetto residents and the different agencies of the city government. They serve as "one-stop" information centers, where the individual can get answers to questions about municipal services and can present complaints against particular agencies. The persons manning the neighborhood centers refer these grievances to the officials involved, and try to see that remedial action is taken, as justified.

Commenting on the absence of major disorders in New York

[3] See "Community Relations for Government," Management Forum, *Public Administration News*, Chicago: American Society for Public Administration, *VIII*, No. 9 (November, 1958).

City after the assassination of Dr. Martin Luther King, Jr., the *New York Times* praised the work of "neighborhood task forces in which top-level city officials administering programs in their areas meet with local leaders of poverty agencies, civil rights groups, community councils, churches, and other organized units. . . . To slum residents they mean a direct line of communication to City Hall and some assurance that dirty streets will be swept or an abandoned car removed or a dark park lighted or play streets marked off. To city government they mean an understanding of ghetto problems."[4]

Police community relations is being particularly emphasized; in New York City, a separate group at police headquarters oversees the activities of community councils in each precinct. These councils are concerned with the problems of all groups in the community, not only youth. As one example, in Spanish-speaking areas Spanish-speaking residents have been recruited on an around-the-clock basis to serve as interpreters in police stations. The National Advisory Commission on Civil Disorders, however, evaluates most police-community programs as "disappointing."[5] While admitting that great results could not be expected overnight, the Commission noted such deficiencies as "minimum participation by ghetto residents . . . infrequent meetings . . . [and] lack of patrolmen involvement. . . ." The Commission was particularly critical of those programs that appeared to be aimed at improving the "department's image in the community," rather than being genuine efforts to achieve better community relations.[6]

Effective use of press outlets

Finally, in developing its public relations program, a good agency management makes effective use of press and other outlets. It is well aware that bungling in contacts with newspaper reporters and other representatives of the mass communications media can do great damage to its program. An information director with an extensive background in journalism understands the point of view of the press and knows when it is apt to be offended by officials who are well-meaning but who have no "public relations sense." Later in this chapter we will discuss a very sensitive area as far as the press is concerned: withholding of information by government officials. This is where a good information director can save the management from making serious mistakes.

Press relations must be managed well, and an agency management that underrates the importance of this may quickly find itself in publicity difficulties. The Presidency illustrates the po-

[4] *New York Times,* editorial, April 12, 1968.
[5] *Report of the National Advisory Commission on Civil Disorders,* New York: Bantam, 1968, p. 319.
[6] *Ibid.*

tential and the pitfalls, for while the Chief Executive is in a very good position to get favorable publicity, he can make serious mistakes from the public relations standpoint or simply prove ineffective in communicating his message.

LEGITIMATE INFORMATION VERSUS PROPAGANDA

In a democracy—indeed, in any kind of government—it is necessary that the people be well informed, and this is not possible unless the government tells them what it is doing and how the citizenry will be affected. Yet there has been no general agreement as to exactly how much and what kinds of information should be released by the various agencies. Legislators distinguish between "legitimate" public information activities and "propaganda." However, the difficulty lies in defining whether or not something is legitimate. Furthermore, what one person brands as propaganda, another may sincerely argue as essential for developing public understanding and support of agency programs.

Critics of the administration in power are suspicious of increases in expenditures for "information" purposes (the word *publicity* is avoided precisely to placate these critics). The dilemma for the opposition is that "the more efficient the official information services are in facilitating administration and increasing popular understanding of government policies, the more they will add to the reputation of the administration of the day."[7] The "ins" are also in a good position to organize "seminars," conferences, and other meetings to propose the extension of existing programs or the initiation of new ones. The "outs" often challenge such use of government funds, arguing that this is "propaganda" intended to perpetuate the rule of the "ins." Since the policy-formulation role of administrators is acknowledged even by many of the strongest critics of "bureaucracy," such complaints usually are to no avail. In any event, those in control generally are careful not to be extravagant with such expenditures.

A recent newspaper survey showed that the federal government spends $425 million annually for information purposes, not including an estimated $200 million charged the government by Defense and space program private contractors for their public relations activities. Furthermore, an estimated additional $125 million is spent on printing costs for information materials. These sums are large, but so is the government; how much is unnecessary is a matter of opinion. That officials must be wary with information expenditures is seen in the following comment: "Government

[7] J. A. R. Pimlott, *Public Relations and American Democracy*, Princeton, N.J.: Princeton University Press, 1951, pp. 96–97.

agencies will come up readily with such abstruse information as how many cases of Maine sardines there are on store shelves on a given date, or how much is spent on the poor of Barry County, Missouri. But it is a different matter when they are asked how many employees are engaged in their public relations programs and how much it costs. The study turned up few officials willing or able to be specific."[8]

Legislation and information release

The legislature actually defines the responsibilities of some agencies in such a way as to make "large-scale" information programs necessary. The Department of Agriculture was established in 1862 "to acquire and diffuse among the people of the United States information on subjects connected with agriculture in the most general and comprehensive sense of that word." The statute creating the Office of Education in 1867 requires it to "diffuse such information as shall aid the people of the United States in the establishment and maintenance of efficient school systems, and otherwise to promote the cause of education."

Disseminating information and enlisting public support is one of the functions of many executive agencies at all levels of government. Health departments could hardly function effectively without programs of health education; the public must be educated to recognize health hazards and to cooperate in governmental programs to reduce the incidence of disease. In other programs, paid advertising and other forms of publicity must be used if the legislative mandate is to be carried out successfully. Public agencies responsible for promoting tourism place such advertisements and make the same appeals to the spending public as private entrepreneurs. Similarly, state and local development commissions carry out systematic promotional efforts to attract new industries. Anyone who makes even a passing examination of the advertisements that appear in magazines and the Sunday issues of newspapers will have no trouble finding some that describe the advantages of a particular state or locality as a place in which to start a business.

Sometimes it is said that government information programs should be limited to disseminating factual information, and that efforts to *persuade* should not be permitted because they are *propaganda*. The examples just given show clearly that it is impractical to try to make such a distinction. The public-health department cannot consider its job ended when it advises the public of an outbreak of disease; it must also *persuade* the citizen to take

[8] *New York Times,* March 19, 1967.

certain action, such as participating in a mass immunization program. Federal and state officials in agricultural programs similarly try to convince the farmer to use the technical advice that they give him. Diffusion of information, in and of itself, could hardly be considered sufficient, particularly when success in obtaining the desired results depends on the cooperation of many citizens.

If the governmental activity meets with general public approval, few people question the need for persuasion. It is only when an element of controversy is injected into the picture that the cry of propaganda is likely to be heard. Suppose that there is an alarming increase in the number of polio cases. Appeals in the newspapers, on radio and television, and in leaflets urge those who have not yet done so to obtain polio shots—these activities by the public-health authorities are considered proper. Suppose, however, that a group of citizens is urging the local government to fluoridate its water supply. How far can the health department go in urging public support for obtaining the legal authorization to provide fluoridation? Some people are strongly opposed to fluoridation, but practically everybody is in agreement with immunization against polio. It is when people are against a program that they complain the most about propaganda.

A SENSITIVE CASE: THE CIGARETTE CONTROVERSY

The current controversy over "smoking and health" poses a particularly sensitive problem: Should the government launch a public information program to dissuade people from smoking? The Public Health Service thinks so; in mid-1967 it followed up its first extensive report on the subject[9] with another one emphasizing that the question no longer was whether smoking *was* harmful but *how* harmful. The first report linked smoking to lung diseases, including cancer; the second found that cigarette smokers have substantially higher (earlier) rates of death and disability than nonsmokers.

As the result of the first report, Congress passed a law requiring the following warning on each cigarette package: "Caution: Cigarette smoking may be hazardous to your health." The law also provided that the Federal Trade Commission (FTC) could not require similar health warnings in cigarette *advertising* until July 1, 1969. The background here is that the FTC had been preparing to forbid some kinds of cigarette advertising, rigorously regulate other kinds, and require the warning on the packages to read that cigarette smoking "may cause death." The $8-billion-a-year tobacco industry, which spends about $229.3 million a year

9 *Smoking and Health*, Report of the Advisory Committee to the Surgeon General of the Public Health Service, Washington, D.C.: Government Printing Office, 1964.

on radio and TV advertising, had won an initial victory. The federal government is in an embarrassing position because it obtains some $2 billion annually in cigarette taxes, and state governments, of course, also obtain substantial revenues from the same kind of tax. At the same time that the Public Health Service and the FTC were trying to discourage cigarette smoking, the Agriculture Department was spending money to advertise American-made cigarettes abroad.

In releasing the second report, the FTC recommended that Congress pass legislation requiring a strong health warning in all cigarette advertisements, and that more federal funds be made available for educating the public about the health hazards. The Commission charged that the broadcasters had failed to implement their voluntary advertising code, and that the industry continued to use cigarette advertising with special appeal to younger people. The FTC has also issued a rule applying the "fairness doctrine" to cigarette advertising, and has suggested an informal ratio of one anti–cigarette-smoking message to every three cigarette commercials. The broadcasting industry has filed a court appeal, and the expectation is that the issue will ultimately be decided by the Supreme Court. Since the FTC has a very limited staff for monitoring broadcasting (only three people in early 1968), in practice, conformance with this rule is voluntary with the broadcasters. The latter have appealed the rule in court, and the expectation is that the issue will eventually come before the Supreme Court.

A young attorney, John Francis Banzhaf, petitioned the FTC for equal time for anti-smoking ads, and when this was rejected, also appealed to the courts. Banzhaf has been the citizen leader in the anti-smoking battle, and has demonstrated, like Ralph Nader in the case of highway safety, how one man can significantly affect public policy.

In July, 1969, the tobacco industry offered to end all cigarette advertising on radio and TV by September, 1970, if Congress would grant such action immunity under the antitrust laws. Anti-smoking forces in the Senate were so strong that approval in that chamber of a bill passed by the House to continue the ban on health warnings in cigarette advertising seemed unlikely. The FTC, which had been expected to require prominent health warnings on *all kinds* of cigarette advertising, announced that, if the tobacco industry did stop the radio and TV ads, it would suspend judgment for two years on whether to require the warnings in newspaper and other written advertisements.

WITHHOLDING INFORMATION

There has been much criticism in recent years of the tendency to *withhold* information from the public. Specifically, the complaint has been that some administrative officials refuse to release information that ought to be made known to the public. How can we say that we have a truly democratic system if the people are denied the facts needed for making intelligent judgments about government policies? The very idea of secrecy in the government is repugnant to most Americans.

The press has been much concerned because "freedom of information" is the very basis of its operations. It naturally becomes concerned when government officials appear unjustifiably to deny them access to important information. Such organizations as the American Society of Newspaper Editors, the American Newspaper Publishers Association, and the Associated Press Managing Editors Association have protested the withholding of information. Most of this criticism has been leveled at the federal government, and sometimes at the President himself, but state and local officials have not escaped similar criticism.

This situation has existed throughout American history since George Washington's Administration, but since World War II the issue has arisen in sharper form because of the increasing complexity of our society and the consequent "vast range of information"[10] that officials have been able to keep secret. Newspapermen and others have exposed some of the ridiculous examples, such as the Defense Department's examining for security clearance a "review of a Civil War book entitled *Destruction and Reconstruction*, written by a Confederate Army General and first published in 1879."[11] As late as 1960, despite the efforts to reduce overclassification, it was reported that the "Pentagon was wielding secrecy stamps at a rate which created each week a stack of classified documents higher than the Empire State Building."[12]

The Defense Department was by no means the only agency withholding much information; the practice was widespread throughout the government. For three years the Public Housing Administration refused to release the names of its employees; until 1953 the Department of Agriculture kept secret the names of persons receiving drought aid.[13] As can be seen from the examples, secrecy had become the pattern, to the point where even routine data, the release of which could not conceivably injure the agency or its clientele, was being withheld.

Furthermore, existing laws could easily be so interpreted as

[10] Francis E. Rourke, *Secrecy and Publicity*, Baltimore: Johns Hopkins, 1961, p. 11.

[11] See Senate Judiciary Committee, 86th Congress, 1st Session, *Executive Privilege (General Accounting Office)*, Washington, D.C.: Government Printing Office, 1959, p. 171.

[12] Rourke, *op. cit.*, pp. 76–77.

[13] *Executive Privilege (General Accounting Office)*, *op. cit.*, p. 170.

to justify the secrecy. One example is the Housekeeping Act of 1789, which authorized "the head of each department to prescribe regulations, not inconsistent with law, for the government of his department, the conduct of its officers and clerks, the distribution and performance of its business, and the custody, use, and preservation of its records, paper, and property appertaining to it." Over the years, this statute was frequently invoked by officials to keep confidential any sort of information if it suited their purposes. As the result of pressure by Congressional opponents of administrative secrecy, in 1958 this ancient law was amended as follows: "This section does not authorize the withholding of information from the public or limiting the availability of records to the public."[14] Yet the House Subcommittee on Government Information later had to admit that the amendment had not proved an effective check on secrecy.

Section 3 of the Administrative Procedure Act of 1946 deals with public access to the rules and regulations of the government. It was so loosely drawn that it also sanctioned much secrecy. It permitted withholding information if "any function of the United States requiring secrecy in the public interest . . ." was involved; also, if the data were ". . . held confidential for good cause found."[15]

The doctrine of executive privilege also permits the President to refuse to give information to the Congress when he believes the national interest so requires.[16] Sometimes subordinate administrative officials have claimed the same right, but President Kennedy established the precedent, continued by Presidents Johnson and Nixon, that the Chief Executive alone would invoke the doctrine.[17] Congress has also disliked "executive privilege" because it has sometimes been interpreted to give the President uncontrolled discretion to withhold data and records[18] and, in any event, can deprive the legislators of information they strongly feel should be disclosed in the public interest. Under the American system of separation of powers, the Presidents appear to be firmly ensconced behind this doctrine. The late Senator Hennings of Missouri argued that the claim of executive privilege had to be weighed against a fundamental constitutional protection—the people's "right to know." This right, he believed, was protected by the First Amendment, along with the guarantees of freedom of speech and thought, and, indeed, he was confident that the Supreme Court would eventually interpret the First Amendment in this way and allow the government to deprive the people of its "right to know" only if it could prove a clear and present danger.[19]

14 Rourke, *op. cit.*, pp. 59–60.

15 *Clarifying and Protecting the Right of the Public to Information*, 89th Congress, 2nd Session, House of Representatives, Report No. 1497, May 9, 1966, p. 4.

16 See Senate Judiciary Committee, 85th Congress, 2nd Session, *The Power of the President to Withhold Information from the Congress*, Washington, D.C.: Government Printing Office, 1958.

17 *Clarifying and Protecting the Right of the Public to Information, op. cit.*, p. 3.

18 *The Power of the President to Withhold Information from the Congress, op. cit.*, pp. 3–4.

19 *Executive Privilege (General Accounting Office), op cit.*, pp. 106–117.

The freedom of information act

Legislation was passed in June of 1967, however, with the expectation that eventually it will eliminate most of the unjustified secrecy.[20] It gives *any* person the right to request information from the administrative agencies, and provides that if the request is denied, the individual can file action in federal court where the case will be tried "de novo and the burden is on the agency to sustain its action." The court can enjoin the agency from withholding records, order the release of any records improperly withheld, and punish the "responsible official" for contempt if its orders are disregarded. The only exceptions are materials:

1. specifically required by Executive order to be kept secret in the interest of the national defense or foreign policy;
2. related solely to the internal personnel rules and practices of an agency;
3. specifically exempted from disclosure by statute;
4. trade secrets and commercial or financial information obtained from a person and privileged or confidential;
5. interagency or intraagency memorandums or letters which would not be available by law to a party other than an agency in litigation with the agency;
6. personnel and medical files and similar files, the disclosure of which would constitute a clearly unwarranted invasion of personal privacy;
7. investigatory files compiled for law enforcement purposes, except to the extent available by law to a party other than an agency;
8. contained in or related to examination, operating, or condition reports prepared by, on behalf of, or for the use of an agency responsible for the regulation or supervision of financial institutions;
9. geological and geophysical information and data, including maps, concerning wells.[21]

The new legislation, however, does not attempt to abrogate "executive privilege." The law became effective on July 4, 1967, so that the experience with the new requirements is still recent. While there is agreement that secrecy-minded officials now find it more difficult to deny information, there are many criticisms that some officials are successfully evading the law. Note this report: "The whole attitude of government information officers was summed up beautifully at a recent seminar. The audience was made up of information officers. The subject was freedom of information. The meeting was closed to the press."[22]

A number of court suits have been filed since the effective

[20] Public Law 90-23, 90th Congress, H.R. 5357, June 5, 1967.
[21] *Ibid.*, p. 2.
[22] *Federal Times*, editorial, December 20, 1967.

date of the new law, but very few have been decided. Concern is expressed that the news media have initiated a relatively low proportion of the appeals made to agencies to reverse initial decisions not to disclose information. Some of the examples of information withheld are just as incomprehensible as those cited prior to passage of the new law. It was obvious that Congress would have to "monitor" the legislation, and that compliance would "rest upon the extent to which the act is used by the general public, by the press and media, by grantees and citizen groups."[23] It was pointed out that "Congress itself is less than a model for open decisions openly arrived at," for in 1967 Congressional committees still held 39 percent of their meetings in private. "All 383 House Appropriations Committee meetings were closed."[24]

TRUTHFULNESS IN PUBLIC RELATIONS

In evaluating information for release, the agency should consider whether or not the release of it is purely a matter of propaganda in its own behalf, and, on the other hand, whether the withholding of it is purely a matter of fear of public criticism. The agency must ask itself if this information—whether it is favorable or unfavorable—*really* is in the public interest. In order to do this, the agency should be willing to recognize its own shortcomings and to make whatever improvements are necessary. Where it is failing, chances are that attempts to hide its faults by withholding information or to offset them by releasing propaganda publicity will only add to its poor public image. Yet once the agency has completed an honest self-examination, it is in a position to improve its operations and, consequently, the image the public has of it. As Appley puts it, "Knowing what we are, we next want to know what we ought to be; how to get there; and how to get people to believe it."[25] Unfortunately, all too frequently such frank and honest appraisals are not made.

THE "CREDIBILITY GAP"

Indeed, in the last few years much concern has been expressed over the "credibility gap . . . the degree of refusal by the public to accept at face value what the Government says and does."[26] Despite public indignation over the seizure of the *Pueblo*, many people, both in the United States and abroad, were skeptical that the intelligence-gathering vessel had not ventured into North Korean waters. They remembered that in 1960 the Eisenhower Administration had at first denied that a U-2 plane shot down deep in Soviet territory was carrying out a "spy" operation for

23 Joseph A. Loftus, "New Freedom of Information Law: Fact-Seekers Testing Its Effectiveness," *New York Times*, February 18, 1968.

24 *Ibid.*

25 Appley, *op. cit.*, p. 54.

26 Walter Lippmann, "Truth and the White House," *San Francisco Chronicle*, March 28, 1967.

the Central Intelligence Agency.[27] Under President Kennedy, Adlai Stevenson, "deceived by his own government," had told the UN that the air raids over Cuba before the Bay of Pigs invasion were by Cuban defectors, not American pilots.[28] Then, in February, 1965, the Johnson Administration, reacting to a statement by UN Secretary-General Thant that Hanoi made a peace-feeler in 1964, had "insisted there were 'no meaningful proposals' then before the government."[29] Yet when Eric Sevaried wrote in November, 1965, that during the 1964 Presidential campaign U Thant had informed Adlai Stevenson of his obtaining Hanoi's agreement to meet with an American representative in Rangoon, Washington admitted that there had been such a proposal. The "offer," it now said, was too "nebulous" to take seriously.

In August, 1965, the State Department had denied a charge by Lee Kuan Yew, prime minister of Singapore, that five years previously a CIA agent had offered him a $3.3 million bribe. When Lee produced a letter to him from Dean Rusk apologizing for the attempted bribe, the State Department changed its story, saying that "the man issuing the denial hadn't known the facts."

Earlier in 1965, when U.S. armed forces landed in the Dominican Republic, the explanation given was that the lives of thousands of Americans and other civilians were threatened by local disorders. President Johnson said at a news conference that "some 1,500 innocent people were murdered and shot or their heads cut off." Shortly, this version was changed, and the American public was told that the action had been taken to prevent a seizure of power by the Communists, as in Cuba. Apparently the American Embassy in the Dominican Republic had relayed unverified reports of mass atrocities. The Senate Foreign Relations Committee later heard secret testimony on the U.S. intervention, and Chairman Fulbright criticized the Administration for "lack of candor" and for relying on exaggerated reports both of the atrocities and the danger of a Communist takeover.[30]

Incidents of this type are not limited to foreign affairs. After the Apollo tragedy, the National Aeronautics and Space Administration was reluctant to release the full text of the Phillips' report. General Phillips was very critical of the performance of NASA's principal contractor, the North American Aviation Company. In fact, he had written in this report, prepared long before the fire that killed the astronauts, "Even with due consideration of hopeful signs, I could not find a substantive basis for confidence in future performance."[31] Representative William F. Ryan of New York, using his own contacts, obtained a copy of the report and made it public. Ryan charged that NASA did not want to release

[27] See Rourke, *op. cit.*, p. 6.

[28] Erwin D. Canham, "To Lie for One's Country," editorial page, *Christian Science Monitor*, November 20, 1965.

[29] Saul Pett, "The Government's Right to Lie," *Philadelphia Sunday Bulletin*, March 6, 1966.

[30] *Ibid.*

[31] "Is NASA Covering Up?," editorial, *Christian Science Monitor*, May 2, 1967.

the report because it had failed to clear up the deficiencies discovered by General Phillips. When James E. Webb, then NASA Administrator, was asked by the Senate Space Committee whether North American had been the first choice of NASA's Source Evaluation Board, he replied in the affirmative. Quizzed again on this a few days later by Senator Margaret Chase Smith, he then "revealed for the first time that he and a few of his colleagues had overruled the technical experts and picked North American for the rich Apollo contract."[32] The *New York Times* wrote: "The contradiction between Mr. Webb's testimony on the two occasions would be bad enough in isolation. But against the record of these months of investigation into the Apollo tragedy it strongly supports the belief that neither Congress nor the American people have been treated with full candor in NASA's reporting of what is going on in the space program."[33]

Writers such as Walter Lippmann, James Reston, and Erwin D. Canham have concurred that the news was being "managed." Lippmann wrote that granted there was "an inherent conflict between public officials and reporters. . . . The conflict today has degenerated to the point where there is no longer much pretense that the news is not being manipulated in order to make Congress, the newspapers, the networks, and the public at large support the President."[34] About Defense Secretary McNamara's denial of any connection between the Johnson Administration's decision to sell its stockpiled aluminum and the industry's prior decision to raise prices, Reston wrote: "The number of people who believe in this extraordinary coincidence could be gathered together comfortably in any Washington telephone booth."[35] Canham said: "A free government cannot really have it both ways. It cannot live both in the shadow and in the light. It can retain some privacy, withhold certain facts, but sooner or later it must admit its accountability to public opinion and let the people know what has been going on."[36]

Herbert G. Klein, named by President Nixon as Director of Communications for the entire federal executive branch, has defined his function as that of "eliminating any possibility of a credibility gap."[37] Reminding that in the relationships between the Government and the press, "mistrust is as mutual and old as the Presidency itself," Max Frankel observed: "Government and press need one another and manipulate one another, yet an immutable conflict of interest colors the relationship. For every charge of secrecy there is a reply of ignorance, and for every complaint about the misuse of information [by the press] there is a reply of prejudice in its handling."[38]

[32] "NASA Candor Needed," editorial, *New York Times*, May 11, 1967.

[33] *Ibid*.

[34] Lippmann, *op. cit*.

[35] James Reston, "Washington: 'Candor Compels Me to Tell You . . . ,'" editorial page, *New York Times*, November 17, 1965.

[36] Canham, *op. cit*.

[37] "Minister of Information," editorial, *New York Times*, November 27, 1968,

[38] Max Frankel, "Nixon and the Press," *New York Times*, November 27, 1968.

EVALUATING THE PUBLIC RELATIONS PROGRAM

It should be stressed that a discerning management is well aware that the *quantity* of the publicity it receives is not necessarily related to success in its public relations program. Naturally the agency hopes that the press will publish its news releases and not neglect to report its accomplishments. However, counting up the inches of space that it has received in the newspapers does not, in and of itself, prove anything. Newspapers are swamped with requests to publish different material. Generally speaking, they ward off the publicity-seekers and try to print only that information which is genuinely newsworthy. Usually, then, efforts to get into the newspapers every day or with great regularity do not meet with success anyway, and even if the agency does get better than average coverage because of its persistence, this does not mean that the reading public necessarily pays any attention to the articles in question. Discriminating readers come to identify the "blurbs" from the items with real substance. Then again, mere publicity-seeking can boomerang. By being in the public eye too much, the agency may find itself criticized all the more severely when something goes wrong with its programs.

"We are not getting enough publicity" is a common complaint. Perhaps the reverse question should be asked, "Are we seeking too much publicity?" One of the valuable services that the information director can perform is to caution the management about placing too much emphasis on the quantity of publicity as such. The real test of success is the agency's skill in dealing with its various publics, and this will be measured in terms of the reactions of these publics, rather than the volume of information releases.

BIBLIOGRAPHY

Altshuler, Alan A., (ed.), *The Politics of the Federal Bureaucracy*, New York: Dodd, Mead, 1968, pp. 381–412.

Cater, Douglass, *The Fourth Branch of Government*, Boston: Houghton Mifflin, 1959.

Cohen, Bernard C., *The Press and Foreign Policy*, Princeton, N.J.: Princeton University Press, 1963.

Friedman, Robert S., Klein, Bernard W., and Romani, John H., "Administrative Agencies and the Publics They Serve," *Public Administration Review*, XXVI, No. 3 (September, 1966).

House Committee on Government Operations, *Freedom of Information Act* (Compilation and Analysis of Departmental Regulations Implementing 5 U.S.C. 552), 90th Congress, 2nd Session, Washington, D.C.: Government Printing Office, 1968.

Mosher, Frederick C., (ed.), *Governmental Reorganizations: Cases and Commentary*, Indianapolis, Ind.: Bobbs-Merrill, 1967.

Pimlott, J. A. R., *Public Relations and American Democracy*, Princeton, N.J.: Princeton University Press, 1951.

Rourke, Francis E., "Administrative Secrecy: A Congressional Dilemma," *American Political Science Review*, *LIV*, No. 3 (September, 1960).

Rourke, Francis E., *Secrecy and Publicity*, Baltimore: Johns Hopkins, 1961.

Rowat, Donald C., (ed.), *Basic Issues in Public Administration*, New York: Macmillan, 1961. Chapter VIII.

Senate Committee on Aeronautical and Space Sciences, *Apollo 204 Accident*, 90th Congress, 2nd Session, Report No. 956, Washington, D.C.: Government Printing Office, 1968.

Senate Subcommittee on Constitutional Rights, *Executive Privilege* (Parts I and II), 86th Congress, 1st Session, Washington, D.C.: Government Printing Office, 1959.

Senate Subcommittee on Constitutional Rights, *The Power of the President to Withhold Information from the Congress*, 85th Congress, 2nd Session, Washington, D.C.: Government Printing Office, 1958.

CHAPTER 11
LEADERSHIP

FREQUENTLY THE COMPLAINT is heard that an organization "lacks leadership." What is meant is that action of some sort should have been taken, but no one assumed the initiative in trying to get others to see the need for action, and thus nothing was accomplished. In other cases the criticism is that the organization does not have "good leadership." Decisions are made and action taken, but those responsible for persuading others to accept their ideas lead them in the wrong direction. These statements reveal both the *nature* and the *importance* of leadership. The essence of leadership is influencing the actions of others; the essential quality of the leader is that he is convinced something must be done, and he persuades others to help him get it done. Where no effort is made to influence the thoughts and actions of others, there is a default of leadership.

Why complain about lack of leadership if the work results are reasonably good? Why expect spectacular accomplishments from the employees every day? Of course, only the humanly attainable should be expected, but questions such as these may reflect either lack of understanding or resistance to being spurred to greater accomplishment, or both. To be a leader is not to be a superman; it is simply to do what the word "leader" indicates—lead. An organization does not have good leadership when its officials sit back and let things drift. The factor of lethargy comes in when there are no serious penalties for failing to improve operations. So long as the work gets done without complete breakdowns of the administrative machine, why should the official embark on ambitious schemes for improvement? Why should he look ahead, when it is so much easier to look back and simply be assured that things are no worse than they were before? The one who looks ahead is the leader; the one who looks back has no desire to become one—and, unfortunately, there are too many of the latter type in modern bureaucracy. Actually, it is no more unreasonable to require good leadership than it is to insist on satisfactory physical facilities like buildings and offices. Obviously, it is easier to obtain the latter, but the element of demanding the best applies in both cases.

APPROACHES TO LEADERSHIP

The trait approach

Not too long ago even learned discussions of leadership, as distinguished from popular discussions, had a certain mystic quality. The leader was conceived of as someone blessed with certain qualities that made it relatively easy for him to bend others to his will. Nobody was really sure of the exact complement of leader personality traits, but it was generally assumed that many of these characteristics were inherited.

The trait approach, however, failed to hold up under the testing of research, such as that conducted by one scholar who compiled a long list of traits identified in one or more studies as distinguishing characteristics of leaders as opposed to nonleaders. He found that only 5 percent of the traits so identified were common to four or more of the studies. Such a low percentage of agreement could hardly substantiate the claim that leaders basically have the same personality qualities. The findings of this scholar have not been disproved in later studies,[1] and for some years now, most social scientists have accepted the following summarization by Cartwright and Zander:

> On the whole, investigators in this field are coming to the conclusion that, while certain minimal abilities are required of all leaders, these are also widely distributed among nonleaders

[1] Dorwin Cartwright and Alvin Zander (eds.), *Group Dynamics, Research and Theory*, New York: Harper & Row (second edition), 1960, p. 490.

as well. Furthermore, the traits of the leader which are necessary and effective in one group or situation may be quite different from those of another leader in a different setting. This conclusion, if adequately substantiated, would imply that the selection of leaders must consider a man's suitability for the type of functions he is to perform in a given situation and it would raise questions about the desirability of formal arrangements which maintain the responsibilities of leadership in the same person regardless of the changing task of the group and the changing requirements upon leaders.[2]

The situational approach

Accordingly, most writers now support this situational approach, although actually it is not new. Long before the term "situational approach" came into usage, Mary Parker Follett was calling attention to the emergence in American life of "leadership by function." In the late 1920s this wise lady, whose writings are classics in management literature, gave several lectures on leadership.[3] In these lectures she noted that in scientifically managed organizations three types of leadership could be distinguished: the leadership of position, of personality, and of function. There was nothing new about the first two, because they represented the accepted views on leadership. The man holding a position that gave him formal authority over others obviously could make himself a leader. If he had a forceful personality, he could do this much more easily. This kind of individual combined the leadership of position with that of personality.

Something was absent, however, in such a conception of leadership. It failed to take into account the possibility that some persons, in fact quite a few in modern specialized organizations, exercised leadership because of their expert knowledge. The organization depended on them to give sound technical advice to their superiors. In many situations these experts actually did the "leading," because others were influenced by their judgments. Miss Follett stressed that "we have people giving what are practically orders to those of higher rank. The balance of stores clerk, as he is called in some places, will tell the man in charge of purchasing when to act. The dispatch clerk can give 'orders' even to the superintendent. The leadership of function is inherent in the job and as such is respected by the president of the plant." She noted that "the man possessing the knowledge demanded by a certain situation tends in the best managed businesses, and other things being equal, to become the leader at that moment."[4]

In Chapter 8 of this book, a distinction was made between

[2] *Ibid.*, p. 491. See also John Paul Jones, "Changing Patterns of Leadership," *Personnel*, XLIV, No. 2 (March–April, 1967), 8–15, and William G. Scott, *Organization Theory: A Behavioral Analysis for Management*, Homewood, Ill.: Irwin, 1967, pp. 207–218.

[3] See Mary Parker Follett, "Some Discrepancies in Leadership Theory and Practice," in Henry C. Metcalfe and L. Urwick (eds.), *Dynamic Administration*, New York: Harper & Row, 1940, pp. 270–294. See also in this same collection of her papers, the essay "Leader and Expert," pp. 247–269.

[4] *Ibid.*, p. 277.

formal authority and *power*. Formal authority is the basis for what Miss Follett called leadership of position. Sometimes someone in a position of formal authority is unable to persuade others to accept his ideas, the explanation being that he does not possess "the knowledge demanded by the situation." In any event, we saw in Chapter 8 that not all power is concentrated in the hands of a few persons at the top of the organization. Subordinates frequently exercise power because they "know best" about a particular operation. Harlan Cleveland's excellent analysis was cited to show how specialization has diffused decisionmaking throughout modern organizations. Cleveland stated that the real leaders are the "experts on complexity," in other words, the persons who understand what is needed in a particular situation.

It should be made clear that Miss Follett did not consider that the leadership of function and the leadership of personality could not be combined in the same person. Nor did she deny that personality played a very large part in leadership. She did believe, however, that leadership of function was becoming more important than leadership of personality. She felt that the success of an organization depended on its being "sufficiently flexible to allow the leadership of function to operate fully—to allow the men with the knowledge and the technique to control the situation."[5] Miss Follett makes an interesting point about Joan of Arc. This great woman possessed leadership of personality because of the "ardour of her conviction and her power to make others share that conviction." Yet it is also related that "no trained artillery captain could excel Joan of Arc in the placement of guns."[6]

CHANGES IN LEADERSHIP REQUIREMENTS

What are some other factors that affect the requirements for leadership, apart from expertise in a particular subject matter field? A change in the work situation may call for a different kind of leader. One kind of individual may be an excellent leader in launching new government programs, but fail to impress when asked to keep a going program functioning. Likely, he saw a challenge in the first kind of assignment, but could not get really interested in the second one. Possibly he is the "promoter" type, of great value in sparking new endeavors but out of place for less exciting work. Similarly, there is the university president who is effective for increasing enrollments, getting gifts, and putting up buildings, but too little interested in academic matters to be the man for the job when the period of physical growth is over and the emphasis is on the scholastic side.

The characteristics of the followers obviously constitute an-

5 *Ibid.*, p. 278.

6 *Ibid.*, p. 172.

other variable influencing the leadership needs. The competent head of a public agency might be unsuited for a leadership role in a church group, yet a minor employee in the same public agency might be admirably equipped to lead the church group. Within the church, one person might be excellent for work with preschool children, another for youth activities, and so on. It takes one kind of person to lead a labor gang, another to direct professional activities. Within the professional ranks, supervisors lacking certain formal qualifications deemed essential by the subordinates will prove ineffectual; a dean without a Ph.D. will not command the respect of many of the university professors. If the leadership assignment requires conciliation of various groups, the individual's personal background can eliminate him from consideration, as in an international agency where the person's nationality might make him unacceptable to one or more parties to a dispute. These are only a few of the ways in which the situation can vary, thus altering the requirements for leadership.

HUMAN MOTIVATIONS AND LEADERSHIP

Before discussing in specific terms the kinds of leadership techniques that should be used in given circumstances, it is advisable to briefly review some of the theories of human motivation. Depending on their concepts of worker motivation, one person may select one leadership pattern, another may choose a very different one. Anyone who seeks to lead others must be concerned with such questions as: What are the desires of people who work in organizations? What do they want from the management and its representatives? How do they want their superiors to treat them? What causes them to respect or not respect the management? What are the needs of human personality? There are various theories, but no agreement on the answers to these questions.

Theories of motivation

Without any pretense of being exhaustive in the treatment of this profound subject, we will present the different views on motivation.

WORK AS A MEANS TO CONSUMER ACTIVITIES

According to one interpretation, the job is not the primary source of the individual's satisfactions in life. In most cases he is much more interested in his after-hour activities, such as in clubs, social groups, and other voluntary organizations. The eminent sociologist Robert Dubin believes that most workers, far from being tyrannized by the work situation, tolerate it and even perform efficiently despite their general apathy. So long as the management makes clear what is expected of them and provides the requisite financial incentive, they can be counted on to do satisfactory work. This, to Dubin, is the "magic of social organization—the ability to sustain required behaviors even when the institution is not central to the actors' interests."[7] Dubin's view, then, is that most workers never really become so involved in their jobs as to experience the frustrations they are supposed to have. It must be made clear, however, that he does not deny that some people do make work a central life interest. Any activity, whether it be required—such as working for one's livelihood—or voluntary— such as participation in a church group—can become an individual's most absorbing interest. Dubin's point is that the most absorbing interest does not have to be the work situation, and looking at our society as a whole, he finds "nothing about the organization of productive work, or the supervision of people while doing it, that is so antithetical to human personality needs as to result only in frustration and disappointment."[8]

Supporting this viewpoint, Michael Schwartz states that "work today has come to have a fairly clear-cut 'means orientation' "; it "provides the individual with resources that enable him to engage in consumer activities which, in turn, permit him to present himself to others in terms of, say, an appropriate life style."[9] While he does satisfy some of his social needs through contacts with fellow workers during the day, he has many more ways of satisfying these needs off the job. What motivates him is not intrinsic interest in the work as such, but rather the amount of his earnings and what this symbolizes in the culture.

The reader will recall Frederick W. Taylor's belief (see Chapter 4) that it was "high wages" the worker sought mostly. Although modern managers have developed sophisticated techniques not known in Taylor's time, many basically still seek to motivate the worker through *external* rewards that he receives in exchange for his work, rather than any internal rewards that he experiences in doing the work.[10] External rewards include: compensation; job security; the prestige attached to a particular occupation, job, or employer; pleasantness of working conditions; and the nature of the interpersonal relationships. Internal rewards include: achievement; recognition; satisfactions in the job tasks; learning new techniques or information; perfecting skills; and solving problems.[11]

If this interpretation is correct, "job enlargement" (described

[7] Robert Dubin, "Persons and Organization," in Robert Dubin (ed.), *Human Relations in Administration,* Englewood Cliffs, N.J.: Prentice-Hall, 1961, p. 80.

[8] *Ibid.*, p. 79.

[9] Michael Schwartz, "Why They Don't Want to Work," *Personnel Administration,* XXVII, No. 2 (March–April, 1964), 7.

[10] Saul W. Gellerman, *Management by Motivation,* New York: American Management Association, 1968, p. 31.

[11] *Ibid.* Listing of external and internal rewards based on Gellerman, and from Frederick Herzberg, "The Motivation-Hygiene Concept and Problems of Manpower," *Personnel Administration,* XXVII, No. 1 (January–February, 1964), 3–7.

in Chapter 4) would in many cases not be necessary. Why try to make the job more interesting to someone who basically seeks his satisfactions elsewhere? Since there are limits anyway to making more interesting the narrow kind of assignment that has evolved through specialization, such efforts can easily boomerang. The leader should understand worker apathy for what it is and not expect total involvement in their jobs by the majority of the workers.

On the other hand, this analysis does not mean that the management need not concern itself with making *any* of the jobs challenging, apart from the financial inducements. While the great bulk of the production line and clerical personnel may not be concerned on this score, those in professional and executive jobs often are. The professional typically is absorbed in his specialty and reacts as a distinctive individual with definite needs that he feels the organization should satisfy. The executive, whether the junior just starting or the senior man seeking to cement his position, is typically concerned with the image of himself as a "success." He looks to the organization to satisfy his psychological needs so that he will feel that he is a "success" or on the road to becoming one.

WORK AS THE CENTRAL LIFE INTEREST

Another theory is just the opposite: It predicates that work is the central life interest of most people, and that, as already mentioned in Chapter 4, even mass-production workers and those on routine assignments prefer variety and more challenge in their jobs. An outstanding exponent of this view (although by no means the only one) is Chris Argyris, already mentioned in Chapter 8.

Based on his studies of the development of the human personality, Argyris believes that "people, in our culture, develop from a state of high dependence on others as an infant, to a state of independence, and finally, to a state of interdependence in their society as an adult," and that the individual enters the world of work just when he feels a strong desire to be self-reliant and to obtain the free expression of his personality. He wants to have something to say about the work situation, not simply to be the passive agent of others. He wants to be able to express his "needs, sentiments, and personal goals."[12]

The tragedy is that most modern organizations require the worker to be passive and dependent upon the management's wishes; the worker is regarded generally as a tool of production, to be manipulated as the management sees best. The scientific-

12 Chris Argyris, *Personality Fundamentals for Administrators,* New Haven, Conn.: Labor and Management Center, Yale University, 1953, pp. 46–47.

management point of view takes into account "primarily the physical and biological properties of man," and in many respects is even "diametrically opposed to the development of a healthy personality in our culture."[13] Argyris believes that most workers today are permitted "little control over their work-a-day world. [The] developmental processes and end result of the individual and organization are, at crucial points, fundamentally different and even antagonistic."[14] The individual seeks "self-actualization," that is, to be able to satisfy the needs of his personality, whereas the management is obsessed with trying to make the worker behave rationally. It even assumes that "individual differences in the human personality may be ignored by transferring more skill and thought to machines."[15] The task specialization of scientific management permits the individual to use only a fraction of his abilities. New work procedures based on even greater specialization, which management hails as a great improvement, make the workers feel even more frustrated. They find their role in the organization narrowed even more. Like Golembiewski (see Chapter 4), Argyris believes that fundamental modifications in work assignments and processes, as well as in management practices, are needed if the organization is to be adapted to meet human needs and replace worker apathy with real involvement. Management's reliance on rigid controls to assure compliance with its mandates—and on a multiplication of such controls when nonconformance is detected—boomerangs; such restrictive and punitive policies simply motivate the worker *not* to cooperate.[16]

Frederick Herzberg's "satisfiers-dissatisfiers" theory of motivation, much discussed in recent years, supports Argyris.[17] Based on research conducted with 200 engineers and accountants in the Pittsburgh area, Herzberg concluded that some factors (pay, working conditions, supervision, interpersonal relationships, and company policy and administration) can cause employee dissatisfaction, but even when the conditions complained about are corrected by the management, "contribute very little to job satisfaction."[18] Conversely, while the presence of other factors (achievement, recognition for achievement, intrinsic interest in the work, responsibility, and advancement) produce satisfaction, their absence causes very little dissatisfaction. The big mistake management typically makes is to emphasize the first set of factors, on the mistaken assumption that attention to them will positively stimulate the employees to put forth their best efforts. The real motivators, the second set of factors, are given lip service only. As a result, "from a

[13] *Ibid.*, p. 46.

[14] *Ibid.*, p. 48.

[15] Chris Argyris, "Personal vs. Organizational Goals," in Robert Dubin (ed.), *Human Relations in Administration*, Englewood Cliffs, N.J.: Prentice-Hall, 1961, p. 72.

[16] See Chris Argyris, *Personality and Organization*, New York: Harper & Row, 1957, p. 137.

[17] See Frederick Herzberg, Bernard Mausner, and Barbara Block Snyderman, *The Motivation to Work*, New York: Wiley, 1959.

[18] Frederick Herzberg, "The Motivation-Hygiene Concept and Problems of Manpower," *Personnel Administration*, XXVII, No. 1 (January–February, 1964), 4.

lifetime of diverse learning, successive accomplishment through the various academic stages, and periodic reinforcement of efforts, the entrant to our modern companies finds that rather than work providing an expanding psychological existence, the opposite occurs; and successive amputations of his self-conceptions, aspirations, learning, and talent are the consequences of earning a living."[19] Whether or not Herzberg's theory about the unipolarity of the "satisfiers" and the "dissatisfiers" is correct, his belief that the "external" factors are overstressed, at the expense of the psychological needs of the individual, is consistent with Argyris' analysis.

OTHER VIEWS OF MOTIVATION

Other theorists are critical of many traditional management practices, but they cannot accept the view of the entire working population as consisting overwhelmingly of strongly independent-minded individuals anxious to self-actualize on the job. Whereas Argyris believes the mature individual starting his working career does not relish a passive role, Robert Presthus believes that many adults accept a status of dependency on their superiors.

Presthus bases his interpretation on Harry Stack Sullivan's interpersonal psychiatry theory. According to Sullivan, the individual's personality forms in definite ways as he reacts to the pressures of those with whom he comes in contact. From childhood on, he seeks to release tension by deferring to certain "authority figures," such as parents, teachers, and, in later years, the supervisor in a work situation. The cause of the tension is anxiety: He is anxious to obtain the approval of these authority figures. Presthus quotes Sullivan as saying: "I believe it fairly safe to say that anybody and everybody devotes much of his lifetime, and a great deal of his energy . . . to avoiding more anxiety than he already has, and, if possible, to getting rid of some of this anxiety."[20] Presthus does not challenge the view that, to be effective, the superior's authority must be accepted by the subordinate, but he does question the implication that the subordinate has much choice in the matter. As he sees it, the subordinate must relieve his anxiety tensions by bowing to the wishes of his superior officer, just as all through his life he has sought inward peace by yielding to other authority figures.

The desire for dependency may be very great. Robert N. McMurry cites the banking industry, which in his opinion prefers the passive individual who can be expected to conform in every way with his superiors' concepts of how he should

19 Ibid., 6.

20 Robert Presthus, The Organizational Society, New York: Knopf, 1962, p. 104.

behave. The preferred kind of addition to the staff is often someone who as a child was never completely weaned emotionally from overprotective parents. Sometimes he is someone who grew up in a "loveless and threatening environment [and] never dared to become self-reliant."[21] When he enters the world of work and gets a job where he is expected to accept responsibility, he is frightened and looks for "parental surrogates among persons who have power, strength, and authority." Such persons, Mc-Murry believes, react very well to the authoritarian kind of supervision practiced in some banks; they are relieved to be in a position where they need take no risks and can depend on others to worry about what should be done. "As employees they repeat their childhood behavior pattern; they become the 'good soldiers,' the loyal conscientious workers."[22]

CHANGES IN MOTIVATION

It is further questioned that the individual's state of motivation is as static as some implicitly describe it. According to A. H. Maslow, there is a hierarchy of human needs, each level of which must be satisfied, although not completely, before the next level asserts itself. In ascending order, these needs are: physiological (food, rest, and protection from the elements); safety or security (not only protection from danger and deprivation but also from arbitrary action of others); social needs (such as friendships and acceptance by others); egoistic needs (status, recognition, and respect); and self-fulfillment needs (to realize one's potential). Since satisfied needs are no longer motivations, one must know the present needs level of the person whom he wants to motivate.[23]

The aging process, as described by Harry Levinson of the Industrial Health Division of the Menninger Foundation, also has its impact. He calls attention to the "male menopause," meaning the period of middle age that for many men is one of "acute psychological loss" and thus really a "change of life." At 45 a man realizes that very likely he has fewer years ahead of him than behind him. Usually he must realistically anticipate that in all probability he will remain in much the same economic and social position for the rest of his life as he occupies in middle age. Some executives at this stage in their life build a "psychological cocoon" about themselves. They lose their old fight and fall into a rut. They fear younger men as threats and may even refuse to train them. Instead of continuing as assets to the organization, they become a drag on it. Levinson explains that these are not aberrations of weak individuals but common

21 Robert N. McMurry, "Recruitment, Dependency, and Morale in the Banking Industry," *Administrative Science Quarterly*, III, No. 1 (June, 1958), 92–93.

22 *Ibid.*

23 A. H. Maslow, *Motivation and Personality*, New York: Harper & Row, 1954.

experiences of men who have reached middle age. Understanding this, the management can deal sympathetically with executives who suddenly seem to have lost their vitality, and by providing them with new challenges, it can help them regain their confidence.[24]

Implications for leadership

Where has this analysis of theories of human motivation taken us? Is it not inconclusive, in view of the differences of opinion reported? First, let it be made clear that the basic purpose was to indicate the complexity of the problem of human motivation. A subject that has so many ramifications cannot honestly be painted as relatively simple. It would be marvelous to be able to say, categorically, what all or most members of any organization can be expected to want in terms of leadership behavior by their superiors. It would simplify matters enormously if all the authorities espoused identical theories. The fact, however, is that they do not. From one standpoint it is well that they do emphasize different needs of the human personality: People are different, and no one person is exactly like another. All kinds of people will be found in any one organization, and each person is not always the same.

Actually, Argyris, Dubin, and Presthus do not claim that their theories apply to all individuals. Argyris admits that some workers have no desire to feel independent. Such workers, he states, must be classified as "not mature." He does not attempt to tell us what proportion of the working population is "mature" or "immature" in these terms for the simple reason that he cannot.[25] No statistical measures are available of the psychological makeup of millions of workers. Furthermore, as indicated, no one can predict exactly how many "mature" and "immature" workers will be found in any one organization. Similarly, Dubin does not say that all individuals look for their satisfactions off the job; and at no point does Presthus say that all employees feel the same strong urge to satisfy their anxiety tensions by deferring to the authority of others. The point, rather, is that each has a general theory of human motivation, which amounts to no more than an expectation as to what may probably be found in dealing with large numbers of workers. None denies that the supervisor must adapt his leadership pattern in accordance with the kinds of subordinates he has under him. Treatment that satisfies one employee may offend another. General theories

[24] Harry Levinson, "The Executive's Anxious Age," Management Forum, *Public Administration News*, XII, No. 3, Chicago: American Society for Public Administration (August, 1962).

[25] Argyris, *Personality Fundamentals for Administrators, op. cit.*, pp. 47–48.

are helpful, but they can never relieve the supervisor of the need to understand the variations in human personalities.

LEADERSHIP STYLE

Usually three types of leadership styles or patterns are identified: authoritarian, democratic, and laissez-faire. Because democracy is so important a value to Americans, it will disturb some people that democracy may not be feasible with some work groups and in some work situations. Therefore it is advisable to make clear at once in any discussion of leadership style that, as Golembiewski states, "the research literature does not consistently support any one leadership style."[26] On the other hand, while Pfiffner and Sherwood also recognize this to be so, their analysis is that "most of the research has seemed to support the desirability of moving toward the democratic type."[27] At this point, it seems wise to refer to some of these research studies.

RESEARCH FINDINGS ON LEADERSHIP

One of the most famous of these experiments was conducted with a group of 10-year-old boys at the University of Iowa in the late 1930s.[28] Four adult leaders were "trained to proficiency" in each of the three different leadership styles—authoritarian, democratic, and laissez-faire. The specific leadership behavior under each style is shown in Figure 8. Each of these adult leaders was assigned to direct the activities of a boys' club consisting of five boys who met after school to engage in hobby activities. The boys in each of the four groups were roughly similar in terms of social and economic background and mental, physical, and personality characteristics. The adult leaders were shifted every six weeks from one club to another, and every time they switched to a new group they changed to a different leadership style. All the boys' clubs met in the same places and carried out the same activities under the same conditions. During these meetings, observers were present to study the boys' behavior in detail. The boys themselves were later interviewed to determine their reaction to each leadership style. Home visits were also made to the parents to discover what the impact of each leadership pattern had been on the boys' conduct at home.

The basic findings were as follows:

1. Under laissez-faire supervision, the boys proved less efficient. Furthermore, they did not like the club activities as much as when they were treated democratically. They did less

26 Robert T. Golembiewski, "Three Styles of Leadership and Their Uses," *Personnel,* XXXVIII, No. 4 (July–August, 1961), 35. See also Erwin S. Stanton, "Which Approach to Management—Democratic, Authoritarian or . . .?" *Personnel Administration,* XXV, No. 2 (March–April, 1962), 44–47.

27 John M. Pfiffner and Frank P. Sherwood, *Administrative Organization,* Englewood Cliffs, N.J.: Prentice-Hall, 1960, p. 364.

28 The description of these experiments is from Ralph White and Ronald Lippitt, "Leader Behavior and Member Reaction in Three 'Social Climates,' " in Cartwright and Zander, *op. cit.,* pp. 527–553.

Fig. 8.   Characteristics of the three treatment
variables. From Ralph White and Ronald Lippitt,
"Leader Behavior and Member Reaction in
Three 'Social Climates,'" in D. Cartwright
and A. Zander (eds.), Group Dynamics,
Research and Theory, New York:
Harper & Row, 1960, p. 528.

Authoritarian	*Democratic*	*Laissez-faire*
1. All determination of policy by the leader	1. All policies a matter of group discussion and decision, encouraged and assisted by the leader	1. Complete freedom for group or individual decision, with a minimum of leader participation
2. Techniques and activity steps dictated by the authority, one at a time, so that future steps were always uncertain to a large degree	2. Activity perspective gained during discussion period. General steps to group goal sketched, and when technical advice was needed, the leader suggested two or more alternative procedures from which choice could be made	2. Various materials supplied by the leader, who made it clear that he would supply information when asked. He took no other part in work discussion
3. The leader usually dictated the particular work task and work companion of each member	3. The members were free to work with whomever they chose, and the division of tasks was left to the group	3. Complete nonparticipation of the leader
4. The dominator tended to be "personal" in his praise and criticism of the work of each member; remained aloof from active group participation except when demonstrating	4. The leader was "objective" or "fact-minded" in his praise and criticism, and tried to be a regular group member in spirit without doing too much of the work	4. Infrequent spontaneous comments on member activities unless questioned, and no attempt to appraise or regulate the course of events

work and poorer work than when under democratic supervision. The complete freedom they had under laissez-faire conditions led them to play more than when under either democratic or authoritarian supervision.

2. If efficiency is evaluated both in terms of work production and social satisfactions, democracy was clearly superior to both

laissez-faire and autocracy. The boys worked as efficiently under authoritarian as they did under democratic supervision, but they enjoyed themselves more under democracy.

3. There was a significant difference in the boys' behavior when a democratic, as contrasted with a dictatorial, adult leader temporarily left the room. The boys in democracy kept right on working, but those under iron rule "stopped working as if glad to be relieved of a task which they 'had' to do." Work production went down precipitously during leader-out periods under autocracy, whereas the decline was only slight under democracy.

4. The boys showed more originality and creative thinking under democracy than under either laissez-faire or autocracy, for "there was a larger amount of creative thinking about the work in progress than in autocracy, and it was more sustained and practical than in laissez-faire."[29]

5. Autocracy can create much hostility and aggression, including aggression against scapegoats. "Dominating ascendance," meaning imperious treatment of one boy by another, illustrated by such language as "shut up," took place more often in the autocratically managed groups. Real hostility between the boys and aggressive demands for attention were also more characteristic of the autocratic groups. Destruction of work materials and property was not unusual when the meetings of the autocratic groups ended, but it did not take place at all in the democratic groups.

As to scapegoat behavior, it was evidenced in the autocratic, but not in the democratic, groups. Held down by the adult leader when he was playing the authoritarian role, the boys vented their spleen on some innocent member of the group. They took out on him their accumulated resentments against the adult leader. They could not openly defy the leader, so they directed their "aggressions" against other club members who had done nothing to them.

Upon return to democratic or laissez-faire treatment after autocracy, the boys sometimes released their "bottled-up tensions." The change to relative freedom after repressive control resulted in their breaking loose and engaging in much aggressive behavior, with the democratic adult now the scapegoat. The boys appeared to say to themselves, "Aha! *Now* I can do what I've been wanting to do in this club!"[30] After a couple of days, however, the "thrill of new-found freedom" wore off, and the boys again exhibited the "spontaneous interest" characteristic of democracy.

---

[29] *Ibid.*, p. 541.
[30] *Ibid.*, p. 545.

6. There was more group-mindedness and friendliness in democracy. The pronoun "we" was used much more often in the democratic than in the autocratic groups. The kinds of remarks made by the boys in the democratic groups indicated the existence of greater group cohesion than under autocracy. "Friendly playfulness" was more pronounced, and there was a greater readiness to share group property.

A number of studies made with adult workers have also shown that democratic supervision produces better results. Frequently cited are those made some years ago by the Institute for Social Research of the University of Michigan. The major finding was that work output was directly correlated with the amount of freedom the supervisor gave the worker. A comparison was made between the production achieved by groups of clerical workers functioning under "close" or "general" supervision. Close supervision meant that the supervisor "watched" the subordinates and checked constantly on how they were carrying out their tasks. Under general supervision, the supervisor put the workers on their own and employed an honor system. It was found that production was highest in work units headed by supervisors who practiced general supervision. Furthermore, the high supervisors, in terms of production, in most cases themselves received general rather than close direction from their own superiors. Finally, the high supervisors were generally content to leave the detailed performance of the work to their subordinates, and to concentrate on their supervisory responsibilities. In this respect they were "people-oriented." The low supervisors tended to neglect their supervisory responsibilities and to spend too much time actually trying to do a share of the production job themselves. Accordingly, they were considered to be "work-oriented."[31]

More recent studies at Michigan have shown that it takes about two years or even longer for changes in supervisory style to have their full impact. If management changes to "pressure-oriented supervision," operating efficiency will improve in the short-range, but in the long-run it will appreciably decline. Conversely, if management changes to more "people-oriented" patterns, there will either be no change in efficiency, or even a *decrease;* however, in the long-range there will be an appreciable improvement in the work results. In the first situation, production goes up because unused physical capacity is used and costs are cut. But the employees, who are waiting to see what the change means, cooperate only passively. When they find that the new policies are not meant to be temporary, they either quit or

[31] Daniel Katz, Nathan Maccoby, and Nancy C. Morse, *Productivity, Supervision, and Morale in an Office Situation,* Ann Arbor, Mich.: Survey Research Center, Institute for Social Research, 1950.

in various ways resist the management, causing production to drop sharply. In the second situation, the employees are at first skeptical, so they do not respond with enthusiasm. But when they see that the management is continuing the new policy, their morale steadily improves to the point where new highs in production are reached.[32]

Gellerman warns that although it "is probably optimal" for most workers, employee-centered supervision should not be a "panacea for all supervisors."[33] Some employees "dislike ambiguity and prefer a clear-cut set of do's and don'ts to general guidelines that leave too much room for their own judgment."[34] Therefore "the most effective approach to sustained productivity is neither the production-centered nor the employee-centered style in its 'pure' form, but a mixed or flexible style that continually adapts itself to changing conditions."[35]

Selecting the appropriate leadership style

In a most stimulating essay, Robert Tannenbaum and Warren H. Schmidt take up the problem of selecting leadership style.[36] Their analysis is particularly valuable because they organize it around the central question of decisionmaking. Figure 9 reproduces a continuum that they have prepared showing the range of possible leadership behavior available to the manager. They explain each of the "behavior points" shown on the bottom line of the continuum as follows:

1. *The manager makes the decision and announces it.* Here the executive gives his subordinates no opportunity to participate directly in the decisionmaking process. He decides what the problem is, determines the possible courses of action, selects one of them, and then tells the subordinates to carry it out. In making his decision, he may or may not take into account how the employees will react to it. He may or may not use coercion in getting them to do as he says.

2. *The manager "sells" his decision.* There is no difference between this and 1., except that the manager does try to persuade the subordinates to accept the decision. He recognizes that some employees may not like the decision and may try to resist it, so he is careful to make clear what they will gain by accepting it. Note that the area of authority exercised by the manager remains large.

3. *The manager presents his ideas and invites questions.* The difference between this and 2. is that the manager gives the subordinates the opportunity to explore with him the implications of the decision. Instead of simply explaining why they should accept

[32] Rensis Likert, *The Human Organization: Its Management and Values,* New York: McGraw-Hill, 1967.

[33] Gellerman, *op. cit.,* p. 38.

[34] *Ibid.*

[35] *Ibid.,* p. 39.

[36] Robert Tannenbaum and Warren H. Schmidt, "How to Choose a Leadership Pattern," *Harvard Business Review,* XXXVI, No. 2 (March–April, 1958), 95–101.

it, he invites them to ask questions, and he takes the time to go into some detail about "his thinking and his intentions." At this point on the continuum, the "area of freedom for subordinates" begins to look significant.

4. *The manager presents a tentative decision subject to change.* Here for the first time, the subordinates are allowed to have some influence on the decision. The executive retains responsibility for identifying the problem and developing a proposed

Fig. 9. Continuum of leadership behavior. From Robert Tannenbaum and Warren H. Schmidt, "How to Choose a Leadership Pattern," Harvard Business Review, XXXVI, *No. 2 (March–April, 1958), 96.*

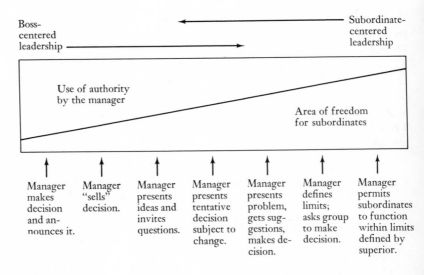

solution, but only on a tentative basis. Before making a final decision, he asks the subordinates to give their frank reactions, but he also makes clear that he is retaining the right to decide the question as he sees fit.

5. *The manager presents the problem, gets suggestions, and then makes his decision.* In 1. through 4. above, the manager in every case makes the decision himself, although in 4. it is a tentative one. In 5., he asks the subordinates for their opinions before he makes any decision, final or tentative. He respects their knowledge of operating problems and knows that they may be

able to suggest solutions that would not occur to him. After evaluating their ideas, as well as his own, he "selects the solution that he regards as most promising."

6. *The manager defines the limits and requests the group to make a decision.* Here the manager delegates to the subordinates the authority to make a certain decision. He states exactly what the problem is and makes clear the restrictions on what the employees can decide. As a hypothetical example, the manager tells the subordinates that a new parking lot will be built for the use of the employees. A ceiling figure of $100,000 for the construction costs has been fixed. So long as this figure is not exceeded, the group can decide to build whatever kind of lot it wants, an underground one or a surface one with multilevel facilities. The management may not like the employees' decision but will accept it within the financial limit.

7. *The manager permits the group to make decisions within prescribed limits.* The difference between 6. and 7. is that in 7. a general grant of decisionmaking power is made, not limited to any one problem. The example given is of teams of managers or engineers whose responsibility is not only to identify problems but also to decide what to do about them. The only limits on what the group can do are those specified by the official to whom the team leader reports. This leader may or may not himself participate in the making of the decision. If he does, he has no more authority than any other team member. He commits himself in advance to support whatever decision the group makes.[37]

Under 6 and 7, the subordinates' "area of freedom" widens greatly. The question remains, however, as to which of the leadership behaviors shown on the continuum is appropriate at a particular time. Tannenbaum and Schmidt identify three sets of factors that bear upon this question:

forces in the manager
forces in the subordinates
forces in the situation[38]

FORCES IN THE MANAGER

By "forces in the manager" Tannenbaum and Schmidt mean his own preferences, based on his past history and experiences. Is he the type who strongly believes that people should participate in decisions that affect them as individuals? Or is he someone who has long been convinced that the supervisor must stoically assume the burden of making the decisions himself because he is paid to do so? How much confidence does he have in other people in general and in his present subordinates in particular? Some managers are so constituted that they become uneasy

[37] *Ibid.,* 97.
[38] *Ibid.,* 98.

if there appears to be an element of risk and uncertainty in the operations they supervise. This kind of executive is better off if he frankly acknowledges to himself that he is not the person to make delegations of authority as broad as those shown on behavior points 6. and 7. of the continuum.

FORCES IN THE SUBORDINATES

"Forces in the subordinates" refers to the expectations of the employees as to how the supervisor should behave in his relations with them. It also means the personality requirements of each individual in the group as these bear upon the question of the kind of direction he responds to best. The executive can allow greater freedom to subordinates under the following conditions:

1. The subordinates have relatively high needs for independence.
2. They *want* to assume responsibility, rather than to avoid it.
3. They have a "relatively high tolerance for ambiguity," meaning they would rather receive broad instructions than to be tied down by clear-cut instructions.
4. They are interested in the problem and believe that it is important.
5. They understand the goals of the organization and identify with them.
6. They have the necessary knowledge and experience to be able to deal with the problem.
7. They are accustomed to sharing in decisionmaking. This is what they expect and are prepared for, rather than being denied such a role.[39]

If these conditions do not exist, there may be no alternative to running a "one-man show." Depending on his assessment of these factors, the executive may on one occasion decide to make the decisions himself, on another to let the subordinates participate. If the manager has the respect of the subordinates, they will understand why in the one case he brings them in and in the other he does not.

FORCES IN THE SITUATION

"Forces in the situation" refers to the "critical environmental pressures" that surround the manager, stemming from "the organization, the work group, the nature of the problem, and the pressures of time."[40]

As to the organization, it has values and traditions that condition the manager's behavior. Someone newly appointed from the outside "quickly discovers that certain kinds of behavior are approved while others are not." There is a great compulsion

[39] *Ibid.*, 99.
[40] *Ibid.*, 100.

for him to select that kind of behavior on the continuum that conforms to his superiors' concepts of how he should conduct himself. Sometimes this is referred to as the "management climate" in the agency; in other words, the lower ranking executives tend to imitate the behavior of the higher ones. The latter are a very important part of the "situation."

Other organizational factors influencing the extent of employee participation include the size of the organization units, their geographical distribution, and whether or not information about work plans must be kept confidential. In a very large and dispersed organization, it may be impossible to have as much employee participation as the management would like. If the activity is one involving national security, work plans and other information obviously cannot be communicated as freely to the employees.

"Group effectiveness" is another consideration. Before he gives a problem to the work of the group to solve, the manager must be convinced that it is equal to the task. Has the group functioned effectively in the past? Does it seem confident of its ability to cope with this kind of assignment?

The "nature of the problem" also sets limits on the extent to which the manager can safely delegate. Perhaps the problem is one with which the work group is not familiar, so he must handle it himself. There is no virtue in asking any one subordinate or a group of workers to take on responsibilities they are not ready to assume. Yet the executive wants to be sure that he is making full use of the special knowledges and abilities of his staff. Tannenbaum and Schmidt suggest that the manager should ask himself, "Have I heard the ideas of everyone who has the necessary knowledge to make a significant contribution to the solution of this problem?" If he asks this question and answers it honestly, he is more likely to select the most appropriate leadership pattern.

"Pressure of time," meaning the need to act quickly, may force the manager to make the decision himself, without consulting with his subordinates. Leisurely consideration of every problem is not possible in the swift-moving environment of government. The manager does not by any means have full control of his time schedule; his own supervisors set deadlines for him. Unforeseen situations arise that make it necessary for him to make the best decision possible in very short period of time. Under such circumstances, all he can do is consult with as many subordinates as possible.

The great value of the preceding analysis is that it makes

clear the different considerations that should influence the decision as to leadership style. If the "boss-centered" type is used on occasion, this does not mean that the managers in question must be tyrants at heart. Of course, some may have such tendencies, evidenced by their use of "boss-centered" leadership even when it is not necessary. The point is that the manager should use the leadership pattern called for by the particular situation.

BIBLIOGRAPHY

Argyris, Chris, *Personality Fundamentals for Administrators*, New Haven, Conn.: Labor and Management Center, Yale, 1953.

Argyris, Chris, *Personality and Organization*, New York: Harper & Row, 1957.

Argyris, Chris, "The Individual and Organization: Some Problems of Mutual Adjustment," *Administrative Science Quarterly, II*, No. 1 (June, 1957).

Argyris, Chris, *Understanding Organizational Behavior*, Homewood, Ill.: Irwin, 1960.

Bavelas, Alex, "Leadership: Man and Function," *Administrative Science Quarterly, IV*, No. 4 (March, 1960).

Bennis, Warren G., "Leadership Theory and Administrative Behavior: The Problem of Authority," *Administrative Science Quarterly, IV*, No. 3, (December, 1959).

Blake, Robert R., and Mouton, Jane S., "Three Strategies for Exercising Authority: One-Alone, One-to-One, One-to-All," *Personnel Administration, XXVII*, No. 4 (July-August, 1964).

Bowers, David G., and Seashore, Stanley E., "Predicting Organizational Effectiveness with a Four-Factor Theory of Leadership," *Administrative Science Quarterly, II*, No. 2 (September, 1966).

Cartwright, Dorwin, and Zander, Alvin, (eds.), *Group Dynamics, Research and Theory*, New York: Harper & Row, 1960. Part Five.

Friedlander, Frank, and Walton, Eugene, "Positive and Negative Motivations Toward Work," *Administrative Science Quarterly, IX*, No. 2 (September, 1964).

Gellerman, Saul W., *Management by Motivation*, New York: American Management Association, 1968.

Ginzberg, Eli, "Perspectives on Worker Motivation," *Personnel*, *XXXI*, No. 1 (July, 1954).

Golembiewski, Robert T., "Three Styles of Leadership and Their Uses," *Personnel*, *XXXVIII*, No. 4 (July-August, 1961).

Halpin, Andrew W., *The Leadership Behavior of School Superintendents*, Columbus, Ohio: College of Education, The Ohio State University, 1956.

Hieronymous, George H., "The Job's the Thing, II," *Personnel Administration*, *XXVII*, No. 4 (July-August, 1964).

Hills, R. Jean, "The Representative Function: Neglected Dimension of Leadership Behavior," *Administrative Science Quarterly*, *VIII*, No. 1 (June, 1963).

Jones, John Paul, "Changing Patterns of Leadership," *Personnel*, *XLIV*, No. 2 (March-April, 1967).

Katz, Daniel, and Kahn, Robert L., *The Social Psychology of Organizations*, New York: Wiley, 1966. Chapter 11.

Lee, H. C., "Do Workers Really Want Flexibility on the Job?" *Personnel*, *XLII*, No. 2 (March-April, 1965).

Likert, Rensis, *New Patterns of Management*, New York: McGraw-Hill, 1961.

Likert, Rensis, *The Human Organization, Its Management and Value*, New York: McGraw-Hill, 1967.

Livingstone, John Leslie, "Management Controls and Organizational Performance," *Personnel Administration*, *XXVIII*, No. 1 (January-February, 1965).

McGregor, Douglas, *The Human Side of Enterprise*, New York: McGraw-Hill, 1960.

McMurry, Robert N., "The Case for Benevolent Autocracy," *Harvard Business Review*, *XXXVI*, No. 1 (January-February, 1958).

Rodney, Thomas C., "Can Money Motivate Better Job Performance?" *Personnel Administration*, *XXX*, No. 2 (March-April, 1967).

Sorcher, Melvin, and Meyer, Herbert H., "Motivation and Job Performance," *Personnel Administration*, *XXXI*, No. 4 (July-August, 1968).

Thompson, Arthur A., "Employee Participation in Decision Making: The TVA Experience," *Public Personnel Review*, *XXVIII*, No. 2 (April, 1967).

Wager, L. Wesley, "Leadership Style, Hierarchical Influence, and Supervisory Role Obligations," *Administrative Science Quarterly*, *IX*, No. 4 (March, 1965).

PART IV
PERSONNEL
ADMINISTRATION

CHAPTER 12

EVOLUTION

OF PUBLIC

PERSONNEL

ADMINISTRATION

IN THE UNITED

STATES

T HE RELATIONSHIP between good administration and high-quality personnel is by
no means a discovery of the modern age.
Indeed it was recognized in the earliest civi-
lizations. In Plato's *Republic*, there occurs this interesting bit of
dialogue between the narrator, Socrates, and Glaucon, one of the
auditors:

> Do you know, I said, that governments vary as the disposi-
> tions of men vary, and that there must be as many of the one as
> there are of the other? For we cannot suppose that States are
> made of "oak and rock," and not out of the human natures which
> are in them, and which in a figure turn the scale and draw other
> things after them?

> Yes, he said, the States are as the men are; they grow out of
> human characters.[1]

Since governments "grow out of human characters," the
quality of that human element is of decisive importance. John
M. Gaus is reported to have said that the *Republic* is really a

[1] Plato, *The Re-
public* (trans.
Benjamin Jow-
ett), New
York: Vintage
Books, Random
House, p. 293.

treatise on personnel administration, concerned as Plato is with a comprehensive plan for selecting and training the philosopher-kings. Of course, Plato's specific program is impractical for the modern age, but that the "states are as the men are" is just as true today as it was in his time. In fact, centuries later the American philosopher John Dewey wrote, "The state is as its officials are." Dewey believed, just as did Plato, that public officials could not be "mean, obstinate, proud, and stupid, and yet the nature of the state which they serve remain essentially unimpaired."[2] Here is the great challenge of personnel administration; it deals with the key human element, and how to make it equal to the greatly increasing public-service needs of the people.

In the United States, public personnel administration as it exists today is the product of a long evolution. Let us briefly examine this background with the intention simply of identifying the main strands in the public personnel movement.[3]

RECORD OF FIRST SIX U.S. PRESIDENTS

The first six Presidents of the United States have frequently been praised for maintaining good standards in the selection of federal employees. Paul P. Van Riper, the leading authority on the history of the federal civil service, recounts that, in the main, these first Presidents did give a good deal of weight to merit principles in making their appointments. He stresses, however, that they also took political factors into account to some extent. George Washington, for example, emphasized job fitness, but in choosing from among the candidates he was careful to select individuals who were friendly to the Federalist cause, and Jefferson made no bones about removing men from posts for political reasons. It should be made clear, however, that both under the Federalists and the Jeffersonians most government jobs were filled by persons with an upper middle-class background. Under Jefferson, there was no program of replacing such persons with embodiments of the common man. Comments Van Riper: "American government in the early years of the nineteenth century was still the prerogative of those with considerable means."[4]

THE SPOILS SYSTEM (1829–1883)

The class composition of federal employees changed drastically with the advent of Andrew Jackson to the Presidency, for he

[2] John Dewey, *The Public and its Problems*, New York: Holt, Rinehart and Winston, 1927, pp. 68–69.

[3] The following historical account is from Paul P. Van Riper, *History of the United States Civil Service*, New York: Harper & Row, 1958.

[4] *Ibid.*, p. 24.

strongly felt that no one social class should have a monopoly of the public service. Such a monopoly was not only undemocratic, it also was unnecessary in terms of governmental efficiency. In his opening message to Congress in December, 1829, Jackson said: "The duties of all public officers are, or at least admit of being made, so plain and simple that men of intelligence may readily qualify themselves for their performance; and I can not but believe that more is lost by the long continuance of men in office than is generally to be gained by their experience."[5] For these reasons, Jackson believed that rotation in office was highly desirable. Under such a policy, holdovers from previous administrations are swept out, and, acting accordingly, Jackson made numerous removals. Van Riper and others have stressed that Jackson had good intentions about the public service and did not want to damage it. He was not the machine politician who is intent on building personal power and is indifferent to the harmful effects on the government. Nevertheless, with his new policies he did open the gates for the spoils politicians at the national level.

Approximately in 1800, the spoils system began to take hold in state and local governments. Under the spoils system, the party winning the election reasons that to the victor belongs the spoils, so it makes gifts of government jobs to party workers. By 1829 this policy was strongly entrenched in many states, particularly in New York and Pennsylvania. Political parties were just emerging, replacing the former mere factional groupings. The professional politician was being born, and it was not long before he discovered that gifts of government jobs could be used to lubricate the party machinery. Such men were motivated not by the egalitarian ideals of Jacksonian democracy, but rather by considerations of the raw struggle for political power.

Historians differ about who was personally responsible for bringing the unadulterated spoils system to Washington. Some blame it on Martin Van Buren, the clever New York politician whom Jackson made his first Secretary of State, but Van Buren's biographers dispute this.[6] In any case, the unmitigated spoils system had started in other parts of the country, and it naturally spread to Washington and the federal service when Jackson adopted the new policy of rotation in office. Under the Presidents who followed Jackson, political removals were made on a more extensive basis, and by 1860 the original opening provided by Jackson had produced a spoils system with an "adhesive . . . grip upon the political machinery of the United States."[7]

[5] *Ibid.*, p. 36.

[6] See Felix A. Nigro, "The Van Buren Confirmation Before the Senate," *Western Political Quarterly, XIV, No. 1* (March, 1961), 148–159.

[7] Van Riper, *op. cit.*, p. 42.

Van Riper describes in specific terms what was involved in terms of obligations and rewards:

> That politics was often a touchstone to success in private enterprise via land grants, franchises, and government contracts only heightened interest in public office. In return, however, public servants were expected to contribute their votes and a portion, often substantial, of their time, energy, and income to the political party to which they were indebted for their employment. All this was not a matter of contract, though such might be implied. Rather, it was usually a recognition of a sort of partnership, often entered into with considerable enthusiasm by all concerned. Loyalty to one's political party was as appropriate, and just about as frequently assumed, as loyalty to the nation, a church, or an individual state. Most frequently the penalty for both administrative and political failure was removal. In addition, however, one might be cut off from any access to other types of political favors, both those directly at the command of the party, such as nominations, and those available only through governmental channels, such as contracts. On the whole, the motivations and methods of private enterprise were those of the spoils system.[8]

Under Lincoln, the "spoils system reached new heights." In order to develop support in the North for carrying on the war with the Confederacy, Lincoln was forced to make numerous appointments for political reasons. In fact, he made the "most complete sweep of offices" of any President up to that time. From a personal standpoint, however, Lincoln found the spoils system distasteful. One day, observing a crowd of office-seekers in his outer office, he remarked that "the spoils system might in the course of time become far more dangerous to the Republic than the rebellion itself."[9] But to the man in the street there was nothing wrong with the spoils system. In Lincoln's time and during the immediate post-Civil War period, most Americans still agreed with the Jacksonian view that the duties of public office were so simple that they could be entrusted to almost anyone.

THE CIVIL SERVICE
REFORM MOVEMENT

However, important changes were taking place in American society, and the role of government was being expanded as the country became increasingly industrialized. Government jobs no longer were as simple as they used to be, so some people became concerned that the government could not discharge

---

[8] *Ibid.*, p. 46.
[9] *Ibid.*, pp. 43–44.

its responsibilities effectively with personnel chosen for political reasons and not for merit. Not enough people were concerned about governmental efficiency, however, for this to become the primary moving force for civil service reform. It was the evidence of widespread corruption in the federal service, tied in with the spoils system, that gave civil service reform its real impetus.

The scandals in the Grant Administration, involving some members of the Cabinet, aroused a public that had become increasingly aware of the connection between the spoils system and graft. Those who obtained appointments as a reward for political service were willing allies of predatory outside interests in different kinds of frauds perpetrated against the government, as in the awarding of contracts. The moral argument for civil service reform soon caught hold in an America which, at that time, thought largely in moral terms. The spoils system was an evil that had to be extirpated from American society if standards of decency were to be maintained, and this became the battle cry of a small group of dedicated individuals, known as the "civil service reformers."

These men were mostly from the eastern part of the country, representing the "top strata of politics, law, business, journalism, and education."[10] They had the personal means to devote their time to developing public interest in civil service reform. Their crusade had proved so successful by 1872 that both the Republican and Democratic parties picked up civil service reform as an issue in the election campaigns for the Congress. One year previously, in March, 1871, Congress had actually voted authorization for President Grant to establish a merit system. This came in the form of a last-minute rider to an appropriations bill; the motivation was the desire of the Republican-controlled Congress to improve its position with the electorate after losses suffered by the Republicans in the mid-term elections of 1870. Grant established a Civil Service Commission that developed a set of civil service rules and administered competitive examinations in some federal departments. In 1873 Congress failed to vote any further funds for this Commission, and it was forced to suspend its operations.

The Pendleton Act

When a disappointed job-seeker assassinated President Garfield in 1881, many Americans previously not moved by the pleas of the civil service reformers now could see that "spoils equaled

---

[10] *Ibid.*, p. 80.

murder." Van Riper believes that Congress would have acted to adopt a civil service system even if this tragedy had not occurred. The Republicans suffered a disastrous defeat in the mid-term election of 1882. They feared that the next President would be a Democrat, and that he would turn out all the Republican officeholders. Although in December, 1880, Senator George H. Pendleton of Ohio introduced a bill providing for adoption of a civil service system, which he later replaced with one sponsored by the New York Civil Service Reform Association, no action was taken in the Senate until Garfield's assassination and the Republican reverses in the 1882 elections. Faced by the possibility that the Democrats would win in the 1884 Presidential elections, the Republicans now decided to support Pendleton's bill. It was passed by Congress in December, 1882, and signed by the President on January 16, 1883. Van Riper writes, "As a later observer cynically put it in 1888, 'the devil was sick, and the devil a monk would be.' "[11]

The civil service reformers and Pendleton were much influenced by the example of the English civil service system. Dorman B. Eaton, a leading figure in the reform movement, had been commissioned by President Hayes to visit England and make a study of the English system. Eaton served as the second chairman of the Grant Commission and later became the first chairman of the United States Civil Service Commission created by the Pendleton Act. The British had had their spoils system, no less venal than the American, but by 1870 the merit system was beginning to function in England and attracted the attention of Americans such as Eaton, anxious to prove to the American people that the spoils system was not a necessary evil.[12]

It was Eaton who persuaded Pendleton to introduce his second bill, so it is not surprising that the Pendleton Act incorporated certain features of the English civil service system as it then existed. Three basic elements were borrowed: (1) use of competitive examinations for entrance into the public service, (2) relative security of tenure, with removals for political reasons forbidden, and (3) guarantee of the political neutrality of the civil servant by providing that he cannot be coerced to make political assessments and to contribute his services to political campaigns. All three principles represented important changes from existing practices in the federal service. It took some years to make the ban on political removals and assessments effective, but the legislative intent in the matter was clear enough.

[11] *Ibid.*, p. 94.
[12] See *The Civil Service Vol. 1 Report of the Committee 1966–68 Chairman, Lord Fulton,* London: Her Majesty's Stationery Office, June, 1968.

There is, however, another feature of the British system that was originally included in the Pendleton bill but was rejected by Congress: the principle of the closed career service. In England, recruitment to the public service has been articulated with the educational system, in accordance with a definite plan whereby the best products of the latter have been tapped for the entrance jobs in each line of work. In general, the principle of initial recruitment to the bottom rungs of certain career ladders has been followed; to be eligible for appointment to a beginning position in one of these career progressions, the individual had to complete a certain level of education. In the British system what is known as "late entry" has been kept to a minimum, and very few opportunities have been available for entering one of the career ladders at one of the intermediate steps or at the top rung *after* having had outside work experience.[13] The British career system has been a closed one, because it has discouraged free movement of individuals, no matter what their age and education, from private to public employment.[14] All of this is in the past, however. In June, 1968, Prime Minister Wilson announced that he had accepted all the principal recommendations of the Fulton Committee, including "no restriction on the levels to which suitably qualified and experienced people from outside the Service can be directly appointed."[15]

In his bill, Pendleton proposed that entrance into the public service be permitted only "at the lowest grade." This provision met with a decidedly adverse reaction on the part of most of his colleagues in the Senate. The found it contrary to one of the most treasured values of American society: The right of anyone, no matter what his formal schooling, age, or past work history, to demonstrate his ability in any walk of life. Eliminating the spoils system was one thing; making federal employment the virtual monopoly of persons with a certain educational background was another. The United States was a democracy, an open society with no class distinctions like those in Britain. The "efficient" features of the British system should be borrowed, but not those that seemed undemocratic. This is why Van Riper calls the Pendleton Act an "Americanization of a foreign invention."

The opposition was so strong to this provision in Pendleton's bill that Pendleton himself made a motion to eliminate it. The motion was overwhelmingly adopted, and as a result, "from 1883 to this day, one may enter the American public service at almost any level and at almost any age."[16] As we shall see in the next chapter, strong efforts are being made to make govern-

13 *Ibid.*, pp. 43–44.
14 *Ibid.*, pp. 108–131, for texts of Northcote-Trevelyan and Macaulay reports, upon which the British civil service system was established. The Northcote Trevelyan report is also reproduced in *Public Administration*, XXXII (Spring, 1954), 1–16.
15 *Ibid.*, p. 44.
16 Paul P. Van Riper, "Adapting a British Political Invention to American Needs," *Public Administration*, XXXI (Winter, 1953), 321–322. See also his "The Tap Roots of American Personnel Management," *Personnel Administration*, XXV, No. 2 (March–April, 1962), 12–16, 32.

ment service a highly desired career for young persons, but the feeling remains as strong against any closed system. Open career systems, with plenty of late entry, are the goal, and it is a goal consonant with American values. Now the British are borrowing from this feature of the American system!

The Pendleton Act created a three-member commission, with members to be appointed by the President subject to Senate confirmation. Of these three members, not more than two may be adherents of the same political party. By not placing the new agency directly under the President and by including this requirement for bipartisanship, Congress clearly indicated its desire to keep the civil service system free from partisan Presidential control. On the other hand, the debates in committee and on the floor of Congress clearly show that "Congress did not intend the Commission to be so independent as to prohibit executive responsibility for administering the civil service."[17]

With respect to coverage, the Act provided for immediately placing under the competitive service only about 10.5 percent of all federal jobs. Furthermore, these were mainly clerical positions in Washington and in post offices and customs houses in the field service. To obtain approval of any civil service measure at that time, it was necessary to proceed slowly. Despite public pressures, there was still considerable opposition in Congress to adopting the merit system. Actually, the Civil Service Commission was not equipped anyway to administer examinations for any large proportion of federal positions. It needed time to get started. Within the limitations of its modest budget, it found it difficult enough to develop a satisfactory program even for the small proportion of employees originally placed under its jurisdiction. Total employment in the federal service averaged about 140,000 in the 1880s.

Extension of the Civil Service system (1883–1969)

The Pendleton Act did give the President the authority by executive order to bring additional positions under civil service as he saw fit. Without this provision, the civil service reformers would not have won much of a victory. Once the Pendleton Act was passed, they could and did renew pressure on the Chief Executive to make the civil service system more inclusive. Presidents still found it necessary to retain a certain number of spoils positions to use as a means of persuading recalcitrant Congressmen to accept their legislative leadership. On the other hand,

[17] Senate Committee on Post Office and Civil Service, *Administration of the Civil Service System*, Washington, D.C.: Government Printing Office, 1957, p. 44.

it was now good politics to demonstrate to the electorate positive support of the civil service principle by including large numbers of additional positions.

Political self-interest marched hand in hand with civil service idealism. When a President of one party was leaving the White House to turn over direction of the government to a successor elected by the opposing party, he found it convenient, as one of his last acts, to bring many additional jobs under civil service. These jobs had been filled with individuals friendly to his Administration, so the departing Chief Executive both protected the position of his party and advanced the cause of civil service. This process is known as "blanketing in." To qualify to retain their jobs, all the incumbent had to do was pass a noncompetitive examination, consisting of a review by the Civil Service Commission of his service record on the job. Practically anybody could pass this kind of examination, since they already had some experience in the job.

Lest a cynical view be formed of Presidents such as Cleveland, Theodore Roosevelt, and Franklin Roosevelt, who "blanketed in" thousands of additional jobs, it should be made clear that at heart they did not relish using the "club" of spoils positions. Carl Russell Fish, the historian, came to the conclusion that throughout the nineteenth century the President's patronage proved an indispensable weapon for overcoming the obstacles to Presidential leadership inherent in a system of separation of powers.[18] In the twentieth century, however, the picture had changed. Congress itself took positive action in 1940 with the Ramspeck Act to encourage President Franklin Roosevelt to bring under civil service by far the greater number of positions still outside the merit system. When the New Deal first appeared, the Democrats, out of power for twelve long years, were hungry for patronage. Positions in the flock of new agencies created in the effort to fight the Depression were usually exempted from civil service.

By 1940 the situation was different. No longer harried by the same pressures, FDR gladly issued the executive orders that clinched the victory for the merit system in the federal service. Specifically, FDR "covered in" some 200,000 positions formerly exempted by law. By 1943 approximately 85 percent of all federal personnel were within the permanent civil service. Since approximately the same percentage is covered today, for almost 30 years now civil service has covered the great bulk of federal jobs. In early 1969, President Nixon issued an executive order

[18] See Carl Russell Fish, *The Civil Service and the Patronage*, Cambridge, Mass.: Harvard University Press, 1904.

placing under merit procedures the jobs of the some 70,000 post-masters and rural letter carriers, the "last great pool of patronage in the federal government service."[19]

Interestingly enough, the Pendleton Act as it still stands makes it possible for the President to remove positions from civil service as well as to place them under it. That no recent President has sought to capitalize on this authority and remove large numbers of positions is testimony to the strength that the civil service principle now has at the national level. Presidents still have some patronage jobs to dispense, such as those of federal district attorneys and marshalls, but the argument that the national government could not be satisfactorily admin-istered without large numbers of spoils jobs to give out is now accepted by very few people, inside and outside Congress. As a simple reading of the newspapers shows, a much more effective control over Congressmen is to threaten them with curtailing expenditures for new post offices and other federal projects in their home constituencies.

Civil Service in the states and cities (1883–1969)

Progress in obtaining civil service in the state governments has not been nearly as great. Thirty-three of the 50 states have adopted comprehensive merit systems, meaning that a large proportion of the positions in the state service is covered. New York (1883) and Massachusetts (1884) were the first to follow the federal example. As late as 1958, only 23 states had comprehensive merit systems, so in the last decade the picture has brightened considerably. The outlook is even better, how-ever, because a merit system functions in all state agencies administering federally aided programs for public welfare, public health, employment security, and civil defense. This began with 1939 amendments to the Social Security Act, followed by extension of the same principle to later authorized federal grant programs.[20] Thus there is no state in the country in which the merit system does not function in some part of the executive branch. Furthermore, if the proposed Intergovernmental Man-power Act is passed, the President could extend the same merit system requirements to any and all state and local programs financed in whole or in part by federal funds.[21]

In the nation's counties, civil service coverage is still quite small, with less than one-tenth of the nation's some 3050 counties having "merit system laws worthy of the name."[22] The picture is much better in the cities, where about 75 percent of the em-

[19] News from the National Civil Service League, March 28, 1968.

[20] Remarks of Senator Edmund S. Muskie on the Intergovernmental Personnel Act of 1967. Congres-sional Record, January 26, 1967.

[21] See Senate Subcommittee on Intergovernmen-tal Relations, Intergovernmen-tal Personnel Act of 1967, Intergov-ernmental Man-power Act of 1967, Hearings on S. 699 and S. 1485, Washing-ton, D.C.: Gov-ernment Printing Office, 1967, p. 4.

[22] Paul P. Van Riper, "Personnel Opinions," Public Personnel Re-view, XXVII, No. 4 (October, 1966), 279.

ployees (outside education) are covered. Most cities over 100,000 in population have civil service systems. Although two-thirds of all public employees are employed by state and local governments, not considering those in education, only about half are under civil service.[23]

Reviewing the entire picture in state and local governments, it can hardly be said that the spoils system is dead. In many state and local jurisdictions it obviously still thrives. A *New York Times* mid-1968 survey of patronage in New York state and local government found it "vastly expanded," but it did define patronage to include all kinds of favors besides jobs.[24] Local politicians argue that the political machine needs the patronage to survive. Getting merit systems approved in these jurisdictions constitutes some of the toughest unfinished business on the personnel front. The battle is just as hard in many places as it was for the original civil service reformers.[25]

THE MODERN CONCEPT OF PERSONNEL ADMINISTRATION

For many years after the passage of the Pendleton Act, not only in the federal government but also in the state and local jurisdictions that followed suit by adopting civil service laws, success was measured by the degree to which political influence was kept out of appointments and promotions. This was the significant consideration, rather than whether the persons appointed or promoted were of high quality. The essential requirement was to give competitive tests to candidates who presented themselves, and to refuse to relax the standards to suit the politicians. It is unfair to judge the personnel procedures then in use on the basis of the more sophisticated techniques we have today, but the basic point remains that it was a limited, negative type of program that these first civil service agencies conducted. Apart from giving examinations and maintaining records, they did little else. Efforts were not made to search out the best available candidates. Clerks, rather than trained personnel technicians, held most of the jobs in these agencies.

Such limited programs were understandable in the first years after the adoption of civil service. Appropriations were generally very small, and much time had to be devoted to staving off the attempts of the politicians to undermine the merit system. Even today, personnel administrators in places that have had civil service for many years do not assume that a reincidence of the spoils system is impossible. Realistically, they recognize

[23] Jean J. Couturier, "Patronage Versus Performance—The Balance Sheet of Civil Service Reform," *Good Government,* LXXXIV, No. 3 (Fall, 1967), 14.

[24] Martin Tolchin, "Political Patronage Rising at Fast Rate, Study Finds," *New York Times,* June 17, 1968.

[25] For a more sanguine view, see Frank J. Sorauf, "The Silent Revolution in Patronage," *Public Administration Review,* XX, No. 1 (Winter, 1960), 28–34.

that some attention must be given to the "protective function"—standing ready to fight any spoils threats. The trouble is that too many of the early civil service agencies continued to spend much of their time on the protective function long after the merit system had become firmly established in these jurisdictions. Their programs were not updated to meet a new situation, one in which the test of success is the ability to staff the public service with the high-quality personnel needed to carry out government activities of an increasingly complex character.

Leaders in the personnel field began to urge their brethren to adopt a broader view and to develop truly "modern" personnel programs. By a modern program, they meant one that was positively oriented toward the goal of recruiting and retaining efficient public employees. They envisioned the creation of personnel offices staffed with professionally trained individuals rather than clerks. Their objective was the development of a broad-gauged personnel program, not one limited merely to giving examinations and keeping records.

Some jurisdictions began to broaden their programs, but in general the following list describes public personnel administration in the country as a whole in the late 1930s:

1. A preponderance of the daily working hours devoted to the routine aspects of appointments, records, and position classification.
2. Centralization of most important personnel decisions in the civil service commission or board, and normal delays of several weeks in placing someone on the departmental payroll.
3. Very little in-service training activity.
4. Only scattered evidence of interest in improved personnel practices being developed in private industry, despite the obvious importance of some of these techniques and the possibility of using them in the government.
5. Very little career planning in the line departments, despite the rush of college graduates, attracted by the New Deal, to Washington.
6. Very few personnel directors with any real voice in the management policies of their agencies.
7. Almost a complete neglect of the importance of good supervision and of the personnel responsibilities of line officials in general.
8. Little attention to employee welfare and health, apart from some low-priced cafeterias, emergency rooms, bowling leagues, and softball.[26]

26 Felix A. Nigro, "Public Personnel: Agenda for the Sixties," *Public Administration Review,* XXI, No. 4 (Autumn, 1961), 191–192.

In 1938, FDR issued an executive order requiring all major departments and agencies to establish bona fide, professionally staffed personnel offices. Previously, personnel functions had mainly been entrusted to high- and low-ranking clerks. They kept records and maintained liaison with the Civil Service Commission on appointments and other personnel actions requiring Commission approval.

Issuance of the executive order ushered in a new era in federal personnel management, marked by emphasis on developing a true merit system. Progress was not spectacular, but it was steady. Procedures were speeded up, and college-trained persons replaced the clerks. Important delegations of authority were made by the Commission to the operating departments, inaugurating a decentralization movement that led in a relatively few years to departmental responsibility for making the great bulk of the appointments, without any requirement of prior Commission approval. This decentralization took place through agency Boards of Civil Service Examiners, since replaced by 65 Interagency Boards, located in the major metropolitan centers.[27] The unimaginative and restricted recruiting programs of the past were replaced with intensive efforts to attract good candidates. Liaison with educational institutions was improved, to the point where in 1967, federal government recruiters visited about 1100 colleges and universities, including virtually every school with 500 or more students.[28] After experimenting with several approaches, the Commission developed the highly successful Federal Service Entrance Examination to attract college students. The FSEE, as it is known, will be mentioned again in the next chapter.

Training programs, too, received a great stimulus with passage by Congress of the Government Employees Training Act of 1958. This legislation extended authority for the first time to *all* federal agencies to expend funds on the training of their employees, both by sending them to outside facilities such as universities, and by organizing programs using the agency's own personnel and facilities. With the passage of this legislation, federal training activity greatly increased. Then in April, 1967, President Johnson, acting upon the recommendation of his Task Force on Career Advancement, issued Executive Order 11348, which directed the Civil Service Commission and the agencies to expand further the training activities.[29] During fiscal year 1967, more than one-third of all federal civilian employees received eight or more hours of formal classroom training.

Early in 1962, President Kennedy issued an executive order providing a new basis for employee-management relations in the federal service. As a result, the whole role of public-employee

[27] See John W. Macy, Jr., "Personnel Panorama —1966, Personnel Developments on the U.S. Federal Level," *Public Personnel Review*, XXVIII, No. 1 (January, 1967), 8.

[28] Tom Woodall, "College Recruiting Review Scheduled," *Federal Times*, March 6, 1968.

[29] See John W. Macy, Jr., "Personnel Developments on the U.S. Federal Level," *Public Personnel Review*, XXIX, No. 2 (April, 1968), 88.

unions is being expanded, opening an entire new chapter in the history of personnel administration in the government. In October, 1962, Congress passed new pay legislation designed to make federal salaries more competitive with private industry rates than they have been in the past, and in subsequent legislation it provided for achievement of full comparability with such rates by July, 1969.[30] All these developments are treated in some detail in the chapters that follow.

State and local governments also have substantially improved their personnel programs. In fact, in some areas the states and cities moved ahead of the federal government in introducing more enlightened practices. Paid advertising was used by quite a few state and local governments long before the United States Commission announced in late 1957 that in the future federal agencies would be permitted to use such advertising in recruiting for scientists and engineers. Formal programs and machinery for dealing with management-employee union relationships had already been developed and were functioning in cities such as Philadelphia, New York, and Cincinnati before President Kennedy issued his executive order. Before passage of the new federal pay legislation, California, Georgia, Illinois, Michigan, New York, Ohio, and Pennsylvania had all established higher top career salaries than those paid in the federal service. The same was true of Los Angeles City and County, Denver, Detroit, St. Louis, San Francisco, and Philadelphia.

In other areas, state and local governments have lagged behind. Training as a personnel activity of real importance has been developed in relatively few state and local jurisdictions. In most such jurisdictions nothing comparable to the Federal Service Entrance Examination has been developed. In many cases, recruiting methods are unimaginative, and the personnel program is still of an essentially negative character. On the other hand, in the past few years notable improvements have taken place in quite a few state and local agencies.[31]

CHALLENGES OF THE PRESENT PERIOD

In the 1960s it became clear that public personnel administration needed to develop a new and more positive orientation: identification with the goals of government policies, and assumption of a leadership role in attaining those goals. For one thing, the accelerated technological and social change made it imperative that public personnel agencies develop and maintain up-to-date projections of future manpower requirements, and step up train-

[30] See Public Law 90-206, 90th Congress, H.R. 7977, December 16, 1967.

[31] See recent issues of *Public Personnel Review* and *Personnel News*, published by the Public Personnel Association, 1313 East 60th St., Chicago, Ill. 60637.

ing and retraining programs for a working force constantly threatened with skill obsolescence. As A. D. P. Heeney has said:

> In many parts of the world . . . many of the solutions to problems of personnel management—legislative and otherwise— that were developed between the two world wars and refined in the immediate post-war period are no longer capable of dealing with the social, economic, and technical changes in our society. And these elements of change are gaining in strength, forcing the pace of change and renovation.[32]

The personnel man was deeply involved with two social movements, each characterized by strife: equal opportunity for minority groups, and collective bargaining for public employees. Never before had social awareness been so important for personnel workers; purely technical training could no longer suffice. As to equal opportunity, at all levels of government, efforts were being made to recruit and promote much larger numbers of workers from the disadvantaged groups, with the success of these efforts naturally depending greatly on the effectiveness of the personnel offices. No easy problem, the objective, stated so well by Chester A. Newland, was to make the merit system "inclusive" rather than "exclusive," without lowering employment standards.[33] As to collective bargaining, the employee militancy grew out of deep resentments long felt over grievances now deemed intolerable. The ensuing chapters also deal with both these problems.

BIBLIOGRAPHY

"A Basic Bibliography in Public Personnel Administration," *Public Personnel Review*, XXII, No. 4 (October, 1961).

Berlin, Seymour S., "Is Centralized Control of Personnel Management on the Upswing?" *Personnel Administration*, XXX, No. 1 (January-February, 1967).

Chapman, Brian, *The Profession of Government*, London: G. Allen, 1959.

The Civil Service Vol. 1 Report of the Committee 1966–68 Chairman, Lord Fulton, London: Her Majesty's Stationery Office, June, 1968.

Fish, Carl Russell, *The Civil Service and the Patronage*, Cambridge, Mass.: Harvard University Press, 1904.

Goode, Cecil E., *Personnel Research Frontiers*, Chicago: Public Personnel Association, 1958.

[32] A. D. P. Heeney, "The Environment of Public Personnel Administration," *Public Personnel Review*, XXVIII, No. 4 (October, 1967), 211.

[33] Chester A. Newland, "Variety: A Public Personnel Approach," *Public Personnel Review*, XXVIII, No. 4 (October, 1967), 231–236.

Hall, Chester G., Jr., "The U.S. Civil Service Commission: Arm of the President?" *Public Personnel Review*, *XXVIII*, No. 2 (April, 1967).

Hoogenboom, Ari, *Outlawing the Spoils: A History of the Civil Service Reform Movement, 1865–1883*, Champaign-Urbana, Ill.: University of Illinois Press, 1961.

Jones, Roger W., "Developments in Government Manpower: A Federal Perspective," *Public Administration Review*, *XXVII*, No. 2 (June, 1967).

Jones, Roger W., "The Merit System, Politics, and Political Maturity: A Federal View," *Public Personnel Review*, *XXV*, No. 1 (January, 1964).

Mosher, Frederick C., *Democracy and the Public Service*, New York: Oxford University Press, 1968.

Muskie, Edmund S., "The State and Local Manpower Crisis," *Personnel Administration*, *XXIX*, No. 6 (November-December, 1966).

Nigro, Felix A., "Can Personnel Practice Change?" *Personnel Administration*, *XXIX*, No. 1 (January-February, 1966).

Senate Subcommittee on Intergovernmental Relations, Intergovernmental Personnel Act of 1967, Intergovernmental Man-Power Act of 1967, 90th Congress, 1st Session, Hearings on S. 699 and S. 1485, Washington, D.C.: Government Printing Office, 1967.

Sorauf, Frank J., "Patronage and Party," *Midwest Journal of Political Science*, *III*, No. 2 (May, 1959).

Sorauf, Frank J., "The Silent Revolution in Patronage," *Public Administration Review*, *XX*, No. 1 (Winter, 1960).

Stanley, David T., "New Patterns in Public Personnel Administration," *Public Personnel Review*, *XXV*, No. 2 (April, 1964).

Van Riper, Paul P., *History of the United States Civil Service*, New York: Harper & Row, 1958.

Van Riper, Paul P., "The Tap Roots of American Public Personnel Management," *Personnel Administration*, *XXV*, No. 2 (March-April, 1962).

Waldby, H. O., *The Patronage System in Oklahoma*, Norman, Okla.: Transcript Company, 1950.

CHAPTER 13
RECRUITMENT
AND SELECTION

T HE *New York Times* recently published a very significant article about the "Depression Virtuosos," many of whom were about to retire and whose departure would leave a "talent gap that city officials believe cannot be filled." Originally numbering some 25,000, only about 2500 remained. "These top civil servants are the people who really run New York City," said Budget Director Frederick R. Hayes. "Many of them are fantastic guys who came to the city because of the absence of other opportunities during the Depression. They're vastly better than the people who came before and since."[1] In this respect New York City is by no means unique: Elsewhere, many highly qualified persons, easily recruited during the Depression, are now retiring, with "no second echelon to take their places."[2] The Depression not only made it easy to recruit talent, it also caused a decline in the birth rate. As a result, there will be very little increase during the 1970s in the age group 25–44, which has been the chief source of administrative, professional, and technical personnel.[3]

[1] *New York Times*, September 17, 1967.

[2] *Ibid.*

[3] Paul P. Van Riper, "Governmental Personnel Mobility, Basic Factors and Issues," *Public Administration Review*, XXVII, No. 4 (November, 1967) 365.

It is true that during the Depression examining techniques were not as good as they are today and that frequently the lesser qualified candidates—rather than the better—were appointed. Nonetheless, there were numerous candidates and consequently no serious problem of competition with industry. Furthermore, at that time fringe benefits (meaning benefits in addition to salary, such as pension rights and paid vacations) were generally superior in the public service to those offered by most private companies. This was before passage of the Social Security Act of 1935 and before the great growth in the strength of the unions. Public service as a career by no means enjoyed great prestige, but with employment prospects in private business so slim, government jobs definitely had their attractions. There was never any justification for simply waiting for applicants to present themselves, but because of the loose labor market it is understandable why so many civil service agencies decided that this was all that was necessary. They were under no pressure to improve their recruiting techniques. The jobs might not be filled with top-quality people, but still they would be filled.

That these "bargain days" are over is clearly seen when we look at the present labor market. Despite the persistence of some unemployment and the constant threat of layoffs, as in the defense industry, job security for most Americans is far from the problem that it was during the Depression. A whole generation of young Americans never even experienced the Depression. Jobs have been plentiful in industry, and they now pay much better. Furthermore, private companies have greatly improved fringe benefits, to the point that there is now general agreement that these benefits are at least as good as in government. Naturally, this varies with the company, but most business concerns offer far better pension, leave, and other rights than used to be the case. A 1968 Bureau of Labor Statistics survey showed that fringe benefits now account for 24.5 percent of total employee compensation in industry, compared to 23.8 percent in the federal government.[4] Most state and local jurisidictions do not provide as good benefits as the federal government.

To cap it all, defense contractors now offer challenging jobs in many professional fields. Government has rarely been able to capitalize on the vital and interesting nature of its work as a recruitment incentive, and now it must compete for talent with the defense industry it supports with multimillion dollar contracts. Since civil servants "are working side-by-side with contractor employees, their salaries, fringe benefits, and other job attractions must be 'in the same ballpark.' "[5] When to all this is

[4] Harold Harris, "Industry Still Leads In Fringe Benefits," *Federal Times*, December 18, 1968.

[5] David T. Stanley, "New Patterns in Public Personnel Administration," *Public Personnel Review*, XXV, No. 2 (April, 1964), 91.

added the inflexibility of government salaries in periods of rapidly rising living costs, it can be appreciated how handicapped public agencies have been in competing with private employers in the postwar period.

LOW PUBLIC SERVICE PRESTIGE

The salary situation will be discussed shortly, but first let us examine the question of low public service prestige. This problem is fundamental, because the public will not support higher salaries and other measures to make government service more effective if it continues to hold public employees in low esteem.

Studies of public service prestige have not been numerous, but a sufficient number have been made, some recently, to enable certain conclusions to be formed. Leonard D. White pioneered with this kind of study in the 1920s, and in later years others made similar investigations to see whether the picture had changed.[6] Basically, they found the same condition described by White: a distinctly more favorable opinion of private than of public employment on the part of the general public. Furthermore, like White, they report an inverse correlation between level of income and education, and favorable attitudes toward public employment.

According to the 1964 landmark study *The Image of the Federal Service*, jobs in the federal government are ranked higher by persons with less than high school education and by those making less than $4000 a year, than by those with more education and higher incomes.[7] Negroes rate federal service higher than whites rate it. The authors' conclusion is that the federal government is in a reasonably good position to recruit janitors, maintenance workers, and postal employees, but not in a good position in the case of scientists, engineers, and executives.[8]

In a 1966 survey of 1424 University of Maryland beginning government students, private employment was found to be more appealing to them than jobs at *any* level of government.[9] However, there was "only a small difference . . . between the appeal of federal and private work." Local government was ranked lowest, with the "state governments . . . slightly more and the national government appreciably more appealing."[10] As to the students' reasons for their preferences, the "strongest determination of the appeal of work for a private firm was . . . [their] perceptions of the chances of 'being really successful.' " Among those with positive views toward federal work, impressions about getting ahead and being really successful were not as influential

[6] Leonard D. White, *The Prestige Value of Public Employment in Chicago*, Chicago: University of Chicago Press, 1929.

[7] Franklin K. Kilpatrick, Milton C. Cummings, Jr., and M. Kent Jennings, *The Image of the Federal Service*, Washington, D.C.: Brookings Institution, 1964.

[8] *Ibid.*

[9] H. George Frederickson, "Understanding Attitudes Toward Public Employment," *Public Administration Review*, XXVII, No. 5 (December, 1967), 411–420.

[10] *Ibid.*, 414.

as the impression that federal jobs were not routine and monotonous. In terms of expectations of success, local government appeared the "most hampered," business the "most advantaged," with the state and federal governments "falling in between."[11] On the one hand, it "doubtless is a great aid in federal civil service recruiting" that "those who are interested in the national civil service are interested because they feel it will not be dull"[12]; on the other hand, it is unfortunate that the "reservoir of individuals who indicate a favorable perception of the appeal of government work is made less rich by the absence of students who are strongly motivated toward success and who see little possibility of achieving it in government work."[13]

Frank K. Gibson and George A. James, in their survey of 89 high school students in Athens, Georgia, and 258 University of Georgia students, found that attitudes toward all three levels of government become increasingly unfavorable as age increases.[14] Those in the 16–18 age category, consisting entirely of high school students, had the most favorable views, graduate students the least favorable. Those whose parents are professionals, proprietors, or skilled workmen "gave a higher percentage of unfavorable responses" than those whose fathers are clerks, operators, and laborers. Negro students (all of them from the mostly Negro high school in Athens) had "the smallest percentage of unfavorable responses toward federal and local government services and the highest percentage of unfavorable responses toward the state service of all other groups in the sample." This is explained by the role of the federal government in protecting civil rights, welfare services of local governments, and the conservative attitude of the Georgia state government.

Reasons for low prestige

Why is it that Americans do not hold more favorable opinions of public employment? Chapter 2 indicated that we live in a business civilization and that young people are reared in an environment in which the accomplishments of the businessman are much admired. In Chapter 3 we saw how the reverse situation exists in some other countries of the world where government service is a high-prestige occupation. Clearly our history and traditions are such that it would be surprising if most young people preferred public to private employment. No one suggests that young Americans as a group should shun private employment and believe that the only good job is one in government. What is a legitimate source of worry, however, is that so many people in the

---

[11] *Ibid.*, 418.

[12] *Ibid.*, 419.

[13] *Ibid.*, 418.

[14] Frank K. Gibson and George A. James, "Student Attitudes Toward Government Employees and Employment," *Public Administration Review*, XXVII, No. 5 (December, 1967), 429–435.

community, young and old, have such mistaken ideas about the nature of government employment. Far too many people are discouraged from seeking government employment because of the persistence of these erroneous notions.

One widely held belief is that government agencies are very inefficient and that public employees put out very little work. "Parasites" and "tax-eaters" are favorite epithets that some sections of the press hurl at the government worker. Young persons grow up in homes and communities where the truth of these statements is taken for granted. Undoubtedly, many people make the public employee the scapegoat. They resent the extension of government services into so many new areas. This means more government control and higher taxes. They basically know that these new services are necessary in present-day society, but someone has to be blamed, and the easiest scapegoat is the government worker; somehow or other, he must be responsible. Of course, if he administers an unpopular program like tax collections, he easily becomes a special object of scorn.

Nor is this kind of reaction unique to this country. In England, public employees are also frequently severely criticized. As one group of prominent Englishmen stated in a report made some years ago to the Chancellor of the Exchequer: "The urge to 'shoot the man at the piano' often arises not so much from the demerits of his performance as from dislike of the tune."[15] The "tune" in many countries today is too much government. In the United States, with its strong tradition of suspicion of the executive power, this tune is all the more irritating.

In defense of government service

Quite a few businessmen have tried to correct some of the erroneous opinions about government employees. These company executives have served in the government themselves. In some cases they entered the government fully expecting to find evidence of widespread inefficiency and to be surrounded by more than a sprinkling of incompetents. Instead they were pleasantly surprised to find that the career public servants were both industrious and efficient. Witness this statement by Marion B. Folsom, a director of the Eastman Kodak Company, who served from 1955 to 1958 as Secretary of Health, Education, and Welfare:

> I found in my experience here that there are very able people in the government, civil service executives who do a fine and understanding job and who put in long hours of work. And I can testify from first-hand experience in both government and a

[15] Report of the Committee on the Training of Civil Servants, reproduced in Felix A. Nigro (ed.), *Public Administration: Readings and Documents*, New York: Holt, Rinehart and Winston, 1951, p. 255.

large business organization that the top ranks of civil service constitute a high level of skill, competence, and loyalty capable of holding their own with those in equivalent ranks in the business world. I do not think that the country as a whole appreciates the work our civil service people are doing.[16]

Men like Folsom have been more than willing to cooperate with government spokesmen in the intensified efforts now being made to dispel these myths about public employees and to create more favorable attitudes toward government service. Increasingly, business organizations are giving strong support to efforts to improve the pay and other conditions of work of public employees. A leading example is the Committee for Economic Development (consisting of 200 leading businessmen and educators), which published a report calling for "Improving Executive Management in the Federal Government."[17]

THE SALARY PROBLEM

[16] Marion B. Folsom, "The Most Effective Way to Improve Government Administration," *Good Government*, *LXXIX*, No. 6 (June, 1962), 27. See also W. Lloyd Warner et al., "A New Look at the Career Civil Service Executive," *Public Administration Review*, *XXII*, No. 4 (December, 1962), 188–194.

[17] *Improving Executive Management in the Federal Government*, A Statement on National Policy by the Research and Policy Committee of the Committee for Economic Development, New York, July, 1964.

The problem of inadequate salaries has been particularly serious in the postwar period. A chief difficulty has been the rigidity of government pay rates. Private companies are able to raise salaries and wages just as fast as the management takes to make up its mind. It is true that in the past few years the government has urged the unions not to seek inflationary wage agreements and the companies not to increase prices too much. The fact still remains, however, that in peacetime there are no laws to prevent private firms from adjusting compensation rates upwards as fast as they see fit.

The situation is different in government because, for the great majority of public employees, changes in pay scales are not possible until the legislative body of the jurisdiction decides to act. This means delay, sometimes of a prolonged character. In the postwar period, legislatures have raised the salaries of government workers, but not nearly as fast as increases by private companies. It takes time for the legislature to meet and deliberate. Furthermore, because this is the political environment, points of view generally not found in the realm of private management are manifested. Many rural legislators cling to the suspicion that government employees are already paid too much. They are unconcerned that industry pays more, because to them the executive branch is at best a necessary evil. There is also the understandable reluctance to authorize top salaries that exceed those paid the legislators themselves. The discrepancy between salaries of top executives in government at all levels and those received in industry for comparable work has been enormous. The legislators usually are much more generous with the employees in the lower ranks. They sympathize more with these "little people," particularly since there are so many more of them and they can exert great pressure on the legislature. Voters themselves can be just as unsympathetic: Recently the mayor of Denver, Colorado, resigned to accept a much better paying position with an airline. His salary in Denver was $14,000. Three times, within a three-year period, Denver voters refused to approve higher salaries for the mayor and other city officials.[18]

Blue-collar workers versus white-collar workers

Until passage of the Federal Salary Reform Act of 1962, briefly mentioned in the preceding chapter, federal compensation policy was more inflexible than that of some state and local governments.[19] In recent years, salary increases received by public employees at all levels of government have not only been less frequent but also less substantial than those received by workers in industry. However, quite a few state and local jurisdictions have made annual or biennial adjustments in rates in accordance with the principle of trying to pay salaries equal to those paid for comparable positions by private employers.

Until Congress acted in 1962, the national government was not pledged to paying industry-prevailing rates. There was one important exception to this: blue-collar workers, numbering some 800,000 out of the total of close to three million federal employees. These blue-collar workers are employed in trades and crafts jobs, almost 80 percent of them being in the Defense Department. For many years their wages have been set by local boards that continuously study industrial rates in the particular areas and recommend changes in federal pay to keep it on a par with what private firms are currently paying. Changes in pay rates, authorized by the heads of the agencies concerned after reviewing the proposals of the local boards, do not require prior approval of Congress. As a result, federal pay for blue-collar workers has been competitive with industrial rates for such jobs. Although sound in principle, the wage board system did have serious weaknesses, which are now being corrected. Uniform job standards and pay scales for the same occupations in the same locality did not exist, because each agency with wage board employees operated its system independently. Under the new Coordinated Federal Wage

[18] See *New York Times*, editorial, December 13, 1968.

[19] Federal Salary Reform Act of 1962, Public Law 87-793, 87th Congress.

System, now being implemented, trades and labor employees performing similar work in the same local wage area receive the same rates of pay in all federal agencies.[20]

In the case of white-collar workers, Congress alone could raise rates of pay, and it chose to do this generally every few years. There was no fixed policy, as in many local jurisdictions, of reviewing the adequacy of the rates each year at budget time. A few state governments, such as Michigan, Illinois, and California, had even acted to delegate to the executive branch the authority to fix the salary scales and to make changes in them, without any need for prior approval by the legislature. Significantly, in the last few years other state legislatures, as in Wisconsin, have delegated the authority to the executive branch to fix salary schedules and individual rates for executive and certain other classes of employees.[21] In such cases, the only participation in setting salaries by the lawmakers is to provide the appropriations required to finance any increases. No one suggests that the legislature should abandon its control of the purse, but delegating to the executive branch the authority to set the salary scales and to make changes in them in accordance with the movement of industry rates provides very desirable flexibility. The first Hoover Commission strongly recommended that Congress adopt a similar policy. It proposed that Congress "limit its participation to establishing the minimum and maximum rates of payment within which all general adjustments in federal compensation"[22] would be made. Congress would set the salary floor and ceiling, and subject to approval by the President, the Civil Service Commission would fix the individual pay scales within this framework, making annual adjustments as necessary.

Establishing pay comparability

Experience since passage of the federal Classification Act of 1923 had clearly shown that equal pay for equal work could not be guaranteed unless the prevailing-rate principle was also enacted into law. It was small solace for federal employees to receive equally *inadequate* salaries for the same work. Unfortunately, this is what equal pay for equal work meant in practice. Positions of approximately the same difficulty and responsibility were placed in the same pay grades. The incumbents did receive the same pay, but often got a lot less than persons holding similar jobs in industry. In the 1962 legislation, Congress for the first time accepted the principle of paying prevailing private rates for all kinds of federal jobs. The law stated this in no uncertain terms:

[20] See John W. Macy, Jr., "Personnel Panorama—1966: 11. Personnel Developments on the U.S. Federal Level," *Public Personnel Review*, XXVIII, No. 1 (January, 1967), 9–10.

[21] *Information Bulletin*, Citizens Conference on State Legislatures, 4722 Broadway Building, Kansas City, Missouri, 64112, September 11, 1968.

[22] Commission on Organization of the Executive Branch of the Government, *Personnel Management*, Washington, D.C.: Government Printing Office, 1949, pp. 27–28.

"Federal salary rates shall be comparable with private enterprise salary rates for the same levels of work."[23] The President was directed to report annually to Congress on the relationship between private and federal pay and to recommend the changes in the federal scales needed to keep them on a par with those in industry.

The recommended adjustments in federal rates are based on the annual survey now made by the Bureau of Labor Statistics of professional, administrative, and technical salaries in industry, with the national average of the private rates followed rather than the pay in each locality. Uniform pay scales for federal white-collar workers on a nationwide basis are still the rule, but the objective was for the scales to be periodically adjusted to keep up with the national average of rates paid by private employers for comparable positions. Federal pay had lagged so far behind that Congress could not immediately vote funds sufficient for achieving "comparability" for all salary grades; however, in the Postal Revenue and Federal Salary Act of 1967, it directed the President to adjust the rates in two stages so that after July 1, 1969, they would be equal, "as nearly as practicable," with private rates.[24]

Based on the Bureau of Labor Statistics survey covering the period between June, 1967, and June, 1968, it was estimated that top federal career pay (refers to those under the Classification Act) after July 1, 1969, would be $34,950; this assumed that Congress would change a provision of the 1967 legislation, which put a ceiling of $28,000 on career pay.[25] There are 18 salary grades under the Classification Act; three of these, Grades 16 through 18, known as the "super-grades," were added after World War II. Separate legislation (the Federal Executive Salary Act of 1964) governs the pay of top executives not under the Classification Act, such as Cabinet members, other agency heads, undersecretaries, assistant secretaries, chairmen and members of boards and commissions, and bureau heads.[26] These are political policymaking positions, filled by the President or the department heads at their discretion. The highest Classification Act pay, which means for Grade 18, cannot exceed that for the lowest level, Level 5, of the Federal Executive Salary Schedule.

One of the stickiest problems is how to arrange matters so that legislative pay can be increased without the lawmakers incurring the displeasure of their constituents. If legislative pay cannot be raised, career pay is depressed under a ceiling far too low to make possible comparability with private sector rates.

The 1967 legislation copes with this problem by establishing a

[23] Federal Salary Reform Act of 1962, *op. cit.*
[24] Public Law 90–206, 90th Congress, H.R. 7977, December 16, 1967, Section 212.
[25] *Ibid.*, Section 215 (c).
[26] This is Title III of the Government Employees Salary Reform Act of 1964, Public Law 88–426, 88th Congress, H.R. 11049, August 14, 1964.

Commission on Executive, Legislative, and Judicial Salaries.[27] Its responsibility, beginning with the 1969 fiscal year and thereafter every fourth fiscal year, is to review the compensation of Congressmen, federal judges, and those under the Federal Executive Salary Schedule, and make recommendations to the President. The President, after reviewing these recommendations, makes his own in his budget, submitted to Congress in January. His recommendations, as a whole or in part, become effective within 30 days after submission of the budget, provided neither House of Congress enacts legislation disapproving all or part of his proposals, and that Congress has not passed a law authorizing salary rates differing from his recommendations. In late 1968 the Commission (three of whose members are appointed by the President, and two each by the President of the Senate, the Speaker of the House of Representatives, and the Chief Justice of the Supreme Court), in its first report to the President, recommended some very substantial pay increases. The President recommended slightly lower scales that went into effect when they were not disapproved by Congress.

Some states are also creating special commissions with substantial powers for determining legislative, judicial, and executive pay. An amendment passed in 1968 by the Michigan legislature and approved by the voters created a Commission on Executive, Judicial, and Legislative Compensation. The Commission's recommendations go into effect unless overruled by a two-thirds vote of the legislature.[28] In Michigan, as in many other states, "pay increases approved by the legislators for themselves had raised a public outcry."[29] A Legislative Compensation Board with power to set legislative pay without action by the legislature was also established in 1968 in Oklahoma.[30]

For the nation as a whole, David T. Stanley's statement, made several years ago, still holds: "The idea that public employees should be paid and 'fringed' as well as employees of commerce and industry is becoming less of a vision and more of a reality."[31] The pressures of public employee unions (see Chapter 15) are now providing much of the impetus.

DIFFICULTIES IN ATTRACTING POLITICAL POLICYMAKING OFFICIALS

As President-elect Nixon began filling the political policymaking positions (referred to above) in his Administration, the importance of this aspect of public recruitment was brought out once

[27] Public Law 90-206, 90th Congress, *op. cit.*, Section 225.

[28] *Information Bulletin*, Citizens Conference on State Legislatures, *op. cit.*

[29] *New York Times*, December 1, 1968.

[30] *Information Bulletin*, Citizens Conference on State Legislatures, *op. cit.*

[31] Stanley, *op. cit.*, 92.

again. In the Committee for Economic Development report, cited earlier in this chapter, it is stated:

> Political selection, whether accomplished by the President, his personal staff, or key appointees, is difficult for several reasons. Prompt action on major posts is essential. Lesser positions can be filled at a more leisurely pace, but these have less prestige and are less attractive to acceptable candidates. . . .
>
> Public attention given to the President's early struggles with political selection tends to mask an essential characteristic of the process—the need to continue to recruit capable political executives throughout the life of the administration, as the terms of Board and Commission members expire. . . .[32]

Many political policymaking positions of this same type are found in state governments and in the larger municipalities and counties. These jurisdictions have the same trouble in not being able to offer sufficiently high salaries, so this is by no means a unique problem of the federal government. A principal recruitment source in filling these positions at all levels of government has been private industry, for in its ranks are men with tested ability to direct large-scale operations. Businessmen as a social group are not preferred as such; it is rather a question of the experience that they have. Universities and colleges, private foundations, labor unions, farm organizations, and quasi-public agencies have also been tapped. While many able persons have been recruited from these sources, it usually has taken a good deal of persuading to secure and retain their services.

As we have just seen, the inadequate salaries have been a major deterrent, but there are other reasons. It would be unrealistic to assume that all that needs to be done to attract high-grade executives is to offer better pay. Some companies frown on their men "getting into politics," which is what some senior company executives think is entailed if they let a junior official accept a policymaking position in government. "Keep out of the government mess" is what they often advise the younger man. The Task Force of the second Hoover Commission made an impassioned plea for the leaders of the business world to encourage their best young men to accept government assignments.[33]

The conflict of interest problem

A hindrance of significant proportions in attracting private-sector personnel has been the conflict-of-interest statutes. (See Part VI of this book, "Administrative Responsibility.") Congress acted

[32] *Improving Executive Management in the Federal Government, op. cit.,* p. 23. See also Commission on Organization of the Executive Branch of the Government, *Task Force Report on Personnel and Civil Service,* Washington, D. C.: Government Printing Office, 1955, p. 39, and W. Lloyd Warner *et al.,* "Federal Political Executives— A New View," *Good Government, LXXX,* No. 1 (January, 1963).

[33] *Task Force Report on Personnel and Civil Service, op. cit.,* p. 46.

in October, 1962, to bring these anachronistic statutes up-to-date. The new legislation retains essential protections for the government against possible abuses of their public trust by industry officials on government assignments.[34] It also eliminates certain "absurdities," as they were called by the Senate Subcommittee on National Policy Machinery.

One example will demonstrate this. Before the statutes were revised, part-time consultants employed by the government were subject to the same restrictions as those placed on regular employees. This meant, for one thing, that they could not assist private parties for pay in transactions involving the government. Consequently, many people refused to accept such consulting assignments. As the Subcommittee said: "A consultant working for the Government a week or two a year can scarcely sever his economic ties with his regular business or profession."[35] The new law makes a distinction between regular and "special" employees who serve not more than 130 days in a year's time. As a special employee, the part-time consultant is not subject to the prohibitions on outside compensation. A lawyer who is a part-time consultant can represent private parties in such routine matters as income tax appeals. Under the statutes as they stood previously, he could not do so.[36]

Other deterrents

Even if they were offered better salaries and if conflict-of-interest complications were removed, many businessmen would still hesitate to accept government assignments. The executive in mid-career is risking a good deal when he leaves his company even for a few years. Vacancies that develop in higher ranks while he is on government leave must be filled notwithstanding. The company can protect his pension rights and similar privileges, but it cannot agree to hold up all promotions until he returns.[37] Certainly an executive on the rise cannot be blamed if he is unwilling to leave his firm at this critical stage in his career. Yet, as the Senate Subcommittee stressed: "The person in mid-career is in many ways the private citizen whose services the Government needs the most. He is at the very height of his vigor and powers. He is bold and innovative." The Subcommittee concluded that "any improvement of this situation depends primarily upon employers—not the Government." They should contribute to the best interests of the nation by "releasing some of their best personnel for national service, and welcoming them back."[38] The best way of welcoming them back, of course, would be to reward

[34] Public Law 87-849, 1963, 87th Congress.

[35] Senate Subcommittee on National Policy Machinery, 87th Congress, 1st Session, Organizing for National Security, The Private Citizen and the National Service, Washington, D.C.: Government Printing Office, 1961, p. 3.

[36] On need for further changes in conflict-of-interest policy, see Improving Executive Management in the Federal Government, op. cit., p. 26.

[37] See Organizing for National Security, Mobilizing Talent for Government Service, Hearings before Senate Subcommittee on National Policy Machinery, 86th Congress, 2nd Session. Washington, D.C.: Government Printing Office, May, 1960, p. 480.

[38] Organizing for National Security, The Private Citizen and the National Service, op. cit., pp. 6–7.

them with more responsible posts, in recognition of their enhanced value to the company.

Dan H. Fenn, Jr., who served as staff assistant to President Kennedy in the filling of top-level administrative posts, stresses the "re-entry syndrome," the "anxiety that they [the possible candidates] could not perform as successfully in government as they had in the private sector. . . ."[39] He reports:

> In addition, even extraordinarily able men become anxious when faced with the prospect of moving into a world with which they are unfamiliar. They wonder whether they will succeed; they are concerned about how they will get back into the private sector on at least the same level they have left. There are no formal "outplacement" services offered by any governmental unit of which I am aware, and, though they recognize the statistics are in their favor, they wonder whether they really will return to business or education at a higher echelon than they would have reached had they stayed at their desks.[40]

As part of a broad program for increasing mobility of personnel, and with the specific purpose of fostering better understanding between government and business, President Johnson established a 30-member panel to develop a program for the interchange of young executives in government and business. Before left office, Johnson, acting upon this panel's advice, established by executive order a permanent commission on personnel interchange, to be staffed by the Civil Service Commission. A study of the post-service attitudes of businessmen recruited by Presidents Truman and Eisenhower has shown that many of them left with increased respect for federal career personnel.[41]

If too gloomy a picture of the possibilities of attracting high-grade industry executives seems to have been presented, it should be remembered that quite a few of them have made a personal decision to take government jobs anyway. Despite the lower pay, the irksome restrictions, and the uncertainty as to what awaits them when they return to private industry, they have been attracted by the challenges and great responsibilities of government work. As Fenn states: "The best recruiting tool in the hands of any President is the quality of the posts he has to offer. At these upper reaches of the federal service, no office is routine, unimportant, or without great opportunities to have an impact on program and policy." Unfortunately, top jobs in state and local government often are much less appealing because of the "fragmentation of jurisdictions, uncertainty of the political leadership, confusion or even lack of programs, and drabness of the surroundings in terms of colleagues and support services. . . ."[42]

[39] Dan H. Fenn, Jr., "Governmental Personnel Mobility: A View of the Practical Problems," *Public Administration Review, XXVII*, No. 4 (November, 1967), 376.

[40] *Ibid.*

[41] Alan H. Schechter, "The Influence of Public Service on Businessmen's Attitudes Toward the Federal Government," *Public Administration Review, XXVII*, No. 5 (December, 1967), 458.

[42] Fenn, *op. cit.*

IMPROVEMENTS IN RECRUITMENT

In the previous chapter, brief mention was made of the improvements being made in government recruitment procedures. Let us now give additional examples, because some public agencies now conduct much more aggressive recruiting campaigns as the competition for the available manpower becomes increasingly keen.

Artificial barriers to recruitment are being removed, new employment sources are being opened up, information about openings is being supplied to job applicants much more conveniently, bolder methods of attracting candidates are being used, and recruits are being placed on the payrolls much more rapidly. Examples of "unnecessary hurdles" are filing fees for civil service examinations, once required in more than a few places but now rare, and residence requirements, now increasingly abandoned.

As to new sources of labor supply, systematic efforts are being made to recruit members of minority groups, such as Negroes and Mexican-Americans. In April, 1968, just two years after President Johnson's issuance of Executive Order 11246 launching a "new affirmative-action" Equal Employment Opportunity program, the Civil Service Commission reported that employment of Negroes had reached a new high of 496,672 (of 2.6 million full-time positions surveyed), representing 14.9 percent of the work force, as compared with 13.9 percent in 1966. Similar gains were reported for other minority groups.[43] The Commission works closely with national and local organizations of Negroes, Mexican-Americans, and other ethnic groups, and has developed special arrangements to make these cooperative relationships effective. As one example, it recently hired a number of Spanish-speaking Community Liaison Specialists to serve in locations in the Southwest where there are many Mexican-Americans living in the vicinity of the federal installations in that area. Working out of the Commission's regional offices, their assignment is to provide job information to local organizations and the schools, counsel applicants, and generally strengthen service to the Spanish-speaking community on federal employment matters.[44]

In Savannah, Georgia, the city receives applications continuously so that members of all ethnic groups can apply at any time. The city also advertises all vacancies, including in the Negro weekly newspaper and on the local radio station to which many in the Negro community listen; sends copies of all job announce-

[43] *Civil Service News*, U.S. Civil Service Commission, Washington, D.C., 20415: April 24, 1968.

[44] See address by John W. Macy, Jr., at 20th National Convention of the American G.I. Forum of the United States, Corpus Christi, Texas, August 9, 1968. Complete text reported in *Civil Service News* of the same date.

ments to the predominantly Negro Savannah State College; and notifies all city employees of openings "so they can tell friends and neighbors in the Negro community of opportunities with the City."[45] Quite a few local government recruiters now go directly into the ghettoes, sometimes with "job-mobiles," to explain what jobs are available and who can qualify for them.

The federal government, and some state and local jurisdictions, also have affirmative programs for the employment of more women. Based on Executive Order 11375, signed by President Johnson in October, 1967, equal opportunity now includes women, and a comprehensive program is in effect to recruit more women.[46] Finding that the specifications for some 300 job classes arbitrarily restricted employment to men, and finding that under a rule entitled "Certification by Sex," appointing officers could make a special request for male candidates only for positions in the 1900 other classes, the Michigan Department of Civil Service reduced the classes having a male-or-female-only restriction to 135. The men-only limitation now applies only to positions such as guards, forest fire officers, and those requiring moving and lifting of heavy objects.[47] It is urged that the example of the Canadian Civil Service in making part-time jobs available to married women be followed also in the United States.

Regarding convenience to applicants, each of the Interagency Boards of Civil Service Examiners referred to in the previous chapter (see page 259) serves as a one-stop Job Information Center. Each Center provides "information on all examinations open to persons in the area, regardless of whether the jobs offered are local or in other parts of the country."[48] In some places, examinations are given at night. For some time now, a number of civil service agencies have been administering them in the schools, for example, when recruiting typists and stenographers from secretarial schools, high schools, and junior colleges.

Appointment procedures are being speeded up, and it is being demonstrated that merit system requirements can be met even though some steps in the traditional procedures are being omitted or shortened. "Rapid recruitment," as it is sometimes called, has numerous forms. Candidates can visit the civil service agency, fill out applications, take tests, and receive offers, all in the course of one visit to the agency's premises. This fast process is most often used for stenographers, engineers, accountants, planners, and other jobs of a "hard-to-fill" nature.[49] In some jurisdictions, application forms have been shortened and made much easier to complete. Written examinations are graded much more quickly than used to be the case, and the interval between date of receipt

[45] E. Frank Walls, Jr., "Public Employment in Savannah, Georgia," *Public Personnel Review*, XXIX, No. 2 (April, 1968), 98.

[46] See John W. Macy, Jr., "Personnel Developments on the U.S. Federal Level," *Public Personnel Review*, XXIX, No. 2 (April, 1968), 89–90.

[47] Dudley Anderson and Charles S. Pearson, "Changing Sex Requirements in Michigan Class Specifications," *Public Personnel Review*, XXVIII, No. 3 (July, 1967), 153–155.

[48] Macy, "Personnel Panorama—1966: 11. Personnel Developments on the U.S. Federal Level," *op. cit.*, 8.

[49] See Arvin N. Donner, Jr., "Instant Certification: The Answer to Hiring Clerical Applicants," *Public Personnel Review*, XXVIII, No. 2 (April, 1967), 102–104, and Thomas Lewisohn, "New Approaches to Recruitment and Examination," *Public Personnel Review*, XXIX, No. 1 (January, 1968), 13–16.

of the candidates' applications and the preparation of the civil service registers has been greatly reduced. Use of automated equipment for scheduling and grading examinations, and other personnel processes, has contributed greatly to the time savings. Illustrative of the faster time schedules is that the goal in Kansas City "has been to have qualified applicants processed and on the job within three weeks from the time they see" the job advertisement.[50] In Kansas City, candidates usually are notified of the results within two working days from the examination date; if they pass, they generally are called for an interview the day after receiving the results.[51]

Despite these examples, it would be wrong to give the impression that all or most public personnel agencies have highly developed programs of positive recruitment. As the Municipal Manpower Commission reported, many lag far behind, others are just beginning to make progress.[52] As indicated in Chapter 1, no government agency will ever function exactly like a private company. However, there is no reason to think that civil service recruitment cannot be fast, efficient, and truly competitive with industry.

THE GOAL OF CAREER SERVICE

A paramount objective is to create a true career service, as against simply recruiting to fill individual jobs. In such a career service, the recruits, whether fresh from college or already possessing some work experience, would be guaranteed the opportunity to move up the line as they demonstrate their capacity. Ultimately, the best of them would fill the highest ranking positions. They would have every inducement to continue in the government service, instead of leaving after a few years because of the lack of a planned system of career development for them.

In the past, for many people in the United States, government service has tended to be a mere episode that precedes or follows private employment. Movement in and out of the service has been too great. Late entry is desirable, but not if it means that people are constantly shuttling in and out of the government. This, again, is unfortunately what has happened too often in the past. Promising young persons entered government service and decided that they wanted to make a life work of it; but they had been recruited for individual jobs, not for careers. The responsibility generally devolved on them to locate promotional opportunities and prepare themselves for posts of higher responsi-

[50] Lewisohn, *Ibid.*, 16.

[51] *Ibid.*

[52] Municipal Manpower Commission, *Governmental Manpower for Tomorrow's Cities*, New York: McGraw-Hill, 1962.

bility. Typically, this meant making "contacts" and shopping around for better jobs. Many of them did make careers for themselves, but in spite of the personnel system, not because of it.

Success of the FSEE

Today many government agencies are recruiting people for careers instead of individual jobs. Mention was made in the previous chapter of the Federal Service Entrance Examination (FSEE). It represents one important phase of career-service planning at the federal level. It provides the entrance gate for college students, a broad one because it is open to all college majors with only a few exceptions. Separate entrance examinations are now given only for engineers, physicists, chemists, accountants, and a few other technicians.

The existence of this main entrance gate clearly shows the college student how to get started on a federal career. He need not enroll in a special collegiate program of study to be able to qualify. All he has to do is pursue his major; indeed, seniors and graduates with either a grade point average of 3.5 or "top-10-percent-of-class" standing may establish eligibility without taking the written test. First given in 1955, the FSEE is given such widespread publicity that it is hard to see how any college student can claim that he does not know about it.

The successful candidates are appointed not only to staff jobs, such as in personnel and budget work, but also to positions in program administration, such as in housing management, food and drug inspection, transportation, business analysis and regulation, social security administration, and agriculture and the natural sciences. This is significant, because it means that careers are opened up not only in the staff jobs but also in the administration of the many different substantive fields in which the government now functions. In previous years, those interested in careers in administrative work were mostly restricted to the "housekeeping" kind of job. The FSEE makes it possible for persons with broad collegiate training to qualify for careers in program administration. In the past, most administrative jobs of this kind have been filled by persons trained in technical specialties such as engineering, medicine, and law. Some of them have performed capably in such assignments, but many have proved far too narrow in their approach. The FSEE seeks to develop in the lowest ranks of the federal service a corps of generalist trainees who, it is hoped, will eventually fill many of the program administration posts.

Making good on the "career contract"

The FSEE, like any examination, constitutes only one part of career planning. It is the beginning. The rest consists of training and promotion programs that make it possible for the recruit to climb up the ladder as he proves his ability. Such programs are now being developed through the joint efforts of the Civil Service Commission and the line agencies. Training and promotion are discussed in the next chapter, but they are mentioned here as an essental part of what Henry Reining, Jr., calls the "career contract," which entails assuming responsibility for the recruit's development after he passes the entrance examination.[53] It is not fair from the college student's standpoint if he is given an entrance job but then required to shift for himself. It is clear that some federal agencies are delivering on the career contract, and consequently their recruits are staying with them. Much remains to be accomplished before a true career service comes into being throughout the entire federal executive branch, but definite progress is being made in that direction.

Only a few state and local governments give an examination that is in any way comparable to the FSEE. There are exceptions, but the Municipal Manpower Commission found no general evidence in urban governments of a real career service based on selection, training, and promotion of individuals on a merit basis.[54] Some state and local jurisdictions, however, have excellent career programs.

Comparison with the British

Publication of the Fulton report, referred to in the previous chapter, should reassure Americans about the soundness of career planning in this country. Many Americans have long thought that we should emulate, or closely follow, the British system, despite the protestations of some Englishmen that they were not satisfied with the suitability of that system for modern times. The Fulton report finds the basic premise of the British system no longer acceptable: namely, the "cult of the generalist."[55] The administrative class, a relatively small group for whom the top administrative policymaking positions have been reserved, best illustrates this preference for the generalist or "all-rounder." The belief has been that broadly educated individuals with first-class minds, recruited directly after university graduation, would in

[53] Henry Reining, Jr., "The FSEE: The University Point of View," *Public Administration Review, XVI*, No. 1 (Winter, 1956), 11–14.

[54] Municipal Manpower Commission, *op. cit.*, p. 116.

[55] *The Civil Service Vol. 1 Report of the Committee 1966–68 Chairman: Lord Fulton*, London: Her Majesty's Stationery Office, June, 1968, p. 11.

time make better administrators than persons with more specialized preparation and previous work experience.

The Fulton Committee rejects the concept of the "ideal administrator" who ". . . is still too often seen as the gifted layman who, moving frequently from job to job within the Service, can take a practical view of any problem, irrespective of its subject matter, in the light of his knowledge and experience of the government machine."[56] While recognizing that this frequent job rotation gives the generalist administrators "proficiency in operating the government machine, and in serving Ministers and Parliament," the Committee bluntly states:

> But many lack the fully developed professionalism that their work now demands. They do not develop adequate knowledge in depth in any one aspect of the department's work and frequently not even in the general area of activity in which the department operates. Often they are required to give advice on subjects they do not sufficiently understand or to take decisions whose significance they do not fully grasp.[57]

It also believes the questions on the examinations for the administrative class are not sufficiently "relevant" for the problems of the modern world, and that recruits should be attracted "from a wider range of degree subjects than those from which administrators have traditionally been drawn."[58] Furthermore, the Committee is of the opinion that administrative class occupants are not sufficiently trained in management as such, and that the denial, with few exceptions, of administrative posts to those with specialist backgrounds (that is, scientists, engineers, and lawyers) deprives the government of a valuable source for filling directive posts. With adequate training in management, these specialists would be better administrators than "all-rounders."

In the United States, at all levels of government, subject-matter specialists have usually been promoted to the top administrative jobs, and concern has been felt over the "narrowness" of their preparation. This concern has been justified, because a very narrow subject-matter specialist, without any aptitude for or training in management, is as undesirable as the "all-rounder" who administers a program about which he knows very little. With such in-service training programs as those currently functioning in progressive U.S. jurisdictions, subject-matter specialists are being better prepared to carry out their administrative responsibilities. At the same time, broadly trained college students are being taken in through such exams as the FSEE, and then given

---

56 *Ibid.*
57 *Ibid.*, p.18.
58 *Ibid.*, p. 28.

intensive training in both program content and management science. In all, it would seem that, assuming implementation of the Fulton report, the British and American systems will grow together, with the same comprehension of the need for good administrators who also know in detail what they are administering.

THE SELECTION PROCESS

The selection process will be best understood if it is described in step-by-step sequence. The first step is for the candidate to file his application. Before he does this, he studies the examination announcement to see whether he possesses the minimum qualifications; these are the experience, training, and other requirements that the individual must meet if his application is to be accepted. There is no point in his applying if he does not have these qualifications. The civil service agency cannot be expected to incur the expense of having to examine any and all candidates. On the other hand, too often more has been required than is actually needed for successful performance in the jobs concerned. This has been particularly true with respect to formal schooling, the reasoning being that while the level of education prescribed was not absolutely necessary for doing the job, it was good policy to require it anyway. Sometimes, minimum qualifications included in position specifications prepared during the Depression were continued without much change into the post-World War II period, despite the shrinkage in the labor supply.

Accordingly, as part of their equal opportunity programs, public personnel agencies are eliminating "any requirements that are not specifically related to the duties and responsibilities" of the positions being filled.[59] In Detroit, the following changes in police recruitment were recently made: height requirement lowered by one inch to 5 feet 7 inches; age range extended from 21 to 33; sight requirements lowered slightly; absolute weight requirements dropped; and rules rescinded disqualifying men with divorces or separations pending, or with traffic, misdemeanor, felony, or juvenile records. (Those with police records may be disqualified, but do not have to be.) Such changes, properly administered, do not weaken the merit system, but others sometimes evoke sharp protests. In Portland, Oregon, the Police Chief announced his intention to hire six more Negro recruits, but on a temporary basis, without their having to take the regular civil service examination immediately (although they would be sub-

[59] Macy, address before G.I. Forum of the United States, *op. cit.*

jected to rigid physical and psychological tests and searching background investigations). When they were sufficiently trained, they would be required to take and pass the civil service examination. The Portland Police Association went to court in an effort to block the hiring of the new men, arguing that the "appointment of temporary personnel not subject to Civil Service procedures would hurt the morale and efficiency of the police."[60]

Assuming that his application is accepted, the next step is for the candidate to take the examination. This usually consists of several different tests, with weighted scores to produce the individual's final grade. Usually there is no justification for using only one test, for in most cases no single test has sufficient validity in measuring ability to perform well in the kind of position for which the individual is examined. The reason for this will become clear as the different kinds of tests are discussed in turn.

In most cases the candidate is required to take a written test. This is administered by the personnel agency at a location where the candidates assemble to take the examination. For this reason, this is known as an assembled examination. State and local jurisdictions have always made great use of assembled examinations. The examination load in the federal government is so heavy that it sometimes has not been able to give assembled examinations and has had to give unassembled examinations. In the unassembled type, candidates mail in their applications, together with supplemental sheets on which they describe their work background in detail. It is these applications that are scored and given a numerical grade, just like a written test. Furthermore, written tests of acceptable validity have been lacking in testing for some high-level professional and administrative posts.

Kinds of written tests

What kinds of written tests are given? From the standpoint of content, there are two principal types: achievement and aptitude tests. The first kind measures the candidate's ability to perform the duties of the position immediately upon appointment, without the need for extended training. Traditionally, this has been the preferred kind of test in the United States as far as community opinion is concerned. Civil service laws and regulations commonly require that "practical tests" be given. A "practical test" in effect means one that measures what the candidate already knows about the duties and responsibilities of the job.

[60] *New York Times,* August 18, 1968.

By contrast, aptitude tests measure the applicant's potentialities, not his immediate ability to do the job. In recruiting for career service, aptitude is what really counts: the individual's evidence of ability to master the duties of jobs of increasing difficulty, not his immediate equipment to fill just one job.

In practice, both achievement and aptitude tests are frequently combined in the same written examination. This is a good compromise solution because, while personnel agencies usually would like to make more extensive use of tests of general ability than public opinion permits, some use of the aptitude kind of question is better than none at all.

Most civil service tests are of the multiple-choice variety. Essay tests are given on occasion, but besides requiring much more time to grade, they can, of course, include only a limited number of questions. Multiple-choice tests, consisting as they frequently do of dozens of items, permit a much wider sampling of the candidates' knowledge and aptitudes. True-false questions are sometimes given, but they are generally avoided because of the high guessing factor. Furthermore, experience has shown that it is very difficult to frame questions that are completely true or false.

The evaluation of training and experience

If the position is one that requires experience, another part of the examination will consist of an evaluation of training and experience. The examination announcement states the weight to be assigned to this evaluation in comparison with other parts of the examination. Those possessing the minimum qualifications usually receive the minimum passing score on the evaluation of training and experience. They are given additional points based on the examiners' appraisal of the quantity and quality of their training and experience.

There has been much criticism of this part of the examination, but few persons question that it is needed for positions requiring experience. Basing everything on the written test would mean placing 100 percent faith in its validity. Experience shows that this is too much to expect of any written test. The evaluation of training and experience entails many subjective judgments, but in practice it has served as a desirable supplement to the written test. It is the unassembled examination that has been criticized the most, since the individual's final grade is based entirely on the evaluation of training and experience unless an oral examination is also given.

The oral examination

The oral as a weighted part of the examination is usually required only for positions above the entrance level, although in some cases it is also included in competition for jobs not requiring previous experience. State and local jurisdictions have made much greater use of the oral as a weighted part of the examination than has the federal government. The much heavier examining load at the federal level has made it impossible to include the oral as a routine matter in the competition for all higher level posts. Where time and funds permit, however, it is given, and in recent years it has been used more often than used to be the case.

Usually the purpose of the oral is to evaluate the individual's personality characteristics. Sometimes it is used, however, to evaluate the candidate's training and experience, as well as his personal traits. In the past there was a good deal of suspicion about the oral for fear that bias and hasty judgments by the members of the interviewing panels would lead to breaking down the merit system. With all their shortcomings, it was argued, written tests can be scored objectively. Answers to multiple-choice questions are either right or wrong; the machine that scores these answers can have no favorites. Undoubtedly the oral has many subjective elements, but, for that matter, all tests are subjective. Multiple-choice questions can be graded objectively, but that does not mean that there will be perfect agreement that the answers in the scoring key are really the most correct. Preparation of the scoring key is itself a subjective process, to some extent at least. The essential point is that evaluation of a candidate's personal qualities is necessary, particularly for higher level positions and those requiring frequent contacts with the public. The oral cannot be eliminated as part of the examination process simply because it has subjective elements.

Although criticisms of the oral continue, as they should until this examining device is further improved, there is increasing awareness that the government cannot, as one congressional subcommittee put it, "buy a pig in a poke."[61] Many people fail on the job, not because they lack technical knowledge and skills but because they do not get along well with the persons with whom they must deal, inside and outside the government. Very few employees in modern complex organizations function in relative isolation from other persons. Usually they must work together closely, and it is a rare worker who has nothing to do with the public.

61 Senate Subcommittee on Federal Manpower Policies, 83rd Congress, 1st Session, *Personnel Recruitment and Employment Practices in the Federal Government*, Senate Document No. 37, Washington, D.C.: Government Printing Office, 1953, pp. 37–38.

In recent years public personnel agencies have made significant improvements in the oral. Greater care has been exercised in selecting the interviewers, and they are given intensive training. Interview rating forms have been developed that define more precisely the meaning of the characteristics on which candidates are to be evaluated.

An innovation that has aroused considerable interest is the group oral. Rather than appearing singly before an interview panel, the candidates are assembled in small groups and assigned a topic for discussion. To the side, seated at a distance of some five to ten feet from the candidates, are several representatives of the oral examining staff of the personnel agency. They do not ask the candidates any questions. Instead they observe intently what goes on during the discussion. After the participants have withdrawn, the examiners then either individually rate the candidates, or jointly agree on the final rating to be given each candidate. The principal advantage of the group oral is that it gives the examiners an opportunity to judge how the candidates might conduct themselves in a group situation. The word "might" needs to be emphasized, because, like any interview, the group oral represents an artificial situation. The participants might interact differently in a real work situation. All the same, the examiners do see the candidates perform with others present.

In the traditional panel-type interview, the candidate simply *says* how he would react in a group situation. He is unable to provide the panel with a sample of his behavior, even if synthetic. On the other hand, in a group oral the individual may fail to impress simply because he has had the bad luck of being assigned to a truly outstanding group. Conversely, he may appear to be much better than he really is when the others happen to be mediocre. Both kinds of orals have their advantages, so some personnel agencies have the candidates submit to a panel interview and a group oral. Their feeling is that the individual's composite rating on both kinds of orals will tell more about his personality than his score on just one of them alone.[62]

[62] See Milton M. Mandell, *Employment Interviewing*, Washington, D.C.: U.S. Civil Service Commission, 1956, Personnel Methods Series No. 5, pp. 1–103.

The reference check

Although it is not a weighted part of the examination, a reference check is also a standard part of the selection procedure. Sometimes it consists of a routine mail inquiry sent to previous employers and to personal references listed by the applicant. This may be supplemented by telephone inquiries and, in some cases, by visits by trained investigators who ask detailed questions about the candidates. Sending out investigators to previous employers is highly desirable because they can ferret out significant information about the candidate's personal qualities, as well as the kind of work experience he has had. What former employers say about the way the candidate works with others is often much more reliable than the impressions he gives during an interview. Unfortunately, in the past, funds have been too limited for personnel agencies to make intensive investigations of this kind except for a relatively few top positions.

Control of cultural bias in testing

The efforts of the California State Personnel Board illustrate the attention being given in progressive jurisdictions to reducing the cultural bias in testing. Many people believe that "cultural differences—in education, use of language, and attitudes toward employment—put members of minority groups at a severe disadvantage when they take examinations designed for the dominant group."[63] It is maintained that because of their inferior educational preparation they do not read as well, so they score low on written tests despite good innate ability. Furthermore, there are words and expressions in the tests that are easily understood by members of the dominant culture, but not the minority one. Also, because they do not remain in school as long, minority-group members are not as accustomed to taking tests; "they therefore tend to be more confused by the various answer sheets, the differing and sometimes sketchy instructions, and the multiplicity of item forms."[64]

Because it found that "written tests were more of a bar to employment of minorities than any other phase of the selection process,"[65] the Board now makes more frequent use of nonverbal aptitude tests, that is, those that measure reasoning ability by means of geometric figures. Consultants were called in to help locate in the instructions and the tests any "language or cultural demands beyond the required education or . . . the demands of the job," such as hard-to-follow directions, complex sentences, and difficult vocabulary.[66] Some instructions were found to be too complicated, and were accordingly simplified; inappropriate vocabulary in test items was eliminated and more common words substituted. Some written examinations were replaced with tests of actual performance, as in the printing and building trades, which were believed to have greater validity and, in any case, are more acceptable to minority-group candidates. As to the oral exam, competent minority-group representatives were placed on the interview panels for a large number of examinations; con-

[63] See Vernon R. Taylor, "Cultural Bias in Testing: An Action Program," *Public Personnel Review, XXIX,* No. 3 (July, 1968), 168.

[64] *Ibid.*

[65] *Ibid.,* 170.

[66] *Ibid.,* 172.

sequently, this phase of the competition is now more acceptable to minority groups.

Preparation of examination registers

The successful candidates are ranked in the order of their final scores on the examination as a whole. Most jurisdictions follow the "rule of three" in making appointments. This means that the central personnel agency, when it receives a request for the names of eligibles to fill a vacancy in one of the departments, "certifies" the names of the three persons at the top of the register. The civil service law or rules specify the number of names to be certified. For many years, the United States Civil Service Commission elected to use the rule of three. The Pendleton Act did not require it, but the rule of three was later made a matter of law, and it is now binding on the Commission.

In recent years a few jurisdictions have liberalized the certification procedures. There is widespread feeling among the personnel experts themselves that the appointing officer should have more leeway. Frequently, eligibles are bunched so closely together on the civil service registers that they are separated by only a point or two, perhaps by only a fraction of a point. The tests used do not possess sufficient validity to justify the conviction that such small differences in scores really indicate significant differences in the capacities of the eligibles. On the other hand, fear is expressed that if the appointing officer is given too wide latitude, he may pass over the best qualified persons and then appoint some personal favorite or some other person whose abilities he overrates.

The jurisdictions that have liberalized the certification procedures use different systems. In some, the rule of five or six is followed. The Minnesota Civil Service Department certifies the top three names plus those of any others whose scores are within three points of the top-ranking eligible on the list at the time. Vermont certifies the names of the persons attaining the highest three scores, no matter how many people have the same numerical grade. Some small cities are following the practice of certifying the entire list. Such a procedure would, of course, be difficult to administer in large jurisdictions with very long eligible lists— the appointing officer would have to interview far too many people. Minority groups in some places have urged the rule of one as a means of preventing passing over someone because of his ethnic origin.[67]

[67] See Erwin Baker, "Rules Tightened for City Civil Service Selections," *Los Angeles Times*, July 17, 1968.

The probationary period

The final stage in the selection process is the probationary period. Since tests are not perfect, and since in any case there is no assurance that individuals will work up to their abilities, this trial period is necessary. Unfortunately, in most jurisdictions the probationary period is not taken very seriously. Only a tiny percentage of appointees are dropped, even though in most places all the appointing officer has to do is file a report that the probationer's services are not satisfactory. As nonpermanent employees, the probationers usually do not have the same appeal rights as those who have permanency. Greater efforts should certainly be made to persuade supervisors to make real use of the probationary period. However, as in private industry, the human tendency not to want to dismiss anyone has been noted.

The duration of the probationary period varies according to the jurisdiction. In the federal government it is one year. In some state and local governments it is the same, although others require only six months. In recent years some jurisdictions have authorized the central personnel agency to use a working test period of variable length, depending on the nature of the position, in the interests of flexibility. In Wisconsin the director of the Bureau of Personnel now has the authority to establish a probationary period of up to two years for some positions over a certain salary level.[68] The rationale is that it takes longer to judge the effectiveness of persons in responsible jobs than it does for those with routine duties.

It should be stressed that good selection is the key to good personnel administration. If the recruits are of high quality, promotion, training, and other programs stand a much better chance of being successful than when the new appointees are of poor caliber. With good people coming into the service, prospects are excellent for developing a really efficient public service.

BIBLIOGRAPHY

Caiden, G. E., *Career Service*, London: Melbourne University Press, 1965.

Chapman, Brian, *The Profession of Government*, London: G. Allen, 1959. Chapter 2.

The Civil Service Vol. 1 Report of the Committee 1966–68 Chair-

[68] *Personnel News*, Public Personnel Association, Chicago, Ill., *XXVIII*, No. 2 (February, 1962), 10.

man, Lord Fulton, London: Her Majesty's Stationery Office, June, 1968.

"Comparative Career Systems," *Public Personnel Review, XXVI*, No. 2 (April, 1965). Bibliography prepared by Library of U.S. Civil Service Commission.

Corson, John J., and Paul, Shale R., "Men Near the Top: Filling Key Posts in the Federal Service," Baltimore, Md.: Johns Hopkins Press, 1966.

Cummings, Milton C., Jr., Jennings, M. Kent, and Kilpatrick, Franklin P., "Federal and Nonfederal Employees: A Comparative Social-Occupational Analysis," *Public Administration Review, XXVII*, No. 5 (December, 1967).

Donovan, J. J. (ed.), *Recruitment and Selection in the Public Service*, Chicago: Public Personnel Association, 1968.

"Electronic Data Processing in Public Personnel Management," *Public Personnel Review, XXVII*, No. 2 (April, 1966). Bibliography prepared by Library of U.S. Civil Service Commission.

French, Wendell L., "Psychological Testing: Some Problems and Solutions," *Personnel Administration, XXIX*, No. 2 (March-April, 1966).

Hackett, Bruce, *Higher Civil Servants in California*, Davis, Calif.: Institute of Governmental Affairs, 1967.

Kilpatrick, Franklin P., Cummings, Milton C., Jr., and Jennings, M. Kent, *The Image of the Federal Service*, Washington, D.C.: Brookings Institution, 1964.

Mosher, Frederick C., "Careers and Career Services in the Public Service," *Public Personnel Review, XXIV*, No. 1 (January, 1963).

Municipal Manpower Commission, *Governmental Manpower for Tomorrow's Cities*, New York: McGraw-Hill, 1962.

Otten, Dorothy W., "How to Take a Civil Service Examination," *Public Personnel Review, XVI*, No. 2 (April, 1955).

"Recruitment for the Public Service," *Public Personnel Review, XXII*, No. 1 (January, 1961). Bibliography prepared by Library of U.S. Civil Service Commission.

Stanley, David T., and associates, *Professional Personnel for the City of New York*, Washington, D.C.: Brookings Institution, 1963.

Stanley, David T., *The Higher Civil Service: An Evaluation of Federal Personnel Practices*, Washington, D.C.: Brookings Institution, 1964.

Stanley, David T., Mann, Dean E., and Doig, Jameson W., *Men Who Govern*, Washington, D.C.: Brookings Institution, 1968.

Warner, W. Lloyd, Van Riper, Paul P., Martin, Norman H., and
Collins, Orvis F., *The American Federal Executive*, New
Haven, Conn.: Yale University Press, 1963.

What Research Says to the Supervisor Using Personnel Tests,
Society for Personnel Administration, 14th and F. Streets,
N.W., Washington, D.C.

CHAPTER 14
THE IN-SERVICE
PERSONNEL
PROGRAM

IN MANY WAYS, the real challenge in personnel administration begins after the selection process has been completed and the appointments of new employees have been made. The formidable task then facing the jurisdiction is to provide the incentives that will induce these new appointees to make a career of public service. Specifically, this requires the development of training, promotion, and other programs to meet the needs of the employees at the various stages during their employment. The new recruit represents a valuable resource, an investment that will yield dividends only if careful attention is given to his development. The time and money spent on the search for high-quality recruits will be wasted if the in-service personnel program —that is, actions taken after the initial appointment—is uninspired.

IN-SERVICE TRAINING

In Chapter 12 it was noted that as late as the end of the 1930s, in-service training was a weak activity in most government agencies. The atmosphere simply was not one in which persons desirous of improving their capabilities could count on much help from the government as employer. Legislative bodies, and the public generally, considered that the employee should meet the costs of any after-hours instruction, such as in the evening programs of local educational institutions. If the employee felt that after-hours instruction was not enough and that he should enroll as a full-time day student in a local or other institution, it was expected that he would request a leave of absence *without* pay. Naturally, very few people could afford to do this; moreover, it was far from certain that their request for leave would be approved. Many supervisors were skeptical about the value of further formal instruction either for themselves or their subordinates, and there was no policy that required them to view the matter any differently.

In the federal government, rulings of the General Accounting Office (GAO) severely limited the kinds and amount of inservice training activity that could safely be attempted. The Comptroller-General made it very clear that payments of the salaries and other expenses for employees' training at nonfederal facilities would be disallowed unless Congress had specifically granted legal authority to the agency to make such expenditures. The appropriations acts of the Defense and State Departments, and of a few other agencies, regularly carried such authorization. For all other federal establishments, however, *external training,* as it is called, was prohibited. This meant that if the agency could not itself provide the needed training—using its own buildings, personnel, and other facilities—the employee and the agency were simply out of luck. This was a serious limitation, because in many kinds of work the skilled instructors and the necessary equipment for proper training do not exist in the government.

Even when the agency did organize *internal training* programs—those using its own facilities—it had to proceed with great caution: GAO rulings stated that any training given, such as in classes, discussion sessions, and work shops, had to be directly related to the *present* official duties of the participating employee. Furthermore, the GAO cautioned that only a "reasonable amount" of internal training would be regarded as legal in any case. While only nominal sums might have been spent on supplies, materials, travel, and other items, the salary payments of the participants covering the hours during which they were away from their jobs ran into substantial sums, which the GAO could rule had been illegally expended. With this possibility always existing whenever internal programs of any real scope or duration were proposed, it is no wonder that agency heads reluctantly decided to cancel the programs and take no chances with the GAO.[1]

The current situation

The picture is much improved today. The Government Employees Training Act of 1958, referred to in Chapter 12, represented a substantial mental revolution because it *required* federal agency heads to provide for the training of their employees, using both governmental and nongovernmental facilities. Training gained standing previously lacking as a necessary part of the personnel function, and training activity soon developed a momentum it has since never lost. With the stimulus of the Civil Service Commission, a pattern developed of offering much of this training on an interagency basis, with agencies specializing in certain kinds of programs opening them up to employees of other agencies as well. With training so meagre prior to passage of this legislation, the new programs seemed very sizeable by comparison. Since the law authorized payment of salary, travel, subsistence, tuition, and other expenses of employees approved for external training, growing numbers of them soon were taking after-hours courses in local educational institutions, and some were sent to educational and other organizations for full-time training.

The 1967 report of President Johnson's Task Force on Career Advancement constitutes another landmark, because it made numerous recommendations for further development of the training function.[2] Executive Order 11348 (April 20, 1967), issued by President Johnson upon the recommendation of this Task Force, contains very positive statements of responsibilities of the Civil Service Commission and the agencies for planning and carrying out an improved, more comprehensive training program. The Commission is instructed to counsel with agency officials "on the improvement of training"; identify needs for new or expanded interagency training, either providing the training itself or seeing to it that the agencies offer it; encourage agencies to use appropriate external training facilities; disseminate findings on training methods and conduct research in this area or assign this function to the agencies.

The agencies are required, at least annually, to reevaluate the effectiveness of their methods for identifying training needs; review periodically *each* employee's training needs in relation to program objectives; and check up on the effectiveness of the

[1] See Arthur D. Kallen, "Training in the Federal Service—170 Years to Accept," *Public Administration Review,* XIX, No. 1 (Winter, 1959), 36–46.

[2] *Investment for Tomorrow: A Report of the Presidential Task Force on Career Advancement,* Washington, D.C.: Government Printing Office, 1967.

training, as well as the stimulus to the employee's desire for self-development.[3] The Task Force had found that interagency training was still too limited; it was particularly concerned that few agencies had "sound executive development programs," and that many subject-matter specialists moving into administrative positions were not sufficiently prepared for such assignments.[4]

To meet its responsibilities under the executive order, the Commission has created a new Bureau of Training, and Regional Training Centers throughout the country. Acting upon another recommendation of the Task Force, President Johnson in May, 1968, authorized creation of the long-desired Federal Executive Institute, which began its first course in October, 1968. Located in Charlottesville, Virginia, it provides in-residence training for top-level executives (those in General Schedule Grades 16 through 18). Studies at the Institute concentrate on the major problems facing government, how these problems should be dealt with, and how to improve the administration of federal programs. Earlier the Commission had established similar centers for middle-level managers (Grades 13 through 15) at Kings Point, New York, and Berkeley, California.

Some state and local jurisdictions have recently started programs,[5] but for the country as a whole, training activity is still deficient.[6] In his remarks on the proposed Intergovernmental Personnel Act, Senator Muskie cited a recent survey of the International City Managers' Association showing that "most of the states have no training or development programs for administrative, technical, and professional personnel." Senator Muskie said:

> . . . No city has anything approaching a model training program. Most existing training is still designed to improve the skills of routine office-workers, policemen, and firemen. Moreover, training programs stimulated by Federal grants-in-aid are largely geared to specific functional specialties. Such in-service training and educational leave are valuable . . . but they do not meet the growing requirements of state and local governments for more and better administrative, professional, and technical talent.[7]

The proposed Intergovernmental Manpower Act, mentioned in Chapter 12, authorizes: (1) any federal agency to admit state and local government employees to its training programs for technical, adminstrative, and professional personnel; (2) any federal agency administering a grant program for state and local governments, to establish and conduct special training programs for state and local employees working in such program, and authorize state and local governments to use program grant funds

[3] Executive Order 11348 Providing for the Further Training of Government Employees, April 20, 1967.

[4] *Investment for Tomorrow, op. cit.*, p. 2.

[5] As only one example, see Donald F. Reilly, "Upgrading Employee Skills in Massachusetts," *Public Personnel Review,* XXVIII, No. 3 (July, 1967), 182–183.

[6] See Gladys M. Kammerer, "Opportunities Missed: The 'Little Hoover Commission' Reports," *Public Personnel Review, XXI,* No. 4 (October, 1960), 239, and Municipal Manpower Commission, *Government Manpower for Tomorrow's Cities,* New York: McGraw-Hill, 1962, p. 73.

[7] Congressional Record, Vol. 112, May 25, 1966, No. 86.

to provide the training themselves; (3) the Civil Service Commission to provide state and local governments with training grants, up to 75 percent of the costs when training is not adequately provided for under grant-in-aid or other statutes. It also establishes a plan for Government Service fellowships for state and local employees, for periods of full-time graduate-level study not exceeding two years.[8] The Higher Education Amendments Act of 1968 contains a title, "Education for the Public Service," which authorizes the Secretary of Health, Education, and Welfare to "establish a program of grants and fellowships to improve the education of students attending institutions of higher education in preparation for entrance into the service of state, local, or federal governments, and to attract such students to the public service." Not yet funded, this title provides for grants to educational institutions for developing or expanding programs preparing students for the public service, as well as for public-service fellowships for graduate or professional study, for periods not to exceed three years.[9]

Kinds of training programs

The various kinds of training activities have been described so far only in very general terms. Let us now turn to a description of some of the programs currently carried on in "training-conscious" agencies.

Orientation programs of one sort or another are now very common. Too often in the past, new appointees were ushered to their desks, given some hasty instructions, and told to start. Today, however, public agencies realize that it is a wise investment to help the new employee get oriented. Instead of requiring him to go to work immediately, a period of a week or two or at least of some days can profitably be devoted to telling him about the agency and its work. Furthermore, it is appreciated that "when a person goes to a new job, especially a younger person, he is now more open to attitude-building suggestions and instruction in ways of doing work than he is likely to be later."[10] Orientation programs in government now typically include such activities as special classes and discussion groups, films depicting the work of the agency, tours of work locations, and distribution of employee manuals describing the workers' privileges and responsibilities.

On-the-job training—instruction the individual receives while he carries out his regularly assigned duties—is, in many cases, the most important kind of help that can be given to the

[8] *Intergovernmental Personnel Act of 1967, Intergovernmental Manpower Act of 1967*, 90th Congress, 1st Session, Hearings on S. 699 and S. 1485, pp. 18–20.

[9] Public Law 90–575, 90th Congress, S. 3769, October 16, 1968, Title IX.

[10] *Investment for Tomorrow, op. cit.*, p. 18.

worker. There is nothing new about on-the-job training, for it has been traditional for many years in such vocations as the skilled trades, where apprentices receive instruction from the journeymen. The supervisor, as the experienced worker, observes the performance of the beginner and shows him how to correct his mistakes. On-the-job training, or "coaching" as it is sometimes called, is also practiced in white-collar and professional positions. In fact, the Johnson Task Force said it was "still the most important and effective means of developing professional, administrative, and technical employees."[11]

Increased attention is being given to training the supervisors themselves in supervisory skills. This is sometimes referred to as "training the trainers," that is, instructing supervisors in how to teach the subordinates to do the job. Much emphasis is given to training the supervisors in human-relations skills: how to treat the employee and to motivate him to improve his work performance. Formerly it was all too often assumed that the most technically skilled individual worker in the group should be named the supervisor, but now it is recognized that the ability required of a supervisor is usually only partly technical, and that the key to his success in his new role will be his ability to deal effectively with subordinates.

The shortage of administrative talent has led to the introduction in government of executive development programs, long a familiar training activity in the private sector. The Johnson Task Force did not believe it pure coincidence that "all 10 of the companies found by a jury of 300 highly placed industry executives to be the best managed in the United States have active, continuing management development programs."[12] The objective of executive development programs is to broaden the individual's perspective and to improve his understanding of such problems as planning, coordination, communications, decisionmaking, delegation, headquarters-field relationships, and public relations. Much use is made of external facilities, such as educational institutions, foundations, and the management institutes of professional associations. The results of a survey made by the United States Civil Service Commission of the academic preparation of federal service executives showed that only 12 percent had majored in government and public administration, whereas "much larger numbers" had majored in "business and commerce, economics, law, engineering, and the physical sciences." The Commission commented, "Therefore, while career executives need acute perceptions of the broad role of the Federal Government as a major institution in society,

[11] *Ibid.*

[12] *Ibid.*, p. 12.

few have had an opportunity to gain such perceptions through academic work or in previous assignments."[13]

Internship is another important kind of training activity. For the young person just completing his academic training, it is the bridge between theoretical and "live" work. By "live" work is meant actual exposure to practical situations on the job where the intern can gain valuable experience. The essence of the internship is that the beginner is given the opportunity to learn the particular job or function with the help of experienced workers who counsel him. The intern is more than an observer, for he is given actual work assignments. He is getting started on the work phase of his career, and he receives the benefit of the advice of those with long work experience.

Internships may be in technical, professional, or administrative work, and they may take place as part of preentry training for the public service or after college graduation. Quite a few educational institutions arrange for, and even require, students to work as interns in public agencies to supplement particular academic programs; the students may or may not receive course credit or compensation for such assignments. A larger purpose is to interest them in government career service; in the state government of Georgia, "the long-range goal of the program is to instill in these future community leaders a concern about state government so that as citizens, even if not state employees, they will be of service to their state."[14] Frequently the "supervised practice" received in the public agency is supplemented by some night courses in nearby educational institutions, and by seminars and discussions with public officials.

In the federal government, most agencies have their own intern training programs for new recruits, such as those selected from the Federal Service Entrance Examination registers. Some state and local governments also have good intern programs. The Ford Foundation is currently financing a program of career education for promising young administrators at all levels of government. The participants are persons who already have some government service; after a special period of on-the-job training in their agencies designed to meet their particular developmental needs, they are given leave to study for a year in selected educational institutions offering broad training in public administration and government. Costs of tuition and other expenses are met from the Ford grant.[15]

Another kind of training program—for foreign nationals— is now offered not only by the federal government but also by many state and local jurisdictions.[16] A brief description of this

13 University-Federal Agency Conference on Career Development, held May 4–5, 1962, at Berkeley, Calif. Washington, D.C.: U.S. Civil Service Commission, 1962, pp. 8a, 9a.

14 Augustus B. Turnbull III, "Government Summer Interns: The Georgia Experience," Public Personnel Review, XXIX, No. 3 (July, 1968), 158.

15 See Personnel News, Public Personnel Association, Chicago, Ill.: XXVIII, No. 9 (September, 1962), 47.

16 See Albert Lepawsky (ed.), Agenda for International Training, Vancouver, Canada: Publications Centre, University of British Columbia, 1962.

kind of program will illustrate the variety of instructional techniques used in training efforts. Since the developing countries lack trained personnel in the different fields required to support programs of economic development, they have sent many of their nationals to the developed countries to obtain required training. National governments, international organizations such as the United Nations and its specialized agencies, private foundations, and individual corporations have for many years been providing special training for these foreign nationals. They have also helped the governments of the developing countries establish and operate training facilities of their own, thus obviating the need for sending some of their nationals abroad for training. Up to now, most of the developing countries have had to be satisfied by sending trainees abroad, but real progress is being made in the development of indigenous training facilities.

Training for foreign nationals takes various forms. Some of it is provided by their admittance as degree-seeking undergraduate and graduate students in the programs of academic institutions. Frequently, it consists principally of observation training, supplemented by evening courses at educational institutions in the host countries. Observation training simply means that the foreign national is escorted on guided tours of work installations, during which he has the opportunity to observe in detail how certain programs are conducted. He listens to explanations of these programs by the officials in charge of them, asks questions, digests reading materials, and generally learns from the opportunity to make these first-hand observations. In other cases the foreign national is assigned to work under supervision for a period of time in public or private agencies in the host country.

Evaluation of training programs

As training programs have been expanded, increasing concern has been expressed over the difficulty of measuring the benefits in tangible terms. In such areas as typing, taking dictation, and other activities where performance prior to and after the training can be measured concretely, the evaluation process presents no great difficulties. But objective units of measurement, such as typing speed, are lacking in most kinds of government work. This is illustrated in supervisory and executive training programs, because strong doubts have been expressed that the participants really profit from such programs. It is standard procedure to request the executive trainees, upon completion of the program, to fill out questionnaires giving their opinions as to the effectiveness of the training. These comments are of limited value, however, because no matter how favorable the individual's reaction, there is no certainty that he will actually practice what he has learned. Furthermore, the participants themselves often disagree widely as to the value of the different training courses and sessions. An added limitation is that there is a definite tendency on the part of some of them to praise the program simply for reasons of courtesy even though they are not required to sign their names to the questionnaires.

A method generally felt to be more reliable is to obtain some measure of the individual's work performance sometime after he returns to his agency. However, since this is done by checking with his superiors, his colleagues, and even his subordinates, here again the method remains subjective, so the results of the evaluation can be regarded with some skepticism. Nonetheless, in the past too little evaluation of any kind was made of training programs, and subjective as these evaluations may be, they are better than none at all.

PROMOTIONS

If a true career service is to be created, staffing patterns should be developed showing the succession of progressively responsible posts to which the new recruit can in time be promoted depending on his performance. The employee should know exactly what he has to do in order to earn promotion to each of these higher ranks. Furthermore, only the best qualified of the candidates should be promoted, just as in original recruitment only those ranking highest on the entrance lists receive appointments. These requirements are easy to state. In practice, as past experience clearly indicates, they are very difficult to achieve.

One of the biggest stumbling blocks has been undue emphasis on seniority. Pressure for the seniority principle is generally strong in all kinds of organizations, private or public. There is a strong suspicion that if promotions are decided on the basis of merit, too many subjective judgments will be introduced that would probably lead to decisions based on favoritism. Older workers also reason that long service must indicate the development of a more mature viewpoint and of greater skill on the job. There is no question about the objectivity of the seniority rule. All that has to be done is add up the years of service. An English scholar clearly expresses what is wrong with this principle:

The trouble with the seniority system is that it is so objective that it fails to take any account of personal merit. As a system it is fair to every official except the best ones; an official has nothing to win or lose provided he does not actually become so inefficient that disciplinary action has to be taken against him. Thus, although it is fair after a fashion to the officials themselves, it is a heavy burden on the public and a great strain on the efficient handling of public business.[17]

Promotions in the federal government

Until 1959, most federal agencies had no formal system of competition for filling promotional jobs. The supervisory officer simply selected one of his subordinates, and if this person met the Civil Service Commission's *minimum* qualification standards for the kind of job in question, the promotion was approved by the agency personnel office. Enjoying this great discretion, appointing officers tended to follow the time-honored practice of seniority and to promote the man with the longest service. As a result, too often it was the mediocre employee who was promoted.

In 1959, however, the Civil Service Commission required federal agencies to establish formal promotion systems. Specifically, it issued guidelines requiring the agencies to make promotions on the basis of merit from among the best-qualified candidates. Each agency was directed to establish a promotion plan consistent with these standards, and the Commission reviewed the functioning of these plans under its inspection program. While promotion policy was much more defensible thereafter, some weaknesses existed in practice. Therefore, after a thorough study, the Commission announced a new program to be complied with by the agencies by July 1, 1969. The new system functions on the same decentralized basis, with the agencies developing their own promotion plans, subject to Commission post-audit for compliance with the new standards. The new program requires:

1. Consideration of qualified candidates from as broad a segment of the agency as possible to assure maximum opportunities for promotion.
2. Ranking procedures to be based upon appropriate job-related criteria.
3. Length of service or length of experience to be used as a ranking factor only when clearly and positively related to performance.

[17] Brian Chapman, *The Profession of Government,* London: G. Allen, 1959, p. 164.

4. Written tests to be used for promotion only when approved in advance by the Commission, or found necessary by it for in-service placement.
5. An employee to be selected from a regular civil service examination register to fill a higher grade position in his own agency only when he would rank among the best qualified under competitive promotion procedures.
6. In filling positions by transfer from another federal agency, or by reinstatement of a former federal employee, the agency must assure that the person so selected ranks with the best qualified agency employees if the position has known promotion potential.

Employee organizations were particularly critical of the rule on seniority; one spokesman said, "The Commission has treated seniority as a dirty word."[18] Chapter 15 discusses the impact of collective bargaining on merit policies.

The purpose of the new Executive Assignment System, fully operational since November, 1967, is to assure the widest possible search in filling all executive positions in the top General Schedule Grades (16, 17, and 18). The Commission's Bureau of Executive Manpower, created to administer the program, has prepared an inventory of federal executive personnel in these grades, plus qualified persons outside the government, to be used in attracting the "right executive to the right job at the right time."[19] In making these executive assignments, the agencies are required to use their merit promotion programs and the Commission's special facilities in locating highly qualified persons from inside and outside the service.

Practices in state and local jurisdictions

In state and local merit systems, competitive procedures have long been used in filling promotional positions. Written examinations are given and eligible registers prepared, just as in the case of the competition for original entrance. Sometimes, however, the candidates' scores are augmented with additional points for length of service. Furthermore, competition is often narrowly limited, giving the advantage to persons holding jobs in the same department or even smaller organizational units where the vacancy is being filled. Despite the existence of formal competition, seniority may, in practice, be a decisive factor.

An encouraging development is the action of some jurisdictions to broaden the area of competition greatly. For example, some

[18] Tom Woodall, "Merit Plan Shifts Blasted by Unions," *Federal Times,* September 11, 1968.

[19] *Civil Service News,* U.S. Civil Service Commission, November 17, 1967.

jurisdictions accept applications for a promotional examination from any employee who meets the minimum requirements for the position. The practice of always requiring experience in the next lower grade is being dropped, because there is no reason why everyone should be required to serve time in every grade. If the promotional examination is a good one, those with inadequate experience will either not pass or will not rank as high as those with better backgrounds.

Promotion from within or without

Should individuals not in the government be allowed to compete for vacancies in the higher jobs, along with existing public employees? The law and the regulations of the federal service do not prohibit this. The individual agency can frame its promotion policy in such a way as to permit making judicious use of appointments of outsiders. Flexibility also exists in state and local merit systems, because the central personnel agency is often given the discretion to open the competition to outsiders. The Municipal Manpower Commission found, however, that most urban governments are rarely willing to fill middle and top positions with outsiders.[20]

What should be done is to strike the proper balance between promotion-from-within and promotion-from-without. Too much promotion-from-within leads to inbreeding and resultant stagnation. Some promotion-from-without is desirable to provide the stimulation of new ideas and to counteract any tendency toward excessive "conformism." On the other hand, too free a policy of filling the higher posts with outsiders can damage the morale of those passed over for promotion despite their being well qualified for the jobs in question. As discussed in Chapter 13, the British appear to have had too little reinvigoration through late entry, and in the United States there has on occasion been too much movement in and out of the public service.

Many people support the principle that no one should be appointed from outside the government, or from outside the particular agency, unless he has qualifications clearly superior to those of the best qualified aspirant for the promotion within the agency. This is both fair and logical, but as a guiding principle it falls down in practice at the point of measuring the qualifications of the individuals concerned. Whether the outsider is better qualified or not can be and frequently is a matter for dispute.

[20] Municipal Manpower Commission, *op. cit.*, pp. 76–78.

Comparison with private companies
and foreign governments

Imperfect as government promotion procedures have been in the past, disillusionment over practices in industry has been far greater. Articles and research findings recently published paint a picture of favoritism, chance, scheming, and other extraneous factors as the decisive ones in obtaining promotions. The senior executive often prefers to advance the man who most resembles him in his work habits and personal characteristics. The junior executive who is the "carbon copy" of his boss gets the promotion. Of course, this is not true in all companies, but it does appear to be widespread.[21]

Foreign governments have also wrestled with the problem and come up with some solutions, which, however desirable in their environments, would probably be rejected by most Americans. Some European countries establish a quota of higher jobs to be filled on the basis of seniority alone, and another quota of the same jobs to be awarded on the basis of merit. In Italy, for example, the "posts of *primo segretario* in the *carriere di concetto* (executive class) are filled for a quarter by competitive examinations amongst those in the class below, and for three quarters by *ideoneitá*: that is, promotion from seniority amongst those who have satisfactorily passed a test of competence."[22] There is no precedent for establishing such a quota system in the American public service. Nevertheless, study of foreign experience and other research in the area of promotional systems should be highly desirable, for existing American practices have been used too long without critical examination.

SERVICE RATINGS

From the employees' standpoint, it is essential that they know whether they are doing their work satisfactorily and how they can improve their performance. Naturally, they also want appropriate recognition for the quality of the services they render. As to the management, it wants to help the employees achieve the highest possible levels of performance. It is glad to reward superior performance and to treat the employees fairly, in accordance with an accurate evaluation of their respective value to the organization. Again, what should be done is easy to state in terms of broad principles. Achieving the result is in this case more difficult than in many other areas of personnel administra-

[21] See Charles H. Coates and Roland F. Pellegrin, "Executives and Supervisors: Informal Factors in Differential Bureaucratic Promotion," *Administrative Science Quarterly*, II, No. 2 (September, 1957), 209–215. Also Robert N. McMurry, "The Executive Neurosis," *Harvard Business Review*, XXX, No. 6 (November-December, 1952), 33–47.

[22] Chapman, *op. cit.*, p. 170.

tion. This "accurate evaluation" of the employees' services is exceedingly difficult to make: a quick survey of the experience to date with service ratings will show the reason.

Public rewards or penalties

The outstanding characteristic of service rating plans in government has been what the first Hoover Commission termed the system of mandatory *public rewards or penalties*.[23] The employees are given adjective ratings by their supervisors, such as "excellent," "very good," "good," "fair," and "unsatisfactory." These ratings have controlled the individual's work destinies, favorably or unfavorably. One of the best examples of this is eligibility for a within-grade increase. This is not the same as a promotion. A promotion is a movement from a position in one class to another ranked higher in the salary plan; the within-grade increase means a raise from a lower to a higher rate in the salary scale for the *same* class of positions. The scales typically consist of several intermediate rates besides the minimum and maximum. The supervisor knows that unless he gives the employee the minimum rating required by law, he will be depriving him of his next "increase." Similarly, the last service rating frequently has at least something to do with the individual's ranking on reduction-in-force and reemployment registers. It is sometimes even weighted in promotional examinations and, if the rating is low enough, immediate dismissal action against the employee may be required.

There is nothing wrong with rewarding good employees and penalizing poor ones. The trouble is that the mandatory system of public rewards or penalties has by no means produced this result, since the supervisor hesitates to give ratings that will adversely affect the employee. The situation has sometimes been complicated by the innumerable appeal rights granted to the employees. Rather than be tied up in time-consuming hearings, the supervisor simply decides to give the subordinate an acceptable rating. Furthermore, many employees regard any rating of less than "excellent" or "very good" as reflecting on their performance. The net result is that the ratings tend to be far too high.

Recommendations of the Hoover Commissons

Both Hoover Commissions recommended that the system of public rewards or penalties be ended. Instead supervisors would

[23] Commission on Organization of the Executive Branch of the Government, *Task Force Report on Federal Personnel*, Washington, D.C.: Government Printing Office, 1949, pp. 60–62, 71–72.

be required to make periodic reports of a confidential nature on the performance of their subordinates and their growth potential. These reports would be used within the agency as the basis for granting or denying within-grade increases and taking any other actions. Employees would be continuously evaluated, but summary adjective ratings would not be given. The supervisor would call the employee in for frequent confidential chats, during which he would give his reactions to his work performance.

Would not the employee who is denied his "increase" or otherwise treated adversely resent the rating? Very likely he would, but no service rating system can be expected to eliminate hard feelings. The important thing is to create a situation in which the supervisor is encouraged to take the job of evaluating his subordinates seriously. The confidential talks, it is hoped, will produce such an atmosphere. Furthermore, with the final adjective ratings eliminated, the employees would not be constantly making the invidious comparisons that poison the atmosphere.

In making this recommendation, both Hoover Commissions were influenced by the example of private companies that have achieved good results without summary ratings and other characteristics of the system of public rewards or penalties. The Civil Service Commission has supported these recommendations, but up to now no such change has been made in the Performance Rating Act of 1950. However, the Federal Salary Reform Act of 1962 definitely severs the connection between the last service rating and the within-grade increases. It provides that the employee will be eligible for an increase, after a specified period of time at his existing salary rate, if "his work is of an acceptable level of competence as determined by the head of the department."[24] There is no requirement that this determination by the head of the department must be based on the last service rating. Previously, within-grade increases had to be granted to all employees who got a service rating of "satisfactory." In practice, however, this new provision of law does not seem to have made any real change. Department heads have been reluctant to state that the employee's services are not acceptable. This would raise the question of why the employee was not dismissed. As we shall see later in this chapter, appointing officers are reluctant to bring dismissal actions for fear that they will be reversed when the employee appeals.

For some years, several state and local governments have disassociated within-grade increases and other personnel actions from the ratings, but it is now clear that this represents no trend.

[24] Section 701 (a)(B) Public Law 87-793, 87th Congress.

David T. Stanley noted that "there are still far too many systems which require an overall rating. . . . Anybody who tells you that such a system is working well is kidding you and himself. What is really happening is that genuine evaluations of performance are being made, informally, subjectively, and confidentially for a variety of purposes."[25]

Trait-rating plans

The rating process itself is very difficult no matter what kind of evaluation system is used. The most common kind of plan used in the past in both government and industry is known as "trait rating." There are several variations of this plan, but essentially it consists of rating the individual on aspects of his personality, such as industry, initiative, intelligence, dependability, courtesy, cooperation, and tact. If the graphic trait scale is employed, the employee is rated according to the degree to which he possesses certain qualities.

This kind of plan is simple to administer, because large numbers of employees can be rated rapidly by simply making the appropriate marks in the indicated spaces. It is, however, highly subjective for two important reasons. First, there is no common agreement on what the traits in question mean. What does a characteristic like "cooperativeness" really mean? Sometimes brief definitions of each trait are given on the rating form, but usually they consist of descriptive phrases and adjectives that again do not have the same meaning to all raters. Secondly, the best intentioned raters will disagree, sometimes sharply, as to whether an employee possesses a given trait, and to what degree. How do we know when an employee is "very cooperative" rather than just "cooperative"?

Performance standards

In an effort to reduce this subjectivity, some public agencies have developed rating systems based on performance standards. Under this kind of system the employee is rated not on his personality traits but on his performance in carrying out the different tasks in his job. This creates the necessity, however, of breaking the job down into its essential components and of rating the employee's performance on each. It is undoubtedly an educational process for superior and subordinate to identify the job components and to agree on the performance standards. The performance standard is the minimum acceptable level of perform-

25 David T. Stanley, "New Patterns in Public Personnel Administration," *Public Personnel Review, XXV,* No. 2 (April, 1964), 95.

ance by the employee on each task, measured in terms of both quantity and quality of work. Still it is a laborious undertaking to list the tasks and determine the performance standards for each and every task, in hundreds and thousands of positions. When every employee has to be rated on how he performs each task in his job, this is a time-consuming process except in very small organizations.

Some agencies do not require the preparation of written performance standards, but they do instruct the supervisors to base their evaluations on the employee's work performance rather than on vague personality traits. The supervisor is urged to make entirely clear to the subordinate what his job is and what work results are expected of him. If the supervisor believes that the subordinate's performance is not up to the desired standards, he is expected to show him in specific terms why this is so. When the emphasis is on performance, the supervisor can set work improvement targets for the subordinate to try to meet by the time of the next evaluation conference. This gives the conferences themselves a constructive character and presents the worker with a challenge. He sees the superior as someone personally interested in his developing, not as a judge on high who gives him no real help but is quick to lecture him on his deficiences. When this kind of evaluation system is employed, it is immaterial whether a rating form as such is used or whether the superior simply prepares a memorandum or other report for the official records in which he gives his latest observations on the subordinate's performance. The essential element is that the evaluation is based on a careful definition of the employee's responsibilities and of his progress in meeting the work goals mutually agreed upon between himself and his superior. Quite a few private companies have in recent years switched from trait rating to performance evaluation conducted on this basis, and they are better satisfied with the results. In government there has also been a noticeable attempt to shift the emphasis to rating specific work performance rather than personality characteristics.

Need to train supervisors in rating

No matter how good the service rating system, it will fail if the supervisors do not understand it. For this reason it is unfortunate that such inadequate attention has been given in the past to training supervisors in rating. Very few jurisdictions schedule enough supervisory training conferences for this purpose. What happens too often is that the rating time arrives and the supervisor is ill-prepared to do his job as rater of so many subordinates. Sometimes, because of the pressure of other duties, he leaves this chore for the last minute. The night before the ratings are due, he puts the forms in his briefcase and does the job at home that night. Ratings prepared so hurriedly naturally could be greatly improved if the supervisors devoted more time to this important task. It is the agency's responsibility to explain the system to the supervisors and to stimulate them to do the best possible job of rating.

Both in industry and government there is marked dissatisfaction with the results obtained to date with service rating systems. The need to improve ratings has definitely emerged as a high-priority objective, as the meagre accomplishments of past years are viewed in retrospect. In the case of government, it now seems clear that really good service rating systems will not be developed unless legislative bodies and the public recognize that much more money must be invested in this part of the personnel function than at present. At with tests, evaluation of employee performance requires a great deal of study and experimentation, which costs money. If this had been recognized a long time ago, much better results would undoubtedly have been achieved in this area.

DISMISSALS

The dismissal procedure is naturally a very sensitive matter. The workers justifiably want to be protected against arbitrary action by the supervisors. In turn, the latter understandably do not want unreasonable obstacles placed in the way of their discharging clearly unfit subordinates. As to the public, it wants "deadwood" eliminated and is concerned about the often heard statement that "you can't fire anyone" in government. Two policies with respect to dismissals have been followed in the public service. They are known as the "open back door" and the "closed back door."

The "open back door"

Under the "open back door" policy, the decision of the appointing officer in discharging an employee for reasons of inefficiency cannot be cancelled by the central personnel agency. Any employee who has completed his probationary period has the right to appeal to the Civil Service Commission, just as he has the right to appeal the dismissal first within his own agency. All the Civil Service Commission can do, however, is to recommend to the appointing officer that he reinstate the dismissed employee. If the appointing officer still feels that he is right, he does not have to follow this recommendation. The law sometimes permits the Commission to place the employee's name on the reemployment list for the class of positions involved, but that is as far as it can go. It should be made clear that under the "open back door" the employee is protected against dismissal for political, religious, or racial reasons. If the Commission is convinced that the action was taken for such a reason, it can order the reinstatement of the employee.

The "closed back door"

Under the policy of the "closed back door," the central personnel agency can order the appointing officer to restore the employee to his position. In state and local jurisdictions, the "closed back door" policy is more common than the "open back door." In the federal service, the Pendleton Act as originally passed provided for the "open back door." It is interesting that, anxious as they were to eliminate the spoils system, the civil service reformers still did not want to make it hard to get rid of the incompetents. The Veterans Preference Act of 1944, however, made an important change. It provided for special treatment of veterans in dismissal cases and gave them the protection of the "closed back door." Specifically, they were allowed to appeal a dismissal action to the Civil Service Commission, and the latter was given the power to reverse it. Nonveteran employees, as before, could not appeal to the Commission unless they could show that the action was taken for political, religious, or racial reasons, or that the appointing officer, in making the dismissal, had failed to comply with the procedural steps required by law and the Commission's regulations. In Executive Order 10988, President Kennedy extended to nonveterans the same appeal rights given the veterans under the 1944 act. The "closed back door" now applies to all federal employees under civil service. The President's purpose was to make the policy uniform, without favored treatment for any group of employees.

The pros and cons of each policy

Those who favor the "closed back door" argue that it is always possible that an appointing officer may be prejudiced against an employee and want to fire him simply because he does not like him. Accordingly, protection against dismissal for political, religious, or racial reasons is not enough. Since past experience suggests that a few supervisors, at least, can be expected to abuse their authority, there must be a court of higher appeal to which the employee can take his case. True, the central personnel agency, after conducting its hearing and weighing the evidence for and against the employee, may err and order the reinstatement of someone whose dismissal was fully justified. This is unfortunate, but it is better than making it possible for unjust supervisors to dismiss perfectly good employees. All the appointing officer is being asked to do is justify the dismissal. If he cannot do this to the central personnel agency's satisfaction, then he probably was wrong.

Advocates of the "open back door" argue that the appointing officer is in a much better position than the central personnel agency to make a judgment as to the efficiency of the employee. The management of the agency in which the employee has been working has direct knowledge of his work performance and conduct. For the central personnel agency to disagree with the supervisor and tell him that the employee must be taken back creates an impossible situation. The supervisor is responsible for the work of the unit. If he is to be forced to keep someone he is convinced is incompetent, he is denied the support that he deserves. Of course, the reinstated employee can be assigned to a different supervisor. The point still remains, however, that an outside group, in no way responsible for the work of the agency, is interfering with the agency's management determinations. The authority of the agency management before the other employees can only suffer when they see the vindicated worker return to the agency.

Furthermore, what control can the agency exercise over the reinstated employee? Is he not apt to feel that he is now free to behave as he pleases? It is also argued that the record clearly shows that central personnel agencies let the employees play upon their sympathies and all too easily come to the conclusion that the supervisor was too tough in resorting to dismissal action. The civil service commissioners who hear the employee's defense can afford to be more lenient than the supervisor. Once they decide the case, their contacts with the employee are ended. This is not so in the case of the supervisor if the employee's reinstatement is ordered. He and the agency management must still deal with the employee for every minute of the working day.

Under the "open back door" a few employees may be dismissed without adequate justification, but a much larger number of incompetents will be gotten rid of than under the "closed back door." No system can be expected to guarantee perfect justice to all employees. The "open back door" is better because appointing officers are much more likely to take action against unsatisfactory employees. The probability of a time-consuming hearing before the central personnel agency, with the possibility always present of being overruled, discourages many a supervisor from initiating dismissal proceedings against even the most patently incompetent employees.

Accurate statistics probably could not be obtained on just how many supervisors have been so discouraged; it appears, however, that civil service commissions reinstate relatively few dismissed employees. A study of the Philadelphia Civil Service Commission showed that in a 10-year period it sustained only 17 percent of the dismissal appeals.[26]

The public-employee unions generally support the "closed back door." Professional organizations such as the National Civil Service League and the American Municipal Association strongly recommend the "open back door."[27] The second Hoover Commission was very critical of the provision of the Veterans Preference Act of 1944 that gave the veterans special appeal rights. It said that appeals by veterans in dismissal cases heard by the Civil Service Commission resembled a "judicial-criminal proceeding," with the appointing officer as much on trial as the employee. For the first time in the history of civil service, "Civil Service Commission control of the power of a department head to discipline his staff" had been introduced.[28]

The Hoover Commission recommended that the special appeals rights of veterans be limited to the first five years after the date of honorable discharge. Congress did not accept this recommendation, and, as previously mentioned, President Kennedy's solution was to extend the same appeals rights to non-veterans. In the absence of action by Congress to restore the "open back door" for all employees, the President elected to make the procedure uniform on the basis of the "closed back door."

[26] William B. Boise, "Civil Service Commission Appeals—The Management Approach," *Public Personnel Review*, XXV, No. 2 (April, 1964), 113.

[27] See the *Model State Civil Service Law*, revised edition, 1953, prepared jointly by these two organizations.

[28] Commission on Organization of the Executive Branch of the Government, *Task Force Report on Personnel and Civil Service*, Washington, D.C.: Government Printing Office, 1955, pp. 95–96.

BIBLIOGRAPHY

Boise, William B., "Civil Service Commission Appeals—The Management Approach," *Public Personnel Review*, XXV, No. 2 (April, 1964).

Booker, Gene S., and Miller, Ronald W., "A Closer Look at Peer Ratings," *Personnel*, XLIII, No. 1 (January-February, 1966).

Chapman, Brian, *The Profession of Government*, London: G. Allen, 1959. Chapters 3 and 8.

Coleman, Charles J., "Avoiding the Pitfalls in Results-Oriented Appraisals," *Personnel*, XLII, No. 6 (November-December, 1965).

"Executive Development in the Public Service," *Public Personnel Review*, XXVIII, No. 3 (July, 1967). Bibliography.

Foreman, Wayne J., "A Study of Management Training Techniques Used by Large Corporations," *Public Personnel Review*, XXVIII, No. 1 (January, 1967).

Foundation for Research on Human Behavior, *Performance Appraisals: Effects on Employees and Their Performance*, Ann Arbor, Mich: 1141 E. Catherine Street, P.O. Box 1261, 1963.

Handbook of Training in the Public Service, New York: Department of Economic and Social Affairs, Public Administration Branch, United Nations, 1966.

Harmon, Francis L., and Glickman, Albert S., "Managerial Training: Reinforcement Through Evaluation," *Public Personnel Review*, XXVI, No. 4 (October, 1965).

House Subcommittee on the Federal Civil Service, 83rd Congress, 2nd Session, *Performance Rating Plans in the Federal Government*, Washington, D.C.: Government Printing Office, 1954.

International City Managers' Association, *Post-Entry Training in the Local Public Service*, Washington, D.C.: 1963.

Investment for Tomorrow: A Report of the Presidential Task Force on Career Advancement, Washington, D.C.: Government Printing Office, 1967.

Lopez, Felix M., Jr., *Evaluating Employee Performance*, Chicago: Public Personnel Association, 1968.

Michael, Jerrold M., "Problem Situations in Performance Counselling," *Personnel*, XLII, No. 5 (September-October, 1965).

Paine, Frank T., and Bassin, William M., "Sensitivity Training: Theory and Practice," *Public Personnel Review*, XXVI, No. 2 (April, 1965).

Risen, Isidore L., "Discipline and Appeals in the Federal Service," *Personnel Administration*, XXIX, No. 6 (November-December, 1966).

Schinagl, Mary S., *History of Efficiency Ratings in the Federal Government*, New York: Bookman Associates, 1966.

Self and Service Enrichment Through Federal Training: An Annex to the Report of the Presidential Task Force on Career Advancement, Washington, D.C.: U.S. Civil Service Commission, 1967.

Tickner, Fred J., *Modern Staff Training*, London: University of London Press, 1952.

Varela, Jacobo A., "Why Promotions Cause Trouble—And How to Avoid It," *Personnel, XLI*, No. 6 (November-December, 1964).

CHAPTER 15
COLLECTIVE BARGAINING IN THE PUBLIC SERVICE

IN THE PAST FEW YEARS the newspapers have been full of stories about disputes between public employee unions and public management. A great change in labor relations in government has taken place in a relatively few years, which is why some people have called the 1960s the "decade of the public employee." Whereas "as recently as 1959, public employees were damned for picketing a state Governor during nonworking time," in 1967 "over 300 full-scale strikes of public employees—including policemen and firefighters—racked public services across the nation."[1] As late as 1965 there were only 42 public employee strikes. From 1956 to 1966, union membership increased 88 percent in federal, state, and local governments (from 915,000 to 1,717,000), compared to only 12 percent in the private sector.[2]

A thoroughgoing report published in June, 1957, states that "group participation of any kind in the formulation of terms and conditions of employment for the civil servant is not yet the prevailing fashion."[3] Ten years later, the executive com-

[1] Jean J. Couturier, "Bargaining Faces Crisis and Change," *Federal Times*, November 13, 1968.

[2] Irwin Ross, "Those Newly Militant Government Workers," *The Public Employee*, XXXIII, No. 9 (September, 1968), 6. Condensed from an article in *Fortune* magazine.

[3] Ida Klaus, *Report on a Program of Labor Relations for New York City Employees*, New

mittee of the National Governor's Conference published a report that began: "One of the most significant developments in public administration during the past decade is the growth of collective bargaining in the public service."[4] The governors considered the matter so important they obtained a foundation grant to finance an intensive task-force study. Prominent in the report of the task force is the following statement: "While collective bargaining in the public service is not now and probably never will be a universal practice, it is definitely expanding."[5]

DEVELOPMENTS IN STATE AND LOCAL GOVERNMENTS

Prior to 1959, relatively few collective bargaining agreements were in force in state and local governments. In 1959 Wisconsin passed a law *requiring* local governments to bargain collectively with their employees, and by the end of 1967 nine other states— Connecticut, Delaware, Massachusetts, Michigan, New York, Oregon, Rhode Island, Vermont, and Washington—had approved similar legislation for state and/or local government employees. Three other states—Alaska, Missouri, and New Hampshire—*permit* collective bargaining. In several other states, collective bargaining is required or permitted only for certain groups of employees, such as firemen, policemen, teachers, and nurses.

In California, Hawaii, and Minnesota, employees are given the right to "meet and confer" with management, but management unilaterally makes the final decision.[6] While this is not the same as collective bargaining, the essential characteristic of which is that decisions over wages, hours, and conditions of employment are *jointly* reached by management and the employees' representatives, it does require management to hear the employees and give consideration to their proposals. The California statute imposes a mutual obligation on both sides "to endeavor to reach agreement on matters within the scope of representation." However, it also states that if an agreement is reached, it cannot be "binding."[7] In collective bargaining as practiced in the private sector, and under the mandatory state legislation referred to previously, the agreement is binding, and failure to respect it is an unfair labor practice. "Meet-and-confer" arrangements sometimes prove a transitional state toward full-blown collective dealings.

In quite a few of the remaining states, although there is no collective bargaining legislation, collective agreements are being signed anyway. As will be explained below, the public employee

York: Department of Labor of the City of New York, June, 1957, p. 17.

[4] *Report of Task Force on State and Local Government Labor Relations, 1967: Executive Committee, National Governors' Conference*, Chicago: Public Personnel Association, 1967, p. vi.

[5] *Ibid.*, p. 3.

[6] *Ibid.*, pp. 29–30.

[7] Richard Salik (ed.), *The Right to Meet and Confer—Laws and Policies*, Chicago: Public Personnel Association, Public Employee Relations Library, No. 10, 1968, p. 24.

unions, joined by some management officials themselves, are maintaining that the bargaining is legal if not prohibited by law, and in the absence of court tests and rulings to the contrary, the contracts are respected on a *de facto* basis. In some states without statutes, the bargaining takes place on the basis of a municipal ordinance, as in Baltimore, Maryland.[8] The combined effect of the mandatory and permissive state legislation, the local ordinances, and the *de facto* bargaining rights has been the signing of thousands of collective agreements, with no indications of any generalized successful movement to wipe out the bargaining rights once granted. In many places there is still strong resistance to collective bargaining and it is not being allowed, but the movement is definitely not being contained, for it continues to spread.

Characteristics of bargaining arrangements

Furthermore, in state and local governments the scope of the bargaining is broad, usually including salaries and wages and, frequently, hours of work, fringe benefits, and other conditions of employment. In the private sector, collective bargaining means signing an agreement with an exclusive bargaining agent that represents the majority of the workers in the bargaining unit; once signed, the contract applies to all workers in the unit, whether or not members of the majority union. In most cases, the state and local government bargaining is with exclusive bargaining agents, so that the resemblance with industrial practice under the Taft-Hartley Act is close. In California, under the Winton Act (which applies to school districts only), the negotiating takes place with councils on which seats are allocated according to the number of members the rival teachers' organizations have in proportion to the total number of organized certificated employees in the district. However, such an arrangement is unusual; furthermore, it is reported that the councils have not developed in practice as effective negotiating bodies.[9]

The administrative machinery for regulating the collective bargaining varies.[10] In some states the state agency performing labor relations functions for the private sector has been given the same role for government; examples are Connecticut, Michigan, and Wisconsin. In two states, Oregon and Washington, the civil service agencies are in charge of the programs. In other cases a new state entity is created, as in New York where an independent, three-member Public Employment Relations Board, appointed by the governor, is responsible for implemen-

[8] Ordinance 251, approved September 6, 1968.

[9] Salik, *op. cit.*, p. 18.

[10] See Felix A. Nigro, *Management-Employee Relations in the Public Service*, Chicago: Public Personnel Association, 1969, pp. 121-132.

tation of the Public Employees' Fair Employment Act of 1967. New York City has its own Office of Collective Bargaining (OCB), established by ordinance; the unusual feature is that the employee organizations select two of the seven members of the board of collective bargaining, an important part of the OCB.[11]

In cities such as Cincinnati and Philadelphia, where exclusive bargaining agents have been recognized for years, there is no separate labor relations machinery as such. In Cincinnati a City Council resolution authorizes the city manager to bargain collectively with employee organizations that can prove majority representation in appropriate bargaining units; since passage of the ordinance, the city managers have recognized District Council 51 of the American Federation of State, County, and Municipal Employees (AFSCME) as the exclusive agent for all city employees. The city manager, aided by the personnel officer, negotiates the agreements for the city. The city and District Council 51 carry out the labor relations program. In Philadelphia, an ordinance authorizes the mayor to enter into an agreement with District Council 33 of the AFSCME, designated in the ordinance as the exclusive bargaining agent for "certain" civil service employees. An agreement with District Council 33 was then entered into by the personnel director, signing for the city; he and District Council 33 are mutually responsible for the collective bargaining arrangements.

If collective bargaining is to be successful, both management and the employee organizations must observe certain rules, commonly referred to as "fair labor practices." The Taft-Hartley Act lists unfair labor practices by both sides. An example is refusal to bargain collectively. Complaints of unfair labor practices are made to the National Labor Relations Board (NLRB), which investigates. If it finds the complaint justified, but the guilty party refuses to desist from the practice in question, it issues a cease and desist order, enforceable in federal court. Both the union and management can appeal NLRB rulings in the courts.

In states such as Michigan and Wisconsin, unfair labor practices by public management or public employee unions are policed and enforced in much the same way as in industry.[12] Delaware law contains an unfair practices section, but says nothing about enforcement. Some local government units have employee relations policies that include statements of unfair practices,[13] but these essentially are statements of intentions only. However, such statements should not be deprecated, since

---

11 *Ibid.*, pp. 130–132.

12 *Ibid.*, p. 142–145.

13 Salik, *op. cit.*, pp. 38–39.

they represent pledges in writing and may in practice be scrupulously observed.

Many of the collective contracts being signed in state and local governments do provide for binding arbitration of disputes over the enforcement of the contract terms. This means that neither side can simply refuse to respect its commitments under the contract; the grievance procedure in the contract provides for resolution of such conflicts by independent, outside arbitrators, as in industry. Management must pay the overtime rate pledged; the union cannot make management give the union stewards more time off the job to investigate grievances of union members than that specified in the contract. Where collective bargaining has been long practiced, as in the private sector, deliberate noncompliance with the contract is rare; usually the problem is one of differing interpretations of the meaning of contract provisions.

THE FEDERAL LABOR–MANAGEMENT COOPERATION PROGRAM

In the federal service, with very few exceptions, collective agreements were not signed until issuance of President Kennedy's Executive Order 10988, in January, 1962.[14] (A prominent exception was the Tennessee Valley Authority (TVA).) The Lloyd-La Follette Act of 1912 had established the right of federal employees to organize; however, as stated by former U.S. Civil Service Commission Chairman John W. Macy, Jr., "Before 1962, Federal employee organizations existed on sufferance and by grace, welcomed in some agencies and hardly tolerated in others."[15]

Pressures had been building for union recognition and bargaining rights in the federal service, and Kennedy made a campaign pledge to grant such rights. The examples of states and cities that had already started collective bargaining programs was a stimulus for federal action; in turn, the Kennedy order then influenced other states and local governments to adopt collective bargaining. Whereas the Lloyd-La Follette Act had been limited to protecting the bare right of organization, Executive Order 10988 greatly strengthened the role of the employee organizations by stating that "the efficient administration of the Government and the well-being of the employees require that orderly and constructive relationships be maintained between employee organizations and management officials."[16] Some 762,000 individuals, or approximately one-third of the total federal work

[14] See Kenneth O. Warner and Mary L. Hennessey, *Public Management at the Bargaining Table,* Chicago: Public Personnel Association, 1967, pp. 349–358.

[15] John W. Macy, Jr., "A Long-Standing Partnership in Progress," address before National Convention of National Federation of Federal Employees, Miami Beach, Fla., September 13, 1966.

[16] Warner and Hennessey, *op. cit.,* p. 349.

force, were members of employee organizations before the Order; by the end of 1967, this had increased to 1,500,000, or more than half the total employment.[17] By November, 1967, a total of 1,238,748 employees were covered under exclusive representation.[18]

Bargaining arrangements in federal service

The scope of negotiations in federal service is more restricted than in state and local governments with collective bargaining because the agreements "are governed by the provisions of any existing or future laws and regulations," which includes both Civil Service Commission and agency regulations.[19] This means that salaries, wages, hours of work, and fringe benefits cannot be bargained, because for most federal employees they are prescribed by Congress. It also means that personnel policies and procedures provided for by law or by regulations of the Civil Service Commission are not subject to negotiation; the same holds for agency regulations if the management insists that the matters involved are "management prerogatives."

While many of the employee organizations are unhappy about the scope of the bargaining as defined in the Order, in practice the negotiations include many items of significance to the employees, such as tours of duty, lunch periods, locker facilities, sanitation, vacation scheduling, rest periods, subcontracting, health services, and training and recreation programs. Furthermore, those phases of the personnel program that are delegated by the Civil Service Commission to the agencies can, at the latter's discretion, be negotiated with the employee organizations. This represents a considerable area for bargaining because, as noted in Chapter 12, the Commission has delegated much authority to the agencies.

The Kennedy Order provides for formal and informal recognition, as well as exclusive recognition. Informal recognition is available to employee organizations that do not have enough members in the bargaining unit to entitle them to formal or exclusive recognition. It confers the right to meet with the management and express views on matters of concern to its members, but the management is under no obligation to accept these opinions or to consult with the organization before formulating personnel policies. Formal recognition is granted organizations that, although not qualified for exclusive recognition, have a stable membership of 10 percent or more of the employees in the unit. It guarantees that the management will "consult with

[17] Harold Harris, "Union Membership Shows Steady Rise," *Federal Times,* March 6, 1968.

[18] *Civil Service News,* U.S. Civil Service Commission, March 5, 1968.

[19] Warner and Hennessey, *op. cit.,* p. 354.

such organization from time to time in the formulation and implementation of personnel policies and practices, and matters affecting working conditions that are of concern to its members."[20] The right to negotiate a contract is reserved for organizations that can show that they represent more than 50 percent of the employees in the unit. Once signed, the agreement applies to all employees in the unit, as in private-sector collective bargaining. When an organization is granted exclusive recognition, none other can be given formal recognition, no matter what its membership.

One of the recommendations in a draft report of a committee named by President Johnson in September, 1967, to study the federal program was to abolish informal recognition. (In releasing this report before he left office, Secretary of Labor Willard Wirtz emphasized that it had no official standing, was only a draft report, did not have the approval of the review committee, and had not been submitted to the President.) In view of the extensive amount of formal and exclusive recognition already granted, the committee believed that informal recognition was no longer necessary, that it encouraged fragmentation and placed "an undue administrative burden on management," and that "unions with such recognition lack the strength to contribute substantially to stable labor relations."[21] The committee favored retaining formal recognition, but that it confer only the right to consult on proposed changes in personnel policy of concern to members of the particular organization. Discussion of matters pertaining to the implementation of personnel policies and practices, and of matters affecting working conditions of concern to employees, would be reserved to organizations holding exclusive recognition.

DECENTRALIZED NATURE OF FEDERAL PROGRAM

From the standpoint of administration, the federal program is decentralized, with each agency responsible for issuing rules and regulations for the implementation of the Executive Order. There is no labor relations agency responsible for overseeing the program throughout the federal service, and for performing functions comparable to those of the National Labor Relations Board for the private sector.

Each agency defines the bargaining units and determines which employee organizations qualify for the three levels of recognition provided for in the Order. The agency or a qualified employee organization seeking exclusive recognition can request the Secretary of Labor to nominate qualified arbitrators from

[20] *Ibid.*, p. 352.
[21] Special Supplement, Bureau of National Affairs, Washington, D.C., January 20, 1969.

a national panel maintained by the Federal Mediation and Conciliation Service, to render advisory opinions as to the "appropriateness of a unit for purposes of exclusive recognition,"[22] and/ or which employee organization, if any, should be the exclusive agent. The Civil Service Commission functions in an advisory capacity; its responsibility under the Order is to establish and maintain a "program to assist in carrying out the objectives" of the Order.[23] The Commission and the Labor Department were required jointly to propose both a set of Standards of Conduct for Employee Organizations and a Code of Fair Labor Practices, promulgated by President Kennedy in May, 1963. The Standards are the requirements that employee organizations must meet to quality for recognition, and the Code lists prohibited practices on the part of either the agency or the employee organization, the list being very similar to that in the Taft-Hartley Act.[24]

The objection many of the employee leaders have to these arrangements is that the agency head essentially determines how fair the agency has been in meeting its responsibilities under the Order. If, for example, the agency is charged with an unfair labor practice, it decides in its discretion whether there is a "substantial" basis for the complaint. If it should decide that the "substantial" requirement has been met, it is required to hold a hearing—but the agency head does not have to accept the findings of the hearing officers. Similarly, each agency makes the final decision as to whether to grant, deny, suspend, or withdraw recognition. Remembering also, as previously noted, that the agency does not have to agree to advisory arbitration of bargaining unit and representation disputes, the total picture to the employee leaders is one of an overconcentration of power in management's hands, incompatible with the industrial concept of bargaining between "equals." Furthermore, since the Order makes no provision for "third-party" resolution of bargaining deadlocks, the employee leaders complain that the management can, whenever it wants, close the negotiations, arguing that it has done all it can to come to an agreement. The Civil Service Commission has urged the use of mediation and other impasse settlement techniques, and these have been used. However, there has been no panel or other body to which the parties could refer the dispute when still unable to come to an agreement.

It is recommended in the draft report of the Johnson review committee that the Assistant Secretary of Labor for Labor-Management Relations should be empowered to issue decisions in bargaining unit, representation, unfair labor practice, and standards of conduct cases, with a limited right of appeal by

[22] Warner and Hennessey, *op. cit.*, p. 355.
[23] *Ibid.*, p. 356.
[24] See Nigro, *op. cit.*, pp. 134–141.

either party, on major policy issues, to a Federal Labor Relations Panel.[25] The Panel would consist of the chairman of the Civil Service Commission as Panel chairman, the Secretary of Labor, and the chairman of the National Labor Relations Board, and either or both parties could also request its services when voluntary techniques had failed to settle bargaining impasses. The Panel could suggest further use of voluntary methods, or itself assume jurisdiction, with the power to issue final and binding solutions.[26] The Assistant Secretary of Labor for Labor-Management Relations, and the proposed Federal Labor Relations Panel, would constitute the "third-party" machinery missing in the present decentralized arrangements.

REASONS FOR EMPLOYEE MILITANCY

Fundamentally, the new militancy of public employees is part of the social change taking place in the United States. Many public officials have been caught by surprise, and have difficulty understanding why government workers are behaving in this strange way, which explains some of the mistakes that have been made in dealing with the employee organizations.

One mistaken belief is that "labor" (meaning the AFL-CIO and other unions) is responsible for the new militancy. According to this analysis, the unions are desperate over a long-term trend of declining membership in the private sector. Thus the "unions" are making an all-out effort to find new recruits in that biggest growth industry of all—government—and have poured in the funds and otherwise provided the motivating force for the increased unrest of public employees. Undoubtedly, the sharp decline in blue-collar jobs and the shift to a labor force consisting mostly of white-collar workers have influenced the labor leaders to step up organizing efforts in government.

Clearly, the rapid membership increases in such AFL-CIO affiliated employee organizations as the American Federation of State, County, and Municipal Employees has been aided by the financial and other support of the AFL-CIO. However, the influence of organized labor has been only one element in the picture. The increases have resulted from other factors, such as discontent with existing conditions. As *Newsweek* has commented, ". . . but civil servants have been the sporadic targets of union organizers for years; their new militancy is a change more in them than in the unions."[27] Public employees are in no sense captives of "labor." One clear indication of this is the tendency of the rank and file to reject as inadequate agreements

[25] Special Supplement, Bureau of National Affairs, *op cit.*, p. 3.
[26] *Ibid.*, pp. 3, 5.
[27] *Newsweek*, September 29, 1966.

recommended by their leaders, duplicating the experience in industry. Unions are not creating the dissatisfactions of either private or public workers, nor are the union leaders as aggressive as much of the rank and file. Younger union members have high expectations: They remember no depression and are impatient for change, just like many college students.

Public employees now look at themselves differently. They see no reason why, in an affluent society, they should be discriminated against and expected to accept without complaint salaries and working conditions worse than those of private workers. The *Newsweek* article previously quoted put government workers in the same category as other groups left behind in the economic boom, such as farm laborers and the poor in the ghettoes.[28] The motivations, however, are ideological and psychological, as well as economic: Public employees have the same desire as workers in the private sector to participate in management decisions, to be treated with dignity. When government launches far-reaching programs such as the war against poverty, and justifies them in terms of the goal of justice for all Americans, public employees do not see why they, too, should not be treated with justice. In a period of social upheaval, as one group succeeds in making gains other groups are bound to try to improve their status also, and to imitate the tactics used. Note this statement:

> Teachers, too, have often viewed themselves as oppressed; they have viewed their treatment by society as being far less than commensurate with the importance of their contribution to the general welfare. Apparently, the activism of the civil rights movement and the effectiveness of that activism have had a significant impact upon the behavior patterns of teachers who have aspired to improve their status.[29]

To a large extent, the union movement in government is a revolt of professional workers who are redefining their role and remaking their self-image. Government, of course, employs huge numbers of professional workers, and will have to hire many more. Welfare workers, nurses, doctors, and other degree holders, many in organizations not affiliated with the labor movement, are very active in the current militancy. The welfare workers protest about having to spend most of their time on clerical work; they see first-hand the inadequacies of the present welfare system, yet no one seems to listen to them. Nurses want better-administered hospitals; in their opinion, money is

28 *Ibid.*

29 T. M. Stinnett, Jack H. Kleinmann, Martha L. Ware, *Professional Negotiation in Public Education,* New York: Macmillan, 1966, p. 6.

wasted that could be used to increase salaries and otherwise improve working conditions. They claim that they are not treated with proper respect, that their training is much under-utilized, and that they are not allowed to participate in decisions where they could make a real contribution. Many other examples could be given, but the resentments, of course, are not limited to the professionals. Policemen and firemen, exposed to death and injury in the problem-ridden cities, are deeply resentful over what they consider the community's failure to appreciate their contributions.

Public employees also sense their strength from the great increase in the size of their ranks and the fact that in many cases their services are in short supply. Census Bureau figures showed that in October, 1967, there were 12 million federal, state, and local government employees, comprising about 15 percent of the civilian labor force. As one newspaper columnist has written, "In talking of public employees these days, one no longer refers to a small cadre of 'dedicated public servants.' "[30] He points out that in California about one in every six persons is employed by some agency of government, and notes the "struggle . . . developing among unions and other employee groups to organize and lead this potent force."[31] Furthermore, in many cases the services of the public employees are desperately needed. As governments increase their commitments to the citizens with such programs as hospital and medical insurance, the necessary number of nurses, doctors, and laboratory and other technicians must be induced to stay on the job, and there are numerous vacancies to fill.

Another factor not to be overlooked is that of momentum. There may have been a point early in the 1960s when the union movement in government could have been held back, but the first big breakthroughs, like the signing in 1961 of the first collective contract between the New York City Board of Education and the United Federation of Teachers, fed upon themselves. Once they had successfully tested their power in such confrontations, public employees sensed they could go on to other victories. When this element of momentum estab-lishes itself, the possibility that any drive will be checked is greatly reduced. Of course, the pace of advance is not uniformly the same. Labor's influence in the state legislatures fluctuates, which has an important bearing on the chances for passage of the many public-worker collective bargaining bills now before the lawmakers.

30 Tom Goff, "Public Strike Answers Sought," editorial section, *Los Angeles Times*, October 10, 1966.
31 *Ibid.*

FALLING OF THE LEGAL BARRIERS

The developments described earlier in this chapter could not have taken place without the removal of certain legal barriers to collective bargaining in the public service. Analysis of how these barriers are crumbling provides an interesting case study of the effect of social pressures on court decisions and long-established dogma.

The right to enter into collective agreements

Until very recently, the argument that government would be giving away its "sovereignty" if it signed collective agreements was little questioned. Basically the concept has been that as the "sovereign employer," the government cannot be compelled to accept any commitment, or to respect one it has made if it later decides that it cannot or should not. The origins of this view of the government's rights are in the English common law doctrines that the king could do no wrong and that no individual could sue the state without its consent.[32] Although these beliefs were carried over into the legal system of the American colonies, we know that, based on legislation passed over the years by the Congress and by the state legislatures, private individuals can sue the "government" for redress of alleged injuries. Nonetheless, the courts formerly consistently ruled that since terms of employment are at bottom a matter of legislative policy, it was an illegal delegation of legislative power—and thus the abdication of sovereignty—for administrative officials to sign collective agreements with employees.

For example, in a 1943 case a court in New York State said, "Collective bargaining has no place in Government service. The employer is the whole people. It is impossible for administrative officials to bind the Government of the United States or the State of New York by any agreement made between them and representatives of any union."[33]

What did emerge from the court decisions, however, was the dictum that collective bargaining was legal if authorized by statute; as late as 1959, however, no state had passed such legislation. Apparently the courts recognized that, in a democracy, sovereignty resides in the people, and that the state legislature represents the people. Therefore, if the legislators authorized collective bargaining, a big mistake might be being made, but the responsibility was the electorate's. In many of the states

[32] See Wilson R. Hart, *Collective Bargaining in the Federal Service*, New York: Harper & Row, 1961, pp. 38–54.

[33] Herbert W. Cornell, "Legal Aspects of Collective Bargaining by Public Employee Groups," a paper presented at the Central Regional Conference of the Public Personnel Association, St. Louis, May 12, 1958. The case quoted is *Railway Mail Association vs Murphy*, 44 N.Y. Supp. (2), 601.

without authorizing legislation, public officials still refuse to bargain collectively, arguing that they have no legal authority to do so; in other states they are entering into collective agreements on the assumption that it is legal if there is no statute *prohibiting* it.

The Chicago Board of Education at first refused to bargain collectively, alleging legal incapacity. The Board then changed its mind and agreed with the American Federation of Teachers (AFT) that since by state law it was empowered to make contracts and do all things "necessary and proper" for the operation of the schools, it could negotiate agreements with the teachers.[34]

While court rulings in one state do not bind other state courts, a break in long-prevailing doctrines sets the stage for a spreading of the new interpretations, particularly when the social climate in the country as a whole is changing. Attorneys General in some of the states without legislation are now ruling that a statute is desirable but not necessary. Illustrating how convinced some administrators now are that legislation is not needed, the Wilmington (Delaware) School Superintendent agreed to collective bargaining despite an adverse ruling by the Delaware State Attorney General. The city's legal advisers sided with the superintendent, so a struggle developed between the old and the new legal views on collective bargaining in government. There are now so many states without legislation where the bargaining nevertheless takes place, without any apparent danger of being stopped by successful court tests, that it seems likely that the newer doctrine will continue to spread. The Georgia State Nurses Association is seeking legislation giving nurses the right to organize and bargain collectively, but meanwhile it maintains that the Georgia Health Code gives both private and public hospitals "broad contractual powers sufficient . . . to contract with the nurses, either individually or collectively."[35]

The union and agency shops

Under the union shop, new employees are required to join the union within a specified time period, frequently 30 days. The Taft-Hartley Act legalizes the union shop except in states that elect to pass laws prohibiting it. Nineteen states now have such "right-to-work" legislation. In an agency shop there is no requirement to join the union, but all employees must pay the union dues. Organizations such as the American Federation of State, County, and Municipal Employees (AFSCME) believe, as do the unions in the private sector, that compulsory member-

[34] See John Ligtenberg and Robert G. Andree, *Collective Bargaining in the Public Schools: A Handbook of Information and Source Materials on Teacher Rights and Teacher Obligations*, Chicago: American Federation of Teachers Educational Foundation, 1966, pp. 188–198.

[35] Christina Bledsoe, "Nurses Push Bargaining for Private, Public Hospitals," *Atlanta Journal and Constitution*, February 9, 1969.

ship is essential to build up the membership and thus strengthen the union in the bargaining sessions with management. If the union shop cannot be obtained, then the agency shop is appropriate, because nonunion members are "free-riders" who pay no dues but benefit from the contract gains won by the exclusive bargaining agent.

The traditional court view has been that the union shop is illegal in the public service in the absence of specific statutory authorization; nonetheless, numerous such agreements are now being signed. For these agreements to be rescinded, they must successfully be challenged in court, but there are few such challenges.

In 1968 the New Hampshire Supreme Court ruled against the Berlin, N.H., police chief when he and two other officers of the city's force questioned a union contract as an "abdication and surrender of municipal sovereignty." The court reasoned that there was no state statute prohibiting the union shop, and emphasized that the union could not cause the discharge of an employee even if it expelled him from union membership so long as he paid the dues.[36] The latter point has long been stressed by labor leaders in the private sector, to erase the widespread misunderstanding that under the union shop they can order the removal from the employer's payroll of dissidents and other members they do not like. Under Taft-Hartley, they cannot. Whether other state supreme courts will rule similarly is impossible to predict; furthermore, there is no evidence of a rush to the courts to invalidate or prevent union shop agreements.

Just a few years ago the agency shop was rare in the public service, but it now is a frequent bargaining demand. AFSCME President Jerry Wurf recently said, " . . . We are now achieving more and more contracts with agency shop clauses."[37] Detroit recently agreed to the agency shop,[38] after a ruling by the Michigan Labor Mediation Board that the agency shop was a mandatory subject for collective bargaining under the state's Public Employment Relations Act.[39] In his testimony before the Johnson review committee, AFL-CIO President Tom Meany asked for the agency shop in the federal service,[40] but no such recommendation appeared in the unofficial, draft report referred to earlier in this chaper.

Binding Arbitration

The thinking about binding arbitration is also changing. Many of the collective agreements now being signed in government

[36] *The Public Employee,* March, 1968, pp. 1, 3.

[37] *The Public Employee,* January, 1969, p. 2.

[38] *The Public Employee,* May, 1968, p. 3.

[39] *The Public Employee,* January, 1968, p. 1.

[40] David R. Jones, "Meany Urges U.S. to Revise Its Labor Policies," *New York Times,* October 24, 1967.

provide for binding arbitration of disagreements over the interpretation and application of the contract terms. Since this means that outside arbitrators can make decisions binding upon the government, the courts have also considered this a surrender of sovereignty, as well as illegal delegation of governmental power to private parties. The counterargument is that governments have long signed contracts with construction companies, suppliers, and others containing clauses for binding arbitration of disputes over compliance with the contract terms. While to labor lawyers this smashes the illegal delegation-of-power argument, others argue that contracts with employee organizations are "different."

A County Circuit Court in Michigan recently ruled that while Michigan did not have a statute expressly permitting or preventing school districts and other public employers from agreeing to binding arbitration, there was the implied power to do so in the Michigan Public Employment Relations Act. The Benton Harbor School District had signed an agreement with a municipal employee union providing for binding arbitration as the final step in the grievance procedure, but when the union requested arbitration of certain grievances, the school board backed out, saying it had no legal authority to submit to arbitration. The court reasoned that if the legislature had intended for the words "collective bargaining" not to embrace binding arbitration within the terms of collective agreements, it could have specifically so stated in the statute. It dismissed the illegal delegation argument as follows:

> This is not a situation of passing to an individual [the arbitrator] the rights and duties of the state legislature or of the board of education of the defendant school district. It is an amicable and more efficient means than resignation, walkout or strike by the employees to resolve any difficulties within a contract previously acceptable to and executed by the parties.[41]

That the views about binding grievance arbitration are changing is also seen in the recommendations of prominent study groups. The Governors' Task Force on State and Local Government Labor Relations recommended it as a "more practical, logical, equitable, and less costly way of settling disputes than the strike."[42] Under the federal program the agencies have been free to refuse to arbitrate grievances, or to accept the arbitrators' decisions. The draft report of the Johnson review committee urges acceptance by both parties of the arbitrators' awards, subject, however, to challenges that would be "sustained only on grounds similar to

41 "Michigan Court Rules in Favor of Grievance Arbitration for Public Employees," *The Public Employee*, November, 1967, p. 5.
42 *Report of Task Force on State and Local Government Labor Relations, op. cit.*, p. 5.

those applied by the courts in private sector labor-management relations."[43]

It is now even maintained that binding settlement of bargaining impasses is legal, which means that the arbitrators in effect determine the tax rate with their salary, wage, and fringe-benefit awards. The recent widely publicized garbage strike in New York City was finally settled only through voluntary referral by both parties to an arbitrator whose decision they agreed in advance to accept. When New York's Mayor Lindsay said that the arbitration was legal, he contradicted previous statements by city officials[44]—but no one could doubt that something had to be done about 100,000 tons of uncollected garbage. Both management and labor usually oppose binding arbitration of bargaining impasses, based on their conviction that it discourages real bargaining. The dangers of strikes in essential services is creating some sentiment, however, for last-resort, agreed-upon binding arbitration.

THE STRIKE QUESTION

The courts have long ruled that public employee strikes are illegal, whether or not prohibited by statute. The reasoning is that such statutes are merely declaratory of the common law. The dominant court view is that such strikes are against the people themselves and therefore cannot be tolerated.

Before the end of World War II, the only anti-strike legislation consisted of local ordinances and some state laws applying only to certain classes of employees. After the war ended there were major strikes in private industry, as well as a "rash of public employee strikes."[45] This led to inclusion of a provision in the Taft-Hartley Act (1947) making it illegal for federal employees to strike, under penalty of immediate removal, loss of civil service status, and a three-year ban against reemployment. This Taft-Hartley provision was repealed by Public Law 84-330, passed on August 9, 1955, which makes it a felony for federal employees to strike or assert the right to do so, the penalty being a fine of not more than $1000 or imprisonment of not more than one year and a day, or both.

Beginning with Virginia in 1946, some 18 states have passed legislation prohibiting strikes by all state and local government employees; in two other states the prohibition covers state employees only. One state outlaws strikes in the political subdivisions only, and in several other states the strike ban is restricted to particular kinds of employees (policemen, firemen, teachers).[46] The collective bargaining laws mentioned at the beginning of this

[43] Special Supplement, Bureau of National Affairs, op. cit., p. 4.
[44] Maurice Carroll, "Arbitration Plan Lauded by Mayor As Breakthrough," New York Times, February 19, 1968.
[45] Public Employee Labor Relations, Springfield, Ill.: Illinois Legislative Council, November, 1958, p. 6.
[46] Report of Task Force on State and Local Government Labor Relations, op cit., pp. 89–90.

chapter typically contain offsetting anti-strike provisions, so this has added to the total. In these state laws the "prevalent pattern is to secure compliance by a threat of discharge . . ."[47]; later reinstatement is permitted, but the employee must serve a substantial period of time under a new probationary period and without salary increases.

Changed attitude of employee organizations

Despite the anti-strike legislation, public employees are now much less willing than in the past to commit themselves to a policy of *never* striking. Not only do some of the AFL-CIO affiliated groups claim the ultimate right to strike, but some of the independent organizations have recently dropped their anti-strike pledges.

The AFSCME, whose position on this matter is the same as that of the AFL-CIO Executive Council, insists that the strike is necessary as a "final-resort" weapon to be used "only under the most extreme provocation" or when the "employer acts in an irresponsible manner"; however, it is against strikes by police and other law enforcement officers. In the private sector, it is accepted—and, of course, the law—that collective bargaining, by definition, includes the right to strike. So it is not surprising that labor-affiliated government unions should reason that they also should possess this ultimate weapon. Until the recent "militancy," however, they, along with the other public employee organizations, generally did not assert the right to strike, although "before 1940 there had already been more than 1000 authenticated cases of actual strikes by public employees,"[48] and at least 743 government strikes during the years 1942–1961.[49]

Now some of the nonlabor affiliated groups agree that the employee representatives cannot have real strength at the bargaining table if the management knows they cannot or will not call a strike. They are particularly resentful that there seems to be no reward for their not threatening walkouts; indeed, they are punished for their loyalty because the unions which threaten to strike, and do, get better settlements for their members.

The International Association of Fire Fighters, the Civil Service Employees Association in New York State, the California Nurses Association, and the Los Angeles County Employees Association—all with large memberships—have recently dropped their no-strike pledges. While this does not put them in the same camp on the strike issue as such AFL-CIO affiliates as the AFSCME and the AFT, it gives warning that for them strikes no longer are out of the question. The National Education Association (NEA),

[47] *Public Employee Labor Relations, op. cit.,* p. 7.

[48] Donald Gallagher, "The Legal Aspects of Collective Bargaining for California Public Employees," Sacramento: California State Employees Association, November, 1959, p. 26.

[49] U.S. Department of Labor, Bureau of Labor Statistics, BLS Report No. 247, *Work Stoppages, Government Employees, 1942–61,* Washington, D.C., 1963.

which for years distinguished itself from the AFT by supporting "professional sanctions" instead of strikes, now supports strikes, and in fact quite a few of the teacher walkouts are by NEA affiliates.[50]

In the federal service, the United Federation of Postal Clerks, the National Postal Union, the National Alliance of Postal and Federal Employees, and the National Association of Government Employees have also eliminated the no-strike clauses from their constitutions. The definition of "employee organization" in Executive Order 10988 excludes organizations asserting the right to strike; furthermore, any strike activity is proscribed under the Code of Fair Labor Practices. The aforementioned organizations that have removed the no-strike pledges from their constitutions have kept their recognition and other rights under the Order because they have not *asserted* the right to strike. Very few walkouts have taken place in the federal service; the principal walkout was a jurisdictional strike in August, 1962, by some 80 TVA sheetmetal workers. They were dismissed. In October, 1968, there was a four-day strike of 50 cafeteria workers (called by the Laundry and Dry Cleaners Union, AFL-CIO) at the Hunters Point naval shipyard in San Francisco.[51] Yet the "militant mood of postal workers" influenced the Post Office Department in the summer of 1968 to distribute to regional directors and postmasters at first-class offices a four-page Contingency Plan for Work Stoppages.[52] There seems to be no immediate danger of federal service strikes to the same extent as in state and local government, but some people are predicting that eventually this will happen.

The experience with anti-strike legislation

Recent events such as the teachers strikes in New York City in the fall of 1968 continue strongly to suggest that anti-strike legislation is ineffective. Not all people agree, for some think such statutes have failed because they lacked certain provisions. Let us examine New York State's experience because it provides a good case study.

THE CASE OF NEW YORK STATE

In 1947, after a teachers' strike in Buffalo, the New York state legislature, at the request of Governor Dewey, passed a statute (the Condon-Wadlin Act) containing penalties that Dewey considered "moderate but firm."[53] In practice, however, these penalties proved too drastic to make the anti-strike ban effective. The

[50] On sanctions, see Stinnett, Kleinmann, and Ware, *op. cit.*, pp. 121–151.

[51] *Federal Times*, November 6, 1968.

[52] Court Gifford, "Post Office Maps Anti-Strike Action," *Federal Times*, September 25, 1968.

[53] New York State Joint Legislative Committee on Industrial and Labor Relations, *Report, 1960–1961*, Legislative Document (1961), No. 17, Albany, New York: 1961, p. 32.

punishment was to dismiss any employee who participated in a strike; he could be reemployed, but not at a salary higher than the one he was making immediately prior to violating the law. Furthermore, his pay could not be increased until three years after reemployment, and he had to serve a new probationary period of five years.

The law proved ineffective because employees in important services knew the public employer was in no position to fire all of them if they went out on strike. In its entire 20-year history, the Condon-Wadlin penalties were invoked in very few cases. The 12-day subway strike which began on New Year's Eve, 1966, demonstrated the impracticality of the legislation; there were no qualified persons in sufficient number available whom the Transit Authority could have employed as replacements. As part of the settlement, the Transit Authority agreed not to invoke the Condon-Wadlin penalties against the strikers, but a taxpayer sued to force the courts to apply the penalties. Obviously no one wanted another subway shutdown, so the state legislature hurriedly approved "forgiveness legislation" retroactively exempting the strikers from Condon-Wadlin penalties.[54]

After the subway strike, Governor Rockefeller appointed a panel headed by Professor George W. Taylor of the University of Pennsylvania to make recommendations for new legislation. For many months after release of this group's report, differences of opinion between the Democrats and Republicans in the legislature prevented passage of a new law. Finally, in the last hours of the 1967 legislative session, the Public Employees' Fair Employment Act of that year was approved.[55] The new statute (also known as the Taylor Law) followed one of the main recommendations of the Rockefeller panel: the strike penalties should be shifted from the employees to the unions. While employees who went out on strike were made subject to disciplinary action, including dismissal, the principal penalty was a court fine against the union equal in amount to one week's dues collections from its members, or $10,000, whichever was less, for each day of a strike. Union leaders disobeying court orders were made subject to a fine of not more than $250, or to imprisonment for not more than 30 days, or to both.

TESTS OF THE 1967 ACT. The first test of the Taylor Law came quickly. In the fall of 1967, New York City schoolteachers struck for 14 days. Although the city's Corporation Counsel, in accordance with the new law, requested the State Supreme Court to punish the United Federation of Teachers (UFT), and although

[54] For a complete account of the subway strike, see Nigro, *op. cit.*, pp. 53–75.

[55] Public Employees' Fair Employment Act, Chapter 392 of the Laws of 1967 of the State of New York.

Supreme Court Justice Emilio Nunez rejected the UFT's contention that the teachers had merely resigned en masse and that a strike was not in progress, Nunez recessed the court hearings several times in order to allow UFT President Albert Shanker to return to the bargaining table. Obviously, at this stage the judge thought the important thing was to get the strike settled, not to punish Shanker and the UFT.

After the teachers returned to work, Shanker was fined $250 and sentenced to 15 days in jail, and the UFT was fined $150,000. This amounted to about $3 a member, so it did not hurt the union very much. More serious to the UFT was the loss of the dues checkoff privileges for a period of 18 months, ordered by the Public Employment Relations Board pursuant to another provision of the new legislation. It proved very costly for the UFT to make arrangements through a private computer service to bill the teachers directly, but the clear message of the whole episode was that the new penalties had not in the slightest deterred the UFT from striking.[56]

The schoolteacher strikes in the fall of 1968, in the emotion-charged atmosphere of the school decentralization controversy, again evidenced the ineffectiveness of the 1967 legislation. This time the UFT was fined $220,000, and Shanker was again fined and served another 15-day jail sentence. AFL-CIO President George Meany announced that the AFL-CIO would raise the money to pay the fine. State Supreme Court Justice Bloustein, who levied the fine, said he could have made it $620,000, in view of the duration of the strikes, but had not done so because of the "extreme provocation" for the strike by representatives of the city's Board of Education and others "in official office."[57]

There was a more profound message from the 1968 strikes: the opposing parties were too deeply divided by disagreements over fundamental principles for the normal give-and-take of the collective bargaining process to take place. In bargaining over economic benefits, there is much room for maneuver; management, for example, can offer more fringe benefits to induce the union to lower its wage demands. Compromise *is* possible and *does* take place. Between the position of the governing board of the Ocean Hill-Brownsville experimental school and all the groups strongly supporting community control of the schools, and on the other hand the determination of the UFT to fight to the finish to protect the job rights of the teachers, very little bargaining could take place. As A. H. Raskin, the *New York Times* labor editor, wrote:

---

[56] See Nigro, *op. cit.*, pp. 117–118.

[57] Joseph A. Loftus, "Labor Federation to Raise $220,000 for U.F.T. Fine," *New York Times*, February 5, 1969.

The Bloustein decision amounted to a confession of judical impotence to administer true justice in a situation growing out of profound social upheaval, where the penalties available by law were all against one side, but the guilt for forcing things to the explosion point was universal. . . .

Fear was the engine on both sides—union fear of a destruction of job security and a takeover of the schools by black extremists, community fear of a union desire to wreck school decentralization and strip parents of any effective voice in running their neighborhood schools. To Justice Bloustein, the tragedy was that nobody in authority used the year or more in which deep trouble was brewing to set up the necessary machinery for adjustment and reconciliation.[58]

ROCKEFELLER'S NEW PROPOSALS.   Before the 1968 New York City school strikes, Governor Rockefeller had argued that two or three years of additional experience with the Taylor Law were needed before any changes should be made in it. In November, 1968, there were strikes at four state mental hospitals, the first strikes of state employees during Rockefeller's governorship. When the Republicans gained control of both houses of the legislature, and legislative sentiment for more effective curbs on public employee strikes increased, the Governor recommended removing the ceiling on the fines, so that the judges could levy any amount per day they saw fit. He also made a number of other recommendations to improve the dispute-settlement procedure, but it was clear that he had decided on a tougher approach toward the unions.[59] Labor experts such as the well-known mediator Theodore W. Kheel did not think that the unlimited fines would have much effect. Kheel had argued all along that the mere inclusion of an anti-strike provision in effect dares the unions to strike, and that the soundest approach is the positive one of trying to improve the bargaining process. Feeling in the legislature against public employee strikes was so strong, however, that a new law was hastily passed providing not only for unlimited fines against the unions but also for financial penalties against individual strikers.

EXPERIENCE ELSEWHERE

In general, the experience with anti-strike laws in other states, such as Ohio with its Ferguson Act, has been the same as in New York. The best indication of this is the way the judges are following something of a pattern in first trying to get the strikes settled, then punishing the strikers and/or the union. As Arthur J. Goldberg has said, there is no magic formula for settling

[58] A. H. Raskin, "A Tougher Law is Only a Partial Answer," New York Times, editorial section, Feb. 9, 1969. Also see Martin Mayer, The Teachers Strike New York 1968 New York: Perennial Library, Harper & Row, 1968.
[59] Ibid.

strikes, either in the private or public sector.[60] The best that can be done is to remove the conditions that might cause them, and to provide the best machinery available for settling those disputes that do pose strike threats.

COLLECTIVE BARGAINING AND THE MERIT SYSTEM

Is collective bargaining compatible with the merit system? This question is critical, because if the price of collective bargaining is the discarding of the basic principles fought for by the civil service reformers, then many people would say that collective bargaining, whatever its good points, was not worth it.

In analyzing this problem, it is first necessary to have a clear understanding of the word "merit" in the civil service context. In practice, merit systems—meaning the programs of civil service agencies—have often been unimaginative, inflexible, and unresponsive to the real needs of the employees. Outmoded policies and procedures, actually harmful to the employees, have been perpetuated in the name of "merit." The staunchest defenders of civil service do not deny that "merit systems" have often failed to live up to their promise. They agree that many of the procedures and requirements are unnecessary and even self-defeating, but they are concerned that some public employee union leaders would eliminate the merit principle itself—that of hiring and promoting only the best qualified persons.

Points of conflict

Let us analyze the different points of potential and actual conflict between collective bargaining and "merit," as defined above, namely, competitive ranking of the candidates.

Since union and agency shops create requirements unrelated to qualifications for the job, (that is, union membership or at least payment of the union dues), they conflict with the merit principle as traditionally conceived. The employee organizations have able theoreticians of their own arguing that, since the union and agency shops make the union strong in terms of members and financial resources, the long-run effect will be to increase the employees' voice and thus to improve the merit system. For example, the stronger the union, the more effective it will be in improving pay and fringe benefits. The employee leaders ask, "How can you call this a merit system when the pay is so unfair compared with private rates for the same jobs?" In truth, the

[60] Arthur J. Goldberg, address to the Seminar on Collective Bargaining of the Federal Mediation and Conciliation Service, Washington, D.C., January 9, 1967. Unpublished.

union shop does not seem to have done the damage many people feared. It was expected that many new and present employees would refuse to join the union and thus have to give up their jobs. With few exceptions, however, they are joining the union, often expecting it to do more for them than "civil service." In Philadelphia, which has a modified union shop, Personnel Director Foster B. Roser reports that relatively few employees use the "escape" clause that permits them to drop out of the union at a certain time each year. When they do leave the union, usually it is because they believe it has not done enough for them.[61]

To many of the employee leaders, civil service is synonymous with unilateralism and paternalism, which means the "boss," no matter how well-intentioned, imposes his rule on the employees. Because they are appointed by the "boss" (governor, mayor, or other chief executive), civil service commissioners are viewed as "management-oriented"; in a showdown, they almost always back up the supervisors and agency heads, as in disciplinary hearings. Binding arbitration of grievances by outside arbitrators is the only guarantee of justice. Essentially, under civil service, the "boss" decides how fair he has been to the employee. The position of some of the labor-affiliated unions apparently is that ultimately civil service should be limited to initial hiring of employees; all other phases of the personnel system, or most all, would be governed by collective contracts. The goal seems to be to make as many aspects of the personnel system as possible subject to bargaining and thus inclusion in the contracts. Unions seem to recognize, however, that the complete replacement of civil service statutes and rules by such contracts is unlikely.

The labor-affiliated unions do not all have exactly the same attitudes toward civil service; the American Federation of State, County, and Municipal Employees, for example, is more critical than some of the others. The independent associations, while dissatisfied in many respects with the accomplishments of merit systems, generally tend to identify with the civil service movement; in many cases, they oppose outright the introduction of industrial-type collective bargaining in the public service.

WHICH ITEMS SHOULD BE BARGAINED?

The difficult question is which phases of merit systems should be determined by collective bargaining and which should not be so determined. There is much support for negotiation of salaries, wages, and fringe benefits, although, as we have seen, these are not subject to bargaining at the federal level and likely will not be for the foreseeable future. Although it is still early and much

[61] See Nigro, *op. cit.*, p. 96.

research still needs to be done, clearly the introduction of collective bargaining has brought substantial improvements in the pay of teachers, nurses, law enforcement officers, and other underpaid public employees. The principle of salary standardization suffers, however, when pay scales are determined by the strength of the different unions at the bargaining table. While the union spokesmen support the principle of "equal pay for equal work," they naturally try to get the best pay possible for the particular groups of employees they represent. Furthermore, the same union is not always the bargaining agent for the same kinds of workers in *all* departments; thus the rates negotiated in one department may be different from those in another.

As to recruitment, promotions, grievances, and other aspects of the personnel program, it all depends upon the particular policy or procedure. There is so much disagreement on some matters, even among experts, that it seems indefensible to refuse to open them to negotiation. An example is the length of the probationary period. So long as whether or not there is a probationary period is not bargainable, there is little danger that negotiating its length would damage the merit system. The same can be said for details of the promotion, reduction-in-force, and other procedures. The grievance procedure is another example, provided the employee cannot grieve such basic merit determinations as the requirement for ranking candidates on promotion registers according to ability, as determined by written tests and other measurement devices.

The insistence of many of the employee organizations on seniority as the basis for promotions represents, in the opinion of this author, the greatest threat to the merit principle. Some of the agreements now being signed in government provide that the promotion shall go to the most senior qualified man, with "qualified" defined to mean meeting the *minimum* qualifications only. With all their deficiencies, civil service agencies generally have not promoted on so indiscriminating a basis. While they have given weight to seniority—perhaps too much weight—they have required competition between all those candidates who meet the minimum qualifications, just as in initial recruitment. Research evidence shows that really good workers perform far better than those who simply meet minimum standards.

THE REAL CHALLENGE

The viewpoints of the employee organizations on the merit system are still in the process of formation. Within the unions themselves there is lack of consistency in the statements of the various officials. For the country as a whole, it does not appear that the collective bargaining process has done much damage to basic merit principles. The threat of such damage, however, clearly exists. The challenge is to infuse merit systems with the dynamic element of collective dealings, but at the same time to preserve the basic principle of recruitment and promotion of the best-qualified individuals.

CODETERMINATION OF POLICY

Collective bargaining is not only changing public personnel administration, but it is also influencing the administrative policy-making process. The employee organizations do not solely seek participation in the determination of personnel policies. Increasingly, they want to extend the bargaining to program questions such as the work of the agency. Experience in the private sector clearly reveals that there is a dynamic to collective bargaining, namely, to make more and more subjects, previously considered "management prerogatives," subject to negotiation. The same dynamic is now apparent as collective bargaining progresses in government; again there are benefits and perils.

Examples of codetermination

In quite a few school districts it is now established practice to negotiate such aspects of the instructional program as maximum class size limits, teacher preparation periods, teacher participation in textbook selection, and even the school calendar. Social workers have been successful in obtaining contracts with maximum caseload limits, and nurses have secured pacts with limitations on the nonnursing duties to which they can be assigned. Some contracts make management and the union jointly responsible for the planning and conduct of in-service training programs.

All of the above have a clear justification, although many administrators, pressed by budgetary limitations, would prefer not to have to negotiate such matters as class size and caseload limits. The employee organizations have many good ideas, and they perform a very useful function in stimulating management to improve the agency's program. The problem is how far management can and should go in agreeing to negotiate program questions. When social workers in New York City wanted to negotiate the clothing and other allowances to be received by welfare families, the Welfare Commissioner pointed out that he did not have the authority to do so, since these disbursements are controlled by federal and state regulations. He could consult, but not negotiate, with the employees on such matters; he would be abdicating his responsibility for the welfare program if he agreed to codetermination in these areas.[62]

The same problem arose when the New York Patrolman's Benevolent Association wanted a contract guarantee that patrol cars would be staffed with two men. The Association was worried that the Police Department might return to the practice of assigning only one man to each car, a practice that had been abandoned when police fell "easy prey to thugs in some neighborhoods."[63] The Police Commissioner refused to bargain this question, on the ground that it was management's responsibility, not the employees', to decide how to carry out the police function.

The trouble is that the policies desired by some employee groups would not be in the public interest. Some firemen in New York City moonlight, taking off-duty jobs in the neighborhoods where their fire stations are located. The Fire Commissioner started a new policy of shifting companies from lower Manhattan to nighttime duty in heavily populated areas such as Brownsville and the Bedford-Stuyvesant section of Brooklyn. His reasoning was that after business hours some of the fire equipment in the business district could be spared and used to make fire prevention more effective in other parts of the city. The Uniformed Firemen's Association protested the new policy, because the firemen did not want to leave the neighborhoods in which they had obtained these part-time jobs. The *New York Times* strongly supported the Fire Commissioner for refusing to agree to bargain the deployment of fire companies and equipment throughout the city.[64]

Thus, while codetermination can breathe new life into many programs, it can also damage others. Many management rights have been preserved in industry; public management should hold the line at certain vital boundary points beyond which it is convinced that codetermination would not serve the best interests of the citizens.

[62] Thomas R. Brooks, "The Caseworker and the Client," *New York Times Sunday Magazine*, January 29, 1967, 73.

[63] *New York Times*, October 11, 1966.

[64] *New York Times*, editorial, September 9, 1966.

BIBLIOGRAPHY

Bureau of National Affairs, Inc., *Government Employee Relations Report*, Washington, D.C. 20037: 1231 25th St., N.W. Weekly publication.

Committee on Manpower and Labor Relations, National Governors' Conference, *1968 Supplement to Report of Task*

Force on State and Local Government Labor Relations,
Chicago: Public Personnel Association, 1968.

Hart, Wilson R., *Collective Bargaining in the Federal Service,*
New York: Harper & Row, 1961.

Lieberman, Myron, and Moskow, Michael H., *Collective Nego-
tiatons for Teachers: An Approach to School Administration,* Chicago: Rand McNally, 1966.

McCart, John A., Murphy, Richard J., and Nigro, Felix A.,
Labor-Management Relations—Where Do We Stand?" *Civil
Service Journal, VIII,* No. 1 (July-September, 1967).

Moskow, Michael, *Teachers and Unions,* Philadelphia: University
of Pennsylvania, Wharton School of Finance and Commerce,
1966.

Nigro, Felix A., (ed.), "Collective Negotiations in the Public
Service," Symposium, *Public Administration Review, XXVIII,*
No. 2 (March-April, 1968).

Nigro, Felix A., *Management-Employee Relations in the Public
Service,* Chicago: Public Personnel Association, 1969.

Perry, Charles R., and Wildman, Wesley A., "A Survey of Collective Activity Among Public School Teachers," *Educational Administration Quarterly,* University Council for Educational Administration, Ohio State University, *II,* No. 2
(Spring, 1966).

President's Task Force on Employee-Management Relations in
the Federal Service, *Report of the President's Task Force on
Employee-Management Relations in the Federal Service,*
November 30, 1961. Washington, D.C.: Government Printing Office, December, 1961.

Public Employee Relations Library, Chicago: Public Personnel
Association. First issue published in 1968. A series of studies
and reports on employee-management relations in government.

*Report of Task Force on State and Local Government Labor
Relations, 1967: Executive Committee, National Governors'
Conference,* Chicago: Public Personnel Association, 1967.

*Report of the Preparatory Committee on Collective Bargaining in
the Public Service,* Ottawa: Queen's Printer, July, 1965.

Research Division, National Education Association, *Negotiation
Research Digest.* Published 10 times a year. Reports developments in collective bargaining in public education.

Shils, Edward B., and Whittier, C. Taylor, *Teachers, Administrators, and Collective Bargaining,* New York: Crowell, 1968.

Somers, Gerald E., (ed.), *Collective Bargaining in the Public*

Service, Proceedings of the 1966 Annual Spring Meeting, Industrial Relations Research Association, Madison, Wisc., 1966.

Stinnett, T. M., Kleinmann, Jack H., and Ware, Martha L., *Professional Negotiation in Public Education,* New York: Macmillan, 1966.

Warner, Kenneth O., (ed.), *Collective Bargaining in the Public Service: Theory and Practice,* Chicago: Public Personnel Association, 1967.

Warner, Kenneth O., and Hennessey, Mary L., *Public Management at the Bargaining Table,* Chicago: Public Personnel Association, 1967.

Van de Water, John R., "Union-Management Relations in Public and Private Education," *The Journal of the College and University Personnel Association,* XVII, No. 1 (November, 1965).

Vosloo, Willem B., *Collective Bargaining in the United States Federal Civil Service,* Chicago: Public Personnel Association, 1966.

PART V
FINANCIAL ADMINISTRATION

CHAPTER 16
RESPONSIBILITY
FOR FINANCIAL
ADMINISTRATION

F INANCIAL ADMINISTRATION is of special importance today for the simple reason that
while there seems to be no limit to what we
may ask of government, there is always a
limit to the funds available. Determining the spending priorities
and finding the money is difficult enough in peacetime, particularly when domestic wars, such as that against poverty, are being
waged. There are backlogs of urgently needed projects, with the
rising expectations of the people creating pressures for massive
programs and quick results. The financial pinch created by the
Vietnam War has made the determination of financial policies and
budget decisions particularly vexatious. New techniques are being
developed to improve financial administration, such as planning-
programming-budgeting, which is given extensive treatment in
the next chapter. In the immediate years ahead, it is likely that
financial practices of the national, state, and local governments
will undergo some very significant changes.

The components of financial administration are budgeting,
accounting, auditing, purchase and supply management, tax ad-

ministration, and treasury management. The last two are specialized fields of administration not appropriate for detailed treatment in an introductory textbook. Broadly speaking, financial administration also includes fiscal policy and the government's role with respect to economic stabilization. Since courses in public finance take up these problems from a substantive standpoint, we will be concerned with them only in terms of the adequacy of the budget and accounting systems as tools for carrying out whatever economic policies the government adopts.

ASSIGNMENT OF FINANCE FUNCTIONS

Finance functions should be so assigned as to promote coordination of effort, under the general direction of the chief executive (President, governor, or mayor). The chief executive should have a financial plan for the entire jurisdiction; he should control the preparation and execution of the budget, as well as the financial reporting and related systems for measuring program accomplishment. He cannot be expected to carry out this overall responsibility without a competent, well-organized finance organization under him. Although good results are not necessarily guaranteed by sound organization arrangements, past history demonstrates that certain errors in assigning finance responsibilities create serious problems and prevent effective executive leadership.

Adoption of the executive budget, meaning one controlled by the chief executive, did not take place in the federal government until 1921 with the passage of the Budget and Accounting Act.[1] The executive budget was introduced in some state and municipal governments before then; it is now found in most of them.[2] In many states and cities, however, the legislators participate in one way or another in the formulation of the budget, thus weakening the chief executive's role. In numerous county and rural governments, the governing body prepares the budget; for example, in many counties a committee of the board of supervisors receives expenditure estimates directly from the department heads and puts together the budget. In these jurisdictions there is no one administrative officer responsible for the budget, and its execution, once approved, is left to the spending departments.[3] The legislature should have a strong role in reviewing the chief executive's budget and in making its own independent evaluations of program results achieved by the spending agencies.[4] The executive budget does not mean executive domination, with no real role for the legislators. Rather, it is based on the principle

[1] For the text of this Act and important financial legislation later passed by Congress, see *Financial Management in the Federal Government*, 87th Congress, 1st Session, Senate Document No. 11, Washington, D.C.: Government Printing Office, 1961. Part VIII: "Appendixes," pp. 275–369.

[2] See *State Expenditure Controls: An Evaluation*, New York: Tax Foundation, Inc., 1965, pp. 18–27, and Jesse Burkhead, *Government Budgeting*, New York: Wiley, 1956, pp. 12–29.

[3] Burkhead, *Ibid.*, p. 86.

[4] See *Budgeting for National Objectives*, New York: Committee for Economic Development, 1966, pp. 41–49.

of executive leadership, which means entrusting the formulation of the estimates, and the execution of the budget, as approved by the legislature, to the chief executive. In this way the legislature is better able to hold him to account for any deficiencies in financial procedures, as well as for disappointing program results.

Besides the failure to establish executive responsibility, now largely corrected, there has been an unfortunate history of scattering of finance functions, with consequent duplication and lack of coordination. A strong belief in "checks and balances" led many state and municipal governments to assign parts of the finance responsibility to a number of different elective officials, each independent of one another and none subject to effective control by the chief executive of the jurisdiction. The theory was that these officials would watch over one another, to the resultant benefit of the public. This scheme for enforcing accountability through divided responsibility and the ballot box did not prove effective; in practice, these independent finance officials "were able to detect only the gross violations of fiscal provisions, so crude were their methods and records in most cases."[5] Before the second decade of this century there was no real financial administration, meaning efficient procedures and concentrated responsibility, in most state and municipal governments.

THE INTEGRATED FINANCE DEPARTMENT

Beginning around 1913, some city and state governments acted to concentrate responsibility for financial administration in an integrated department of finance, placed under the direct control of the chief executive. It was during this period that the concept of financial administration as part of management planning began to emerge. The public was requesting expanded public services, the tax burden was rising, and it was no longer possible to tolerate poor financial practices and waste in government. Professional reform groups joined with the business community in demanding honest, efficient financial administration. Budget offices were created for the first time, and progress was made in correcting the diffusion of finance responsibilities. Since achievement of the goal of an integrated finance department was delayed in many jurisdictions, efforts toward that end are still being pushed vigorously in many parts of the country.

Today most governmental experts recommend the creation of such departments, as shown in Figure 10, which is based on the Model City Charter of the National Municipal League.[6] This document is often consulted by charter-review and other groups

[5] *Municipal Finance Administration*, Washington, D.C.: International City Managers' Association, 1962, p. 21. For an example, see Margaret G. Oslund, "The Guardians of La Loma," in Frederick C. Mosher (ed.), *Governmental Reorganizations: Cases and Commentary*, Indianapolis, Ind.: Bobbs-Merrill, 1967, pp. 375–376.

[6] *Model City Charter*, Fifth edition, New York: National Municipal League, 1941, pp. 36–45. The sixth edition (1964) does not give the internal organization of the municipal departments; it is recommended that their detail be embodied in an administrative code. The principle of the integrated finance department is still favored, however.

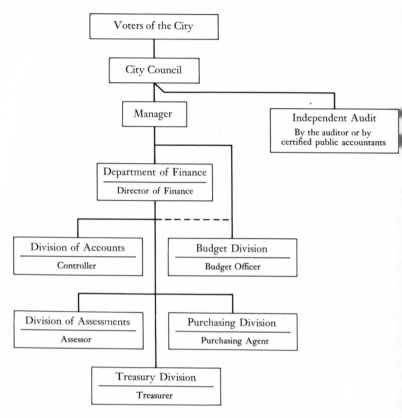

Fig. 10. Organization chart, Department of Finance. Based on Model City Charter Plan (Large City). From Municipal Finance Administration, Chicago: International City Managers Association, 1962, p. 23.

charged with making proposals for changes in existing municipal governments or for establishing new ones. Reviewing the essential elements of this plan, we see that it clearly establishes the responsibility of the city manager as the chief executive for finance matters. In mayor-council cities, the same principle would be followed, with the department of finance under the mayor. The department is broken down into five divisions: accounts, budget, assessments, purchasing, and treasury. The department head is appointed by the manager and serves at his pleasure; division chiefs are selected by the department head. In smaller cities, some of the functions, such as accounting and budgeting, would probably be combined.

Some cities prefer to place the budget staff directly in the chief executive's office. It is argued that this is necessary to ensure that the chief executive maintains as close control as possible over the budget function. In other cities, effective working relationships have been established between the chief executive and the budget staff in the Department of Finance. Either plan for location of the budget function may work satisfactorily, depending on the circumstances in the particular jurisdiction.

In a state government an integrated finance department would have the following bureaus or divisions: (1) budget, (2) accounting, (3) treasury, and (4) purchasing. In smaller states the department might also include a division of taxation to administer the state tax system; in the larger states, a separate tax department would be required. While several states have located the budget function directly in the governor's office, this generally is the case when no integrated finance department exists. When one is established, the budget staff is usually transferred to it.[7]

ARRANGEMENTS AT THE NATIONAL LEVEL

In the national government there is no one department in which the principal finance functions are placed. When originally created in 1921 by the Budget and Accounting Act, the Bureau of the Budget was placed in the Treasury Department. Franklin D. Roosevelt's Committee on Administrative Management recommended that it be placed directly under the President, so that it could be coordinated with other staff services, and it was transferred in 1939 to the newly formed Executive Office of the President. Since then there has been no strong movement to return it to the Treasury, although this was recommended by a Task Force of the first Hoover Commission.

This Task Force wanted the Treasury Department to "be so reorganized that it would be a real department of finance."[8] All nonfiscal units, such as the Coast Guard, the Bureau of Narcotics, and the Secret Service, were to be transferred to other departments. The reorganized Treasury Department would be responsible only for genuine finance functions, on an integrated basis. In addition to budgeting, it would have control over the administrative accounting system of the government. This would have meant removing this function from the General Accounting Office (GAO), a change that has never been made and could only

[7] *Model State Constitution,* fifth edition, New York: National Municipal League, 1948, pp. 40–44. In the sixth edition, published in 1963, the detailed structure of the administrative branch is left to be determined by statute.

[8] Commission on Organization of the Executive Branch of the Government, *Task Force Report on Fiscal, Budgeting, and Accounting Activities,* Washington, D.C.: Government Printing Office, 1949, p. 2.

be accomplished by amending the Budget and Accounting Act of 1921, which established both the Budget Bureau and the GAO. The Treasury Department would retain its responsibility for collection of taxes, custody and disbursement of funds, operation of the Mint and the Bureau of Engraving and Printing, and management of the debt. These recommendations were accepted by neither the Hoover Commission nor Congress. The Treasury Department still retains the aforementioned nonfiscal functions, except for the Coast Guard, which in 1967 was made a part of the new Department of Transportation; the Treasury Department has neither gained nor lost any finance functions.

Purchasing and supply in the federal government originally was also a responsibility of the Treasury Department, but it is now one of the functions of the General Services Administration (GSA), which was established in 1949, largely as the result of a recommendation of the first Hoover Commission. It is responsible for providing a variety of general administrative services to the other agencies. (We will be concerned with its purchase and supply operations in Chapter 19.) Among its other responsibilities are those for the national archives, records administration, public buildings, and transportation and communications services. The GSA is not a part of the Executive Office of the President. It is one of numerous independent offices and establishments, responsible directly to the President. Proposals have been made to place it in the Executive Office where it could be integrated with other staff services, but there seems to be no immediate prospect that such action will be taken. It has clearly been established, however, that the President has overall responsibility within the executive branch for financial planning and administration. Better arrangements for the financial functions under him may be made in the future, but the basic problems of finance in the federal government today are not questions of internal assignment of responsibilities within the executive branch. The fundamental need is for improvements in the financial-planning process itself, a subject dealt with in succeeding chapters.

BIBLIOGRAPHY

Budgeting for National Objectives, New York: Committee for Economic Development, 1966.

Commission on Organization of the Executive Branch of the Government, *Task Force Report on Fiscal, Budgeting, and Ac-*

counting Activities, Washington, D.C.: Government Printing Office, 1949.

Financial Management in the Federal Government, 87th Congress, 1st Session, Senate Document No. 11, Washington, D.C.: Government Printing Office, 1961.

Harris, Joseph P., *Congressional Control of Administration*, Garden City, New York: Doubleday, 1964. Chapter 3.

International City Managers' Association, *Municipal Finance Administration*, Chicago, Ill.: 1962. Chapter 2.

Lepawsky, Albert, (ed.), *Administration, the Art and Science of Organization and Management*, New York: Knopf, 1949. Chapter 15.

National Municipal League, *Model City Charter*, New York, 1941.

National Municipal League, *Model State Constitution*, New York, 1948.

Nigro, Felix A., (ed.), *Public Administration, Readings and Documents*, New York: Holt, Rinehart and Winston, 1951. Chapter V.

President's Committee on Administrative Management, *Report with Special Studies*, Washington, D.C.: Government Printing Office, 1937.

CHAPTER 17
CONCEPTS
OF BUDGETING

T HE EXECUTIVE budget is only the beginning step; in and of itself it does not answer the questions: What kind of budget shall be prepared? What purposes shall it serve? The chief executive can lead, but his comprehension of the uses of the budget may be too limited or otherwise deficient. Frequently budgets are defined as work plans, but, as we shall see, there are different conceptions of what is meant by a work plan. Budgetary concepts are not fixed; they evolve in accordance with new needs. As indicated in the previous chapter, the present period is one of important reformulations of budgetary objectives.

THE HISTORICAL BACKGROUND

The control emphasis

In general, the first executive budgets in the United States placed primary emphasis on controlling expenditures, to prevent overspending, waste, and misuse of the taxpayers' money.[1] A good

[1] See Allen Schick, "The Road to PPB: The Stages of Budget Reform," in "Planning-Programming-Budgeting System: A Symposium," *Public Administration Review*, XXVI, No. 4 (December, 1966), 243–258.

budget system should meet several objectives, and expenditure control certainly is one of them. The question is one of emphasis; despite the advocacy of the executive budget as the vehicle for making budgets meaningful statements of work programs, in practice this objective usually was relegated to the background because of the pressures to develop the protections mentioned above.

The budget-reform movement was a crusade against dishonest and loose financial practices. Overspending was common in the absence of orderly budget procedures and systematic expenditure controls, and legislatures were frequently requested to grant deficiency appropriations. When public treasuries were full and citizen demands for services could be met without great difficulty, these conditions could be tolerated, much as they were disliked by many people. With the attainment of the executive budget, however, public expectation was that immediate steps should be taken to institute and enforce controls to eliminate past spending abuses. Another factor is that the introduction of the first executive budgets was quickly followed by the post-World War I emphasis upon "normalcy" and economies in government. In this atmosphere, keeping expenditures down, rather than reshaping the budget to make it an instrument of forward work planning, was the pragmatic approach for political leaders.

This description applies to all levels of government; possibly the most striking evidence is Charles G. Dawes' statement that "the Bureau of the Budget is concerned only with the humbler and routine business of Government" and "with no question of policy, save that of economy and efficiency."[2] Dawes was the first director of the Bureau. Furthermore, the national government did not conceive of the budget as a vital instrument for fiscal planning to stabilize economic conditions and promote full employment. Interestingly, in 1887 President Cleveland had warned Congress that the large surpluses brought in by the protective tariff were making the Treasury "a hoarding place for money needlessly withdrawn from trade and the people's use, thus crippling our national energies . . . and inviting schemes of public plunder."[3]

LINE ITEM BUDGETING AND OBJECTS OF EXPENDITURE

The control emphasis is associated with *line item budgeting* and *objects-of-expenditure*. In its most rigid form, line item budgeting means listing every single position and piece of equipment on separate lines in the expenditure estimates. The individual items are stricken out or approved by the legislature; if allowed, the

[2] *Ibid.*, 248.
[3] Jesse Burkhead, *Governmental Budgeting*, New York: Wiley, 1956, p. 12.

money may be spent only for the item and not for any other purpose, even if it be to hire a clerk instead of a janitor or buy a typewriter rather than an adding machine.

In another form, a listing of every job or purchase is not required, but the appropriated funds may not be transferred from one category of expense to another, such as from the salary to the equipment account. Category is the same as object-of-expenditure: the "object" is what the money is used for, such as personal services, supplies and materials, equipment, travel, printing and binding, and rental of buildings. In the eyes of many legislators and others, the line item approach, in a budget prepared on an object-of-expenditure basis, provides maximum control. Line item budgeting, in one form or another, is still found in many state and local governments.[4]

LUMP-SUM BUDGETING

Some believe that lump-sum budgeting can judiciously be used, provided that the object method of presentation is kept. Under lump-sum budgeting, transfers of funds may be made not only between objects but also between organization units and approved work activities. As expenditure abuses were corrected in the first years of executive budgets, some use was made of the lump-sum principle. In the federal government, lump-sum budgeting has been used for many years; it is not unusual, however, for Congress to restrict the amounts that can be spent for certain purposes, such as administrative expenses or those for printing and binding.

Advent of the management approach

It was not until the 1930s that the original promise of the executive budget as a vehicle for "work planning" began to produce results. With the oncome of the New Deal, new concepts were in the air, such as "administrative management," a term used in the report of Franklin D. Roosevelt's Committee on Administrative Management. The focus was now a positive one: achieving work results, under strong executive leadership.

This came to be known as the "management approach" to budgeting. Expenditure control was not disregarded; indeed, in some ways it was more effectively applied, as, for example, by instituting a system of apportionments of the funds appropriated by the Congress whereby the President and the Bureau of the Budget control the rate of agency spending.[5] Both purposes could be combined, with the guiding orientation the positive one of

[4] See *State Expenditure Controls: An Evaluation*, New York: Tax Foundation, Inc., 1965, pp. 33–35.
[5] See Burkhead, *op. cit.*, pp. 101–102, 353–354.

achieving concrete work results, as measurable as possible. Far from being restricted to "humbler and routine business," the staff of the Bureau of the Budget was greatly increased, and its director became a key policy adviser to the President. Agency estimates were critically reviewed in terms of efficiency, and a beginning was made in developing work units to measure program results. In the agencies, efforts were made to improve the preparation of the estimates; gradually the finance responsibilities passed into the hands of "management-minded" individuals, frequently newly recruited, who replaced the narrow-gauged accountants with their "unbending attitude, indiscriminate concern with minutia, and exaggerated impersonality."[6] At the same time, economic theory became much more significant in the President's budget recommendations. Although tax and spending policies were not conceived together and presented through the budget as they have been in the last few years, the fiscal-planning implications of the budget were evident throughout the New Deal period, as the Roosevelt Administration adopted "pump-priming" measures.

In most state and local governments, the "budget" had simply been a collection of figures, a subsidiary of the accounting system. A number of them now adopted the management approach, at least in principle, and employed trained budget examiners for the first time. Most state and local jurisdictions, however, clung to the negative control approach; indeed, they still do, as Allen Schick has convincingly documented in the case of state government.[7]

Furthermore, prior to World War II, at all levels of government, with very few exceptions the estimates continued to be prepared on an object-of-expenditure basis, which meant that the really important question was left unanswered: Exactly what work was proposed and what accomplishments were anticipated, compared with those realized in the past? A typical budget consisted of a detailed listing of the positions to be filled, followed by the recommended amounts to be spent on each object of nonpersonal services. Three columns of figures frequently were shown: first, the actual expenditures for each object in the last complete fiscal year; second, the estimated amounts to be expended on them during the current fiscal year; and third, the sums desired for each object for the future fiscal year.

A budget of this type could quickly be put together without the need for careful planning of future work programs. All that was necessary was to obtain a list of the existing positions, make the usual request for some additional ones and for certain salary increases, and then make some quick and usually quite liberal

[6] Joseph Pois, "Evolutionary Role of the Financial Manager," *The Federal Accountant*, XI, No. 3 (March, 1962), 38–39.

[7] Allen Schick, "Control Patterns in State Budget Execution," *Public Administration Review*, XXIV, No. 2 (June, 1964), 97–106.

guesses as to what would be needed for such objects as travel, supplies, and equipment. The head of the agency and his principal lieutenants could quickly hammer out a budget in this way. Particularly in the relationships with the central budget staff for the jurisdiction, this became more a bargaining than a planning process. Estimates were frequently padded in anticipation of the cuts of the "hatchet boys" in the budget bureau. The process was highly unscientific, to say the least. Object-of-expenditure budgeting in practice becomes rule-of-thumb budgeting. A division head who is asked to present his estimates in terms of what he needs to spend for individual positions, telephone service, and the like does not have to develop detailed plans. Previous years' expenditures as recorded in the accounts provide him with the basis for his estimates for the future fiscal period.

Certainly, what is spent on travel, telephone service, and the other traditional objects of expenditures is important, and extravagant expenditures on these items should not be tolerated. However, the detailed estimates of such expenses belong in the supporting schedules of the budget estimates, preceded by a clear statement of exactly what work is to be performed. What security is there in increasing or decreasing travel and other expenses if there is no way of knowing what impact such increases or decreases will have on the work programs of the agency? Legislators tend to feel that object-of-expenditure budgeting provides them with the detailed control that is essential. Actually, it may give them very little control over what should be of most concern: the overall effectiveness of the agency program.

Performance budgeting

After World War II, attempts to make the management approach really effective were intensified, and "performance budgeting" was urged. There was nothing new about the concept, for it meant emphasizing the budget as a "work plan." What was new was the progress made in switching from budget presentations on an object basis to presentations on a program basis. Work objectives were defined, even if in many cases inadequately, and the cart (items and services purchased) was no longer before the horse (the program). Much of the stimulus came from the first Hoover Commission, which reported:

> The Federal budget is an inadequate document, poorly organized and improperly designed to serve its major purpose, which is to present an understandable and workable financial plan for the expenditures of the Government. The document has grown

larger and larger each year as the Government's requirements have increased, but its general framework and method of presentation have not changed.

The Commission noted that the budget for 1949–1950 contained 1625 closely printed pages, with about 1,500,000 words. Exactly what all this detail meant in terms of work proposed and accomplished was far from clear. Accordingly, the Commission recommended that "the whole budgetary concept of the Federal Government should be refashioned by the adoption of a budget based upon functions, activities, and projects," and designated this the "performance budget."[8] The term "program budget" came to be used by many people to mean the same thing.

In 1949, Congress approved an amendment to the National Security Act providing for performance budgeting in the Defense Department, and in January, 1950, President Truman sent to Congress the first budget for the entire federal administrative branch prepared on such a basis.[9] With budgets as large as they now are, even in the best of circumstances conversion from one system to another takes a great deal of time. Although within a few years the " 'green sheets' of detailed personnel requirements," long used in traditional federal budgeting on an object basis, came to be "included merely as an appendix to the President's budget,"[10] in many agencies the budget estimates were not significantly more meaningful. Proposed expenditures were grouped by categories, and substantial progress was made in defining work measurements, but just why expenditures were requested for certain purposes and not for others was often not clear.

The same limitations were true of performance budgeting in those few states and cities where it was employed. Using public health as an example, expenditures for activities such as well-baby clinics might be separately shown, instead of being lumped together with those for other programs, and cost data might even be included, such as the cost per patient visit. Why such clinics were recommended, instead of other ways of improving infant health in low-income areas, would not be explained, nor would any material be included on past effectiveness of the clinics in reducing illness.[11]

RELATIONSHIP TO PLANNING-PROGRAMMING-BUDGETING

Performance budgeting did represent a forward step. The previous period of almost universal use of unmodified object-of-expenditure budgeting was incongruous with announced objectives of making the budget a management tool. Valuable experience was gained in developing work measurements and cost data. The

[8] Commission on Organization of the Executive Branch of the Government, *Budgeting and Accounting*, Washington, D.C.: Government Printing Office, 1949, pp. 7–8.

[9] *Financial Management in the Federal Government*, 87th Congress, 1st Session, Senate Document No. 11, Washington, D.C.: Government Printing Office, 1961, pp. 332–333.

[10] Arthur Smithies, "Conceptual Framework for the Program Budget," in David Novick, (ed.), *Program Budgeting . . . Program Analysis and the Federal Budget*, Washington, D.C.: Government Printing Office, 1965, p. 8.

[11] *The Planning-Programming-Budgeting System: Progress and Potentials*, Subcommittee on Economy in Government of the Joint Economic Committee, 90th Congress, 1st Session, Washington, D.C.: Government Printing Office, 1967, p. 124.

evolution from performance budgeting to planning-programming-budgeting (PPB), to which we now turn, is clear and direct, and it would be untrue to say that PPB has no resemblance to performance budgeting.[12] Indeed, one of PPB's greatest accomplishments is that, with strong Presidential backing, it has made genuine program budgeting a requirement in the Federal service, and has been the stimulus for state and local governments to move more rapidly in the same direction.

PLANNING-PROGRAMMING-BUDGETING

PPB is broader than budgeting, because basically it attempts to make decisionmaking on governmental activities as rational as possible.

Components of PPB

There is nothing new about each of the components—planning, programming, and budgeting—taken separately; what is claimed to be new is the total pattern of ideas into which they are fitted. *Planning* is the determination of the basic goals of the organization and the selection of the programs best calculated to achieve these goals. *Programming* entails the scheduling and execution, as efficiently as possible, of the specific projects required to implement these programs. *Budgeting* is the process of converting the goals, programs, and projects into money estimates for review within the administrative branch and final action by the legislature.

To illustrate these terms, an example of a *goal* is to raise per capita income; of a *program* toward that end, industrialization; and of a *project*, a steel mill. Since this goal, like so many others in government, covers so much, it embraces many other programs, such as fisheries, natural resource development, and vocational training. Furthermore, within each program there will be numerous projects reflecting the different choices in executing the program.

Comparison with past practices

In the past, say the PPB advocates, the planning, programming, and budgeting that has taken place in governments has often been disjointed, with little attention given to the weighing of the relative merits of alternative goals, programs, projects, and the different ways of carrying them out. Typically, each agency

[12] See Frederick C. Mosher, "PPBS: Two Questions," reproduced from *Public Administration Review*, XXVII, No. 1 (March, 1967) in *Planning-Programming-Budgeting, Selected Comment*, Senate Subcommittee on National Security and International Operations, 90th Congress, 1st Session, Washington, D.C.: Government Printing Office, 1967, pp. 23–28.

has planned its own future operations, with varying degrees of care, and then asked for as big a budget as it dared request, usually inflating the estimates to protect against anticipated reductions. The expenditure estimates have not been presented in such form that the reviewing officials could determine exactly what programs and projects would be undertaken and why they had been chosen, as compared with other possibilities. Accordingly, arbitrary spending totals have been imposed on the agencies, without any real knowledge of what would be desirable in terms of the merits of the work activities being conducted.

The effort has been to hold down costs, which is logical because there is much pressure from the agencies to spend more and more. However, while total expenditures may be controlled in this way, there is no check on the effectiveness with which the funds granted are used, or any certainty that they might not better be spent on other activities. Under such procedures there is no set of coordinated plans to guide all activities of the government, and annual budgets are not developed as an integral part of such central plans. One of the unfortunate consequences, of course, is that individual departments, carrying out activities within the same basic programs, such as land and water use, sometimes do not cooperate as they should; in fact, they may work at cross-purposes.

In many governments, when the estimates are reviewed the existing program base is seldom changed: it is assumed that the agency should get at least as much as it has in previous years. As governments have grown in size, limitations of time make it impossible to reexamine each year every activity for which funds have been granted in the past. Besides, there is the force of tradition: what has already been approved many times deserves to be continued. So the major attention is given to analyzing the requests for increases in the existing programs, and for financing of completely new activities. Sometimes desirable programs are rejected while deficient old ones are routinely reapproved. PPB, in its widest application, would expose the program bases to as much scrutiny as the requests for increases and for new programs, because its essence is to raise questions about what public policies should be pursued and which programs and projects offer the best promise of achieving the newly determined or the reconfirmed goals. Not only does it call for careful consideration of known policy alternatives, but for the framing of new ones if none of the existing choices is satisfactory.

As to performance budgeting, because of its limitations mentioned above, PPB enthusiasts do not believe it was much help to top executives in basic policymaking.[13] The budget experts and the officials preparing estimates on a performance basis were not thinking in terms of improving the decisionmaking process for determining and executing policies, but rather of improving the budget process, taking it as it was. They did not ask the basic question "Why?" and usually accepted existing programs and levels of expenditure as "givens." PPB, the argument continues, is much more innovative, because it rejects traditional procedures that interfere with the development of the most rational policy-making possible. It defines efficiency in terms of the most logical allocation of the government's scarce resources, in the interests of all the citizens. Budgeting must contribute to that end; if it does not, it is deficient, even if it is called "performance" or "program" budgeting.

The PPB supporters also question that performance budgeting really measured agency "outputs." In PPB the output is a good or service produced for the public—a school, health center, park, etc. The input represents the personal services, materials, and other elements going into the production of the output. The supporters say performance budgeting frequently quantified work processes, such as documents or reports prepared, which at best are "intermediate" or "contributory" outputs.[14] PPB, it is further argued, provides for the discipline of constant, intensive analysis of program results, in terms of these outputs. Note this statement:

> Business managers are regularly forced to sit down and take stock—particularly if things go bad—because the system provides regular feedback on whether each program or product is performing badly, mediocre, or well. . . . This discipline is frequently lacking in the administration and management of Government programs. Consequently, it is not always easy to get agencies to take a really critical analytic look at their various programs.[15]

Origins of PPB

PPB has its roots in industry, where it was practiced by General Motors as early as 1924 and in the War Production Board's Controlled Materials Plan, in effect during World War II.[16] In its present form in government, it originated in weapon systems' research performed for the Defense Department (DoD) by the Rand Corporation during the 1950s. In making these studies, Rand applied *systems analysis*, which means presenting "decision-makers with a systematic and comprehensive comparison of the costs and benefits of alternative approaches to a policy goal, taking advantage of techniques variously described as operations re-

[13] See Schick, "The Road to PPB: The Stages of Budget Reform," *op. cit.*, pp. 250–253.

[14] Samuel M. Greenhouse, "The Planning-Programming-Budgeting System: Rationale, Language, and Idea Relationships," in "Planning-Programming-Budgeting System: A Symposium," *Public Administration Review*, XXVI, No. 4 (December, 1966), 274–275.

[15] *The Planning-Programming-Budgeting System: Progress and Potentials*, *op cit.*, p. 193.

[16] David Novick, "Origin and History of Program Budgeting," Rand Corporation Paper No. 9-3427, October, 1966, reproduced in *Planning-Programming-Budgeting, Selected Comment*, *op. cit.*, pp. 28–31.

search or cost-effectiveness studies."[17] Rand was convinced that weapon systems should be compared in terms of their social, political, and economic implications, such as their impact on the U.S. economy, as well as on the basis of traditional performance factors such as speed and payload. This is an example of how systems analysis widens the consideration of alternatives.

When the Rand Corporation, using this approach, attempted to compare, for example, different kinds of bombers, it discovered that the budgeting and accounting system then in effect could not provide it with the necessary cost and other information. At this time, it will be remembered, performance budgeting had been "adopted" in DoD, but Rand found it necessary to propose what it considered a true program budget, based on "program packages" (explained in detail below).[18] The Air Force did not accept Rand's recommendations, but when Robert McNamara became Secretary of Defense, he adopted PPB for the entire Department. By fiscal 1964 (July 1, 1963–June 30, 1964) it was fully operative in Defense.[19]

Upon the recommendation of the Budget Bureau, President Johnson on August 25, 1965, issued a directive calling for the extension of the system on a government-wide basis.[20] By August, 1967, the Bureau of the Budget had applied it to 21 agencies, with the ultimate goal being 36 in all.[21] As a result of the federal example, it has been adopted by, and is being implemented in, several state and city governments.[22] It appears, however, that some of them had skipped performance budgeting and are now employing program categories for expenditures and appropriations for the first time, which means that their full attainment of PPB may be delayed for some time.

The specific nature of PPB can be illustrated by describing in more detail its origins and development in the Defense Department. Its use in other federal agencies will then be discussed, followed by the arguments of its critics and defenders.

PPB in the Defense Department

At the time of the aforementioned Rand studies, the following budget breakdowns were in effect in DoD: Military Personnel; Operation and Maintenance; Procurement; Military Construction; and Research, Development, Test, and Evaluation. Although this described what was proposed in general terms, as David Novick of Rand pointed out, such a budget "did not provide either the Secretary of Defense, the Executive, or Congress with any way of sorting out these major categories of resources and relating them to

[17] *Planning-Programming-Budgeting*, Hearings Before Senate Subcommittee on National Security and International Operations, 90th Congress, 1st Session, Part 1, Washington, D.C.: Government Printing Office, 1967, p. 12.

[18] Novick, "Origin and History of Program Budgeting," *op. cit.*, pp. 31–32. See also his paper, "The Department of Defense," in *Program Budgeting . . . Program Analysis and the Federal Budget, op. cit.*, pp. 50–71.

[19] *Planning-Programming-Budgeting*, Hearings Before Senate Subcommittee on National Security and International Operations, 90th Congress, 1st Session, Part 2, Washington, D.C.: Government Printing Office, 1967, p. 80.

[20] *Planning-Programming-Budgeting, Official Documents*, Senate Subcommittee on National Security and International Operations, 90th Congress, 1st Session, Washing-

such major military objectives as defense of the continental United States or strategic offensive capability."[23] As early as 1954, Novick argued that what was urgently needed was the definition of the different programs of the Department and of the "program packages," namely the combinations of personnel, installations, equipment, and other resources required for accomplishing missions within programs, such as B-52 wings, infantry battalions, and attack submarines. In this way the role of each service command would be made clear, with the emphasis, of course, on coordination.

When McNamara accepted the principle of PPB, nine major programs were identified; they have since been reworked somewhat and now include: Strategic Forces, General Purpose Forces, Specialized Activities (such as intelligence), Airlift and Sealift, Guard and Reserve Forces, Research and Development, Logistics, Personnel Support, and Administration. Each of these major programs is broken down into subprograms; for example, under Strategic Forces are shown Offensive Forces, Defensive Forces, and Civil Defense.[24] In turn, each subprogram is divided into "program elements" such as (continuing with the above example) Aircraft Forces; Missile Forces, Land-Based; and Missile Forces, Sea-Based.

The program elements are a key consideration in PPB, because they are supposed to compete for funds on the basis of a comparison of their respective advantages and costs. Thus the Navy's Polaris missiles compete with the Titan and the Minuteman, as the planners in DoD decide which weapon system is more effective at a given level of use for a given purpose. Before the adoption of the new system, the requests for Polaris were considered in relation to competing claims within the Navy Department for its other activities, such as aircraft-carrier construction and antisubmarine warfare. Since the purposes were different, there was no real basis for comparison.[25]

ROLE OF COST-EFFECTIVENESS ANALYSIS

As Secretary McNamara said, it is not simply a question of wanting the very best for our military, but, more particularly, of deciding whether the additional capability requested is really required and, if so, whether the resource use proposed represents the least costly way of achieving it. He gave the example of two tactical fighter aircraft, identical in performance except that one can fly ten miles an hour faster than the other. Aircraft A costs $10,000 more per unit than Aircraft B, so if 1000 more planes are needed, the total additional cost would be $10 million. If the problem is

ton, D.C.: Government Printing Office, 1967, pp. 1–3.

[21] *Planning-Programming-Budgeting,* Hearings Before Senate Subcommittee on National Security and International Operations, Part 1, *op. cit.,* p. 25.

[22] "The Planning-Programming-Budgeting System: Progress and Potentials," *op. cit.,* pp. 86–127, pp. 243–251.

[23] Novick, "The Department of Defense," *op. cit.,* pp. 52–53.

[24] *Planning-Programming-Budgeting, Official Documents, op. cit.,* pp. 21–23.

[25] Novick, "The Department of Defense," *op. cit.,* pp. 55–56.

approached in terms of a given amount of resources, the additional combat effectiveness made possible by the greater speed of Aircraft A should be weighed against that produced if the same $10 million were applied to other defense purposes, such as more Aircraft B, more or better aircraft munitions, more ships, or even more military family housing. Assuming, however, that it is approached from the standpoint of a given amount of combat capability, then it must be decided whether that given amount can be achieved at less cost by perhaps buying more of Aircraft B or more aircraft munitions or more missiles. The fact that Aircraft A flies ten miles faster than Aircraft B is not conclusive: The question still remains whether the greater speed is worth the greater cost, the kind of determination that is *"the heart of the planning-programming-budgeting or resources allocation problem within the Defense Department."*[26]

This process is commonly known as cost-effectiveness analysis; it is also often called "cost-utility" or "cost-benefit" analysis. It includes the following: (1) evaluation and comparison of alternative courses of action for achieving a specified objective; (2) framing of additional alternatives if none examined is believed suitable; (3) for each alternative, the assessment of the economic resource cost and of the utility (benefits to be gained); and (4) projection of the analysis over a substantial period of time, at least five years and possibly ten years or longer. The PPB advocates say that previously, not only in Defense but also in the other departments, the annual expenditure estimates have included the initial installments of projects that cost a good deal over a period of years but are approved by budget reviewers who do not realize this. This is known as "foot-in-the-door financing," which the Assistant Secretary of Defense (Systems Analysis) told a Senate subcommittee is being curbed under the PPB system. He cited the Skybolt missile-carrying plane project: Original estimates made by the Air Force in 1960 were about $890 million, but at the time the project was abandoned after cost-effectiveness analysis, the cost threatened to be about $3 billion.[27]

PROGRAM PLANNING AND THE BUDGET

Prior to 1961, substantive military planning was virtually divorced from budgeting; military strategists in each service command decided their future requirements for weapon systems and forces on the basis of their own assessments of national security needs and what they should do to meet the dangers. They then presented the Secretary of Defense with spending estimates, typically so high as to warrant being called "wish lists,"[28] and he had to reduce

[26] Gene H. Fisher, "The Role of Cost-Utility Analysis in Program Budgeting," in *Program Budgeting . . . Program Analysis and the Federal Budget, op. cit.,* p. 34.

[27] *Planning-Programming-Budgeting,* Hearings Before Senate Subcommittee on National Security and International Operations, Part 2, p. 78.

[28] *Planning-Programming-Budgeting, Selected Comment, op. cit.,* p. 12.

them drastically to make them conform with dollar totals separately determined by the Bureau of the Budget and the President.

As for the programming, once each service command was allocated its share of the defense budget by the Secretary, it used the funds as it saw fit, emphasizing its favorite projects without fitting its decisions into a coordinated operations plan for the Department as a whole. So great was the lack of coordinated planning that in 1961 the Air Force was preparing for a short nuclear war and the Army for a long, conventional war. To boot, neither was doing its planning on an adequate long-range basis: "Because the land and tactical air forces were being planned for different kinds of wars, they were not ready to fight either."[29]

THE NEW PROCEDURES

Under the new system, each spring the Joint Chiefs of Staff and the service commands send the Secretary of Defense their detailed recommendations on military force requirements. After reviewing these recommendations, the Secretary returns his comments in the form of Draft Presidential Memoranda that "summarize the relevant information on the threat, our objectives, the effectiveness, and cost of the alternatives he has considered and his tentative conclusions."[30] The Joint Chiefs are given a month to review and comment on these drafts in detail. They meet with the Secretary when it is necessary, and finally agreement is reached on both substantive programs and budget figures. The results of this process are summarized in a Five Year Defense Program, and an eight-year projection of costs, manpower, procurement, construction, and some other components. The Five Year Program is considered tentative; basically it is "an official set of assumptions"[31] about the military forces for which funds will be requested in the future, and as such is the reference point for those preparing the budget requests to support these forces. Each year the Five Year Program is reviewed, revised as necessary, and projected one more year into the future. The net result is that substantive planning is coordinated, projected over a long period, and united with the annual budget preparation process.

The complete PPB system includes periodic accounting and other data to show what is being spent on the different programs and how effectively. (The accounting aspects will be discussed in Chapter 19.) Because of the massive undertaking it represents, this information system has not yet been completed in Defense, but it can answer the kind of question Lyndon B. Johnson, then

29 *Planning-Programming-Budgeting,* Hearings Before Senate Subcommittee on National Security and International Operations, Part 2, *op. cit.,* p. 97.

30 *Ibid.,* p. 71.

31 *Ibid.*

chairman of the Senate Preparedness Investigating Subcommittee, once asked. He wanted to know how much money was being spent during fiscal 1959 for defense against manned bombers, but the Department of Defense could not provide the information.[32]

PPB in other federal agencies

REQUIREMENTS FOR BUDGET SUBMISSSIONS

The Bureau of the Budget's instructions to the federal agencies (including Defense) on PPB require three kinds of submissions: (1) program memoranda (PM), (2) the multiyear Program and Financial Plan (PFP), and (3) Special Analytic Studies (SAS's).[33] A concise memorandum must be prepared for each program category involved in a Major Program Issue (the MPI is defined as "a question requiring a decision in the current budget cycle, with major implications in terms of either present or future costs, the direction of a program or group of programs, or a policy choice"[34]). Each PM defines the program and makes clear "why particular choices have been made, by identifying agency objectives in a measurable way, and comparing alternative programs in terms of their costs and who pays them, and their benefits and the group benefitted." Taken together, they "show what choices the agency head has made . . . the major program recommendations of the agency for the upcoming budget, and . . . strategy underlying those program recommendations."[35]

The PFP is a tabular presentation, projected into the future, showing outputs, costs, and other pertinent data for all the programs, broken down by subcategory. This information is shown for the previous fiscal year, the current one, the budget year (that is, next fiscal period), and at least four additional years. The years beyond the budget year are included primarily to show the future implications of current (past and present) decisions. The PFP is not meant as a complete set of estimates for the entire period covered, because it does not show any future new programs or changes in spending levels for existing programs, decisions about which are not part of the current budget cycle. During the time for budget preparation each year, program plans are reviewed and altered as deemed necessary, and new programs may be approved. One of its purposes is to prevent "foot-in-the-door" financing; it feeds into the annual budget submissions a record of the present and future budgetary and output consequences of the current year's decisions. Special Analytic

[32] *Ibid.,* p. 68.

[33] Bureau of the Budget Bulletin No. 68-9, April 12, 1968, reproduced in *Planning-Programming-Budgeting: Budget Bureau Guidelines of 1968,* Senate Subcommittee on National Security and International Operations, 90th Congress, 2nd Session, Washington, D.C.: Government Printing Office, 1968.

[34] *Ibid.,* p. 2.

[35] *Ibid.,* p. 5.

Studies are supporting analyses made in depth, normally for each Major Program Issue (MPI's).[36]

THE CROSSWALK. Long-range substantive planning, the programming of individual projects, and the annual budget process are thus joined together. Because of Congressional reluctance to make appropriations on a program basis, the agencies must also complete a form, known as a "cross-walk," in which they convert the program data into the traditional appropriation items. Congress now makes numerous separate appropriations on the basis of an organization unit rather than a program. For example, the Department of Health, Education, and Welfare has in the past received funds from 116 separate appropriations.

Many programs, whether or not shared by different agencies, are supported by quite a few different appropriations, all of which means that the principle of program budgeting is not carried into the legislative expenditure-authorizing process. Many Congressmen feel strongly that the present appropriation structure must be retained to guarantee them effective expenditure control. The "cross-walk" is philosophically accepted by PPB supporters as a necessity until Congress sees the advantages and decides to put the appropriations on a program basis.

PRESIDENTIAL SUPPORT

It was recognized from the very start that expert analysts in sufficient number would be required to implement PPB. In his original directive to the agency heads, President Johnson said: "Each of you will need a central staff for program and policy planning accountable directly to you. To make this work will take good people, the best you now have and the best you can find.[37] Evidencing his continued interest, on November 17, 1966, he followed up with a memorandum in which he instructed them to "train and recruit the necessary staff"; he advised them that he was having the Budget Director make an "objective analysis" of the effectiveness of the agency PPB systems and that in the future the Budget Director would report to him quarterly "on the progress of your implementation of my directive."[38]

On March 17, 1967, he issued another statement in which he urged Congress to *approve the funds for PPBS requested in the budgets of the various Federal agencies.*[39] Congress is not granting all the positions requested, but it is obvious that PPB is receiving the strong Presidental support never accorded to performance budgeting. The latter was endorsed in principle by the Presidents, but never insisted upon and followed up in the same way.

[36] *Ibid.*, p. 6.

[37] *Planning-Programming-Budgeting, Official Documents, op. cit.,* p. 2.

[38] *Ibid.*, p. 4.

[39] *Ibid.*, p. 6.

THE ACCOMPLISHMENTS

Some indications of the progress achieved with PPB appears in the printed hearings of Senator Proxmire's Subcommittee on Economy in Government, which has listened to testimony from federal officials and others on the new system. It was frankly stated that PPB is not adapted to making "grand decisions," such as how much money should be spent on education rather than welfare. The Assistant Secretary (Program Coordination), HEW, said, "No amount of analysis is going to tell us whether the nation benefits more from sending a slum child to pre-school, providing medical care to an old man, or enabling a disabled housewife to resume her normal activities." These, he said, were "questions of value judgments and politics."[40] Those who had pioneered with PPB in Defense knew that it was "difficult to compare the relative merits of an additional military division and an additional university," but they did think it was feasible to "compare the relative merits of spending an additional billion dollars in one direction or the other."[41] Some of its proponents hope that PPB will at some future date also be helpful in making these "large choices."

Apparently, agencies are doing much more hard thinking about their objectives. The Interior Department's Deputy Under Secretary for Programs confided, "When PPB came along, it gave us the framework we were looking for, and . . . has given us a new opportunity to look at the present, and more particularly the future, and see the needs of the country," and "define . . . objectives in very specific terms to remove, if you will, the mother-love type of objective that has tended to be with conservation, and to get some very specific goals and objectives."[42]

The effect of PPB has been to sharpen the administrative policymaking discussed in Chapter 1; frequently, when legislative and administrative goals remain on the "mother-love" basis (meaning very general and simply identified with "virtue"), programs that produce real "outputs" for the public are never defined and executed. The broad legislative mandate, although stated in inspiring terms, often remains vague. A wider range of policies is being considered, and in some cases new alternatives being framed. As one example, research is being conducted into the relative merits of the different sources of energy production, such as oil, coal, natural gas, oil shale, uranium, and hydroelectric power, "to determine which alternative actions will best achieve national energy goals consistent with appropriate consideration for the preservation of the quality of the environment . . . and proper

[40] *The Planning-Programming-Budgeting System: Progress and Potentials,* op. cit., p. 5.
[41] *Smithies, op. cit.,* p. 3.
[42] *The Planning-Programming-Budgeting System: Progress and Potentials,* op. cit., p. 55.

coordination with other national resource, economic, and national security factors."[43]

Coordination is built into the PPB process because the intensive program analysis required of the agency brings out the interrelationships with activities of other agencies in the same general area. The connecting points for both intradepartmental and interdepartmental cooperation are more prominently revealed. Much more than in the past, plans are being projected into the future:

> . . . Until this year, long-range planning in the Department [HEW] was sporadic and generally not departmentwide. No mechanisms existed for focusing attention on longer range objectives, deciding which types of programs should be given highest priority over the next several years and then drawing up a budget consistent with those objectives and priorities.[44]

The in-depth evaluation of program results required under PPB is producing some interesting, albeit tentative, conclusions. In the past, little has been known about the effectiveness of disease-control programs, but HEW's studies are now producing some definite conclusions, such as that cervical cancer detection and treatment programs have "high payoff," the cost per life saved being estimated from $2200 to above $4000. With an effective car seat belt program, the same cost was estimated at as little as $87.[45] In other cases, for reasons discussed next, the conclusions are much more tentative, but PPB evaluation studies are just beginning.

PPB in state and local governments

[43] *Ibid.*, p. 62.
[44] *Ibid.*, p. 9.
[45] *Ibid.*, pp. 6–7.
[46] *Ibid.*, p. 95. See Selma J. Mushkin, "PPB in Cities," in "Planning-Programming-Budgeting System Reexamined: Development, Analysis, and Criticism," *Public Administration Review*, XXIX, No. 2 (March-April, 1969), 167–177.

The Proxmire subcommittee was told that perhaps 8 to 10 states and a dozen big cities have PPB. In most cases, as mentioned previously, these jurisdictions have adopted program budget classifications but have not as yet developed complete PPB systems, including intensive "output" analysis. New York City, believing it impractical to try to put into effect quickly a program budget and account classifications for the entire city, decided instead to concentrate on cost-effectiveness analysis in "sectors of high apparent yield," such as police and fire protection, health services, and waste disposal.[46] For example, it has been testing the theory that the effectiveness of police surveillance can be measured by the number of patrol units.

Since state and local agencies receive substantial funds from the federal government under various "categorical" aid programs, it is argued that this greatly reduces the scope of possible application of PPB. While the federal money is unavailable for purposes other than those specified, thus limiting the spending options of the state and local officials, the federal officials may reject grant applications if evidence is lacking that alternative ways of spending the desired funds, within the categorical aid program, were considered adequately. The same holds for state aid to the localities; yet it would be unrealistic to deny that existing state constitutional limitations on indebtedness and taxing powers place obstacles in the way of PPB. The widespread use in state governments of special funds and earmarked appropriations, in some cases removing as much as 60 percent of the expenditures from central budget control, presents another problem.[47] Obviously, state and local government financial reform should accompany PPB.

Criticisms of PPB

In late summer of 1967, Senator Henry M. Jackson's Subcommittee on National Security and International Operations issued a staff report highly critical of PPB.[48] It later held hearings during which it quizzed the Budget Director and the Assistant Secretary for Defense (System Analysis) in detail. What follows below is a discussion of the principal criticisms of PPB made by legislators, scholars, and others.

THE QUESTION OF VALUES

Legislators and others suspect that PPB, in its pursuit of rationality, seeks to eliminate politics from decisionmaking. Professor Frederick C. Mosher, author of *Program Budgeting: Theory and Practice*, published in 1954, believes that some PPB advocates ignore, and possibly even have contempt for, "democratic values and processes."[49] Within the administrative agencies and Congress, it is suspected that PPB experts want to impose their judgments as to *which* policies and programs the government should pursue. Highly respected Vice Admiral H. G. Rickover believes "politicians . . . saw the truth before the cost accountants," and that their judgment "is at least as meritorious as the pronouncements of social scientists."[50]

PPB defenders contend they are "on the side of the politicians,"[51] because budget presentations on a program basis, accompanied by output evaluation data, enable the legislators to exercise more effective control. They know that ultimately budget decisions must be the result of the democratic bargaining process and the pull-and-haul of various groups and individuals, inside

[47] *State Expenditure Controls: An Evaluation, op. cit.,* p. 11. See William M. Capron, "PPB and State Budgeting," and Frederick C. Mosher, "Limitations and Problems of PPBS in the States," in "Planning-Programming-Budgeting System Reexamined: Development, Analysis, and Criticism," *Public Administration Review,* XXIX, No. 2 (March-April, 1969), 155–167.

[48] *Planning-Programming-Budgeting, Initial Memorandum,* Senate Subcommittee on National Security and International Operations, 90th Congress, 1st Session, Washington, D.C.: Government Printing Office, 1967.

[49] Mosher, *op. cit.,* pp. 25–26.

[50] *Planning-Programming-Budgeting, Selected Comment, op. cit.,* p. 42.

[51] *Planning-Programming-Budgeting,* Hearings Before Senate Subcommittee on National Security and International Operations, Part 2, *op. cit.,* p. 102.

and outside of the executive branch and Congress. They would not change this; rather, they would improve the process by giving the political policymakers more adequate information as to available choices. Realistically, "log-rolling"—whereby legislators customarily support one another's public works projects—must be expected to continue. However, some of the projects now usually approved might be thrown out because their utter unsuitability would be revealed by the comparisons required under PPB procedures. In any case, they clarify that PPB was never intended to be the basis for such decisions as whether or not to recognize a foreign government, go to war, or pull out of Vietnam.

Yet it is not denied that PPB can influence political decisions, such as the one made to cancel the Skybolt missile-carrying plane project despite the British orders for such aircraft. The Jackson subcommittee questioned whether the Defense Department had considered the "impact on the British Government and perhaps on French policies in Atlantic and West European affairs." The answer: "Skybolt was kept alive for many months and millions of dollars longer than it otherwise would have been precisely because of the British interest. But, it finally got to the point that the expected effectiveness of Skybolt fell so low, and the projected cost rose so high in relation to competing systems, such as Minuteman, that the President and the Secretary of Defense reached the conclusion that Skybolt would not be satisfactory for the British, and was clearly unsatisfactory for us. Continuation of Skybolt would have only postponed the political problem, not avoided it"[52]

POSSIBLE DIMINUTION OF LEGISLATIVE CONTROL

A related criticism is that the Bureau of the Budget and the agencies unjustifiably withhold from Congress information used during the PPB deliberations within the executive branch. It is true that Congress is not given a complete set of PPB documents prepared within the agencies. As the Budget Director has explained, the agencies would not make frank evaluations of their programs if "everything they put on paper" were given to Congress. However, Congress is provided with agency budget justifications that incorporate the work data and, in the opinion of the President and his advisers, conceal nothing that the legislators need to know.[53] Furthermore, Congressional committees may request copies of the complete program-evaluation studies, except for material not released for security reasons.

Still, legislators remain uneasy about a decisionmaking process that on the face of it relegates them to the role of receiving for review the results of cold logic within the executive branch.

[52] *Ibid.*, pp. 77–78.

[53] *Planning-Programming-Budgeting,* Hearings Before Senate Subcommittee on National Security and International Operations, Part 1, *op. cit.*, p. 49.

How can a legislator challenge a recommendation of the Chief Executive presented as the "best" of all alternatives? Besides, the executive branch's experts, like everyone else, are not omniscient; they may make mistakes in their analyses. It has been suggested that Congress employ an "analytical capability" of its own, to carry out some studies independently, prod the agencies "to be more critical in their own self-examinations," and "appraise the technical aspects" of the agency analyses.[54]

Empirical studies of federal expenditures for the 1948–1963 period, made by Professors Otto A. Davis, M. A. H. Dempster, and Aaron Wildavsky, support the conclusion that Congressional budget control is generally a fiction anyway. They found that the pattern is for the spending agencies to ask for a certain percentage more than last year's budget, which is what the Bureau of the Budget and Congress expect, so they in turn cut the requests somewhat. This procedure, long witnessed by those on the federal scene and also firmly embedded in state and local governments, is referred to as "creeping incrementalism." They found it to be even more characteristic of Congress than of the Bureau of the Budget, from which they deduce that the legislators have adopted this unscientific approach because "the traditional budget . . . simply does not give them an adequate basis upon which to make . . . an evaluation of how well agencies are doing."[55]

In PPB neither expenditures nor revenues are treated as "givens." What was done before is not automatically continued. Of course, political realities and past decisions are limiting factors; former Budget Director Charles L. Schultze, who strongly defended PPB before the Jackson subcommittee, had told the House Appropriations Committee that $29.4 billion, or roughly half the amount recommended for nondefense purposes in the budget for fiscal 1968, represented "uncontrollable major programs, such as interest on the public debt, veterans compensation and pensions, payments to the medicare trust fund, public assistance, farm supports, and the like." As he also stressed, no expenditure is "absolutely uncontrollable"[56]; Congress can reduce or eliminate these programs, but the pressures supporting their continuation are so great that this is unlikely. PPB is being applied to both the "controllable" and "uncontrollable" programs; the latter can be improved through more adequate consideration of alternatives and cost-effectiveness analysis.

THE "CENTRALIZING BIAS"

PPB also has a "centralizing bias" that offends some people. If integrated planning is to predominate, there must be a master

[54] *The Planning-Programming-Budgeting System: Progress and Potentials, op. cit.,* pp. 193–194.

[55] *Ibid.,* p. 208. See also pp. 323–341 for reproduction of Otto A. Davis, M. A. H. Dempster, and Aaron Wildavsky, "A Theory of the Budgetary Process," *American Political Science Review,* LX, No. 3 (September, 1966).

[56] *The Budget for 1968,* Hearings Before the Committee on Appropriations, House of Representatives, 90th Congress, 1st Session, Washington, D.C.: Government Printing Office, 1967, p. 86.

...ally is developed by the Chief Executive and
...n a predominant role also for the department
...eir agencies. The basic policies must be determined
...taking into account, it is true, information and view-
...smitted from below, but without allowing each de-
...t, and the subdivisions thereof, to control the spending
...ons. To many Congressmen this means too much power for
...President and the department heads. They fear that the
...argaining process, whereby bureau heads and others within the
agencies can freely express their points of view, is severely
curtailed. "A consequence, whether intended or not, is that it
may be more difficult for voices of doubt and dissent at lower
levels to make themselves heard at high levels."[57] The use of PPB
in the Defense Department has revived fears that the Secretary and
his civilian advisers are unduly restricting the military, and that
"Defense programs may . . . be more nearly tailored to one estimate of the future and to one cost benefit calculus than in a
period when decisionmaking was less centralized."[58] Alarm has
also been expressed that because PPB emphasizes comprehensive-
ness, meaning that all program interrelationships must be taken
into account, it will lead to a further erosion in the autonomy of
state and local governments. For example, it is feared that master
plans in education, traditionally regarded as a state and local
responsibility, will be made in Washington.

The Bureau of the Budget states that its instructions to the
agencies, described earlier, provide for full consultation by agency
heads with those at the lower levels. The substantive military plans
originate with the heads of the service commands, and the
Secretary does not act until he has received their detailed comments on his Draft Presidential Memoranda. Still, the military
planning is now coordinated under the direction of the Secretary
and the President, rather than completely decentralized in the
service commands, and this worries Congressional "friends" of
branches of the military. It also perturbs others who may not be
worried about curbs on the military, but who, like Aaron Wildavsky, conclude that a "more useful tool for increasing his [the top
executive's] power to control decisions vis-à-vis his subordinates
would be hard to find." In Wildavsky's opinion, "*that all decisions ought to be made by the most central person in the most
centralized body capable of grabbing hold of them is difficult to
justify on scientific grounds . . . the qualifications of efficiency experts for political systems analysis are not evident.*"[59] His reasoning is that PPB experts basically will be dealing with many political issues, and that to evaluate political choices mostly in eco-

[57] *Planning-Programming-Budgeting,* Hearings Before the Senate Subcommittee on National Security and International Operations, Part 1, *op. cit.,* p. 14.

[58] *Ibid.*

[59] Aaron Wildavsky, "The Political Economy of Efficiency: Cost-Benefit Analysis, Systems Analysis, and Program Budgeting," *Public Administration Review,* XXVI, No. 4 (December, 1966), 305, reproduced in *Planning-Programming-Budgeting, Selected Comment, op. cit.,* pp. 50–72.

nomic terms overlooks the "political costs and benefits," such as losing some votes and gaining others.

THE BARGAINING AND THE HIERARCHICAL APPROACHES. Fundamentally, the issue is differing theories of decisionmaking, with the PPB critics believing in the "bargaining" as against the "hierarchical" approach.[60] Essentially, the former posits that "independent, partisan decisionmakers can be coordinated in several ways in the absence of a central coordinator; that such partisan mutual adjustment is characteristic of the real world; that complex decisionmaking is necessarily fragmented, disjointed, and incremental; that having a multiplicity of interacting quasi-independent decisionmakers promotes rationality; that central decisionmaking doesn't work very well; that partisan mutual adjustment facilitates agreement on values and actions; and that the process promotes consent to democratic government."[61] The latter emphasizes "hierarchies of objectives, lines of authority, division of labor among organization units, coordination of policies and programs, and systems efficiency."[62]

Henry S. Rowen, president of the Rand Corporation, while not accepting the "strict hierarchical view," does not believe that good "technical and economic decisions will be made, or even taken into account, by a system operating primarily in a partisan mutual adjustment mode." His first reason is the "remarkable inertia" of large bureaucracies that keeps them moving in the same directions, the result being the suppression of options and the concealing of "possibilities that don't conform." Second, not only does the bargaining power of the competing organizations vary greatly, but also power "is not necessarily very highly correlated with the information or the power to take relevant action to accomplish objectives with a high degree of efficiency." The Bureau of Public Roads has power with Congress and others, but Rowen questions that it is sufficiently well-informed to "shape the structure of cities differently than it now does through its urban highway programs. . . ."[63] Third, even where countervailing power is present, government agencies can strike bargains harmful to the public interest, just like private firms and the unions. One of the examples he gives here is "our maritime policies which have traditionally been worked out via the bargaining mode" and "include an operating subsidy . . . structured so as to create a positive incentive to overmanning of ships."

While examples of this kind may illustrate how the political system transfers income to different groups, they are frequently "as much due to . . . bureaucratic inertia, random differences in

[60] Henry S. Rowen, paper delivered at Annual Meeting of the American Political Science Association, September 6–10, 1966, reproduced in *Planning-Programming-Budgeting, Selected Comment, op. cit.,* pp. 44–49.

[61] *Ibid.,* p. 45.

[62] *Ibid.,* p. 44–45.

[63] *Ibid.,* p. 47.

bargaining power, absence of market forces, unregulated intra-governmental monopolistic practices."[64] Rowen believes that the PPB kind of analysis is needed as well as the bargaining, that the bargaining itself does not "work well if left to chance," and that "action from a higher level" is required. He is optimistic that "more systematic analysis" will "narrow the vast areas in which governmental action is uninformed, arbitrary, and based on un-enlightened opinion rather than data and analysis."[65]

As to the concern that Washington will use PPB to extend federal controls, the point is made that there is nothing in the new system that would change the existing, voluntary, cooperative relationship between federal, state, and local governments. In many areas of crisis, the national interest demands coordinated efforts by all levels of government and cooperating private groups; if PPB assists this process, as it should, it will be serving another useful purpose.

QUANTIFICATION

The objection that intangible factors are overlooked is implicit in the criticisms already presented. It is charged that PPB places exaggerated emphasis on numbers, statistical computations, and quantification in general. Quoting Admiral Rickover again: "The basis for using cost-effectiveness studies as the rationale on which to make a decision is the assumption that the important factors can be expressed in numerical form. . . . I have no more faith in the ability of the social scientists to quantify military effectiveness than I do in numerologists to calculate the future."[66]

The PPB experts say they use quantitative analysis only where appropriate, but that for some problems, such as choice of weapon systems, "non-quantitative judgment is simply not enough."[67] The statement that "nuclear power for surface ships offers a major in-crease in effectiveness" is not very helpful when a choice has to be made, let us say, between eight conventional or six nuclear ships. The performance of each kind of vessel, when measured on various missions, justifies being much more precise and saying that nuclear power offers "something between X and Y percent more effectiveness per ship." How much more effective a given amount of money budgeted for nuclear ships would be than the same sum invested in conventional ones can then be computed. The principle is that "where a quantitative matter is being discussed, the greatest clarity of thought is achieved by using numbers instead of by avoiding them, *even when uncertainties are present*."[68]

If, however, the costs or benefits are intangible, PPB does not employ mathematical techniques and seek to "measure the im-

[64] *Ibid.*, p. 48.

[65] *Ibid.*, p. 49.

[66] *Ibid.*, p. 36.

[67] *Planning-Programming-Budgeting,* Hearings Before Senate Subcommittee on National Security and International Operations, Part 2, *op. cit.,* p. 156.

[68] *Ibid.*, pp. 156–157.

measurable."[69] An example of such an intangible is the loss in scenic beauty to be offset against the shorter automobile routes made possible by new highways. The courts are granting damage claims arising from sonic boom, but the money is hardly compensation enough for a wage earner's discomfort and lack of sleep. A good PPB analyst lists and describes such factors; he includes them in his total analysis, leaving them out of his mathematical calculations only. The guiding principle is "open and explicit analysis," meaning that "the objectives and alternatives are clearly defined, and all of the assumptions, factors, calculations, and judgments are laid bare so that all interested parties can see exactly how the conclusions were derived, how information they provided was used, and how the various assumptions influenced the results."[70]

Nonetheless, Rickover insists the analysts pay careful attention to anticipated expenditures but tend to reject claims of benefits that they find difficult to measure or of which they are skepical. He states that when they decided that nuclear-propelled ships were too expensive, they were assuming that oil for conventional ships is readily available, and that logistic support forces would not be subject to attack. The "history of war," he says, "is replete with examples of major military defeats . . . brought about by the inability of military forces to maintain a supply of propulsion fuel to the forces in combat."[71]

Some of the critics have said that PPB represents decisionmaking by computers. Noting that the Navy has in its laboratories computers "which can perform approximately a million operations per second," Rickover observes, ". . . the numerical answer cannot be any more accurate than the assumptions on which the calculation was based and the accuracy of the data available for inputs to the calculation."[72] The advanced information technology represented by the computers has undoubtedly contributed to the development of PPB; the machines make possible analyses that in the past could never have been completed in time to be of use in decisionmaking. Rickover simply does not think that the computers are being properly used.

The promise of PPB

PPB is complex, ambitious, and imaginative. It rejects complacency, blind insistence on past practices, and the aversion for central planning long expressed by many groups and individuals. Basically, it is a theory of how greater rationality can be introduced into public-policy decisionmaking. Not too long ago there

69 Planning-Programming-Budgeting, Hearings Before Senate Subcommittee on National Security and International Operations, Part 1, op. cit., p. 25.

70 Planning-Programming-Budgeting, Hearing Before Senate Subcommittee on National Security and International Operations, Part 2, op. cit., p. 73.

71 Planning-Programming-Budgeting, Selected Comment, op. cit., p. 37.

72 Ibid.

was little expectation that something as big as government in the United States would attempt such a transformation. Today, despite the criticisms, it holds great promise.

FISCAL POLICY AND THE BUDGET

Although concepts of how to achieve economic stabilization had influenced government spending policies and thus the budget, only in recent years has the budget come to be recognized as the "key instrument in national policymaking."[73] After World War II, as combined federal, state, and local expenditures rose, the impact on the economy became progressively greater. Government spending now represented so large a proportion of total economic activity that those responsible for government budgets increasingly thought in terms of the impact of their decisions on employment and other economic conditions.

The "new economics"

President Kennedy's budget for fiscal 1964 represented a significant change. For one thing, he stressed his revenue recommendations, presenting them in the opening paragraphs of his budget message. Previously, the Presidents scarcely dealt with tax policy in these messages. Furthermore, the Kennedy budget was presented in two parts, the first consisting essentially of data significant for economic analysis, and the second presenting the detailed supporting schedules that in previous years had constituted the "budget document." John D. Millett wrote, "This . . . reveals a major development in federal government budgeting. It acknowledges the special importance of the federal budget as an instrument of economic policy, and endeavors to contribute to an examination of the impact of federal government receipts and expenditures upon the American economy."[74] Kennedy stressed tax policy in this message, because he wanted Congress to reduce taxes in order to stimulate the economy. In the following year, after his death, Congress took such action, and the "New Economics," whereby government uses its spending and tax powers to steer the economy, had been launched. Imperfectly applied since then, because of the political difficulties in obtaining tax increases in time to prevent "overheating" of the economy, it is still opposed by many Congressmen and other "balanced-budget" advocates. That fiscal policy implications are paramount is seen in the fact that when the House Appropriations Committee holds its preliminary hearings on the budget as a whole, it listens to

[73] *Report of the President's Commission on Budget Concepts,* Washington, D.C.: Government Printing Office, 1967, p. 11.

[74] John D. Millett, "Governmental Budgets and Economic Analysis," *Public Administration Review,* XXIII, No. 3 (September, 1963), 125.

testimony by the Secretary of the Treasury and the Budget Director, who speak largely in terms of how the proposed expenditures will affect such questions as inflation and the balance of payments. The Committee members themselves ask many probing questions in this area.[75]

Need for better budget presentation

President Johnson began his budget message to Congress for fiscal 1968 by saying:

> A Federal budget lays out a two-part plan of action:
> - It proposes *particular programs,* military and civilian, designed to promote national security, international cooperation, and domestic progress.
> - It proposes *total expenditures and revenues* designed to help maintain stable economic prosperity and growth.[76]

The President announced in this same message that he would name a special commission to make a "thorough review of the budget and recommend an approach to budgetary presentation which will assist both public and congressional understanding of this vital document."[77] Since no one form of presentation could satisfactorily serve the different purposes served by the budget, several methods were being used, but not without some dawbacks.

THE ADMINISTRATIVE, CONSOLIDATED CASH, AND NATIONAL INCOME ACCOUNTS BUDGETS

Previously the "administrative budget" had been employed as the "principal financial plan for conducting the affairs of Government."[78] It covers receipts and expenditures of funds owned by the federal government but excludes trust funds, such as those for old-age and survivors insurance, unemployment insurance, federally aided highway construction, medicare, and civil service retirement. These trust funds are controlled by Congress, which makes frequent changes in them, such as in tax rates and contribution and benefit formulas. In theory, however, the government acts only as trustee for them.

Whereas at one time the administrative budget accounted for the bulk of federal financial activity, the trust funds have grown so large that they must be taken into account in gauging the total effect of government operations on income levels and other aspects of the economy. An increase in Social Security benefits as surely adds to purchasing power as a

[75] See *The Budget for 1969,* Hearings Before the Committee on Appropriations, House of Representatives, 90th Congress, 2nd Session, Washington, D.C.: Government Printing Office, 1968. Note comment by Chairman Mahon on p. 9.

[76] Quoted in *Report of the President's Commission on Budget Concepts, op. cit.,* p. 12.

[77] See *The Budget for 1968, op. cit.,* p. 74.

[78] *Ibid.,* p. 4.

rise in government employment. For this reason, prior to the Johnson Administration, two additional forms of presentation had been added, the *consolidated cash budget* and the *national income accounts budget*. The consolidated cash budget combines "administrative budget transactions with those of trust funds . . . to show the flow of cash between the Federal Government and the public.[79] It shows all payments to and receipts from the public. The national income accounts budget (NIA) is "a measure of receipts and expenditures of the Federal Government sector of the national income and product accounts [maintained by the Department of Commerce]. It includes federal trust fund transactions, but excludes loans and similar transactions since they consist of the exchange of financial assets or physical assets which are not newly produced and therefore do not contribute to current 'income.' "[80] Loans are included in the administrative and consolidated cash budgets, but a loan is not like any other government expenditure because the borrower assumes the responsibility to repay. While economists are generally agreed on the way in which taxes and expenditures other than loans affect the economy, they differ about the effect of loans and, therefore, have generally felt that the NIA was the best measure of the federal government's economic impact.

In presenting his budget for fiscal 1968, the President used all three forms of budget presentation, but emphasized the NIA. Because there usually are more payments into the trust funds than out of them, whereas the anticipated deficit under the administrative budget was $8.1 billion, it was $2.1 billion under NIA.[81] This illustrates the inadequacy of the administrative budget for fiscal policy planning, but it was retained because it shows proposed agency spending and thus provides Congress with its best instrument for control of the individual programs for which it is asked to make appropriations.

THE UNIFIED BUDGET

Essentially, what the President's Commission on Budget Concepts recommended is a *unified budget*, consisting of two complementary components: a *receipt-expenditure account* and a *loan account*. The receipt-expenditure account includes as receipts all tax revenue, trust fund receipts, and other current receipts of the government; the difference between these receipts and expenditures, called the expenditure-account surplus (or deficit), measures the economic impact of the budget. The loan account shows net lending, which is derived by deducting loan repay-

[79] *Report of the President's Commission on Budget Concepts, op. cit.,* p. 101.
[80] *Ibid.,* p. 99.
[81] *The Budget for 1968, op. cit.,* p. 71.

ments and sales from gross loan disbursements during the year. Net lending, added to the expenditures-account deficit, equals the total budget deficit.[82]

President Johnson accepted this recommendation, and his estimates for fiscal 1969 were prepared on this basis. Separate breakdowns were shown for the administrative, consolidated cash, and NIA budgets, but these were to be discontinued in future years.[83] The new budget format neatly solves the problem of how to serve both the fiscal-policy and expenditure-control uses of the budget.

In recent years economic analysis has also played a more important part in state government budgets.[84] While no one state's budget is big enough to have anywhere near the impact of federal activities on the economy, some are now in the billion-dollar category and have a great effect on economic conditions within the state. The same is true of budgets in the large cities and the big urban counties; to a more limited extent it is true in the smaller ones. No longer can budgeting be viewed only as a management device, an important "tool" of the top executives. Particularly at the federal level, budgeting now serves "simultaneously as an aid in decisions about both the efficient allocation of resources among competing claims and economic stabilization and growth."[85]

BIBLIOGRAPHY

Budgeting for National Objectives, New York: Committee for Economic Development, 1966.

Burkhead, Jesse, *Government Budgeting*, New York: Wiley, 1956.

Golembiewski, Robert T., (ed.), *Public Budgeting and Finance, Readings in Theory and Practice*, Itasca, Ill.: F. E. Peacock Publishers, 1968.

Mosher, Frederick C., *Program Budgeting: Theory and Practice*, Chicago: Public Administration Service, 1954.

Novick, David, (ed.), *Program Budgeting . . . Program Analysis and the Federal Budget*, Washington, D.C.: Government Printing Office, 1965.

"Performance Budgeting: Has the Theory Worked?" *Public Administration Review*, XX, No. 2 (Spring, 1960). Symposium of articles reporting experiences in public agencies using performance budgeting.

"Planning-Programming-Budgeting System: A Symposium,"

[82] *Report of the President's Commission on Budget Concepts, op. cit.*, p. 5.

[83] *The Budget for 1969, op. cit.*, pp. 45–55.

[84] Arlene Theuer Shadoan, "Developments in State Budget Administration," *Public Administration Review*, XXIII, No. 4 (December, 1963).

[85] *Report of the President's Commission on Budget Concepts, op. cit.*, p. 12.

Public Administration Review, XXVI, No. 4 (December, 1966).

"Planning-Programming-Budgeting System Reexamined: Development, Analysis, and Criticism," Symposium, *Public Administration Review, XXIX*, No. 2 (March-April, 1969).

Report of the President's Commission on Budget Concepts, Washington, D.C.: Government Printing Office, 1967.

Senate Subcommittee on National Security and International Operations, *Planning-Programming-Budgeting Official Documents*, Washington, D.C.: Government Printing Office, 1967.

Sherwood, Frank P., *The Management Approach to Budgeting*, Brussels: International Institute of Administrative Sciences, 1954.

State Expenditure Controls: An Evaluation, New York: Tax Foundation, 1965.

Wildavsky, Aaron, *The Politics of the Budgetary Process*, Boston: Little, Brown, 1964.

CHAPTER 18
STEPS
IN THE BUDGET
PROCESS

THE DETAILED procedure for the preparation and approval of a budget varies greatly depending on the place. Two examples will be used: New Castle County (Delaware) and the federal government.

NEW CASTLE COUNTY

Like many other local governments, New Castle County (Delaware) has both a *capital* and an *operating* budget.[1] The capital budget is part of the long-range planning of the physical facilities of the county, such as drainage systems, sewers, buildings, and parks. The county maintains a *capital program*, which is a schedule of capital improvement projects for the next six years, showing their priority, estimated costs, and sources of financing. (Capital improvement is defined as any permanent physical improvement with a normal life of 10 years or more.) Each year the capital program is extended for another fiscal year; beginning with July 1, 1968, the period covered was 1969–1974. The *capital budget* is a detailed list of capital expenditures to be incurred during

[1] The legal basis is *An Act Providing for the Reorganization of the Government of New Castle County and Amending and Repealing Existing Laws Pertaining Thereto,* Chapter 11, Part II, Title 9, Delaware Code.

the next fiscal year (which is the new first year of the six-year plan). The *operating budget* shows all anticipated expenditures during the next fiscal year for non-capital expenditures such as salaries and materials and supplies (current expense).

The capital budget

In New Castle County, there is an elective county executive, and a chief administrative officer (CAO) appointed by the county executive. Under the direction of the executive, the

Fig. 11. Capital Budget Procedure, New Castle County, Delaware. (Procedure followed in preparing for Fiscal 1969.)

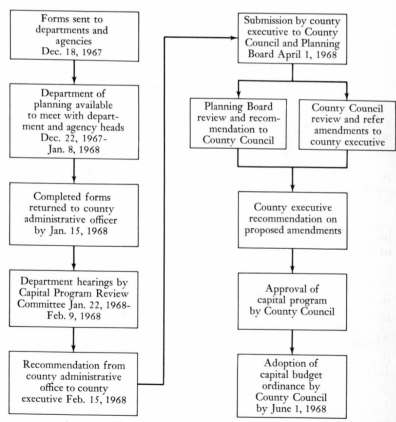

CAO is responsible for preparing the capital program and capital budget, and for ensuring that they are in conformance with the comprehensive development plans prepared by the Department of Planning. Figure 11 shows the detailed steps in the capital budget procedure; the Capital Program Review Committee, shown in the fourth step, consists of the CAO, the Director of Planning, and the Director of Finance. After it has held hearings during which the departments and agencies justify their requests, the CAO consults with the other members of the Committee, as well as with the Planning Board, before presenting his recommendations to the county executive. The latter reviews these recommendations at the same time that he goes over the operating budget requests (see Figure 12). The law requires the county executive to submit his recommendations on the capital program by April 1 to both the County Council and the Planning Board.

Fig. 12. Operating Budget Procedure, New Castle County, Delaware.

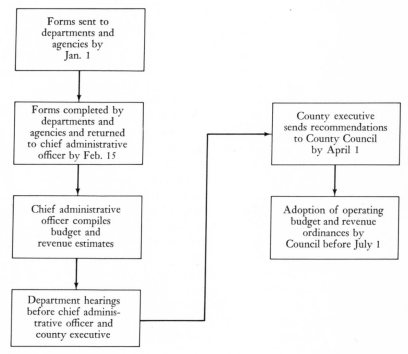

The operating budget

The CAO is required to distribute the budget estimate forms no later than January 1, and the departments and agencies to return them by February 15. The budget data is requested both on a program and object expenditure basis. The CAO puts together the budget estimates and forwards them to the county executive together with forecasts of receipts to be received from the various sources of revenue to be used to finance the budget. After the departmental budget hearings, the county executive makes his recommendations to the County Council in the form of a budget message "accompanied by proposed revenue and operating budget ordinances to give effect to the budget as presented." If estimated revenue is insufficient for balancing the budget, he must "recommend revenues sufficient to achieve a balanced budget."[2] The operating budget ordinance provides appropriations by object of expenditure for each "office, department, or board to which appropriations are made";[3] both ordinances must be submitted to the Council by the first of April.

THE FEDERAL GOVERNMENT

No separation of capital and current expenditures

The federal government does not have a separate capital budget, nor are the estimates for capital and current expenditures shown separately. The budget document does include special tabulations of expenditures of an investment nature. The lumping together of capital and current expenditures has long been criticized, because capital investment expenditures are treated as current expenses, with the entire cost for an expensive project sometimes charged to one year's operations, thus making deficits much larger than they otherwise would be. This is contrasted with private business, where capital outlays are not charged against current sales in estimating a firm's profit or loss. Furthermore, the future-year implications of items included in any one year's budget as single installments on projects that will take years to complete are obscured.

President Johnson's Commission on Budget Concepts recommended, however, against excluding "*outlays for capital goods from the total of budget expenditures . . . used to compute the budget surplus or deficit.*" Its reasoning was that the "current draft by the government on the economic resources of the

[2] Delaware Code, Title 9, Section 1132(d).

[3] Ibid., Section 1132(e).

private sector" would be seriously understated. It feared further that the institution of a capital budget might lead to over-emphasis on "brick-and-mortar" projects by comparison with those in areas such as health and education, where the future benefits cannot be capitalized. Notwithstanding, the Commission strongly supported better estimating of capital costs and cost-benefit analysis at the agency level.[4] The Program and Financial Plans referred to during the discussion of PPB in the preceding chapter now indicate the future-year costs of the different programs; thus one of the criticisms of lack of segregation of capital and current expenditures is apparently being met to some extent.

Budget preparation within the executive branch

Under the new PPB system (see Chapter 17, pages 358–376), in January the individual agency reviews its special study program and submits to the Bureau of the Budget a proposed list of such studies for the calendar year. In February the Bureau advises the agencies of the Special Analytic Studies it believes desirable and of the issues to be covered in the Program Memoranda for the next fiscal year. Between February and July the agencies complete their Special Analytic Studies and prepare drafts of the program memorandums; from April through August the Bureau of the Budget reviews these materials and gives the agencies its comments. From July to September the agency heads make final decisions on their program recommendations, and the draft Program Memoranda are revised, with another year added.[5] The agency budget estimates, made on the "cross-walk" basis referred to in the preceding chapter, must be in the hands of the Bureau of the Budget as early as possible in September, and in no event later than September 30.[6]

If considered desirable by the Bureau or the agency, arrangements are then made for formal hearings that "enable the agency to supplement the written material submitted, with an oral statement of the issues involved."[7] The Budget Director then makes his recommendation to the President as to the agency's estimates. The Bureau advises the agency of the President's decision, and the agency then revises its estimates accordingly.[8] This process is completed for all the agencies by the end of December.

Meanwhile, the Bureau of the Budget has received the latest estimates of revenues from the Treasury Department. With the expenditure and revenue information now ready, the Bureau

[4] Report of the President's Commission on Budget Concepts, Washington, D.C.: Government Printing Office, 1967, pp. 33–34.

[5] Planning-Programming-Budgeting, Official Documents, Senate Subcommittee on National Security and International Operations, 90th Congress, 1st Session, Washington, D.C.: Government Printing Office, 1967, p. 16.

[6] Instructions for the Preparation and Submission of Annual Budget Estimates, Executive Office of the President, Bureau of the Budget, Circular No. A-11, July, 1967, Section 11.3.

[7] Ibid., Section 11.7.

[8] Ibid., Section 11.8.

puts the budget document together. Usually the President sends his budget message and the accompanying estimates to Congress in the third week in January.

Review and action in congress

In Congress, programs must be authorized by legislation before appropriation bills providing funds for the activities in question can be passed. The authorization bills are considered by the standing committees with jurisdiction in the particular field of legislation; increasingly, the authorization is for one year only and must be reviewed with each new fiscal year. The appropriations are usually made on an annual basis, with the agencies being allowed to carry over unexpended funds from one fiscal year to another. Although there is one budget, Congress takes action by approving a number of different appropriation bills, in recent years totaling about 15 bills. It also passes legislation providing the agencies with obligational authority, which means that they can enter into commitments requiring the federal government to pay out money up to a specified total sum. Unobligated balances from such authorizations can also be brought forward from prior years. About $39.3 billion of fiscal 1968's administrative budget of $135 billion represented estimated disbursements to be made in that fiscal year from unspent authorizations enacted in previous years.[9]

The budget goes first to the House Appropriations Committee. Article 1, Section 7, of the Constitution requires that all revenue measures be initiated in the House, but it does not so require in the case of appropriations. The practice has been traditional, however, for spending bills also to originate in the House. The House Appropriations Committee may, as in recent years, hold an "overall budget hearing" at which the Budget Director and the Secretary of the Treasury are questioned in detail about the budget as a whole.[10] The budget is then broken down and the various parts sent to subcommittees that specialize in the consideration of the estimates of given agencies.

The subcommittees hold hearings at which the departments concerned have another opportunity to be heard. Representatives of the Bureau of the Budget usually do not testify at these hearings; the task of defending the estimates is left to the departmental budget officer and other top officials of the department. Witnesses are almost always "official," that is, they represent government agencies, not the general public. When these hearings are over, the subcommittee meets in a closed session to

[9] *The Budget for 1968,* Hearings Before the Committee on Appropriations, House of Representatives, 90th Congress, 1st Session, Washington, D.C.: Government Printing Office, 1967, p. 66.

[10] *Ibid.,* p. 1.

agree on its recommendations to the Appropriations Committee and draft the appropriation bill. Usually the Appropriations Committee will register no serious objections; it is recognized that the subcommittee members have made a detailed study of the estimates, whereas the full committee has not.

After the full committee acts on the draft appropriation bill, it is reported for consideration on the floor of the House, where it is treated like any other piece of legislation. The House of Representatives itself usually makes few important changes in the Appropriations Committee's recommendations, and thus the opinions and attitudes of the subcommittee and committee chairmen are important.

After House action is completed, the appropriation bill is sent to the Senate where it is referred to that body's Appropriations Committee. The same procedure of referral to the appropriate subcommittee is followed. The Senate subcommittees usually hold brief hearings, during which they concentrate on agency appeals from House action. As any newspaper reader knows, in recent years the Senate has often incurred the wrath of the House by restoring substantial portions of the cuts made in the lower chamber. Almost always the House and Senate versions of the appropriation bill will not coincide. This necessitates a conference committee, made up of representatives from the House and Senate Appropriations Committees designated by their respective chairmen.

After the conference committee makes its report to both Houses, each House decides whether it wants to accept or reject. Either House may reject the report and request that the bill be sent back to conference for further consideration, but this seldom happens. By this time the old fiscal year is just about to conclude, and there is great pressure to approve the appropriation bills for the next fiscal year. After action by both Houses on the conference committee recommendations, the bill is sent to the President. Under the Constitution, he must reject or approve the bill as a whole. He does not have the item veto, which means that he cannot eliminate individual items in the bill; thus Presidents almost never veto appropriation bills, since to do so would mean leaving the agencies altogether without funds when the new fiscal year begins. Time is not available to start the machinery of legislative consideration of the appropriation bill all over again. In signing, though, Presidents do not hesitate to indicate their disapproval of any expenditures they believe unwise. If the appropriation bill has not been enacted by June 30, Congress passes a continuing resolution permitting expenditures at the rate of the old fiscal year until the new appropriation act is passed. Concern has been expressed over the frequency with which such continuing resolutions have been necessary; the appropriation acts have sometimes not been approved until the end of December.[11]

With respect to the above procedure, it should be noted that revenue measures follow the same route, except that they are first considered in the House by its Ways and Means Committee, and in the Senate by its Finance Committee. Within Congress, consideration of expenditures and tax measures is not coordinated.

PROPOSALS TO IMPROVE CONGRESSIONAL REVIEW

A number of proposals have been made to improve Congressional consideration of the budget. One is to end annual program authorizations and make them, where possible, on a permanent basis or at least for periods of three to five years.[12] Proponents of this change argue that annual authorization means competition every year between the legislative committees and subcommittees, on the one hand, and the Appropriations Committees and subcommittees on the other, evidenced in the fact that frequently the sums appropriated are substantially less than those authorized. They also believe that the present annual system makes for piecemeal rather than long-range planning, and that in programs such as foreign aid, it harms our relations with other nations. Finally, they point to the delays in the passage of the appropriation acts, the extra work for Congress, and the damaging effect on employee morale in administrative agencies whose continuance is in jeopardy every year. Congress, however, remains reluctant to make authorizations for longer periods and has done so in very few cases.

A second proposal would make it possible for Congress to control the amount of spending during the fiscal year for which funds are appropriated. This would be accomplished by requiring that all bills be paid and accounts settled by the end of the year, with the unexpended balances reverting to the Treasury. Only the funds needed in each fiscal year would be appropriated, but agencies would be authorized to enter into contracts requiring expenditures over a period of years by a provision either in the legislation authorizing the program or in the initial appropriation. It is argued that under the present system of huge "carryovers" Congress has lost effective expenditure control, and that the change proposed would enable it every year to reconsider spending authority already granted.

[11] See *Budgeting for National Objectives,* New York: Committee for Economic Development, 1966, pp. 60–65.

[12] *Ibid.,* p. 21, pp. 44–45.

The counterargument is that the appropriations committees get full reports on the unexpended balances and take these into account in making their recommendations on new appropriations; furthermore, Congress can at any time change the obligational authority previously granted. Congress apparently must feel that the present system is tolerable, for it has not made this change, although it was recommended by the second Hoover Commission.[13]

Many people feel that spending could be better controlled, or its implications more clearly grasped at the time of authorization, if early consideration were given to coordination of the expenditure and revenue sides of the budget. Congress sought to deal with this problem with Section 138 of the Legislative Reorganization Act of 1946.[14] This section provides that the House Ways and Means and Appropriations Committees, and the Senate Appropriations and Finance Committees, shall annually meet jointly and, by February 15, report to their respective Houses a "legislative budget for the ensuing fiscal year, including the estimated overall Federal receipts and expenditures for such year." Specifically, they are to recommend the "maximum amount to be appropriated for expenditure in such year." If the estimated receipts exceed the estimated expenditures, their report must contain a "recommendation for a reduction in the public debt." The report is to be accompanied by a resolution providing for its adoption by Congress. If the proposed expenditures exceed the estimated revenues, the resolution must include the following language: "That it is the sense of the Congress that the public debt shall be increased in an amount equal to the amount by which the estimated expenditures for the ensuing fiscal year exceed the estimated receipts, such amount being $——."[15]

The maximum amount approved by Congress in this concurrent resolution was to guide the Appropriations Committees of both Houses in acting on the appropriation bills. Section 138 has not been repealed, but only on one occasion has Congress approved a legislative budget. This was for fiscal year 1949, but even then Congress failed to keep within the ceiling amount, exceeding it by $6 billion. Congress found the legislative budget unworkable because it requires setting a limit on total expenditures very early in the session, long before a detailed review of the spending proposals of the executive agencies has been finished. A further objection was that it was unrealistic to put a ceiling on expenditures in view of the many unpredictable circumstances that may create the need for Congress to

[13] See Joseph P. Harris, *Congressional Control of Administration*, Garden City, New York: Doubleday, 1964, pp. 125–127.

[14] *Financial Management in the Federal Government*, 87th Congress, 1st Session, Senate Document No. 11, Washington, D.C.: Government Printing Office, 1961, pp. 29–32.

[15] *Ibid.*, p. 30.

vote additional funds later in the session. The time allowed for preparation of the legislative budget is short, and the joint committee, an unwieldy group of more than 100 members, was not adequately staffed to do its job.

Since the failure of the legislative budget, strong efforts have been made to obtain the creation of a Joint Committee on the Budget.[16] Senator McClellan of Arkansas introduced a bill for this purpose which was passed by the Senate in 1957 but not approved by the House. McClellan's bill would have created a Joint Committee on the Budget composed of 14 members, with the House and Senate Appropriations Committees each having seven representatives.

In general, it was hoped that such a committee would function in much the same manner as the Joint Committee on Internal Revenue Taxation, which is made up of members of the House Ways and Means and Senate Finance Committees, and which has a permanent professional staff that studies revenue proposals and gives the committee members expert advice. This professional staff has provided a valuable service, and it is felt that Congress could use similar help on the expenditures' side.

Specifically, the proposed Joint Committee was to study the budget estimates in detail and make recommendations thereon to the Appropriations Committees. Similarly, it was to analyze the available information relating to the revenue side of the budget and propose a fiscal program that would meet essential spending requirements within the anticipated income. Not only was the Joint Committee to provide the Appropriations Committees with these analyses, but it was also to lend them the services of its staff during the periods when appropriation bills were being considered. The Appropriations Committees do have some professional staff of their own, which is one reason the House Appropriations Committee objected to the McClellan bill. Its argument was that the Appropriations Committees of both Houses already had the authority to employ any additional staff needed. Some members of the House also feared that the Senate-approved McClellan bill might be an effort by the second chamber to have a say in introducing appropriations measures.

A modified plan has been suggested whereby the House Appropriations Committee would invite the House Ways and Means Committee to sit with it during the "overall" budget hearing. Both committees would then adopt a joint resolution, or separate resolutions, outlining revenue and expenditure targets for the next fiscal year. These targets would guide both

16 *Ibid.*, pp. 195–218.

committees in their deliberations, and they "would also be useful to the legislative committees in evaluating the nation's ability to afford new programs."[17]

Still another proposal callls for an omnibus appropriation bill. Under the procedure of approving a number of different spending bills, neither the Appropriations Committees nor the members of each House know what the full tab for expenditures will be at the end of the session. The advantage of the omnibus bill is that it would make this total bill clear, even if it proved impossible to keep expenditures down to the level some Congressmen want. Legislation has been introduced in recent years to provide for an omnibus appropriations bill, but although this proposal was twice approved in the Senate, it was not passed by the House.

The House Appropriations Committee did decide to try the single-package bill on a voluntary basis when considering the budget requests for the 1951 fiscal year. On March 21, 1950, it reported a single bill to the House, which approved it on May 10, 1950. The Senate Appropriations Committee reported the bill to the Senate on July 8, 1950. It was approved with amendments by the Senate on August 4, sent to conference committee where it was considered for three weeks, and finally signed by the President on September 6, 1950.

Although the House Appropriations Committee chairman favored using the omnibus approach again in 1951, the committee decided to drop it. For one thing, it was argued that Congressmen were in a much better position to vote against individual appropriation bills than to defeat a single measure containing such an enormous number of items. Another objection was the excessive delay inevitably associated with an omnibus bill, because neither House could take any action on expenditures until its Appropriations Committee had finally completed consideration of the mammoth measure. Individual members of Congress were asked late in the session to vote on a single appropriation bill that they had no real time to study. Under the existing procedure of considering several different bills separately, the Congressman has time to study the reports of the Appropriations Committees on each bill and inform himself better on the issues.[18]

Another objection to the omnibus bill is that it puts the President in the position of having to approve or disapprove *all* expenditure requests for the fiscal year in question. As previously mentioned, the President does not have the item veto whereby he may delete items from expenditure bills; as Article 1, Section 7, of the Constitution is worded, he must approve or

[17] *Budgeting For National Objectives, op. cit.,* p. 43.

[18] *Financial Management in the Federal Government, op. cit.,* pp. 229–236.

reject the bill *in toto*. By contrast, in 39 of the 50 states the governor now possesses the item veto.[19] Consequently, the legislatures in these states tend to follow the governor's expenditure proposals much more closely than the national Congress does the President's, for a governor can delete any items added to his budget of which he does not approve. The great majority of state governments do employ the omnibus appropriation bill.[20]

Numerous proposals have been made in Congress to give the President the item veto. Some of these have sought to accomplish the objective through the ordinary route of passing a new law. Others have been made in the form of a proposed amendment to the Constitution on the assumption that this was necessary. Those in favor argue that if he could eliminate or reduce items in appropriation bills, the President could save the taxpayers much money. They have in mind "log-rolling," the practice whereby Congressmen mutually help one another to obtain approval of spending projects desired by local constituents. Those opposed claim that the item veto would give the President too much power. Congressional control over the purse would be weakened, to the detriment of the nation. The Chief Executive might even use the item veto to intimidate Congressmen by threatening them with disallowing expenditures in their home districts unless they supported his policies.[21] Obviously, the item veto would strengthen the Presidency. Since this is the case, it is understandable why many Congressmen are reluctant to give the Chief Executive this power.

EXECUTION OF THE BUDGET

Once the appropriation bill or bills are passed by the legislative body, the budget must be executed. In some foreign governments the legislative authorizations are not made directly to the administrative agencies but to the ministry of finance or budget office. The latter then controls the release of funds to the agencies and may reserve portions of the appropriations whenever it considers this necessary in the light of changing conditions affecting the nation's finances.[22] In the United States, with few exceptions, the funds are voted directly to the administrative agencies.

Control over expenditures, however, is exercised by the central budget office or staff through a system of apportionments. The United States Bureau of the Budget, exercising powers granted to it by law,[23] requires the departments to sub-

[19] *State Expenditure Controls: An Evaluation,* New York: Tax Foundation, 1965, p. 50.

[20] *Ibid.,* p. 47.

[21] *Financial Management in the Federal Government, op. cit.,* pp. 236–249.

[22] *Government Accounting and Budget Execution,* New York: United Nations, 1952, p. 14.

[23] Section 3679, Revised Statutes. Reproduced in *The Budget for 1968, op. cit.,* pp. 55–57.

mit requests for apportionments before any of the funds voted by Congress for the next fiscal year can be used. Legal provisions in state and local governments also typically provide for an apportionment system. In the federal service, the apportionments are usually made for a quarterly period; in some states and cities they are made on a monthly basis. In New Castle County (Delaware), the county administrative officer, with the approval of the county executive, is authorized to "establish such allocation or allotment procedures" as he deems "appropriate for a proper administration of the [operating] budget."[24] The purpose of the apportionments is to control the rate of spending so as to make deficiency appropriations unnecessary. Without such control, an agency might exhaust its funds before the end of the fiscal year. Another reason for having an apportionment system is that it makes it possible to time expenditures with collection of taxes and receipt of other income. In this way spending can be kept within income throughout the entire fiscal year, and there is no need to seek short-term loans in anticipation of later revenue.

If an agency does not spend all of its apportionment for a particular period, it is usually allowed to carry over the unused portion for expenditure in future periods. The Model City Charter authorizes the city manager to revise the apportionments at any time during the budget year "for any reason."[25] In New Castle County, the county executive is required to direct changes in the allotments when necessary to keep "expenditures within the revenues received or anticipated."[26]

The controversy over impounding funds

In the federal government, the Bureau of the Budget has from time to time impounded funds, that is, placed them in reserve not for reasons of insufficient income but because the President does not believe it wise to make the particular expenditures. Recently, for reasons of economy, it has also been withholding appropriations made by Congress in excess of the amounts requested by the President, and also reducing other appropriations or deferring the making of expenditures from them.[27] The justification given for impounding funds is that an appropriation is an authorization—not a mandate—to spend for a particular purpose. The Bureau has been sharply criticized by some Congressmen who dispute its legal authority to withhold appropriated funds for any reason; it is argued that in this way the

[24] *An Act Providing for the Reorganization of the Government of New Castle County and Amending and Repealing Existing Laws Pertaining Thereto, op. cit.,* Section 1133(b).

[25] *Model City Charter*, Sixth edition, New York: National Municipal League, 1964, p. 40.

[26] Delaware Code, Title 9, Section 1133(d).

[27] *The Budget for 1968, op. cit.,* pp. 45–54.

President is really usurping the power of item veto. Congressional sensitivity has been greatest in the area of defense appropriations and, in particular, weapons systems.

On repeated occasions Congress has voted more funds for development or production of manned bombers than the Presidents have thought necessary. One example was the controversy over the desirability of putting more money into the development of the RS-70, the projected 2000-mile-an-hour bomber. The position of President Kennedy and Defense Secretary McNamara was that more money should not be spent on this project, because by the time the RS-70 was operational, it would be obsolete due to expected further developments in missile warfare. Representative Carl Vinson, then chairman of the House Armed Services Committee, not only disagreed but also proposed that the House insert a provision in the appropriation bill ordering the Secretary of the Air Force to spend the sum Congress considered necessary on this project. A compromise agreement was later reached whereby Vinson dropped his request for such appropriation language, but the President also agreed to restudy the RS-70 question. Congress then voted funds for development of a number of RS-70 prototypes, but the Air Force later lost its enthusiasm for the RS-70. The constitutional question raised is: Does Congress' control of the purse give it the right to decide which weapons systems should be developed? But if Congress, and not the President, makes the decisions on weapons systems, how can the Chief Executive function effectively as Commander-in-Chief of the armed forces? If his opinions on such matters are not followed, how can he be held responsible for the nation's security? Basically, the issue really is academic; there is no way of forcing the President and the executive agencies to spend funds appropriated by Congress if they do not choose to do so. As Lippmann has said, "Congress cannot go to court."[28]

BIBLIOGRAPHY

Budgeting for National Objectives, New York: Committee for Economic Development, 1966.

Burkhead, Jesse, *Governmental Budgeting*, New York: Wiley, 1956. Part III.

Financial Management in the Federal Government, 87th Congress, 1st Session, Document No. 11, Washington, D.C.: Government Printing Office, 1961.

[28] *St. Louis Post-Dispatch*, editorial page, March 14, 1962.

Government Accounting and Budget Execution, New York: United Nations, 1952.

Harris, Joseph P., *Congressional Control of Administration*, Garden City, N.Y.: Doubleday, 1964. Parts 3 through 5.

Wildavsky, Aaron, *The Politics of the Budgetary Process*, Boston: Little, Brown, 1964.

CHAPTER 19
ACCOUNTING,
AUDITING,
AND PURCHASING

G OVERNMENTAL FINANCIAL systems should be so devised as to facilitate program planning and safeguard the use of the public's funds. This brings us to three important aspects of fiscal management: (1) accounting, (2) auditing, and (3) purchasing and supply.

ACCOUNTING AND AUDITING

Accounting is the art of recording and summarizing the activities of an organization in terms of money, and of interpreting the results thereof. Without a good system of accounts and comprehensive financial reports derived from the accounting data, no agency, public or private, could function effectively. Expenditures must be kept within the approved budget totals; the accounting reports show what has been paid out or committed, and thus overspending is prevented. Important as controlling overspending is, this should be a minimum objective only, for the accounting system should also serve to help carry out management policies with maximum effectiveness. Planning-Programming-Budgeting (PPB), described in Chapter 17, could not succeed without accurate allocations of costs to the different programs and program elements. When budgeting was a subsidiary of the accounting system and the emphasis was primarily on controlling governmental outlays, refined cost data was not needed. Cost-utility analysis, one of the pillars of PPB, could not be undertaken without such data.

Auditing is an analysis of proposed or past expenditures with respect not only to their legality but also to their desirability. Accounting data provides much of the information upon which audits are made. Auditors examine expenditure vouchers and other documents showing proposed or past financial transactions. If the audit takes place prior to payment of an obligation, it is known as the *pre-audit*. Usually the pre-audit is conducted within the executive branch. This is logical because the purpose is for those in government administration to exercise a control on the use of funds by subordinate officials. If an external group, such as auditors responsible directly to the legislature, was responsible for the pre-audit, the managers of the executive branch would not be making the decisions as to how best to use the available funds. In effect, the external auditors would be the managers of the executive branch.

The *post-audit* takes place after payment, in fact sometimes many months afterwards. There are numerous past financial transactions to review, so the auditors frequently have a big backlog of work. The purpose of the post-audit is to check upon the judgments made by the responsible officials in the executive branch. Perhaps in some cases they erred or authorized illegal expenditures. The legal provisions governing the use of funds are numerous, complicated, and sometimes subject to several different interpretations. Did the agency concerned respect the intent of the law? Legislators are naturally very much concerned about this; they want the funds spent as they intended. They also want to be sure that efficient use was made of the funds. Money can be spent legally but foolishly, and thus the post-audit should be broad enough to encompass the question of efficiency. Not too many years ago, the post-audit was very narrowly conceived in the federal government and in many other jurisdictions: it was limited to catching financial irregularities, frequently in the expenditure of very small sums.

Since the post-audit is a check on the administrative branch, it should be performed by persons outside that branch. The logical arragement is for the auditors to be responsible to the legislature and to report their findings directly to it. The objectivity of post-auditing could not be trusted if it were carried out by representatives of the same branch that authorized the expenditures in the first place. It follows that it is illogical to put the same official in charge of both pre-auditing and post-auditing. If someone approves an expenditure in the pre-audit, he naturally will not be inclined to question his own judgment when he makes the post-audit. Indeed, such a combination of functions is apt to put temptation in the way of any weak character who functions in both roles. He could, as one example, accept bribes from vendors, approve overpayments to them, and later certify the transaction as having met legal requirements.

A few years ago Illinois voted to separate the responsibilities for pre- and post-auditing, after an official responsible for both functions was found to have embezzled millions of dollars from the state. Post-auditing in that state is now the responsibility of an Auditor-General appointed by the legislature, who submits audit reports to a Legislative Audit Commission that reviews them for the legislature. Only a minority of the states, however, have legislative auditors, which explains the comment that "organization of the post-audit function in most states appears to be unsatisfactory."[1] A majority of the states have "either an elected auditor independent of both the legislature and the executive, or one within the executive branch."[2]

[1] *State Expenditure Controls: An Evaluation,* New York: Tax Foundation, Inc., 1965, p. 12.

[2] *Ibid.* See also pp. 71–73.

[3] "Protecting the Taxpayer's Dollar," address by the Comptroller General of the United States, Elmer B. Staats, to the 80th Annual Meeting of the American Institute of Accountants, Portland, Oreg., September 26, 1967, p. 2.

The case of the federal government

It was noted in Chapter 16 that the Budget and Accounting Act of 1921, besides establishing the Bureau of the Budget, also created the General Accounting Office (GAO). The head of the GAO—whose title is the Comptroller General—is appointed by the President, subject to Senate confirmation, for a period of 15 years. He may not be removed by the President for *any* reason. Only Congress can remove him, either for cause as stated in a joint resolution or through impeachment proceedings. As the present Comptroller General has said, "The General Accounting Office is an agency of the Congress."[3]

The Budget and Accounting Act did not limit the GAO to post-auditing; it also gave it the power to "prescribe the forms, systems, and procedure for administrative appropriation and fund accounting in the several departments and establishments, and for the administrative examination of fiscal officers' accounts and claims against the United States."[4] This meant that control of agency accounting systems and the pre-audit were also the responsibility of the GAO. In 1937, stressing that accounting was a "tool of management" and that the pre-audit was an executive function, Franklin D. Roosevelt's Committee on Administrative Management recommended that the GAO's accounting functions be transferred to the Treasury Department, along with the authority to settle claims for or against the government. In the Committee's opinion, the GAO was not doing a good job in either accounting or auditing; it was spending its time mostly on the detailed checking of expenditure vouchers and supporting documents for each and every financial transaction in the administrative agencies, no matter how small the amounts involved. Once the "executive" functions mistakenly assigned to it were removed, it could concentrate on making genuine post-audits, that is, critical reviews of the efficiency of agency operations and the wisdom of spending decisions.[5] Roosevelt accepted these recommendations, but Congress rejected them; the legislators saw this as an attempt to increase the Chief Executive's powers at their expense.

In 1948 the Joint Program for Improving Accounting in the Federal Government was initiated, the participants being the GAO, the Treasury Department, and the Bureau of the Budget. The purpose was to unite their efforts in a systematic attempt to meet the need for an integrated pattern of accounting and financial reporting for the government as a whole. The first Hoover Commission agreed with its Task Force on Fiscal, Budgeting, and Accounting Activities that a voluntary arrangement of this kind was unsatisfactory, but it did not want to see the GAO completely removed from the field of accounting. It proposed a compromise arrangement whereby an Accountant-General would be established in the Treasury Department "with authority to prescribe general accounting methods and enforce accounting procedures," but with the Comptroller General's approval required before "these methods and procedures" could go into effect.[6] Significantly, Congress flatly rejected even this compromise. The Senate Committee on Government Operations stated a view widely held in Congress: the GAO's role in accounting was "essential to legislative control of appropriations and expenditures in the executive branch."[7] If anything, the Congressional view of the GAO as its "own agency" is even stronger today, particularly in view of the many services it now renders to the legislators. However, what the GAO

[4] See *Financial Management in the Federal Government*, 87th Congress, 1st Session, Document No. 11, Washington, D.C.: Government Printing Office, 1961, pp. 275–289, for text of the Act.

[5] *Ibid.*, pp. 13–18.

[6] Commission on Organization of the Executive Branch of the Government, *Budgeting and Accounting*, Washington, D.C.: Government Printing Office, 1949, p. 38.

[7] *Financial Management in the Federal Government, op. cit.*, p. 67.

agrees to delegate to the administrative agencies is its own business; so long as it retains its ultimate control over the administrative accounts, most Congressmen will apparently be satisfied.

THE CHANGE TO COMPREHENSIVE AUDITS

Other recommendations of the first Hoover Commission were accepted and led to significant improvements. One was that the GAO stop requiring the agencies to send to it in Washington the supporting documents for each and every financial transaction; freightloads of vouchers from all over the country were being hauled to Washington for central examination in the GAO, and this work was consuming about half the GAO's entire budget. The Commission recommended that, as in private enterprise, the post-audit be conducted at the work locations where the transactions had taken place and that business-type audits be made, with the emphasis on reviewing the efficiency of agency operations.

Since then the GAO has been conducting most of its audits at the agency locations, and its goal, increasingly better realized in recent years, has been to make "what is usually described as *management audits*, including in some cases program evaluations or reviews of Federal programs."[8] In accordance with new legislation passed in 1950, the Budget and Accounting Procedures Act, it concentrates on reviewing agency internal control systems, reports on the conditions found, and makes recommendations for improvements.[9] Obviously, in some cases the GAO auditors also do make intensive examinations of individual transactions, as when they detect evidences of gross fraud or waste. Its auditing is selective, because it is not staffed to review every agency's operations every year. It makes audits in those agencies where it believes they are most needed, and it gives priority to audit requests of Congressional committees and individual Congressmen.[10]

One of its most important functions is "the continuing review of policies, procedures, and practices followed by Government departments and agencies in the negotiation and award of contracts and in the administration of contract terms and conditions."[11] Recently the federal government has been awarding contracts for the procurement of property and services at the annual rate of $50 billion, including about $35 billion in Defense alone for weapon systems and equipment and supplies. About 80 percent of these are negotiated contracts, permitted by law in cases where the use of advertised bids and award procedures are deemed impracticable or inappropriate. Since negotiated

8 "Protecting the Taxpayer's Dollar," *op. cit.,* p. 8.

9 For text of Budget and Accounting Procedures Act of 1950 (64 Stat. 832, 834), see *Financial Management in the Federal Government, op. cit.,* pp. 289–295.

10 "The Role of the General Accounting Office in Business-Government Relationships," address by Elmer B. Staats, the Comptroller General of the United States, at ceremonies marking Dean's Day, New York University, New York, N.Y., December 2, 1967.

11 *Comptroller General of the United States, Annual Report 1967,* Washington, D.C.: Government Printing Office, 1967, p. 103.

prices must be based largely on actual or estimated prices for producing the equipment and articles in question, the cost information used by the contractors must be accurate if the government is not to be overcharged.[12] GAO audit findings that some contractors were obtaining unreasonably high prices for defense materials were an important factor in Congress' passage in 1962 of Public Law 87-653, the "Truth-in-Negotiations Act." It requires that suppliers submit cost and pricing data with their estimates, together with a certification that the information given is accurate, complete, and current.[13] Of course, the GAO is not always right in its audit findings and recommendations; this is for the agencies and Congress to decide, except that GAO decisions on legal questions relating to the awarding of government contracts are final and binding on the executive branch.

ACCRUAL ACCOUNTING, COST-BASED
BUDGETING, AND PPB

The first Hoover Commission also recommended that the government adopt the *accrual* basis of accounting for both expenditures and revenues. When the accounts are on an accrual basis, revenues are posted when they are earned, rather than waiting until the money is collected. Similarly, expenditures are recorded when the commitments are entered into, rather than delayed until the payments are made to those supplying the goods or services. (Under the cash system of accounting, entries are not made in the accounts until money is actually paid out or received.) Furthermore, under accrual accounting the cost of materials and supplies is charged to expense in the period when they are consumed, rather than charging the whole cost at the time when the entire shipment of the commodity is received.

Using the illustration of the Task Force: ". . . if several months' supply of coal is purchased and received during one fiscal year, but will not completely be consumed until the next fiscal year, it would be improper to charge all of the cost of the coal as expense of the year in which it is purchased and received."[14] Similarly, in the case of fixed assets such as plant and equipment, which have a useful life beyond the current budget period, the cost is spread over all the periods benefited.

Accrual accounting is essential for what is known as "cost-based budgeting." Under such budgeting, the estimates show exactly what costs will be incurred during the fiscal year in question. It is not enough simply to show the requests for new authorizations to spend money during the budget period. Supplies, materials, and equipment already on hand will be used,

[12] *Ibid.*

[13] *Ibid.*, pp. 106–108.

[14] See Felix A. Nigro (ed.), *Public Administration, Readings and Documents*, New York: Holt, Rinehart and Winston, 1951, p. 368.

as well as resources that become available during the budget period from orders placed during prior years. As noted in the previous chapter, the true cost of operations for a given period is not accurately measured by the estimates for new obligations to be entered into during that period. Cash accounting cannot provide the data needed for cost-based budgeting and the cost-benefit analyses that are a vital part of PPB.

It was not until 1956, however, that Congress amended the Budget and Accounting Procedures Act of 1950 to require the heads of each agency to maintain their accounts on an accrual basis, in accordance with principles and standards prescribed by the Comptroller General.[15] Progress by the agencies in installing and implementing such systems has been slow, and is of increasing concern to those who want to see PPB fully functioning as quickly as possible. In May, 1966, the President sent a memorandum to all agency heads urging them to use " 'businesslike financial systems' in support of PPB."[16]

In early 1968 the GAO, which under the Budget and Accounting Procedures Act of 1950 issues statements of accounting principles and then reviews agency systems for conformance, had been able to approve only 75 of the government's total of 154 accounting systems. Only one of the 18 within the Defense Department, where PPB was first introduced, had been cleared. Representative Betts of Ohio, estimating that it could take 22 years for all the systems to be approved, introduced a bill that would prevent agencies from installing PPB until they had obtained the GAO's approval of their accrual accounting systems.[17] The delays were partly attributable to resistance to both accrual accounting and PPB, but also to the complexities of developing the required cost data in administrative establishments of such large size.

PRESENT STATUS OF JOINT PROGRAM

The cooperative program, started in 1948 and made a legal requirement by a provision in the Budget and Accounting Procedures Act of 1950, has been broadened and renamed the Joint Financial Management Improvement Program. It is coordinated by a steering committee composed of one representative each for the GAO, the Bureau of the Budget, and the Treasury Department. Because of the difficulties in recruiting, training, and retaining finance personnel, a representative of the Civil Service Commission meets with and advises the committee on personnel problems. The other administrative agencies of the government designate representatives to act as liaison with the

[15] *Financial Management in the Federal Government, op. cit.,* p. 291.

[16] *The Joint Financial Management Improvement Program Annual Report Fiscal Year 1966,* Washington, D. C.: Government Printing Office, 1967, pp. 17–18.

[17] H. R. 12998, 90th Congress, 1st Session.

committee.[18] As an example of its role, the committee has been stimulating the preparation, for the benefit of all agencies, of case materials describing how individual agencies have actually benefited from better cost and financial information.[19]

PURCHASING AND SUPPLY

Purchasing and supply management is important because the required materials, supplies, and equipment must be on hand if the agency's programs are to be carried out successfully. The public is naturally concerned when it hears the claim that millions and even billions of dollars could be saved annually with more efficient procedures. We will be concerned later with the details of these criticisms; it is first advisable to describe briefly the essential elements of an efficient system of purchase and supply management. Just as there has been a budget-reform movement, so has there been a purchase-reform movement. The same forces that impelled public jurisdictions to adopt the executive budget have led many of them to modernize their purchasing and supply operations.

Essentials of efficient purchase and supply management

The first essential of efficient purchase and supply management is the establishment of a central purchasing agency, headed by a technically trained purchasing agent. If the government is to obtain full value for the commodities it buys, expertise on the part of those who make the purchases is indispensable, just as it is in private companies. When operating officials in each department contact the vendors directly and make their own purchases, the result is usually inefficiency and waste. There is no attempt to standardize quality and to consolidate requisitions in order to obtain the lower unit prices available when bulk purchases are made.

The central purchasing office should itself make the purchases for all using departments, subject to whatever delegations of authority to the departments it believes appropriate. For example, it may be advisable to have the public hospitals purchase perishable commodities directly. In state and local governments there usually should be few exceptions to the rule of centralized purchasing. In fact, in many cases it is advantageous for local governments to enter into joint purchasing programs for various articles of supply. Dozens of such cooperative agreements have been in force for years. Because of its great size, decentral-

18 *The Joint Financial Management Improvement Program Annual Report Fiscal Year 1966, op. cit.*, p. 1.

19 *Comptroller General of the United States Annual Report 1967, op. cit.*, p. 41.

ization of purchase authority must be practiced on a much wider scale in the federal government. The special case of the federal government will be discussed later.

Specifically, what are the expert services provided by the central purchasing agency? One of the most important is the preparation of commodity specifications. Just as the class specification in personnel administration defines the kind of job and the qualifications needed to fill it, so does the commodity specification describe in detail the characteristics of the article to be purchased. The magnitude of this task will be appreciated when it is remembered how many thousands of items of different kinds are procured by public agencies. Fortunately, by this time many sets of specifications have been published and can be consulted. State and local governments, for example, can adapt specifications available from the Federal Supply Service in the General Services Administration. Another important source is the National Bureau of Standards. Leaders in the purchasing movement have stressed that preparing the specifications should be a cooperative enterprise of the central purchasing office and representatives of the using agencies. The help of chemists, engineers, and other technicians in the line departments is valuable in developing specifications for materials and equipment to be used on construction and other projects.

Stimulation of real competition among the bidders is another important responsibility of the central purchasing agency; indeed, it is of anyone who is authorized to make the purchases. The usual procedure is to require the vendors to submit sealed bids and for the order to be placed with the lowest bidder. Usually the legal provisions are worded flexibly, however, so as to make it possible to reject a bid even though it is the lowest one. Based on past experience, the purchasing office may not have confidence in the integrity of the vendor or in the quality of his merchandise. Further, when commodities are available from only one vendor, the formality of bids is unnecessary.

There have been cases where an unscrupulous individual in the position of purchasing officer has dispensed with competition so as to favor certain vendors. He may do this in open violation of the law or because there are loopholes in it. For purchasing agents who violate the law, criminal penalties are usually provided in the statutes. Civil action can also be instituted to recover money lost by the jurisdiction because of irregularities. Several years ago the purchasing agent of one state government resigned after publication of a series of articles in a leading newspaper charging that he had accepted gifts from vendors and had otherwise violated the law.[20] Such cases are exceptional, but they do serve as a constant reminder of the indispensable requirement of high integrity on the part of those in purchasing operations.

Inspection and testing of goods when received from the vendors is another essential element of good purchasing procedure. Some vendors will ship inferior merchandise if they know that it will not be checked carefully upon delivery. Goods may be damaged in transit, or errors made by the vendors' shipping clerks in counting the items shipped. They may even send the wrong goods. Just as any shopper should open and check deliveries from the local stores as soon as they are received, so should public agencies.

When deliveries are made by the vendors directly to the using department, the usual procedure is to require someone to open the packages, check the materials, and advise the central purchasing office of any discrepancies or deficiencies in the goods received. If the deliveries are made to warehouses and other supply centers maintained by the central purchasing agency, the shipments are inspected there. To relieve the pressure on storage facilities, agreements are often made with the vendors for them to make partial shipments at designated periods of time. A commitment is made to buy from them large quantities of certain commodities so as to obtain lower unit prices. The vendor, however, does not ship all the goods immediately, but ships stipulated quantities at the times agreed until finally the entire order is filled. In this way the government gets the vendor to supply the storage facilities.

Certain kinds of commodities should undergo careful testing upon receipt. Mere counting and inspection for damage is not enough. In such cases, the purchasing office arranges for the use of existing test facilities in the laboratories of the governmental jurisdiction, or it contracts with private companies to perform this work. Without a central purchasing office to see to it that this testing takes place, a jurisdiction may, without knowing it, accept costly shipments of goods that really do not meet the standards.

An efficient system of warehousing and of supply management is also essential. Stock levels should be sufficient to meet needs, but not so high as to make it necessary later to declare much material surplus. The inventory records should accurately show the quantity of the stocks on hand of each item stored.

[20] *St. Louis Post-Dispatch*, November 29, 1959.

If they are inaccurate, materials may have been over- or under-ordered. Furthermore, all government property should be protected against theft, fire, or other loss or damage. Finally, there should be an orderly procedure for declaring property surplus and disposing of it on the best terms available to the government. The same kind of material that is being purchased by one agency should not be disposed of as surplus by another. So small a return is received on sales of surplus property that it is gross waste to dispose of items at only a tiny fraction of their cost when exactly the same article is needed by another agency.

Purchasing functions in the federal government

21 Commission on Organization of the Executive Branch of the Government, *Task Force Report on the Federal Supply System*, Washington, D.C.: Government Printing Office, 1949 p. 1.

22 See Commission on Organization of the Executive Branch of the Government, *Office of General Services*, Washington, D.C.: Government Printing Office, 1949.

23 Commission on Organization of the Executive Branch of the Government, *Surplus Property*, Washington, D.C.: Government Printing Office, 1955, p. xii.

As stated in Chapter 16, the General Services Administration (GSA) was established largely as the result of the recommendations of the first Hoover Commission. One of the latter's Task Forces stated that "the problem of supply is treated all too casually by the United States Government."[21] It believed that greater centralizatian of responsibility for purchasing and supply management in the federal government was needed.[22] The legislation establishing the GSA gave it general servicewide responsibility for purchasing and supply management, and its Federal Supply Service functions more effectively than did the Bureau of Federal Supply in the Treasury Department which it replaced. The GSA does not, however, attempt to do all the purchasing for the federal government. Under the law, it delegates purchasing authority to the administrative agencies, and, because of the great size of many of them, it has made many such delegations. The original legislation also provided that, depending on the discretion of the department head or of the President, some agencies such as the Veterans Administration and the Defense Department could elect to remain outside the GSA's jurisdiction or to come under it only partly.

When the second Hoover Commission made its studies, it had some strong criticisms of government supply operations, particularly in the Defense Department. "The Government," it said, "has mountainous accumulations of property which it would not have bought if it had a good inventory system. It is estimated that with proper inventory control and more realistic stock levels from $10 billion to $25 billion of supplies now in Government warehouses could be eliminated."[23] Fantastic examples of overbuying and waste were cited. In some military depots, supply items easily obtainable from the manufacturers were being stocked in quantities sufficient to meet needs for 20, 30, and, in one case, even 128 years.[24] In many cases, property was declared surplus by one branch of the military when the same items were being purchased in the open market by other branches. Since property sold as surplus produced a return of only 5 to 7 percent of its original cost, millions of dollars were being squandered. For that matter, property procedures throughout the government were inefficient. Civilian agencies were also buying and selling the same items as surplus at the same time.

The Commission's recommendations for tightening up supply operations led to improvements, and, when Robert McNamara became Secretary of Defense, he established the Defense Supply Agency (DSA), which is in charge of purchasing and supply operations for the Department of Defense as a whole.[25] McNamara estimated that the DSA's creation would result in savings of at least $3 billion a year, since previously each individual service command had conducted its own purchase and supply operations. The Defense Department later also arranged to turn over to the GSA the responsibility for buying all its nonmilitary supply items.

Unfortunately, evidence of waste in military and other supply operations still continues. The GAO and Congressional committees maintain constant vigilance in this area and prod the agencies to make further improvements. In 1967 a subcommittee of the House Armed Services Committee started a broad review of military procurement policies, procedures, and practices. In one of its first reports, issued on January 23, 1968, it stated that suppliers were overcharging the government, and in one case had "fleeced" it of more than $114,000 over a three-year period. Significantly, it found that besides deficiencies in the Defense Department's procedures, the cause was poor quality of the Department's procurement personnel, including some of the supervisors.[26] When so many billions of dollars are spent, under pressures like that of the Vietnam build-up, some waste is inevitable. However, just as the spoils system became intolerable when the functions of government became more complex, so too is the "casual" approach to purchasing outmoded. Where faithfully applied, the principles of the purchasing movement have clearly proved their value. Wider application of these principles constitutes one of the areas of unfinished business for public administration in the years ahead.

[24] *Ibid.,* pp. 6–7.

[25] *United States Government Organization Manual, 1968–69,* Washington, D.C.: Government Printing Office, June, 1968, pp. 205–208.

[26] *Defense Procurement Policies, Procedures, Practices, Part II—Small Purchases,* Report of the Subcommittee for Special Investigations of the House Committee on Armed Services, 90th Congress, 2nd Session, Washington, D.C.: Government Printing Office, 1968, pp. 3–4.

BIBLIOGRAPHY

Commission on Organization of the Executive Branch of the Government (First Hoover Commission), Washington, D.C.: Government Printing Office, 1949.
> *Task Force Report on Fiscal, Budgeting and Accounting Activities.*
> *Budgeting and Accounting.*

Commission on Organization of the Executive Branch of the Government (Second Hoover Commission), Washington, D.C.: Government Printing Office, 1955.
> *Task Force Report on Budget and Accounting.*
> *Budget and Accounting.*
> *Surplus Property.*

Financial Management in the Federal Government, 87th Congress, 1st Session, Senate Document No. 11, Washington, D.C.: Government Printing Office, 1961.

Forbes, Russell, *Purchasing for Small Cities*, Chicago: Public Administration Service, 1951.

Government Accounting and Budget Execution, New York: Department of Economic Affairs, United Nations, 1952.

Harris, Joseph P., *Congressional Control of Administration*, Garden City, N.Y.: Doubleday, 1964. Chapter 6.

Lewis, Robert B., "General Accounting Office—Background, Organization and Functions," *Federal Accountant*, XIV, No. 4 (Summer, 1965).

Staats, Elmer, "The General Accounting Office and American Business, *Public Administration Review*, XXVI, No. 3 (September, 1966).

PART VI
ADMINISTRATIVE
RESPONSIBILITY

CHAPTER 20
THE PROBLEM
OF ADMINISTRATIVE
POWER

PUBLIC OFFICIALS must act responsibly. Although it is recognized that reliance must be placed upon administrative officials to cope with the many complex problems of our day, there is much concern as to the adequacy of the controls over these officials. All criticisms of the "bureaucrats" cannot simply be dismissed as propaganda by people opposed to the governmental programs concerned. Some men will misuse their authority; this is true in any kind of organization, public or private. One is reminded here of James Madison's remark in one of the *Federalist* papers: "If men were angels, no government would be necessary. If angels were to govern men, neither external nor internal controls on government would be necessary."[1] It is with these external and internal controls on administrative officials that we will deal in this part of the book. In this chapter the possible abuses will be described, and the next chapter will deal with the available means of control.

[1] Alexander Hamilton, James Madison, and John Jay, *The Federalist*, Cambridge, Mass.: Harvard University Press, 1961, p. 356.

POSSIBLE ABUSES

Criticisms of public officials are sometimes made in general, even sweeping, terms, without any specific indication of the wrongs that have been committed. From such statements it is difficult to define the real problem, so we will present a number of examples as a factual basis for the discussion of control measures in the next chapter. In this identification of areas of possible abuse, some illustrations will be given that are already familiar to anybody who reads the newspapers and follows current events to some extent at least. Other illustrations will deal with possible misuses of authority that are less well known to the average citizen and may even be of no particular concern to him as an individual, yet they are sources of deep preoccupation to economic and other groups in their relations with the government, as well as to legislators and others interested in preventing the abuses in question.

Dishonesty

First, and most obvious, some public employees may be dishonest. They may steal from the government, as when a bridge toll collector pockets some of the money he receives and then falsifies the records of receipts. Many different employees receive government funds, or otherwise have control over them. Embezzlement may be in small or large amounts, perpetrated by low- or high-ranking officials. It is, however, only one of many different kinds of fraud that can be practiced in government programs.

The employee may accept bribes for either minor or major favors. The first instruction New York City Buildings Commissioner Charles G. Moerdler received from Mayor Lindsay was to investigate collusion between building inspectors and slumlords. Moerdler, convinced that some inspectors were accepting bribes for issuing "certificates of occupancy," appealed to the public to write him confidentially about cases of such bribery about which they had knowledge.[2] Later, Fire Commissioner Robert O. Lowery suspended 12 of the Fire Department's 13 electrical inspectors for allegedly taking payoffs from companies that install fire alarm and sprinkler systems in schools, factories, hospitals, and nursing homes. Apparently it had been common practice for more than 20 years for payments ranging from $5 to $150 to be made.[3] In the Sanitation Department, dishonest supervisors manipulated the rule of three so as to force the eligibles on promotion lists to pay them money before they would promote them.[4]

[2] New York Times, January 17, 1966.

[3] Bernard Weinraub, "Lowery Suspends 12 Fire Inspectors in 'Payoff' Inquiry," New York Times, September 1, 1966.

[4] McCandlish Phillips, "Sanitation Scandal Sparks Debate on Civil Service," New York Times, November 13, 1966, and Morris Kaplan, "2 Sanitationmen Admit 34 Payoffs," New York Times, October 18, 1968.

The bribes in the aforementioned cases all involved relatively small amounts of money; the conviction of James L. Marcus, the City's Commissioner of Water Supply, Gas and Electricity, for accepting a "kickback" of $16,000 from a private firm in return for awarding it an $840,000 reservoir-cleaning contract, caused much more comment.[5] Nor is New York City's case exceptional, as seen in the following statement:

> There is little question that the Marcus case was simply the beginning of a series of federal and state cases that will, in the opinion of people with access to as yet undisclosed facts, disgust and depress not only New Yorkers but Americans in general. The boundaries of future cases are not proscribed by any local limits but are national in scope.[6]

In California, state officials estimated that at least $200 million in potential tax revenues had been lost because of underassessments often made by elective tax assessors who were bribed by tax consultants representing the corporations owning the property concerned.[7]

Unethical behavior

The second illustration concerns officials who may keep within the letter of the law and do nothing for which they could be criminally prosecuted, yet their behavior is such as to raise a serious question about their ethics. Sometimes there are convenient loopholes in the law that make it possible for someone lacking integrity to engage in practices that defeat the intent of the legislation. This is like the thief who finds the front gate firmly secured but is able to slip in through a hole in the wire fence. As Ralph Eisenberg has said: "The area of concern today is the oft-cited 'gray zone'—that lying between behavior that is 'clean as a hound's tooth' and behavior obviously improper and illegal, involving such things as bribery, embezzlement, and theft."[8]

The whole field of conflict of interest illustrates this very well. In general terms, a conflict of interest exists when a "public official is placed in a position where, for some advantage to be gained for himself, he finds it difficult or impossible to devote himself with complete energy and loyalty to the public interest."[9] With some conflict-of-interest situations the law can deal in no uncertain terms. It can, for example, make illegal the acceptance of any payment in cash or in services from contractors with whom the government does business. But this is only one kind of conflict of interest, for the official may accept no money but may

5 John J. Goldman, "Marcus Case Leads to Extensive Investigation," Los Angeles Times, July 2, 1968.

6 Barnard L. Collier, "The Marcus Case: Many More Indictments Ahead," New York Times, June 23, 1968.

7 New York Times, December 4, 1966.

8 Ralph Eisenberg, "Conflicts of Interest Situations and Remedies," Rutgers Law Review, XIII, No. 4 (Summer, 1959), 666.

9 Report Submitted by the Legislative Research Council Relative to Conflict of Interest, Boston: Commonwealth of Massachusetts, May, 1961, p. 15.

make decisions that favor personal friends or political allies. The purchasing agent may decide that the lowest "best" bid is the one submitted by an old friend. Those awarding government contracts may prefer firms that have made substantial contributions to the political party in power.

Some years ago the head of the General Services Administration justified making insurance brokerage awards on a political basis, because to him "practical politics" required that the business should not go to firms that "did not help this administration get into office."[10] He resigned because of adverse public reaction to his views on this matter, but the point remains that legislation cannot be framed to eliminate all such possibilities of favoritism.

Overriding the law

Third, although personally honest, some officials may act without legal authority, or otherwise violate the law. Here the official seeks no bribe or other personal gain. Perhaps he is very strong-minded and has decided that he is going to take certain action no matter what doubts may later be raised about its legality. A Senate subcommittee that investigated ethical standards in government some years ago made this observation:

> Heads of agencies commonly turn to legal officers whom they appoint for rulings as to whether or not they can proceed in a given manner. The resulting opinions are not unbiased. They commonly tell the administrators what they want to hear. Undoubtedly they are leading to an undue expansion of administrative power under which administrators are changing or creating law, and hence usurping legislative functions.[11]

In recent years, criticism has intensified that administrative officials, through their rule-making powers and daily actions, in effect make "new law." In his testimony before the Senate Subcommittee on Separation of Powers, Senator Hartke of Indiana claimed that by negotiating an antidumping code at Geneva, the Johnson Administration had not only attempted to modify the Antidumping Law of 1921 but also to "write entirely new law in that field."[12]

Another example Senator Hartke gave was an internal revenue regulation of April 14, 1967, "supposedly based on an act of Congress 17 years ago," which "would tax the profits from advertising in publications of certain tax-exempt organizations. . . ." In his opinion, the 17-year-old law did not have the "slightest connection" with this issue; the Internal Revenue Service simply

[10] *St. Louis Post-Dispatch*, March 15, 1960.

[11] Senate Subcommittee on Labor and Public Welfare, 82nd Congress, 1st Session, *Ethical Standards in Government*, Washington, D.C.: Government Printing Office, 1951, p. 32.

[12] *Separation of Powers*, Hearings Before the Senate Subcommittee on Separation of Powers, 90th Congress, 1st Session, Washington, D.C.: Government Printing Office, 1967, p. 9.

had wanted to establish new policy. Congress, he felt, should legislate before such an important change in tax policy was made. He remarked, "Particularly when one looks at some of the proceedings of the IRS, it makes one think of Biblical exegetes gone mad. All I can say is, I'm very glad the IRS is not interpreting the Bible."[13]

Appearing before the same subcommittee, Senator Stennis of Mississippi charged that contrary to a very clear stipulation in the Civil Rights Act of 1964, the U.S. Office of Education was issuing school desegregation guidelines that were not of general applicability and did not have the President's approval. Further, although Congress had provided that federal funds should not be cut off until "there has been an express finding on the record, after opportunity for hearing, of a failure to comply," payments to some school districts were being "deferred," that is, delayed, without any hearing at all.[14]

He also told how upon one occasion the Administration proposed to the Senate Armed Services Committee the appointment of the Commandant of the Marine Corps as a member of the Joint Chiefs of Staff for two years, although the term stated in the enabling legislation for this body is four years: "So I called over there. They said, 'Yes it is true the law says four, but four includes two, so four or anything less than four. . . . So two is legal because it is less than four.' "[15]

Sometimes an official may think he is proceeding legally, but he may inadvertently omit some procedural step required by the law or the regulations issued under it. In other cases, whether he acted legally or not will depend upon the interpretation given to the facts. Was there "probable cause" for arrest? Was the arrested person really given a "prompt" preliminary hearing or arraignment? Were the civil rights demonstrators creating a public disturbance? The courts to which such cases are appealed examine the facts, because this is the only way of determining whether or not the action taken by local enforcement authorities was proper under the laws and the relevant constitutional principles. In some cases the official may be strongly biased and have taken action on the assumption that it would not be possible to prove in court or otherwise that his interpretation of the "facts" was prejudiced.

Unfair treatment of employees

Fourth, some agency decisions may violate principles of fair play in relations with their own employees. Someone may be dismissed

[13] *Ibid.*, p. 21.
[14] *Ibid.*, p. 37.
[15] *Ibid.*, p. 33.

allegedly for inefficiency, but the true motivation for the action is otherwise. Perhaps he was too outspoken in his criticisms of his superiors; perhaps he is a holdover from a previous administration that blanketed him in under civil service. The new regime would like to replace him with someone whose name is on the civil service lists but whose political and personal loyalty is more certain. There is nothing about government that ensures that all its decisions affecting its employees will be justifiable; the management can act arbitrarily, just as it can in private companies.

The early history of the loyalty program in the federal service illustrates how government employees may be dealt with summarily. There is no question about the right of the government to dismiss individuals who are guilty of subversive activities. The difficulty is in making defensible decisions as to who should be fired as a security risk. According to one point of view, once frankly stated by high-ranking federal officials, if there is any doubt at all about the employee's loyalty he should be dismissed. During the first years after World War II, quite a few employees were summarily dismissed or suspended, without even knowing the nature of the charges against them. The Supreme Court, however, ruled in 1956 that the loyalty procedures being used could only be applied in the case of "sensitive positions," namely those in which the individual because of the nature of his duties can adversely affect the security of the United States.[16] This has greatly reduced the scope of the loyalty program, because it previously had been extended to cover all employees, whether or not in sensitive positions.

Under present procedures, reflecting the latest court decisions, no employee who has completed his probationary period may be dismissed for security reasons without first receiving a written statement of the charges against him. He is entitled to answer the charges, request a hearing by a duly constituted agency authority, and obtain a review of his case by the agency head before a final decision is made. Furthermore, no agency may issue a letter of charges without first consulting the Department of Justice to assure that the rights of the employee are respected. Justice advises the agencies as to whether the charges are fully supported, and on the extent to which confrontation and cross-examination of witnesses will be required. It has ruled that it is improper to furnish security hearing boards or heads of agencies with investigative information not made available to the employee.[17]

16 Cole *v.* Young, 351 U.S. 536 (1956).

17 *Federal Personnel Manual,* United States Civil Service Commission, Chapter 732, Personnel Security Program, Subchapter 4, Security and Related Determinations, and Subchapter 1, General Provisions, 1–7.

Violations of procedural due process

Fifth, some agency decisions violate principles of procedural due process in relationships with outside parties. In general terms, procedural due process, based on the Fifth and Fourteenth Amendments to the Constitution, means that public officials at all levels of government must be fair in their dealings with private citizens and groups. In specific terms, it means that certain procedural safeguards must be observed. The right of confrontation illustrates procedural due process as it relates to proceedings against an individual. In this fifth point, however, we have primarily in mind the relationships of government regulatory agencies with business and other groups.

Congress and individual states have sought to deal with this problem by passing what are known as Administrative Procedure Acts. Congress passed such a law in 1946, and there has been considerable discussion and much disagreement about its adequacy ever since. Much of the controversy revolves around technical points that are most appropriately dealt with in courses in administrative law. For our purposes, it should suffice to say that legislation of this kind seeks to establish fair procedures to govern both administrative rulemaking and the quasijudicial decisions made by administrative agencies when they decide whether or not a private individual or group has violated any of the agency's rules or the provisions of the law itself. The legislation often requires advance notice of issuance of the rule and the opportunity for interested parties to make their reactions known.

As to the quasijudicial proceedings, it spells out the details of the adjudicatory procedure, covering "such matters as specifying issues and giving adequate notice, admissibility of evidence, opportunities for cross-examination, and the process by which decisions are reached."[18] The federal law deals with the problem of impartiality in deciding such cases by making the Civil Service Commission, not the individual agencies, responsible for the appointment of the hearings examiners. The latter "preside in cases not heard by agency heads" and "issue initial or recommended decisions."[19]

Failure to respect legislative intent

Sixth, public officials may keep within the law and respect procedural due process, yet fail to respect legislative intent or to

[18] See Ferrel Heady, "The New Reform Movement in Regulatory Administration," *Public Administration Review*, XIX, No. 2 (Spring, 1959), 91.

[19] Ferrel Heady and Eleanor Tabor Linenthal, "Congress and Administrative Regulation," *Law and Contemporary Problems*, XXVI, No. 2 (Spring, 1961), 247.

consider the viewpoints of all the groups in a community affected by their decisions. The administrative agency may fully understand what the legislative intent was and decide not to be guided by it. In Chapter 18, instances were cited where the President and the Secretary of Defense have refused to spend additional funds voted by Congress for certain weapons systems. In such cases the executive branch disregards the legislative intent, because it is convinced that the lawmakers have exceeded their powers.

As we saw in Chapter 1, in many areas all the legislature can do is to state broad policies in the law and leave their application in individual cases to the administrative agencies. In so doing, the agency's decisions may infuriate individual legislators. The action taken, the latter charge, was not what Congress intended; or on the other hand, action that the legislation plainly called for was deliberately avoided by the agency.

The Federal Communications Commission (FCC) is a case in point. Its function is to regulate radio and television stations in the "public interest," but there are varying interpretations of what this means. Under one view, the FCC should merely function as an "electronic traffic cop," limiting its responsibilities to assigning radio frequencies and television channels. Under another interpretation, it should construe its function to extend also to assuring that the broadcasters provide balanced programming and that they improve the quality of the programs.[20] For years, station licenses were renewed as a matter of course; there was very little critical review of the programming.

President Kennedy's first chairman of the FCC, Newton N. Minow, frankly stated that he thought that the television stations and the commercial sponsors had too low an opinion of the public's tastes, and under Minow, the FCC initiated a new policy where renewal of station licenses was no longer virtually automatic. More careful scrutiny was made of the broadcaster's past programming to determine whether or not it really was in the "public interest." Robert W. Sarnoff, Chairman of the Board of the National Broadcasting Company, immediately challenged Minow's interpretation of the public interest. He said that the FCC's authority to license stations did not give it the "responsibility of raising viewers' tastes or broadening their interests to conform to its own views on what those tastes and interests should be."[21] Disagreeing with Sarnoff, one editorial writer asked, "What is that public interest, if not in 'raising viewers' tastes' and 'broadening their interests'?"[22]

Recently the FCC has been taking a very positive view of

[20] See *Broadcasting and Government Regulation in a Free Society,* Center for the Study of Democratic Institutions, Santa Barbara, Calif.: 1959.

[21] *St. Louis Post-Dispatch,* editorial page February 3, 1962.

[22] *Ibid.*

its powers. Chapter 10 mentioned the FCC's ruling requiring broadcasters to carry free anti–cigarette-smoking messages. The major tobacco manufacturers appealed to the Supreme Court, arguing that the FCC overstepped its authority because there is no law requiring it to make the broadcasters "balance" their cigarette advertising. In early 1969, the FCC took away Boston's Channel 5 from the Boston Herald-Traveler Corporation, a newspaper company that had operated it since 1957 as a Columbia Broadcasting Company affiliate, and gave it instead to Boston Broadcasters, Inc. This was the first time that a major television license had been both cancelled and reassigned at renewal proceedings after the expiration of a license (licenses are granted for three-year periods). In taking this action, the FCC sought to diversify media control, in the interests of independent local control of broadcasting companies. Established broadcasters were concerned that the FCC might be establishing a new policy of treating license holders and new applicants as equals; in making its decision in this case, the FCC stated that past record was meaningful only if it represented better-than-average performance.

The regulatory commissions are by no means the only agencies that function under general mandates, making possible the charge that they have disregarded legislative intent. Decisions of the Secretary of the Interior are sometimes criticized as favoring special interests, such as the private power companies, mining concerns, and the livestock grazers. Partisans of public power, the conservation of natural resources, and the improvement of recreation facilities for the general public have allies in Congress who can and do raise the charge of failure to observe legislative intent. As we saw in Chapter 10, there are numerous "publics" that the same administrative agency must serve. Of course, there are some clear-cut cases where by no stretch of the imagination can administrative decisions be said to conform with policies specifically stated in the law. Frequently, however, the decisions can be justified by the agency as obeying part of its legislative mandate and being in direct conflict with no other provision of the law.

Gross inefficiency

Seventh, some public officials or their subordinates may prove grossly incompetent, and, as a result, the public suffers. No matter how good their intentions, if the administrative agencies fail to get their job done properly they have not met their responsibilities. The legislators and the public should not, and usually do not, expect perfect performance. If millions and even billions of dollars are wasted because of carelessness, this is hardly excusable. Some mistakes and some inefficiency will be tolerated as inevitable; gross inefficiency, however, falls in a different category.

An official indifferent to the need for efficiency is an irresponsible official, no matter how honest he is. Observing the law means not only respecting the statutes dealing with improper activities, but also those requiring completion of the work within designated time periods. If it is humanly impossible to meet these deadlines, that is another matter. Sometimes the/legislature itself is to blame, because it refuses to authorize the money needed to hire all the staff required to do the job adequately. It is sometimes very difficult to pinpoint responsibility for administrative failures, as charges and counter-charges are made by administrative officials, the legislators, the press, and others. An administrative agency with a proven record of efficient operations in the past is in the best position to come out on top in such disputes.

Covering up mistakes

Eighth, some officials may try to cover up their mistakes and errors, or refuse to cooperate with the legislative body or the public, as was shown in detail in Chapter 10. As we saw, whether the official has refused to cooperate is often a matter of opinion. The staunchest defenders of the public interest sometimes refuse to accede to certain demands of the legislators. What the infuriated legislator brands irresponsible conduct, the press and much of the public may regard as great courage on the part of the official concerned.

Failure to show initiative

Ninth, some public officials fail to make positive decisions and to exercise the discretion they have under the law. Primarily this means the unwillingness of public officials to take action, not because they do not sympathize with the laws they administer, but basically because they lack initiative. A number of examples will make this clear. The official may be afraid of criticism if he takes a certain action, even though the circumstances clearly call for it. He decides to play it safe by doing nothing, and, in a good many cases, no one will criticize him. Indeed, his superiors may never even know that there was action that he could have taken had he been more courageous. As another possibility, the official may decide it is too much work to find out whether something can be done. He saves himself from this "extra work" by saying "no" to the solicitor. The latter may be another employee asking about some privilege, or a member of the public asking for a certain service. Of course, complaints can be made about officials who evade their responsibilities in this way. Often, however, the solicitor does not have the necessary knowledge to question the validity of the denial of his request. Furthermore, many people are reluctant to complain. Many who do get nowhere with superior officers who treat the complaints perfunctorily and give them small consideration.

This ninth and final point is of particular importance because too often responsibility is thought of in negative terms only. Unless he commits an overt wrong, the public employee cannot be said to have failed to fulfill his public trust. This is faulty reasoning, because the employee should contribute a maximum, not a minimum, of service.

Charles S. Hyneman writes: "It is possible that government in America fails to accord with the will of the people fully as much because administrative officials fail to rise to these demands for initiative and leadership as because they overextend the authority that is given them."[23] V. O. Key, Jr., wrote:

> The danger of the rise of a bureaucracy aggressively grasping for unwarranted power is probably much less than the danger of drifting into a condition in which the bureaucracy is purely a negative force. A seasoned bureaucracy, without heroic measures to the contrary, tends to become attached to the time-honored ways of doing things, hostile toward innovation, lacking in initiative, and timid. These qualities are admirable at the right time and place, but the next few decades in the United States will hardly be the time and place for pleasant habituation to the customary.[24]

BIBLIOGRAPHY

Altshuler, Alan A., (ed.), *The Politics of the Federal Bureaucracy*, New York: Dodd, Mead, 1968. Chapter IV, B.

Bailey, Stephen K., "Ethics and the Public Service," *Public Administration Review*, XXIV, No. 4 (December, 1964).

Congressional Oversight of Administrative Agencies (National Labor Relations Board), Hearings Before the Senate Subcommittee on Separation of Powers, Parts 1 and 2, 90th Con-

[23] Charles S. Hyneman, *Bureaucracy in a Democracy*, New York: Harper & Row, 1950, p. 33.

[24] V. O. Key, Jr., *Politics, Parties, and Pressure Groups*, 4th ed., New York: Crowell, 1958, pp. 763–764.

gress, 2nd Session, Washington, D.C.: Government Printing Office, 1968.

Davis, Kenneth C., *Administrative Law in Government*, St. Paul, Minn.: West Publishing Company, 1960.

"Ethics in the Public Service," an annotated bibliography, *Public Personnel Review*, XXIII, No. 4 (October, 1962).

Friendly, Henry J., *The Federal Administrative Agencies: The Need for Better Definition of Standards*, Cambridge, Mass.: Harvard University Press, 1962.

House Subcommittee on the Federal Aid Highway Program, 87th Congress, 1st Session, *Relationship Between Road Contractors and State Personnel in Florida*, Washington, D.C.: Government Printing Office, 1961.

Redford, Emmette S., *Administration of National Economic Control*, New York: Macmillan, 1952.

Schubert, Glendon A., " 'The Public Interest' in Administrative Decision-making," *American Political Science Review*, XLI, No. 2 (June, 1957).

Senate Subcommittee on Administrative Practice and Procedure of the Committee on the Judiciary, 86th Congress, 2nd Session, *Report on Regulatory Agencies to the President-Elect*, Washington, D.C.: Government Printing Office, 1959.

Separation of Powers, Hearings Before the Senate Subcommittee on Separation of Powers, Part 1, 90th Congress, 1st Session, Washington, D.C.: Government Printing Office, 1967.

Special Subcommittee on Legislative Oversight of the House Committee on Interstate and Foreign Commerce, 85th Congress, 2nd Session, *Independent Regulatory Commissions*, Washington, D.C.: Government Printing Office, 1959.

CHAPTER 21
ENFORCING
ADMINISTRATIVE
RESPONSIBILITY

I N DESCRIBING the possible abuses of administrative power, some of the methods of administrative control were mentioned in the previous chapter. What now follows is a more complete discussion of these controls, as well as a critical examination of their effectiveness.

LAWS AGAINST FRAUDULENT ACTS

As to embezzlement, accepting bribes, and similar acts of dishonesty, the control problem is relatively simple as far as punishment is concerned. As one example, federal law makes it a crime for anyone who "corruptly gives, offers, or promises anything of value to any public official or person who has been selected to be a public official . . . with intent to influence any official act; or to influence such public official or person who has been selected to be a public official, to commit or aid in committing, or collude in, or allow, any fraud, or make opportunity for the commission of any fraud, on the United States. . . ."[1] The employee who accepts the "thing of value" is also guilty of fraud under the law.

All the states have laws against bribery and graft.[2] Thus the public employee who is tried in court and found guilty of fraud will be given a jail term, like any other criminal. Naturally, not all acts of fraud are detected in government, any more than they are in industry. It sometimes also happens that while the evidence of malfeasance is clear enough, it is not sufficient to obtain a conviction in court. In such cases, however, the employee concerned can be dismissed.

CLOSING THE LOOPHOLES IN CONFLICT-OF-INTEREST STATUTES

Sometimes the laws have loopholes; they may even require punishment of lesser offenses but permit no action to be taken against those guilty of major ones. For many years this was true of the federal conflict-of-interest statutes. Before these laws were changed recently, a former federal official was barred for a period of two years after his separation from the service from handling any claim that was pending anywhere in the government when it employed him. The courts interpreted the word *claim* to mean demands for money only. Actually, much of the influence-peddling, by present or former employees, has to do with applications for federal licenses and contracts that run into millions of dollars. A former government lawyer could not help a client with a claim for an income tax refund, but he could use his contacts in the government to influence the awarding of contracts involving very large sums of money. A recently passed statute[3] corrects this lamentable omission by covering not only claims but any application or matter before the government. However, it excludes Congressmen from its coverage, a very big loophole indeed, in view of the stock holdings, law practices, and other private interests of the lawmakers.

State governors urging passage of conflict-of-interest laws sometimes find a singular lack of interest on the part of the legislators, because the latter fear that the legislation will be so drafted as to include them along with officials of the administrative branch. Much of the practice of lawyer members of state legislatures consists of representation of private individuals before state licensing and other agencies. One governor who urged that a comprehensive conflict-of-interest law be passed in his state had this to say:

[1] Section 201, Public Law 87-849, 87th Congress.

[2] *Report Submitted by the Legislative Research Council Relative to Conflict of Interest,* Boston: Commonwealth of Massachusetts, May, 1961, p. 28.

[3] Public Law 87-849, 1963, 87th Congress.

I certainly do not believe the argument that lawyer members of the legislature will lose large parts of their law practice has any cogency, because I believe that if a large part of their law practice is of a nature to be affected by this action, they have the practice not because they are lawyers but because they are legislators.[4]

PREVENTING UNETHICAL CONDUCT

Those drafting conflict-of-interest statutes realize that they cannot be so worded as to identify and proscribe every kind of possible influence-peddling. The opening section in the statute passed in 1960 in Kentucky reads: "The purpose of this Act is to prescribe standards to guide public officers and employees in the conduct of their offices or employment, and to proscribe improper conduct *to the extent which such conduct may be sufficiently described to enable statutory prohibitions against it to be properly enforced* [Italics added]."[5] As previously indicated (see pages 273–274), the dilemma is that if the conflict-of-interest statutes are too tightly drawn, they may have the effect of deterring perfectly honest persons from accepting government jobs.

Conflict-of-interest situations, however, are not the only ones in which public employees may be guilty of unethical conduct. Favoring one of the agency's "publics" over the others does not exemplify high integrity. Other illustrations could be given, but suffice it to say that a faulty sense of ethics accounts for much of the censurable behavior by public employees.

Codes of ethics

This brings us to the consideration of codes of ethics.

A code of ethics is best defined as a statement of acceptable standards of behavior for government officials and employees. The code may be embraced in a statute or merely in departmental regulations or in a legislative resolution. It serves the purpose of clearly stating to public officials and to the public what is acceptable behavior. A code too may carry with it sanctions—although the sanctions are seldom criminal. Dismissal from office is a common sanction associated with codes of ethics. Implicit in the promulgation of a code of ethics, however, is the notion that each situation in the future will be evaluated on its particular merits.[6]

A number of state and municipal governments have passed legislation providing for codes of ethics. New York State has

[4] *St. Louis Post-Dispatch*, March 20, 1962.

[5] *Report Submitted by the Legislative Research Council Relative to Conflict of Interest*, op. cit., p. 37.

[6] Ralph Eisenberg, "Conflicts of Interest Situations and Remedies," *Rutgers Law Review, XIII*, No. 4 (Summer, 1959), 672.

a Public Officers Law which, in addition to a section on conflicts of interest, includes a code of ethics. The code prescribes standards of conduct, some fairly specific and others very general. As an illustration of a general standard, it is stated that the public employee "should endeavor to pursue a course of conduct which will not raise suspicion among the public that he is likely to be engaged in acts that are in violation of his trust."[7] This makes clear one of the limitations of codes of ethics. Descriptions of the desired conduct are couched in such general terms that the employee can easily justify his behavior as proper. Nonetheless, many people are strong partisans of the codes, and they are increasingly being adopted, sometimes through the voluntary action of professional organizations of public employees, sometimes in the form of executive order and departmental regulations, as in the federal service.

"LEGISLATING MORALITY"

An oft-repeated argument against the codes is that you cannot "legislate morality." If people do not have it in their hearts to adhere to high ethical standards, no code of ethics will reform them. The counterargument is that organized society has always legislated morality:

> A defensive view that "You can't legislate the Ten Commandments" overlooks the fact that wherever the Ten Commandments are held in high regard, legislative bodies have found it necessary to elaborate and enforce their basic principles. It is the function of a considerable part of the penal code to deal in more detail with matters which are specifically prohibited by the Ten Commandments. Every civilized people supplements its moral code with an extensive criminal code and with a vast body of civil law.[8]

Another objection is that you cannot expect the ethics of public officials to be any higher than those of the public as a whole. The Senate subcommittee just quoted acknowledged that "the clever man who makes a 'fast buck' gets a certain amount of acclaim, provided he makes enough of them. The political trickster frequently can claim his rewards—if he wins. There is a tolerance in American life for unscrupulous methods which bring immediate rewards, even though those methods, if they should become universal, would destroy the very society in which they are tolerated."[9] The subcommittee pointed out that there is a two-way relationship between standards of conduct in public affairs and those prevailing in the country generally. If the people are not too much concerned about ethical considerations, this

[7] *Report Submitted by the Legislative Research Council Relative to Conflict of Interest,* op. cit., p. 43.

[8] Senate Subcommittee on Labor and Public Welfare, 82nd Congress, 1st Session, *Ethical Standards in Government,* Washington, D.C.: Government Printing Office, 1951, p. 14.

[9] *Ibid.,* p. 9.

will be reflected in the behavior of many public officials. Conversely, if the latter go about setting an example of high integrity, this should raise the standards of the public. Those in positions of public leadership can inspire the citizen to follow certain principles—provided they themselves practice them.[10]

After all, the codes can do no harm, and their potentialities for doing good may be great. If they were totally ineffective, it is hard to see why for so long doctors, lawyers, engineers, businessmen, and many others have placed such great reliance on them. While it is true that individual members of these groups have been guilty of unethical conduct, it can hardly be claimed that for the professions as a whole the codes are dead letters. In the main, they serve the very important function of reminding the individual of his professional obligations.

THE INNER CHECK

Some people place great emphasis on what they call the *inner check*, by which they mean the individual's own sense of responsibility to the public. As John M. Gaus has written: "Professional standards and ethics may seem external; yet they operate on the thought and feeling of the individual, opening new vistas of action and objective, creating a warmth of personal association in a corporate enterprise."[11] Others are frankly skeptical; human nature being what it is, they are convinced that the main reliance must be placed on external controls over the employee. The disagreement is basically a question of emphasis, for those who emphasize the inner check fully appreciate that external controls are also needed. They believe, however, that every effort should be made to influence the employee "from within."

The official's sense of responsibility is, of course, the product of his entire previous history. This is why discriminating practices in the original selection of personnel are so essential. No code of ethics will make much of an impact on someone who for long has been convinced that the smart man does not let his conscience bother him about the methods he uses in attaining his ends.

CONTROLLING OFFICIALS WHO EXCEED THEIR POWERS

Several kinds of controls are available for officials who are personally honest but exceed their legal authority. If it is a clear case of an *ultra vires* act, that is, one not within the official's powers as defined in the law, the injured party can appeal to the courts and

[10] *Ibid.*, p. 7.

[11] John M. Gaus, *Reflections on Public Administration*, University, Ala.: University of Alabama Press, 1947, pp. 115–116.

get the action rescinded. If the official has jurisdiction but uses his authority in such a way as to violate the constitutional rights of the citizen, recourse can also be had to the courts.

An example is police officers who arrest demonstrators for "disturbing the peace." This action is within the scope of their powers, and they may be sustained in the local courts. When such cases reach the federal courts on appeal, however, the convictions will be set aside as a violation of freedom of speech and assembly when the courts are convinced that the demonstrators were behaving peaceably.

PREVENTING INJUSTICE TO THE EMPLOYEE

With respect to unfair treatment by the agency of its own employees, this may, in part, be avoided or corrected by control agencies within the executive branch. An employee who is dismissed allegedly for inefficiency, but actually because he is disliked because of his political views, can appeal to the Civil Service Commission. If it decides that the removal was really made for political reasons, it will order the employee restored to his position. Furthermore, punitive action may be taken against the official responsible for the dismissal. The Model State Civil Service Law provides for a punishment of forfeiture of position and of ineligibility for reappointment in the state service for a one-year period.[12]

Perhaps the situation is different. The case might be one of a federal employee who has lost his job as the result of a reduction in force. He claims the agency did not correctly interpret the law and the relevant regulations when it terminated his services. Let us assume that he appeals to the Civil Service Commission, but the latter decides in favor of the agency. The employee can still take his case to the courts, which may decide in his favor. The legal provisions governing reduction in force and many other personnel actions are complicated and susceptible to different interpretations. Palpable injustices are seldom committed by the agency managements, and they are almost always rescinded by the central personnel agency. When appeals do go to the courts, they will not hesitate to uphold the employee if they are convinced that the action taken against him was arbitrary, capricious, and without foundation in law.

Binding grievance arbitration, discussed in Chapter 15 (see pages 328–330), should have the effect of discouraging arbitrary and harsh action by the public employer. It assures "due process" for the employee.

12 See Felix A. Nigro, *Public Personnel Administration,* New York: Holt, Rinehart and Winston, 1959, Appendix A, p. 460.

ENSURING OBSERVANCE OF
PROCEDURAL DUE PROCESS

As to failure to observe procedural due process in relations with business and other groups, the injured party can appeal the agency's action to the courts. There would be no purpose in passing administrative procedure acts if the regulatory agencies were not required to observe the detailed requirements spelled out in such legislation. These are questions of law, and the courts will go into them thoroughly. Such appeals from actions of the national regulatory commissions are heard by the United States Circuit Courts of Appeal. They will set aside the commission's decisions if they find any violations of procedural due process. Furthermore, they will also do so if they believe the decisions to be "unsupported by competent, material, and substantial evidence in view of the entire record as submitted."[13] This means that the courts will examine questions of fact as well as of law, and administrative rulings may be nullified on both grounds.

Since judicial remedies have already been mentioned several times in this chapter, it is appropriate at this juncture to quote Don K. Price on their limitations in practice:

> Many administrative agencies, in matters of adjudication, deal with questions that have to be answered immediately in order to prevent hardship, or that individually do not justify the cost of legal proceedings. Thus an unsuccessful claimant for a small social security benefit will usually not hire a lawyer to contest a doubtful case, simply because the odds are not worth the cost. A grower will not take to court a decision by an examiner of the United States Department of Agriculture condemning a carload of perishable commodities, for his goods will decay before they could be introduced as evidence. A securities broker will find little satisfaction in appealing from an adverse decision of the Securities and Exchange Commission on the listing of a security, for the opportunity to sell it profitably may have gone.
>
> To depend mainly on judicial review in these cases would be futile. The chief problem is how to organize on a fair basis the system of rendering the original decision. The volume of administrative decisions alone would make it unwise to rely too extensively on review by the courts. . . . What the courts can do, however, is to protect the fundamental rights of citizens to fair treatment in the hearing of their cases, and to maintain the basic political and constitutional relationship between the administrative agency and other branches of government. . . .[14]

[13] Ferrel Heady, "The New Reform Movement in Regulatory Administration," *Public Administration Review*, XIX, No. 2 (Spring, 1959), 91.

[14] Don K. Price, "The Judicial Test," in Fritz Morstein Marx (ed.), *Elements of Public Administration*, Englewood Cliffs, N.J.: Prentice-Hall, 1959, pp. 488–489. See also Norman John Powell, *Responsible Public Bureaucracy in the United States*, Boston: Allyn and Bacon, 1967, pp. 70–80.

PROTECTING THE INTERESTS OF THE WHOLE PUBLIC

Responsible administration takes place only if all groups in the community with a legitimate interest in the agency's program are given the opportunity to make their views known. The provisions in the administrative-procedure acts requiring public notice of intention to issue rules and giving interested parties the opportunity to offer objections are useful in this connection, but they are no guarantee that the agency will give appropriate weight to all the points of view expressed. Furthermore, many decisions, such as in letting contracts, making loans, and deciding which programs within a multipurpose agency to emphasize, are not, and should not, be covered in administrative-procedures legislation.

Use of advisory committees

One technique used a great deal is the creation of advisory committees on which the different interest groups are represented. Sometimes the legislation requires the establishment of such committees; in other cases the head of the agency decides that he needs outside advice and voluntarily sets up the committee. The advantage of the advisory committee is that it can make known to the administrator points of view of which he otherwise might not be aware. Policies proposed by the agency's expert staffs may overlook practical difficulties that might arise in putting them into effect. The members of the advisory committee can save the agency some mistakes by warning of these difficulties.

If, as authors Maass and Radway suggest, one of the criteria for judging administrative responsibility should be the extent to which the agency succeeds in "winning group consent," proper use of advisory committees can contribute greatly to that objective. At the same time, another of their criteria is that the agency should equalize "opportunities to safeguard interests" and give "equitable treatment" to each of the major interests affected by its program.[15] It is here that in practice advisory committees often fail to function as they should, for the more powerful groups represented on them may dominate their deliberations. In such case the committee will "provide the administration with a distorted view of interest opinion and provide a focus through which the strong and strategically-located interests may exert a disproportionate amount of influence."[16]

[15] Arthur A. Maass and Lawrence I. Radway, "Gauging Administrative Responsibility," in Dwight Waldo (ed.), *Ideas and Issues in Public Administration,* New York: McGraw-Hill, 1953, p. 445.

[16] Emmette S. Redford, *Administration of National Economic Control,* New York: Macmillan, 1952, p. 262.

Actually there is no foolproof way of assuring that administrators equalize "opportunities to safeguard interests." It is frequently a matter of opinion whether or not an agency is pursuing policies that benefit one interest group as against another. Individual legislators themselves often exert pressure on the agency heads on behalf of *one* particular group. Each legislator represents the voters in his constituency, not the entire public. Administrators, it can be argued, are in a better position to consider the needs and desires of the whole public.[17] In any event, in some cases it will be clear that the agency is not giving "equitable treatment" to a certain group or groups. The legislators can investigate and put pressure on the Chief Executive to correct such situations, or the latter may take the initiative in the matter and even remove the agency head if he believes this necessary. In many instances, however, conclusive proof will be lacking that the agency failed to act in accordance with the "public interest," and the offended groups will achieve no success with their protests.

ELIMINATING GROSS
INCOMPETENCE AND APATHY

The most effective control mechanism to prevent gross incompetence on the part of public employees is a good personnel program. The personnel offices in the line departments and the central personnel agency should exert positive leadership to raise levels of performance. Although the key factor is the quality of the personnel recruited, other staff groups besides the personnel men can make important contributions to efficiency. Administrative analysts, now employed in many agencies, make detailed studies of organization and procedures, with the purpose of eliminating delays, waste, and other inefficiency. Efficiency is, however, more than a question of good organization and procedures; it is also the product of the attitudes and values of the public employees. This is why the discussion of administrative responsibility overlaps at so many points. The inner check can provide the will to be efficient. The best management studies will not result in substantial improvements if the employees feel no great urge to perform up to their abilities.

(The subject of officials who try to cover up their mistakes was dealt with in detail in Chapter 10, Public Relations; thus it will not be discussed here.)

As to the individual who lacks initiative, the greatest need here is an administrative leadership that encourages and rewards

[17] See Peter Woll, *American Bureaucracy,* New York: Norton, 1963, pp. 138–141.

employees who show initiative and creativity. If those in the top positions demonstrate that they really want employees with ideas and energy, then the organizations they direct come alive. This is why legislative bodies err so grievously when they put into the laws detailed requirements that narrow the administrative officials' discretion. As Woodrow Wilson so wisely said:

> If to keep his office a man must achieve open and honest success, and if at the same time he feels himself intrusted with large freedom of discretion, the greater his power the less likely is he to abuse it, the more is he nerved and sobered and elevated by it. The less his power, the more safely obscure and unnoticed does he feel his position to be, and the more readily does he relapse into remissness.[18]

EVALUATION OF LEGISLATIVE CONTROLS

Throughout this chapter, reference has been made to some of the methods used by legislatures to control administration. Various control devices were mentioned, but there was not an opportunity to refer to all of the principal ones. An evaluation was previously made in this chapter of judicial remedies. What are the strengths and weaknesses of the legislative controls?

The principal legislative controls now used are:

1. passage, amendment, and possible repeal of the enabling legislation under which administrative agencies function
2. review and approval or disapproval of budgetary requests
3. investigations by standing or select committees of the conduct of agency programs
4. direct participation in agency decisionmaking, in line with the doctrine of codirectorship discussed in Chapter 1
5. performance of *case work* for constituents, also mentioned in Chapter 1
6. the action taken in confirming or not the appointment of high-ranking officials

Changing the enabling legislation

If Congress is displeased with the policy decisions of executive officials, it can tie their hands by writing certain prohibitions into the law. The President can be directed by law not to make foreign aid available to certain countries;[19] the Federal Communications Act can be amended so as to make entirely clear what policies Congress wants the FCC to follow with respect to pay television. It is a post-control, however, and may be criti-

18 Waldo, *op. cit.*, p. 73.

19 *Separation of Powers*, Hearings Before the Senate Subcommittee on Separation of Powers, Part I, 90th Congress, 1st Session, Washington, D.C.: Government Printing Office, 1967, p. 44.

cized also for placing too many shackles on the administrators. In many programs the administrators must be left with certain discretion, and there is no way of predicting with certainty what kinds of policy decisions they will make. Furthermore, the legislators themselves disagree as to whether the administrators' decisions were correct or not. This greatly reduces the possibilities of passage of amendments to the enabling legislation. Too, it may be that the administrators were right, and that the legislature would be wrong if it amended the law. The press has often criticized legislative decisions that reverse administrative policies and argued that the people should vote such legislators out of office at the next elections.

If the legislature has serious doubts about the agency's program, it can authorize it only for a limited period of time, subject to renewal. Norman J. Powell notes that whereas before World War II Congress "would approve the authorization of new programs without time or money limitations," it now tends to place "stringent limits on authorized expenditures, including one year authorizations." In 1965 "about one third of the money in the executive budget could not be appropriated until Congress had passed eight or more authorization bills, good for only one year."[20] Sometimes the authorizing legislation provides for total expenditures that are reduced drastically in the appropriation bill as finally enacted. V. O. Key, Jr., wrote:

> Legislation enacted to be in effect only for one year or some other determinate period assures congressional review of administrative policy and performance when an extension of power is sought. For months preceding the renewal of such an act, its administrators walk warily, perhaps fearing to take steps of urgent importance lest some group in Congress be annoyed. They must wage battle for renewal when the expiration dates of such statutes approach, and the difficulty of obtaining positive action from Congress gives to opponents of a policy based on short-term legislation tactical advantages they would not enjoy if they had to seek outright repeal.[21]

Inability to make long-term commitments may, however, make it difficult or even impossible for a program to be successful. How can foreign aid be effective when the recipient countries are urged to develop long-range economic-development programs but told at the same time that assurances about grant funds can only be made for a 12-month period? And how can the employees of the Agency for International Development keep their morale up when the future of the agency for which they work is in constant doubt?

[20] Powell, *op. cit.*, pp. 49–50.
[21] V. O. Key, Jr., "Legislative Control," in Marx, *op. cit.*, pp. 313–314.

Of course, if the Congressman is not enthusiastic about foreign aid, these arguments will fail to convince him. Legislative control means control by the dominant group in the legislature at a particular time. Unfortunately, it cannot always be equated either with correct policies from the standpoint of the national interest or with accurate reflection of what the people of the country really want. This suggests that the people themselves should make more positive efforts to ensure that legislative and administrative policies are responsive to their desires.

When the legislature is convinced that an administrative agency no longer serves a useful purpose, it can abolish it outright. Scores of agencies have been abolished, many of the emergency variety. Once created, agencies typically struggle to survive. Franklin D. Roosevelt's Committee on Administrative Management said, "There is among governmental agencies great need for a coroner to pronounce them dead, and for an undertaker to dispose of the remains."[22]

Again, however, there may be a strong difference of opinion as to whether the agency is really dispensable. When Congress finally abolished the National Resources Planning Board in 1943, it decided not to take a chance on the agency rising from the dead. It specifically provided in the legislation terminating the Board that no similar agency could be created by Executive Order of the President.[23] Many people felt at the time that it was a mistake to abolish this central planning agency, so here again we have an example of how an act of "control" by the legislature is defensible or indefensible, depending on the point of view. In many cases, any threat to abolish an entire agency is out of the question. Perhaps the agency has existed for decades and its services must be continued because of the public's demand for them. A much more frequent threat is to reduce the agency's scale of operations or to fail to provide funds for certain of its programs. This brings us to the appropriation process, regarded by many as the most effective weapon in the arsenal of legislative controls.

Control through action on budget requests

In Chapter 17 it was seen that the form in which the executive branch presents the estimates has much to do with the legislators' understanding of what is being proposed. Efficient budgetary procedures within the executive branch will promote more effective legislative review of proposed expenditures.

22 *Administrative Management in the Government of the United States,* Washington, D.C.: Government Printing Office, 1937, p. 34.

23 John D. Millett, *The Process and Organization of Government Planning,* New York: Columbia University Press, 1947, p. 150.

Perhaps a Joint Committee on the Budget with its professional staff would help Congressmen make sounder judgments about the justification for the Executive's requests for funds. Yet even if this and other recommended improvements were adopted and proved to have the advantages their proponents claim for them, the task of the legislature in reviewing the budget requests would still remain a difficult one. Governmental programs are now so large and complex that the legislator does not have the time to make a thorough appraisal of all the budget proposals. This, of course, is no argument for their not trying to make the best possible review under the circumstances. It is rather a statement of the practical limitations of legislative budgetary control under present conditions.

At the national level more than half the spending requests are for national defense and related purposes. Although many Congressmen have, on occasion, claimed that defense expenditures could be cut, in practice Congress is generally reluctant to make large reductions in this part of the budget. Many Congressmen believe that they are in no position to substitute their judgment for that of the President and his civilian and military advisers on the security needs of the nation. Thus the tendency is to try to economize on such programs as foreign aid and to hold the line on expenditures for domestic programs, such as new federal grants to the states.

In desperation, legislators sometimes propose "across-the-board" cuts, that is, a straight percentage reduction in all programs. They want economies but are not sure where they can be found, so they resolve the problem "equitably" by applying the same percentage reduction to all the agencies. This is frequently referred to as the *meat-axe* approach. The butcher's knife trims the agency programs in a neat, straight line, but in budgeting this means penalizing the efficient programs along with the inefficient ones. Of course, to some legislators no program is so desirable and so well managed that it should be spared from the meat-axe. Admittedly, the meat-axe may reflect the legislators' conviction that the "empire-builders" in the executive branch habitually submit inflated expenditure requests. The way to protect against this abuse, however, is to identify the agencies that are guilty of such practices, and not to punish the innocent along with the guilty.

Legislators often clamor for economy and demand that the executive's budget be reduced drastically, yet they will ask for more funds to be spent in their own districts. This is not a characteristic of American legislators alone, because a British financial authority reportedly said, "If you want to raise a certain cheer in the House of Commons, make a general panegyric on economy; if you want to invite a sure defeat, propose a particular saving."[24] Once a spending program is started in a Congressman's district, pressure quickly builds up for him to see to it that it is continued. When he runs for reelection, it is standard practice to remind the constituents of the federal money he has obtained for the district. Members of the state legislatures are also judged largely on the basis of the state funds they get allocated to their home districts. Since this is the role in which the legislator is cast, he cannot be expected to make entirely objective judgments in his votes on spending measures. Yet it can be argued that the legislator's dedication to local interests has its beneficial aspects as well:

> An individual Congressman looks at the budget with concern for the welfare of his region, or district, or state, as well as with concern for national interests. The combined views of many Congressmen will thus reflect an approach to budgeting that is broader geographically but narrower functionally than the approach to budgeting which the President will employ. Both approaches are necessary in a society that is complex and dedicated to pluralistic values. Either one alone could give rise to provincialism or distortion.[25]

Most observers believe that Congress and legislative bodies in general could do a much better job of reviewing spending proposals. Some critics emphasize the need for legislatures to organize themselves more efficiently for purposes of budget review. Others stress the desirability of expanded professional staffs to help the legislators make more thorough analyses of the estimates. Still others express the view that the legislators would be able to exercise more effective control if they stopped trying to go into so much detail, as when they insist on budget presentations on an object-of-expenditure basis. Others see the solution in strengthened party discipline and reorganization of Congress as a whole to make it function more efficiently.

Yet, with all its imperfections, legislative budget review does put the administrators on guard, and remind them that "somewhere there are limits beyond which the bureaucrats may not transgress."[26] They must be prepared to justify their requests before sharp inquisitors who can ask many embarrassing questions. Few administrative officials are foolish enough to go to legislative budget hearings expecting clear sailing; most of them do their "homework" well before they make their appearance.

[24] Jesse Burkhead, *Governmental Budgeting,* New York: Wiley, 1956, p. 323.

[25] *Ibid.,* p. 321.

[26] Powell, *op. cit.,* p. 56.

Legislative investigations

The legislative investigation is a much-used tool of legislative control. It is safe to say that whenever allegations are made of serious wrong-doings in the administrative agencies and there seems to be some foundation for the charges, legislatures will promptly investigate. In 1967, Congress spent a record $10 million for investigations.

If the purpose of the investigation is simply to dig out the facts and the committee members are not inspired by partisan motives, the inquiry can serve a very useful purpose. A recent example is the investigation of the Apollo 204 tragedy by the Senate Committee on Aeronautical and Space Sciences.[27] Although on the same day of the accident (January 27, 1967), National Aeronautics and Space Administration (NASA) administrator James E. Webb named a review board to investigate the causes of the fire that killed the three astronauts, on the following day the Senate Committee announced that it would conduct its own investigation. The Apollo review board had eight members, five from NASA, because "in the judgment of the Administrator, the complexity of the Apollo program required Board members thoroughly familiar with the Apollo system and with the NASA management procedures to make an orderly and accurate investigation of the accident. . . ."[28]

The Senate Committee did not object to the composition of the review board; it did believe it necessary in its hearings to question not only NASA officials and representatives of the contractor (North American Aviation, Inc.) but also the review board members. It concluded that the review board did make an exhaustive and objective investigation of the accident, as attested "by the critical findings the Board made of certain National Aeronautics and Space Administration management and technical operations."[29] The Committee's verdict was that "everyone associated with the design and test of the spacecraft simply failed to understand fully the danger and the cooperative effect of an ignition source, the combustible materials, and the pure oxygen atmosphere in the sealed spacecraft cabin."[30] It did not recommend setting back the target date for a moon landing, but it did say that "safety must be considered of paramount importance in the manned space flight program even at the expense of target dates."[31] It expressed its displeasure that the NASA administrator had failed to inform it of the difficulties with the contractor or of the Phillips' report (see page 218 of this book),

27 *Apollo Accident,* Hearing Before the Senate Committee on Aeronautical and Space Sciences, 90th Congress, 1st Session, Parts I and II, Washington, D.C.: Government Printing Office, 1967.

28 *Apollo 204 Accident,* Report of the Senate Committee on Aeronautical and Space Sciences, 90th Congress, 2nd Session, Report No. 956, p. 2.

29 *Ibid.*

30 *Ibid.,* p. 3.

31 *Ibid.,* p. 10.

and it "urged" NASA "to keep the appropriate congressional committees" better informed in the future.[32]

The public would not have been satisfied with an investigation by NASA only, particularly in view of the disclosures about NASA's attempt to keep the Phillips' report secret. Self-investigation has never proved itself effective in correcting errors or evils of any kind. Numerous examples could be given of legislative investigations that have spurred the administrative agencies to function more efficiently.

On the debit side, some legislators are far more interested in getting publicity for themselves than they are in being impartial fact-finders. The legislator who makes sensational charges can usually count on getting his name in the headlines; in reasoning that politics is politics, he may not worry about the fairness of his allegations. The Chief Executive's enemies in the legislature often try to use legislative investigations to embarrass him and to gain partisan advantage. They are not interested in an objective analysis of the facts but rather in finding anything that can be used to persuade the electorate that "it is time for a change." Nor is this the tactic of the opposing party only. It is also freely employed by members of the Chief Executive's own party who dislike his policies. Pious statements by legislators about the value of a "vigilant" opposition may mask the desire to make it *seem* that the administration has made a mistake. If enough of the public believe it, then their objective is accomplished. There is evidence, however, that citizens are increasingly aware of the political biases of many of the legislative "investigators." Some of the abuses of investigating committees have become so patent that the supposed beneficiary, the public, is skeptical that it is being served as faithfully as the legislator-sleuths would have it believe.

Powell makes a balanced statement when he evaluates legislative investigations as follows:

> Any time there is an investigation of whatever it may be, some people are subjected to scrutiny and on occasion brought into disrepute. Charges are not proof, of course, and the work of any modern major investigating committee is praised as well as condemned. What remains is the fact that alleged wrongdoing and bureaucratic functioning must be investigated, that in the process some people may be tarred who are pure by any standard.[33]

[32] *Ibid.,* p. 11.

[33] Powell, *op. cit.,* p. 58.

The pros and cons of codirectorship

The principal criticism of codirectorship is that it injects Congress into the details of day-by-day administration, a function it is ill-equipped to discharge. Codirectorship is based on the belief that the administrative agencies should be under the direct control of the legislature. While, as we saw in Chapter 1, the Constitution permits this interpretation, many people are convinced that the lawmakers exercise more effective control when they accept the principle of "indirect responsibility," namely, that "an administrative agency should be responsible to the legislature, but only through the chief executive, and primarily for broad issues of public policy and general administrative performance."[34]

If codirectorship means meddling in details and decisions that competent administrators should be trusted to make, it can justifiably be viewed as interference rather than desirable collaboration. Questionable acts of administrators can be criticized during the annual budget reviews and in the course of the legislative investigations referred to previously. On the other hand, codirectorship may serve the constructive purpose of clarifying legislative intent and preventing erroneous interpretations of the law by the agency heads. If it is true that the bureaucrats sometimes stretch the law, it can be argued that it is desirable to give Congressional committees veto power over certain kinds of proposed administrative action. The difficulty, of course, is in defining which administrative decisions are important enough to fall in this category.

This issue came up in the controversy over the application of the 160-acreage limitation to the federal-state contract for joint construction of California's San Luis water project. Long-standing federal policy, as required by law, is to extend the benefits of irrigation projects only to landowners with tracts of land within this limitation. Secretary of the Interior Udall, relying upon an opinion issued in 1933 by Secretary of the Interior Ray Lyman Wilbur, approved the San Luis water contract without the acreage limitation. Attorney-General Kennedy offered no objection to this decision, but made the qualifying suggestion that Congress itself should review the matter, since in his opinion there was an area of doubt. Under federal law, such contracts go into effect unless disapproved within a 90-day period by either the Senate or House Interior Committee. Both did approve the contract, despite allegations of Senator Morse of Oregon that suspension of the acreage limitation in effect meant a "giveaway"

---

[34] Waldo, *op. cit.*, p. 446.

to the big landowners.[35] Udall later decided that the Wilbur interpretation was wrong, and in January, 1967, the Justice Department filed suit to enforce the statutory limitation.[36] Of course, Congress can, if it wishes, settle the question by changing the law and making clear what policy the Interior Department should follow.

Codirectorship, as revealed in this incident, supplies at least a temporary answer as to legislative intent. So long as the basic legislation cannot cover all contingencies, direct administrative responsibility to legislative committees can be defended as serving a useful function.

Casework

As to casework, it appears to be an indispensable part of the system of administrative responsibility. If administrators were perfect, no constituent would ever have to ask his Congressman for help. On occasion, citizens may not receive the treatment they deserve from administrative officials. Court remedies, as we have seen, are frequently too slow or not even available to correct the particular abuse. Time and time again legislators have intervened to obtain remedial action on justifiable complaints. Of course, many of the complaints are groundless. In such cases, most legislators will be satisfied with the evidence the administrative agency gives them to show that they have acted properly. It also goes without saying that legislative intervention to obtain special favors for constituents is indefensible.

Confirmation of appointments

Legislative confirmation of appointments to certain high-ranking posts is practiced at all levels of government. In the federal government, positions such as those of department heads, undersecretaries, assistant secretaries, members of regulatory commissions and boards, and ambassadors and ministers are filled by the President, with the advice and consent of the Senate. As explained by Alexander Hamilton in *The Federalist*, the requirement for Senate approval would "tend greatly to prevent the appointment of unfit characters from State prejudice, from family connection, from personal attachment, or from a view to popularity."[37] The President might sometimes slip and make a poor appointment. Presidents sometimes yield to political and personal pressures and nominate persons of mediocre quality. Sometimes they appoint men of undoubted competence but whose past connections make

35 *Los Angeles Times,* April 3 and 4, 1962.
36 *New York Times,* January 13, 1967.
37 See Felix A. Nigro (ed.), *Public Administration, Readings and Documents,* New York: Holt, Rinehart and Winston, 1951, pp. 443–444.

it seem unlikely that they could be counted on to enforce the laws with vigor.

An example is Calvin Coolidge's appointment in 1925 of Charles Warren as Attorney General. Despite Coolidge's landslide victory in the elections of 1924, the Senate rejected Warren, not once but twice, when Coolidge resubmitted the nomination. Warren had been connected in various ways with the "Sugar Trust," and opposition Senators did not see how someone with such a background could be trusted to carry out the Attorney General's responsibility for prosecuting the monopolies.[38]

On the other hand, the Senate sometimes objects to nominees for the opposite reason, namely, because their record indicates that they would press for strong enforcement of the laws. The Senate refused to confirm Truman's reappointment of Leland Olds to the Federal Power Commission (FPC) because of the stand he had taken in favor of FPC regulation of natural gas rates.[39] Hamilton predicted that the Senate would refuse to confirm only for "special and strong reasons," and he assumed that it would carefully scrutinize the nominees' qualifications. In practice, partisan considerations greatly influence a Senator's reaction to a Presidential nomination. If the Senator is of the opposing party, or of a wing in the majority party that does not like the President's policies, he may fight the appointment simply to get at the Chief Executive.[40] Conversely, if he is a loyal follower of the President, he may close his eyes to obvious shortcomings of the appointees.

In practice, legislative confirmation of appointments gives the lawmakers a second opportunity to hold the Chief Executive in check. Even if they do not defeat his legislative proposals, they may be able to cripple their enforcement by rejecting his nominees for key administrative posts. Whether the public has been injured or benefited after the votes have been counted and the nominee accepted or rejected will naturally remain a matter of opinion. Did the people want Charles Warren? Coolidge certainly thought so. But while the people had elected Coolidge, they had also elected the Senate that rejected Warren. Commented the old *New York World*, "If the public elects a Senate which will not confirm the President's nomination, and a President who makes a nomination unsatisfactory to the Senate, it must be assumed that the public is getting what it wants."[41]

THE OMBUDSMAN

Reviewing the material presented so far in this chapter, we see that there is an imposing array of devices for enforcing administra-

[38] Felix A. Nigro, "The Warren Case," *Western Political Quarterly*, XI, No. 4 (December, 1958), 835–856.

[39] See Joseph P. Harris, "Senatorial Rejection of Leland Olds: A Case Study," *American Political Science Review*, XLV, No. 3 (September, 1951), 677.

[40] Felix A. Nigro, "The Van Buren Confirmation Before the Senate," *Western Political Quarterly*, XIV, No. 1, Part 1 (March, 1961), 148–159.

[41] Nigro, "The Warren Case," *op. cit.*, 854. For effects of Senate confirmation at State level, see Ronald Sullivan, "Jersey Senators to End Blackball," *New York Times*, November 30, 1965.

tive responsibility. Nonetheless, there still remains no guarantee that the individual employee or citizen will be treated fairly, or that the government agencies will function efficiently. Of course, since humans are not perfect, no absolute guarantee of this kind could ever be given. The present system of administrative responsibility, however, leaves much to be desired; there is clearly room for much improvement.[42]

Court remedies, as we have seen, are frequently of little or no practical use; besides, they are usually costly to invoke and therefore largely unavailable to persons of modest means. Laws to punish dishonest employees exist, as do codes of ethics to inhibit unethical behavior, but the dishonesty may not be detected, and more than a few employees will not respect the codes. Legislators can do much to require compliance with legislative intent, but the enormous number of government transactions means that inevitably many questionable administrative rulings will go unchallenged. Noting that most state legislatures meet biennially and even then are in session only for limited periods of time, Ralph Nader states bluntly, "State legislative oversight of the administrative agencies is non-existent in many cases, highly sporadic and superficial in others."[43] Even the most conscientious Congressmen, and those with sizeable office staffs, cannot investigate thoroughly all of the numerous complaints referred to them by constituents.

It is not simply that government has grown so very big, it is also that citizens today are very conscious of their rights—as they should be. Thus citizen expectations have gone up, at the same time that the great growth in government programs has multiplied the "likelihood of friction."[44] Therefore it is not surprising that in the past few years such great interest should be shown in the possibilites of adapting the Scandinavian office of the *Ombudsman* to the American environment. Many other countries have also been studying the experience in countries with Ombudsmen, and some already have established Ombudsman systems of their own.

"The Ombudsman is an officer of Parliament who investigates complaints from citizens that they have been unfairly dealt with by government departments and who, if he finds that a complaint is justified, seeks a remedy."[45] Until recent years, Sweden's 1809 institution of an Ombudsman attracted little attention elsewhere, although Finland established one in 1919. Countries recently creating an Ombudsman are Denmark (1955) and Norway and New Zealand (1962). In 1967 Great Britain established the position of Parliamentary Commissioner for Administration

[42] See testimony before Senate Subcommittee on Administrative Practice and Procedures, *Regional Ombudsman Proposal*, 90th Congress, 2nd Session, Washington, D.C.: Government Printing Office, 1968.

[43] Ralph Nader, "Ombudsman for State Governments," in Donald C. Rowat (ed.), *The Ombudsman: Citizen's Defender*, Toronto: University of Toronto Press, 1965, p. 241.

[44] David Winder, "Ombudsman Urged as Best for N.Y.," *Christian Science Monitor*, November 22, 1966. Interview with Professor Walter Gellhorn of Columbia University.

[45] Rowat, *op. cit.*, p. 7.

(PCA). In effect, the PCA is a weak Ombudsman, because he can only act on complaints referred to him by members of Parliament, and his jurisdiction is very limited. Complaints against the nationalized industries, local government, the police, the armed services, and the health service and hospitals are all excluded from his competence.[46]

In the United States, Ombudsman bills have been introduced in Congress, as well as many state legislatures and local governing bodies. So far, Hawaii has been the only state to establish such an office by legislation. In Nassau County, New York, in June of 1966, the county executive issued an executive order naming former Judge Samuel Greason to the vacant office of Commissioner of Accounts and directed him in effect to function as an Ombudsman, pending establishment of such a position on a permanent basis. In November, 1967, a charter referendum including the permanent Ombudsman failed, but the position is being continued by the county executive on the same temporary basis. Some jurisdictions have established, or are considering establishing, administrative arrangements of different kinds providing for "Ombudsman" type functions. In New York City, where Ombudsman bills have been introduced in the City Council but none has passed to date, the mayor has for some years maintained Post Office Box 100 as the place to which citizens can send their complaints.[47]

How an Ombudsman functions

Ombudsmen in the various countries function in much the same way, although there are some differences. Sweden and Denmark will be used here as examples.[48]

OMBUDSMAN IN SWEDEN

In Sweden there is an Ombudsman for Civil Affairs and one for Military Affairs; we will be concerned with the former. He is elected for a four-year term by a body of 48 electors, the latter elected by Parliament (24 from each House). In practice, he is entirely independent of the Government and Parliament; he decides what he should investigate and what action to take after investigation. Parliament does not try to influence him; "political parties in Parliament always try to unite" in his selection in order to demonstrate to the public the "political independence" of the office.[49]

His duties are to "supervise how judges, government officials, and other civil servants observe the laws, and to prosecute

[46] For authoritative descriptions of Ombudsman in Sweden, Finland, Denmark, Norway, and New Zealand, see Rowat, *ibid*. On Britain, see Melita Knowles, "British Ombudsman Handles Limited Field," *Christian Science Monitor*, April 1, 1967, and "British Ombudsman Gains Public Favor," *Christian Science Monitor*, March 30, 1968.

[47] Fritz Morstein Marx, "The Importation of Foreign Institutions," in Rowat, *op. cit.*, p. 262.

[48] Sources are principally Alfred Bexelius, "The Ombudsman for Civil Affairs," and Miss I. M. Pedersen, "Denmark's Ombudsman," in Rowat, *op. cit.*, pp. 22–44 and 75–94 respectively.

[49] Bexelius, *ibid.*, p. 26.

those who have acted illegally or neglected their duties."[50] His competence extends, with few exceptions, to both national and municipal officials. He has access to all documents, including secret ones, and has "the right to be present at all deliberations at which judges or administrative officials make their rulings."[51] All officials must comply with his requests for information or for assistance in making an investigation, and all prosecuting attorneys must undertake any prosecution he directs. He does *not* have the power to change the decisions of courts or administrative officials, and, as to prosecutions, in practice he requires them only "in cases of undue interference or errors on the part of the nation's officialdom."[52] If he investigates and determines that something is wrong, usually all the action he finds necessary is a public reprimand or criticism of the erring official.

Nor does he investigate only after receiving complaints; he carefully reads government reports and the newspapers and often initiates investigations on the basis of information from these and similar sources. In addition, he makes periodic inspection tours of jails, hospitals, and other public facilities, and investigates in detail when he notes undesirable conditions or practices. In all his work he looks not only for cases of failure to follow the law or to use fair procedures in dealing with employees and citizens, but also for evidences of inconsistency in the application of the law to individual cases. Finally, as he deems necessary, he suggests changes in the laws themselves to make them more defensible, and he makes a comprehensive annual report to Parliament. The press publicizes his reports and contributes greatly to the acceptance of his recommendations and advice.

OMBUDSMAN IN DENMARK

In Denmark the Ombudsman is elected by the legislature (Folketing) at the time of each general election. His jurisdiction covers both civil and military administration, and extends to the municipalities although, as in Sweden, the municipal councils in their collective capacities are generally excluded from his control. Administrative tribunals, but not the courts, are under his competence.

If he believes that an official has committed a criminal offense, he can order a criminal prosecution, and if he believes that a civil servant should be disciplined, he may require the "competent administrative authorities to start such proceedings. . . ."[53] Actually, he has never used either power; he has found it sufficient to state his views on a case and indicate the action that he believes should be taken by the proper authority. In cases of major mistakes and

---

[50] *Ibid.*, p. 24.
[51] *Ibid.*, p. 25.
[52] *Ibid.*
[53] Miss I. M. Pederson, in Rowat, *op. cit.*, p. 81.

acts of negligence, he also makes a report to the appropriate minister and to the Folketing.

As in Sweden, the legislature refrains from subjecting him to any partisan pressures. He investigates cases both upon receipt of complaints and on his own initiative. Officials under his jurisdiction are required to provide him with the information and the documents he requests, and he is often given access to internal minutes of the administrative authorities. The wide range of his functions is seen in the legal requirement that he "keep himself informed as to whether any person under his jurisdiction pursues unlawful ends, makes arbitrary or unreasonable decisions or otherwise commits mistakes or acts of negligence in the discharge of his duties."[54] With this authority he criticizes officials for failure to be consistent in their rulings on similar cases, for bias in their decisions, failure to inform citizens of their rights, undue delays, and anything else he believes should be corrected.

Results achieved by Ombudsmen

In Sweden, Denmark, and the other countries having a full-fledged Ombudsman, the record of accomplishments has been good. His recommendations are accepted in most cases, and he exerts a constructive influence in improving the public service. In most cases he finds the complaints unjustified, which provides support for conscientious officials, and he reduces the workload of the government offices by investigating complaints for them. By distributing his reports widely, he calls attention to errors made in some departments that can be avoided in others. Naturally, his reports sometimes are resented, but in the main his function is accepted within the bureaucracy.

As to the citizen, he is protected from illegal, arbitrary, and otherwise undesirable acts. Although many of the errors the Ombudsman corrects can be classified as relatively minor, still these are matters that disturb and alienate the public and might continue if there were no Ombudsman. He persuades officials to change their decisions and conduct, in a relationship that does not menace but rather leads them toward the common goal of better service to the public.

Possibilities of adopting the Ombudsman in the United States

In 1963, cases arising from complaints or from the Ombudsman's own initiative were as follows: Sweden (Ombudsman for Civil

---

[54] *Ibid.*, p. 84.

Affairs), 1781; Denmark, 1130; Finland, 1441; and Norway, 1275.[55] These are small countries, which is why doubt is expressed that a single Ombudsman could cope with the much larger number of cases to be anticipated in the huge federal government of the United States, or in the largest state and local governments. While the Ombudsman in each of the aforenamed countries has some staff, it is small, numbering just a few people; furthermore, much of his effectiveness derives from the fact that he deals personally with each case. He has succeeded in Scandinavia and New Zealand largely because of his personal prestige and human appeal as a contrast with the faceless bureaucracy. To give an Ombudsman a large staff is to bureaucratize his function and thus defeat the purpose of his office.

To answer this objection, federal regional Ombudsmen have been suggested, but an Ombudsman working out of Denver or Philadelphia or Chicago would have a hard time putting himself on the same basis with the people living in the large areas served as the Ombudsman in a small country. In addition, there are cultural differences; the populations of the Scandinavian countries are homogeneous and they have civil services "with a strongly professional orientation."[56] Samuel Krislov stresses:

> Denmark's heaviest population density centers around a metropolitan region containing 25 percent of the total population of the country. The existence and effectiveness of a national press under these conditions and a national audience for the announcements of the Ombudsman are therefore assured. . . . The competition facing an American Ombudsman for publicity in our diffuse news system may well prove to be an overwhelming disadvantage.[57]

As we have seen, the Ombudsmen in Scandinavia function on a strictly nonpartisan basis. It is conceivable, but not likely, that American legislators would eschew partisan political considerations in their views of the Ombudsman's role and in their relationships with him. All countries now with Ombudsmen have the parliamentary form of government, characterized by fusion of legislative and administrative powers, as contrasted with our system of separation of powers. The long-standing rivalry between the executive and legislative branches in the United States raises doubts that the Ombudsman could function as effectively in his relationships with administrative officials. We saw in Chapter 10 (see pages 214–217) how much resistance there is in the executive branch to releasing information to Congressmen and the general public. This has been remedied somewhat by passage of the Freedom of Information Act, but to give the Ombudsman

[55] Rowat, *op. cit.*, pp. 329–337.
[56] Samuel Krislov, "A Restrained View," in Rowat, *ibid.*, p. 249.
[57] *Ibid.*, pp. 250–251.

access to all government files, including secret ones, as in Sweden and Denmark, would require a great change in present attitudes and practices. If the President can, as he sometimes does, deny information to the General Accounting Office under the doctrine of executive privilege, he is not likely to make any exceptions for an American-type Ombudsman.

Some American legislators, anxious to keep their "casework," also fear that an Ombudsman would make their constituents less dependent upon them for favors. This reportedly is one of the reasons why an Ombudsman bill, based on recommendations of the Bar of the City of New York, was not approved by the City Council.[58] The Ombudsman was to be appointed by the mayor, with the advice and consent of two-thirds of the City Council. The Democratic-controlled Council has been at odds with Republican Mayor Lindsay, not an uncommon situation in the American political environment and one which illustrates the difficulty in establishing the Ombudsman on a nonpartisan basis. Professor Walter Gellhorn, who has published two books on the Ombudsman, believes that the office can be appointive, either by legislative action or by executive order; to him, the "mechanism of appointment is less significant than the spirit on which the mechanism operates."[59]

Some people believe that an Ombudsman is more feasible for state and local governments; they further argue that it is more needed at these levels than in the federal government where standards of administration are higher despite the complications of size. In this connection, the good results achieved in Nassau County with its Ombudsman are cited as proof that the institution is practical for local government.[60]

In truth, no one knows how successful the Ombudsman would be at any level of government; all of this is speculation, and the answers will only be provided after experimentation. Former Senator Edward V. Long of Missouri introduced a bill providing for a two-year pilot project for a Regional Ombudsman who would be based in Missouri and investigate complaints about federal agencies by residents of that state only.[61] Representative Reuss of Wisconsin named one of his office staff as his own Ombudsman, and stationed him in Milwaukee to attend to complaints from constitutents relating to all public services in the city.[62] Similar experiments undoubtedly will be undertaken, because the interest in the Ombudsman continues strong.

Evidence that the Ombudsman is not considered visionary on the American scene is seen in the following recommendations of Columbia University's American Assembly:

[58] Paul Hofmann, "Ombudsman Finds Most Complaints Unfounded," *New York Times,* June 20, 1967.

[59] David Winder, *op. cit.*

[60] George H. Favre, "A County Ombudsman Ends Year," *Christian Science Monitor,* July 19, 1967.

[61] *Regional Ombudsman Proposal, op. cit.,* pp. 1–4.

[62] *Milwaukee Sentinel,* February 9, 1967.

We recommend that Ombudsman offices be established in American local and state governments. We do not recommend the establishment of a single office of Ombudsman for the entire federal government, but we do recommend that applications of the concept be undertaken at the federal level. . . .

Since American local governments vary greatly in size, population, and legal structure, no uniform design need be followed and advantages are to be derived from experimentation. Such experimentation should include meaningful accessibility to the Ombudsman by all sectors of society.[63]

In any event, the persistence of interest in the Ombudsman discloses the discontent with the existing means for enforcing administrative responsibility. As Nader states, "The development of the administrative state has undermined deeply the effectiveness of the old institutions of check embodied in the principle of separate powers."[64] The search undoubtedly will go on for discovery, testing, and refinement of new means for making administration responsive to public and individual citizen needs. Here again, the opportunity for creativity and innovation is great.

BIBLIOGRAPHY

Anderson, Stanley V., *Canadian Ombudsman Proposals*, Berkeley, Calif.: Institute of Governmental Studies, 1966.

Anderson, Stanley V., (ed.), *Ombudsman for American Government?*, Englewood Cliffs, N.J.: Prentice-Hall, 1968.

Anderson, Stanley V., "Ombudsman Proposals: Stimulus to Inquiry," *Public Affairs Report*, Berkeley, Calif.: Bureau of Public Administration, *VII*, No. 6 (December, 1966).

Anderson, Stanley V., "The Ombudsman: Public Defender Against Maladministration," *Public Affairs Report*, Berkeley, Calif.: Bureau of Public Administration, *VI*, No. 2 (April, 1965).

Chapman, Brian, *The Profession of Government*, London: G. Allen, 1959. Chapters 9–13.

Gellhorn, Walter, *Ombudsmen and Others: Citizens' Protectors in Nine Countries*, Cambridge, Mass.: Harvard University Press, 1966.

Gellhorn, Walter, *When Americans Complain: Governmental Grievance Procedures*, Cambridge, Mass.: Harvard University Press, 1966.

[63] American Assembly, Columbia University, *The Ombudsman*, Report of the Thirty-second American Assembly, October 26–29, 1967, Arden House, Harriman, N.Y., pp. 6–7.

[64] Nader, *op. cit.*, p. 241.

Harris, Joseph P., *Congressional Control of Administration*, Garden City, N.Y.: Doubleday, 1964.

Key, V. O., "Legislative Control," in Marx, Fritz Morstein, (ed.), *Elements of Public Administration*, Englewood Cliffs, N.J.: Prentice-Hall, 1959.

Maass, Arthur A., and Radway, Lawrence I., "Gauging Administrative Responsibility," *Public Administration Review*, IX, No. 3 (Summer, 1949).

The Mexican "Amparo" as a Supplemental Remedy for the Redress of Citizen Grievances in California, Berkeley, Calif.: Institute for Local Government, 1967.

Nigro, Felix A., (ed.), *Public Administration, Readings and Documents*, New York: Holt, Rinehart and Winston, 1951. Chapter VII.

Powell, Norman John, *Responsible Public Bureaucracy in the United States*, Boston: Allyn and Bacon, 1967.

Redford, Emmette S., *Democracy in the Administrative State*, New York: Oxford University Press, 1969. Chapter VI.

Rosenthal, Albert H., and Rowat, Donald C., "An 'Ombudsman' for America?", "The Ombudsman—Swedish 'Grievance Man,'" and "Ombudsmen for North America," *Public Administration Review*, XXIV, No. 4 (December, 1964).

Rowat, Donald C., (ed.), *The Ombudsman: Citizen's Defender*, Toronto: University of Toronto Press, 1965.

Schaller, Lyle E., "Is the Citizen Advisory Committee a Threat to Representative Government?" *Public Administration Review*, XXIV, No. 3 (September, 1964).

Senate Subcommittee on Administrative Practice and Procedure, *Regional Ombudsman Proposal*, 90th Congress, 2nd Session, Washington, D.C.: Government Printing Office, 1968.

Separation of Powers, Hearings Before the Senate Subcommittee on Separation of Powers, Part I, 90th Congress, 1st Session, Washington, D.C.: Government Printing Office, 1967.

Waldo, Dwight, (ed.), *Ideas and Issues in Public Administration*, New York: McGraw-Hill, 1953. Chapters 18 and 19.

PART VII
INTERNATIONAL
ADMINISTRATION

CHAPTER 22
INTERNATIONAL
ADMINISTRATION

TODAY INTERNATIONAL AFFAIRS loom much larger in the consciousness of the people, both young and old. Many college students show great interest in the possibilities of careers in international agencies or in the foreign services of their own countries. Similarly, quite a few persons who already have substantial work experience are also attracted to overseas employment. They want to do their part to see to it that the "social invention of international cooperation" is perfected to the point that the peoples of the world can live in peace and in general enjoy a happier existence. The Peace Corps has atracted many persons, in all age groups, to tours of duty on very useful projects. For these reasons, this textbook would not be complete without some discussion of international service.

THE EXPANDED WORLD COMMUNITY

Multination agencies are by no means new. They are, however, much more numerous today because of a basic change that has taken place in the methods of diplomacy:

Traditional diplomacy, with its conventions and accepted practices, assumed that relations between states would normally be carried out on a bilateral basis. Today, account must also be taken of a complex of international and regional machinery, most of it created since World War II. In addition to the United Nations itself, there are many permanent international organizations operating in such specialized fields as agriculture, health, banking, investment, communications, and labor. Beyond these are a variety of regional organizations such as the North Atlantic Treaty Organization, the Southeast Asia Treaty Organization, the Organization of American States, the Intergovernmental Committee for European Migration, and others; and there are countless other multilateral arrangements of one or another type—temporary, *ad hoc*, periodic. Indeed, part of the challenge of diplomacy today lies in the invention of new forms and structures of international relations to meet emerging problems.[1]

Because of the recent great increase in the number of independent nations, the United Nations is now a much bigger organization than it used to be. When it was created in 1945, it had 50 member states; as of 1969 it had 126 members, many admitted in the past few years. The new nations have also increased the membership of the specialized agencies that work closely with the UN, such as the World Health Organization, the Food and Agriculture Organization, the International Labour Organization, and the International Civil Aviation Agency (which has been pondering how to stop the hijacking of planes). Pressures of the developing nations have led to the creation of new international machinery such as the UN Conference on Trade and Development, a forum where the poorer nations can argue their case for special trade concessions. With the increased importance of the underdeveloped world, new regional international machinery has been created, such as additional UN regional economic commissions,[2] while at the same time the movement for European integration has produced three now well-established European Communities (the Common Market, the Coal and Steel Community, and the Atomic Energy Community), merged since July, 1967, into a "single giant body" with a civil service of nearly 8000 employees.[3]

The greater scope of international administration is also evidenced in the innumerable conferences now held between the chiefs of state, foreign ministers, scientists, and other prominent figures of the different nations of the world. Today almost every issue of the daily newspaper contains a report of an international conference of some kind. Domestic matters have become inextricably intertwined with international affairs, with the result that leading officials of national governments must frequently

[1] *Personnel for the New Diplomacy,* Report of the Committee on Foreign Affairs Personnel, Washington, D.C.: Carnegie Endowment for International Peace, December, 1962, pp. 3–4.

[2] See Gerard J. Mangone (ed.), *UN Administration of Economic and Social Programs,* New York: Columbia University Press, 1966.

[3] Clyde H. Farnsworth, "Staff of Market in Europe Frets," *New York Times,* February 23, 1968.

travel abroad. Some officials actually "commute" between their nation's capital and the sites of conferences abroad, and it is generally appreciated that this is what their jobs require. In 1965 the United States government participated in 650 conferences; during one typical week, a State Department list printed at the order of Secretary of State Dean Rusk showed 11 conferences in session and 12 scheduled to begin during the week.[4]

PROBLEMS OF OVERSEAS PERSONNEL

Many problems of persons serving abroad are much the same, whether they are employed by international organizations or the foreign services of their own countries. Employees of private companies, representatives of missionary groups, and persons working abroad for numerous voluntary agencies are also exposed to the same problems. This is why the word *overseasmanship* has come into our vocabulary. It means the ability to be effective in relationships with the nationals of the country in which one is stationed. We are not limiting our discussion in this chapter to the problems of staff members of international agencies only. Since people-to-people contacts are so important in international relations today, a general discussion of overseasmanship is in order. At the same time, it is recognized that employees of international agencies such as the United Nations do have certain peculiar problems. Working for an international agency, as will be elaborated, is never completely the same as being an employee of the government of one's own country.

Many factors make the problem of adjustment difficult. Before we discuss some of the most important factors, however, let it be clear that overseas employment has great attractions and is ardently desired by many people. The sense of accomplishment after achieving even limited success in a foreign program is a great satisfaction to persons highly motivated to make a contribution in this kind of work. Furthermore, as we shall see, some of the adjustment problems can be solved, at least in part. The challenge in international service, after all, is that it is difficult and different. If everything were cozy, the challenge, and consequently the interest in the job, would be far less.

Social isolation

A. Loveday, an Englishman who served for 20 years in the secretariat of the League of Nations, mentions first the unhappy circumstance of *social isolation*. No matter how well received

[4] *Christian Science Monitor*, November 4, 1966.

he is by the local population, the international civil servant always remains a guest:

> The international official very rarely becomes completely integrated in the local society in which he lives, and the international society of which he forms a part never affords full scope for the natural development of the individual personality from its own cultural roots. It is a society based originally on certain tacitly accepted restrictions on self-expression and gradually developing from the common experience of its members, a common experience, however, which is in each case divorced from childhood and educational background. The individual, therefore, dumped, as it were, in a community of which he can never form an integral part and limited in self-expression, must find either in his work or in some other way an outlet for whatever part of his personality is thus suppressed. If he fails to do so, he gradually shrivels up.[5]

The degree of isolation depends upon the kind of contacts international officials can establish with the local society; some are more successful than others. The smaller the group, the better are its chances of being integrated into the local community. It is not that the local population has an aversion to the international officials, although this may be a contributing factor in the case of some officials who irritate and offend some local residents simply because they are "foreigners." Even in large cosmopolitan settings such as New York, Paris, and Rome, the condition of social isolation exists despite the sophistication of the local society:

> Whatever the country, however, the international official must remain external to the society in which he lives. He is not a working partner; he can play no part in either municipal or national politics. He must accept the social organization for better or worse as he finds it. . . . The international official finds himself therefore with his home, school, and college roots cut and prevented from striking new tap roots. At best he may live as a houseleek lives. He is in consequence forced to join with his colleagues in forming a distinct social group—a quasi-independent and quite artificial community. . . .[6]

[5] A. Loveday, Reflections on International Administration, Oxford, England: Clarendon Press, 1956, p. 3.

[6] Ibid., p. 4.

Members of national foreign services face the same difficulties as far as integration with local societies is concerned as do international officials. In fact, their situation is worse if they happen to be representatives of countries disliked or viewed with distrust by the local population. Americans are in a somewhat disadvantageous position from this standpoint. In terms of per capita income, the American has an abnormally high standard of living. Desperately poor people are not noted for feelings of friendship toward the extremely wealthy. Americans are generous in giving foreign aid, but this does not make us liked any the more in some countries.

In some parts of the world, historical factors also contribute to resentments. Latin America remembers the "big-stick diplomacy" of the United States in the early part of the century. No matter how much concrete evidence we have given that we have mended our ways, the stereotypes of "dollar diplomacy" and of Yankee conceptions of superiority still dominate the thinking of millions of Latin Americans.

The United States is not by any means the only nation plagued by errors and circumstances of the past. The former dependent areas of Africa and Asia have no love for nationals of the powers that once ruled them. Extreme nationalist sentiment in some countries produces animosities toward small neighboring states deeper on occasion than the antipathy toward the United States and other big powers. Of course, the countries that are disliked are also represented in the international organizations. Being a staff member of such organizations does not immunize the official from being the object of prejudice because of his nationality. Nonetheless, there are sometimes distinct advantages in being the representative of a multinational agency rather than of a foreign government. Those serving in the United States technical-assistance programs quickly become aware that in some countries aid from the United Nations is preferred. No nation likes to put itself in any position that can in the slightest be interpreted to mean that it has become the "satellite" of another power. To accept help from an international organization of which the country is a member and to which it contributes financial support is respectable. There are no "strings" attached to aid on a multilateral basis. Accepting help from a government that seems to be making the offer in order to gain "friends" in competition with a rival power offends many countries.

Foreign officials, whether employed by national or international agencies, are forced to live generally apart from the local population. Sometimes they do this to the point of forming "national compounds." This is a familiar criticism of the American communities abroad of servicemen, diplomats, and technicians of different kinds. Mottram Torre makes this interesting observation:

This kind of segregation has been criticized by those who believe that American policy is best advanced by maximum personal contact which serves as a bridge for mutual understanding and sympathy. However, compound living has its advantages for Americans who are overwhelmed by a foreign environment and can make only marginal adjustments. Their contacts with the "outside" population are painful and unsuccessful and do not contribute to good public relations. They are much happier when surrounded by fellow-employees and located close to post exchanges, central mess hall, and other American amenities.[7]

This should not be interpreted to mean that Torre favors the idea of compound living. It is a much more satisfactory situation if the Americans can make some cordial contacts with the local residents rather than sealing themselves off almost completely from them. He points out that the flexible American, even if he lives in a compound, will have many contacts "outside the walls" and can contribute to good public relations.

Climate and physical location

A second problem of adjustment has to do with climate and physical location. It is sometimes said that the person who cannot make a satisfactory adjustment to his work and other environment is quick to convince himself that the cause is something outside his control rather than his own inability to maintain an internal personal equilibrium. While this is undoubtedly true in some cases, there is ample evidence to show that some of the most balanced personality types find it difficult to maintain their health and vitality in certain climates. For those who have lived all their lives in tropical climates, assignment to such places as United Nations headquarters in New York City may produce health problems, in addition to general discomfort. New York does not pose a health hazard in terms of the sanitation and disease problems found in tropical areas, yet it can prove to be a very unhealthy place to live for someone who comes from the tropics.

The element of personal danger in certain locations also cannot be denied. The overseas employee (and his family) sometimes must reside or travel in areas where bandits and guerillas are a menace, and some employees have been murdered. Nor is this a problem in remote places only, as the problem of crime in New York City illustrates very well. U.S. agencies offer special pay and benefits for service in "hardship" posts, but most of the international agencies do not. " 'After all,' " an official said, " 'the world is the parish of these organizations . . . why should they pay a hardship allowance?' "[8]

[7] Mottram Torre, "Personality Adjustment in Overseas Service," in Harlan Cleveland and Gerard J. Mangone (eds.), *The Art of Overseasmanship,* Syracuse, N.Y.: Syracuse University Press, 1957, p. 86.

[8] Mike Causey, "The Federal Diary," *Washington Post,* December 5, 1966.

Inadequate housing facilities

Inadequate housing facilities contribute to the health problem, both from physical and psychological standpoints. Much has been written and said about the luxurious quarters of Americans and some other foreign officials stationed abroad. Americans in some posts do live in houses they could not afford to rent or buy at home. In many foreign locations, however, the only suitable housing is in the very high-price ranges. Since the middle class is usually very small or scarcely existent in the underdeveloped countries, the local housing industry is geared to building the kind of large, sometimes fancy residence that only the wealthy can afford. The mass of the population lives in dwellings that American families in the income groups represented in our missions simply do not occupy in the United States. In such countries the housing and utility allowances paid by the government in addition to salary may be considered a fortuitous circumstance for the mission member and his family. Yet this contributes to the lack of enthusiasm shown them by representatives of the foreign governments with whom they deal. These men, despite high positions in their governments, frequently live in much more modest quarters than their foreign advisers.

Yet in many overseas locations, Americans and their families are forced to live in very unsatisfactory quarters, simply because nothing else is available, even in metropolitan centers. It was reported that in Paris two-thirds of the apartments have no bathtubs, half have no private toilets, and only one-sixth are less than 25 years old.[9] Most international agencies do not pay housing allowances as high as those provided by U.S. agencies. Buildings and other facilities where the overseas employees work are also often inadequate, and, illustrating that Americans are not always better off, Congress has on occasion been unwilling to provide funds for air-conditioning and other conveniences. Undoubtedly, some of the reductions Congress makes in the requests for such outlays at certain posts are justified, yet the inability of so many Congressmen to understand how serious the living problems are at some posts does adversely affect the morale of many overseas employees. Economies possible in domestic programs cannot realistically be expected in certain phases of foreign operations.

The feeling of insecurity

Insecurity and tensions of various kinds also complicate the adjustment problems of persons serving overseas. Job insecurity is

[9] *New York Times*, August 22, 1965. See also House Subcommittee on Civil Service Commission and Personnel Programs, 84th Congress, 1st Session, *Personnel Programs and Policies of the Federal Government*, Washington, D.C.: Government Printing Office, 1956, pp. 93–94, and John D. Montgomery, *The Politics of Foreign Aid*, New York: Praeger, 1962, pp. 8–9.

one disturbing factor. This point is brought home as we look at the United Nations today. To much of mankind it is unthinkable that the United Nations should suffer the same fate as the League of Nations. Nobody can be sure what the future holds, but one thing is certain: Unstable conditions plague the United Nations and will probably continue to do so indefinitely. In truth, by its very nature this is an inherent characteristic of this most important of international organizations. Its deadlocks and financial worries reflect the unresolved issues of world politics.

Actually, most of the permanent employees of the United Nations are not worried about losing their jobs. Still they feel insecure, because they are in a real sense actors on a world stage with shaky foundations. As the organization reels under the impact of its crises, so does its staff. The instability of international organizations in a world still groping to make effective the machinery for international cooperation inevitably has an adverse effect on staff morale. As Loveday states: "To the great majority of them the world in which they live is seemingly more unstable and insecure than is the world of, for instance, a farmer or even a businessman or a factory hand, and the world—not the state of the weather or of the markets—is what immediately affects their life and work."[10]

APPOINTMENT PROBLEMS

In our discussion of personnel administration (see pages 278–282) we saw that the establishment of a true career service was essential for maintaining good staff morale. Application of the career principle in overseas service is just as essential, but there are some special difficulties. The career principle is applied in the UN by making most of the appointments to positions in the Secretariat permanent ones, but in recent years the percentage of posts filled on a fixed-term basis has been more than the 25 percent limit considered desirable by Secretary-General Thant.

It was recognized from the very beginning of the UN that some use of *secondment*, that is, appointing officials of member states for limited periods of time, was desirable to introduce "a certain amount of freshness" of viewpoint.[11] However, concern is now expressed that the pressures of the new states on the one hand, and of the Soviet Union on the other, for larger numbers of fixed-term appointments may in the end make UN career service the exception rather than the rule. The new states want to be represented equitably in the Secretariat without undue delay (the principle of geographical representation, as provided for in the UN Charter, is discussed in detail later). By limiting the

[10] Loveday, *op. cit.*, p. 13.

[11] Tien-Cheng Young, *International Civil Service: Principles and Problems*, Brussels, Belgium: International Institute of Administrative Sciences, 1958, pp. 141–150. Quoted words are from p. 145.

term of appointments, more jobs are made available; an analysis made in a recent one-year period "suggests that the policy of the Secretary-General for achieving better geographical distribution was to allocate vacancies roughly on a fifty-fifty basis between internal promotion and outside recruitment and, of the vacancies allocated for outside recruitment, to use about 75 percent for fixed-term appointments and the rest for probationary permanent appointments."[12]

The Soviet Union has long been against permanent appointments, a position it recently reiterated when its representative came out for appointments of not more than 10 years, on grounds that persons with permanent contracts may "come to do mediocre or even bad work."[13] All along it has taken the position that limited-term appointments are necessary to assure adequate representation of " 'varying political tendencies and social systems,' " which some observers interpret to mean it wants an *intergovernmental* service, rather than an independent, *international* service.[14]

While the danger of having too many fixed-term appointments is a real one, it is also true that in "some cases the prospect of a career service may result not in attracting the best candidates but in discouraging them."[15] Some urgently needed individuals simply do not want to move their families to New York or to accept any permanent appointment in a foreign country. Considering other factors, such as the inability of the new UN members to "spare permanently the services of their qualified nationals,"[16] it may well be that a higher proportion of limited-term appointments is functional for international, as compared with national, agencies.

UNCERTAINTIES OF TECHNICAL ASSISTANCE PROGRAMS

In the technical assistance programs of the UN and its specialized agencies, career service has not been a practical objective since these programs are financed on a short-term basis. Most appointments are made for a one-year period, but some continuity is achieved through the frequent reemployment of the same experts on the same or new projects without break in service. The case is even cited of a port planning expert sent out on his first field assignment in 1952 who was still with the UN on a similar mission in another country in 1961.[17] The temporary nature of the employment, and the uncertainties of contract renewal, create problems as follows:

> What actually happens in the case of many projects is that the short-term contracts of on-the-job experts are if possible

12 Leland M. Goodrich, "The Secretariat of the United Nations," in Mangone, *op. cit.*, p. 29.

13 *Budget Estimates for the Financial Year 1969: Report of the Committee on the Reorganization of the Secretariat: Note by the Secretary-General*, United Nations General Assembly, Agenda Item 74, 27 November 1968, p. 63.

14 Goodrich, *op. cit.*, p. 21.

15 *Ibid.*, p. 30.

16 *Ibid.*

17 Yonah Alexander, *International Technical Assistance Experts: A Case Study of the U.N. Experience*, New York: Praeger, 1966, p. 159.

renewed, or new experts have to be engaged, or both. In proportion as new personnel is introduced into a going project, at frequent intervals, lost motion and lack of continuity in project direction may result. To be sure, the infusion of some fresh blood into a project team may be desirable but unless substantial overlap in the membership of a project mission can be assured the chance of successful implementation may be prejudiced or, at best, unduly delayed. The point is relevant to one-man projects as well—all the more because few foreign experts are able to orient themselves effectively in the local, cultural, political, or administrative environment short of several weeks or even months, particularly if they have no previous trans-cultural experience.[18]

If the expert received definite advice about the renewal of his contract well in advance, the situation would be improved. Unfortunately, the matter often remains in doubt until near the end of the contract expiration date. Budgetary uncertainties are not the only reason for this; sometimes the host government is slow in deciding whether or not to retain the services of the expert. Often it is plain "bureaucratic slowness" on the part of both the international agency and the host country that keeps the issue in doubt. Whatever the explanation, it has sometimes happened that in the absence of a definite word as to their retention, experts have decided to go ahead and wind up their affairs in the particular country. After selling their automobiles and household effects and getting everything in order to leave, they suddenly receive an offer of a contract renewal. As Sharp states: "Experienced field experts are lost in the shuffle simply because they cannot arrange at the eleventh hour to stay on—or to return later." He quotes the remark of one experienced mission chief: "The expert is asked to take all the risks while the organization takes none."[19] International-agency headquarters officials are well aware of this problem and its disastrous impact on the morale of the experts. They would like to give earlier assurances of contract renewal, indeed, to put more of the appointments on a long-term basis. Unfortunately, up to now this has been impossible.[20]

Employment and other uncertainties have also plagued the administration of United States technical assistance programs. The recent budget cuts and reductions-in-force in the Agency for International Development (AID) are merely another chapter in its unstable history. Most of AID's professional overseas personnel hold appointments that are made for the duration of its operations. However, so long as foreign aid continues under constant attack inside and outside Congress, "duration of opera-

18 Walter R. Sharp, *Field Administration in the United Nations System,* New York: Praeger, 1961, pp. 162–163.

19 *Ibid.,* p. 165.

20 For a detailed discussion of the appointment procedure, see Alexander, *op. cit.,* pp. 131–155.

tions" can hardly leave the staff member without any doubts at all as to his future employment. AID has been a much-reorganized agency, with every new year like the last one: constant necessity to convince Congress that its programs should be continued.

In 1962 the Secretary of State's Committee on Foreign Affairs Personnel proposed the establishment of a career system for core personnel of AID, similar to that of the State Department's Foreign Service. The AID career group was to consist of a cadre of some 1500 persons "to be used in filling positions of mission directors and deputy directors and in providing the core professional staffs of country program offices, administrative, financial, and logistical support sections, and the directing positions in each of the major functional specialties."[21] Unfortunately, Congress did not accept this recommendation, although in August, 1968, it did pass legislation establishing a career service for foreign information officers of the United States Information Agency (USIA), along the lines also recommended by the Secretary of State's Committee.[22] The latter's full plan was for a "family" of career services for AID, USIA, and the State Department's Foreign Service, to be "governed by uniform statutory provisions regarding personnel management."[23] In a recent report the American Foreign Service Association, now dominated by "not-so-young 'Turks,'" made several recommendations for more coordinated personnel policies for State, AID, and USIA.[24]

Conflicts between nationality groups

The problem of understanding the culture of the country in which an official is stationed was explored in detail in Chapter 3, Administration and Culture. There is no need, therefore, to say much more on this subject, but a few words on the special problems of the staff members of international agencies are in order.[25] These men must adjust during every workday to the ways and points of view of colleagues who represent many different nationalities. In bilateral programs the cultural problem, difficult as it is, is appreciably less complicated than in an international agency. It takes a high order of leadership to weld the members of these different nationality groups into a real team. The big danger is that the staff will form national blocs, that is, join together with other employees from their own country or part of the world.

There are, however, common interests that do tend to unite

[21] *Personnel for the New Diplomacy, op. cit.*, pp. 26–27.

[22] Public Law 90–494, 90th Congress, S. 633, August 20, 1968.

[23] *Personnel for the New Diplomacy, op. cit.*, p. 28.

[24] *Federal Times,* December 11, 1968.

[25] See Francis C. Byrnes, *Americans in Technical Assistance: A Study of Attitudes and Responses to Their Role Abroad,* New York: Praeger, 1965, pp. 42–45.

the members of the different nationality groups. In specialized agencies such as the Food and Agriculture Organization, the World Health Organization, the International Civil Aviation Organization, and the World Meteorological Organization, the scientists and other specialists generally work together quite well. In these lines of work, similar professional interests submerge antagonisms based on nationality. Note this statement:

> The technical experts of the Mekong project go right on as "technicians" in spite of the fact that a shooting war goes on literally next door among the "political" representatives of the very same nations that these technicians are also from; these technicians are committed, mainly, to their professional loyalties, while their fighting co-nationals hold, shall we say, non-technical loyalties, loyalties that make consensus difficult on them because of the very complex nature of questions that these loyalties raise.[26]

However, "where the organization has many facets professional interests tend rather to divide the whole society into separate groups than to unite it."[27] Of course, this is also true in national governments. The more numerous the groups of specialists, the more difficult it usually is to achieve administrative coordination. Where international-agency programs involve value judgments in decisionmaking, and consequently a large area in which national biases can color the thinking of the different staff members, then cooperation is even more difficult to achieve.

Social and economic programs of different kinds are a good example. An English meteorologist may find it relatively easy to get along with a Spanish or Latin American meteorologist, yet he may find it difficult to understand the ideas of Spaniards and Latin Americans as to how national civil services should be organized. Furthermore, the more political the implications of the problem under discussion, the more likely it is that national biases will influence the thinking of the participants.

Counteracting these divisive forces is the keen realization of the consequences of failure in the missions of the international agencies. High morale and great enthusiasm can be sensed in meetings of international agency personnel, responding to the appeals of their directors, just as it can be in similar meetings in national agencies. Certainly it would be erroneous to present a picture of the international agency as one paralyzed by the internal bickerings of its staff members. Furthermore, bureaucratic rivalries in national governments sometimes create power blocs that do more damage to total program objectives than the national blocs in international organizations.

26 Latheef N. Ahmed, "The Multiple Loyalties Hypothesis and the International Civil Servant (ICS)," paper presented at the 1968 Annual Conference of the American Society for Public Administration, Boston, March 27–30, 1968, p. 40. Mimeographed.

27 Loveday, *op. cit.*, p. 5.

The language problem

The language barrier is another serious problem; in fact, some persons serving abroad have said that this is their principal problem. The writer recalls one conversation with the deputy head of an American technical-assistance mission who frankly stated that his lack of a real grasp of the language spoken in the host country had greatly limited his effectiveness. AID does much more than its predecessor agencies to give language training to new personnel before sending them out on foreign assignments, yet in Latin America, as one example, only a few United States government representatives are really fluent in the use of the Spanish language. The basic reason is that most adults have great difficulty mastering a foreign language. This is true in any country; it is not a special characteristic of Americans. Absolute command of the language is usually obtained only when it is learned during childhood and then not allowed to lapse completely. The only occasion on which the writer heard any appreciable number of adult Americans speak Spanish perfectly, with all the right intonations and not the slightest trace of an accent, was during a party held in the home of an executive of an American company that has operated in Latin America for many years. These Americans had been reared and largely educated in Latin American countries. Some of the sons had followed their fathers into the service of the company, and the net result was that there was no language difficulty whatsoever. But, of course, it would be impossible for the government to duplicate those conditions.

In the great majority of cases, those recruited for American overseas posts are born in the United States and have had no opportunity to gain perfect command of a foreign language. Of course, such perfection is not necessary, except in the case of interpreters and translators. An incorrect accent is inevitable when the language is learned as an adult. Foreign accents jar the national sensibilities of some people in any country, but effective communication can take place even if the foreigner speaks with an accent. What counts is his feeling for the language and the national psychology it represents, and his consequent ability to put across his ideas. If the necessary effort is made, and the employing agency gives encouragement and help, a fair proportion of adults can achieve a very acceptable control of the local language. It goes without saying that previous study of foreign languages in college, high school, and even primary school should prove very useful.

In some parts of the world many government officials and the educated groups in general have a good command of English. This, of course, largely eliminates the language barrier. French was thought to be decreasing in importance, but suddenly a whole new group of African nations in which that language is spoken became part of the international scene. Suffice it to say that the language problem remains a difficult one to solve. In overseas programs the individual who combines professional competence with language proficiency is rare. Frustration over inability to communicate in the local language is sometimes the chief cause of psychological difficulties of overseas personnel. They find themselves profoundly disliking both themselves and the people of the country concerned. If language deficiency can create such feelings, it is worth careful remedial action, just as in the case of the other major adjustment problems.

Ideally, every staff member in international agencies should have adequate command of one of the official languages of the organization. Yet because as many member nations as possible must be represented on the secretariats, some persons must be appointed who do not have a satisfactory knowledge of one of the official languages. They must try to learn it on the job. The services of translators and interpreters are available, but in the committee meetings where so much of the work of international agencies is conducted, "a perfect command of one of the official languages is of real advantage, and those who possess it are likely to advance more rapidly than those who do not."[28] Many United Nations experts have been just as ineffective as Americans in trying to communicate with the local population. The advantage enjoyed by the United Nations, however, is that its experts come from many countries, and thus from cultures or regions in which a particular language fluency or potential can be found. However, even the United Nations is frequently desperate in its efforts to find experts with the requisite language ability. On the other hand, to appoint someone with a meagre technical background simply because of his language fluency may be worse than sending a well-qualified person who does not know the language. The fluent but otherwise poorly qualified "expert" may do more harm than good, for he may teach the wrong things. Even though his effectiveness is limited by having to communicate through interpreters, the individual who is thoroughly competent in his field may at least get some of the desired aims accomplished.

---

[28] *Ibid.,* p. 77.

PROBLEMS OF PERSONNEL POLICY

In the process of describing these adjustment problems of over-seas personnel, it was necessary to refer from time to time to questions of personnel policy, such as tenure. The rest of the chapter will be devoted to various other personnel matters that have an important bearing on the morale of persons serving abroad.

Geographical distribution of positions

The principle of geographical representation in making appointments to the staffs of the international agencies has already been mentioned. The United Nations and its specialized agencies follow this policy, but it is not new; the precedent already had been firmly established by the League of Nations. Article 101, paragraph 3, of the United Nations Charter reads:

> The paramount consideration in the employment of the staff and the determination of the conditions of service shall be the necessity of securing the highest standards of efficiency, competence, and integrity. Due regard shall be paid to the importance of recruiting the staff on as wide a geographic basis as possible.

Let us describe in detail how the system of geographical representation is now applied in the United Nations. First, most employees in the lower salary brackets—such as messengers, guards, and clerks—are recruited locally from among nationals of the country where the international agency has its offices. This excludes these positions from geographical representation, the explanation being that "the experiences of every international organization has shown that it is not feasible to go beyond the local area for the recruitment of substantial numbers of staff members in the lower levels."[29] (The quoted words are from a report of the International Civil Service Advisory Board, which was created by the United Nations General Assembly in 1946, and advises the United Nations and the specialized agencies on recruitment and other personnel policies.) Local recruitment is the more practical policy for lower-level positions, because "financial considerations such as cost of transportation, various allowances, home leave, etc. weigh heavily."[30] The Board was expressing a generally accepted opinion when it stated that "the value to the organization of geographical distribution in these levels does not outweigh the difficulties."[31] As Tien-Cheng Young comments, it is not necessary to make messenger posts subject to worldwide recruitment in order to give the agency secretariat a

[29] International Civil Service Advisory Board, *Report on Recruitment Methods and Standards for the United Nations and the Specialized Agencies,* New York: United Nations, 1950, p. 11.

[30] *Ibid.*

[31] *Ibid.*

"truly international character."[32] Yet the UN recently has had so much difficulty recruiting typists in New York City that it has started bringing them in from abroad, particularly the Philippines. This has led to another problem: "The recruits come in on visas that require them to remain in United Nations employ or leave the country—a kind of indentured worker, some complain."[33]

As to positions for which a certain language qualification is indispensable, recruitment must be limited almost entirely to the countries in which that language is the mother tongue. This, therefore, also removes these positions from allocation on a geographical basis.

With these exclusions, the number of positions in the United Nations subject to geographical allocation becomes quite small compared with the total work force. It consists principally of posts of a professional or administrative character. Since these positions are so few, they are highly coveted, and consequently the pressures from the numerous members states to place as many of their nationals as possible in them are exceedingly intense.

Originally, as developed by Trygve Lie, the first Secretary-General, the UN made "financial contribution the basic consideration for the number of nationals from each member state in the Secretariat. . . ."[34] The precedent was also established of avoiding an inflexible formula for the allocation of the positions; the device of "permissible ranges," giving much leeway, was adopted. By 1960 the admission of many new but poor states had led to strong dissatisfaction with the financial-contribution criterion, and in 1962 the General Assembly, by resolution, instructed the Secretary-General to take into account population as well. As a result, the proportion of positions assigned to African, Asian, Latin American, and Middle Eastern nations has increased substantially, with a corresponding decline for Eastern and Western Europe and North America.[35]

By 1969 the United States, long dissatisfied with its representation, was openly complaining that its nationals were being slighted while other countries such as India, the United Arab Republic, and Czechoslovakia were already overrepresented. Although the desirable range for the United States was 361 to 552, it only held 360 jobs, whereas India with a range of 26 to 31 had 65. One of the U.S. representatives suggested that the UN consider cutting off recruitment for a year in the case of countries already seriously overrepresented; he warned that many young persons interested in careers with the United Nations would despair and look for jobs elsewhere.[36]

A UN panel of seven experts, themselves selected on a

[32] Tien-Cheng Young, op. cit., p. 104.

[33] Kathleen Teltsch, "U.N. Study Urges Recruiting Drive," New York Times, December, 3, 1968.

[34] Goodrich, op. cit., p. 20.

[35] Ibid., p. 24, for chart showing distribution as of end of 1964.

[36] Kathleen Teltsch, "U.S. Charges Bias in Hiring by U.N.," New York Times, December 15, 1968.

geographic basis, said in their report that there was "a need for greater discipline and stricter application of the policy of not recruiting from countries which are over the upper limit of their desirable range, save in truly exceptional cases and with the Secretary-General's special authorization in each such case." However, "nothing should be done to compromise the earliest achievement of the desired equitable geographical distribution."[37]

THE POLITICS OF GEOGRAPHICAL APPOINTMENTS

Geographical representation also introduces a political element in the decisions made on appointments by the international agency head. Member governments cannot dictate appointments to him; in theory he exercises independent judgment. In practice, however, to win support for his policies and to keep the organization working together, he may have to yield to a member state's pressure to appoint one of its nationals to a high post.

> Certain attitudes of member states and some practices followed by the Secretariat under political pressure have undoubtedly resulted in a lowering of general competence and efficiency. . . . The appointment of persons from outside the Secretariat to higher posts, usually for fixed terms—what the "under-represented" countries usually want—limits promotional opportunities and weakens morale.[38]

Some observers believe, however, that even from the efficiency standpoint the advantages of geographical distribution outweigh its disadvantages. Tien-Chen Young notes:

> A person is not *simply* efficient or inefficient. He is efficient or inefficient for a given purpose, and efficiency for one purpose may mean inefficiency for another. For example, in negotiation with the British Foreign Office, an ex-English Foreign Service man may be extremely efficient, but for negotiation with Egyptian authorities he may be terribly inefficient. An international establishment staffed with Frenchmen might be highly efficient in its dealing with the French public, but it would be totally inadequate for functioning effectively on a world-wide scale.[39]

The point is well taken, but nothing is said about the man appointed for geographical reasons who simply lacks the technical qualifications for the job in question. One can agree with the statement that "a slightly incompetent man's nationality may make him more useful than a more expert civil servant of inappropriate nationality."[40] But what if, as sometimes happens, the appointee is more than "slightly incompetent" for the job? Loveday philosophically states that the directors must accept the fact

[37] *Budget Estimates for the Financial Year 1969: Report of the Committee on the Reorganization of the Secretariat, op. cit.,* p. 36.

[38] Goodrich, *op. cit.,* pp. 25–26.

[39] Tien-Cheng Young, *op. cit.,* pp. 93–94.

[40] Inis L. Claude, Jr., *Swords into Plowshares,* New York: Random House, 1956, p. 200.

that they will have to "carry a certain proportion of relatively incompetent officials."[41]

RECOMMENDATIONS OF THE INTERNATIONAL
CIVIL SERVICE ADVISORY BOARD

The International Civil Service Advisory Board made several suggestions, adoption of which it felt "would go a long way toward attaining proper balance between competence and geography."[42] One of these was to adopt a "sound career system under which recruitment at the junior level in under-represented countries" would be emphasized.[43] The logic behind this proposal is to recruit young people on the basis of their aptitudes and train them in the skills and knowledges required in the different higher-level posts in the secretariat. The Board was "convinced that while some nations of the world cannot at this time produce or spare highly trained persons in certain special fields, there is no country in which young persons with all the educational and intellectual qualifications which make for career international civil servants of outstanding quality cannot be found."[44] This, however, is a long-run solution and, in any case, "there will be a considerable number of posts requiring practical experience which cannot be filled in this way." Furthermore, "recruits from certain countries where the level of education is low are unlikely to make the grade even when no experience is demanded."[45]

Another of the Board's recommendations was to develop a program of in-service training for new appointees. This, it was hoped, would make "recruiting on a geographical basis much more feasible," by repairing "the inevitable flaws" in such recruitment.[46] In-service training is highly desirable in any organization, but some skepticism can be expressed about the Board's hope that recruitment deficiencies could be remedied in this way. Training programs can reduce the margin of incompetence in some cases and eliminate it in others; that is about all one can expect. It must be concluded that geographical recruitment is a political necessity in international organizations and makes strict adherence to merit principles impossible.

Selection methods

What methods should be used in selecting persons for overseas service? Taking the international agencies first, the "desirability of selection of international staff by competitive examination" has been recognized since 1921, when a League of Nations report recommended that, with very few exceptions, staff be employed

[41] Loveday, *op. cit.*, p. 45.

[42] *Report on Recruitment Methods and Standards, op. cit.*, p. 8.

[43] *Ibid.*, p. 10.

[44] *Ibid.*

[45] Loveday, *op. cit.*, p. 45.

[46] *Report on Recruitment Methods and Standards, op. cit.*, p. 10.

in the future on the basis of "competitive selections." The Preparatory Commission of the United Nations was of the same opinion, and the General Assembly, at its sixth session, recommended selection of staff through competitive examinations wherever possible.

Despite these statements of policy, however, the use of competitive examinations in international organizations has been limited principally to positions requiring language ability and to clerical and secretarial jobs. Objection to competitive examinations is based largely on the contention that they could not be administered successfully because of the wide differences in the educational systems of the member states.[47] Yet the International Civil Service Advisory Board must have believed that this difficulty could be surmounted, for it recommended written competitive examinations as "the normal avenue of entry for persons in the professional category." It expressed the opinion

> . . . that all the agencies can and should find within their organization a group of posts which would constitute the commencement to a professional career, and which should be filled by professional examination of young persons with no excessive degree of specialization. Even where specialized study at this level is required, the setting of papers in various fields which must be written only by the candidates seeking employment in those fields should enlarge the usefulness of this type of examination.[48]

By conducting examinations for one country at a time or on a regional basis, the problem of differing educational systems could be solved. "Competitive selection" does not require that written examinations be given in every case. The Board applauded the practice of some agencies, such as the International Labour Organization, of filling posts above the junior professional level through open competition even though written examinations were not considered practicable. Remembering the analysis of selection techniques in Part IV of this book, this would mean unassembled examinations, supplemented by oral interviews and throughgoing reference checks and qualifications appraisals. The panel of seven experts previously mentioned recommended that the International Civil Service Advisory Board should, in consultation as appropriate with UNESCO, make a "comparative evaluation of degrees and diplomas awarded by institutions of higher learning in countries of different educational systems and of different cultural backgrounds."[49]

Of course, the international agencies do have personnel offices that evaluate the qualifications of the applicants and seek

[47] Tien-Cheng Young, *op. cit.*, p. 100.
[48] *Report on Recruitment Methods and Standards, op. cit.*, pp. 28–29.
[49] *Budget Estimates for the Financial Year 1969: Report of the Committee on the Reorganization of the Secretariat, op. cit.*, p. 37.

to obtain the employment of only those most qualified. They do not have to follow uniform policies, however, and in general it can be stated that the principle of merit is followed only to the extent that the Personnel Office is successful in insisting on it. For this reason it has been suggested that an International Civil Service Commission be created with jurisdiction over the United Nations and all the specialized international agencies. Tien-Cheng Young favors the establishment of such a Commission, not only because it would enforce common personnel policies but also because he believes it would eliminate political pressures in appointments. The members of such a Commission, he suggests, should be *elected* for fixed terms by the member states.[50] The danger in this proposal is that the politically elected members of such a Commission might engage in logrolling and similar horse-trading. Yet, since so many of its recommendations have not been adopted, the purely advisory character of the International Civil Service Board leaves much to be desired. Prospects of establishing an International Civil Service Commission, however, appear remote. Greatest reliance will have to continue to be placed on the individual international agency to maintain the highest personnel standards it can under present circumstances.

U.S. FOREIGN AFFAIRS PERSONNEL

Turning to selection of staff for United States government posts abroad, the State Department, AID, and USIA have each functioned under different systems for the selection of foreign service personnel. The State Department has usually given an examination each year aimed at attracting young college graduates; in recent years junior-officer appointments have accounted for approximately 80 percent of the Department's foreign-service appointments.

By contrast, the AID has mostly recruited persons from inside and outside the government who already have the experience to qualify for positions in the middle and top grades. USIA has followed a policy that "falls in between," making more appointments by lateral entry than does State to the middle and top posts, but having "a positive junior professional-recruitment program similar to that of the State Department."[51] With its new career foreign service information corps, USIA gave an examination in May, 1969, intended to fill about 50 junior positions in the corps. In December, 1969, it gave a joint junior officer examination with the State Department; such joint examinations had been given in the past but were suspended in 1968 because of reductions-in-force in overseas personnel required

50 Tien-Cheng Young, *op. cit.*, pp. 59–60.

51 *Personnel for the New Diplomacy*, *op. cit.*, p. 66.

as part of the program to reduce the deficit in the balance of payments.

The Secretary of State's Committee on Foreign Affairs Personnel not only recommended a single written examination, with appropriate options for all three agencies, but also the establishment of a joint Board of Examiners, to replace the State Department's Board of Examiners for the Foreign Service. The function of the proposed joint Board, on which the Civil Service Commission was also to be represented, would be to develop "standards and precepts to govern the examinations for career appointments in the family of foreign affairs services, including written, oral, and other examinations at all levels of entry."[52] Although this proposal—part of the Committee's previously mentioned plan for a "family of career services" (see page 463)— was not acted upon by Congress, different ideas for a unified foreign service personnel program are being presented. The American Foreign Service Association proposes a joint recruitment program for all three agencies, and a joint foreign affairs career examination to result in a single eligible register for use by all three agencies. It believes, however, that the written examination should be de-emphasized, and that there should be greater use of special recruitment programs for minority groups, as well as an expansion of university contacts and intern programs.[53]

As to lateral entry, the Secretary of State's Committee believed it essential that all three agencies make systematic provision for the appointment of competent persons "to meet specialized needs that are not satisfied through appointments at the bottom levels."[54] The way to do this was for each agency to review its personnel needs at least once a year and decide how many career officers it needed at each level. Naturally the number of persons needed by lateral appointment would depend upon the intake of junior officers, and this would vary from agency to agency and year to year. Whatever the number of lateral appointments, the Committee was adamant that mid-career entry standards be "exacting." No one should be appointed who was not highly qualified for the work in question. Instead of the essentially noncompetitive examinations now generally used as the basis for making lateral appointments, "the examining procees should be competitive." Besides a "searching" analysis of the candidates' previous backgrounds, a "thorough oral examination" should be used. Furthermore, consideration should be given in some cases to the use of written tests and the "review of other evidence indicating the candidate's ability to apply his knowledge

[52] *Ibid.*, pp. 71–72.

[53] *Federal Times,* December 11, 1968.

[54] *Personnel for the New Diplomacy, op. cit.,* p. 75.

to problem-solving situations, and his ability to write effectively."[55] In other words, the Committee wanted formal, not informal, procedures for evaluating the qualifications of applicants for mid-career appointments.

In early 1969 the USIA was preparing examination procedures for evaluating the qualifications of present employees interested in lateral appointment to the new Foreign Service Information Officer corps; some 350 to 400 employees were expected to apply. Candidates were required to qualify by passing comprehensive mental and physical requirements prescribed by the State Department's Board of Examiners, after which panels of examiners were to rate them for appropriate openings on the basis of their backgrounds of training and experience.[56]

Salary problems

Just as in domestic employment, the salary problem is a difficult one in recruiting for overseas personnel. The pay legislation mentioned in Chapter 13 provided salary increases for the foreign services of the State Department, USIA, and AID, along with those for the other federal employees. Thus there has been some improvement, although there is room for more, particularly at the highest levels.

The international agencies have certain unique salary problems. Salaries paid by national governments vary greatly. Although the pay of United States public employees has lagged behind that in industry, it is much higher than that received by government workers in many other countries. Nor need the United States be used as the only example: such countries as Great Britain, Sweden, West Germany, and many others pay both public and private workers much more than in lesser-developed nations.

Since all member states are entitled to representation in the secretariats of the international agencies, on what basis should the salary scales be set? How high should the scales be set in relation to pay for comparable work in the public services of the member countries? Should the principle of equal pay for equal work be followed, regardless of the nationality of the employee? In answer to these questions, the United Nations follows the same policy as did the League of Nations. It is to pay salaries that compare favorably with those of the member governments that pay the highest salaries. The same salary is paid for comparable work, regardless of the nationality of the individual. This means that an employee who comes from a country with

[55] *Ibid.*, p. 78.
[56] *Federal Times,* February 19, 1969.

low wage levels earns much more than he could in his home environment: in fact, he may double or even treble his earnings, depending on how low the salaries are in his country. To establish salary scales below the pay rates of the countries paying the most would not be realistic, for the best available talent must be drawn from all the member states. Furthermore, the national from a poor country who does the same work as someone from a much more prosperous nation is entitled to be paid what others get for the same work.

A system of differential salary rates based on nationality would have a disastrous effect on staff morale. During part of its existence, the United Nations Relief and Rehabilitation Administration used such a system. Salaries were set sufficiently high to attract qualified staff, but they varied at the same work location. For the same kind of job, an American might get $1000 a year more than a Frenchman, and the Frenchman $1000 more than someone from India. The only equality was that all received the same cost-of-living allowance.

The trouble with this kind of policy is that despite its economies, "it would destroy the very foundations of the international civil service and consequently reduce an international secretariat to a name only."[57] Actually, there is a clear justification for paying salaries even higher than those of the best-paying member governments. The official incurs additional expenses when he lives outside his home country. The extra costs of expatriation are usually very substantial, even not taking into account "the losses caused by lack of personal and professional contacts and from being remote from normal spheres of employment."[58] In actual practice, the international organizations take the expatriation factor into account in fixing the salary levels. They also give special grants in addition to salary, such as an installation allowance when the official takes up residence at his post, and a termination indemnity when he is returned home.

International loyalty versus national loyalty

A final personnel problem meriting discussion is that of international loyalty versus national loyalty. No one expects an international civil servant to cast off his sentiments of patriotism and affection for his home country. Once he joins the staff of an international agency, however, he must regard it as his *sole* employer. His country of origin may not like the policies he carries out as a staff member of the international agency, but he must not allow this to influence him in discharging his duties.

[57] Tien-Cheng Young, *op. cit.*, p. 131.

[58] *Ibid.*, p. 130.

Like the League of Nations, the United Nations requires the new employee to take an oath of office in which he pledges that he will not seek or accept instructions from any government or other authority external to the organization. Any international civil servant who accepted such instructions clearly would be disloyal to the organization. Such cases have occurred, but the problem goes deeper than this. The individual may accept no outside instructions, but still be greatly influenced by national biases in the opinions he expresses within the organization and in the contacts he has with other members of the secretariat. So long as he and other employees maintain such a narrow attitude, the work of the organization will not progress as it should. What is needed is what the International Civil Service Advisory Board dubs an "international outlook." The Board is very clear about the ingredients of such an outlook:

> It involves willingness to try to understand and be tolerant of different points of view, different cultural patterns, and different work habits. It also entails willingness to work without prejudice or bias with persons of all nationalities, religions, and cultures. It means a readiness to be continually conscious of how proposals, events, and statements of opinion may appear to a very wide range of nationalities. It involves conduct of the highest type and exercise of judgment and restraint in all expressions of view whether public or private; any expressions which could be construed as biased or intolerant, particularly in respect of national interests or political issues with which the organization is confronted, must be scrupulously avoided.[59]

This is no easy order, for "there is nothing so difficult as transforming one's outlook, uprooting prejudices, replacing feelings and emotions, dictated by egoism, in favor of feelings which may lead to the love of one's neighbor and to living in harmony with peoples of other cultures, languages, and races."[60] Cliques based on nationality and similar cultural bonds easily form in international organizations. No matter how stern the statements in the Charter and the staff regulations about the obligation to maintain international loyalty, the individual staff member can easily rationalize that he is "right" in his opinions and not evidencing any national prejudices. Frequently he is totally unaware of his biases. He expects others in the secretariat to behave as his fellow countrymen do in his home government. This to him is correct behavior; any other comportment is wrong. Such an official has failed to acquire the quality of international-mindedness. In the opinion of the International Civil Service Advisory Board, every "true international civil servant" must

---

[59] International Civil Service Advisory Board, *Report on Standards of Conduct in the International Civil Service*, New York: United Nations, 1954, p. 4.

[60] Tien-Cheng Young, *op. cit.*, p. 22.

develop this quality, not only in his work contacts with the other members of the secretariat but also in his social relations with them.[61]

In at least one international agency, the European Communities, application of the principle of geographical distribution appears to have worked toward international-mindedness. "For instance, a bureau chief may be Italian, his deputy French, and the latter's subordinate a Dutchman. This principle thus tends to prevent officers from ganging up into national cliques, and the matter of nationality is largely forgotten on the job."[62]

Political activities of international officials

What about the political activities of international officials? One of the United Nations' regulations states that "staff members may exercise the right to vote but shall not engage in any political activity which is inconsistent with or might reflect upon the independence and impartiality required by their status as international officials."[63] It is up to the Secretary-General to decide when a staff member has exceeded permissible bounds in his political activities.

The United Nations has no elaborate set of regulations such as those developed by the United States Civil Service Commission under the Hatch Acts. In general, the guiding policy is as stated by the International Civil Service Advisory Board. The international official is not expected to be a political eunuch. In fact, the Board encourages him to "take a lively interest in the important public questions of the day." However, such activities as the following are considered improper: candidature for public office of a political character and the holding of such office; public support of a political party by speeches, statements to the press, or written articles; the holding of political party office; membership on any political campaign committee; acceptance or solicitation of any financial contributions for political purposes; and initiation or signature of petitions involving political candidates or political issues.

The Board did not think it was possible to lay down a fixed rule on membership in a political party. However, it did say that it was "inadmissible" for the staff member to belong to a party that was illegal in his country, and ruled out "membership in any group, whether political or not, which imposes on the staff member an obligation to action incompatible with his oath of office and responsibilities as an international civil servant."[64]

The problem of membership in illegal parties is not a simple

[61] *Report on Standards of Conduct in the International Civil Service, op. cit.*, pp. 5–6.
[62] Werner J. Feld, "Personnel Administration of the European Communities," *Public Administration Review,* XXV, No. 1 (January, 1964), 35–36.
[63] Tien-Cheng Young, *op. cit.,* p. 35.
[64] *Report on Standards of Conduct in the International Civil Service, op. cit.,* p. 11.

one. What if the party was legal when the staff member joined the international organization, but there is a change in regimes at home and the party is outlawed? Under such circumstances it is not fair to dismiss him, but it is correct to require him not to engage in political activities aimed at overthrowing the new regime. Furthermore, he should be expected not to show hostility to the new government's delegation to the United Nations. In practice, it is difficult for the United Nations and the other international agencies to check so closely upon the activities of staff members to be sure that they are not involved in clandestine efforts to dislodge the new regime. The United Nations has on occasion hired political exiles who have at least given moral support to movements to overthrow the governments that sent them into exile. So long as changes in governments through use of force occur with any regularity, this problem will remain delicate.

BIBLIOGRAPHY

Alexander, Yonah, *International Technical Assistance Experts: A Case Study of the U.N. Experience,* New York: Praeger, 1966.

Bailey, Sidney D., *The Secretariat of the United Nations,* New York: Carnegie Endowment, 1962.

Byrnes, Francis C., *Americans in Technical Assistance: A Study of Attitudes and Responses to Their Role Abroad,* New York: Praeger, 1965.

Canonici, Aldo, "Management Training Overseas: 1. In Developed Nations," *Personnel, XLV,* No. 5 (September-October, 1968).

Cleveland, Harlan, and Mangone, Gerard J., (eds.), *The Art of Overseasmanship,* Syracuse, N.Y.: Syracuse University Press, 1957.

Cleveland, Harlan, Mangone, Gerard J., Adams, John Clarke, *The Overseas Americans,* New York: McGraw-Hill, 1960.

Fielder, Frances, and Harris, Godfrey, *The Quest for Foreign Affairs Officers—Their Recruitment and Selection,* New York: Carnegie Endowment, 1966.

Hayden, Spencer, "Problems of Operating Overseas: A Survey of Company Experience," *Personnel, XLV,* No. 1 (January-February, 1968).

Hopper, Jerry R., and Levin, Richard I., "Management Training

Overseas: 2. In Developing Nations," *Personnel, XLV*, No. 5 (September-October, 1968).

Loveday, A., *Reflections on International Administration*, Oxford, England: Clarendon Press, 1956.

Mangone, Gerard J., (ed.), *UN Administration of Economic and Social Programs*, New York: Columbia University Press, 1966.

Personnel for the New Diplomacy, Report of the Committee on Foreign Affairs Personnel, New York: Carnegie Endowment, 1962.

Report on Recruitment Methods and Standards for the United Nations and the Specialized Agencies, New York: United Nations, 1950.

Sharp, Walter R., *Field Administration in the United Nations System*, New York: Praeger, 1961.

Young, Tien-Cheng, *International Civil Service: Principles and Problems*, Brussels, Belgium: International Institute of Administrative Sciences, 1958.

INDEX

71 72 73 7 6 5 4 3

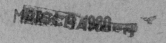
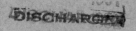